Third Edition

Principles of Incident Response & Disaster Recovery

MICHAEL E. WHITMAN
PH.D., CISM, CISSP

HERBERT J. MATTORD
PH.D., CISM, CISSP

INFORMATION
SECURITY

T0198297

❖ Cengage

Australia • Brazil • Canada • Mexico • Singapore • United Kingdom • United States

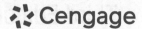

***Principles of Incident Response & Disaster Recovery**, 3rd Edition*
Michael Whitman and Herbert Mattord

SVP, Higher Education Product Management: Erin Joyner

VP, Product Management: Thais Alencar

Product Team Manager: Kristin McNary

Associate Product Manager: Danielle Klahr

Product Assistant: Tom Benedetto

Director, Learning Design: Rebecca von Gillern

Senior Manager, Learning Design: Leigh Hefferon

Learning Designer: Mary Clyne

Vice President, Marketing – Science, Technology, & Math: Jason Sakos

Senior Marketing Director: Michele McTighe

Marketing Manager: Cassie Cloutier

Product Specialist: Mackenzie Paine

Director, Content Creation: Juliet Steiner

Senior Manager, Content Creation: Patty Stephan

Senior Content Manager: Brooke Greenhouse

Director, Digital Production Services: Krista Kellman

Digital Delivery Lead: Jim Vaughey

Developmental Editor: Dan Seiter

Production Service/Composition: SPi Global

Design Director: Jack Pendleton

Designer: Erin Griffin

Cover image(s): Kolonko/ShutterStock.com

For product information and technology assistance, contact us at
Cengage Customer & Sales Support, 1-800-354-9706 or support.cengage.com.

For permission to use material from this text or product, submit all requests online at **www.copyright.com.**

Library of Congress Control Number: 2020917514

ISBN: 978-0-357-50832-9

Loose-leaf Edition:
ISBN: 978-0-357-50833-6

Cengage
200 Pier 4 Boulevard
Boston, MA 02210
USA

Cengage is a leading provider of customized learning solutions with employees residing in nearly 40 different countries and sales in more than 125 countries around the world. Find your local representative at: **www.cengage.com.**

To learn more about Cengage platforms and services, register or access your online learning solution, or purchase materials for your course, visit **www.cengage.com.**

Notice to the Reader

Printed at CLDPC, USA, 03-24

To Rhonda, Rachel, Alex, and Meghan, thank you for your loving support.

—MEW

To my granddaughters, Julie and Ellie. Always stay strong.

—HJM

BRIEF CONTENTS

TABLE OF CONTENTS

PREFACE

As global networks expand the interconnection of the world's technically complex infrastructure, communication and computing systems gain added importance. Information security has gained in importance as a professional practice, and it has also emerged as an academic discipline. Ongoing security events, such as malware attacks and successful hacking efforts, have pointed out the weaknesses inherent in unprotected systems and exposed the need for heightened security of these systems. In order to secure technologically advanced systems and networks, both education and the infrastructure to deliver that education are needed to prepare the next generation of information technology and information security professionals to develop a more secure and ethical computing environment. Therefore, improved tools and more sophisticated techniques are needed to prepare students to recognize the threats and vulnerabilities present in existing systems and to design and develop secure systems. Many years have passed since the need for improved information security education was recognized, and as Dr. Ernest McDuffie, Lead of NIST NICE, points out:

> While there is no doubt that technology has changed the way we live, work, and play, there are very real threats associated with the increased use of technology and our growing dependence on cyberspace. . . .
>
> Education can prepare the general public to identify and avoid risks in cyberspace; education will ready the cybersecurity workforce of tomorrow; and education can keep today's cybersecurity professionals at the leading edge of the latest technology and mitigation strategies.

The need for improvements in information security education is so great that the U.S. National Security Agency (NSA) has established Centers of Academic Excellence in Information Assurance, as described in Presidential Decision Directive 63, "The Policy on Critical Infrastructure Protection" (1998):

> The goal of the program is to reduce vulnerability in our national information infrastructure by promoting higher education and research in cyber defense and producing professionals with cyber defense expertise.

Academics who want to focus on delivering skilled undergraduates to the commercial information technology (IT) sector need teaching resources that focus on key topics in the broader area of information security.

APPROACH

This resource provides an overview of contingency operations and its components as well as a thorough treatment of the administration of the planning process for incident response (IR), disaster recovery (DR), and business continuity (BC). It can be used to support course delivery for information security-driven programs targeted at information technology students, as well as IT management and technology management curricula aimed at business or technical management students.

Features

To ensure a successful learning experience, this product includes the following pedagogical features:

- *Module Objectives*—Each module in this book begins with a detailed list of the concepts to be mastered within that module. This list provides you with a quick reference to the contents of the module as well as a useful study aid.
- *Module Scenarios*—Each module opens and closes with a case scenario that follows the same fictional company as it encounters various contingency planning or operational issues. The closing scenario also includes discussion questions to give students and the instructor an opportunity to discuss the issues that underlie the content. New in this edition is an example of an ethical decision that extends the opportunity to discuss the impact of events in the scenario.
- *Boxed Examples*—These supplemental sections, which feature examples not associated with the ongoing case study, are included to illustrate key learning objectives and technical details or extend the coverage of plans and policies.
- *Learning Support*—Each module includes a Module Summary section, definitions of key terms, and a set of open-ended review questions. These are used to reinforce learning of the subject matter presented in the module.
- *Real-World Exercises*—At the end of each module, Real-World Exercises give students the opportunity to examine the contingency planning arena outside the classroom. Using these structured exercises, students can pursue the learning objectives listed at the beginning of each module and deepen their understanding of the text material.
- *Hands-On Projects*—Virtual labs are now available through the MindTap that accompanies *Principles of Incident Response and Disaster Recovery*. These labs have been designed by the authors to help students develop valuable practical skills. They can be accessed in the Practice It folder in MindTap or through the instructor's learning management system (LMS).

New to This Edition

This edition extends the work from the previous edition by adding more detail and examples, specifically in the examination of incident response activities. It continues to track the evolution in approaches and methods that have been developed at NIST. Although the material on disaster recovery, business continuity, and crisis management has not been reduced, the text's focus now follows that of the IT industry in shifting to the prevention, detection, reaction to, and recovery from computer-based incidents and avoidance of threats to the security of information.

Several modules have been reorganized, with a new module on incident detection that has an increased focus on IDPSs, security information and event management systems (SIEMs), and security event correlation.

Structure

The narrative is organized into 12 modules. Appendices and other materials are available with the instructor resources online and in MindTap. Here are summaries of each module's contents:

Module 1, *An Overview of Information Security and Risk Management*, defines the concepts of information security and risk management and explains how they are integral to the management processes used for incident response and contingency planning.

Module 2, *Planning for Organizational Readiness*, focuses on how an organization can plan for and develop processes and staffing appointments needed for successful incident response and contingency plans.

Module 3, *Contingency Strategies for Incident Response, Disaster Recovery, and Business Continuity*, explores the relationships among contingency planning and the subordinate elements of incident response, business resumption, disaster recovery, and business continuity planning. It also explains the techniques used for data and application backup and recovery.

Module 4, *Incident Response: Planning*, expands on the incident response planning process to include processes and activities that are needed as well as the skills and techniques used to develop such plans.

Module 5, *Incident Response: Organizing and Preparing the CSIRT*, presents a detailed explanation of the actions that the CSIRT performs and how they are designed and developed.

Module 6, *Incident Response: Incident Detection Strategies*, describes IR reaction strategies and how they are applied to incidents.

Module 7, *Incident Response: Detection Systems*, describes IDPSs, security information and event management systems (SIEMs), and security event correlation.

Module 8, *Incident Response: Response Strategies*, describes how an organization plans for and executes the recovery process when an incident occurs.

Module 9, *Incident Response: Recovery, Maintenance, and Investigations*, explores how organizations recover from incidents. It also expands on the steps involved in the ongoing maintenance of the IR plan as well as the IT forensics process.

Module 10, *Disaster Recovery*, presents the challenges an organization faces when engaged in disaster recovery and how such challenges are met.

Module 11, *Business Continuity*, covers how organizations ensure continuous operations even when their primary facilities are not available.

Module 12, *Crisis Management in IR, DR, and BC*, covers the role of crisis management and recommends the elements of a plan to prepare for crisis response. The module also covers the key international standards that affect IR, DR, and BC.

Three appendices in the instructor's resources and MindTap present sample BC and crisis management plans and templates.

MINDTAP

MindTap activities for *Principles of Incident Response and Disaster Recovery* are designed to help you master the skills you need in today's workforce. Research shows that employers need critical thinkers, troubleshooters, and creative problem-solvers to stay relevant in this fast-paced, technology-driven world. MindTap helps you achieve this goal with assignments and activities that provide hands-on practice with real-life relevance.

All MindTap activities and assignments are tied to defined learning objectives. Readings with spaced knowledge checks support the course objectives, while hands-on labs provide practice and give you an opportunity to troubleshoot, explore, and try different solutions in a secure sandbox environment. Videos, Review Questions, and Real-World Exercises will help you reinforce your understanding of each module's concepts, and Security for Life assignments will prompt you to explore industry-related news and events.

Use the interactive Flashcards and PowerPoint slides in each module to help you study for exams. Measure how well you have mastered the material by taking the Review Quizzes and completing the Case Exercises at the end of each module. Finally, the Post-Assessment Quiz helps you assess all that you have learned throughout the course, see where you gained deeper knowledge, and identify the skills where you need additional practice!

Instructors can use the content and learning path as they are, or choose how these materials wrap around their own resources. MindTap supplies the analytics and reporting so you can easily see where the class stands in terms of progress, engagement, and completion rates. To learn more about shaping what students see and scheduling when they see it, instructors can go to *www.cengage.com/mindtap/*.

INSTRUCTOR RESOURCES

Instructors can access a robust set of teaching resources tailored to this product at Cengage's Companion Site. An instructor login is required. Please visit *instructor.cengage.com* to request access or log in to your existing account. There, you will find the following instructor-specific resources:

- *Instructor's Manual*—The Instructor's Manual that accompanies this resource includes additional instructional material to assist in class preparation, including suggestions for classroom activities, discussion topics, and additional projects.
- *Solution Files*—The solution files include answers to selected end-of-module materials, including the review questions and some of the hands-on projects.
- *Test Bank*—Cengage Testing, powered by Cognero, is a flexible, online system that allows you to do the following:
  - ○ Author, edit, and manage test bank content from multiple Cengage solutions.
  - ○ Create multiple test versions in an instant.
  - ○ Deliver tests from your LMS, your classroom, or wherever you want.

  The generous question sets developed for this edition include a variety of question types tagged to core learning objectives and narrative topics.
- *PowerPoint Presentations*—This edition includes Microsoft PowerPoint slides for each module. These are included as a teaching aid for classroom presentation. They can also be made available to students on the network for module review, or they can be printed for classroom distribution. Instructors should feel free to add their own slides for additional topics they introduce to the class.
- *Hands-On Projects*—The virtual labs provided with this resource can help students develop practical skills that will be of value as they progress through the course. These author-developed lab projects are available via MindTap or at the Companion Site for LMS integration.
- *Information Security Community Site*—Stay secure with the Information Security Community Site! Connect with students, professors, and professionals from around the world, and stay on top of this ever-changing field.
  - ○ Visit *www.cengage.com/community/infosec*.
  - ○ Download resources such as instructional videos and labs.
  - ○ Ask authors, professors, and students the questions that are on your mind in our Discussion Forums.
  - ○ See up-to-date news, videos, and articles.
  - ○ Read author blogs.
  - ○ Listen to podcasts on the latest information security topics.

AUTHOR TEAM

Long-time college professors and information security professionals Michael Whitman and Herbert Mattord have jointly developed this text and MindTap to merge knowledge from the world of academic study with practical experience from the business world.

Michael Whitman, Ph.D., CISM, CISSP, is the Executive Director of the KSU Institute for Cybersecurity Workforce Development (ICWD, *cyberinstitute.kennesaw.edu*) and a Professor of Information Security and Assurance at Kennesaw State University, Kennesaw, Georgia. Dr. Whitman has over 30 years of experience in higher education, with over 20 years of experience in designing and teaching information security courses. He is an active researcher in information security, fair and responsible use policies, and computer-use ethics. He currently teaches graduate and undergraduate courses in information security and cybersecurity. He has published articles in the top journals in his field, including *Information Systems Research, Communications of the ACM, Information and Management, Journal of International Business Studies*, and *Journal of Computer Information Systems*. Under Dr. Whitman's leadership, Kennesaw State University has been recognized by the National Security Agency and the Department of Homeland Security as a National Center of Academic Excellence in Information Assurance/Cyber Defense Education four times. Dr. Whitman is also the coauthor of *Principles of Information Security; Management of Information Security; Readings and Cases in the Management* *of Information Security; Readings and Cases in Information Security: Law and Ethics; The Hands-On Information Security Lab Manual; Roadmap to the Management of Information Security for IT and Information Security Professionals; Guide to Firewalls and VPNs; Guide to Firewalls and Network Security;* and *Guide to Network Security,* all published by Course Technology (now Cengage). Prior to his career in academia, Dr. Whitman was an officer in the United States Army.

Herbert Mattord, Ph.D., CISM, CISSP, completed 24 years of IT industry experience as an application developer, database administrator, project manager, and information security practitioner before joining the faculty of Kennesaw State University in 2002. Dr. Mattord is a Professor of Information Security and Assurance and the Director of Undergraduate Education and Outreach at the ICWD. During his career as an IT practitioner, Dr. Mattord has been an adjunct professor at Kennesaw State University; Southern Polytechnic State University in Marietta, Georgia; Austin Community College in Austin, Texas; and Texas State University: San Marcos. He currently teaches undergraduate and graduate courses in information security and cybersecurity. He was formerly the manager of corporate information technology security at Georgia-Pacific Corporation, where much of the practical knowledge found in this text was acquired. Professor Mattord is also the coauthor of *Principles of Information Security; Management of Information Security; Readings and Cases in the Management of Information Security; Readings and Cases in Information Security: Law and Ethics; The Hands-On Information Security Lab Manual; Roadmap to the Management of Information Security for IT and Information Security Professionals; Guide to Firewalls and VPNs; Guide to Firewalls and Network Security;* and *Guide to Network Security,* all published by Course Technology (now Cengage).

ACKNOWLEDGMENTS

The authors would like to thank their families for their support and understanding for the many hours dedicated to this project—hours taken in many cases from family activities.

Reviewers

We are indebted to the following individuals for their contributions of perceptive feedback on the initial proposal, the project outline, and individual learning modules:

- Paul Witman, California Lutheran University
- Humayun Zafar, Kennesaw State University
- Randall Reid, University of West Florida

Special Thanks

The authors wish to thank the editorial and production teams at Cengage. Their diligent and professional efforts greatly enhanced the final product:

- Danielle Klahr, Associate Product Manager
- Amy Savino, Senior Product Manager
- Mary Clyne, Learning Designer
- Brooke Greenhouse, Senior Content Manager
- Dan Seiter, Developmental Editor

In addition, several professional and commercial organizations and individuals have aided the development of the text and MindTap by providing information and inspiration, and the authors wish to acknowledge their contributions:

- Bernstein Crisis Management
- Continuity Central
- Information Systems Security Associations

- Institute for Crisis Management
- National Institute of Standards and Technology
- Oracle, Inc.
- Purdue University
- Rothstein Associates, Inc.
- SunGard
- Our colleagues in the Department of Information Systems and the Michael J. Coles College of Business, Kennesaw State University

Our Commitment

The authors are committed to serving the needs of the adopters and readers. We would be pleased and honored to receive feedback on the textbook, MindTap, and supporting materials. You can contact us through Cengage.

AN OVERVIEW OF INFORMATION SECURITY AND RISK MANAGEMENT

Upon completion of this material, you should be able to:

1. Define and explain information security
2. Describe the role of information security policy in the organization
3. Identify and explain the basic concepts and phases of risk management

An ounce of prevention is worth a pound of cure.

— Benjamin Franklin

Opening Scenario

Paul Alexander and his boss, Amanda Wilson, were sitting in Amanda's office discussing the coming year's budget when they heard a commotion in the hall. Hearing his name mentioned, Paul stuck his head out the door and saw Jonathon Jasper ("JJ" to his friends) walking quickly toward him.

"Paul!" JJ called again, relieved to see Paul waiting in Amanda's office. "Hi, Amanda," JJ said, then, looking at Paul, he added, "We have a problem." JJ was one of the systems administrators at Hierarchical Access LTD (HAL), a Georgia-based cloud services firm.

Paul stepped out into the hall, closing Amanda's door behind him. "What's up, JJ?"

"I think we've got someone sniffing around our credentialing services platform," JJ replied. "I just looked at the log files, and there is an unusual number of failed login attempts on accounts that normally just don't have that many, like yours!"

Paul answered, "Sounds like we need to investigate," then paused a moment.

"That system is configured to allow off-premises VPN access," he finally said to JJ. "Are there corresponding entries in the reverse proxy server or the VPN logs?"

JJ shook his head "no."

Paul sighed. "Which means it must be internal."

"Yeah, that's why it's a problem," JJ replied. "We haven't gotten this kind of thing since we partitioned the credentialing platform. It's got to be someone in-house."

JJ looked exasperated. "And after all that time I spent conducting awareness training!"

"Don't worry just yet," Paul told him. "Let me make a few calls, and then we'll go from there. Grab your incident response plan and meet me in the conference room in 10 minutes. Grab Tina in network operations on the way; she's on call for today."

contingency planning (CP)

The actions taken by senior management to specify the organization's efforts and actions if an adverse event becomes an incident or disaster. This planning includes incident response, disaster recovery, business continuity, and crisis management efforts, as well as preparatory business impact analysis.

security

A state of being secure and free from danger or harm. Also, the actions taken to make someone or something secure.

INTRODUCTION

This book is about being prepared for the unexpected—being ready for events such as incidents and disasters. We call this contingency planning (CP), and the sad fact is that most organizations don't incorporate it into their day-to-day business activities, so they are often not well prepared to offer the proper response to a disaster or security incident. By December 2019, Internet World Stats estimated that there were over 4.5 billion people online, representing well over half of the world's 7.8 billion population.[1] Each one of those online users is a potential threat to any online system. The vast majority of Internet users will not intentionally probe, monitor, attack, or attempt to access an organization's information without authorization; however, that potential does exist. If even less than one-tenth of 1 percent of online users make the effort, the result would be over four and a half *million* potential attackers.

In the weeks that followed the September 11, 2001 attacks in New York, Pennsylvania, and Washington D.C., the media reported on the disastrous losses that various organizations were suffering. Still, many organizations were able to continue conducting business. Why? They were prepared for unexpected events. The cataclysm in 2001 was not the first attack on the World Trade Center (WTC). On February 26, 1993, a car bomb exploded beneath one of the WTC towers, killing 6 and injuring over 1,000. The attack was limited in its devastation only because the attackers weren't able to acquire all the components for a coordinated bomb and cyanide gas attack.[2]

Still, this attack was a wake-up call for the hundreds of organizations that conducted business in the WTC. Many began asking, "What would we have done if the attack had been more successful?" As a direct result, many of the organizations occupying the WTC on September 11 had developed contingency plans. Although thousands of people lost their lives in the attack, many were able to evacuate, and many organizations were prepared to resume their businesses in the aftermath of the devastation.

In a Forrester survey called "The State of Disaster Recovery Preparedness," only about 55 percent of respondents were either prepared or very prepared to recover their data center in the event of a disaster or site failure, and only 54 percent had a formal enterprise disaster recovery program.[3] According to the Syncsort State of Resilience Report, "Nearly half of businesses experienced a failure requiring a high availability/disaster recovery solution to resume operations. 35% lost a few minutes to an hour of data, 28% lost a few hours and 31% lost a day or more."[4] According to the U.S. Federal Emergency Management Agency, between 40 and 60 percent of small businesses affected by a disaster either never reopen or go out of business following the event.[5] Thus, having a disaster recovery and business continuity plan is vital to sustaining operations when catastrophes strike. Considering the risks, it is imperative that management teams create, implement, train, and rehearse test plans to deal with incidents and disasters. For this reason, the importance of information security and contingency planning has been steadily growing and is now taken more seriously by senior management and boards of directors.

Before we can discuss contingency planning in detail, we must introduce some critical concepts, of which contingency planning is an integral part. The first of these, which serves as the overall disciplinary umbrella, is information security. This term refers to many interlinked programs and activities that work together to ensure the confidentiality, integrity, and availability of the information used by organizations. This includes steps to ensure the protection of organizational information systems, specifically during incidents and disasters. Because information security is a complex subject that includes risk management as well as information security policy, it is important to have an overview of that broad field and an understanding of these major components. That is the purpose of this first module. Contingency planning is an important element of information security, but before management can plan for contingencies, it should have an overall strategic plan for information security in place, including risk management processes to guide the appropriate managerial and technical controls.

This module serves as an overview of information security, with special consideration given to risk management and the role that contingency planning plays in (1) information security in general and (2) risk management in particular.

AN OVERVIEW OF INFORMATION SECURITY

In general, security means being free from danger. To be secure in this context is to be protected from the risk of loss, damage, unwanted modification, or other hazards. Achieving an appropriate level of security for an organization depends on the implementation of a multilayered system that works to protect information assets from harm, unwanted access, and modification. Security is often achieved by means of several strategies undertaken simultaneously or used in combination. Many of those strategies will focus on specific areas of security, but they also have many elements in common. It is the role of management to ensure that each strategy is properly planned, organized, staffed, directed, and controlled.

These efforts contribute to the information security program as a whole. This textbook derives its definition of information security from the standards published by the Committee on National Security Systems (CNSS), chaired by the U.S. Secretary of Defense. **Information security (InfoSec)** focuses on the protection of information and the characteristics that give it value, such as confidentiality, integrity, and availability. These characteristics, known as the **C.I.A. triad**, include the technology that stores, processes, and transmits information through a variety of protection mechanisms such as policy, training and awareness programs, and technology. This definition is illustrated in Figure 1-1.

Information assets have the characteristics of **confidentiality** when only the people, agents, or computer systems with the rights and privileges to access them are able to do so. Information assets have **integrity** when they are not exposed (while being stored, processed, or transmitted) to corruption, damage, destruction, or other disruption of their authentic states; in other words, the information is whole, complete, and uncorrupted. Finally, information assets have **availability** when authorized users, agents, or computer systems are able to access them in the specified format without interference or obstruction. In other words, the information is there when it is needed, it comes from an authentic source, and it is in the format expected.

Key Information Security Concepts

This book uses many terms and concepts that are essential to a discussion of information security. Some of these terms are illustrated in Figure 1-2; all are covered in greater detail in this and subsequent modules.

- *Access*—A subject or object's ability to use, manipulate, modify, or affect another subject or object. Authorized users have legal access to a system, whereas hackers must gain illegal access to a system. Access controls regulate this ability.
- *Asset*—The organizational resource that is being protected. An asset can be logical, such as a Web site, software information, or data. An asset can also be physical, such as a person, a computer system, hardware, or other tangible objects. Assets, particularly information assets, are the focus of what security efforts are attempting to protect.

information security (InfoSec)

Protection of the confidentiality, integrity, and availability of information assets, whether in storage, processing, or transmission, via the application of policy, education, training and awareness, and technology.

C.I.A. triad

The industry standard for computer security since the development of the mainframe. The standard is based on three characteristics that describe the utility of information: confidentiality, integrity, and availability.

confidentiality

An attribute of information that describes how data is protected from disclosure or exposure to unauthorized individuals or systems.

integrity

An attribute of information that describes how data is whole, complete, and uncorrupted.

availability

An attribute of information that describes how data is accessible and correctly formatted for use without interference or obstruction.

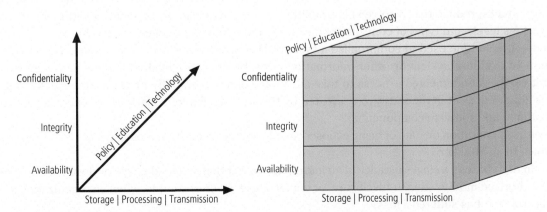

Figure 1-1 CNSS security model[6]

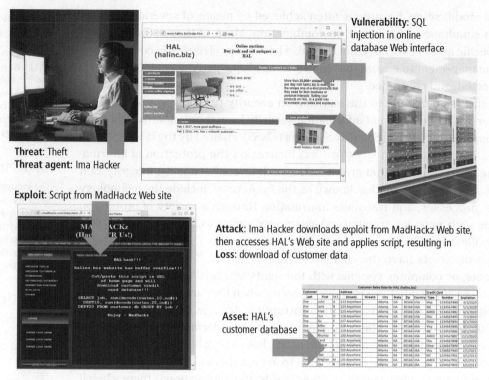

Figure 1-2   Key concepts in information security

Source: The photo at top left is from © iStock.com/TommL. The photo at top right is from © iStock.com/nerminmuminovic.

- *Attack*—An intentional or unintentional act that can damage or otherwise compromise information and the systems that support it. Attacks can be active or passive, intentional or unintentional, and direct or indirect. Someone who purposefully copies valuable data to re-sell commits an *active attack*, while a person who casually reads sensitive information not intended for his or her use is committing a *passive attack*. A hacker attempting to break into an information system is an *intentional attack*, while a lightning strike that causes a building fire is an *unintentional attack*. A *direct attack* is perpetrated by a hacker using a PC to break into a system, but an *indirect attack* is a hacker compromising a system in order to use it only to attack other systems—for example, as part of a botnet (slang for robot network). This group of compromised computers, running software of the attacker's choosing, can operate autonomously or under the attacker's direct control to attack systems and steal user information or conduct distributed denial-of-service attacks. Direct attacks originate from the threat itself. Indirect attacks originate from a compromised system or resource that is malfunctioning or working under the control of a threat.
- *Control, safeguard, or countermeasure*—Security mechanisms, policies, or procedures that can successfully counter attacks, reduce risk, resolve vulnerabilities, and otherwise improve security within an organization. The various levels and types of controls are discussed more fully in the following modules.
- *Exploit*—A technique used to compromise a system. This term can be a verb or a noun. Threat agents may attempt to exploit a system or other information asset by using it illegally for their personal gain. Or, an exploit can be a documented process to take advantage of a vulnerability or exposure, usually in software, that is either inherent in the software or created by the attacker. Exploits make use of existing software tools or custom-made software components.
- *Exposure*—A condition or state of being exposed; in information security, exposure exists when a vulnerability is known to an attacker.
- *Loss*—In this context, a single instance of an information asset that suffers damage or destruction, unintended or unauthorized modification or disclosure, or denial of use. As one example, when an organization's information is stolen, it has suffered a loss.
- *Risk*—The probability of an unwanted occurrence, such as an adverse event or loss. Organizations must minimize risk to match their risk appetite—the quantity and nature of the risk they are willing to accept.

- *Subjects and objects of attack*—A computer can be either the subject of an attack—an agent entity used to conduct the attack—or the object of an attack: the target entity. A computer can also be both the subject and object of an attack. For example, it can be compromised by an attack (object) and then used to attack other systems (subject).
- *Threat*—Any event or circumstance that has the potential to adversely affect operations and assets. The term *threat source* is commonly used interchangeably with the more generic term *threat*. The two terms are technically distinct, but to simplify the discussion, the text will continue to use the term *threat* to describe threat sources.
- *Threat agent*—The specific instance or a component of a threat. For example, the threat source of *trespass or espionage* is a category of potential danger to information assets, while an *external professional hacker* (like Kevin Mitnick, who was convicted of hacking into phone systems) is a specific threat agent. A lightning strike, hailstorm, or tornado is a threat agent that is part of the threat source known as *acts of God/acts of nature*.
- *Threat event*—An intentional or unintentional act that can damage or otherwise compromise information and the systems that support it. An example of a threat event might be damage caused by a storm. This term is commonly used interchangeably with the term *attack*.
- *Threat source*—A category of objects, people, or other entities that represents the origin of danger to an asset—in other words, a category of threat agents. Threat sources are always present and can be purposeful or undirected. For example, threat agent *hackers*, as part of the threat source *acts of trespass or espionage*, purposely threaten unprotected information systems, while threat agent *severe storms*, as part of the threat source *acts of God/acts of nature*, incidentally threaten buildings and their contents.
- *Vulnerability*—A potential weakness in an asset or its defensive control system(s). Some examples of vulnerabilities are a flaw in a software package, an unprotected system port, and an unlocked door. Some well-known vulnerabilities have been examined, documented, and published; others remain latent (or undiscovered).

The 12 Categories of Threats

Table 1-1 shows 12 general categories of threats that represent a clear and present danger to an organization's people, information, and systems. Each organization must prioritize the threats it faces based on the particular security situation in which it operates, its organizational strategy regarding risk, and the exposure levels of its assets. You may notice that many of the examples in the table could be listed in more than one category. For example, a theft performed by a hacker falls into the category of *theft*, but it can also be considered an example of *espionage or trespass* as the hacker illegally accesses the information. The theft may also be accompanied by defacement actions to delay discovery, qualifying it for the category of *sabotage or vandalism*.

Table 1-1   The 12 Categories of Threats to Information Security[7]

Category of Threat	Attack Examples
Compromises to intellectual property	Piracy, copyright infringement
Deviations in quality of service	Internet service provider (ISP), power, or WAN service problems
Espionage or trespass	Unauthorized access and/or data collection
Forces of nature	Fire, floods, earthquakes, lightning
Human error or failure	Accidents, employee mistakes
Information extortion	Blackmail, information disclosure
Sabotage or vandalism	Destruction of systems or information
Software attacks	Viruses, worms, macros, denial of service
Technical hardware failures or errors	Equipment failure
Technical software failures or errors	Bugs, code problems, unknown loopholes
Technological obsolescence	Antiquated or outdated technologies
Theft	Illegal confiscation of equipment or information

intellectual property (IP)

Original ideas and inventions created, owned, and controlled by a particular person or organization; IP includes the representation of original ideas.

software piracy

The unauthorized duplication, installation, or distribution of copyrighted computer software, which is a violation of intellectual property.

availability disruption

A reduced level of service in an element of the critical infrastructure.

service level agreement (SLA)

A document or part of a document that specifies the expected level of service from a service provider. An SLA usually contains provisions for minimum acceptable availability and penalties or remediation procedures for downtime.

noise

The presence of additional and disruptive signals in network communications or electrical power delivery.

faults

Short-term interruptions in electrical power availability.

spikes

Short-term increases in electrical power availability, also known as swells.

surges

Long-term increases in electrical power availability.

sags

Short-term decreases in electrical power availability.

brownouts

Long-term decreases in the quality of electrical power availability.

Compromises to Intellectual Property

Many organizations create or support the development of intellectual property (IP) as part of their business operations. Intellectual property can be trade secrets, proprietary processes, copyrights, trademarks, and patents. IP is protected by copyright and other laws, carries the expectation of proper attribution or credit to its source, and potentially requires the acquisition of permission for its use, as specified in those laws. For example, the use of a song in a movie or a photo in a publication may require a specific payment or royalty. The unauthorized appropriation of IP constitutes a threat to information security.

Employees may have access privileges to the various types of IP owned by the organization, including purchased and developed software and organizational information. Many employees typically need to use IP to conduct day-to-day business. Compromises to IP typically occur in two primary areas:

- *Software piracy*—Organizations often purchase or lease the IP of other organizations, and must abide by purchase or licensing agreements for its fair and responsible use. The most common IP breach is the unlawful use or duplication of software-based intellectual property, more commonly known as software piracy. Many individuals and organizations do not purchase software as mandated by the owner's license agreements.
- *Copyright protection and user registration*—A number of technical mechanisms—digital watermarks, embedded code, copyright or activation codes, and even the intentional placement of bad sectors on software media—have been used to enforce copyright laws. The most common tool is a unique software registration code in combination with an end-user license agreement (EULA) that is usually displayed during the installation of new software, requiring users to indicate that they have read and agree to conditions of the software's use.

Deviations in Quality of Service

An organization's information system depends on the successful operation of many interdependent support systems, including power grids, data and telecommunications networks, utilities, parts suppliers, service vendors, and even janitorial staff and garbage haulers. Any of these support systems can be interrupted by severe weather, employee illnesses, or other unforeseen events. Deviations in quality of service can result from accidents such as a backhoe taking out an ISP's fiber-optic link or other accidents or disruptions. The backup provider may be online and in service but may be able to supply only a fraction of the bandwidth the organization needs for full service. This degradation of service is a form of availability disruption. Irregularities in Internet service, communications, and power supplies can dramatically affect the availability of information and systems. Some of the subcategories of this threat include the following:

- *Internet service issues*—In organizations that rely heavily on the Internet and the Web to support continued operations, ISP failures can considerably undermine the availability of information. When an organization places its Web servers in the care of a Web hosting provider, that provider assumes responsibility for all Internet services and for the hardware and operating system software used to operate the Web site. These Web hosting services are usually arranged with a service level agreement (SLA).

- *Communications and other service provider issues*—Other utility services can affect organizations as well. Among these are telephone, water, wastewater, trash pickup, cable television, natural or propane gas, and custodial services.
- *Power irregularities*—Irregularities from power utilities are common and can lead to fluctuations such as power excesses, power shortages, and power losses. These fluctuations can pose problems for organizations that provide inadequately conditioned power for their information systems equipment. When power voltage levels vary from normal, expected levels, such as during a blackout, brownout, fault, noise, spike, surge, or sag, an organization's sensitive electronic equipment—especially networking equipment, computers, and computer-based systems, which are vulnerable to fluctuations—can be easily damaged or destroyed. Most good uninterruptible power supplies (UPS) can protect against faults, spikes, surges, sags, and even brownouts and blackouts of limited duration.

Espionage or Trespass

Espionage or trespass is a well-known and broad category of electronic and human activities that can breach the confidentiality of information. When an unauthorized person gains access to information an organization is trying to protect, the act is categorized as espionage or trespass. Attackers can use many different methods to access the information stored in an information system. Some forms of espionage are relatively low tech. One example, called shoulder surfing, is used in public or semipublic settings when people gather information they are not authorized to have. Another is *dumpster diving*, where adversaries rummage in refuse for valuable information. Acts of trespass can lead to unauthorized real or virtual actions that enable information gatherers to enter premises or systems without permission. Sound principles of authentication and authorization can help organizations protect valuable information and systems. These control methods and technologies employ multiple layers or factors to protect against unauthorized access and trespass.

The classic perpetrator of information espionage or trespass is the hacker, who spends long hours examining the types and structures of targeted systems and uses skill, guile, and/or fraud to attempt to bypass controls placed on information owned by someone else. Most hackers are grouped into two general categories—the *expert hacker* and the *novice hacker*. The expert hacker is usually a master of several programming languages, networking protocols, and operating systems, and exhibits a mastery of the technical environment of the chosen targeted system. A new category of expert hackers has emerged over the last decade. The professional hacker seeks to conduct attacks for personal benefit or the benefit of an employer, which is typically a crime organization or government-sponsored operation. The professional hacker should not be confused with the penetration tester, who has authorization from an organization to test its information systems and network defense and is expected to provide detailed reports of the findings. Novice hackers have little or no real expertise of their own but rely upon the skills of expert hackers, who often become dissatisfied with attacking systems directly and turn their attention to writing software. These programs are automated exploits that allow novice hackers to act as script kiddies, *mouse monkeys*, or packet monkeys.

After an attacker gains access to a system, the next step is to increase his or her privileges (privilege escalation). While most accounts associated with a system have only rudimentary "use" permissions and capabilities, the attacker needs administrative or "root" privileges.

blackouts
Long-term interruptions (outages) in electrical power availability.

trespass
Unauthorized entry into the real or virtual property of another party.

shoulder surfing
The direct, covert observation of individual information or system use.

hacker
A person who accesses systems and information without authorization and often illegally.

expert hacker
A hacker who uses an extensive knowledge of the inner workings of computer hardware and software to gain unauthorized access to systems and information. Also known as elite hackers, expert hackers often create automated exploits, scripts, and tools used by other hackers.

professional hacker
A hacker who conducts attacks for personal financial benefit or for a crime organization or foreign government. Not to be confused with a penetration tester.

penetration tester
An information security professional with authorization to attempt to gain system access in an effort to identify and recommend resolutions for vulnerabilities in those systems.

novice hackers
Relatively unskilled hackers who use the work of expert hackers to perform attacks. Also known as neophytes, n00bs, or newbies. This category of hackers includes script kiddies and packet monkeys.

script kiddies
Hackers of limited skill who use expertly written software to attack a system. Script kiddies are also known as skids, skiddies, or script bunnies.

packet monkeys

Script kiddies who use automated exploits to engage in denial-of-service attacks.

privilege escalation

The unauthorized modification of an authorized or unauthorized system user account to gain advanced access and control over system resources.

brute force password attack

An attempt to guess a password by trying every possible combination of characters and numbers in it.

dictionary password attack

A variation of the brute force password attack that attempts to narrow the range of possible passwords by using a list of common passwords and possibly including attempts based on the target's personal information.

rainbow table

A table of hash values and their corresponding plaintext values that can be used to look up password values if an attacker is able to steal a system's encrypted password file.

Password Attacks   Password attacks fall under the category of espionage or trespass, just as lock-picking falls under breaking and entering. Attempting to guess or reverse-calculate a password is often called *password cracking*. There are a number of alternative approaches to password cracking:

- *Brute force*—The application of computing and network resources to try every possible password combination is called a **brute force password attack**.
- *Dictionary attacks*—The **dictionary password attack**, or simply dictionary attack, is a variation of the brute force attack that narrows the field using a dictionary of common passwords and includes information related to the target user, such as names of relatives or pets, and familiar numbers such as phone numbers, addresses, and even Social Security numbers.
- *Rainbow tables*—A far more sophisticated and potentially much faster password attack is possible if the attacker can gain access to an encrypted password file, such as the Security Account Manager (SAM) data file. These files can be quickly searched against a repository of possible encryption values (the **rainbow table**), and the corresponding plaintext value can be located.
- *Social engineering password attacks*—Using an approach commonly referred to as *pretexting*, attackers posing as an organization's IT professionals may attempt to gain access to systems information by contacting low-level employees and offering to help with their computer issues.

Forces of Nature

Forces of nature, sometimes called *Acts of God* or *force majeure*, can present some of the most dangerous threats because they usually occur with little warning and are beyond the control of people. Some typical force of nature attacks include the following:

- *Fire*—The ignition of combustible material; damage can also be caused by smoke from fires or by water from sprinkler systems or firefighters.
- *Flood*—Water overflowing into an area that is normally dry, causing direct damage, and subsequent indirect damage from high humidity and moisture.
- *Earthquake*—A sudden movement of the earth's crust caused by volcanic activity or the release of stress accumulated along geologic faults.
- *Lightning*—An abrupt, discontinuous, natural electric discharge in the atmosphere, which can cause direct damage through an electrical surge or indirect damage from fires. Damage from lightning can usually be prevented with specialized lightning rods and by installing special electrical circuit protectors.
- *Landslide or mudslide*—The downward slide of a mass of earth and rock. Landslides or mudslides also disrupt operations by interfering with access to buildings.
- *Tornados or severe windstorms*—Violent wind effects in which air moves at destructively high speeds, causing direct damage and indirect damage from thrown debris. A tornado is a rotating column of whirling air that can be more than a mile wide. Wind shear is a much smaller and more linear wind effect, but it can have similarly devastating consequences.
- *Hurricanes, typhoons, and tropical depressions*—Severe tropical storms that commonly originate at sea and move to land, bringing excessive rainfall, flooding, and high winds.
- *Tsunami*—A very large ocean wave caused by an underwater earthquake or volcanic eruption; it can reach miles inland as it crashes into landmasses.
- *Electrostatic discharge (ESD)*—Also known as static electricity, and usually little more than a nuisance. However, an employee walking across a carpet on a cool, dry day can generate up to 12,000 volts of electricity, and sensitive electronics can suffer damage from as little as 10 volts.
- *Dust contamination*—Can dramatically reduce the effectiveness of cooling mechanisms and potentially cause components to overheat. Specialized optical technology, such as CD or DVD drives, can suffer failures due to excessive dust contamination inside systems.

Human Error or Failure

This category includes acts performed without intent or malicious purpose or in ignorance by an authorized user. When people use information systems, mistakes happen. Errors also happen when people fail to follow the established policy.

Human error or failure often can be prevented with training, ongoing awareness activities, and controls. These controls range from simple activities, such as requiring the user to type a critical command twice, to more complex procedures, such as verifying commands by a second party. Some common types of human error include the following:

- *Social engineering*—There are several social engineering techniques, which usually involve a perpetrator posing as a person who is higher in the organizational hierarchy than the victim.
- *Advance-fee fraud*—Another social engineering attack called the advance-fee fraud (AFF) involves schemes often using the names of legitimate companies, such as the Nigerian National Petroleum Company, to solicit information with the promise of large sums of money from a bank, government agency, long-lost relative, lottery, or other organization.
- *Phishing*—Some attacks are sent by e-mail and may involve schemes attempting to convince users that a valid organization needs their information. Phishing attacks use two primary techniques, often in combination with one another: URL manipulation and Web site forgery. In URL manipulation, attackers send an HTML–embedded e-mail message or a hyperlink whose HTML code opens a forged Web site. In Web forgery, the attacker copies the HTML code from a legitimate Web site and then modifies key elements.
- *Spear phishing*—While normal phishing attacks target as many recipients as possible, spear phishing involves an attacker sending a targeted message that appears to be from an employer, a colleague, or some other legitimate correspondent to a small group or even one person.
- *Pretexting*—Pretexting, sometimes referred to as phone phishing, is a pure social engineering attack in which the attacker calls a potential victim on the telephone and pretends to be an authority figure in order to gain access to private or confidential information.

Information Extortion

Information extortion, also known as *cyberextortion*, is common in the theft of credit card numbers. It involves the theft of information followed by a request for payment to the information's owner, with the threat of public release unless a demand is met. Recent information extortion attacks have involved specialized forms of malware known as ransomware. This attack is usually implemented with malware that is run on the victim's system as a result of phishing or spear-phishing attacks. (See the following section on software attacks.) The result is that the user's data is encrypted. Paying the adversary a ransom in a digital currency may or may not result in the victim receiving the encryption key to recover the data, which is why the U.S. Federal Bureau of Investigation (FBI) recommends not paying the ransom.[8]

In late 2015, ransomware took on a new level of danger. Prior to that time, organizations could reasonably assume that systems attacked by ransomware could be safely restored from backups, losing only hours or, at worst, days of data. In 2015, persistent and delayed ransomware attacks like those from Locky and Crypto were distributed that would either specifically target backups or remain dormant longer than had been previously seen, allowing the malware itself to be backed up with the rest of the organizations' data.[9] When the attack was triggered and the organizations' systems and data were locked up, recovery from backups only re-installed the ransomware.

---

social engineering

The process of using social skills to convince people to reveal access credentials or other valuable information to an attacker.

advance-fee fraud (AFF)

A form of social engineering, typically conducted via e-mail, in which an organization or some third party indicates that the recipient is due an exorbitant amount of money and needs only a small advance fee or personal banking information to facilitate the transfer. This may also involve prepayment for services with a payment larger than required; the overpayment is returned and then the initial payment is repudiated.

phishing

A form of social engineering in which the attacker provides what appears to be a legitimate communication (usually e-mail), but it contains hidden or embedded code that redirects the reply to a third-party site in an effort to extract personal or confidential information.

spear phishing

Any highly targeted phishing attack.

pretexting

A form of social engineering in which the attacker pretends to be an authority figure who needs information to confirm the target's identity, but the real object is to trick the target into revealing confidential information. Pretexting is commonly performed by telephone.

information extortion

The act of an attacker or trusted insider who steals information from a computer system and demands compensation for its return or for an agreement not to disclose the information. Also known as cyberextortion.

ransomware

Computer software specifically designed to identify and encrypt valuable information in a victim's system in order to extort payment for the key needed to unlock the encryption.

sextortion

A spear-phishing and blackmail attack that demands payment to preclude the distribution of hacked recordings of the target visiting pornographic Web sites.

hacktivists

Hackers who seek to interfere with or disrupt systems to protest the operations, policies, or actions of an organization or government agency. See also *cyberactivists*.

cyberactivists

See *hacktivists*.

cyberterrorism

The conduct of terrorist activities by online attackers.

malware

Computer software specifically designed to perform malicious or unwanted actions.

viruses

Types of malware that are attached to other executable programs. When activated, they replicate and propagate to multiple systems, spreading by multiple communications vectors. For example, a virus might send copies of itself to all users in the infected system's e-mail program.

worms

Types of malware that are capable of activation and replication without being attached to an existing program.

Trojan horses

Malware programs that hide their true nature and reveal their designed behavior only when activated.

polymorphic threat

Malware (a virus or worm) that over time changes the way it appears to antivirus software programs, making it undetectable by techniques that look for preconfigured signatures.

A relatively new attack combines the blackmail of information extortion with spear-phishing attacks and information stored on the "Dark Web" from previous attacks. Sextortion e-mails typically include old passwords found on hacker sites on the Web. The result is a detailed and personalized e-mail threatening revelation of alleged illegal or embarrassing information to the target's associates unless payment is provided.

Sabotage or Vandalism

This category of threat involves acts of vandalism or the deliberate sabotage of a computer system or business to destroy an asset or damage the image of an organization. These acts can range from petty vandalism by employees to organized sabotage against an organization. Organizations can minimize their risk of Web site defacement by backing up their Web sites regularly, closely monitoring their Web sites, and minimizing the use of exploitable software such as scripts, plug-ins, and other application programming interfaces (APIs).

The use of the Internet and Web has moved activism to the digital age:

- *Online activism*—In another form of online vandalism, hacktivists or cyberactivists are activists who hack into a target's online resource, such as e-mail or social media, and then release that information to the public.
- *Cyberterrorism and cyberwarfare*—A much more sinister form of hacking is cyberterrorism, which targets critical computing and communications networks as well as physical and power utility infrastructures. Cyberterrorism is typically conducted by enemies of the state, not individual hackers.
- *Positive online activism*—Not all online activism is negative. Social media outlets, such as Facebook, Twitter, Instagram, and YouTube, are commonly used to perform fundraising, raise awareness of social issues, gather support for legitimate causes, and promote involvement.

Software Attacks

Deliberate software attacks occur when an individual or group designs and deploys software to attack a system. This type of attack is usually part of a campaign that integrates a variety of tools as well as defined tactics, techniques, and procedures (TTP) to merge specially crafted software and social engineering methods that seek to trick users into installing computer code on their systems. After an infection occurs, the software leverages that foothold by attacking other systems that can be reached from the newly infected system. Attacking software agents usually try to spread to connected systems and then may attempt to steal information, become an agent of the attacker for other exploits, or encrypt users' data to be held for ransom (see the earlier discussion on ransomware).

There are several forms of software attacks:

- *Malware*—Malware is the most common form of software attack; it is also referred to as *malicious code* or *malicious software*. Malicious code attacks include the execution of viruses, worms, Trojan horses, and active Web scripts with the intent to destroy or steal information. A polymorphic threat is malware that is capable of evolving, changing its size or other characteristics to elude detection.
- *Back doors*—Using a known or newly discovered access mechanism, an attacker can gain access to a system or network resource through a

back door. Viruses and worms can have a payload that installs a back door or trap door component in a system, allowing the attacker to access the system at will with special privileges. Sometimes these doors are left behind by system designers or maintenance staff and are thus also referred to as a maintenance hook.

- *Denial-of-service (DoS) and distributed denial-of-service (DDoS) attacks*—In a denial-of-service (DoS) attack, the attacker sends a large number of connection or information requests to a target, overloading it and preventing it from responding to legitimate requests for service. The system may crash or simply become unable to perform ordinary functions. In a distributed denial-of-service (DDoS) attack, a coordinated stream of requests is launched against a target from many locations at the same time. DoS and DDoS attacks frequently take over a target and use it to attack other targets, turning the original system into a zombie or bot (short for robot).

- *E-mail attacks*—Unwanted e-mail, especially bulk commercial e-mail or spam, is a common problem for e-mail users. While many consider spamming a trivial nuisance rather than an attack, it has been used as a means of enhancing malicious code attacks. Although phishing attacks occur via e-mail, they are much more commonly associated with a method of social engineering designed to trick users to perform an action, rather than simply making the user a target of a DoS e-mail attack.

- *Communications interception attacks*—Common software-based communications attacks include four subcategories designed to intercept and collect information in transit. These types of attacks include packet (network) sniffers, spoofing, pharming, and man-in-the-middle attacks.

Technical Hardware Failures or Errors

Technical hardware failures or errors occur when a manufacturer distributes equipment containing a known or unknown flaw. These defects can cause the system to perform outside of expected parameters, resulting in unreliable service or lack of availability. Some errors are terminal—that is, they result in the unrecoverable loss of the equipment. Some errors are intermittent in that they only manifest themselves periodically, resulting in faults that are not easily repeated.

Technical Software Failures or Errors

Large quantities of computer code are written, debugged, published, and sold before all their bugs are detected and resolved. Sometimes, combinations of certain software and hardware reveal new failures that range from bugs to untested failure conditions. Sometimes these bugs are not errors, but purposeful shortcuts left by programmers for benign or malign reasons. Collectively, shortcut access routes into programs that bypass security checks are called trap doors, and they can cause serious security breaches.

Technological Obsolescence

Antiquated or outdated infrastructure that has had its level of support reduced or discontinued from the original manufacturer can lead to unreliable and untrustworthy systems. Management must recognize that when technology becomes outdated, there is a risk of losing data integrity from attacks. Management's strategic planning should always include an analysis of the technology currently in use. Ideally, proper planning by management should prevent technology from becoming obsolete, but when obsolescence is clear, management must take immediate action. IT professionals play a large role in the identification of probable obsolescence.

---

back door

A malware payload that provides access to a system by bypassing normal access controls. A back door is also an intentional access control bypass left by a system designer to facilitate development.

trap door

See *back door*.

maintenance hook

See *back door*.

denial-of-service (DoS) attack

An attack that attempts to overwhelm a computer target's ability to handle incoming communications, prohibiting legitimate users from accessing those systems.

distributed denial-of-service (DDoS) attack

A DoS attack in which a coordinated stream of requests is launched against a target from many locations at the same time using bots or zombies.

zombie

See *bot*.

bot

An abbreviation of *robot*, an automated software program that executes certain commands when it receives a specific input. See also *zombie*.

spam

Unsolicited commercial e-mail, typically advertising transmitted in bulk.

packet sniffers

Software programs or hardware appliances that can intercept, copy, and interpret network traffic.

network sniffers

See *packet sniffers*.

spoofing

A technique for gaining unauthorized access to computers using a forged or modified source IP address to give the perception that messages are coming from a trusted host.

pharming

The redirection of legitimate user Web traffic to illegitimate Web sites with the intent to collect personal information.

man-in-the-middle

A group of attacks whereby a person intercepts a communications stream and inserts himself in the conversation to convince each of the legitimate parties that the attacker is the other communications partner. Some man-in-the-middle attacks involve encryption functions.

theft

The illegal taking of another's property, which can be physical, electronic, or intellectual.

policy

In business, a statement of managerial intent designed to guide and regulate employee behavior in the organization; in IT, a computer configuration specification used to standardize system and user behavior.

information security policies

Written instructions provided by management that inform employees and others in the workplace about proper behavior regarding the use of information and information assets.

Theft

The threat of **theft** is a constant. The value of information is diminished when it is copied without the owner's knowledge. Physical theft can be controlled easily using a wide variety of measures, from locked doors to trained security personnel and the installation of alarm systems. Electronic theft, however, is a more complex problem to manage and control. When someone steals a physical object, the loss is easily detected; if it has any importance at all, its absence is noted. When electronic information is stolen, the crime is not always readily apparent. Theft is often an overlapping category with software attacks, espionage or trespass, information extortion, and compromises to intellectual property. A hacker or other individual threat agent could access a system and commit most of these offenses if they downloaded a company's information and then threatened to publish it if not paid.

Some or All of the Above

In today's complex attack environment, most threats do not manifest as a simple effort by only one of the categories listed in the previous sections. Rather, adversaries plan and execute sophisticated campaigns using any and all means of attack to achieve their ultimate objectives. The purpose of these categories is to provide a basis for understanding the threats rather than to pigeonhole each threat or attack exclusively.

 For one of the most concise treatments of what a business manager needs to know about information security, we recommend that you read the *Information Security Handbook: A Guide for Managers* from the National Institute of Standards and Technology (NIST). It provides a broad overview to assist managers in understanding how to establish and implement an information security program. You can find it at *https://csrc.nist.gov/publications/detail/sp/800-100/final*.

THE ROLE OF INFORMATION SECURITY POLICY IN DEVELOPING CONTINGENCY PLANS

Policy represents a formal statement of the organization's managerial philosophy—in the case of **information security policies**, the organization's InfoSec philosophy. The communities of interest within the organization (general management, information technology staff, and user managers) use policy to express their views regarding the security environment of the organization. This policy then becomes the basis for planning, operation, and maintenance of the InfoSec profile. Much of what must be done in CP should be guided by, and reinforce, InfoSec policies. In fact, the outcome of the typical CP process is often a new policy. This reinforces the need for proactive planning for employees and the organization. It also indicates that policy is needed to enforce certain requirements for the protection of information before, during, and after any situation requiring a contingency plan. To better understand this relationship, a brief review of key elements in the policy-making process is in order.

High-quality security programs begin and end with policy.[10] Because information security is primarily a management problem, not a technical one, policy obliges personnel to function in a manner that adds to the security of information assets rather than as a threat to those assets. Security policies are the least expensive control in that they involve only the time and effort of the management team to create, approve, and communicate, but they are the most difficult to implement properly. Shaping policy is difficult because it must never conflict with laws, must stand up in court if challenged, and must be properly administered through dissemination and documented acceptance.

Key Policy Components

After policies are designed, created, approved, and implemented, the technologies and procedures that are necessary to accomplish them can be designed, developed, and implemented. In other words, policies comprise a set of rules that dictate acceptable and unacceptable behavior within an organization. Policies should not specify the proper operation of equipment or software—this information should be placed in other documents called standards, procedures, practices, and guidelines. Policies define what you must do and not do, whereas the other documents focus on the *how*.

Policies must also specify the penalties for unacceptable behavior and define an appeals process. For example, an organization that prohibits the viewing of inappropriate Web sites in the workplace must implement a set of standards that clarifies and defines exactly what it means by "inappropriate," and what the organization will do to stop the behavior. In the implementation of an inappropriate-use policy, the organization might create a standard that all inappropriate content will be blocked and then list the material that is considered inappropriate. Later in the process, technical controls and their associated procedures might block network access to pornographic Web sites. Practices, procedures, and guidelines explain how employees are to comply with the policy. Figure 1-3 illustrates the relationship between policies, standards, practices, procedures, and guidelines.

Types of InfoSec Policies

To produce a complete InfoSec policy portfolio, management should define and implement three types of InfoSec policies:

- Enterprise information security policy (EISP)
- Issue-specific security policies (ISSP)
- Systems-specific security policies (SysSP)

 Another very useful document that covers the role of policy in the practice of information security is *An Introduction to Computer Security: the NIST Handbook* from the National Institute of Standards and Technology (NIST). You can find it at *https://csrc.nist.gov/publications/detail/sp/800-12/archive/1995-10-02*.

standards

Detailed statements of what must be done to comply with the policy, sometimes viewed as the rules governing policy compliance. If the policy states that employees must "use strong passwords, frequently changed," the standard might specify that the password "must be at least 10 characters, with at least one number, one uppercase letter, one lowercase letter, and one special character."

procedures

Step-by-step instructions designed to assist employees in following policies, standards, and guidelines. If the policy states to "use strong passwords, frequently changed," the procedure might advise that "in order to change your password, first click on the Windows Start button, then…."

practices

Examples of actions that illustrate compliance with policies. If the policy states to "use strong passwords, frequently changed," the practices might advise that "according to X, most organizations require employees to change passwords at least semiannually."

guidelines

Nonmandatory recommendations the employee may use as a reference in complying with the policy. If the policy states to "use strong passwords, frequently changed," the guidelines might advise that "we recommend you don't use family or pet names, or parts of your Social Security number, employee number, or phone number in your password."

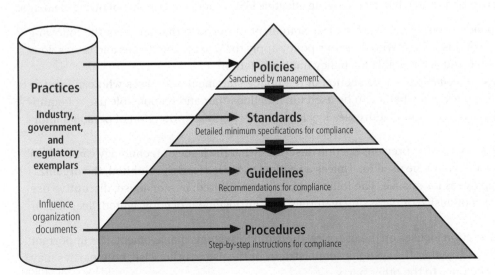

Figure 1-3   Policies, standards, practices, procedures, and guidelines

enterprise information security policy (EISP)

The high-level information security policy that sets the strategic direction, scope, and tone for all of an organization's security efforts. An EISP is also known as a security program policy, general security policy, IT security policy, high-level InfoSec policy, or simply an InfoSec policy.

issue-specific security policy (ISSP)

An organizational policy that provides detailed, targeted guidance to instruct all members of the organization in the use of a resource, such as one of its processes or technologies.

Enterprise Information Security Policy

An **enterprise information security policy (EISP)** is also known as a general security policy, IT security policy, or information security policy. The EISP is a policy based on and directly supportive of the mission, vision, and direction of the organization, and it sets the strategic direction, scope, and tone for all security efforts. The EISP is an executive-level document usually drafted by, or in cooperation with, the chief information officer of the organization. This policy is usually two to ten pages long and shapes the philosophy of security in the IT environment. The EISP does not usually require continuous modification unless there is a change in the strategic direction of the organization.

The EISP guides the development, implementation, and management of the security program. It contains the requirements to be met by the information security blueprint or framework. It defines the purpose, scope, constraints, and applicability of the security program in the organization. It also assigns responsibilities for the various areas of security, including systems administration, maintenance of the information security policies, and the practices and responsibilities of the users. Finally, it addresses legal compliance. According to NIST, the EISP typically addresses compliance by documenting the organizational structures put into place, describing the programs that have been developed, and reviewing the assignment of responsibilities and/or the use of specified penalties and disciplinary actions.[11]

When the EISP has been developed, the CISO (chief information security officer) begins forming the security team and initiating the necessary changes to the information security program.

Issue-Specific Security Policy

As an organization executes various technologies and processes to support routine operations, guidelines are needed to instruct employees to use these technologies and processes properly. In general, the **issue-specific security policy (ISSP)** addresses specific areas of technology and contains a statement about the organization's position on a specific issue. The ISSP requires frequent updating to keep it in alignment with changing technologies.

There are several approaches to creating and managing ISSPs, each with its own set of ISSP documents. Here are the three most common ones:

- Independent ISSP documents, each tailored to a specific issue
- A single comprehensive ISSP document covering all issues
- A modular ISSP document that unifies policy creation and administration while maintaining each specific issue's requirements

ISSPs vary from organization to organization, but in general, an effective ISSP should contain the following elements:

- *Statement of policy*—The policy should begin with a clear statement of purpose that answers the following questions: What is the scope of this policy? Who does this policy apply to? What technologies and issues does it address? Who is responsible and accountable for policy implementation?
- *Authorized access and usage of technology*—This section of the policy statement addresses who can use the technology governed by the policy and what it can be used for. It defines "fair and responsible use" of equipment and other organizational assets, and it addresses key legal issues, such as protection of personal information and privacy.
- *Prohibited usage of technology*—While the previous section describes what the issue or technology can be used for, this section outlines what it cannot be used for. Unless a particular use is clearly prohibited, the organization cannot penalize its employees for misuse. The following can be prohibited: personal use, disruptive use or misuse, criminal use, use of offensive or harassing materials, and infringement of copyrighted, licensed, or other intellectual property.
- *Systems management*—This section focuses on the users' relationship to systems management. It is important to designate all responsibilities to either the systems administrator or the users; otherwise, both parties may infer that the responsibility belongs to the other party.

- *Violations of policy*—This section contains not only the specifics of the penalties for each category of violation, but instructions on how individuals in the organization can report observed or suspected violations without fear of recrimination or retribution.
- *Policy review and modification*—The policy should contain procedures and a timetable for periodic review. This section contains a specific methodology for the review and modification of the policy to ensure that users do not begin circumventing it as it grows obsolete.
- *Limitations of liability*—This final section describes the limitations of the company's liability. It should state that if employees violate company policy or any law using company technologies, the company will not protect them and the company is not liable for their actions.

systems-specific security policies (SysSPs)

Organizational policies that often function as standards or procedures to be used when configuring or maintaining systems. SysSPs can be separated into two general groups—managerial guidance and technical specifications—but they may be written as a single unified SysSP document.

Systems-Specific Security Policy

While issue-specific policies are formalized as written documents, distributed to users, and agreed upon in writing, **systems-specific security policies (SysSPs)** are frequently codified as standards and procedures to be used when configuring or maintaining systems. SysSPs can be written as a combination of two components—managerial guidance and technical specifications. Organizations may write these as separate documents, or they may combine them into a single unified SysSP document.

- *Managerial guidance SysSP*—A managerial guidance SysSP is created by management to guide the implementation and configuration of technology, as well as to address the behavior of people in the organization in ways that support the security of information. These SysSPs are targeted at the technologists responsible for implementation and/or configuration, in order to ensure continuity of intent between management and IT.
- *Technical specification SysSP*—While a manager may work with a systems administrator to create managerial policy, as described in the previous section, the systems administrator may in turn need to create a different type of policy to implement the managerial policy. The manager is primarily responsible for creating the managerial specifications component of the SysSP, and sysadmins may be the primary authors or architects of the technical specification.

In many cases, simply creating a document with the final configuration of the security technology may meet the criteria for a tech-spec SysSP; when filed with the managerial version of the spec, it would meet the need for a comprehensive and well-documented SysSP.

Guidelines for Effective Policy Development and Implementation

How policy is developed and implemented can help or hinder its usefulness to the organization. If an organization decides to punish an employee for a policy violation, the individual(s) affected may sue the organization, depending on the action taken in implementing the penalties or other actions defined in the policy. Employees terminated for violating poorly designed and implemented policies could sue their organization for wrongful termination. In general, a policy is only enforceable and legally defensible if it is properly designed, developed, and implemented using a process that ensures repeatable results. One effective approach has six stages: development (writing and approving), dissemination (distribution), review (reading), comprehension (understanding), compliance (agreement), and uniform enforcement. Thus, for policies to be effective and legally defensible, they must be properly:

1. Developed using industry-accepted practices, and formally approved by management
2. Distributed using all appropriate methods
3. Read by all employees
4. Understood by all employees
5. Formally agreed to by act or affirmation
6. Uniformly applied and enforced

We will examine each of these stages in the sections that follow. But, before reading an explanation about developing policy, you should realize that almost every organization has a set of existing policies, standards, procedures, and/or practices. This installed base of guidance may not always have been prepared using an approach that delivers consistent or even usable results. Most of the situations you find yourself in will actually involve more policy maintenance than policy development. When maintaining policy, all of the complexity of the policy process described here may not be needed. But, when the policy maintenance project gets sufficiently large and complex, it might best be considered as policy redevelopment, and then most of the process described here can come into use. Also note that prior to implementation, a policy should be reviewed by the organization's legal counsel to ensure it is acceptable within the limits of the law and that implementation of the policy and its corresponding penalties would be defensible in the event of a legal dispute.

Developing Information Security Policy

It is often useful to view policy development as a three-part project. In the first part of the project, a policy is designed and written (or, in the case of an outdated policy, redesigned and rewritten). In the second part, a senior manager or executive at the appropriate level and the organization's legal counsel review and formally approve the document. In the third part of the development project, management processes are established to perpetuate the policy within the organization. The first part is an exercise in project management, and the latter two parts require adherence to good business practices and legal regulation.

Writing a policy is not always as easy as it seems. However, the prudent security manager always scours available resources (including the Web) for examples that may be adapted to the organization. Seldom will the manager find the perfect policy, ready to go. Some online sites sell blank policies that you can customize to your organization. In any event, the organization must respect the intellectual property of others when developing policy. If parts of another organization's policy are adapted, appropriate attribution must be made. Most policies contain a reference section where the author may list any policies used in the development of the current document. Even policies that are purchased from policy vendors or developed from a book on writing policies may require some level of annotation or attribution. It is recommended that any policies adapted from outside sources are thoroughly summarized to prevent the need for direct quotations, which can detract from the message the policy is attempting to convey—that "our organization" wants employees to be effective and efficient without undue distractions.

Policy Distribution

While it might seem straightforward, getting the policy document into the hands of employees can require a substantial investment by the organization in order to be effective. The most common alternatives are hard-copy distribution and electronic distribution. Hard copies involve either directly distributing a copy to the employee or posting the policy in a publicly available location. Posting a policy on a bulletin board or in some other public area may be insufficient unless another policy requires the employees to read the bulletin board on a specified schedule (daily, weekly, etc.). Distribution by internal or external mail may still not guarantee that individuals receive the document. Unless the organization can prove that the policy actually reached the end users, it cannot be enforced. Unlike in civil or criminal law, ignorance of an inadequately distributed policy is considered an acceptable excuse. Distribution of classified policies—those containing confidential internal information—requires additional levels of controls in the labeling of the document, in the dissemination and storage of new policy, and in the collection and destruction of older versions to ensure the confidentiality of the information contained in the policy documents.

Another common method of dissemination is by electronic means: e-mail, newsletter, intranet, or document management systems. Perhaps the easiest way is to post current and archived versions of policies on a secure intranet in HTML or PDF (Adobe Acrobat) form. The organization must still enable a mechanism to prove distribution, such as an auditing log for tracking when users access the documents. As an alternative delivery mechanism, e-mail has advantages and disadvantages. While it is easy to send a document to an employee and even track when the employee opens the e-mail, e-mail tracking may not be sufficient as proof that the employee downloaded and actually read any attached policies, and the document can get lost in an avalanche of spam, phishing attacks, or other unwanted e-mail. Perhaps the best method is electronic policy management software, which is described later in the "Policy Management" section. Electronic policy management software not only assists in the distribution of policy documents, it supports the development and assessment of comprehension.

Policy Reading

Barriers to employees reading policies can arise from literacy or language issues. A surprisingly large percentage of the workforce is considered functionally illiterate. In 2017, the U.S. Department of Education's National Center for Educational Statistics (NCES) conducted the Program for the International Assessment of Adult Competencies (PIAAC), which found that 19 percent of American adults between the ages of 16 and 65 scored at a "below basic" level in literacy.[12] Many jobs do not require literacy skills—for example, custodial staff, groundskeepers, or production line workers. Because such workers can still pose risks to InfoSec, however, they must be made familiar with policy even if it must be read to them. Visually impaired employees also require additional assistance, either through audio or large-type versions of the document.

The PIAAC findings translate into approximately 43 million U.S. adults with low literacy levels, "approximately 8.2 million of which could not even be tested due to a language barrier or a cognitive or physical inability to be interviewed."[13] The number of non-English-speaking residents in the United States continues to climb. However, language challenges are not restricted to organizations with locations in the United States. Multinational organizations also must deal with the challenges of gauging reading levels of foreign citizens. Simple translations of policy documents, while a minimum requirement, necessitate careful monitoring. Translation issues have long created challenges for organizations.

Policy Comprehension

A quote attributed to Confucius states: "Tell me and I forget; show me and I remember; let me do and I understand." In the policy arena, this means simply making certain that a copy of the policy gets to employees in a form they can review may not ensure that they truly understand what the policy requires of them. Bloom, Mesia, and Krathwohl define comprehension as "the ability to grasp the meaning of the material. [It] may be shown … to go one step beyond the simple remembering of material and represent the lowest level of understanding."[14]

To be certain that employees understand the policy, the document must be written at a reasonable reading level, with minimal technical jargon and management terminology. The readability statistics supplied by most productivity suite applications—such as Microsoft Word—can help determine the current reading level of a policy. The Flesch Reading Ease test evaluates writing on a scale of 1–100. The higher the score, the easier it is to understand the writing. For most corporate documents, a score of 60 to 70 is preferred. The Flesch-Kincaid Grade Level test evaluates writing on a U.S. grade-school level. For most corporate documents, a score of 7.0 to 8.0 is preferred.

The next step is to use some form of assessment to gauge how well employees understand the policy's underlying issues. Quizzes and other forms of examination can be employed to assess quantitatively which employees understand the policy by earning a minimum score (e.g., 70 percent), and which employees require additional training and awareness efforts before the policy can be enforced. Quizzes can be conducted in either hard-copy or electronic formats. The electronic policy management systems mentioned earlier can assist the assessment of employee performance on policy comprehension.

Policy Compliance

Policy compliance means the employee must agree to the policy. According to "Security Policy: From Design to Maintenance":

> *Policies must be agreed to by act or affirmation. Agreement by act occurs when the employee performs an action that requires them to acknowledge understanding of the policy prior to use of a technology or organizational resource. Network banners, end-user license agreements, and posted warnings can serve to meet this burden of proof. However, these in and of themselves may not be sufficient. Only through direct collection of a signature or the equivalent digital alternative can the organization prove that it has obtained an agreement to comply with policy, which also demonstrates that the previous conditions have been met.*[15]

What if an employee refuses explicitly to agree to comply with policy? Can the organization deny access to information that the individual needs to do his or her job? While this situation has not yet been adjudicated in the legal system, it seems clear that failure to agree to a policy is tantamount to refusing to work and thus may be grounds for termination. Organizations can avoid this dilemma by incorporating policy confirmation statements into employment contracts, annual evaluations, or other documents necessary for the individual's continued employment.

Policy Enforcement

The final component of the design and implementation of effective policies is uniform and impartial enforcement. As in law enforcement, policy enforcement must be able to withstand external scrutiny. Because this scrutiny may occur during legal proceedings—for example, in a civil suit contending wrongful termination—organizations must establish high standards of due care with regard to policy management. For instance, if policy mandates that all employees wear identification badges in a clearly visible location and select members of management decide they are not required to follow this policy, any actions taken against other employees will not withstand legal challenges. If an employee is punished, censured, or dismissed as a result of a refusal to follow policy and is subsequently able to demonstrate that the policies are not uniformly applied or enforced, the organization may find itself facing both punitive and compensatory damages.

One forward-thinking organization found a way to enlist employees in the enforcement of policy. After the organization had just published a new ID badge policy, the manager responsible for the policy was seen without his ID. One of his employees chided him in jest, saying, "You must be a visitor here, since you don't have an ID. Can I help you?" The manager smiled and promptly produced his ID, along with a $20 bill, which he presented to the employee as a reward for vigilant policy enforcement. Soon, the entire staff was routinely challenging anyone without a badge.[16]

Policy Management

Policies are living documents that must be nurtured, given that they are constantly changing and growing. They must be properly disseminated (distributed, read, understood, and agreed to) and managed. To remain viable, security policies must have the following:

- An individual (such as a policy administrator) responsible for the creation, revision, distribution, and storage of the policy; this person should solicit input from all communities of interest in policy development
- A schedule of reviews to ensure currency and accuracy, and to demonstrate due diligence
- A mechanism by which individuals can comfortably make recommendations for revisions, preferably anonymously
- A policy and revision date and possibly a "sunset" expiration date
- Optionally, policy management software to streamline the steps of writing the policy, tracking the workflow of policy approvals, publishing the policy after it is written and approved, and tracking when individuals have read the policy

The need for effective policy management has led to the emergence of a class of software tools that supports policy development, implementation, and maintenance. Sourceforge.net lists a number of policy management software applications (see *https://sourceforge.net/software/policy-management/*). Most share some common features. For example, after development, policies can be approved by management and then published for users to review. The organization can then add links to its training material and create and administer compliance quizzes. All material is electronic, meaning there is no need for hard-copy documents; several of these applications are hosted on the Web and not the company's intranet. In the event of an incident or disaster that disables internal computing infrastructure, critical policies can still be accessed as the organization works to recover. Organizations that are unable to purchase commercial software may want to consider an open source learning management tool like Moodle (*www.moodle.org*). Although Moodle was designed to support classes with students, it's a simple conversion to use the tool to upload policies and quizzes and track employee completion.

Policy Support for Contingency Planning

As you will note in the coming modules, the development of relevant policy is one of the first tasks of a planning team. As stated previously, policy guides the efforts of employees in following managerial intent. Policy guides everything from how employees should behave to how the organization should plan for and react to an incident or disaster. Without the guidance from policy, individual committee members may not sufficiently and efficiently provide detailed plans to support the organization's contingency operations.

OVERVIEW OF RISK MANAGEMENT

risk management (RM)
The entire program of planning for and managing risk to information assets in the organization.

One part of information security is **risk management**, which is the process of identifying and controlling the risks to an organization's information assets. All managers are expected to play a role in the risk management process, but information security managers are expected to play the largest roles. Very often, the chief information officer (CIO) will delegate much of the responsibility for risk management to the CISO.

Given that contingency planning is considered part of the risk management process, it is important to fully understand how risk management works and how contingency planning fits within that process. Risk management is the process of discovering and assessing the risks to an organization's operations and determining how those risks can be controlled or mitigated. This process involves discovering and understanding answers to some key questions with regard to the risk associated with an organization's information assets:

1. Where and what is the risk (risk identification)?
2. How severe is the current level of risk (risk analysis)?
3. Is the current level of risk acceptable (risk evaluation)?
4. What do I need to do to bring the risk to an acceptable level (risk treatment)?

The various components of risk management and their relationships to one another are shown in Figure 1-4.

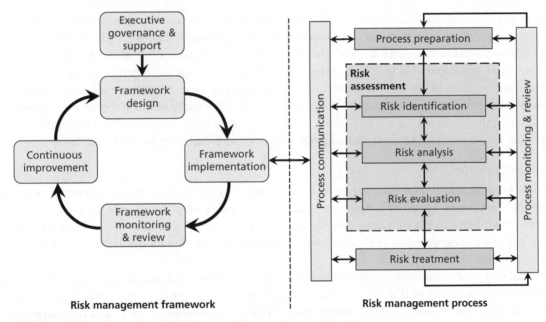

Figure 1-4   The risk management framework and process

Knowing Yourself and Knowing Your Enemy

As an aspiring information security professional, you will have a key role to play in risk management. As part of the management team within an organization, you may find yourself on the team that must structure the IT and information security functions to perform a successful defense of the organization's information assets—the information and data, hardware, software, procedures, and people. The IT community must serve the information technology needs of the broader organization and, at the same time, leverage the special skills and insights of the information security community. The information security team must lead the way with skill, professionalism, and flexibility as it works with the other communities of interest to appropriately balance the usefulness and security of the information system.

Looked at another way, risk management is the process of identifying vulnerabilities in an organization's information systems and taking carefully reasoned steps to ensure the confidentiality, integrity, and availability of all the components of those systems. Each of the three elements in the C.I.A. triad is an essential part of an organization's ability to sustain long-term competitiveness. When the organization depends on technical information systems to remain viable,

RM framework

The overall structure of the strategic planning and design for the entirety of the organization's RM efforts.

RM process

The identification, analysis, evaluation, and treatment of risk to information assets, as specified in the RM framework.

information security and the discipline of risk management move beyond theoretical discussions and become an integral part of the economic basis for making business decisions. These decisions are based on trade-offs between the costs of applying information systems controls and the benefits realized from the operation of secured, available systems.

An observation made over 2400 years ago by Chinese general Sun Tzu is relevant to information security today:

> *If you know the enemy and know yourself, you need not fear the result of a hundred battles. If you know yourself but not the enemy, for every victory gained you will also suffer a defeat. If you know neither the enemy nor yourself, you will succumb in every battle.*[17]

Consider for a moment the similarities between information security and warfare. Information security managers and technicians are the defenders of information. The many threats mentioned earlier are constantly attacking the defenses surrounding information assets. Defenses are built in layers, by placing safeguard upon safeguard. You attempt to detect, prevent, and recover from attack after attack. Moreover, organizations are legally prevented from switching to offense, and the attackers themselves have no need to expend their resources on defense. To be victorious, you must therefore know yourself and know the enemy.

Knowing Yourself

First, you must identify, examine, and understand the information and systems currently in place within your organization. To protect assets, which are defined here as information and the systems that use, store, and transmit information, you must understand what those assets are, how they add value to the organization, and to which vulnerabilities they are susceptible. After you know what you have, you can identify what you are already doing to protect it. Just because you have a control in place to protect an asset does not necessarily mean that the asset is protected. Frequently, organizations implement control mechanisms but then neglect to periodically perform the necessary review, revision, and maintenance of their own systems. The policies, education and training programs, and technologies that protect information must be carefully maintained and administered to ensure that they are still effective.

Knowing Your Enemy

After you know your organization's assets and weaknesses, you can move on to the other part of Sun Tzu's advice: Know the enemy. This means identifying, examining, and understanding all of the threats facing the organization. You must determine the threat aspects that most directly affect the organization and the security of its information assets. You can then use your understanding of these aspects to create a list of threats prioritized by how important each asset is to the organization.

It is essential that all stakeholders conduct periodic asset inventories. On a regular basis, management must verify the completeness and accuracy of the asset inventory. In addition, organizations must review and verify the threats and vulnerabilities that have been identified as dangerous to the asset inventory, as well as the current controls and mitigation strategies. The cost effectiveness of each control should be reviewed as well and the decisions on deployment of controls should be revisited. Furthermore, managers at all levels must regularly verify the ongoing effectiveness of every control that's been deployed. For example, a sales manager might assess control procedures by going through the office before the workday starts and picking up all the papers from every desk in the sales department. When the workers show up, the manager could inform them that a fire drill is under way—that all their papers have been destroyed and that each worker must now follow the disaster recovery procedures. The effectiveness of the procedures can then be assessed and corrections made.

Risk Management and the RM Framework

Risk management is a complex operation that requires a formal methodology. Figure 1-4 explores the entire approach to RM, which involves two key areas: the **RM framework** and the **RM process**. The RM framework is the overall structure of the strategic planning and design for the entirety of the organization's RM efforts. The RM process is the implementation of risk management, as specified in the framework. In other words, the RM framework (planning) guides the RM process (doing), which conducts the processes of risk assessment and risk treatment. The RM framework also assesses the RM process, which in turn assesses risk in the organization's information assets. The RM framework and the RM process are continuous improvement activities. That means they are ongoing, repetitive, and designed to continually assess current performance in order to improve future RM results. The RM framework repeatedly assesses and improves not only how the RM process is evaluating and reacting to risk, it also continuously assesses and improves how well the planning and review activities are being performed—the framework itself.

The left side of Figure 1-4 illustrates the major activities associated with the RM framework. As you have seen with other major InfoSec initiatives, this framework is developed and reviewed by an executive team led by a champion, and organized using effective project management methods. Organizations that have existing RM programs may be able to adapt their operations to the methodology shown here, with minimum impact on their current efforts. Organizations that do not have formal RM programs, or have programs that are unsuccessful, inefficient, or ineffective, need to begin the process from scratch. The RM framework consists of five key stages:

1. Executive governance and support
2. Framework design
3. Framework implementation
4. Framework monitoring and review
5. Continuous improvement

While this framework is provided as an example of how to perform risk management in the organization, it is not by any means the only way to conduct RM. Each organization must decide for itself what works best from the multiple options available. The model shown here is adapted to be in alignment with an ISO standard, while others are based on industry standards or proprietary models. It would not be difficult for an organization to take the general recommendations of this RM framework and process and adapt it to fit the details of another methodology. Only those involved in the process know what's best for their organizations.

Executive Governance and Support

The entire RM program begins with a formal acknowledgment by the organization's most senior governance group that risk management is invaluable and critical to the organization's long-term sustainability and viability. After acknowledging this strategic worth, the group formally commissions the development and eventual implementation of the RM project. This includes:

1. *Forming the RM framework team*, which will be responsible for completing all framework tasks and providing oversight of the process
2. *Supervising the development of the RM policy*, which guides all subsequent efforts
3. *Assigning key responsibilities* for policy, planning, and process team organization and efforts
4. *Developing and communicating priorities and objectives* to the RM team and its leader
5. *Providing resources* to support the RM process

Framework Design

The framework team begins designing the RM process by which the organization will understand its current levels of risk and determine what, if anything, it needs to do to bring them down to an acceptable level in alignment with the risk appetite specified earlier in the process. Designing the RM program means not only defining and specifying the detailed tasks to be performed by the framework team, but those to be performed by the process team. After the framework itself has been designed, most of the work of the framework team involves oversight of the process. Subordinate tasks in this stage include:

1. *Defining the organization's risk tolerance and risk appetite*—As the governance group communicates its intent to the RM framework development team, it also needs to communicate its general perspective

---

risk assessment

An approach to combining risk identification, risk analysis, and risk evaluation into a single strategy.

risk treatment

The selection of a strategy to address residual risk in an effort to bring it into alignment with the organization's risk appetite.

residual risk

The risk to information assets that remains even after current controls have been applied.

risk appetite

The quantity and nature of risk that organizations are willing to accept as they evaluate the trade-offs between perfect security and unlimited accessibility.

risk tolerance

The assessment of the amount of risk an organization is willing to accept for a particular information asset, typically synthesized into the organization's overall risk appetite.

risk threshold

See *risk tolerance*.

risk appetite statement

A formal document developed by the organization that specifies its overall willingness to accept risk to its information assets, based on a synthesis of individual risk tolerances.

risk management plan

A document that contains specifications for the implementation and conduct of RM efforts.

on what level of risk is acceptable and what risk must be reduced or resolved in some fashion. In other words, the RM framework team needs to understand and be able to determine whether the level of controls identified at the end of the risk process results in a level of risk that management can accept. The amount of risk that remains after all current controls are implemented is residual risk. The organization may very well reach this point in the RM process, examine the documented residual risk, simply state, "Yes, the organization can live with that," and then document everything for the next risk management review cycle. The difficulty lies in the process of formalizing exactly what the organization "can live with." This process is the heart of risk appetite. Documenting risk appetite as part of the RM framework development effort is often a vague and poorly understood proposition. A widely used approach to defining risk appetite involves understanding the organization's strategic objectives, defining risk profiles for each major current organizational activity and future strategic plan, defining a risk tolerance (or risk threshold) for each information asset or set of assets, and finally documenting the formal risk appetite statement.

2. *Developing the risk management plan*—The document that contains specifications for the implementation and conduct of the RM efforts is referred to as the risk management plan. The RM plan includes not only the specifications of the RM process but also of the RM framework. The plan is used to conduct the RM process, and is used in conjunction with the RM policy to guide the collection and evaluation of risk information. What is in the RM plan? It contains a detailed set of steps to perform in the conduct of both the RM framework and the RM process, along with supporting information on who performs each step and how. The RM policy focuses on the "who and why" of RM, and the plan is focused on the "who and how." Some organizations may combine the two into a single cohesive document; however, they should be kept separate to better support maintenance and review. The organization typically refers to the developed framework as the plan because it represents the formal documentation of the framework's concepts.

Framework Implementation

After the framework team has finished designing the RM program (framework and process), it begins implementing the program. As with any major project, this involves specifying the project manager for the process and laying out the detailed implementation methodology. The RM process, which is specified in the right half of Figure 1-4, provides general steps to follow in the conduct of risk evaluation and remediation, and is designed to be intentionally vague so it can be adapted to any one of the methodologies available. It is important for the RM framework team to carefully monitor, communicate, and review the implementation so it can detect and address issues before they become threatening to the viability of the program, as discussed in the next section.

Framework Monitoring and Review

After the initial implementation and as the RM effort proceeds, the framework team continues to monitor the conduct of the RM process while simultaneously reviewing the utility and relative success of the framework planning function itself. In the first few iterations, the framework team will examine how successful it was in designing and implementing the RM framework, plan, and RM process, and what issues required adjustments of the plan.

After the RM process is implemented and operating, the framework team is primarily concerned with the monitoring and review of the overall RM process cycle. However, until the framework and plan are implemented and operational, the framework team is also concerned with oversight of the RM framework and plan. The governance group also expects regular feedback on the entire RM program, including information about the relative success and progress of both the framework and process activities.

Continuous Improvement

Continuous improvement is the process of implementing a formal program designed to continuously review and improve any type of organizational effort. Using the methodologies described in Figure 1-4, the organization formalizes its commitment to review the RM plan (both the framework and process) on a regular, recurring basis, to continuously compare outcomes from past and current performance against the desired outcomes, and to make any needed changes to keep the project working toward those desired outcomes. The difference between current outcomes and the ideal outcomes envisioned is commonly referred to as the gap; the assessment between the two is known as a gap analysis.

The performance measures implemented in the RM process provide the data used to assess the performance outcome of the overall RM effort. As the team continues to assess the performance of the RM effort, it can adjust the plans for future RM cycles to improve past performance and increase the probability of success of future iterations.

The RM Process

During the implementation phase of the RM framework, the RM plan guides the implementation of the RM process, in which risk evaluation and remediation of key assets are conducted. The process includes the following tasks:

- Establishing the *context*, which includes understanding both the organization's internal and external operating environments and other factors that could impact the RM process.
- Identifying risk, which includes:
  - Creating an inventory of information assets
  - Classifying and organizing those assets meaningfully
  - Assigning a value to each information asset
  - Identifying threats to the cataloged assets
  - Pinpointing vulnerable assets by tying specific threats to specific assets
- Analyzing risk, which includes:
  - Determining the likelihood that vulnerable systems will be attacked by specific threats
  - Assessing the relative risk facing the organization's information assets, so that risk management and control activities can focus on assets that require the most urgent and immediate attention
  - Calculating the risks to which assets are exposed in their current setting
  - Looking in a general way at controls that might come into play for identified vulnerabilities and ways to control the risks that the assets face
  - Documenting and reporting the findings of risk identification and assessment
- Evaluating the risk to the organization's key assets and comparing identified uncontrolled risks against its risk appetite:
  - Identifying individual risk tolerances for each information asset
  - Combining or synthesizing these individual risk tolerances into a coherent risk appetite statement
- Treating the unacceptable risk:
  - Determining which treatment/control strategy is best considering the value of the information asset and which control options are cost effective
  - Acquiring or installing the appropriate controls
  - Overseeing processes to ensure that the controls remain effective
- Summarizing the findings, which involves stating the conclusions of the identification, analysis, and evaluation stages of risk assessment in preparation for moving into the stage of controlling risk by exploring methods to further mitigate risk where applicable or desired

RM Process Preparation—Establishing the Context

As the RM process team convenes, it is initially briefed by representatives of the framework team, and possibly by the governance group. These groups seek to provide executive guidance for the work to be performed by the RM process team, and to ensure that the team's efforts are in alignment with managerial intent, as documented in the RM policy and plan. The group is briefed on its responsibilities and set to its work. The plan is reviewed and individual assignments given.

risk identification

The recognition, enumeration, and documentation of risks to an organization's information assets.

information asset

Within the context of risk management, any collection, set, or database of information or any asset that collects, stores, processes, or transmits information of value to the organization. Here, the terms *data* and *information* are interchangeable.

media

Hardware, integral operating systems, and utilities that collect, store, process, and transmit information.

The *context* in this phase is the understanding of the external and internal environments the RM team will be interacting with as it conducts the RM process. It also means understanding the RM process as defined by the framework team and having the internal knowledge and expertise to implement it. Finally, it means ensuring that all members of the RM process team understand the organization's risk appetite statement and are able to use the risk appetite to translate that statement into the appropriate risk treatment when the time comes.

NIST's Special Publication 800-30, Rev. 1, "Guide for Conducting Risk Assessments," recommends preparing for the risk process by performing the following tasks:

- Identify the purpose of the assessment;
- Identify the scope of the assessment;
- Identify the assumptions and constraints associated with the assessment;
- Identify the sources of information to be used as inputs to the assessment; and
- Identify the risk model and analytic approaches (i.e., assessment and analysis approaches) to be employed during the assessment.[18]

Understanding the *external context* means understanding the impact that external factors could have on the RM process, its goals, and its objectives. These factors include the business environment, the legal, regulatory, and compliance environment, the threat environment, and the support environment. Understanding the *internal context* involves understanding a number of internal factors that could impact or influence the RM process, such as the organization's governance structure (or lack thereof), internal stakeholders, the organization's culture, the level of maturity of the organization's information security program, and the organization's experience in policy, planning, and risk management in general.

Risk Assessment: Risk Identification

The first operational phase of the RM process is the identification of risk. **Risk identification** begins with the process of self-examination. As Sun Tzu stated, the organization must know itself in order to understand the risk to its information assets and where that risk resides. At this stage, managers must (1) identify the organization's information assets, (2) classify them, (3) categorize them into useful groups, and (4) prioritize them by overall importance. This can be a daunting task, but it must be done to identify weaknesses and the threats they present.

The RM process team has to initially confirm or define the categories and classifications to be used for the information assets after they have been identified. Some organizations prefer to collect the inventory first and then see what natural categories and classifications emerge; those areas are discussed later in this module.

Identification of Information Assets   After the risk management team has been formally organized, it begins with the first major task of risk identification. The process begins with the identification and cataloging of *information assets*, including people, procedures, data, software, hardware, and networking elements. This step should be done without prejudging the value of each asset; values will be assigned later in the process.

One of the toughest challenges in the RM process is identifying information assets with precision for the purposes of risk management. In the most general sense, an **information asset** is any asset that collects, stores, processes, or transmits information, or any collection, set, or database of information that is of value to the organization. For these purposes, the terms *data* and *information* are commonly used interchangeably. In some RM efforts, the information and its supporting technology—hardware, software, data, and personnel—are defined separately, and the decision whether to include a specific category or component is made by the RM process team.

Some commercial RM applications simplify the decision by separating information assets from **media**. Media in this context include hardware, integral operating systems, and utilities that collect, store, process, and transmit information, leaving only the data and applications designed to directly interface with the data as information assets for the purposes of RM. When the application interfaces with an external database or data file (data set), each is treated as a separate, independent information asset. When an application has data that is integral to its operations, it is treated as a single information asset.

For organizations that distinguish between information assets and the media used to access the information, it is important to specify that access. Several applications provide an assessment of the general vulnerabilities that may arise from using various media in association with information assets.

By separating components that are much easier to replace (hardware and operating systems) from the information assets that are in some cases almost irreplaceable, the RM effort becomes much more straightforward. After all, what is the organization most concerned with? Is it the physical server used to host a critical application? Or, is it the application and its data? Servers, switches, routers, and most host technologies are relatively interchangeable. If a server dies, the organization simply replaces it, and then reloads the applications and data that give the server purpose in the organization. If an application dies, the replacement may take a much more substantial effort than simply re-installing an off-the-shelf application. Most core applications are heavily customized or even custom developed for a particular purpose. This is not to insinuate that some assets don't have value to the organization, but they might not necessarily be integral to an RM program.

Some organizations choose to focus narrowly on their initial RM process, then add information assets in later iterations. They may begin with data and core applications, then add communications software, operating systems, and supporting utilities, and finally add physical assets. The bottom line is that the RM process team should decide and define exactly what constitutes an information asset for the purposes of the RM effort, so it can effectively and efficiently manage the scope and focus of the effort. Table 1-2 shows a model outline of some information assets the organization may choose to incorporate into its RM effort. These assets are categorized as follows:

- The people asset can be divided into internal personnel (employees) and external personnel (nonemployees). Insiders can be further divided into employees who hold trusted roles and therefore have correspondingly greater authority and accountability, and regular staff members who do not have any special privileges. Outsiders consist of other users who have access to the organization's information assets; some outsiders are trusted and some are untrusted.

Table 1-2   Organizational Assets Used in Systems

Information System Components	Risk Management Components	Example Risk Management Components
People	Internal personnel	Trusted employees
	External personnel	Other staff members
		People we trust outside our organization
		Strangers
Procedures	Procedures	IT and business-standard procedures
		IT and business-sensitive procedures
Data	Data/information	Transmission
		Processing
		Storage
Software	Software	Applications
		Operating systems
		Utilities
		Security components
Hardware	Hardware	Systems and peripherals
		Security devices
		Network-attached process control devices and other embedded systems (Internet of Things)
Networking	Networking	Local area network components
		Intranet components
		Internet or extranet components
		Cloud-based components

data classification scheme

A formal access control methodology used to assign a level of confidentiality to an information asset and thus restrict the number of people who can access it.

- Procedures can be information assets because they are used to create value for the organization. They can be divided into (1) IT and business standard procedures and (2) IT and business-sensitive procedures. Sensitive procedures have the potential to enable an attack or to otherwise introduce risk to the organization. For example, the procedures used by a telecommunications company to activate new circuits pose special risks because they reveal aspects of the inner workings of a critical process, which can be subverted by outsiders for the purpose of obtaining unbilled, illicit services.

- The data asset includes information in all states: transmission, processing, and storage. This is an expanded use of the term "data," which is usually associated with data sets and databases, as well as the full range of information used by modern organizations.

- Software can be divided into applications, operating systems, utilities, and security components. Software that provides security controls may fall into the operating systems or applications category but is differentiated by the fact that it is part of the InfoSec control environment and must therefore be protected more thoroughly than other systems components.

- Hardware can be divided into (1) the usual systems devices and their peripherals and (2) the devices that are part of InfoSec control systems. The latter must be protected more thoroughly than the former.

- Networking components can include networking devices (such as firewalls, routers, and switches) and the systems software within them, which is often the focal point of attacks, with successful attacks continuing against systems connected to the networks. Of course, most of today's computer systems include networking elements. You will have to determine whether a device is primarily a computer or primarily a networking device. A server computer that is used exclusively as a proxy server or bastion host may be classified as a networking component, while an identical server configured as a database server may be classified as hardware. For this reason, networking devices should be considered separately rather than combined with general hardware and software components.

In some corporate models, this list may be simplified into three groups: People, Processes, and Technology. Regardless of which model is used in the development of risk assessment methods, an organization should ensure that all of its information resources are properly identified, assessed, and managed for risk.

As mentioned previously, the entire set of assets in some risk management programs is divided into RM information assets, such as applications, application-based data, other independent data sets or collections, and media—essentially anything that can collect, store, process, or transmit data. The media are used for grouping access to the asset, but are not valued and evaluated as a critical function of the risk identification step. The simplistic approach may be best for organizations just starting out in RM.

Classifying and Categorizing Information Assets   After the initial inventory is assembled, you must determine whether its asset categories are meaningful to the organization's risk management program. Such a review may cause managers to further subdivide the categories presented in Table 1-2 or create new categories that better meet the needs of the risk management program.

The inventory should also reflect the sensitivity and security priority assigned to each information asset. A **data classification scheme** should be developed (or reviewed, if already in place) that categorizes these information assets based on their sensitivity and security needs. Consider the following classification scheme for an information asset: confidential, internal, and public. Each of these classification categories designates the level of protection needed for a particular information asset. Some asset types, such as personnel, may require an alternative classification scheme that identifies the InfoSec processes used by the asset type.

As you would expect, organizations that need higher levels of security, including certain government agencies, will have very complex data classification schemes. For most organizations, there need be no distinction between multiple levels of information that need security protections, and a simple three-layer *public-internal-confidential* model is sufficient. For organizations that need higher levels of security for very sensitive data, such as that in research and development (R&D), additional levels might be needed.

Classification categories must be *comprehensive* and *mutually exclusive*. "Comprehensive" means that all inventoried assets fit into a category; "mutually exclusive" means that each asset is found in only one category. For example, an organization may have a public key infrastructure certificate authority, which is a software application that provides cryptographic key management services. Using a purely technical standard, a manager could categorize the application in the asset list of Table 1-2 as software, a general grouping with no special classification priority. Because the certificate authority must be carefully protected as part of the InfoSec infrastructure, it should be categorized into a higher-priority classification, such as software/security component/cryptography, and it should be verified that no overlapping category exists, such as software/security component/PKI.

Assessing Value in Information Assets As each information asset is identified, categorized, and classified, a relative value must be assigned to it. Relative values are comparative judgments intended to ensure that the most valuable information assets are given the highest priority when managing risk. It may be impossible to know in advance—in absolute economic terms—what losses will be incurred if an asset is compromised; however, a relative assessment helps to ensure that the higher-value assets are protected first.

As each information asset is assigned to its proper category, posing the following basic questions can help you develop the weighting criteria to be used for information asset valuation or impact evaluation.

- Which information asset is the most critical to the success of the organization?
- Which information asset generates the most revenue?
- Which information asset generates the highest profitability?
- Which information asset is the most expensive to replace?
- Which information asset is the most expensive to protect?
- Which information asset's loss or compromise would be the most embarrassing or cause the greatest liability?

You can use a worksheet, such as the one shown in Figure 1-5, to collect the answers to the preceding list of questions for later analysis.

You may also need to identify and add other institution-specific questions to the evaluation process. Throughout this module, numbers are assigned to example assets to illustrate the concepts being discussed. This highlights one of the challenging issues in risk management. While other industries use actuarially derived sources to make estimates, InfoSec risk management lacks such data. Many organizations use a variety of estimating methods to assess values. Some in the industry question the use of "guesstimated" values in calculations with other estimated values, claiming this degree of uncertainty undermines the entire risk management endeavor. A simplistic method that can be used to value an information asset by determining its "importance" is to simply rank each item on a scale of 1 = not important to 5 = critically important.

System Name: SLS E-Commerce
Date Evaluated: February 2018
Evaluated By: D. Jones

Information assets	Data classification	Impact to profitability
Information Transmitted:		
EDI Document Set 1 — Logistics BOL to outsourcer (outbound)	Confidential	High
EDI Document Set 2 — Supplier orders (outbound)	Confidential	High
EDI Document Set 2 — Supplier fulfillment advice (inbound)	Confidential	Medium
Customer order via SSL (inbound)	Confidential	Critical
Customer service Request via e-mail (inbound)	Private	Medium
DMZ Assets:		
Edge Router	Public	Critical
Web server #1 — Home page and core site	Public	Critical
Web server #2 — Application server	Private	Critical

Notes: BOL: Bill of Lading
DMZ: Demilitarized Zone
EDI: Electronic Data Interchange
SSL: Secure Sockets Layer

Figure 1-5 Sample asset classification scheme

Prioritizing (Rank Ordering) Information Assets The final step in the risk identification process is to prioritize, or rank order, the assets. This goal can be achieved by using a weighted table analysis similar to the one shown in Table 1-3. In this process, each information asset is listed in the first column. Next, the relevant criteria that the organization wants to use to value the assets are listed in the top row. Next, each criterion is assigned a weight or value that typically sums to 1.0, 10, 100, or some other value that is easy to sum. The use of these weights is what gives this analysis its name. Next, the organization assigns a value to each asset, again using a scale of 0–1.0, 0–10, or 0–100, based on the particular value criteria. Table 1-3 uses values from 0.1 to 1.0. Finally, each information asset's cell values are multiplied by the criteria weights and then summed to create the weighted score for that information asset. Sorting the table by the weighted score results in a prioritized list of information assets. Such tables can be used as a method

Table 1-3 Example of Information Assets in a Weighted Factor Analysis Worksheet

Information Asset	Criterion 1: Impact on Revenue	Criterion 2: Impact on Profitability	Criterion 3: Impact on Public Image	Weighted Score
Criterion weight (1–100); must total 100	30	40	30	100
EDI Document Set 1— Logistics bill of lading to outsourcer (outbound)	0.8	0.9	0.5	75
EDI Document Set 2— Supplier orders (outbound)	0.8	0.9	0.6	78
EDI Document Set 2— Supplier fulfillment advice (inbound)	0.4	0.5	0.3	41
Customer order via SSL (inbound)	1	1	1	100
Customer service request via e-mail (inbound)	0.4	0.4	0.9	55

Note: In the table, EDI = Electronic Data Interchange and SSL = Secure Sockets Layer.

threat assessment

An evaluation of the threats to information assets, including a determination of their likelihood of occurrence and potential impact of an attack.

of valuing information assets by ranking various assets based on criteria specified by the organization. This method may prove to be much more straightforward than a raw estimation based on some other more ambiguous assessment.

Threat Assessment As mentioned earlier in this section, the ultimate goal of risk identification is to assess the circumstances and setting of each information asset to reveal any vulnerabilities. Armed with a properly classified inventory, you can assess potential weaknesses in each information asset—a process known as **threat assessment**. As discussed earlier in this module, any organization typically faces a wide variety of threats. If you assume that every threat can and will attack every information asset, then the project scope becomes too complex. To make the process less unwieldy, each step in the threat identification and vulnerability identification processes is managed separately and then coordinated at the end. At every step, the manager is called on to exercise good judgment and draw on experience to make the process function smoothly.

Each of the threats listed in Table 1-1 presents a unique challenge to InfoSec and must be handled with controls that directly address the particular threat and the threat agent's attack strategy. Before threats can be assessed in the risk identification process, however, each threat must be further examined to determine its potential to affect the targeted information asset. In general, this process is referred to as threat assessment.

Not all threats endanger every organization, of course. It is unlikely that an organization can eliminate an entire category of threats, but doing so speeds up the threat assessment process. The amount of danger posed by a threat is sometimes difficult to assess. It may be tied to the probability that the threat will attack the organization, or it may reflect the amount of damage that the threat could create or the frequency with which the attack may occur. The big question every organization wants to answer is: "Which threats represent the greatest danger to our information assets in our current environment?" Posing the following questions can help you find an answer by understanding the various threats the organization faces and their potential effects on an information asset:

- Which threats represent an actual danger to our information assets?
- Which threats are internal and which are external?
- Which threats have the highest probability of occurrence?
- Which threats have the highest probability of success?
- Which threats could result in the greatest loss if successful?
- Which threats is the organization least prepared to handle?
- Which threats cost the most to protect against?
- Which threats cost the most to recover from?

As you will discover later in this module, you can use both quantitative and qualitative measures to rank values. The preceding questions can be used as categories in a weighted table analysis of threats, similar to the asset analysis described earlier in this module. Because information in this case is preliminary, the organization may simply want to identify threats that top the list for each question.

The preceding list of questions may not cover everything that affects risk assessment. An organization's specific guidelines or policies should influence the process and will inevitably require that some additional questions be answered.

Just as it did with information assets, the organization should conduct a weighted table analysis with threats. The organization should list the categories of threats it faces, and then select categories that correspond to the questions of interest described earlier. Next, it assigns a weighted value to each question category, and finally it assigns a value to each threat with respect to each question category. The result is a prioritized list of threats the organization can use to determine the relative severity of each threat facing its assets. In extreme cases, the organization may want to perform such an assessment of each threat by asset, if the severity of each threat is different depending on the nature of the information asset under evaluation.

Vulnerability Assessment   After the organization has identified and prioritized both its information assets and the threats facing those assets, it can begin to compare information assets to threats. This review leads to the creation of a list of vulnerabilities that remain potential risks to the organization. What are vulnerabilities? They are specific avenues that threat agents can exploit to attack an information asset. In other words, they are chinks in the asset's armor—a flaw or weakness in an information asset, security procedure, design, or control that can be exploited accidentally or on purpose to breach security.

A list should be created for each information asset to document its vulnerability to each possible or likely attack. This list is usually long and shows all the vulnerabilities of the information asset. Some threats manifest themselves in multiple ways, yielding multiple vulnerabilities for the asset-threat pair. Of necessity, the process of listing vulnerabilities is somewhat subjective and is based on the experience and knowledge of the people who create the list. Therefore, the process works best when groups of people with diverse backgrounds work together in a series of brainstorming sessions. For instance, the team that reviews the vulnerabilities for networking equipment should include networking specialists, the systems management team that operates the network, InfoSec risk specialists, and even technically proficient users of the system.

The TVA Worksheet   At the end of the risk identification process, an organization should have (1) a prioritized list of assets and (2) a prioritized list of threats facing those assets. Prioritized lists should be developed using a technique like the weighted table analysis discussed earlier.

The organization should also have a working knowledge of the vulnerabilities that exist between each threat and each asset. The lists serve as the starting point for the next step in the risk management process: risk assessment. The prioritized lists of assets and threats can be combined into a Threats-Vulnerabilities-Assets (TVA) worksheet, in preparation for the addition of vulnerability and control information during risk assessment. Along one axis lies the prioritized set of assets. Table 1-4 shows the placement of assets along the horizontal axis, with the most important asset at the left. The prioritized list of threats is placed along the vertical axis, with the most important or most dangerous threat listed at the top. The resulting grid provides a convenient method of examining the "exposure" of assets, allowing a simple vulnerability assessment. We now have a starting point for our risk assessment, along with the other documents and forms.

Before you begin the risk analysis process, it may be helpful to create a list of the TVA "triples" to facilitate your examination of the severity of the vulnerabilities. For example, between Threat 1 and Asset 1 there may or may not be a vulnerability. After all, not all threats pose risks to all assets. If a pharmaceutical company's most important asset is its research and development database and that database resides on a stand-alone network (i.e., one that is not connected to the Internet), then there may be no vulnerability to external hackers. If the intersection of T1 and A1 has no vulnerability, then the risk assessment team simply crosses out that box. It is much more likely, however, that one or more vulnerabilities exist between the two, and as these vulnerabilities are identified, they are categorized as follows:

> T1V1A1—Vulnerability 1 that exists between Threat 1 and Asset 1
> T1V2A1—Vulnerability 2 that exists between Threat 1 and Asset 1
> T2V1A1—Vulnerability 1 that exists between Threat 2 and Asset 1 . . .
> and so on.

In the risk analysis phase discussed in the next section, not only are the vulnerabilities examined, but the assessment team also analyzes any existing controls that protect the asset from the threat or mitigate the losses that may occur. Cataloging and categorizing these controls is the next step in the risk identification process.

Table 1-4   The TVA Worksheet

	Asset 1	Asset 2	Asset 3	...	...	...	...	...	...	Asset n
Threat 1	T1V1A1 T1V2A1 T1V3A1 ...	T1V1A2 T1V2A2 ...	T1V1A3 ...	T1V1A4 ...						
Threat 2	T2V1A1 T2V2A1 ...	T2V1A2 ...	T2V1A3 ...							
Threat 3	T3V1A1 ...	T3V1A2 ...								
Threat 4	T4V1A1 ...									
Threat 5										
Threat 6										
...										
...										
Threat n										
Priority of effort	1	2	3	4	5	6	7	8	...	

These bands of controls should be continued through all asset-threat pairs.

There is a key delineator here between risk identification and risk analysis: In developing the TVA worksheet, the organization is performing risk identification simply by determining whether an asset is at risk from a threat and identifying any vulnerabilities that exist. The extent to which the asset is at risk falls under risk analysis. The fine line between the two is part of the reason that many organizations follow a formal methodology like the one outlined in Figure 1-4 described earlier in this module, then merge risk identification, risk analysis, and risk evaluation into one logical process and just call it risk assessment.

Risk Assessment: Risk Analysis

Assessing the relative risk for each vulnerability is accomplished via a process called **risk analysis**. Risk analysis assigns a risk rating or score to each specific vulnerability. While this number does not mean anything in absolute terms, it enables you to gauge the relative risk associated with each vulnerable information asset, and it facilitates the creation of comparative ratings later in the risk treatment process.

risk analysis

A determination of the extent to which an organization's information assets are exposed to risk.

likelihood

The probability that a specific vulnerability within an organization will be attacked by a threat.

impact

An understanding of the potential consequences of a successful attack on an information asset by a threat.

Estimating risk is not an exact science. Some practitioners use calculated values for risk estimation, while others rely on broader methods of estimation. The goal is to develop a repeatable method to evaluate the relative risk of each vulnerability that has been identified and added to the list.

You can use the simple and popular risk model known as the Risk Management Framework, which was developed and promoted by NIST, to evaluate the risk for each information asset. The model calculates the relative risk for each vulnerability based on existing controls, and calculates the **likelihood** and **impact** of a threat event.

Mitigation of Applicable Controls   If a vulnerability is fully managed by an existing control, the vulnerability can be set aside. If it is partially controlled, you can estimate what percentage of the vulnerability has been controlled. A simplistic approach involves determining what recommended controls have been implemented as part of the security program, and describing the level of implementation. The organization must research each vulnerability to ensure complete understanding of the issues.

You can learn more about NIST's Risk Management Framework, which provides a process that integrates security and risk management activities into the system development life cycle. The framework is a risk-based approach to security control selection and specification that considers effectiveness, efficiency, and constraints due to applicable laws and directives. Read more at *https://csrc.nist.gov/Projects/Risk-Management/Risk-Management-Framework-(RMF)-Overview.*

Determining the Likelihood of a Threat Event   Likelihood is the overall rating—a numerical value on a defined scale—of the probability that a specific vulnerability will be exploited or attacked. This attempt is commonly referred to as a threat event, as described earlier. According to NIST's SP 800-30, Rev. 1:

> *The likelihood of occurrence is a weighted risk factor based on an analysis of the probability that a given threat is capable of exploiting a given vulnerability (or set of vulnerabilities). The likelihood risk factor combines an estimate of the likelihood that the threat event will be initiated with an estimate of the likelihood of impact (i.e., the likelihood that the threat event results in adverse impacts). For adversarial threats, an assessment of likelihood of occurrence is typically based on: (i) adversary intent; (ii) adversary capability; and (iii) adversary targeting. For other than adversarial threat events, the likelihood of occurrence is estimated using historical evidence, empirical data, or other factors.*[19]

A simple method of assessing risk likelihood is to score the event on a rating scale as described in the following section.

Risk Likelihood Scale   Using this scale, the likelihood of a system being damaged by a water leak could be rated as 1, while the likelihood of receiving at least one e-mail that contains a virus or worm in the next year would be rated as 5. Instead of a scale from 1 to 5, you could use a scale of 1 to 10 or 1 to 100, depending on the granularity needed by the organization's process. Whatever rating system you employ for assigning likelihood, use professionalism, experience, and judgment to determine the rating—and use it consistently. Whenever possible, use external references for likelihood values after reviewing and adjusting them for your specific circumstances. For many asset/vulnerability combinations, existing sources have already determined their likelihood. For example:

- The likelihood of a fire has been estimated actuarially for each type of structure.
- The likelihood that a given e-mail will contain a virus or worm has been researched.
- The number of network attacks can be forecast depending on how many network addresses the organization has been assigned.

The use of a risk likelihood scale ranging from 0 to 5 is shown in Table 1-5.

Assessing Potential Impact on Asset Value   After the probability of an attack by a threat has been evaluated, the organization typically looks at the possible impact or consequences of a successful attack. A feared consequence is the loss of asset value. As mentioned in the section on assessing threats, the impact of an attack (most often as a loss in asset value) is of great concern to the organization in determining where to focus its protection efforts. The weighted tables used in risk identification can help organizations better understand the magnitude of a successful

Table 1-5   Risk Likelihood

Rank	Description	Percent Likelihood	Example
0	Not Applicable	0% likely in the next 12 months	Will never happen
1	Rare	5% likely in the next 12 months	May happen once every 20 years
2	Unlikely	25% likely in the next 12 months	May happen once every 10 years
3	Moderate	50% likely in the next 12 months	May happen once every 5 years
4	Likely	75% likely in the next 12 months	May happen once every year
5	Almost Certain	100% likely in the next 12 months	May happen multiple times a year

Source: Clearwater Compliance IRM.

breach. Another good source of information is popular media venues that report on successful attacks in other organizations.

> The level of impact from a threat event is the magnitude of harm that can be expected to result from the consequences of unauthorized disclosure of information, unauthorized modification of information, unauthorized destruction of information, or loss of information or information system availability. Such harm can be experienced by a variety of organizational and non-organizational stakeholders, including, for example, heads of agencies, mission and business owners, information owners/stewards, mission/ business process owners, information system owners, or individuals/groups in the public or private sectors relying on the organization—in essence, anyone with a vested interest in the organization's operations, assets, or individuals, including other organizations in partnership with the organization, or the Nation. Organizations make explicit: (i) the process used to conduct impact determinations; (ii) assumptions related to impact determinations; (iii) sources and methods for obtaining impact information; and (iv) the rationale for conclusions reached with regard to impact determinations.[20]

Most commonly, organizations create multiple scenarios to better understand the potential impact of a successful attack. Using a "worst case/most likely outcome" approach is common. In this approach, organizations begin by speculating on the worst possible outcome of a successful attack by a particular threat, given the organization's current protection mechanisms. After the organization frames this worst-case scenario, it moves on to determine the most likely outcome. The organization uses this approach in most of its planning and assessment activities.

The use of a risk impact scale ranging from 0 to 5, similar to the one used for risk likelihood, is shown in Table 1-6.

After the risk impact has been documented for all TVA triples, it is useful for organizations to retain this information because it can also be used during contingency planning. Attack scenarios play a key role in understanding how the organization needs to react to a successful attack, particularly in its plans for incident response, disaster recovery, and business continuity. Crafting this information at the assessment stage and forwarding it to the contingency planning management team for use in that process saves the organization time and effort.

Table 1-6   Risk Impact

Rank	Description	Example	Number of Records	Productivity Hours Lost	Financial Impact
0	Not applicable threat	No impact	N/A	N/A	N/A
1	Insignificant	No interruption, no exposed data	0	0	0
2	Minor	Multi-minute interruption, no exposed data	0	2	$20,000
3	Moderate	Multi-hour interruption, minor exposure of data	499	4	$175,000
4	Major	One-day interruption, exposure of data	5,000	8	$2,000,000
5	Severe	Multi-day interruption, major exposure of sensitive data	50,000	24	$20,000,000

Source: Clearwater Compliance IRM.

Aggregation   If the RM process begins to overwhelm a small or medium-sized business, the RM team can reduce the process's complexity by merging together or aggregating groups of assets, threats, and their associated risks into more general categories. Larger organizations are usually prepared for the volume of assets, the number of threats, and the multiplicity of risks. As described in NIST 800-30, Rev. 1:

> Organizations may use risk aggregation to roll up several discrete or lower-level risks into a more general or higher-level risk. Organizations may also use risk aggregation to efficiently manage the scope and scale of risk assessments involving multiple information systems and multiple mission/business processes with specified relationships and dependencies among those systems and processes...

In general, for discrete risks (e.g., the risk associated with a single information system supporting a well-defined mission/business process), the worst-case impact establishes an upper bound for the overall risk to organizational operations, assets, and individuals.[21]

Aggregation is one way to assist in the RM process; others include using simpler methodologies with more qualitative approaches (although the method shown here is relatively simplistic), or purchasing applications that guide the organization through the entire process.

Uncertainty   It is not possible to know everything about every vulnerability, such as the likelihood of an attack against an asset or how great an impact a successful attack would have on the organization. The degree to which a current control can reduce risk is also subject to estimation error. A factor that accounts for uncertainty must always be considered; it consists of an estimate made by the manager using good judgment and experience.

> *Uncertainty is inherent in the evaluation of risk, due to such considerations as: (i) limitations on the extent to which the future will resemble the past; (ii) imperfect or incomplete knowledge of the threat (e.g., characteristics of adversaries, including tactics, techniques, and procedures); (iii) undiscovered vulnerabilities in technologies or products; and (iv) unrecognized dependencies, which can lead to unforeseen impacts. Uncertainty about the value of specific risk factors can also be due to the step in the RMF or phase in the system development life cycle at which a risk assessment is performed. For example, at early phases in the system development life cycle, the presence and effectiveness of security controls may be unknown, while at later phases in the life cycle, the cost of evaluating control effectiveness may outweigh the benefits in terms of more fully informed decision making. Finally, uncertainty can be due to incomplete knowledge of the risks associated with other information systems, mission/business processes, services, common infrastructures, and/or organizations. The degree of uncertainty in risk assessment results, due to these different reasons, can be communicated in the form of the results (e.g., by expressing results qualitatively, by providing ranges of values rather than single values for identified risks, or by using visual representations of fuzzy regions rather than points).*[22]

uncertainty

The state of having limited or imperfect knowledge of a situation, making it less likely that organizations can successfully anticipate future events or outcomes.

Risk Determination   After the likelihood and impact are known, the organization can perform risk determination using a formula that seeks to quantify certain risk elements. In this formula, risk equals likelihood of threat event (attack) occurrence multiplied by impact (or consequence), plus or minus an element of uncertainty. Most organizations simply accept the uncertainty factor and go with a simpler formula: Likelihood × Impact. The results provide a range of risk ratings from 1 to 25. The results of this analysis can be summarized in a risk rating worksheet, as shown in Table 1-7. This document is an extension of the TVA worksheet discussed earlier; it shows only the assets and relevant vulnerabilities.

The useful approach shown in Table 1-7 illustrates the use of a weighted factor spreadsheet to calculate risk vulnerability for a number of information assets, using the simpler model of ignoring uncertainty. The columns in the worksheet are used as follows:

- *Asset*—List each vulnerable asset.
- *Vulnerability*—List each uncontrolled vulnerability.
- *Likelihood*—State the likelihood of the vulnerability's realization by a threat agent, as indicated in the vulnerability analysis step. (In our example, the potential values range from 0 to 5.)
- *Impact*—Show the results for this asset from the weighted factor analysis worksheet. (In our example, this value is also a number from 0 to 5.)
- *Risk-rating factor*—Enter the figure calculated by multiplying the asset impact and its likelihood. (In our example, the calculation yields a number ranging from 0 to 25.)

The biggest problem in using a more complex quantitative approach to risk determination is the huge amount of "guesstimation" that must occur to develop discrete values. Very few concrete examples exist to provide the likelihood for a particular threat attack on a more granular scale (say, from 1 to 100), and even fewer examples allow the organization to determine the exact impact on an asset's value from a successful attack (again on a 1–100 scale). For

Table 1-7   Risk Rating Worksheet

Asset	Vulnerability	Likelihood	Impact	Risk-Rating Factor
Customer service request via e-mail (inbound)	E-mail disruption due to hardware failure	3	3	9
Customer service request via e-mail (inbound)	E-mail disruption due to software failure	4	3	12
Customer order via SSL (inbound)	Lost orders due to Web server hardware failure	2	5	10
Customer order via SSL (inbound)	Lost orders due to Web server or ISP service failure	4	5	20
Customer service request via e-mail (inbound)	E-mail disruption due to SMTP mail relay attack	1	3	3
Customer service request via e-mail (inbound)	E-mail disruption due to ISP service failure	2	3	6
Customer service request via e-mail (inbound)	E-mail disruption due to power failure	3	3	9
Customer order via SSL (inbound)	Lost orders due to Web server denial-of-service attack	1	5	5
Customer order via SSL (inbound)	Lost orders due to Web server software failure	2	5	10
Customer order via SSL (inbound)	Lost orders due to Web server buffer overrun attack	1	5	5

the most part, professionals will tell you "It depends." When a method like this is employed in a consistent fashion, it allows making decisions on a relative basis, even when precise values are unknowable.

Any time a calculation is based on pure quantitative numbers of this caliber, the value of the outcome is immediately suspect because the numbers used in the calculations are most likely general estimates. As a result, more and more organizations are turning to qualitative or semi-qualitative assessments, as illustrated in the RM framework and process discussed in this module.

Risk Evaluation   After the risk ratings are calculated for all TVA triples, the organization needs to decide whether it can live with the analyzed level of risk—in other words, the organization must determine its risk appetite. This is the risk evaluation stage. Knowing that a particular threat/vulnerability/asset triple is a 16 out of a maximum of 25 is a start, but is that good or bad? The organization must translate its risk appetite from the general statement developed by the RM framework team (and based on guidance from the governance group) into a numerical value it can compare to each analyzed risk. For some organizations, a level of "10" is acceptable. For others, it may be too high (or too low). This value is then used by the RM team to filter TVAs that do not exceed the value, allowing the process team to focus its efforts on TVAs that do exceed the value.

Although this may seem to be a minor step in the overall risk assessment task, it is a crucial one. There could be severe consequences to the risk analyst or RM process team member who codes this value too high, and as a result leaves key information assets exposed. In the first few iterations of the RM process, the value should be set to a conservative level in the range of 6 to 8, requiring the team to address the risk ratings of assets it might otherwise ignore if the default values were accepted or if a higher level of risk threshold were selected. After the team gains expertise with the process, it can easily adjust this value and streamline the process, with fewer TVAs to review throughout the cycle. The average information asset has dozens of general vulnerabilities; the fewer TVAs the team has to review, the faster it can address those rated as having insufficient levels of current controls.

risk evaluation

The process of comparing an information asset's risk rating to the numerical representation of the organization's risk appetite or risk threshold to determine if risk treatment is required.

Documenting the Results of Risk Assessment   The efforts to compile risks into a comprehensive list allow the organization to make informed choices from the best available information. It is also of value for future iterations of the process to document the results in a reusable form. As these efforts to compile and

Table 1-8   Risk Assessment Deliverables

Deliverable	Purpose
Information asset and classification worksheet	Assembles information about information assets, their sensitivity levels, and their value to the organization
Information asset value weighted table analysis	Rank-orders each information asset according to criteria developed by the organization
Threat severity weighted table analysis	Rank-orders each threat to the organization's information assets according to criteria developed by the organization
TVA controls worksheet	Combines the output from the information asset identification and prioritization with the threat identification and prioritization, identifies potential vulnerabilities in the "triples," and incorporates extant and planned controls
Risk ranking worksheet	Assigns a risk-rating ranked value to each TVA triple, incorporating likelihood, impact, and possibly a measure of uncertainty

assess risk are completed, the results of these steps are documented for current and future use in the list of deliverables, as shown in Table 1-8.

Although the organization may require additional deliverables, the table lists the minimum required to fully document the operations of the RM process team in order to provide continuity for future iterations.

Evaluating Risk

After the risk has been identified and its relative severity against the value of the information asset has been evaluated, the organization must decide whether the current level of risk is acceptable or something must be done. If the RM process team completes its analysis and shares its findings with the framework team and/or governance group, and the executive decision makers state, "We can live with that," then the process moves on to the monitoring and review function, where the organization keeps an eye on the assets, the threat environment, and the known vulnerabilities list for a trigger to restart the RM process anew. If the decision makers indicate that they are not comfortable with the current level of risk, then the next stage of the RM process proceeds: risk treatment.

In most organizations, this is not a simple decision. Instead, it requires extensive input from the RM process team, along with recommendations and cost estimates. This decision process typically requires a formal presentation in which the RM process team provides multiple options if the current level of risk is not acceptable.

Even the decision about whether the current level of risk is acceptable is not a clear-cut choice. Although the governance team provides guidance for general risk appetite, it seldom comes to a simple mathematical comparison, as in "Our risk appetite is a level 10, and the current level of risk in this particular information asset is a 9, so we recommend 'live with it.'"

Another factor that makes this process even more challenging is that the solution for one information asset may positively or negatively affect the level of risk in other information assets. If the simple solution to protect a critical asset is to upgrade the organization's firewall or hire additional firewall administrators, that decision could prove substantially expensive but could very positively impact many other information assets. On the other hand, if the recommendation is to remove an information asset from the threat environment—for example, replacing an overly complex firewall implementation with a simpler alternative that is easier to manage—other information assets could be negatively impacted.

The bottom line is that once the risk is known, it requires extensive deliberation and understanding before the "yea or nay" decision is made. Another step performed during risk evaluation is the prioritization of effort for the treatment of risk, which occurs in the next step of the RM process. The organization can use the asset weighted table analysis performed earlier in the process to make this prioritization, or it can delay the ranking until it has a better understanding of the expected costs and benefits of the various treatment options. Many organizations choose to do a two-pronged approach, developing a draft listing of treatment priorities and then confirming or adjusting that list once the expected costs and benefits are understood. There is also the chance that the organization may think it does not have enough information to decide whether to treat the residual risk in a particular information asset, and may need to request additional information. If this decision is reached by the RM process team, the framework team, or the governance group, then the conduct of additional investigation falls under the risk evaluation phase.

risk control

See *risk treatment*.

defense risk treatment strategy

The risk treatment strategy that attempts to eliminate or reduce any remaining uncontrolled risk through the application of additional controls and safeguards in an effort to change the likelihood of a successful attack on an information asset. Also known as the *avoidance strategy*.

avoidance strategy

See *defense risk treatment strategy*.

transference risk treatment strategy

The risk treatment strategy that attempts to shift risk to other assets, other processes, or other organizations.

Risk Treatment/Risk Control

Risk treatment, also known as **risk control**, is the process of doing something about risk after the organization has identified risk, assessed it, evaluated it, and then determined that the current level of remaining risk—the residual risk—is unacceptable. A variety of options are open to organizations, including removing the information asset from harm's way, modifying how it is currently protected, and passing the responsibility for its protection or replacement to third parties. After the RM process team has identified, analyzed, and evaluated the level of risk currently inherent in its information assets (risk assessment), the team then must treat the risk that is deemed unacceptable when it exceeds the organization's risk appetite. As risk treatment begins, the organization has a list of information assets with currently unacceptable levels of risk; the appropriate strategy must be selected and then applied for each asset. Treating risk begins with an understanding of what risk treatment strategies are and how to formulate them. The chosen strategy may include applying additional or newer controls to some or all of the assets and vulnerabilities found in the tables prepared earlier.

Risk Treatment Strategies

When an organization's general management team determines that risks from InfoSec threats are creating a competitive disadvantage, it empowers the InfoSec and IT communities of interest to treat those risks. After the project team for InfoSec development has identified the information assets with unacceptable levels of risk, the team must choose one of five basic strategies to treat the risks for those assets:

- *Defense*—Applying controls and safeguards that eliminate or reduce the remaining uncontrolled risk
- *Transference*—Shifting risks to other areas or to outside entities
- *Mitigation*—Reducing the impact to information assets should an attacker successfully exploit a vulnerability
- *Acceptance*—Understanding the consequences of choosing to leave an information asset's vulnerability facing the current level of risk, but only after a formal evaluation and intentional acknowledgment of this decision
- *Termination*—Removing or discontinuing the information asset from the organization's operating environment

Defense   The **defense risk treatment strategy** attempts to prevent the exploitation of the vulnerability. This is the preferred approach, and it is accomplished by means of countering threats, removing vulnerabilities in assets, limiting access to assets, and adding protective safeguards. This approach is sometimes referred to as the **avoidance strategy**. In essence, the organization is attempting to improve the security of an information asset by reducing the likelihood or probability of a successful attack.

There are three common approaches to implement the defense risk treatment strategy:

- *Application of policy*—The application of policy allows all levels of management to mandate that certain procedures must always be followed. However, policy alone may not be enough. Effective management always couples changes in policy with the training and education of employees, with an application of technology, or both.
- *Application of security education, training, and awareness (SETA) programs*—Simply communicating new or revised policy to employees may not be adequate to assure compliance. Awareness, training, and education are essential to creating a safer and more controlled organizational environment and to achieving the necessary changes in end-user behavior.
- *Implementation of technology*—In the everyday world of InfoSec, technical controls and safeguards are frequently required to effectively reduce risk.

Risks can be avoided by countering the threats facing an asset or by minimizing the exposure of a particular asset. Eliminating the risk posed by a threat is virtually impossible, but it is possible to reduce the residual risk to an acceptable level in alignment with the organization's documented risk appetite.

Transference   The **transference risk treatment strategy** attempts to shift risk to another entity. This goal may be accomplished by rethinking how services are offered, revising deployment models, outsourcing to other organizations, purchasing insurance, or implementing service contracts with providers. When an organization does not have adequate security management and administration experience, it should consider hiring individuals or organizations that provide expertise in those areas. The key to an effective transference risk treatment strategy is the implementation of an effective service level agreement (SLA). In some circumstances, an SLA is the only guarantee that an external organization will implement the level of security the client organization wants for valued information assets. Of course, outsourcing is not without its own risks. It is up to the owner of the information asset, IT management, and the InfoSec team to ensure that the requirements of the outsourcing contract are sufficient and have been met before problems occur.

Mitigation   The mitigation risk treatment strategy is the treatment approach that focuses on planning and preparation to reduce the impact or potential consequences of an incident or disaster. This approach includes four types of plans, which you will learn about in later modules: the incident response (IR) plan, the disaster recovery (DR) plan, the business continuity (BC) plan, and the crisis management (CM) plan. Mitigation derives its value from its ability to detect and respond to an attack as quickly as possible. The mitigation risk treatment strategy is the focus of this text.

Acceptance   The acceptance risk treatment strategy is the decision to do nothing beyond the current level of protection to keep an information asset from risk, and to accept the outcome from any resulting exploitation. While the selection of this treatment strategy may not be a conscious business decision in some organizations, the unconscious acceptance of risk is not a productive approach to risk treatment.

Acceptance is recognized as a valid strategy only when the organization has:

- Determined the level of risk posed to the information asset
- Assessed the probability of attack and the likelihood of a successful exploitation of a vulnerability
- Estimated the potential impact (damage or loss) that could result from a successful attack
- Evaluated potential controls using each appropriate type of feasibility
- Performed a thorough risk assessment, including a financial analysis
- Determined that the costs to treat the risk to a particular function, service, collection of data, or information asset do not justify the cost of implementing and maintaining the controls

This strategy assumes that it can be a prudent business decision to examine the alternatives and conclude that the cost of protecting an asset does not justify the security expenditure. An organization that decides on acceptance as a strategy for every identified risk of loss may be unable to conduct proactive security activities and may have an apathetic approach to security in general. It is not acceptable for an organization to plead ignorance and thus abdicate its legal responsibility to protect employees' and customers' information. It is also unacceptable for management to hope that if they do not protect information, the opposition will believe it can gain little by an attack. In general, unless the organization has formally reviewed an information asset and determined the current residual risk is at or below the organization's risk appetite, the risks far outweigh the benefits of the acceptance approach.

Termination   Like the acceptance risk treatment strategy, the termination risk treatment strategy is based on the organization's intentional choice not to protect an asset. Here, however, the organization does not want the information asset to remain at risk and so removes it from the operating environment. Sometimes, the cost of protecting an asset outweighs its value. In other cases, it may be too difficult or expensive to protect an asset, compared to the value or advantage that asset offers the company. In either case, termination must be a conscious business decision, not simply the abandonment of an asset, which would technically qualify as acceptance.

Managing Risk

Here are some rules of thumb for selecting a strategy (keeping in mind that the level of threat and the value of the asset should play major roles in treatment strategy selection):

- *When a vulnerability (flaw or weakness) exists in an important asset*—Implement security controls to reduce the likelihood of a vulnerability being exploited.

mitigation risk treatment strategy

The risk treatment strategy that attempts to reduce the impact of the loss caused by an incident, disaster, or attack through effective contingency planning and preparation.

acceptance risk treatment strategy

The risk treatment strategy that indicates the organization is willing to accept the current level of residual risk. As a result, the organization makes a conscious decision to do nothing else to protect an information asset from risk and to accept the outcome from any resulting exploitation.

termination risk treatment strategy

The risk treatment strategy that eliminates all risk associated with an information asset by removing it from service.

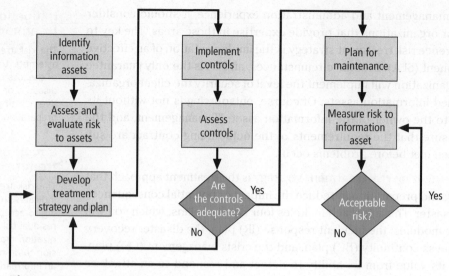

Figure 1-6   Risk treatment cycle

- *When a vulnerability can be exploited*—Apply layered protections, architectural designs, and administrative controls to minimize the risk or prevent the occurrence of an attack.
- *When the attacker's potential gain is greater than the costs of attack*—Apply protections to increase the attacker's cost or reduce the attacker's gain by using technical or managerial controls.
- *When the potential loss is substantial*—Apply design principles, architectural designs, and technical and non-technical protections to limit the extent of the attack, thereby reducing the potential for loss.[23]

After a treatment strategy has been selected and implemented, controls should be monitored and measured on an ongoing basis to determine their effectiveness and to maintain an ongoing estimate of the remaining risk. Figure 1-6 shows how this cyclical process ensures that risks are controlled.

At a minimum, each information threat/vulnerability/asset (TVA) triple that was developed in the risk assessment described earlier should have a documented treatment strategy that clearly identifies any residual risk that remains after the proposed strategy has been executed. This approach must articulate which of the fundamental risk-reducing strategies will be used and how multiple strategies might be combined. This process must justify the selection of the chosen treatment strategies by referencing feasibility studies. Organizations should document the outcome of the treatment strategy selection for each TVA combination in an action plan. This action plan includes concrete tasks, with accountability for each task being assigned to an organizational unit or to an individual. It may include hardware and software requirements, budget estimates, and detailed timelines.

process communications

The necessary information flow within and between the governance group, RM framework team, and RM process team during the implementation of RM.

process monitoring and review

The data collection and feedback associated with performance measures used during the conduct of the process.

Process Communications, Monitoring, and Review

As the process team works through the various RM activities, it needs to continually provide feedback to the framework team about the relative success and challenges of its RM activities. This feedback is used to improve not only the process but the framework as well. It is critical that the process team have one or more individuals designated to collect and provide this feedback, as well as a formal mechanism to submit it to the framework team. These **process communications** facilitate the actions in the **process monitoring and review**. The former involves requesting and providing information as direct feedback about issues that arise in the implementation and operation of each stage of the process. The latter involves establishing and collecting formal performance measures and assessment methods to determine the relative success of the RM program.

Closing Scenario

Events like the one in the opening scenario are part of everyday life for all information system operations. When an alert is brought up for consideration, the proper amount of preparation, planning, training, rehearsal, and experience can turn a potentially harmful event into another minor bump in the road. The lack of those elements can take something that should be handled in stride and turn it into a significant loss event or even a disaster.

Discussion Questions

1. Look at the section and table earlier in this module on the 12 categories of threats. Which of the categories best fits what is going on in the situation JJ described in the opening scenario of this module?
2. How does the exchange between JJ and Paul earlier in this module indicate that this company has thought about contingency planning?

Ethical Decision Making

At the start of this module, suppose Paul's initial response to JJ was, "Thanks for telling me. I'll think about it and get back to you later." When he says this, Amanda looks startled and almost speaks.

Should JJ push the issue or initiate the event review process himself?

MODULE SUMMARY

- Achieving an appropriate level of security for an organization depends on the implementation of a multilayered system that works to protect information assets from harm, unwanted access, and modification. Security is often achieved by means of several strategies undertaken simultaneously or used in combination. It is the role of management to ensure that each strategy is properly planned, organized, staffed, directed, and controlled.

- Information assets have the characteristics of confidentiality when only the people or computer systems with the rights and privileges to access the assets are able to do so. Information assets have integrity when they are not exposed (while being stored, processed, or transmitted) to corruption, damage, destruction, or other disruption of their authentic states; in other words, the information is whole, complete, and uncorrupted. Finally, information assets have availability when authorized users—people or computer systems—are able to access them in the specified format without interference or obstruction.

- Organizations face the 12 general categories of threats that represent a clear and present danger to an organization's people, information, and systems. Each organization must prioritize the threats it faces based on the particular security situation in which it operates, its organizational strategy regarding risk, and the exposure levels of its assets.

- Policy represents a formal statement of the organization's managerial philosophy—in the case of information security policies, the organization's InfoSec philosophy. High-quality security programs begin and end with policy. Because information security is primarily a management problem, not a technical one, policy obliges personnel to function in a manner that adds to the security of information assets rather than as a threat to those assets.

- After policies are designed, created, approved, and implemented, the technologies and procedures that are necessary to accomplish them can be designed, developed, and implemented. Policies must also specify the penalties for unacceptable behavior and define an appeals process.

- An enterprise information security policy (EISP) is also known as a general security policy, IT security policy, or information security policy. The EISP is a policy based on and directly supportive of the mission, vision, and direction of the organization, and it sets the strategic direction, scope, and tone for all security efforts.

- Issue-specific security policy (ISSP) addresses specific areas of technology and contains a statement about the organization's position on a specific issue. The ISSP requires frequent updating to keep it in alignment with changing technologies. Systems-specific security policies (SysSPs) are frequently codified as standards and procedures to be used when configuring or maintaining systems. SysSPs can be written as a combination of two components—managerial guidance and technical specifications.

- One part of information security is risk management, which is the process of identifying and controlling the risks to an organization's information assets. All managers are expected to play a role in the risk management process, but information security managers are expected to play the largest roles. Risk management is more fully defined as the process of identifying vulnerabilities in an organization's information systems and taking carefully reasoned steps to ensure the confidentiality, integrity, and availability of all the components of the organization's information system.

- You must identify, examine, and understand the information and systems currently in place within your organization. After you are informed of your organization's assets and weaknesses, you can move on to identifying, examining, and understanding the threats facing the organization. You must determine which threat aspects most directly affect the organization and the security of the organization's information assets.

- Risk management is a complex operation that requires a formal methodology. The RM framework is the overall structure of the strategic planning and design for the entirety of the organization's RM efforts, which includes the processes of risk assessment and risk treatment. These processes are continuous improvement activities.

- The organization must understand its current levels of risk and determine what, if anything, it needs to do to bring them down to an acceptable level in alignment with the risk appetite specified earlier in the process. This is done by defining the organization's risk tolerance and risk appetite, developing the risk management plan that contains specifications for the implementation and conduct of the RM efforts, and then implementing the program. After the RM process is implemented and operating, the framework team is primarily concerned with the monitoring and review of the overall RM process cycle.

- During the implementation phase of the RM framework, risk evaluation and remediation of key assets are conducted. The process includes establishing the context, identifying risk, and summarizing the findings. Identifying risk includes inventorying, classifying, and valuing information assets as well as identifying threats to them and pinpointing vulnerable assets by tying specific threats to specific assets.

- When an organization's general management team determines that risks from InfoSec threats need attention, it authorizes treatment of those risks using one of five basic strategies: defense, transference, mitigation, acceptance, or termination.

Review Questions

1. What is information security?
2. How is the CNSS model of information security organized?
3. What three principles are used to define the C.I.A. triad? Define each in the context in which it is used in information security.
4. What is a threat in the context of information security?
5. What is an asset in the context of information security?
6. What is an attack in the context of information security?
7. What is a vulnerability in the context of information security?
8. What is a loss in the context of information security?
9. What is intellectual property? Describe at least one threat to this type of asset.
10. What is an availability disruption? Pick a utility service provider and describe what might constitute a disruption.
11. What is a hacker and what are terms used to describe their skill levels?
12. How does a brute force password attack differ from a dictionary password attack?
13. What is phishing, and how is spear phishing different?
14. In general terms, what is policy?
15. What is an enterprise information security policy, and how is it used?
16. Why is shaping policy considered difficult?

17. What are standards? How are they different from policy?
18. What is an issue-specific security policy?
19. List the critical areas covered in an issue-specific security policy.
20. What is a systems-specific security policy?
21. When is a systems-specific security policy used?

22. What is risk management?
23. What are the two main parts of risk management?
24. Who is expected to be engaged in risk management activities in most organizations?
25. What are the basic strategies used to control risk? Define each.

Real-World Exercises

Exercise 1-1

Go to *www.symantec.com/security-center/threat-report*, then download and review the latest Internet Security Threat Report. According to the report, what threats are currently the most dangerous? Which of these top threats represent problems for you and your use of the Internet? Which of these top threats represent problems for your school or business?

Exercise 1-2

Visit your school's Web site and search for any information about a computer policy or Internet security policy used at your academic institution. Compare and contrast this policy with the ones discussed in this module. Are any sections missing? If so, which ones? Does the school's policy contain sections that are not described in this module? Why do you think those sections are included?

Exercise 1-3

Go to *https://cve.mitre.org*. What type of site is this, and what information can it provide? Now, paste in the URL *https://cve.mitre.org/cve*, then click Search CVE List, and enter "Ransomware" in the search field. Click Search again. What information is provided? How would this be useful? Click on one of the named results. What additional information is provided? How could this be useful?

Exercise 1-4

Open a Web browser and search for the "OWASP Top Ten." Visit the site. What information is provided here? What does it mean? How could a security manager use this information?

Exercise 1-5

Open a Web browser and search for "NIST Computer Security Resource Center." Link to the home page. Click the Publications link, then click on the "SP NIST Special Publications" option. Locate SP 800-100. Review the HTML version. What critical information could a security administrator or manager gain from this document? What other documents would be of value to the security manager or technician?

Hands-On Projects

Each module of this resource includes a hands-on project available via Cengage's MindTap platform or your instructor's LMS. In MindTap, the projects can be found in the Practice It folder. These virtual labs will help you develop some practical skills that we think will be of value as you progress through the course.

Also in this section, we will discuss two things that are needed for the labs you will do in later modules. One is how we will use virtualization, and the other is a discussion of the ethical dimension of using information security tools and techniques that many consider to be from the "dark side."

Virtualization

Virtualization is the ability to create a virtual (as opposed to physical) representation of a computing device, such as a network, a computing system, or a storage system. Virtualization is primarily used to create a virtual image of a functioning computer. This virtual image (also referred to as a guest) mimics the behavior of a physical system in almost every way. Guest images reside on a host system and can run at the same time as the host. The host system may run multiple guest images at the same time, if it has enough resources to do so. Virtual systems typically make greater demands on CPU and memory than physical systems, so the host must be robust enough to handle the increased demand. These demands come on top of the usual demand needed to run the host, exclusive of any virtual images.

Before you can actually use virtual images, you must install some type of virtualization software or access a virtualization facility hosted on the Internet. This software will allow you to create (in some cases), maintain, and control each of your guest images. Virtualization software can be integrated with an operating system so that the only functionality provided by the host system is virtualization. Alternatively, some virtualization software can be installed on top of an existing host system that already has an operating system installed. Multiple vendors provide virtualization software, such as VMware, Oracle, Microsoft, Apple, various Linux distros, IBM, and Novell. Some of these software packages are available at no charge, and others are available for a fee.

Your instructor may choose to have you perform hands-on exercises in a local virtual manner or using a private networked platform.

Ethical Considerations in the Use of Information Security Tools

Using the "tools of the trade" in information security can put students (and teachers) in a position to access software and techniques designed to break the rules and allow bad acts to occur. Because each academic community sets certain standards, you need to be aware of how these standards apply in your specific circumstance.

Conforming to standards and exhibiting ethical behavior is required to ensure the unhindered pursuit of knowledge and the free exchange of ideas. Academic integrity means that you respect the right of other individuals to express their views and opinions, and that you, as a student or faculty member, do not engage in plagiarism, cheating, illegal access, misuse or destruction of college property, or the falsification of college records or academic work.

As a member of the academic community, you are expected to adhere to these standards of ethical behavior. You are expected to read, understand, and follow the code of conduct as outlined in your organization's policy and as expressed in graduate and undergraduate catalogs and/or the student handbook. You need to be aware that if you violate these standards, you will be subject to certain penalties as outlined in your college or university's judiciary procedures. These penalties likely range from grade penalties to permanent expulsion.

Read the following White Hat Agreement, and then follow your teacher's instructions for acknowledging your understanding and agreement. You are required to abide by these ethical standards while you are a student. Your agreement indicates that you understand the ethical standards expected of you in this academic community and that you understand the consequences of violating these standards. For those of you in information security/cybersecurity programs, the standard is even higher, given that you will be functioning as one of the guardians of an organization's data.

Are You a White Hat?

As part of this course, you may be exposed to systems, tools, and techniques related to information security. With proper use, these components allow a security or network administrator to better understand vulnerabilities and the security precautions used to defend an organization's information assets. Misuse of these components, either intentionally or accidentally, can result in breaches of security, damage to data, or other undesirable results.

Because these projects will sometimes be carried out in a public network that is used by people for real work, you must agree to the following before you can participate. If you are unwilling to do so, then you cannot participate in the projects.

The White Hat Agreement

If you have questions about any of the following guidelines, please contact your instructor. This agreement may be changed from time to time by your instructor, who will notify you of such changes and may ask you to reaffirm your understanding and agreement.

- Just because you can do something doesn't mean you should.
- As you engage in projects, you will be granted access to tools and training that have the potential to do harm even when they are used to determine or investigate the security of an information system. Use these tools with care and consideration of their impact, and only in the ways specified by your instructor.
- If any question arises in your mind about whether you can or should perform an activity or use a tool in a particular way, stop and ask your instructor for clarification. In information security, it is most definitely *not* easier to ask for forgiveness than for permission.
- You are allowed to use the tools and exercises only if you are currently registered for a grade in the course. An instructor always has the right to ask for appropriate identification if a question arises about the identity of a student.
- Any instance of suspected misconduct, illegal or unauthorized use of tools or exercises, or any action by you that can be construed as outside the guidelines of the course syllabus and instruction will be investigated by the instructor and may result in severe academic and/or legal penalties. Being a student does not exempt you from consequences if you commit a crime.
- We expect all students to follow the ACM Code of Ethics and Professional Conduct *(www.acm.org/about-acm/acm-code-of-ethics-and-professional-conduct)* as well as the following stipulations.
- By acknowledging this agreement, you agree that you *will*:
  - Only perform actions specified by the course instructor for using security tools on assigned systems
  - Report any findings to the course instructors or in specified reporting formats and not disclose them to anyone else
  - Maintain the confidentiality of any private information learned through course exercises
  - Manage assigned course accounts and resources with the understanding that their contents may be viewed by others
  - Hold harmless the course instructors and your academic institution for any consequences or actions should you choose to use course content outside the physical or virtual confines of the specified laboratory or classroom
  - Abide by the computing policies of your academic institution, by all laws governing use of computer resources on campus, and by legal jurisdictions to which you are subject

- By acknowledging this agreement, you agree that you *will not*:
  - Attempt to gain unauthorized access to a system, attempt to increase privileges on any system, or access any data without proper authorization
  - Disclose any information that you discover as a direct or indirect result of any course exercise
  - Take actions that will modify or deny access to any system, data, or service, except those to which administrative control has been duly delegated to you
  - Attempt to perform any actions or use utilities presented in the laboratory outside the confines and structure of the projects or classroom
  - Utilize any security vulnerabilities beyond the target accounts in the course or beyond the duration of the course exercise
  - Pursue any legal action against the course instructors or the university for any consequences or actions should you choose to use what you learn in the course outside the physical or virtual confines of the laboratory or classroom

This agreement has been explained to me to my satisfaction. I have read, understood, and agree to comply with the terms and conditions of this agreement. I agree to abide by the conditions of the ACM Code of Ethics and Professional Conduct and of the White Hat Agreement.

_____

Signature

References

1. Internet World Stats. Accessed 04/29/2020 from *www.internetworldstats.com/stats.htm*.
2. "Lessons of First WTC Bombing." *BBC News*. February 26, 2003. Accessed 12/31/2019 from *http://news.bbc.co.uk/2/hi/americas/2800297.stm*.
3. Balaouras, S. "The State of Disaster Recovery Preparedness 2017." *Forrester Research*. Accessed 12/31/2019 from *http://drj.com/images/surveys_pdf/forrester/2017-Forrester-Survey.pdf*.
4. BusinessWire. "Syncsort State of Resilience Report." Accessed 12/31/2019 from *www.businesswire.com/news/home/20180110005058/en/*.
5. FEMA. "Make Your Business Resilient." Accessed 12/31/2019 from *www.fema.gov/media-library-data/1441212988001-1aa7fa978c5f999ed088dcaa815cb8cd/3a_BusinessInfographic-1.pdf*.
6. "NSTISSI No. 4011: National Training Standard for Information Systems Security (InfoSec) Professionals." National Security Telecommunications and Information Systems Security. June 20, 1994. Accessed 12/31/2019 from *www.cnss.gov/CNSS/issuances/Instructions.cfm*.
7. Whitman, Michael E., and Herbert J. Mattord. "Threats to Information Security Revisited." *Journal of Information Systems Security* (2012).
8. Loshin, P. "FBI ransomware alert: Don't pay; report, defend against attacks." September 23, 2016. Accessed 12/31/2019 from *https://searchsecurity.techtarget.com/news/450304898/FBI-ransomware-alert-Dont-pay-report-defend-against-attacks*.
9. Posey, B. "How ransomware variants are neutralizing data backups." March 2018. Accessed 12/31/2019 from *https://searchdatabackup.techtarget.com/feature/How-ransomware-variants-are-neutralizing-data-backups*.
10. Wood, Charles C., "Integrated Approach Includes Information Security." *Security* 37 (February 2000): 43–44.
11. National Institute of Standards and Technology (NIST). *An Introduction to Computer Security: the NIST Handbook* (SP 800-12, Rev. 1). Accessed 12/31/2019 from *https://csrc.nist.gov/publications/detail/sp/800-12/rev-1/final*.
12. National Center for Educational Statistics 2017 Survey Results. Program for the International Assessment of Adult Competencies (PIAAC). Accessed 12/31/2019 from *https://nces.ed.gov/surveys/piaac/current_results.asp*.

13. National Center for Educational Statistics. "Data Point: Adult Literacy in the United States." Accessed 12/31/2019 from *https://nces.ed.gov/pubs2019/2019179.pdf*.

14. Bloom, Benjamin S., Bertram B. Mesia, and David R. Krathwohl. *Taxonomy of Educational Objectives*. New York: David McKay, 1964.

15. Whitman, M. "Security Policy: From Design to Maintenance." *Information Security Policies and Strategies –* An Advances in MIS Monograph. S. Goodman, D. Straub, & V. Zwass (eds). 2008. Armonk NY: M.E. Sharpe Inc.

16. Ibid.

17. "Sun Tzu's The Art of War." Translated by the Sonshi Group. Accessed 12/31/2019 from *www.sonshi.com/original-the-art-of-war-translation-not-giles.html*.

18. National Institute of Standards and Technology (NIST). "Special Publication 800-30, Revision 1: Guide for Conducting Risk Assessments." 2012. Accessed 12/31/2019 from *http://nvlpubs.nist.gov/nistpubs/Legacy/SP/nistspecialpublication800-30r1.pdf*.

19. Ibid.

20. Ibid.

21. Ibid.

22. Ibid.

23. Ibid.

PLANNING FOR ORGANIZATIONAL READINESS

Upon completion of this material, you should be able to:

1. Discuss key laws, regulations, and standards associated with contingency planning (CP)
2. Explain the contingency planning life cycle, the elements needed to begin the contingency planning process, the initiation of the process, and the composition of the CP management team
3. Discuss how CP policy is used to define the scope of the CP operations and establish managerial intent
4. Define business impact analysis and describe each of its components
5. List the steps needed to create and maintain a budget used for the contingency planning process

> *In preparing for battle, I have always found that plans are useless, but planning is indispensable.*
>
> — Dwight D. Eisenhower

Opening Scenario

It was Thursday evening at Hierarchical Access LTD (HAL). All the employees had left for the day except for a select group of senior staff who were crowded around the conference table with laptops open and index cards in hand. Paul, who was facilitating the contingency planning training exercise, turned to JJ, the acting Incident Manager, and said, "It's your turn."

JJ looked at the next incident card in his deck—a set of possible incidents that HAL was preparing to respond to. He read two words that made him grimace: "Power out."

JJ looked to Paul and asked, "How widespread and for how long?"

"Don't look at me," Paul replied. "That's all you know."

JJ scrolled through the disaster recovery plan on his laptop, finally settling on a section. He looked up, scanning the room for the Communications Coordinator, Susan Lampe. Susan, an experienced systems developer, was assigned responsibility for all communications during this disaster recovery practice session.

"Susan," he said, "please call the power company and ask how widespread the outage is."

Susan, who was reading the same page as JJ, looked up. "Okay, I'll let you know as soon as I have an answer," she said. "Anything else?"

"Uh, yes," JJ said, "just a second." As he was searching his plan for the next step to perform, Ed Michaels, the second shift supervisor, started reading aloud from his screen. "We've got about 45 minutes of battery time," he said, "but the generators need to be manually started at least 15 minutes before that to get them up to speed and load tested. As you know, we'll need continuous power to the on-premises operations so we can maintain connectivity to the cloud providers to keep the Web and network operations up."

"Right!" JJ said. He then turned to Fred, who was representing the building management company that leased space to HAL. "Can you get a team to the generators and keep them going?"

Looking up from his laptop, Fred said, "Yeah. I'm on it."

"We already had the heaters online," Fred added. "It takes 10 to 15 minutes to bring them up from a cold start, and in this weather it's a very cold start. We need five to seven more minutes before we can crank the motor, and three to four minutes more before we can generate power."

Everyone at the table chuckled. Even though the weather outside was 92 degrees and humid, the disaster scenario they were rehearsing was focused on a massive winter storm affecting operations.

"How long will the generators run?" JJ asked.

Fred located and opened a document on his laptop. "Days," he said. "If we have to, we can siphon fuel from your new truck! You told me you got the diesel engine in it. With the on-site tankage supplemented by diesel we can access from employee vehicles, we have plenty of fuel, provided the generator doesn't break down."

"Well, that's a relief," JJ said, smiling as he leaned back in his seat. "Susan, please notify the department heads to begin shutting down non-critical systems and electrical devices." He paused, and then glanced over at Tom Smythe, the acting IT team lead. "How's networking?"

Tom took the note Paul handed him, read it, and frowned. "We've got internal networking, but the primary Internet connection is down. The storm must have taken down an overhead connection. We are on the secondary, low-speed connection now."

JJ sighed and glanced back at Susan "Okay, Susan, activate the emergency employee notification system. Tell everyone who's not on-site to work from home as best they can. Let's coordinate with local police and the highway department to make sure local roads are passable, and see about getting everyone home safe."

"You got it, JJ," Susan said. She simulated contacting the requested agencies. "Done!"

After reviewing the list on his laptop and mentally checking off each action item, JJ glanced over at Paul. "OK, what's next?"

"Good job, everyone," Paul said. "JJ, flip the next card."

INTRODUCTION TO PLANNING FOR ORGANIZATIONAL READINESS

Planning for contingencies is a complex and demanding process. Like any such undertaking, it is improved by using a formal methodology that systematically addresses each challenge an organization might face during an incident, disaster, or other adverse event. Developing contingency plans like the disaster recovery plan used in the opening scenario of this module means taking the time and effort to organize the planning process, prepare the detailed and complete plans, commit to maintaining those plans at a high state of readiness at all times, rehearse the use of the plans with a rigor and diligence usually seen only in military organizations, and then maintain the processes necessary to keep a high state of preparedness.

All this must happen amid the pressures of day-to-day operational demands and the give-and-take of resource allocations common to all organizations. Note that the rehearsal in the opening scenario occurred after normal working hours; an organization and its employees should expect to make such a commitment to contingency planning by training, rehearsing, and testing all plans to ensure they will work as expected. Unfortunately, few organizations can maintain the proper degree of readiness over an extended period of time without a commitment to the process that includes regular rehearsals. This module explores some of the preparatory and foundational actions needed to ensure that the contingency planning process gets off to a solid start.

KEY LAWS, REGULATIONS, AND STANDARDS ASSOCIATED WITH CONTINGENCY PLANNING

As a future InfoSec professional, you will be required to understand the scope of an organization's legal and ethical responsibilities. The InfoSec team plays an important role in an organization's approach to controlling liability for privacy and security risks, especially during and after an incident or disaster. In modern litigious societies, violation of law or ethical misconduct on the part of an organization's managerial team or employees frequently results in a lawsuit, for which plaintiffs can be awarded large civil judgments for damages or to punish defendants. To minimize these liabilities, the InfoSec practitioner must understand the current legal environment and keep apprised of new laws and regulations as they emerge. By educating employees and management about their legal and ethical obligations and the proper use of information technology and information security along with the responsibility of protecting information trusted to the organization, security professionals can help keep their organizations focused on their primary mission.

Beyond that, however, the InfoSec professional has a unique position within the organization. Each is trusted with one of the most valuable assets the organization has: its information. Not only are these professionals responsible for protecting that information, they are privy to the secrets and structures of the systems that store, transmit, use, and protect the information. Thus, they are individuals who must be beyond reproach, with the highest ethical and moral standards. The Roman poet Juvenal, in his work "Satire VI," asked *Quis custodiet ipsos custodes?*"—loosely translated, "Who will watch the watchmen?" This expression has gained unique meaning within the InfoSec community, as InfoSec professionals, above all else, understand the challenges of and need for accountability. Partly for this reason, it is still industry standard practice for organizations to avoid hiring new employees directly into InfoSec positions, unless they have established experience at other organizations where they have proven their trustworthiness. Many organizations value staffing these trusted roles with people who have a track record with their current organization. While this standard is slowly changing, due mainly to the overwhelming demand for security professionals, most organizations still expect new hires to prove themselves worthy of the responsibility associated with this high-trust role. Therefore, it is imperative for you to understand and take to heart this expectation of trust, the expectation of being beyond legal and ethical reproach, as you continue your professional journey into InfoSec.

Ethical Deterrence

It is the responsibility of InfoSec personnel to deter and, where possible, prevent unethical and illegal acts by using policy, education and training, and technology as controls or safeguards to protect the organization's information and technology assets. Most IT professionals understand the use of technology as a means of protection, but many underestimate the value of policy in the creation of durable and reliable information security programs.

There are three general categories of unethical behavior that an organization's management seeks to eliminate:

- *Ignorance*—Ignorance of the law is no excuse, but ignorance of policies and procedures is. The first method of deterrence within an organization involves the security education training and awareness (SETA) program. Organizations must design, publish, and disseminate their policies and information about relevant laws. Employees must be made to understand that they have to abide by these policies. Frequent reminders and training and awareness programs support the retention of this knowledge and, one hopes, compliance.
- *Accident*—Individuals with the authorization and privileges to manage information within the organization have the greatest opportunity to cause harm or damage by accident. Careful placement of security controls can help prevent accidental modification or damage to systems and data. Effective data backup and recovery operations can further support recovery in the event of an accidental loss of information.
- *Malicious intent*—Criminal or unethical intent refers to the state of mind of the individual who commits an infraction. A legal defense can be built on whether the accused acted out of ignorance, by accident, or with the intent to cause harm or damage. Deterring those with malicious intent is best done by means of litigation, prosecution, and technical controls. Intent is only one of several factors to consider when determining whether a computer-related crime has occurred.

Deterrence is the best method for preventing an illegal or unethical activity. Laws, policies, and technical controls are all examples of deterrents. However, laws, policies, and their associated penalties only deter if three conditions are present.

- *Fear of penalty*—Threats of informal reprimand or verbal warnings may not have the same impact as the threat of termination, imprisonment, or forfeiture of pay.
- *Probability of being caught*—There must be a strong possibility that perpetrators of illegal or unethical acts will be caught.
- *Probability of penalty being administered*—The organization must be willing and able to impose the penalty and follow through with punishments.

In the absence of any one of these criteria, employees may not respect or follow policies. Organizations that write policies without explicit penalties are condemning them to irregular compliance and opening themselves to lawsuits should violators be penalized. Only through effective implementation of all three deterrence criteria can organizations expect compliance with established policy.

Laws Germane to Contingency Planning

While the breadth of laws that impact information security is too broad to cover here, there are certain laws that organizations should be cognizant of during contingency planning and associated adverse events, whether incidents or disasters.

Relevant U.S. Laws

While U.S. laws typically apply only to actions that affect federal systems or violations considered a federal crime (such as those involving illegal interstate activities), it is still important to ensure that the organization's contingency planners and responders are aware of laws that could affect employees or other organizational stakeholders should they be violated. Many of these laws also have reporting requirements, which must be followed in the event an organization detects a violation. The most applicable laws include the following:

- **Computer Fraud and Abuse (CFA) Act of 1986** The cornerstone of many computer-related federal laws and enforcement efforts, the CFA formally criminalizes "accessing a computer without authorization or exceeding authorized access" for systems that contain information of national interest as determined by the U.S. government.
- **Electronic Communications Privacy Act (ECPA) of 1986** A collection of statutes that regulate the interception of wire, electronic, and oral communications. These statutes are frequently referred to as the "federal wiretapping acts."
- **Health Insurance Portability and Accountability Act (HIPAA) of 1996** Also known as the Kennedy-Kassebaum Act, this law attempts to protect the confidentiality and security of healthcare data by establishing and enforcing standards and by standardizing electronic data interchange.
- **Federal Trade Commission Act (FTCA)** This law was recently used to challenge organizations that allegedly made deceptive claims regarding the privacy and security of customers' personal information.
- **Gramm-Leach-Bliley (GLB) Act of 1999 (also known as the Financial Services Modernization Act)** This law repeals the restrictions on banks that affiliate with insurance and securities firms; it has significant impact on the privacy of personal information used by these industries.
- **Sarbanes-Oxley (SOX) Act of 2002 (also known as the Public Company Accounting Reform and Investor Protection Act)** This law enforces accountability for executives at publicly traded companies and is having ripple effects throughout the accounting, IT, and related units of many organizations.
- **American Recovery and Reinvestment Act (ARRA) of 2009** In the privacy and security area, this law contains new reporting requirements and penalties for breaches of protected health information (PHI).
- **Health Information Technology for Economic and Clinical Health (HITECH) Act of 2009 (part of ARRA-2009)** This law addresses privacy and security concerns associated with the electronic transmission of PHI, in part through several provisions that strengthen HIPAA rules for civil and criminal enforcement.

- **Disaster Recovery Reform Act of 2018** These reforms acknowledge the shared responsibility for disaster response and recovery, aim to reduce the complexity of the U.S. Federal Emergency Management Agency (FEMA), and build the nation's capacity for the next catastrophic event.

 Many states have similar laws that address privacy, identity theft, and computer crime or cybercrime. Visit the National Conference of State Legislatures (NCSL) pages at *www.ncsl.org/research/telecommunications-and-information-technology/computer-hacking-and-unauthorized-access-laws.aspx* for a listing of state-specific computer crime laws, and at *www.ncsl.org/research/financial-services-and-commerce/identity-theft-state-statutes.aspx* for state identity theft laws.

Breach Laws

Although it is important for information security professionals to be cognizant of all laws pertaining to their organization's operations, professionals responsible for incident management and disaster recovery are particularly interested in laws that address the organization's responsibilities for a successful incident that results in a loss of an organization's data, especially when that data contains customer and/or employee **personally identifiable information (PII)**. Collectively, these laws are referred to as **breach laws**. Most of these laws require some form of after-breach support from the organization, such as free or discounted credit monitoring, progress reports, and a description of actions taken to rectify the incident and prevent reoccurrence.

PII and the healthcare equivalent, **protected health information (PHI)**, are information sets specifically protected by law. In the case of PII, the information could be used to stalk an individual, steal their identity, or enter into fraudulent transactions or contracts. PHI includes health and healthcare information, which may be sensitive in nature and thus is considered protected. A person's PHI includes health records, their healthcare organizations, insurance information, and other related information.

Although the United States currently does not have a national breach law, components of HIPAA and GLB do require breach notices or the explicit protection of PII or PHI. HIPAA requires notification, in writing by first class mail, of individuals who have a loss of PHI within 60 days of detection, unless advised otherwise by law enforcement. While GLB doesn't specifically include breach notification requirements, it does have a formally established set of requirements to fully disclose information regarding a financial institution's responsibility to protect personal financial information, including PII. It also requires these institutions to notify constituents of their responsibilities and policies for protecting private personal information. This requirement has been interpreted as a requirement to notify individuals in the event of a breach, as defined in an *unauthorized disclosure*.

Currently, all 50 states, the District of Columbia, Guam, Puerto Rico, and the U.S. Virgin Islands have breach laws that require notification of affected parties in the event of a data loss. Note that most of these laws have differences; it is up to each organization to be aware of these differences and apply the laws and rules correctly for each customer, based on individual circumstances. For information on a particular state's breach laws, refer to the NCSL Web site at *www.ncsl.org/research/telecommunications-and-information-technology/security-breach-notification-laws.aspx*.

In the state of Georgia, for example, GA Code Section 10-1-910, et seq. requires an organization to notify any person or business whose information they maintain as quickly as possible after a data breach, unless advised by law enforcement otherwise. Further, if the breach affects more than 10,000 residents, they must also notify all consumer credit agencies.

---

personally identifiable information (PII)

Information about a person's history, background, and attributes that can be used to commit identity theft. This information typically includes a person's name, address, Social Security Account Number (SSAN), family information, employment history, and financial information.

breach law

A law that specifies a requirement for an organization to notify affected parties when they detect the loss of a specified type of information. These laws may be state or local or part of an international agreement.

protected health information (PHI)

A set of information about an individual's physical or mental health, healthcare providers, or health insurance.

BEGINNING THE CONTINGENCY PLANNING PROCESS

contingency planning management team (CPMT)

The group responsible for the overall planning and development of the contingency planning process, including the organization of subordinate teams and oversight of subordinate plans.

business impact analysis (BIA)

An investigation and assessment of adverse events that can affect the organization, conducted as a preliminary phase of the contingency planning process, which includes a determination of how critical a system or set of information is to the organization's core processes and its recovery priorities.

The elements required to begin the CP process include forming the **contingency planning management team (CPMT)**; establishing a policy environment to enable the planning process; determining a planning methodology; gaining an understanding of the causes and effects of core precursor activities, known as the **business impact analysis (BIA)**; and ensuring access to financial and other resources, as articulated and outlined by the planning budget. Each of these elements is explained in the sections that follow. The CPMT organizes and performs all of these tasks, so it needs to be formed before any other activities can occur. After the CPMT has been organized and staffed, it begins the development of CP policies and plans. The CP methodology expands the four elements just noted into a multistep contingency process that an organization may apply to develop and maintain a viable contingency planning program. The master CP planning document serves as the focus and collection point for the deliverables that come from the subsequent steps.

The methodology presented adapts and integrates the approaches presented in the National Institute of Standards and Technology's (NIST) Special Publication 800-34, Rev. 1, "Contingency Planning Guide for Federal Information Systems" (2010) and Special Publication 800-61, Rev. 2, "Computer Security Incident Handling Guide" (2012), along with a number of international standards. This provides a complete CP methodology that includes the preliminary steps of organizing the CPMT and performing a BIA, and intermediate steps of formulating policies, plans, and teams. The major stages in this methodology, as illustrated in Figure 2-1, include the following:

1. *Form the CPMT.* Assemble the management team that will guide CP planning and execution. This includes representatives from business management, operations, and the projected subordinate teams.
2. *Develop the CP policy statement.* The CP policy is the formal policy that will guide the efforts of the subordinate teams in developing their plans and the overall operations of the organization during contingency operations.

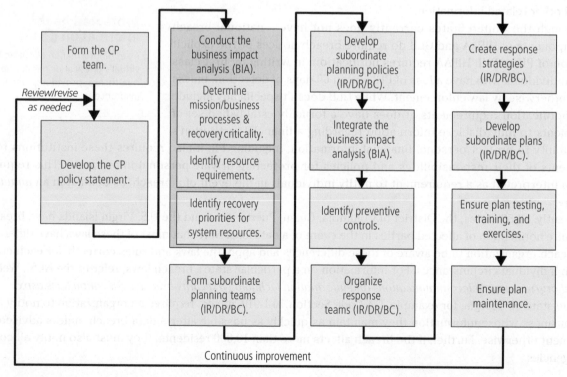

Figure 2-1   Contingency planning life cycle

3. *Conduct the business impact analysis (BIA).* The BIA, described later in this module, helps identify and prioritize organizational functions and the information systems and components critical to supporting the organization's mission/business processes.

4. *Form subordinate planning teams.* For each of the subordinate areas, organize a team to *develop* the incident response (IR), disaster recovery (DR), and business continuity (BC) plans. These groups may or may not contain individuals responsible for *implementing* the plan.

5. *Develop subordinate planning policies.* Just as the CPMT develops an overall CP policy, the newly formed IR, DR, and BC planning teams will begin by developing an IR, DR, and BC planning policy, respectively.

6. *Integrate the BIA.* Each of the subordinate planning teams will independently review and incorporate aspects of the BIA of importance to its planning efforts. As different teams may need different components, the actions and assessments of each team may vary.

7. *Identify preventive controls.* Assess countermeasures and safeguards that mitigate the risk and impact of events on organizational data, operations, and personnel.

8. *Organize response teams.* Specify the skills needed on each subordinate response team (IR/DR/BC), and identify personnel needed. Ensure that personnel rosters are exclusive (no personnel on two different teams) and that all needed skills are covered. These are the individuals who will be called if a particular plan is activated in response to an actual incident or disaster. Some smaller or newer organizations may find that this degree of specialization in planning is difficult to achieve. However, even if an organization cannot currently commit to organized, differentiated, trained, and well-rehearsed teams, it should plan for the day when such teams are possible and the appropriate outlines of training and tracking can be put in place.

9. *Create response strategies.* The CPMT, with input from the subordinate team leaders, will evaluate and invest in strategies that will support the IR, DR, and BC efforts should an adverse event impact business operations. These strategies include data backup and recovery plans, off-site data storage, and alternate site occupancy.

10. *Develop subordinate plans.* For each subordinate area, develop a plan to handle the corresponding actions and activities necessary to (a) respond to an incident, (b) recover from a disaster, and (c) establish operations at an alternate site following a disruptive event.

11. *Ensure plan testing, training, and exercises.* Ensure that each subordinate plan is tested and the corresponding personnel are trained to handle any event that escalates into an incident or a disaster.

12. *Ensure plan maintenance.* Manage the plan, ensuring periodic review, evaluation, and updating.

The discussion of the CPMT, the CP policy, and the BIA completes this module. The other stages are presented throughout the remainder of the text.

Forming the CPMT

To begin the process of planning for contingencies, an organization must first establish an entity that will be responsible for the policies, plans, and teams that emerge from the process. In a small to medium-sized organization, this may be an individual; in large organizations, it may be a team. Some organizations use their own employees; others hire consultants or contractors. Prior to any meaningful planning, people assigned these responsibilities must define the scope of the planning project and identify the resources to be used. Many times, a CPMT is assembled for that purpose. The CPMT is responsible for a number of functions, including the following:

- Obtaining commitment and support from senior management
- Managing and conducting the overall CP process
- Writing the master CP document
- Conducting the business impact analysis (BIA), which includes:
  - Assisting in identifying and prioritizing threats and attacks
  - Assisting in identifying and prioritizing business functions
  - Identifying the systems and resources needed to support the most critical business functions
- Organizing and staffing the leadership for the subordinate teams, including:
  - Incident response planning (IRPT) and response teams
  - Disaster recovery planning (DRPT) and response teams

- ○ Business continuity planning (BCPT) and response teams
- ○ Crisis management planning (CMPT) and its specific response teams, if they are used
- Providing guidance to, and integrating the work of, the subordinate teams, including subordinate plans
  - ○ Incident response plan (IR plan)
  - ○ Disaster recovery plan (DR plan)
  - ○ Business continuity plan (BC plan)
  - ○ Crisis management plan (CM plan; if used)

A typical roster for the CPMT may include the following positions:

- *Leadership*
  - ○ A *champion*—As with any strategic function, the CP project really should have a champion. This should be an executive or a high-level manager with influence and resources that can be used to support the project team, promote the objectives of the CP project, and endorse the results that come from the effort. In a CP project, the champion could be the chief information officer (CIO), chief operations officer (COO), or ideally the chief executive officer (CEO). It is most common, however, for the COO to take overall responsibility for overseeing CP activities.
  - ○ A *project manager*—A champion provides the strategic vision and the linkage to the power structure of the organization, but someone must manage the project. A project manager, possibly a mid-level operations manager or even the CISO, must lead the project and make sure a sound project planning process is used, a complete and useful project plan is developed, and project resources are prudently managed to reach the goals of the project.
- *Team members*—The team members for this project should include:
  - ○ *Representatives from other business units*—Managers from the three communities of interest should be represented. This can include:
    - *Business managers*—Those familiar with the operations of their functional areas, who can supply details on their activities and provide insight into the criticality of their functions to the overall sustainability of the business
    - *Information technology managers*—Those familiar with both the systems that could be at risk and with the subordinate plans that are needed to provide technical content within the planning process
    - *Information security managers*—Those who can oversee the security planning of the project and provide information on the threats, vulnerabilities, and recovery requirements needed in the planning process
  - ○ *Representatives from subordinate planning teams*—Team leaders from the subordinate planning teams should also be included in the CPMT. Additionally, if the organization has a crisis management team, it should be represented.
  - ○ *Representatives from subordinate response teams*—Teams that perform the response activities of the subordinate functional areas also have key functions that are components of the overall contingency planning effort. These response teams should be distinct entities, with one or more representatives on the CPMT—usually the team leaders. The reason these teams are distinct is that their individual functions are very different and may be activated at different times, or they may be activated concurrently. Depending on the size of the organization, the planning teams may be distinct from the response teams. The subordinate teams may include:
    - Incident response reaction teams, also known as computer security incident response teams (CSIRTs), which execute the IR plan by detecting, evaluating, and responding to incidents
    - Disaster recovery response teams, which execute the DR plan by detecting, evaluating, and responding to disasters and by reestablishing operations at the primary business site
    - Business continuity response teams, which execute the BCP by setting up and starting off-site operations in the event of an incident or disaster
    - Crisis management response teams, which mitigate the impact of personal loss and distress on the organization by minimizing the loss of life, ensuring the quick and accurate accountability of personnel, and ensuring the quick and accurate notification of key personnel

Each of the functional areas (IR/DR/BC/CM) may have multiple response teams responsible for different actions during their corresponding adverse events. Those teams are described in detail in later modules.

The relationship between the CPMT and the subordinate teams is shown in Figure 2-2.

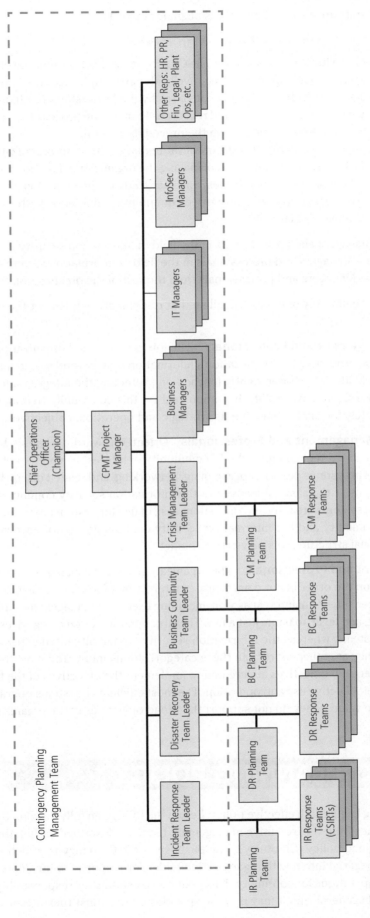

Figure 2-2   Contingency planning management team

Among the most critical start-up tasks of the CPMT is aligning support.

Building Commitment and Support of Senior Management

Like any major project or process within an organization, the CP process will fail without the clear and formal commitment of senior executive management. Only when the executive leadership emphasizes the importance of this process, preferably through personal involvement by the top executive (or by the leadership of a champion), will subordinate managers and employees provide the necessary time and resources to make the process happen. Support should then be gained from the communities of interest mentioned in the preceding section.

For our purposes, a *community of interest* is a group of individuals within an organization who are united by shared interests or values and who have a common goal of making the organization function to meet its objectives. An organization then develops and maintains its own values, and that leads to the evolution of a unique organizational culture. Within the context of this discussion, there are three communities of interest with roles and responsibilities in information security and contingency planning:

- *Information Security*—Managers and professionals in the field of information security
- *Information Technology*—Managers and professionals in the field of information technology
- *Information Consumers*—Managers and professionals from the rest of the organization

In theory, each role (and the community of interest fulfilling that role) must complement the others; in practice, this is often not the case.

Information Security Management and Professionals   The job functions and organizational roles of the InfoSec community of interest focus on protecting the organization's information systems and stored information from attacks. In fulfilling this role, these individuals are often tightly focused on protecting the integrity and confidentiality of systems, and they sometimes lose sight of availability. It is important for this community to remember that all members of the organization are ultimately focused on meeting its strategic and operational objectives.

Information Technology Management and Professionals   Oriented toward designing, building, and operating information systems and associated technologies, the IT community of interest is made up of managers and various groups of skilled professionals in systems design, programming, networking, and related disciplines usually categorized as IT. This community has many of the same objectives as the information security community. However, it focuses more on efficiency and cost of systems creation and operation, ease of use for system users, and transaction response time. The goals of the IT community and the information security community do not always completely align, and depending on the organizational structure, this may cause conflict.

Organizational Management and Professionals   The organization's general management team and other personnel in the organization make up the other major community of interest of information consumers. This large group is almost always made up of other subsets of interest as well, including executive management, production management, human resources, accounting, and legal, to name just a few. The IT community often categorizes these groups as users of information technology systems, whereas the information security community often categorizes them as security subjects. The reality is that they are much more than these categorizations imply. You must focus on the fact that all IT systems and information security objectives are created to implement the objectives of the broader organizational community and safeguard their effective use and operation. The most efficient IT systems operated in the most secure fashion ever devised are of no value if they do not support the broad objectives of the organization as a whole.

CONTINGENCY PLANNING POLICY

Effective contingency planning begins with effective policy. Before the CPMT can fully develop the planning document, the team must receive guidance from the executive management team, as described earlier, then craft that guidance into formal contingency planning policy (CP policy). The purpose of the CP policy is to define the scope of the CP operations and establish managerial intent with regard to timetables for response to incidents, recovery from disasters, and reestablishment of operations for continuity. This policy also establishes responsibility for the development and operations of the CPMT in general, and it may provide specifics on the constituencies of all CP-related teams.

The CP policy should, at a minimum, contain the following sections:

- An introductory statement of philosophical perspective by senior management as to the importance of contingency planning to the strategic, long-term operations of the organization
- A statement of the scope and purpose of the CP operations, specifically stating the requirement to cover all critical business functions and activities
- A call for periodic risk assessment by the organization's risk management team and business impact analysis by the CPMT, typically on a yearly basis, to include identification and prioritization of critical business functions, information assets, and threats to both
- A specification of the CP's major components to be designed by the CPMT, as described earlier
- Identification of key individuals responsible for CP operations and a clear definition of their roles and responsibilities—for example, establishment of the COO as CPMT champion, the deputy COO as CPMT project manager, the CISO as IR team lead, the deputy COO as DR team lead, the manager of business operations as BC team lead, and the legal counsel as crisis management team lead, along with additional details on the responsibilities of those positions (for example, the responsibilities of the CPMT project manager, identified as the deputy COO)
- A call for, and guidance in, the selection of recovery options and business continuity strategies
- A requirement to train, rehearse, and test the various plans on a regular basis (for example, semiannually, annually, or more often as needed)
- Identification of key laws, regulations, and standards that impact CP planning and a brief overview of their relevancy
- A challenge to individual members of the organization, reinforcing their importance as part of the overall CP process
- Additional administrative information, including the original date of the development of the document, dates of any formal revisions, and a schedule for periodic review and maintenance

After the CPMT develops the CP policy and has it approved by the appropriate senior executive, the CPMT lead calls a meeting to begin the planning process in earnest. Each CP meeting should be documented, both to provide guidance for future meetings and to track progress and deliverables set by the committee. The next major step is to plan and then conduct the business impact analysis.

BUSINESS IMPACT ANALYSIS

The business impact analysis (BIA) is an investigation and assessment of the impact that various events or incidents can have on the organization. A crucial component of the initial planning stages, it also provides a detailed identification and prioritization of critical business functions that would require protection and continuity in an adverse event. The BIA, therefore, adds insight into what the organization must do to respond to adverse events, minimize the damage from such events, recover from the effects, and return to normal operations. One of the fundamental differences between a BIA and the risk management processes discussed in Module 1 is that the processes identify the threats, vulnerabilities, and attacks to determine what controls can protect the information. The BIA assumes that these controls have been bypassed, have failed, or were otherwise ineffective in stopping the attack, and that the attack has been successful. In other words, it takes up where the risk assessment process leaves off.

When an organization is undertaking the BIA, Zawada and Evans have noted the following five "Keys to BIA success" that the organization should consider:

1. *Set the scope for the project carefully. Be sure to consider the functional and administrative units to include, the categories of risks to be addressed, and the range of impacts to be considered.*
2. *Initiate a data-gathering process that will find the information senior managers need to make informed decisions.*
3. *Seek out objective rather than subjective data. Subjective data can be useful when used by experienced analysts, but facts are important.*

4. *Determine the needs of higher management prior to the data collection. The final reported risk assessment and BIA must address those needs to be of value.*

5. *Gain validation of the results derived from the risk assessment and BIA from the owners of the business processes being examined, or else the final product may not have their support.*[1]

The CPMT conducts the BIA in three stages:

1. Assessing mission/business processes and recovery criticality
2. Identifying resource requirements
3. Identifying recovery priorities[2]

 For more information on the BIA, including a recommended template, visit *https://csrc.nist.gov/publications/detail/sp/800-34/rev-1/final*. The BIA template is available from the site as supplemental material.

Determine Mission/Business Processes and Recovery Criticality

The first major BIA task is to analyze and prioritize the organization's business processes based on their relationships to the organization's mission. Each business department, unit, or division must be independently evaluated to determine how critical its functions are to the long-term sustainability of the organization as a whole. For example, recovery operations would probably focus on the IT department and network operation before turning to the Personnel department's hiring activities. Likewise, recovering a manufacturing company's assembly line is more urgent than recovering its maintenance tracking system. This is not to say that personnel functions and assembly-line maintenance are not important to the business, but unless the organization's main revenue-producing operations and their supporting technologies can be restored quickly, other functions are irrelevant.

Note that the term *mission/business process* is used throughout this module, given that some organizations that conduct BIAs aren't businesses and thus don't have business processes per se. Don't let the term, which is preferred by NIST, confuse you. It's essentially another way of saying business process, which supports the organization's overall mission.

It is important to collect critical information about each business unit before beginning to prioritize the business units. (See the section titled "BIA Data Collection" later in this module.) The important thing to remember is that the focus of this stage is to avoid *turf wars* and select the business functions that must be sustained in order to continue business operations. Although individual managers or executives might feel that their function is the most critical to the organization, those functions might prove to be less critical in the event of a major incident or disaster. The prioritization of business units is critical in establishing a priority of effort in the event the organization needs to set up temporary operations during a major disaster.

A weighted analysis table can be useful in resolving the issue of which business process or function is the most critical to the organization. Putting together such a table begins by identifying the categories that matter most to the organization. For Hierarchical Access LTD, the company featured in this book's case scenarios, typical processes might include the following:

- Enrolling new customers
- Managing customer accounts
- Providing Internet access
- Providing Internet services
- Providing help desk support
- Advertising services
- Supporting public relations

business process

A task performed by an organization or one of its units in support of the organization's overall mission.

After categories have been identified, weights can be assigned to each category. Typically, the assigned weights add up to a value of 1.0 (as in 100 percent). Table 2-1 shows an example of a weighted factor analysis table. Here, the impact on profitability is assessed at .4 or 40 percent of the value brought to the organization,

Table 2-1 Weighted Ranking of Business Processes

↓Business Process	Impact on Profitability	Contribution to Strategic Objectives	Impact on Internal Operations	Impact on Public Image	Total Weights
Criteria Weight →	.4	.3	.2	.1	1.00
Internet Access Provisioning	5	4	4	4	4.3
Customer Account Management	4	3	3	3	3.4
New Customer Enrollment	4	4	1	3	3.3
Service Advertisement	3	4	2	4	3.2
Help Desk Support	2	3	3	4	2.7
Public Relations Support	2	3	1	5	2.4

Table Instructions:
1. List all business functions in the table.
2. Identify 4 to 5 criteria you will use to evaluate the processes.
3. Assign weights to each criterion in a range of 0 to 1.0 (with 1.0 being most critical to the operations of the organization). View each weight as a portion of a 100 percent total. In other words, the weights must sum to 1.0.
4. For each criterion, assign a value to each business process on a scale of 1 to 5, answering the question "How important is this business process to this criterion?," where 1 = not important at all and 5 = critical. Zero would be used for "Not Applicable."
5. For each business process, multiply each cell value by its criterion weight and total.
6. Sort the business process on the Total Weights column so that the most important business process is at the top.

the contribution to strategic objectives is assessed at .3 or 30 percent, and so on. As you can see in the right-most column, the percentages add up to 1.0 (or 100 percent).

After the criteria have been weighted, the various business functions are identified. For each business process, an importance value is assessed on a scale of 1 to 5 (although it could be almost any range, such as 1–10, 1–100, and so on). After that, the weights are multiplied by the scores in each category. They are then summed to obtain the overall value of the business process to the organization. In Table 2-1, providing Internet services is determined to have a 5-of-5 impact on profitability and a 4-of-5 impact on internal operations. Overall, this business function is given a score of 4.3. Although the number itself does not mean anything in the abstract, it is the highest number of any of the business processes, which means that providing Internet access is the most important business process to this organization, based on the assumptions and evaluations made in this weighted factor analysis.

A useful tool in identifying and collecting information about business processes is the BIA questionnaire, which is discussed later in this module. The BIA questionnaire allows functional managers to directly enter information about their processes, the impacts the processes have on the business and other processes, and the dependencies that exist for the process from specific resources and outside service providers.

NIST Business Process and Recovery Criticality

NIST Special Publication 800-34, Rev. 1 states:

> *FIPS 199 requires organizations to categorize their information systems as low impact, moderate impact, or high impact for the security objectives of confidentiality, integrity, and availability (RMF Step 1). The FIPS 199 category for the availability security objective serves as a basis of the BIA. Further identification of additional mission/business processes and impacts captures the unique purpose of the system.[3]*

Note that large quantities of information are needed in this process and BIA data collection must be done if the BIA is to be made available for use in the overall CP development process. Data collection will be covered later in this module after each of the BIA investigation stages has been discussed. NIST has provided a BIA process and the data collection activities for a sample information system (see Figure 2-3).

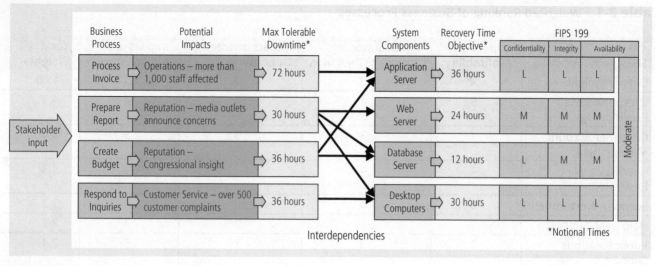

Figure 2-3   Business impact analysis

Key Downtime Metrics   When organizations consider recovery criticality, key recovery measures are usually described in terms of how much of the asset they must recover within a specified time frame. The terms most commonly used to describe this value are:

- **Recovery time objective (RTO)**
- **Recovery point objective (RPO)**
- **Maximum tolerable downtime (MTD)**
- **Work recovery time (WRT)**

The difference between RTO and RPO is illustrated in Figure 2-4. WRT typically involves the addition of nontechnical tasks required for the organization to make the information asset usable again for its intended business function. The WRT can be added to the RTO to determine the realistic amount of elapsed time required before a business function is back in useful service, as illustrated in Figure 2-5.

recovery time objective (RTO)

The maximum amount of time that a system resource can remain unavailable before there is an unacceptable impact on other system resources, supported business processes, and the MTD.

recovery point objective (RPO)

The point in time before a disruption or system outage to which business process data can be recovered after an outage, given the most recent backup copy of the data.

maximum tolerable downtime (MTD)

The total amount of time the system owner or authorizing official is willing to accept for a business process outage or disruption. The MTD includes all impact considerations.

work recovery time (WRT)

The amount of effort (expressed as elapsed time) needed to make business functions work again after the technology element is recovered. This recovery time is identified by the RTO.

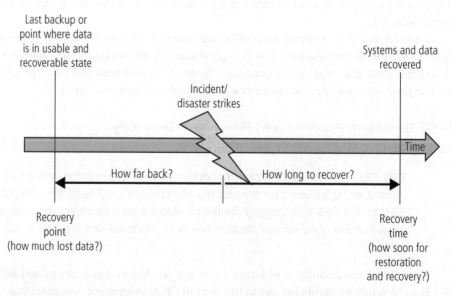

Figure 2-4   RTO vs. RPO

Source: http://networksandservers.blogspot.com/2011/02/high-availability-terminology-ii.html.

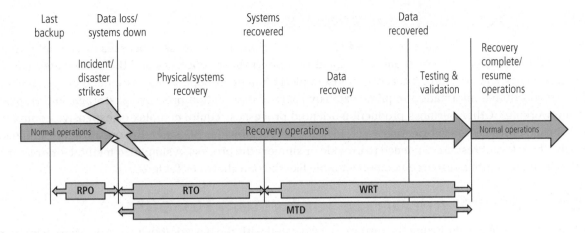

Figure 2-5   RTO, RPO, MTD, and WRT

Source: http://networksandservers.blogspot.com/2011/02/high-availability-terminology-ii.html.

Failing to determine MTD, NIST says, "could leave contingency planners with imprecise direction on (1) selection of an appropriate recovery method, and (2) the depth of detail that will be required when developing recovery procedures, including their scope and content."[4]

When determining the information system resource's RTO, NIST asserts that it is critical to select supporting technologies that optimize the organization's ability to meet the MTD. As for reducing RTO, that requires mechanisms to shorten the start-up time or provisions to make data available online at a failover site. Unlike RTO, RPO isn't part of the MTD but is an indicator of the data loss the organization can tolerate during recovery. Reducing RPO requires mechanisms to increase the synchronicity of data replication between production systems and the backup implementations for those systems.[5]

Because of the critical need to recover business functionality, the total time needed to place the business function back in service must be shorter than the MTD. Planners should determine the optimal cost point for recovering information assets in order to meet BIA-mandated recovery needs while balancing the cost of system inoperability against the cost of the resources required for restoring systems.

The longer an interruption to system availability continues, the more impact and cost it will have for the organization and its operations. When plans require a short RTO, the solutions that will be required are usually more expensive to design and use. For example, if a system must be recovered immediately, it will have an RTO of 0. These types of solutions will require fully redundant, alternative processing sites and will therefore have much higher costs. On the other hand, a longer RTO would allow a less expensive recovery system. Plotting the cost balance points will show an optimal point between disruption and recovery costs. The intersecting point, labeled the cost balance point in Figure 2-6, will be different for every organization and system, based on the financial constraints and operating requirements.[6]

Prioritize Information Assets

As the CPMT conducts the BIA, placing priorities and values on mission/business processes, it is helpful to understand the information assets used by those processes. The presence of high-value information assets may influence the valuation of a particular business process. Normally, this task is performed as part of the risk assessment function of risk management. The organization identifies, classifies, and prioritizes its information assets, placing classification labels on each collection or repository of information in order to better protect it. If the organization has not performed this task, then this is the appropriate time during the BIA to accomplish the task.

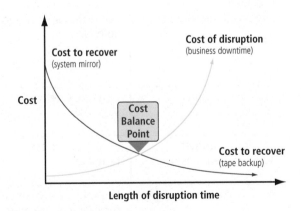

Figure 2-6   Cost balancing

Identify Resource Requirements

After the organization has created a prioritized list of its mission and business processes, it can determine what resources would be needed to recover and subsequently support those processes and their associated information assets. Some processes are resource intensive—for example, IT functions. Supporting customer data, production data, and other organizational information requires extensive sets of information processing, storage, and transmission (through networking). Other business production-oriented processes require complex or expensive components to operate. For each process (and information asset) identified in the previous BIA stage, the organization should identify and describe the relevant resources needed to provide or support the process. A simplified method for organizing this information is to put it into a resource/component table like the one shown in Table 2-2.

Identify Recovery Priorities for System Resources

The last stage of the BIA is prioritizing the resources associated with the mission/business processes, which brings a better understanding of what must be recovered first, even within the most critical processes. With the information from Table 2-2 in hand, the organization can create additional weighted tables of the resources needed to support the individual processes. By assigning values to each resource—for example, using one of the schemes listed below—the organization will develop a custom-designed *to-do* list for use when recovery commences. Whether it is an IR- or DR-scaled recovery or the implementation of critical processes at an alternate site during business continuity, this list will prove invaluable to people tasked with establishing (or reestablishing) critical processes quickly.

In addition to the weighted tables described earlier, simple valuation scales such as Primary/Secondary/Tertiary or Critical/Very Important/Important/Routine can be used. It's important for an organization to avoid getting so bogged down in the process that it loses sight of the objective. A team that finds itself spending too much time developing and completing weighted tables may find a simple classification scheme more suited to its task. However, in a complex process with a large number of resources, a more sophisticated valuation method like the weighted tables may be more appropriate. One of the jobs of the CPMT while preparing to conduct the BIA is to determine what method to use for valuating processes and their supporting resources.

BIA Data Collection

Although the BIA data collection process is not a discrete step in the BIA, it should be used from the beginning and at every step along the way to document the efforts in earlier steps. To effectively perform the BIA, a large quantity of information specific to various business areas and functions is needed. There are a number of methods for collecting

Table 2-2 Processes and Required Resources Arranged in a Resource/Component Table

Mission/Business Process	Required Resource Component	Additional Resource Details	Description
Provide customer support (help desk)	Trouble ticket and resolution application software	Application server with Linux OS, Apache server, and SQL database	Each help desk technician requires access to the organization's trouble ticket and resolution software application, which is hosted on a dedicated server.
Provide customer support (help desk)	Help desk network segment	25 Cat5e network drops, gigabit network hub	The help desk applications are networked and require a network segment to access.
Provide customer support (help desk)	Help desk access terminals	1 Laptop/PC per technician, with Web-browsing software	The help desk applications require a Web interface on a laptop/PC.
Provide customer billing	Customized accounts receivable application software	Application server with Linux OS, Apache server, and SQL database	Accounts receivable requires access to its customized AR software and customer database to process customer billing.

this information. Thus, a data collection plan should be established early on to make the overall process more effective. Methods to collect data include the following:

- Online questionnaires
- Facilitated data-gathering sessions
- Process flows and interdependency studies
- Risk assessment research
- IT application or system logs
- Financial reports and departmental budgets
- BCP/DRP audit documentation
- Production schedules

Online Questionnaires

As an aid in collecting the information necessary to identify and classify business functions and the impact they have on other areas of the organization, an online or printed questionnaire can be quite useful. The questionnaire is a structured method to collect information directly from those who know the most about a business area and its functions.

According to the Texas State Office of Risk Management, the BIA questionnaire should cover the following areas:

- *Function description: A brief description of the function being performed*
- *Dependencies: A brief description of the dependencies of the function; what has to happen or needs to be available before the function can be performed?*
- *Impact profile: Is there a specific time of day, day of the week, week of the month, or month of the year that the function is more vulnerable to risk/exposure or when the impact to the business would be greater if the function is not performed?*
- *Operational impacts: When would the operational impact to the business be realized if the function was not performed? Describe the operational impact.*
- *Financial impacts: When would the financial impact to the business be realized if the function was not performed? Describe the financial impact.*
- *Work backlog: At what point does the backlog of work start to impact the business?*
- *Recovery resources: What kind of resources are needed to support the function, how many are needed, and how soon are they needed after a disruption (phones, desks, PCs, etc.)?*
- *Technology resources: What software and/or applications are needed to support the function?*
- *Stand-alone PCs or workstations: Does the function require a stand-alone PC or workstation?*
- *Local area networks: Does the function require access to the LAN?*
- *Work-around procedures: Are there currently manual work-around procedures in place that enable the function to be performed in the event that IT is unavailable? If so, how long can these work-arounds be used to continue the function?*
- *Work at home: Can the function be performed from home?*
- *Workload shifting: Is it possible to shift workloads to another part of the business that might not be impacted by the disruption?*
- *Business records: Are certain business records needed to perform the function? If so, are they backed up? How? With what frequency?*
- *Regulatory reporting: Are regulatory documents created as a result of the function?*
- *Work inflows: What input is received, either internally or externally, that is needed to perform the function?*
- *Work outflows: Where does the output go after it leaves the functional area, or in other words, who would be impacted if the function were not performed?*
- *Business disruption experience: Has there ever been a disruption of the function? If so, give a brief description.*
- *Competitive analysis: Is there a competitive impact if the function is not performed? When would the impact occur? When would the company potentially start losing customers?*
- *Other issues and concerns: Are any other issues relevant to the success of performing the function?*[27]

In the completion of the BIA, the organization should also address the RTO, RPO, and the dependencies between the BIA and other areas.

Several sample BIA questionnaires are available on the Web to assist the organization in its data collection, including one from TechTarget at *https://searchdisasterrecovery.techtarget.com/tutorial/Business-impact-analysis-questionnaire-template* and one from the U.S. Postal Service at *about.usps.com/who-we-are/privacy-policy/business-impact-assessment-template.rtf*. Related support worksheets are available from organizations like the U.S. Federal Emergency Management Agency at *www.fema.gov/media-library/assets/documents/89526*.

systems diagramming

A common approach in the discipline of systems analysis and design, used to understand how systems operate, chart process and information flows, and understand interdependencies.

Facilitated Data-Gathering Sessions

A focus group, also known as a facilitated data-gathering session, is a commonly used technique for collecting information directly from end users and business managers. If time permits, individuals from a particular business area, along with their managerial team, are brought together to brainstorm answers to the questions posed by the BIA process. Unless steps are taken to ensure a relaxed, productive session, these meetings may not yield the quantity or quality of information desired. Providing a clear structure to the sessions, encouraging dialogue, and restricting the managers' ability to take control are important ways to ensure that users have an opportunity to contribute to the process.

Process Flows and Interdependency Studies

Systems diagramming is commonly used to model operations and information flows in both manual and automated systems. Common diagramming techniques, such as use case diagrams and supporting use cases, are specifically designed to help users understand the interactions between entities and business functions. A sample use case diagram of the interactions between a company's Web commerce functions and its customers is shown in Figure 2-7. Table 2-3 provides descriptions of the ways the business processes are used.

Other modeling techniques drawn from systems analysis and design include Uniform Modeling Language (UML) models such as class diagrams, sequence diagrams, and collaboration diagrams. Other modeling techniques such as traditional systems analysis and design approaches, including workflow, functional decomposition, and dataflow diagrams, may also be useful. Many of these are quite complex, and creating them with the requisite level of detail may be beyond the abilities or resources available to the BIA team. However, if the organization already prepares these types of models as a function of ongoing systems development, then these modeling approaches may provide an excellent way to illustrate how the business functions and may already exist in the IT function of the organization. Figure 2-8 shows a simplified class diagram drawn from the object classes used to support the use case documented earlier. In the context of UML, object classes are entities about which we want to record data and actors are the roles played by people who use the system being modeled.

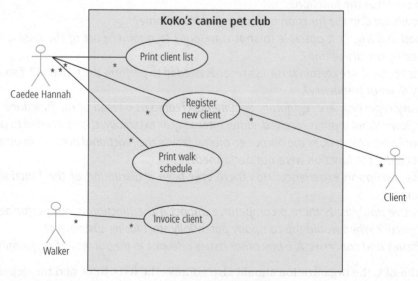

Figure 2-7   Example of a use case diagram

Table 2-3   Description for Sample Use Case Diagram

Use Case Description

Project name: KoKo's Canine Pet Club		Date prepared: 11/21/20
Use case name: Register New Client	ID: 1	Importance level: High
Primary actor: Client	Use case type: Detail, Essential	

Stakeholder and interest:

Client: Wants to get registered in order to use the dog-walking service

Employees: Want more business so they can keep their jobs

Caedee Hannah: Wants as many customers as she can get to increase profit

Brief description:

This use case describes the process by which a new client and pet are registered with the pet club.

Trigger: A new client comes into the store to register

Trigger type: External

Relationships:

    Association: Client

    Include:

    Extend:

    Generalization:

Normal flow of events:

1. A client comes into the store and requests to register with the service.
2. Ms. Hannah sits down with the client to discuss the service.
3. Basic information is collected and entered directly into the system.
4. Fees are negotiated and agreed upon.
5. Preferred walk time and walker are entered into the system.
6. Client and pet are issued a customer number to uniquely identify them.

Subflows:

    None documented

Alternatives/exceptional flows:

    None documented

Figure 2-9 shows a simplified sequence diagram used to document the possible interactions between the actors and object classes shown in Figure 2-8.

Figure 2-10 documents the interactions of the object classes described in Figure 2-8 as the system operates.

Risk Assessment Research

As described earlier, an organization's risk management effort can provide a wealth of information that can be used in the BIA. Although some modification may be necessary, the risk management process is in fact the primary starting point for the BIA. If the organization has not performed a comprehensive risk assessment, some remediation effort will be required. Additionally, the teams may collect information from outside sources on risk assessment.

IT Application or System Logs

When completing the many weighted tables used in the BIA, an IT staff may prove particularly valuable in determining categorical data on frequency of occurrence, probability of success, and so on by providing information from the various logs their equipment maintains. These logs collect and provide reports on failed login attempts, probes, scans, denial-of-service attacks, and malware detected, to name a few. This information can provide an accurate description of the attack environment that the organization faces. In some cases, the BIA team may be able to ask the IT department to collect information from these systems that it is currently not collecting.

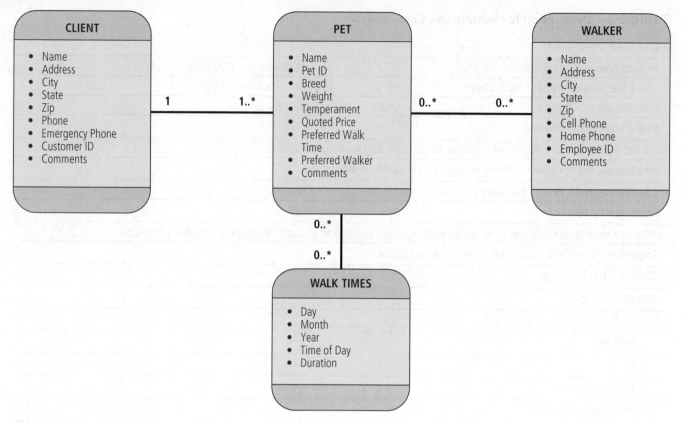

Figure 2-8 Example of a class diagram

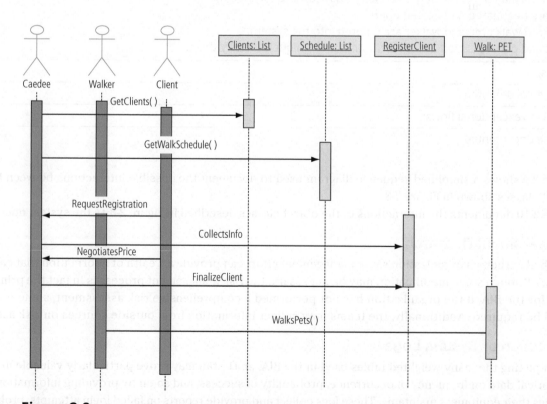

Figure 2-9 Example of a sequence diagram

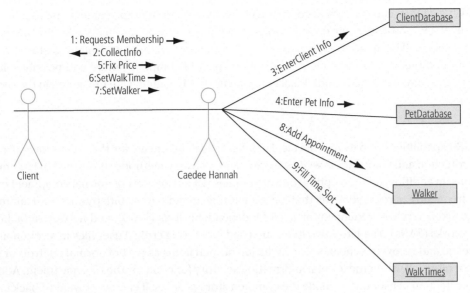

1: Requests Membership
2: CollectInfo
5: Fix Price
6: SetWalkTime
7: SetWalker

3: EnterClient Info
4: Enter Pet Info
8: Add Appointment
9: Fill Time Slot

Client

Caedee Hannah

ClientDatabase

PetDatabase

Walker

WalkTimes

Figure 2-10   Example of a collaboration diagram

Financial Reports and Departmental Budgets

Running a business requires great attention to financial detail. As a normal part of an organization's administration, a number of financial documents are created that can provide insight into the operations of the business, including the costs and revenues provided by each functional area. This information is useful in determining the prioritization of business areas and functions within those areas. It also provides insight into the contribution of each area to the organization's profitability and revenues.

The most common method of calculating business impact is to review financial reports and budgets. Lost sales, idle personnel costs, and other opportunity costs are easily obtained using these documents.

Audit Documentation

As is often the case in larger organizations, especially publicly traded firms, the organization has paid external consultants to audit their functions for compliance with federal and state regulations, with national or international standards, or as part of a proactive, ongoing improvement program. These audit reports can provide additional information for the BIA process.

Production Schedules

Finally, information gained from production schedules, marketing forecasts, productivity reports, and a host of other business documents can also prove valuable in the completion of the BIA. Although the organization may neither have all these sources available nor the desire to include all of them, it is advantageous to include information collected from multiple sources rather than redundantly re-collecting it from the same sources for this process. The important thing to remember is to make sure the information you use is current and accurate, particularly if it is not collected directly by the BIA team. If it is used to make decisions that affect the organization's ability to react and recover from attacks, undated information may often be worse than no information at all, as it adds to confusion.

BUDGETING FOR CONTINGENCY OPERATIONS

As a final component of the initial planning process, the CPMT must prepare to deal with the inevitable expenses associated with contingency operations. Although some areas may not require dedicated budgeting, others will require ongoing expenditures, investment, and service contracts to support their implementation. The simple cost of employee time and effort to conduct testing and training of continuity plans is an expense that can be built into the organization's budget. Many organizations are *self-insured* against some types of losses, such as theft of technology, equipment, or other resources. Ideally, this means that in lieu of payments to an outside insurance organization, the organization puts a set amount each fiscal cycle into a contingency account it can draw upon should replacements be required. With tight budgets and drops in revenues, however, some organizations forego these allocations, instead betting on the probability that such losses, if they occur, will be minimal and can be funded out of normal budgets. The biggest risk is that a disastrous expense could occur and the organization might face the prospect of complete failure and possible closure as a result. Some of the budgeting requirements of the individual components of CP planning are presented in the sections that follow.

Incident Response Budgeting

To a large extent, IR capabilities are part of a normal IT budget. It is customary for the CIO to have his or her managers ensure that data protection and response, as well as backup and recovery methods (described in later modules), are part of normal operations. In addition, uninterruptible power supplies (UPSs) are part of normal equipment expenditures of IT operations. Other frequently purchased items that have an IR role are antivirus, antispyware, and antimalware software, cloud-based data backup services, redundant arrays of independent disks (RAID), and network-attached storage (NAS) or storage area networks (SANs). The latter two items are used for storing critical user files in a common area that can be included in the backup and recovery schemes. The inclusion of such items as part of normal controls or safeguards for IT operations will most often fall within the normal information security function for the IT department. Additional expenses might arise in the protection of user data outside the common storage areas. If end users want to back up their individual data, additional options are needed, such as individualized cloud backup service, tape drives, or writeable DVD systems. When IT systems allow user discretion for where and how data is stored, the users assume responsibility for the backup of documents stored on removable media such as USB devices, which are likely more vulnerable than most users understand.

The only area in which additional budgeting is absolutely required is the maintenance of redundant equipment if there are equipment failures resulting from incidents. The so-called *rule of three* is quite useful in preparing for this inevitability. According to this rule, an organization should keep three levels of computer system environments available: an online production system, an online or very nearly online backup environment with a quality assurance process to serve as a ready reserve for the production systems, and an offline testing and development system to stage software nearing the end of the change management process.

In most organizations, critical equipment has redundancy incorporated into the systems. Online *hot* servers like domain controllers, Web servers, database servers, and e-mail servers frequently have a backup or *warm* server providing redundant functions that are standing by in a near-online state. Should the hot server go down, the warm server steps up to become the hot server and provides the functions needed to the clients. In case the hot server goes down and the warm server is now the hot server, the rule of three requires an organization to maintain a cold server or other equipment to allow the timely creation of a new warm server and provide needed redundancy. The hot server can be taken offline and repaired as needed while there's still redundancy in the system. Some common components, such as network cards and small hubs, may only require a few *shelved* items to provide redundancy for a larger number of in-use items. The key is to ensure that any offline cold server is equipped and configured exactly like the hot and warm versions. In fact, many organizations use the cold server as a test server to ensure that any added patches or upgrades do not negatively affect other applications or services.

Disaster Recovery Budgeting

The primary budgetary expense for DR is insurance. Insurance policies provide for the capabilities to rebuild and reestablish operations at the primary site. Should a fire, flood, earthquake, or other natural disaster strike, the insurance carrier oversees the funding of replacement structures and services until the primary site is restored. Therefore, it is essential that insurance policies be carefully scrutinized to ensure that effective coverage is provided, with the understanding that more comprehensive coverage costs more. Most insurance policies have deductibles, and larger deductibles provide lower monthly premiums. Setting aside a fund specifically dedicated to cover these deductibles ensures that they do not cause financial problems while the organization is getting reestablished.

One problem with insurance is that much of the damage from electronic attacks is not covered in traditional business policies. Fortunately, cyber insurance today is available as an addendum to a business's existing policies. In 2009, for example, Heartland Payment Systems took out a $30 million *cyber insurance policy* specifically designed to cover losses in online commerce. The good news is that they were covered when they suffered a data breach later that year, but the bad news is that the breach resulted in losses estimated at over $145 million. Their insurance company paid the claim—$30 million, as insured.

In 2018, Forrester Research examined cyber insurance policies and found:

- *The cyber insurance market is maturing, but growing pains persist.*
- *Buyers navigate a labyrinth of intertwining providers and partners.*
- *The devil is in the details.*
- *Choose your cyber insurance broker wisely.*[8]

How do you decide if hacker insurance is needed?

- Is your potential liability big enough to justify concern about the possibility of a loss, whether from loss of an asset, loss of access, or loss of prestige?
- Are your online activities a significant part of the business?
- Do you have electronic assets that are valuable proprietary information but are reachable over public networks and might be stolen?
- Would you lose a significant amount of money if your systems were denied access to the Internet?

In an interview with TechRepublic, Jenny Soubra, U.S. head of cyber for Alliance Global Corporate & Specialty, stated:

One of the issues in the cyber market itself is just that there's not consistency across the board from policy to policy, especially in terms of policy language. So different carriers will call the same thing by different names…

And so when the consumer is comparing the different policies, it is hard to figure out what's the same and what is different, which is, of course, where the [insurance] broker comes in.[9]

Many expenses are not covered by insurance—loss of water, loss of electricity, loss of data, and the like. It is important for the BIA to include all the items the organization will need to support operations and then determine which of them are covered by insurance and which are not.

Business Continuity Budgeting

In contingency planning operations, business continuity requires the largest budget expenditure. As you will see in later modules, maintaining service contracts to cover all the contingencies that the organization faces can be quite expensive. The service level agreements (SLAs) for hot sites, for example, require a dedicated duplicate facility complete with servers, networking devices, and telephony devices—essentially everything except data and personnel. The cost to maintain such a high level of redundancy can be staggering. Every level of the continuity plan includes expenses—even mobile services, whose providers are capable of rolling out specially configured tractor-trailers equipped so that the organization can inhabit them until it is ready to move its operations back to the primary site. Unless the organization budgets and contracts for these services well in advance, it may find itself in a financial bind when it finally needs them.

The organization should have a *war chest* of contingency funds set aside to purchase items as they are needed during continuity operations. It can establish safety deposit boxes at a local bank with corporate credit cards, purchase orders, and even cash. Just the expenses associated with office supplies can be quite staggering if the organization has to purchase sufficient materials to maintain its operations, not to mention the staff needed for critical operations, for an extended time.

Another expense not normally budgeted for is employee overtime. Having to reestablish operations at another location inevitably includes extensive overtime for non-salaried employees. Unless a reserve fund is prepared in advance, the expenses associated with late nights, early mornings, and even weekends can quickly mount, unbalancing the organization's precarious finances at a hectic time.

Crisis Management Budgeting

The last item in planning a budget is crisis management. Although the details of crisis management are covered in later modules, it is important to know that the fundamentals of crisis management are focused on the potential for physical and psychological losses associated with catastrophic disasters, like the World Trade Center attacks of September 11, 2001. The primary budget items here are employee salaries, should the employees be unable to come to work. The organization may want to establish a 30-day budget or other minimum budget for paid leave as employees wait at home to see if they have a job to come back to.

Companies may also want to consider budgeting for contributions to employee loss expenses, such as funeral and burial expenses, as well as counseling services for employees and loved ones if they are not specifically covered in the current benefits package.

Closing Scenario

"And the next event in this scenario is . . ."

JJ made a dramatic pause.

"The power came back on 27 minutes after it was terminated," JJ then read from the card.

He looked up at the team, ready to continue the rehearsal.

Discussion Questions

1. In the opening scenario, the group was practicing for a snow emergency. Other than power outages, what incident cards would you expect to see? For each of the incident cards you listed, what would be the proper response of the organization?
2. How often should an organization rehearse its contingency plans?
3. Who should coordinate rehearsal of the contingency plans? Why would that be the appropriate person?
4. What degree of cross-training between the various roles in the plans is most effective? Identify the advantages and disadvantages of such a cross-training plan. What trade-offs do you think exist between extensive and minimal cross-training?
5. The CIO, Amanda Wilson, was not at this rehearsal. Do you think it is important that the CIO, or even the CEO in some cases, participate in this kind of readiness exercise? Why or why not?
6. How can you make progress in contingency planning in the face of resistance from upper management?

Ethical Decision Making

Suppose the CIO of the company, Amanda Wilson, had refused to attend the practice session because she "thought this was a waste of time and unimportant," even though it is a specific requirement of her position by policy.

Should the team that was present inform the CEO that Amanda missed the session?

MODULE SUMMARY

- Contingency planning (CP) is improved by using a systematic methodology that addresses the challenges facing organizations during an incident, disaster, or other crisis. To begin, an organization must establish an entity that will be responsible for contingency policy and plans, such as a contingency planning management team (CPMT), which is a group responsible for the overall planning and development of the CP process. The CPMT is responsible for obtaining commitment and support, managing the overall process, writing documents, conducting the business impact analysis (BIA), organizing and staffing the leadership for subordinate teams, and providing guidance to, and integrating the work of, the subordinate teams. A typical roster for the CPMT may include a champion, a project manager, and a number of additional team members as well as representatives from other business units.
- Effective CP begins with effective policy. The CPMT must receive guidance from executive management through formal CP policy. CP policy should contain an introductory statement of philosophical perspective; a statement of the scope and purpose of the CP operations; a call for periodic risk assessment and business impact analysis; a specification of the CP's major components; a call for, and guidance in, the selection of recovery options and business continuity strategies; a requirement to test the various plans on a regular basis; identification of key regulations and standards that affect CP planning and a brief overview of their relevancy; identification of key individuals responsible for CP operations; and a challenge to the individual members of the organization, asking for their support and reinforcing their importance as part of the overall CP process.
- A BIA is an investigation and assessment of the impact that various events or incidents can have on the organization. It also provides a detailed identification and prioritization of critical business functions that would require protection and continuity in an adverse event. The BIA adds insight into what the organization must

do to respond to adverse events, minimize the damage from such events, recover from the effects, and return to normal operations. A BIA is conducted in three stages: assessing mission/business processes and recovery criticality, identifying resource requirements, and identifying recovery priorities. When organizations consider recovery criticality, they usually think in terms of maximum tolerable downtime, recovery time objective, and recovery point objective. A key element is placing priorities and values on mission/business processes. After the organization has created a prioritized list of its mission and business processes, it can determine what resources would be needed to recover those processes and their associated assets.

- The primary budgetary expense for DR is insurance. Most insurance policies have deductibles, and larger deductibles provide lower monthly premiums. Setting aside a fund specifically dedicated to cover these deductibles ensures that they do not cause financial problems while the organization is getting reestablished after a disaster. In CP operations, business continuity requires the largest budget expenditure. An expense not normally budgeted for is employee overtime. Crisis management budgets consist mostly of employee salaries. Companies may also want to consider budgeting for contributions to employee loss expenses, such as funeral and burial expenses, as well as counseling services for employees and loved ones.

Review Questions

1. List and describe three of the applicable U.S. laws that impact contingency planning.
2. What is the first step in beginning the contingency planning process?
3. What are the primary responsibilities of the contingency planning management team (CPMT)?
4. Which teams may be subordinate to the CPMT in a typical organization?
5. The CP process will fail without what critical element?
6. What are the three communities of interest, and why are they important to CP?
7. What are the elements needed to begin the CP process?
8. What are the major sections in the CP policy document?
9. What is a business impact analysis (BIA), and why is it important?
10. What are the usual stages in the conduct of the BIA?
11. What is a business process?
12. When confronted with many business functions from many parts of the organization, what tool can an organization use to determine which function is the most critical?
13. What are the most common downtime metrics used to express recovery criticality?
14. What is maximum tolerable downtime (MTD)?
15. What is recovery time objective (RTO)?
16. What is recovery point objective (RPO), and how does it differ from recovery time objective?
17. What are the primary means for collecting data for the BIA?
18. What is a facilitated data-gathering session?
19. What are some items usually included in routine IT operations budgets that can be considered part of CP requirements?
20. Beyond the items funded in the normal course of IT operations, what are the additional budgeting areas for CP needs?

Real-World Exercises

Exercise 2-1

Use the Web to search the terms "BP deepwater disaster plan failure." You will find many results. Select one article and identify what the article considers a shortcoming in BP's planning. What part of the contingency planning process came up short (IR, DR, or BC)? How could the shortcoming have been prevented?

Exercise 2-2

Use the Web to search the terms "CitiBank backup tapes lost." You will find many results. Select one article and identify what the article considers a shortcoming in CitiBank's planning. What part of the contingency planning process came up short (IR, DR, or BC)? How could the shortcoming have been prevented?

Exercise 2-3

Use the Web to search the terms "I-35 bridge collapse in Minnesota and response." You will find many results. Review at least three articles about the accident's impact on human life, and then answer this question: Did contingency planning save lives in this disaster?

Exercise 2-4

Visit the article abstract at *www.ncjrs.gov/App/publications/Abstract.aspx?id=246582*. Read the abstract and then answer this question: Do you think having a simulator for training and readiness would help or hinder the quality of response to contingencies? Explain your answer.

Hands-On Projects

The hands-on project for this module can be accessed in the Practice It folder in MindTap or through your instructor's LMS. The virtual labs provided with this resource can help you develop practical skills that will be of value as you progress through the course.

References

1. Zawada, B., and L. Evans. "Creating a More Rigorous BIA." Proceedings of the Contingency Planning & Management West Conference, Vol. 7, p. 24 (2002).
2. Swanson, M., P. Bowen, A. Phillips, D. Gallup, and D. Lynes. Special Publication 800-34, Rev. 1: "Contingency Planning Guide for Federal Information Systems." National Institute of Standards and Technology. Accessed 12/6/2017 from *http://csrc.nist.gov/publications/nistpubs/800-34-rev1/sp800-34-rev1_errata-Nov11-2010.pdf*.
3. Ibid.
4. Ibid.
5. Ibid.
6. Ibid.
7. "Business Continuity Impact Analysis." Texas State Office of Risk Management. Accessed 04/10/2005 from *www.sorm.state.tx.us/Risk_Management/Business_Continuity/bus_impact.php*.
8. Forrester Research for Forrester (2018). "Your 2018 guide to cyber insurance is here." Accessed 10/23/18 from *www.zdnet.com/article/your-2018-guide-to-cyber-insurance-is-here/*.
9. Patterson, J. "Cybersecurity insurance: What to look for when comparing policies." Accessed 10/23/18 from *www.techrepublic.com/article/cybersecurity-insurance-what-to-look-for-when-comparing-policies/*.

CONTINGENCY STRATEGIES FOR INCIDENT RESPONSE, DISASTER RECOVERY, AND BUSINESS CONTINUITY

Upon completion of this material, you should be able to:

1. Discuss the need for strategies to archive and recover critical data and organizational functions in the event of an incident or disaster

2. Describe the alternatives available for data and application availability, backup, and recovery, including how cloud computing has altered the organization's approach to both availability and recovery of critical information assets

3. Explain the strategies employed for resumption of critical business processes at alternate and recovered sites

> *Men at some time are masters of their fates. The fault, dear Brutus, is not in our stars, but in ourselves.*
>
> — William Shakespeare (1564–1616), Julius Caesar (Act I, Scene ii)

Opening Scenario

Bobby was not having a good day. He had started the morning by oversleeping and had clocked in 15 minutes late. Rushing through the mailroom doors, Bobby splashed his coffee into a full cart of mail someone had left near the door. Only heroic blotting kept him from ruining dozens of envelopes. It looked like important stuff, too. As he hurriedly restacked the still damp mail into the cart, a thick yellow envelope slipped from his hand and fell to the floor, exploding into a cloud of white powder that spread over the carpet, the mail cart, all of the mail, and Bobby himself.

"Ooof" was the noise Bobby made as he puffed all the air out of his lungs, mouth, and nose while backing away from the cart and out the mailroom door. Having just gone through the refresher training for emergency procedures in the mailroom, he knew to exhale quickly and get out as rapidly as possible. Everyone else in the mailroom did the same. This was the exact maneuver the team had rehearsed just a week before: Exhale, exit, and hit the big red button that turns off the room's ventilators and sets off the emergency alarm. Bobby stopped after he got out in the hallway and waited with the rest of the mailroom team for the organized chaos he knew would follow.

An hour later, Alan Hake, CEO of HAL, sat with his incident team at the coffee shop across the street. As outlined in their plan, the team consisted of COO Richard Xavier, CFO Rachel Hernandez, and CIO Amanda Wilson. Also present were Roberta Briscoe, manager of corporate security, and Pantoja Martina, supervisor of the administrative staff and the mailroom. They were reviewing the response plan in place for contaminated mail, along with the supporting DR and BC plans, when a man in a fireman's dress uniform walked up to their table and said, "Hi. I'm Deputy Fire Chief Corbett. Are you the folks from HAL?"

"Yes," said Alan. "Please, have a seat." He gestured to an empty chair at their impromptu conference table. Deputy Chief Corbett sat down and said, "The field test, within its limited test range, shows that the white powder in the mailroom is not a pathogen or a contaminant. Normally, at this point, we would send a sample to the forensics lab and ask them to expedite processing. That would give us an answer within six hours."

Alan and the team listened to the deputy chief carefully as he spoke. Now, they smiled as they looked at each other.

"What about the mailroom staff?" Alan asked. "What's your opinion of their reaction?"

"As far as I can tell, they seem to have performed quite well, exactly as your plan specified," Deputy Chief Corbett replied, as he smiled in return. "We isolated them and were preparing them to go through the standard biochemical decontamination protocol. Not very pleasant, nor a very modest activity, but the team was informed that they had just been involved in an unannounced test, right before they had to strip. They're not too happy, but they were greatly relieved. They are currently standing by in isolation suits waiting for the 'final lab results.' As soon as you're ready, we'll release them for your debrief."

He smiled again and then added, "I suggest a long lunch while you let them cool off a bit. And just FYI, if that test was for a real event, and it did come back as contaminated, your office space would probably be off limits for three to four weeks—maybe longer."

Corbett grinned even more as he said, "The fire department thanks you and your staff for your assistance in our Hazmat training program."

Alan shook the chief's hand and turned to his executives. "OK, before we conduct our after-action review with the team, what did we learn other than unannounced tests make our mailroom unhappy?"

INTRODUCTION

As discussed in Modules 1 and 2, contingency planning (CP) encompasses everything done by an organization to prepare for the unexpected. This includes something as trivial as evaluating an alarm from an intrusion detection and prevention system or responding to the never-ending stream of new viruses and worms in e-mail systems, but it can also include an outright catastrophe like the one that could have befallen HAL in this module's opening scenario. The incident response (IR) process focuses on detecting, evaluating, and reacting to an incident, with later phases of the process focusing on keeping the business functioning even if the physical plant is destroyed or unavailable. When the IR process cannot contain and resolve an incident, the company turns to the disaster recovery and business continuity plans (or **business resumption plan** if the organization has a combined DR/BC approach) to help restore normal operations quickly

business resumption plan (BR plan)

The documented product of business resumption planning; a plan that shows the organization's intended efforts in the event of a disaster coupled with the requirement to relocate key business functions to an alternate site until the primary site can be recovered.

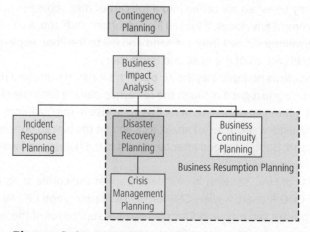

Figure 3-1   Contingency planning hierarchies

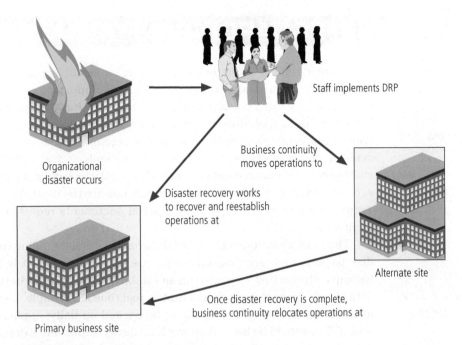

Staff implements DRP

Business continuity
moves operations to

Organizational
disaster occurs

Disaster recovery works
to recover and reestablish
operations at

Alternate site

Once disaster recovery is complete,
business continuity relocates operations at

Primary business site

Figure 3-2   Business resumption

at the primary site or a new permanent site if the old one is no longer viable. The relationships among the various elements of the continuity plan are shown in Figure 3-1.

Most large-scale disasters require the implementation of two key CP plans: the disaster recovery plan (DR plan), which lists and describes the efforts to resume normal operations at the primary places of business, and the business continuity plan (BC plan), which contains the steps for implementing critical business functions at an alternate internal or external location until normal operations can be resumed at the primary site (or at a new location), as illustrated in Figure 3-2.

Note that the DR plan is often technically focused and concerned with recovering the organization's technical capabilities, usually in the context of primary infrastructure. The BC plan is often focused on the business processes supported by technical infrastructure and how to maintain business functionality using resources that are alternatives to this infrastructure.

Some experts argue that the two components of business resumption planning (BRP)—disaster recovery planning (DRP) and business continuity planning (BCP)—are so closely linked that they are indistinguishable. However, each has a distinct place, role, personnel structure, and planning requirement. They may be planned together for efficiency of effort, especially when the organization has insufficient personnel to staff both.

Each of the components of CP (the IR, DR, and BC plans) also comes into play at a specific time in the life of an event, as explained in Module 1. Regardless of the type of response needed (IR, DR, or BC), organizations require a reliable method of restoring information and reestablishing all operations—both IT operations and other business functions. Whether the objective is to recover a backup of a file that has been accidentally deleted or to transfer an entire data center to an alternate facility, there are five key mechanisms that help restore critical information and the continuation of business operations:

- Delayed data protection
- Real-time data protection
- Server recovery
- Application recovery
- Site recovery

The first four of these mechanisms are discussed in the following section; the fifth is covered in a later section.

business resumption planning (BRP)

The actions taken by senior management to develop and implement a combined DR and BC policy, plan, and set of recovery teams.

SAFEGUARDING INFORMATION

data backup

The duplication of systems data to external media or a secondary location to provide recovery capability in the event of data loss.

data archive

The duplication of systems data to external media or a secondary location for the purpose of long-term retention; archival is typically mandated by policy or regulation.

archive

See *data archive*.

data recovery

The restoration of data from a backup or archive to a system or user who needs it.

retention schedule

An organizational policy specifying requirements for data retention, including what must be retained, where it will be stored and for how long, and the method of disposal.

There are a number of methods for making copies of key data in case something happens to the primary storage location. It is important to first understand the difference between a backup and an archive. Data backup typically involves making a copy or snapshot of the data from a specific point in time. Because data is considered volatile and subject to change, multiple copies or versions are usually made at regular intervals. A data archive, or simply archive, involves the long-term storage of a document or data file, usually for legal or regulatory purposes. For data recovery from an incident or disaster, backups are the most common solution. For events that impact backups or for special documents required by policy or law, archives are used.

The most common varieties of data backup include online (or cloud) backup, disk backup, and tape backup, which are discussed here. It is important to use backup methods that are based on an established policy. As a best practice, critical data should be backed up in as close to real time as possible. Less important data files and critical system files should be backed up daily; applications and nonessential files should be backed up weekly. Equally important is determining how long data should be stored. All data storage that involves backups or archives should be based on a retention schedule that guides the location, frequency of replacement, and duration of storage. Some data, such as financial records, is required by law to be retained and stored for years. Data that is not covered by laws or regulations may even be in the organization's best interest to quickly destroy. Management should create a formal policy and plan that includes recommendations from legal counsel for conforming to applicable laws, regulations, and standards. For routine backups of critical data, the organization only needs to retain a few of the most recent copies (daily backups) and at least one off-site copy. (Note that more copies stored at redundant locations are better, as long as the copies themselves are sufficiently protected.) For complete backups of entire systems, at least one copy should be stored in a secure location, such as an encrypted online account, bank vault, security deposit box, or remote office safe.

As suggested by NIST SP 800-34, Rev. 1, "Contingency Planning Guide for Federal Information Systems," alternatives should be considered when designing backup and recovery strategies. Each option should contain planning for the total cost of operation, including establishing and operating costs, downtime estimates, estimates of the security provided by the option, how the option affects the sequence of recovery based on the relative priority of included systems, and how the option fits into broader organizational planning efforts. The information in Table 3-1 can assist in identifying backup and recovery strategies associated with various system priorities.[1]

Table 3-1   Backup and Recovery Strategies Based on System Priority

Information System Target Priority	Backup/Recovery Strategy
Low priority—Any damage to or disruption of such systems would cause little impact, damage, or disruption to the organization	Backup: Tape backup Strategy: Relocate or cold site
Important or moderate priority—Any damage to or disruption of such systems would cause a moderate problem to the organization and possibly other networks or systems	Backup: Optical backup, WAN/VLAN replication Strategy: Cold or warm site
Mission critical or high priority—Any damage to or disruption of such systems would have the most serious impact on the organization, its mission, and other networks or systems	Backup: Mirrored systems and disk replication Strategy: Hot site

Source: NIST Special Publication 800-34, Rev. 1.

The Impact of Cloud Computing on Contingency Planning and Operations

This module explains various technical elements of online Web services, or cloud computing, including ways to back up and restore data as well as emerging trends in provisioning critical contingency services to safeguard data and speed responsiveness in the event of a recovery operation. According to industry reports such as Gartner and IDC, cloud-based backup and recovery services are becoming increasingly popular. Coupled with the trend toward cloud-hosted provisioning of many critical business services, cloud computing has far-reaching consequences for organizations that adopt the technology. This section highlights how the emergence of cloud computing technologies and practices is affecting the world of contingency planning and operations.

Faster Recovery

Taking advantage of cloud technologies could allow companies to react faster to a disaster, which is important because speed of response is a critical element of an effective recovery program. In many situations, businesses can recover from a disaster by using the cloud and automation tools to automate the recovery process. These automated tools are useful because the tasks involved can otherwise be very tedious, with scripts and a lot of manual effort that could significantly delay a response when implementing a disaster recovery solution. Taking advantage of cloud computing in a disaster recovery plan could also mean that businesses can recover their data very efficiently with lower levels of staffing required. This could reduce costs for the company and get them back into production quickly.

Improved Survivability

Using cloud-based production as well as backup and recovery services can improve the organization's ability to survive disasters. When selecting cloud-based services, one criterion is the robustness of the vendor's contingency planning. Smaller and medium-sized organizations can lease cloud-based services from major providers that have the wherewithal to plan, develop, and run a multisite, redundant, continuous operation that will be more effective than what the organization can develop for itself.

When evaluating service providers in this sector, be aware that some resellers use other major vendors without making it obvious to their customers. If your organization has contracted for backup capabilities with Vendor A, it is possible they have subcontracted for those services with Vendor B, which might then subcontract with Vendor C. If your primary supplier is Vendor C and you believe your plan for resilience relies on Vendor A, the plan will fail if Vendor C has a disruption in service at the same time your primary and secondary services fail. Your due diligence must examine which vendors actually provide services to ensure that your plans are resilient.

Efficiency in Providing Services

Companies that use cloud computing for emergency preparedness are often able to create a plan that is relatively inexpensive. Larger organizations may choose to create redundant data centers, even though this option is quite expensive. Others will plan to use specialized third-party data centers for backup capacity. With a cloud-based solution, organizations can manage these virtual data centers themselves, have more flexibility and access to their data, and it can be very economical as well.

Added Flexibility

With cloud computing, businesses have fewer issues in choosing a location for a disaster recovery facility that could be damaged by the same event that damages their main offices. For example, when Hurricane Sandy hit the United States, many New York-based companies saw their disaster recovery centers damaged as well. With a cloud-based solution, that wouldn't be a problem because everything would be in the cloud. A cloud solution also gives businesses the ability to access their data centers anywhere and anytime. This can help businesses be productive no matter where they are.

Cloud Technologies for Backup and Recovery

One of the newest and increasingly common forms of data backup is online backup to a third-party data storage vendor. Several backup software and service providers now offer multiterabyte online data storage that's available anywhere. Even for the home user, companies such as Carbonite (*www.carbonite.com*), Dropbox (*www.dropbox.com*),

Software as a Service

A cloud computing service model whereby applications and the necessary computer resources to run them are provided as a turnkey, on-demand service.

Platform as a Service

A cloud computing service model whereby one or more computing platforms suitable for use in application development and testing are provided as a turnkey, on-demand service.

Infrastructure as a Service

A cloud computing service model whereby an entire computing infrastructure, including computers, operating systems, application software, and any needed network equipment, are provided as a turnkey, on-demand service.

data as a service

A cloud computing service model whereby storage capability for data, data sets, and databases associated with the organization's applications is provided as a turnkey, on-demand service.

storage as a service

A cloud computing service model whereby storage capability for data backup and archiving is provided as a turnkey, on-demand service.

cloud storage

See *storage as a service*.

disaster recovery as a service

A cloud computing service model based on provisioning of both data and computing resources on demand.

Microsoft (through OneDrive at *onedrive.live.com*), Apple (through iCloud at *www.apple/icloud*), and Google (through Google Drive at *www.google.com/drive/*) offer data storage ranging from free accounts with minimal amounts of storage to low-cost, multigigabyte and terabyte solutions.

For the corporate user, cloud services are commonly associated with the leasing of computing resources from a third party. Cloud computing is the provision of a defined range of computing services from an Internet-based service provider. Clients can lease services ranging from an online storage allotment to entire data centers. With the recent advances in virtualization, online services have become increasingly popular both as primary computing resources and as failover systems. Cloud computing was originally described as the provision of three fundamental services:

- **Software as a Service (SaaS)**, in which applications are made available on the Internet (and over the World Wide Web)
- **Platform as a Service (PaaS)**, in which development platforms are made available to developers
- **Infrastructure as a Service (IaaS)**, in which entire computer systems, including OS and application resources, are made available for whatever the organization wants to implement

Over time, the list of as-a-service offerings has increased dramatically. This includes the development of the following:

- *Data as a service*—A service whereby the data associated with an organization's applications is located in the cloud.
- *Storage as a service*—Commonly referred to simply as **cloud storage**, in which the organization stores its data in the cloud. Some argue that cloud storage is the same as data as a service, while others specify the latter as the location of data needed for current operations and associate storage as a service with data backup and data archiving. Regardless of which term you prefer, the data associated with either service can be accessed through specific programming and made available to any system connected to the Internet.
- *Disaster recovery as a service*—Another cloud computing alternative related to disaster recovery, in which both data and computing resources are available to an organization if needed. This option will be explained in additional detail later in this module.

Organizations can lease these types of services, which often include online backup services, and then have data storage needs serviced as part of the package. Currently, the following are the major as-a-service providers:

- Alibaba Cloud
- Amazon Web Services
- Google Cloud Platform
- IBM Cloud
- Microsoft Azure

Clouds are deployed in the following three ways (or a combination that is a hybrid of the three):

- *Public cloud*—The most common implementation, in which a service provider makes computing resources available over the Internet (and World Wide Web) to whoever needs them

- *Community cloud*—An implementation in which several organizations with common interests share computing resources; it can be managed by a third party or by the organizations themselves, and can be hosted internally or externally
- *Private cloud*—An implementation in which computing resources are operated solely by a single organization; an extension of an organization's intranet into the cloud

From a security perspective, the leasing of services from a third party is always a challenge. If you don't own the hardware, software, and infrastructure, you can't guarantee effective security, so you must scrutinize the service agreement and insist on minimal standards of due care.

 Every month, Backup Review, a Web site devoted to providing information about online backup and storage services, presents a list of the "Top 100 Online Backup Companies." To see the latest list, go to *www.backupreview. info/.*

Disk to Disk to Other: Delayed Protection

With the decrease in the costs of storage media, including traditional hard drives, solid-state drives, and tape backups, more and more organizations are creating massive arrays of independent, large-capacity disk drives to store information at least temporarily. In fact, many home users are using similar methods, adding external USB-mounted SATA drives in the 3- to 4-terabyte range and simply copying critical files to these external, portable devices for their routine backups. The use of these types of devices reduces the time-consuming nature of tape backup and avoids the costs and implementation challenges of tape at the individual user level. It also allows quick and easy recovery of individual files and directories, avoiding the tedious method of extracting the data from tape. Some applications like Memeo (*www.memeo.com*) even allow near real-time backup of data, with multiple archived older versions.

The following sections provide an overview of complex disk storage media that have various levels of redundancy. To better understand what goes on during IR or DR data restoration, you need to understand how system backups are created. Data backup is a complex operation that involves selecting the backup type, establishing backup schedules, and even duplicating data automatically using a variety of redundant array of independent disks (RAID) structures.

Disk to Disk to Tape

Individuals and organizations alike can build libraries of local devices—massively connected storage area networks—to support larger-scale data backup and recovery. The problem with this technology is the lack of redundancy if both the online and backup versions fail because of a virus or hacker intrusion. This is why a secondary series of data disks should be periodically backed up to tape—thus, the development of disk-to-disk-to-tape methods. The use of the secondary disk series avoids the need to take the primary set offline for duplication, and it reduces resource usage on the primary systems. The disk-to-disk initial copies can be made efficiently and simultaneously with other system processes.

Disk to Disk to Cloud

Like online data storage, disk-to-disk-to-cloud (also called disk-to-disk-to-online) backup strategies are rapidly gaining acceptance in the consumer and corporate areas. An organization may not need or desire to go directly from disk to cloud; it may want to aggregate all local backups to a central repository and then back up that repository to an online vendor.

From a security standpoint, allowing only a trusted backup server or service to access a company's online data storage reduces the risk of corruption (and therefore threats) to the confidentiality, integrity, and availability of stored online data. Individual users can be allowed to back up their data to a central location using inexpensive software, and then the organization can periodically upload a backup to the online cloud storage repository. Another benefit of cloud data backup is that most commercial backup providers use an encryption process prior to data being transmitted to the cloud storage location. The data is encrypted in transit and is not transmitted in plaintext across the Internet, so it cannot be read by unauthorized parties. Because cloud backup data is available via the Internet, organizations can also easily access that data to restore it to another system in a relatively quick time frame, thus minimizing downtime when systems have to be rebuilt or data has to be reloaded. Another benefit is the ability to automate the cloud backup process, thus removing the need to constantly have employees changing tapes or replacing drives in an array. Automation also allows organizations to back up much more frequently, thus minimizing the potential amount of data lost between backups. Organizations should ensure that their data is being retained in multiple geographical locations to minimize the risk of data loss from natural disaster or hardware failure.

Tape Backup and Recovery: General Strategies

Contrary to popular belief, tape backup isn't dead. While disk backup is recommended for data that needs to be accessed quickly or frequently, tape is still a viable strategy for data archiving for long periods of time, due to its ability to store large amounts of data on a single tape. Traditionally, tape has been able to store larger quantities of data in smaller containers, and it is still a cost-effective method for organizations to maintain large quantities of data. The most common types of tape media for small organizations and individual users are digital audio tapes (DATs), quarter-inch cartridge (QIC) drives, 8-mm tape, and digital linear tape (DLT). For example, one of the newer IBM tapes—the TS 2280—can store up to 30 terabytes of data on a single tape, with a data rate of around 300 megabytes per second and up to 750 MBps with a 2.5:1 compression.[2] Each type of tape has its restrictions and advantages.

The first stage of a tape-based backup and recovery process is the scheduling of the backups, coupled with arranging the storage of the media. The most common schedule is a daily on-site backup, either incremental or differential, with a weekly off-site full backup. Most backups are conducted during off-shift hours when systems activity is lowest and the probability of user interruption is limited.

When addressing the selection of files to back up, a popular method is the *six-tape rotation* method, in which six sets of media are used in rotation. It uses five media sets per week and offers roughly two weeks of recovery capability, as shown in Table 3-2.

When it comes to the recovery stage of the process, the organization first attempts to recover the file(s) using the Monday through Thursday tapes, if they are on hand. If the file that needs to be restored is not contained within the backups that are on hand, the last full backup that was stored off-site is retrieved and the file(s) is recovered from that media. For additional ease of use and for redundancy, an organization may choose to make two copies of each full backup so that an on-site version can be kept in the data center and an off-site set of full backup (Friday) tapes can be sent to the secure storage location. This will avoid the need to retrieve the off-site set unless the needed file(s) cannot be recovered from the backup media available on-site.

Another option is the *Grandparent/Parent/Child* method, which is similar to the six-tape rotation method but retains four full weekly (Friday) backups and adds a full monthly backup, retaining 12 monthly backups. This is considered the most common method of tape rotation. After the monthly backup is created, the four (or five) Friday tapes are reused.

Primary drawbacks of tape backups include the cost of the specialized equipment as well as the media and time required to store and retrieve information. Individual storage tapes can cost hundreds of dollars. Even with multihundred megabyte-per-second backup times, a large data repository can take hours to back up and recover. With dramatically faster and less expensive options of external and internal disk-to-disk data backups now available, the market for consumer-grade tape backups has dwindled to a fraction of its former popularity in the last decade.

Table 3-2   Six-Tape Rotation Method

Week	Monday	Tuesday	Wednesday	Thursday	Friday
1	Incremental BU Tape #1	Incremental BU Tape #2	Incremental BU Tape #3	Incremental BU Tape #4	Full BU Tape #5 stored off-site
2	Incremental BU Tape #1	Incremental BU Tape #2	Incremental BU Tape #3	Incremental BU Tape #4	Full BU Tape #6 stored off-site
3	Incremental BU Tape #1	Incremental BU Tape #2	Incremental BU Tape #3	Incremental BU Tape #4	Full BU Tape #5 stored off-site
4	Incremental BU Tape #1	Incremental BU Tape #2	Incremental BU Tape #3	Incremental BU Tape #4	Full BU Tape #6 stored off-site

Note: Differential or full backups can certainly be used on Monday through Thursday.

How Much to Back Up?

There are three basic backup options when it comes to the question of how much data should be backed up at one time: full, differential, and incremental. The advantage of a full backup is that it takes a comprehensive snapshot of the organization's system. The primary disadvantages are that it requires large quantities of media to store such a large set of data and that the backup process can be time-consuming.

A differential backup works faster and uses less storage space than a full backup, but each daily differential backup is larger and slower than that of the day before. For example, if you conduct a full backup on Sunday, then Monday's backup contains all the files that have changed since Sunday, and Tuesday's backup contains all the files that have changed since Sunday as well, including Monday. By Friday, the file size has grown substantially. If one backup is corrupt, the previous day's backup contains almost all the same information.

An incremental backup requires less space and time to create than a differential backup. The downside to incremental backups is that if an incident occurs, multiple backups need to be restored to restore the full system. In general, incremental backups are designed to complete the backup in the shortest amount of elapsed time. An incremental backup is also economical when accounting for the amount of room needed to store the backup data. Differential backups yield the shortest elapsed time needed to restore files when they must be re-created from the backup media.

A copy backup allows a systems administrator to make sure all files are backed up, but only a subset of them are backed up at a time. It could be considered a partial full backup. A daily backup backs up only files that were modified on that day—a date-specific incremental backup.

Regardless of the strategy employed, all on-site and off-site storage must be secured. It is common practice to use fireproof safes or filing cabinets to store tapes and to use encryption to protect online or cloud data storage. The off-site storage, in particular, must be in a safe location, such as a safety deposit box in a bank or at a professional backup and recovery service. The trunk of the administrator's car is not considered secure off-site storage. It is also important to provide a conditioned environment for off-site physical media—preferably an airtight, humidity-free, static-free storage container. Each off-site media unit must be clearly labeled and write-protected. Because tapes wear out, it is important to retire them periodically and introduce new media.

Redundancy-Based Backup and Recovery Using RAID

Another form of data backup is the use of additional disk drives for redundancy. The usage of redundant array of independent disks (RAID) systems can overcome some of the limits of magnetic tape backup systems. Also, as discussed later in this module, RAID systems provide enhanced capabilities such as a hot swap feature. Unlike tape backups, RAID uses a number of hard drives to store information across multiple drive units. For operational redundancy, this can spread out data; when coupled with checksums, it can also eliminate or reduce the impact of a hard drive failure. There are nine established RAID configurations, which are described along with their capabilities in the following sections. Some approaches offer more than simple data redundancy—they can offer complete systems-level redundancy by using a process that mirrors entire servers to provide server-level fault tolerance (also known as high-availability systems or servers). For example, using Microsoft's Windows Server Failover Clustering, multiple virtual machines are clustered together. If any single server goes down, the remaining systems pick up the load. Although RAID does not address the need for off-site storage like tape-based backups, it does deal with the most common need when restoring from backup, which is recovery from a hard drive failure.

---

full backup

A complete backup of the entire system, including applications, operating systems components, and data.

differential backup

The storage of all files that have changed or been added since the last full backup.

incremental backup

The duplication of only the files that have been modified since the previous incremental backup.

copy backup

A backup of a set of specified files, regardless of whether they have been modified or otherwise flagged for backup.

daily backup

A backup of files that were modified within a defined 24-hour period.

redundant array of independent disks (RAID)

A system of drives that stores information across multiple units to spread out data and minimize the impact of a single drive failure. By storing the data redundantly, the loss of a drive will not necessarily cause a loss of data.

hot swap

A hard drive feature that allows individual drives to be replaced without powering down the entire system and without causing a fault during the replacement.

disk striping

A RAID implementation (typically referred to as RAID level 0) in which one logical volume is created by storing data across several available hard drives in segments called stripes.

disk striping without parity

RAID disk striping without data redundancy to provide error correction.

disk mirroring

A RAID implementation (typically referred to as RAID level 1) in which the computer records all data to twin drives simultaneously, providing a backup if the primary drive fails.

disk duplexing

An approach to disk mirroring in which each drive has its own controller to provide additional redundancy.

disk striping with parity

RAID disk striping that includes redundant data for error correction and allows reconstruction of data if some of the data or parity information is lost.

RAID vendors have come to use a standardized classification model that identifies three types of RAID implementations:

- *Hardware-based RAID*—Organizations can purchase RAID hardware that manages devices attached to a RAID controller, which works as a specialized hard drive controller.
- *Software-based RAID*—Some operating systems are capable of creating a single virtual device from multiple devices, or as a function of the file system in a single drive.
- *Firmware- and driver-based RAID*—Organizations use inexpensive "RAID controllers" based on standard hard drive controllers rather than using expensive RAID hardware to work with the computer BIOS to provide some RAID services. This system is also known as hardware-assisted or hybrid RAID.

The following sections discuss the RAID configurations that are most commonly used in the IT industry.

RAID Level 0

Not considered a form of redundant storage, RAID 0 creates one large logical volume *across* several available hard disk drives and stores the data using a process known as disk striping. When this is done to allow multiple drives to be combined in order to gain large capacity without data redundancy, it is called disk striping without parity. Unfortunately, failure of one drive may make all data inaccessible.

RAID Level 1

Commonly called disk mirroring, RAID 1 uses twin drives in a computer system. The computer records all data to both drives simultaneously, providing a backup if the primary drive fails. A variation of mirroring is called disk duplexing. With mirroring, the same drive controller manages both drives; with disk duplexing, each drive has its own controller. Mirroring is often used to create duplicate copies of operating system volumes for high-availability systems.

RAID Level 2

A specialized form of disk striping with parity was designed as RAID 2 and has been used in later RAID implementations. It uses a specialized parity coding mechanism known as the Hamming code to store stripes of data on multiple data drives and corresponding redundant error correction on separate error-correcting drives. There are no commercial implementations of RAID 2.

RAID Levels 3 and 4

RAID 3 uses byte-level striping of data, and RAID 4 uses block-level striping of data. These approaches use a process in which the data is stored in segments on dedicated data drives and parity information is stored on a separate drive. Similar to RAID 0, one large volume is used for the data, but the parity drive operates independently to provide error recovery.

RAID Level 5

RAID 5 is most commonly used in organizations that balance safety and redundancy against the costs of acquiring and operating the systems. It is similar to RAID 3 and 4 in that it stripes the data across multiple drives, but there is no dedicated parity drive. Instead, segments of data are interleaved with parity data and are written across all the drives in the set.

RAID Level 6

A combination of RAID 1 and RAID 5, RAID 6 provides block-level striping with double-distributed parity and allows systems protected by it to recover from two simultaneous drive failures.

RAID Level 7

This is a proprietary variation on RAID 5 in which the array works as a single virtual drive. RAID 7 is sometimes performed by running special software over RAID 5 hardware.

RAID Level 0+1 & 1+0

These are a combination of RAID 0 and RAID 1. RAID 0 is used for its performance and RAID 1 is used for its fault tolerance. The RAID 0+1 model creates a second striped set to mirror a primary striped set (striping, then mirroring), whereas RAID 1+0 creates a striped set *from* a mirrored set (mirroring, then striping).

RAID Level 5+1

This is another combination of RAID 5 and RAID 1. RAID 5 is used for its robustness, but then the method adds a separate data parity drive not found in RAID 5. (Some vendors market this technique as *RAID 53*.)

Some of the more common implementations of RAID are illustrated in Figure 3-3.

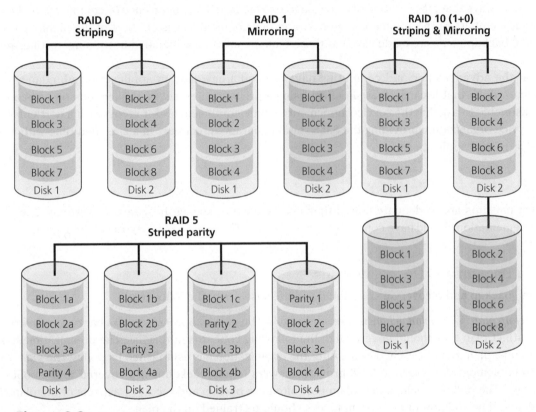

Figure 3-3   Common RAID implementations

Database Backups

Systems that make use of databases, whether hierarchical, relational, or object-oriented, require special considerations when backup and recovery procedures are being planned. Depending on the type of database and the software vendor, it may not be possible to back up the database using the utilities provided with the server operating systems on which the database runs. A further consideration is whether system backup procedures can be used without interrupting the database. With some relational databases, a system backup can work correctly only if all user access to the database is stopped. If these databases must be used while they are being backed up, additional backup tools are needed. Typically, relational database management systems (RDBMSs) or other database management applications contain integral backup applications that allow database managers to schedule and maintain their own backups. Other considerations for properly safeguarding a database include making sure the system administrators know whether there are special journal file requirements used by the database management software, such as run-unit journals or after-image journals, which enable database concurrency functions. If these file systems and their files are not backed up properly, the backup tapes or disk images may be unusable during attempts to restore the prior state of the system.

There are new applications designed to protect databases in near real time. These applications protect data in one of the following ways:

- *Legacy backup applications*—This traditional "lock and copy" approach requires the database to be inaccessible while a backup is created to a local drive.
- *Online (cloud) backup applications*—This is also a "lock and copy" approach, but it provides backups to an online or cloud vendor.
- *Continuous data protection*—This approach copies data in near real time to a second storage location using an application interface. Data is stored within a tolerance of one second or less.

Application Backups

Some applications use file systems and databases in ways that invalidate the customary way of doing backup and recovery. In some cases, applications write large binary objects as files and manage pointers, and they handle internal data structures in ways that make routine backups unable to manage the concurrency or complexity of the application. Make sure that members of the application support and development teams are part of the planning process when these systems' backup plans are made and that these team members are included in training, testing, and rehearsal activities.

Note that the advances in cloud computing have opened a new field in application redundancy and backup. Because organizations that lease SaaS are in effect using a preconfigured set of applications on someone else's systems, it is reasonable to ask that the service agreement include contingencies for recovery. If a particular server goes down, the service organization providing the SaaS should guarantee recovery in a specified time with a comparable (if not identical) set of applications.

Backup and Recovery Plans

Even the best backups are inadequate unless they can be used to successfully restore systems. Each backup and recovery implementation should have complete recovery plans. The plans need to be developed, tested, and rehearsed periodically.

Developing Backup and Recovery Plans

At a minimum, backup and recovery plans should include answers to the following:

- *The backup plan: Who, what, when, where, and how?*—The entire approach to data backup and recovery relies on a distinct plan that should govern all of the following concerns in this list. The organization should have policy and a plan to address each issue. After the organization has established its policy, the plan will explain how to implement the policy and will provide answers to any questions not covered in the policy—mainly the "how." The policy should also explain how often the backup and recovery aspects of the plan should be tested, and how and how often the employees should be trained on the plan.
- *Backup creation: Who, what, when, where, and how?*
  - Who is responsible for backing up each database, data set, and data repository?
  - What data should be backed up?
  - When should it be backed up?
  - Where should it be backed up to?
  - How should it be backed up (method)?

  There should be a formal document with the answers to all of these questions. It's most efficient to have a schedule for backups with the answers to each of these points, including the software or methodology for backups, the appropriate personnel responsible, the backup destination, and the schedule. This also requires that the appropriate personnel are fully trained on the software and/or methodology for creating backups, and that all users are informed of the schedule so that they may work around any needed system downtime.
- *Backup verification: Who, what, when, where, and how?* How will backups be verified so that they are known to be correct and reliable?—"Trust but verify" is the hallmark of security. The organization may trust the software and personnel responsible for backing up its critical data, but unless it's periodically verifying those backups, they may not be usable when needed. Verification is the process of reading a backup immediately

after it has completed and comparing the backup to the original data to confirm its integrity. Effective verification requires not only using the verification function on the backup software, but periodically accessing a data backup and testing it to see if the data is recoverable. Depending on the media and the storage locations, archival backups especially can degrade over time. The same questions asked about performing the backup should be asked about its verification.

- *Data storage: Who, what, where, how, and for how long?*—After the data backup has been performed, there is essentially a duplicate copy of all critical data in one accessible location. Understanding the details of where that location is, who can access it, what is stored where, how it's maintained in the storage location, and how long the data needs to be kept there are all important questions the organization must address, most likely in policy. Also relevant to this set of questions are any special data retention requirements and regulations. Some data must be kept longer than other data—for example, tax records must be retained for at least three years. Some data should be destroyed as soon as it's no longer needed—like e-mail, to prevent issues with legal discovery. Also, how many copies (iterations) of backups will be kept? The backup plan will specify how many archived copies of the data will be retained, and that will become critical should the organization determine that an intrusion was overlooked for an extended period of time and recovery from backup included re-installation of malware or back doors.

- *Encryption: Who, what, when, where, how, and why?*—One last point: If encryption will be used, a complete set of documentation is required to describe who has access to the encryption software and the associated decryption keys, where the keys will be escrowed, and who will have access to them. In addition, the organization should understand any special requirements or regulations associated with the use of certain encryption algorithms, especially if their data is stored outside the United States.

It is imperative that the organization clearly understands the answers to all of these questions. What the organization does not need is to have to guess at this information in the event a backup is needed.

Real-Time Protection, Server Recovery, and Application Recovery

As you have learned, data backups are important, but some strategies are employed in an attempt to improve the robustness of a server or system. One approach that provides real-time protection as well as data backup is the use of mirroring. Mirroring provides duplication of server data storage by using multiple hard drive volumes, as described in the section on RAID level 1. RAID level 1 can be achieved with software or hardware by writing data to other drives, even if they are located on other systems. Mirroring can be extended to the point of vaulting and journaling, which are discussed later in this module.

One strategy for implementing server recovery and redundancy through mirroring servers uses hot, warm, and cold servers. In this strategy, the online primary server (i.e., domain controller) is the hot server, and it provides the services necessary to support operations. The warm server is used as an ancillary or secondary server (i.e., domain controller), and it services requests when the primary server is busy or down. The cold server is the administrator's test platform and should be configured identically as the hot and warm servers. Before a patch, upgrade, or new application is applied to the hot and warm servers, it is first tested on the cold server. Should the hot server go down, the warm server automatically takes over as the hot server, and the cold server can be added as the new warm server while the hot server is taken offline for repair.

Recent advances in server recovery have developed **bare metal recovery** technologies designed to replace operating systems, applications, and data when they fail. These applications allow you to reboot the affected system from a remote drive or removable media and quickly restore the entire set of system software by providing images backed up from a known stable state.

Although Linux and UNIX versions of bare metal implementations abound, the Windows versions are more difficult to come by. Linux and UNIX kernels run easily from small storage locations, but Windows is only just developing a stand-alone bootable CD platform. Under most Windows clients, you can create a system repair disk to use in the event of a corrupted Windows installation. Use of bare metal recovery applications, in conjunction with routine backups, allows the recovery of entire servers quickly and easily. There are many options, including Knoppix and Helix, for Linux/ UNIX users to choose from. A "liveCD," also known as a liveDVD, liveOS, liveDrive, or

bare metal recovery

A data recovery technique whereby the user is able to restore the entirety of a computer's operating system, applications, and data without any requirements of previously installed operating system software, essentially re-creating the computer from "bare metal" (hardware only).

application recovery

A system failover strategy using software to detect the failure of the primary application server and then activate a secondary application server to accept and service client requests.

clustering services

See *application recovery*.

electronic vaulting

A backup method that uses bulk batch transfer of data to an off-site facility; this transfer is usually conducted via leased lines or secure Internet connections.

simply liveDisc, is a bootable image on a CD, DVD, flash drive, or external USB drive that contains systems administration tools and the ability to reinstall the base operating systems. The LiveCD List provides several hundred programs that serve about a dozen purposes, from gaming to network security tools (see *www.livecdlist.com*). Many of these programs have lively support communities where you can engage with other users and often the developers to gain insight into using the programs.

The next level of recovery is **application recovery** or **clustering services** plus replication. The use of software replication can provide increased protection against data loss. Clustering services and application recovery work is similar to the hot, warm, and cold redundant server model described earlier. It is common practice for system administrators to install applications on multiple servers so that if one fails to provide the service, a secondary system steps up and takes over the role. Application recovery expands on this premise for applications: Rather than simple services providing failover capabilities for critical applications, application recovery uses software to detect the failure of the primary application server and to then activate the secondary application server to begin accepting and servicing requests.

As noted earlier, mirroring of data, whether through the use of RAID 1 or alternative technologies, can increase the reliability of primary systems and enhance the effectiveness of business resumption strategies. The techniques of vaulting and journaling dramatically increase the level of protection; they are discussed next.

The bulk transfer of data in batches to an off-site facility is called **electronic vaulting** (see Figure 3-4). This transfer is usually conducted via leased lines or data communications services provided for a fee, although recent developments in online and cloud backups are quickly taking over this market. The receiving server archives the data as it is received. Some DR companies specialize in electronic vaulting services. The primary criteria for selecting an electronic

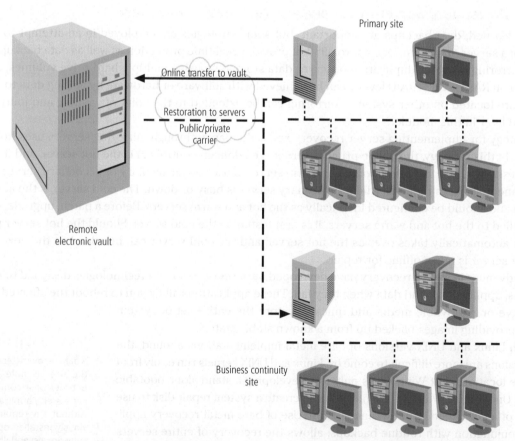

Figure 3-4   Electronic vaulting

vaulting (e-vaulting) solution are the costs of the service, the required and available bandwidth, the security needs for the stored data, and the needed service level for recovery and continuity.

remote journaling

The backup of data to an off-site facility in close to real time based on transactions as they occur.

Because e-vaulting means transferring data off-site, the organization must ensure that it has the capability to do so without affecting other operations. If the organization does not currently have enough bandwidth to support e-vaulting, it must obtain the additional bandwidth through a vendor. It may be advantageous to get the extra bandwidth, regardless of whether the organization feels it is necessary.

E-vaulting used to be more expensive than tape backup and slower than data mirroring; however, the explosion in the online/cloud market has changed this. Solutions for a few hundred dollars per month are now available, with most services based on capacity needs that are measured in gigabytes or terabytes of storage. This allows organizations to scale their purchases according to their needs. Organizations should consider using specialized e-vaulting applications for data that warrants the additional expense, such as critical transactional data and customer databases. If the organization already has a data classification or prioritization scheme, it may already know what data is most critical. These means of categorizing data assets may have been put in place during the BIA or in the development of the risk assessment processes. While e-vaulting can be performed over public infrastructure using VPNs, the data must be encrypted while in transition, which can slow the data transfer rate.

For managed solutions from vendors, a software agent is typically installed on all servers and included in the e-vaulting process. After it is installed, the software initiates a full backup of data to the remote vault and then prepares to continuously copy data as it is created or modified. The vendor is then responsible for the maintenance and protection of the data. Access to the data can be obtained through a Web interface or by using installed software to facilitate restoration or validation of transferred data. Vendors like Amazon, Rackspace, Carbonite, and Barracuda Intronis have facilities and services designed to support an organization's online data backup in this capacity. If the organization desires to transfer data to its own vault, different applications can facilitate the transfer between organizationally owned equipment over public or private communications links. In either case, the routine transfer of data should not have an impact on the organization's networks; however, organizations with network connections below 25 Mbps should consider upgrading to higher-speed Internet connections, given that the current average U.S. Internet speed is approximately 33 Mbps[3], with some states having average speeds over 50 Mbps.[4]

Remote journaling (RJ) is the transfer of live transactions to an off-site facility. Developed by IBM in 1999 for its OS/400 V4R2 operating system, RJ differs from e-vaulting in that only transactions are transferred, not archived data, and the transfer is performed online, in much closer to real time. Although e-vaulting is much like a traditional backup, with a dump of data to the off-site storage, RJ involves online activities on a systems level, much like server fault tolerance, in which data is written to two locations simultaneously. However, this process can be performed asynchronously, if preferred. RJ facilitates the recovery of key transactions in near real time. Figure 3-5 shows an overview of the RJ process.

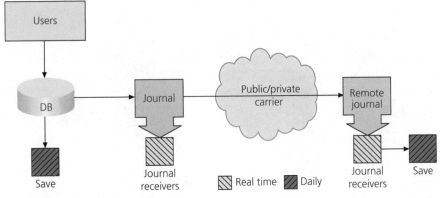

Figure 3-5   Remote journaling

database shadowing

The storage of duplicate online transaction data, along with the duplication of the databases, at a remote site on a redundant server; it combines e-vaulting with remote journaling, writing multiple copies of the database simultaneously in two separate locations.

When journaling is enabled for a given object, the operating system initiates a process that creates a record of the object's behavior. All changes are recorded by the journal in a journal entry, which is stored in a journal receiver, similar to storing a record in a database file. After the journal receiver is full or reaches a preset level, a new journal receiver is linked to the journal, and the full receiver is available for storage to tape, for example. For recovery, the stored receivers can be pulled from tape and applied to the data in the production database, restoring the data to a known stable point. Remote journaling involves the transference of journal entries to a remote journal, which in turn stores them to a remote journal receiver. This remote journal receiver is then transferred to remote tape or other storage when full, creating a virtual real-time backup of the entries.

Database shadowing, also known as *databank shadowing*, is a technology that can be used simply, with multiple databases on a single drive in a single system, or using databases in remote locations across a public or private carrier, as shown in Figure 3-6. Shadowing techniques are generally used for organizations needing immediate data recovery after an incident or disaster. The "shadowed" database is available for reading as well as writing and thus serves as a dynamic off-site backup. Database shadowing also works well for read-only functions, such as the following:

- Data warehousing and mining
- Batch reporting cycles (quarterly and year-end reports, and so on)
- Complex SQL queries
- Local online access at the shadow site
- Load balancing

Database shadowing is performed by having each transactional event written simultaneously to multiple databases. In its original incarnation, database shadowing could only be done to a secondary partition or database on the original drive, or to a secondary drive on the same machine (disk mirroring or duplexing). However, with the introduction of third-party software, these same transactions can be buffered, transmitted across a network, and stored in a shadow database on a remote server.

As each transaction occurs, the primary database and shadowed database both receive the transaction entry, update, or deletion request. Only the primary database responds to the transaction application, but both databases make the requested entry, modification, or deletion. When a problem occurs with the primary database, the secondary database can be accessed to serve as a redundant copy. If the redundant copy is on the same system, the transactions can continue without interruption. If the copies are on a remote system, the copy must be read back to the original system, restoring the data to provide a local copy, in order to prevent latency in the transaction process.

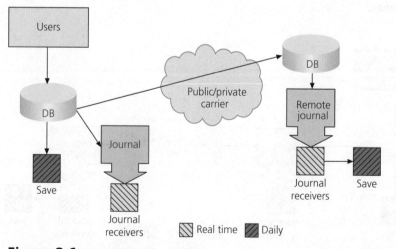

Figure 3-6   Database shadowing

Database replication is a similar strategy to those previously mentioned. There are three types of database replication:

- *Snapshot replication*—Copying data from one database to another
- *Merger replication*—Merging data from multiple databases into a separate database
- *Transaction replication*—Using a master database for regular operations but periodically copying new and updated entries to a backup

E-vaulting, RJ, and database shadowing are quickly becoming functions of various backup applications rather than services unto themselves. Organizations are increasingly focusing on availability of data rather than how it is stored. Selecting online or local backup applications that support the storage of real-time data rather than batched data is more prevalent than examining e-vaulting or RJ methodologies. However, it is important for the organization to select a backup regime that allows it to meet its availability needs without sacrificing its confidentiality and integrity requirements.

Two other advances in data storage and recovery are **network-attached storage (NAS)** and **storage area networks (SANs)**. Though similar in name, the two have different implementations and configurations. Unlike direct-attached storage, NAS is commonly a single device or server that attaches to a network and uses common communications methods—such as Windows file sharing, NFS, CIFS, HTTP directories, or FTP—to provide an online storage environment. Commonly implemented as additional storage space, NAS is configured to allow users or groups of users to access data storage. It does not work well with real-time applications because of the latency of the communication methods.

SANs are similar in concept but differ in implementation. Whereas NAS uses TCP/IP-based protocols and communications methods, SANs use fiber-channel direct connections between the systems that need the additional storage and the storage devices themselves. This difference is shown in Figure 3-7 and described in Table 3-3.[5]

For general file sharing or data backup use, NAS tends to provide a more compatible solution. For high-speed and higher-security solutions, SANs may be preferable. With SANs, only the devices connected to the SAN can access it. With NAS, anyone who can intercept the IP address can access (or attempt to access) it.

database replication

The backup of multiple copies of a database for recovery purposes.

network-attached storage (NAS)

A data storage and recovery system that consists of a single device or server that attaches to a network and uses common communications methods to provide an online storage environment.

storage area network (SAN)

A data storage and recovery system that uses fiber-channel direct connections between the systems that need the additional storage and the storage devices themselves.

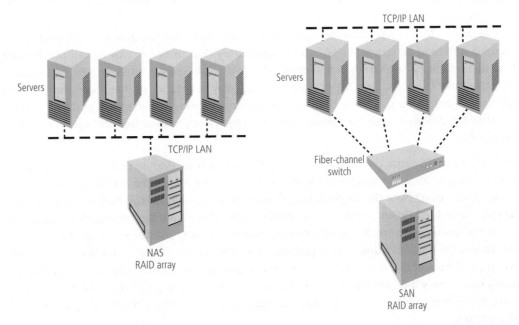

Figure 3-7   NAS versus SANs

Table 3-3   NAS versus SANs

	NAS	SAN
Connectivity	Any machine that can connect to a LAN and use standard protocols (such as NFS, CIFS, or HTTP)	Only server-class devices with SCSI fiber channel; a topology limit of 10 km
Addressing, identification, and file transfer	By file name with NAS handling security, including permissions, authentication, and file locking	By disk block number, with no individual security control
OS support	Greater sharing, especially between differing OSs	OS dependent and not compatible with all OSs
File system	Managed by NAS head unit	Managed by servers
Backups and mirrors	Done on files to save time and bandwidth	Done on blocks; requires destination volumes to have greater storage capacity than source volumes

Source: NIST Special Publication 800-43 Rev.1.

The Future of Backups

What if the organization could eliminate the need for a backup function? By combining the data storage and data backup functions and essentially outsourcing them to a service provider, organizations now can do just that. Two applications commonly used in larger organizations combine off-site data storage and automatic backups for a single price:

- *Dropbox*—Dropbox is an application that syncs the user's data to a cloud server. After Dropbox is set up, an individual user or an entire organization can decide what to sync and where. The software creates a local copy of the data on the user's system, providing access if the user is offline. After the user establishes an Internet connection, their files are synced automatically. From the user's perspective, Dropbox is just another set of file folders under a different header. Dropbox Basic provides a free quantity of storage (2 GB in 2020) to individuals as a trial, with options to upgrade to plans offering 2 or 3 TB of storage for a fee. For organizations, Dropbox Business provides 5 TB of storage and unlimited options on a pay-per-user basis. These services provide between 30- and 120-day file recovery and version histories, which allows older or deleted files to be recovered by the account administrator. For a complete list of options, visit *www.dropbox.com*.

- *Microsoft OneDrive*—Microsoft's data storage application is designed to integrate with both locally installed and online MS Office application suites. For organizations that prefer not to install productivity software directly on their client systems, they can implement all of the Microsoft suite virtually, including data storage and access. Just like Dropbox, OneDrive creates a local copy of data for offline access and syncs seamlessly. Microsoft has plans to offer OneDrive both as a stand-alone, storage-only option and as an integrated set of options within MS Office on a per-user basis. Storage ranges from 5 GB of free storage to 1 TB/user for Office 365 subscribers.

While many other applications do almost the same thing (such as Google Drive), Dropbox and OneDrive are easily integrated into users' desktop and laptop systems, and they provide access to their data anytime, anywhere. What is so special about that? Now the organization doesn't have to manage the backup and recovery of end-user data or—in the case of online MS Office suites—the applications. Many common organizational applications, such as enterprise resource planning software, financial software, and purchasing software, are also being offered by vendors with online and integrated data backups. It is important, however, for the organization to fully understand the who, what, when, where, and how of this data backup, as they are essentially outsourcing their data storage as well as its backup. Because a completely independent organization is storing and managing their data, the organization may find it challenging to get answers to these questions, and may have to rely on the service level agreement (SLA) to provide the needed information.

Virtualization

Critical to any discussion of server or application recovery is the prolific technology known as virtualization. Virtualization is the development and deployment of virtual systems rather than physical implementations of systems and services. A virtual system is a computer operating environment that works within another environment, allowing developers and organizations to develop and deploy a multitude of different applications and environments without requiring a separate hardware platform for each environment or operating system. An organization can use its existing hardware to deploy operating systems and applications using specialized virtualization technologies. It is commonplace to use the term "virtual machine" to refer to a virtualized environment operating in or on a host platform. The host platform (i.e., host machine) is the physical server and operating system that the virtualization application and all virtual machines run on. The virtual machine (also known as the guest) is the hosted operating system or platform running on the host machine. The virtualization application, known as the hypervisor or virtual machine monitor, is the specialized software that enables the virtual machine to operate on the host platform.

Virtualization can occur in a variety of ways:

- *Hardware-level virtualization*—In this setup, a virtual machine acts like an independent computer with its own operating system. Hardware virtual machines also allow the development and deployment of simulated hardware components, not just the OS (including network cards). At this level, the physical host's resources (CPU, RAM, HDD) are divided between the virtual machines and the host itself. This is currently the most common and popular implementation.
- *Operating system-level virtualization (also known as software virtualization)*—In this approach, only one OS is used: the host's OS. The virtualization offers multiple virtual sessions of the OS, and thus each application can be independent of the others. This allows increased controls over resource utilization (CPU, RAM, HDD).
- *Application-level virtualization*—This is a broad term that describes a virtualization approach designed to improve portability and compatibility of applications. The virtualization layer appears to the application as the expected OS, answering all necessary application programming interface (API) calls made by the application. The application perceives that it is interacting with the host OS and the resources managed by it. This approach allows an application to run on a computer that otherwise could not support the application. For example, a Linux OS can emulate certain applications designed to operate in Windows using a virtualization program called Wine.

Within these virtualization environments, memory, storage, data, and networking resources can be virtualized, allowing a differentiation between the physical implementation of the resources and their logical use. For example, virtual machines commonly need multiple networking addresses separate from the host application's physical network interfaces. The physical host and virtual hypervisor provide these by mapping them within the host's equipment.

Although virtualization's roots can be traced back to the 1960s with the development of IBM's CP-40, a virtual machine/memory time-sharing operating system, only in the last 15 years or so has it become commercially prevalent and available. SoftPC was developed and introduced in 1988, Virtual PC was developed in 1997, and VMware was patented in 1998. Currently, the following vendors and products dominate the virtualization market:

- Microsoft's Hyper-V Virtual Server
- VMware's vSphere/ESXi
- Oracle VM VirtualBox
- Citrix XenServer

Most virtualization applications can be traced back to developments by just two companies: Innotek GmbH and Connectix Corporation. They were recognized as industry pioneers in virtualization technologies and were acquired by Sun and Microsoft, respectively.

---

virtualization

The development and deployment of virtual systems rather than physical implementations of systems and services.

host platform

The physical server (and operating system) that the virtualization application and all virtual machines run on.

host machine

See *host platform*.

virtual machine

A hosted operating system or platform running on a host machine.

guest

(in virtualization) See *virtual machine*.

hypervisor

The specialized software that enables the virtual machine to operate on the host platform.

virtual machine monitor

See *hypervisor*.

What makes virtualization important to contingency planning is the ability to easily and accurately back up an entire system and then move it to another hardware platform, usually within minutes. In addition to specialized backup applications that are available with the virtualization technology (for example, VMware's consolidated backup), virtualization allows administrators to create snapshot backups by copying the collection of files that support the particular virtual machine to another location, including online, disk, or tape. That image can then be loaded into a new host that's running the same virtualization application. Then, the image only needs to be mounted to be up, running, and available, all within a much shorter time frame than if a system had to be built from scratch and the data had to be reloaded. Additionally, because multiple virtual systems can run on a single host, organizations do not have to worry about quickly purchasing and setting up multiple pieces of hardware. This quick response and ease of backup is another reason organizations are moving toward virtualization.

Backup of Other Devices

When formulating plans and developing procedures for backups, the focus is usually on computers such as servers, databases, NAS, SANs, desktops, and laptops. However, most organizations use many other kinds of devices that contain valuable data and configuration information. These devices need to be included in an organization's backup and recovery strategies to ensure that they are complete and thorough. Thorough strategies encompass policy and procedures as well as training and rehearsal.

Productivity Devices

Most organizations have personal productivity devices in service, with members using tablets and smartphones to leverage access to company data. The data on these devices may not be included in the backup and recovery plans that protect data on more traditional computing systems. Backup plans might also need to include external storage devices such as USB drives.

Networking Devices

The networking environment spans many types and sizes of devices, including routers, switches, and the myriad elements of intrusion detection and prevention systems, security incident and event management systems, and other elements of a unified threat management environment. Just as data on productivity devices may be overlooked, the configuration information for networking devices is probably a valuable asset for an organization. The configuration of these devices should also be considered in a well-formulated backup and recovery strategy.

SITE RESUMPTION STRATEGIES

Five key procedural mechanisms were introduced earlier in this module. Up to this point, the module has focused on the first four of these: delayed protection, real-time protection, server recovery, and application recovery. The fifth, site recovery, includes the steps needed to plan for and execute the procedure to quickly establish critical capabilities at an alternate site when the organization's primary site or sites are not available.

Providing alternate processing capability may be necessary either to implement a disaster recovery plan when the primary site is temporarily unavailable or as a business continuity strategy to institute operations at an alternate site. In either case, it is sometimes necessary to quickly put a computing environment into operation and make sure it can meet the expected needs. Resumption of IT services, whether at a site under the exclusive control of a responding organization or at a site using shared resources, is discussed in the following sections.

A contingency planning management team (CPMT) can choose from several strategies when planning for business resumption. The determining factor is usually cost. In general, the exclusive control options are hot sites, warm sites, and cold sites; the three popular shared-use options are time-shares, service bureaus, and mutual agreements; and the independent option is mobile sites.

Exclusive Site Resumption Strategies

When an organization wants its operations to resume at a location over which it has exclusive control, it can select from several options. These options are shown and compared in Table 3-4.

Table 3-4   Selection Criteria for an Exclusive-Use Site

Site	Cost	Hardware Equipment	Telecomm-unications	Setup Time	Location
Cold site	Low	None	None	Long	Fixed
Warm site	Medium	Partial	Partial/full	Medium	Fixed
Hot site	Medium/high	Full	Full	Short	Fixed
Mobile site	Dependent	Dependent	Dependent	Dependent	Not fixed
Mirrored site	High	Full	Full	None	Fixed

Hot Sites

Although the actual specifics vary from vendor to vendor, a **hot site** is generally a fully configured computer facility, with all services, communications links, and physical plant operations capable of being established at a moment's notice. Hot sites duplicate computing resources (servers, appliances, and support computers), peripherals, phone systems, applications, and workstations. Essentially, a hot site is a duplicate facility that needs only the latest data backups and personnel to function. Some versions can even be staffed around the clock to transfer control of the data processing almost instantaneously. To do so, the organization must use e-vaulting, RJ, or data shadowing. This creates a virtual mirroring of the core IT functions. It is also the most expensive alternative. Other disadvantages include the need to provide maintenance for all the systems and equipment at the hot site, as well as physical and information security. However, if the organization requires a round-the-clock capability for near real-time recovery, the hot site is the optimum strategy.

Prices for hot sites are based on a number of included options, such as personnel costs, and can cost tens of thousands of dollars per month, depending on the speed of changeover needed. The ultimate in hot sites is a **mirrored site**, which is identical to the primary site and includes live or periodic data transfers. Thus, it is capable of immediate operation. Some organizations may choose to build essential redundancy into the functional specifications of their plant and equipment. This ensures that their environment includes redundant capabilities in locations that are sufficiently isolated to avoid coincidental loss and has sufficient capacity to meet all critical needs, even if one facility is removed from service.

Figure 3-8 provides a conceptual representation of a hot site.

hot site

An exclusive site resumption strategy that consists of a fully configured computer facility, with all services, communications links, and physical plant operations capable of being established at a moment's notice. Hot sites duplicate computing resources (servers, appliances, and support computers), peripherals, phone systems, applications, and workstations.

mirrored site

The ultimate in hot sites; it is identical to the primary site and includes live or periodic data transfers.

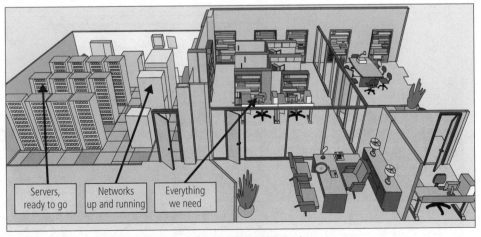

Site includes floor space, HVAC, office furniture, servers (with applications), client workstations, network and telecom connections, office equipment, and possibly on-site staff

Figure 3-8   Hot site

warm site

An exclusive site resumption strategy that provides some of the same services and options as a hot site, but the software applications are typically not included, installed, or configured. A warm site frequently includes computing equipment and peripherals with servers, but not client workstations.

cold site

An exclusive-use resumption strategy that provides only rudimentary services and facilities; no computer hardware or peripherals are provided. All communication services must be installed after the site is occupied, and frequently there are no quick recovery or data duplication functions at the site.

time-share

A shared-site resumption strategy that operates like a hot, warm, or cold site, but is leased in conjunction with a business partner or sister organization.

Warm Sites

A **warm site** provides some of the same services and options as a hot site, but software applications are typically not included, not installed, or not configured. A warm site frequently includes computing equipment and peripherals with servers, but not client workstations. It also has connections or access to data backups or off-site storage to facilitate quick data recovery. A warm site has some of the advantages of a hot site, but at a lower cost. The downside is that it may require several hours or perhaps days to make a warm site fully functional. Prices for warm sites are customized to the needs of the customer but typically cost several thousand dollars per month. It is possible for an organization to make contractual arrangements with an equipment provider that maintains stocks of critical equipment in a central facility so an entire data center can be provisioned with as little notice as 12 hours.

Figure 3-9 provides a conceptual representation of a warm site.

Cold Sites

A **cold site** provides only rudimentary services and facilities. No computer hardware or peripherals are provided. All communication services must be installed after the site is occupied, and it frequently has no quick recovery or data duplication functions. A cold site is an empty room with standard heating, air conditioning, and electrical service. Everything else is an added cost option. Despite these disadvantages, a cold site may be better than nothing. The primary advantage is cost. The most useful feature of this approach is to reduce contention for suitable floor space if a widespread disaster strikes, but some organizations are prepared to struggle to lease new space rather than pay maintenance fees on a cold site. A cold site can typically cost a few thousand dollars per month, so it is not a trivial investment.

Figure 3-10 provides a conceptual representation of a cold site.

Shared-Site Resumption Strategies

When an organization needs to plan for resumption and cannot justify the expense of an exclusive-use strategy, there are three shared-use options it can choose from.

Time-Share

The first of the shared-use options is the time-share. A **time-share** operates like one of the hot, warm, or cold sites described earlier, but it is leased in conjunction with a business partner or sister organization. The time-share allows the organization to provide a DR/BC option while reducing the overall cost. The primary disadvantage is the possibility

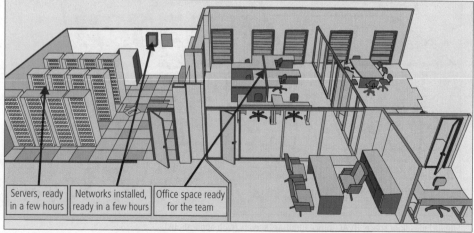

Servers, ready in a few hours | Networks installed, ready in a few hours | Office space ready for the team

Site includes floor space, HVAC, some office furniture, and servers (without applications)

Figure 3-9   Warm site

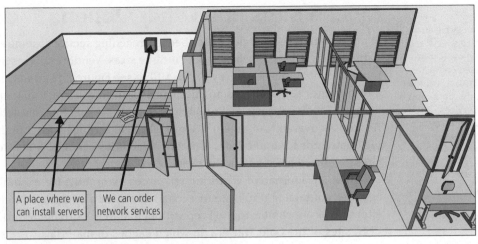

A place where we can install servers

We can order network services

Site includes floor space, HVAC, and some office furniture

Figure 3-10   Cold site

that more than one organization involved in the time-share will need the facility simultaneously. Other disadvantages include the need to stock the facility with the equipment and data from all the involved organizations, the complexity of negotiating the time-share with the sharing organizations, and the possibility that one or more parties will exit the agreement or sublease their options. It is much like agreeing to co-lease an apartment with a group of friends. Organizations must try to remain on amicable terms, given that they could use the same systems, albeit at different times.

Service Bureaus

A service bureau is an agency that provides a service for a fee. In the case of DR/CP, the service is the provision of physical facilities in the event of a disaster. These agencies also frequently provide off-site data storage for a fee. Contracts with service bureaus can specify exactly what the organization needs under what circumstances. A service agreement usually guarantees space when needed, even if this means that the service bureau has to acquire additional space in the event of a widespread disaster. It is much like the rental car provision in your car insurance policy. The disadvantage is that service contracts must be renegotiated periodically and rates can change. This option can also be quite expensive.

One of the most common service bureau approaches involves a partnership with a commercial real-estate broker to provide empty or vacant commercial space as needed. Because disaster recovery may take weeks or even months, commercial real-estate brokers may be willing to provide short-term lease agreements for organizations that have previously contracted with service bureaus.

Mutual Agreements

A mutual agreement is a contract between two organizations for each to assist the other in the event of a disaster. One organization is obligated to provide necessary facilities, resources, and services until the receiving organization is able to recover from the disaster. This arrangement can be a lot like moving in with relatives or friends. It doesn't take long for an organization to wear out its welcome. Many organizations balk at the idea of having to fund duplicate services and resources, even in the short term. Additional irritants can be the need to allow access to a partner's employees and contractors as well as the provisioning of office space.

Still, mutual agreements between divisions of the same parent company, between subordinate and senior organizations, or between business partners may be a cost-effective solution when both parties to the agreement have a mutual interest in each other's continued operations and both have similar capabilities and capacities. When an organization finds itself relying on a mutual agreement for its alternate processing needs, it should use a memorandum of understanding (MOU) to make sure that as many issues as possible are resolved before the need materializes.

service bureau

A shared-site resumption strategy in which a service agency provides physical facilities for a fee in the event of a disaster.

mutual agreement

A shared-site resumption strategy that consists of a contract between two organizations. One is obligated to provide necessary facilities, resources, and services until the receiving organization is able to recover from the disaster.

mobile sites

A site resumption strategy based on a service contract with a specialized vendor capable of deploying portable office facilities based on tractor-trailer recovery units that include integral power, phone, data, and HVAC cabling and services; additional options include furniture, telephones, and computer systems.

service agreement

A contractual document that guarantees certain minimum levels of service provided by vendors.

Mobile Sites and Other Options

In addition to the strategies described in preceding sections, some specialized alternatives are available, such as rolling mobile sites. Vendors such as SunGard AS maintain a fleet of Mobile Recovery Units (MRUs; see Figure 3-11) that can be deployed to any area after a disaster. Companies can use the MRUs to set up temporary facilities at or near their primary facility, such as in their parking lots, until the primary facilities are recovered.[6] An organization might also arrange with a prefabricated building contractor for immediate, temporary facilities—mobile offices on mobile home chassis—brought on-site in the event of a disaster.

Another alternative is storing resources externally; for example, a rental storage area containing duplicate or second-generation equipment can be used. These alternatives are similar to the Prepositioned Materiel Configured to Unit Sets (POM-CUS) sites of the Cold War era, in which caches of materials were stored in case of an emergency or war.

> (i) For more information on the mobile site shown in Figure 3-11, you can watch the following YouTube video from SunGard AS: *www.youtube.com/watch?v=5Gy0CUaQfUc*.

Service Agreements

Whether an organization is making arrangements for an exclusive-use location or a shared-use location, the terms and conditions of that site should be known to all parties through a negotiated service agreement. Service agreements are contractual documents that guarantee certain minimum levels of service provided by vendors. It is imperative that service agreements be reviewed and, in some cases, mandated to support incident, disaster, and continuity planning. If a service provider makes no legal assurances as to the level of performance, the organization will be unable to require replacement, redundant, or alternative forms of services in case the primary site is compromised by a contingency.

An effective service agreement should contain information on:

- What the provider is promising
- How the provider will deliver on those promises
- Who will measure delivery and how
- How service measurements will be calculated and reported; many companies find that averages over time can hide drastically poor performance at peak loads
- What happens if the provider fails to deliver as promised
- How the SLA will change over time

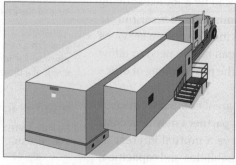

Exterior   Interior

Figure 3-11   Mobile site
Source: SunGard AS.

A typical SLA should include the following major sections:

- Definition of applicable parties
- Services to be provided by the vendor
- Fees and payments for these services
- Statements of indemnification
- Nondisclosure agreements and intellectual property assurances
- Noncompetitive agreements (covenant not to compete)

Definition of Applicable Parties

The introductory paragraph in any legal document serves to identify to whom the document applies. Service agreements, as contractual legal documents, are no different. Note that in many documents, the long formal names of the two parties are replaced with abbreviated names—for example, "the Client," "the Vendor," or "the Service Provider."

Services to be Provided by the Vendor

In this section, the vendor or service provider must specify exactly what the client is to receive in exchange for the payments identified in the following section. A service agreement is a legal document, so if a service is not explicitly identified in this section, the vendor will not be required to provide it. Any verbal agreements, compromises, or special arrangements must be fully documented. The critical elements of this section should include specifications of the services expected from the vendor for the protection and restoration of services if an incident or disaster occurs. Some organizations also include a clause for contingency operations, such as, "For a nominal fee the Vendor agrees to provide additional services to an alternate location within X amount of time following an incident or disaster requiring relocation of the Client's primary business." However, this type of arrangement typically requires a separate agreement, usually called a business continuity service agreement or contract.

In a typical service agreement, there are specific statements about the vendor's agreement to: (a) protect the content of the client, (b) back up the client's content, and (c) restore services after internal or external events. (Internal events include system and software failures.) This information is important in determining whether a separate agreement is needed to ensure compliance with the special needs of the organization for data backup and recovery. Without these specific statements, there is no warranty that the vendor will protect anything but its own software and hardware, and the client is required to conduct its own data backup and restoration.

Fees and Payments for Services

This section indicates what the vendor receives in exchange for the services rendered. Although the most common exchange is financial, it is not unusual to see an exchange of services, goods, or other securities. The terms of contract and any special fees, such as late fees, returned check fees, or discounts for early payment, could be specified here. A common inclusion is "2/10 net 30," indicating a 2 percent discount if payment is made within 10 days, with the net payment (balance) due in 30 days, usually for shipped goods paid by invoice.

Statements of Indemnification

Frequently found in legal documents of this type are statements that the vendor is not liable for actions taken by the client. If the vendor gets sued or incurs other financial liability based on the client's use of the vendor's services, the client is responsible for those costs. So, if a client were to put up an insulting Web site that got the client and the vendor sued, the client would be responsible for any fees or expenses incurred by the vendor. Failure to include such statements may result in additional legal fees from both parties as the vendor sues to recoup its losses.

Nondisclosure Agreements and Intellectual Property Assurances

It is important for both parties to understand the level of agreement that applies to the protection and disclosure of the client's intellectual property. The nondisclosure agreement covers the confidentiality of information from everyone involved unless disclosure is mandated by the courts. Vendors are expected to certify the validity of these documents and then provide the information as required. However, they are prohibited from providing information based on the personal or professional requests of individuals, including law enforcement, without warrant or subpoena.

If the client does not want the vendor to view the contents of its file directory structures, it can ask for that agreement. If the vendor wants to restrict the type of business performed on its systems, it can ask for that agreement. The two parties must formalize the expectations on both sides for protecting the confidentiality of the services and business information to be shared. Even in a breach of contract dispute, a breach of one clause (such as a late or missing fee payment) does not negate the legality of another clause (the disclosure of information); this prevents the vendor from selling off information to recoup financial losses.

Federal law and most state laws permit a service provider to view the contents of its clients' systems in the routine conduct of business and maintenance on those systems. This means that the vendor can review the contents of a file directory, but it does not mean the vendor can review the contents of the files within the directory. These same laws permit network administrators to review the headers of packets but not the packets' data contents. Just because one has access to information does not give one authorization to review the contents. Any expectation or requirement of monitoring should be stipulated in the agreements as well.

Noncompetitive Agreements (Covenant Not to Compete)

Although not essential to a service agreement, it is customary for the client to agree not to use the vendor's services to compete directly with the vendor, and for the client not to use vendor information to gain a better deal with another vendor. One exception is in telecommunications, where federal regulation requires common carriers to offer services even to companies that would use those services to compete with them. In the early days of MCI and Sprint, the companies leased services from AT&T to establish their start-ups and then moved to their own networks. However, outside of the telecommunications and cable television industries, where court orders can mandate specific arrangements between competitive organizations, there is no requirement that an organization allow subleases that can create an advantage for a competitor.

General SLA Requirements

SLAs for alternate sites should cover the following at a minimum:

- Duration
- Costs and fee structures for initiation and use, including fees for occupancy, maintenance, testing, and transportation support as well as payment terms and conditions for payment
- Parameters for declaration of activation
- A priority-setting process for when multiple clients claim access at the same time; this process should include a listing of all clients that subscribe to the same resources and sites, and the total number of site subscribers, as applicable
- How the contract/agreement can be modified or terminated
- Performance and compatibility guarantees
- System requirements for all computing devices, network devices, and channels as well as hardware and software
- Full description of change management and notification requirements for hardware, software, and infrastructure
- Security requirements
- Complete description of support services provided
- Description of support services provided in the facility, such as use of on-site office equipment, cafeteria, and others
- Testing procedures, including scheduling, availability, and duration
- Provision for records management, both on-site and off-site, as well as use of electronic media and hard copy
- Service-level management (performance measures and management of quality of IT services provided)
- Workspace requirements (chairs, desks, telephones, PCs)
- Supplies provided or not provided (office supplies)
- Additional costs not covered elsewhere
- Other contractual issues, as applicable
- Other technical requirements, as applicable

Closing Scenario

Deputy Chief Corbett stood up and returned to the command vehicle that was parked in the street outside the office building.

Alan breathed a sigh of relief, then flipped open his master contingency planning binder.

"At least we don't have to make up a plan," he said. "Let's review our next steps in case our offices are ever inaccessible for a month or more."

Discussion Questions

1. What other crises or catastrophes can happen in a mailroom that could prompt an emergency procedure like the one illustrated here?
2. What goals should be included when planning for the resumption of critical business functions at an alternate site for four weeks? What would be different if the planning horizon were 30 weeks instead?
3. When the organization makes a plan like the one described here, what parts of the plan should be from the contingency planning management team (CPMT) and what parts should come from the subject area experts?

Ethical Decision Making

1. It seems that the company exposed its employees to some stress during the "white powder" drill without telling the employees that it was taking place. While this is almost certainly legal, do you think it was ethical to spring the surprise on the employees as part of a training event?
2. What if a key customer had an urgent special request that the company could not respond to because of this drill? Is it an ethical lapse to fail to meet a customer expectation?
3. What if Bobby had been injured during the drill when the package opened in the mail room? Of course, the company would be responsible for the worker compensation claim, but would it also be guilty of an ethical failure to protect the safety of its employees?

MODULE SUMMARY

- The umbrella term *contingency planning* (CP) addresses everything done by an organization to prepare for the unexpected. CP also addresses later parts of the information security process, which are focused on keeping the business alive.
- A business resumption (BR) plan has two major elements: the disaster recovery (DR) plan, for resuming normal operations at the primary sites, and the business continuity (BC) plan, for activating critical business functions at an alternate site.
- Each of the components of BR planning (the DR plan and the BC plan) comes into play at a specific time in the life of an incident, and overlap between them may occur.
- There are five key mechanisms that help restore critical information and the continuation of business operations: delayed protection, real-time protection, server recovery, application recovery, and site recovery.
- Cloud technologies include methods to back up and recover data as well as emerging trends in provisioning critical contingency services that allow organizations to safeguard data and speed responsiveness in the event of a recovery operation.
- Cloud backups are becoming a popular way to back up and store data in remote locations while ensuring that it is available for quick restoration, if necessary. Cloud computing is a popular way to lease computing resources. It comes in three offerings: Software as a Service (SaaS), in which applications are provided for a fee and hosted over the Internet; Platform as a Service (PaaS), in which development platforms are made available

to developers and hosted by third parties; and Infrastructure as a Service (IaaS), in which the hardware and operating systems resources made available to an organization are hosted by a third party. Clouds can be public, community, private, or a hybrid of the three.

- A backup plan is essential; data files and critical system files must be backed up frequently, and nonessential files can be backed up less frequently. Equally important is the determination of how long data should be stored. There are three basic types of backups: full, differential, and incremental. A full backup is a complete backup of the entire system, including all applications, operating systems components, and data. A differential backup is the storage of all files that have changed or been added since the last full backup. An incremental backup only archives the files that have been modified since the last incremental backup, and thus requires less space and time than a differential backup.

- Another form of data backup is the use of online disk drives for redundancy. RAID systems can overcome some of the limits of magnetic tape backup systems and provide enhanced capabilities. Many organizations are creating massive arrays of independent but large-capacity disk drives to store information and copying critical files to these devices as routine backups.

- When systems make use of databases, whether hierarchical, relational, or object-oriented, they require special considerations when backup and recovery procedures are being planned. Some applications use file systems and databases in ways that invalidate the customary way of doing backup and recovery. In some cases, applications write large binary objects as files and manage pointers, and they handle internal data structures in ways that make routine backups unable to manage the concurrency or complexity of the application.

- Even the best backups are inadequate unless they can be used to successfully restore systems. Each backup and recovery implementation should have complete recovery plans, including testing and rehearsal.

- To provide real-time protection, also known as replication, a popular feature used in server support is mirroring and duplication of server data storage with RAID techniques.

- The bulk transfer of data in batches to an off-site facility is called electronic vaulting (e-vaulting); it is usually conducted with the receiving server archiving the data as it is received.

- Remote journaling is the transfer of live transactions to an off-site facility so that all changes are recorded. Database shadowing, also known as databank shadowing, is the storage of duplicate online transaction data, along with the duplication of databases, at a remote site on a redundant server.

- Several strategies are possible when planning for business resumption, including hot sites, warm sites, cold sites, time-shares, service bureaus, and mutual agreements. A hot site is a fully configured computer facility, with all services, communications links, and physical plant operations capable of being established at a moment's notice. A warm site provides some of the same services and options as a hot site, but software applications are typically not included, not installed, or not configured. A cold site provides only rudimentary services and facilities; no computer hardware or peripherals are provided. A time-share operates like one of the three sites just mentioned, but it is leased in conjunction with a business partner or sister organization. A service bureau is an agency that provides a service for a fee—for example, it might provide physical facilities in the event of a disaster. A mutual agreement is a contract between two organizations for each to assist the other in the event of a disaster.

- Service agreements are contractual documents that guarantee certain minimum levels of service provided by vendors. An effective service agreement should contain a definition of applicable parties, a list of services to be provided by the vendor, fees and payments for these services, a statement of indemnification, nondisclosure agreements and intellectual property assurances, and noncompetitive agreements.

Review Questions

1. What purpose does a business resumption plan serve?
2. What are the two major components of BRP, and how are they related?
3. What is the primary site?

4. What is the difference between a backup and an archive?
5. What is a retention schedule?
6. What are the major types of backups?
7. What is encompassed in a full backup?

8. What is encompassed in a differential backup?

9. What is encompassed in an incremental backup?

10. What is a redundant array of independent disks (RAID), and what are its primary uses? How can it be used in a backup strategy?

11. What is disk striping, and how might it be considered the opposite of disk mirroring?

12. In what way are the backup needs of systems that use databases different from backups to safeguard other systems that don't use databases?

13. Beyond simply identifying what to back up, when to back it up, and how to restore it, what should a complete backup recovery plan include?

14. What is bare metal recovery?

15. What is electronic vaulting, and how is it used in a backup strategy?

16. What is remote journaling, and how is it used in a backup strategy?

17. What is database shadowing?

18. What is virtualization?

19. Explain the site resumption strategy known as exclusive use and how it uses hot sites, warm sites, and cold sites.

20. Explain each of the following shared-use strategies: time-share, service bureau, and mutual agreement.

21. How have cloud computing architectures impacted the backup options available for organizations?

Real-World Exercises

Exercise 3-1

This module's opening scenario illustrates a specific type of event and incident that may turn into a disaster. Do a Web search for information related to preparing an organization for another type of incident: an "active shooter." List two or three key points that contingency planning for active shooters should be sure to include.

Exercise 3-2

Do a Web search for available commercial applications that use various forms of RAID technologies, such as RAID 0 or RAID 5. What is the most common implementation? What is the most expensive?

Exercise 3-3

Not too long ago, tape backup was the industry standard. Is it still? Do a Web search for "What is the best way to back up my office computer." Review the top two or three articles found to determine whether magnetic tape, hard disks, optical disks, or cloud-based backups are the most prevalent approach. What do you think will still be the best practice in five years?

Exercise 3-4

Do a Web search for vendors that provide alternate-site strategies, such as hot sites, warm sites, and cold sites. How prevalent are they? What about mobile sites?

Exercise 3-5

This module explains the components of a typical service agreement. Search for other examples on the Web. How do they differ? What areas are common to all?

Exercise 3-6

Suppose that you work at a small firm and your manager has asked you to investigate using Dropbox to replace a tape drive that backs up a single server system with 12 TB of data. Your manager says the company spent $8,000 six years ago for the tape drive and tapes it uses, and that it pays a vendor $1,200 a month to pick up and deliver backup tapes to a secure facility each week. Would Dropbox be an economical replacement for the current process? Justify your answer based on costs and then based on other benefits.

Hands-On Projects

The hands-on project for this module can be accessed in the Practice It folder in MindTap or through your instructor's LMS. The virtual labs provided with this resource can help you develop practical skills that will be of value as you progress through the course.

References

1. Swanson, M., P. Bowen, A. Phillips, D. Gallup, and D. Lynes. NIST Special Publication 800-34, Rev.1: "Contingency Planning Guide for Federal Information Systems." National Institute of Standards and Technology. May 2010. Accessed 11/5/2018 from *csrc.nist.gov/publications/detail/sp/800-34/rev-1/final*.
2. IBM. "TS2280 Tape Drive." Accessed 1/2/2020 from *www.ibm.com/us-en/marketplace/ts2280/details*.
3. Cable.co.uk. "Worldwide broadband speed league 2019." Accessed 1/5/2020 from *www.cable.co.uk/broadband/speed/worldwide-speed-league/#highlights*.
4. Business Insider. "The 5 Fastest and Slowest States for Internet." Accessed 1/5/2020 from *www.businessinsider.com/map-fastest-and-slowest-internet-speeds-united-states-2019-4*.
5. NAS-SAN.com. "Technology Overview." Accessed 1/5/2020 from *www.nas-san.com/differ.html*.
6. SunGard AS. "Mobile Disaster Recovery." Accessed 1/5/2020 from *www.sungardas.com/en/services/colocation-and-disaster-recovery-centers/workplace-recovery/mobile/*.

INCIDENT RESPONSE: PLANNING

Upon completion of this material, you should be able to:

1. Describe the process used to organize incident response planning

2. Identify the activities and deliverables used in an incident response policy, and explain how policy affects the incident response planning process

3. Describe how policy can be implemented to support incident response practices

4. Discuss the major issues and trade-offs to be managed when assembling the final incident response plan

If you can keep your head when all about you are losing theirs and blaming it on you, if you can trust yourself when all men doubt you, … yours is the Earth and everything that's in it.

— Rudyard Kipling

Opening Scenario

It was 2 a.m. when Paul's cell phone began to buzz. He turned in his bed once, then twice, before finally grabbing for the phone. Seeing the Network Operations Center's number lit up on the display, he answered.

"Sorry to wake you, Paul." It was Susan Carter, the third-shift supervisor. Now that everything was back to normal operation after the Hazmat drill, she was working her usual hours again.

"What's up, Susan?" Paul replied groggily.

"We're getting slammed by a DDoS again," Susan said. She sounded worried.

"I thought these were pretty routine," Paul said. "Have you updated the rules on the outside firewall?"

"I did that already," Susan said. "Now it's coming in on a different port. This is the third one in about 10 minutes. That makes it seem like a live attack rather than a scripted attack, because it's reacting to our defensive efforts as quickly as we can make them. I think this means that the attack is being executed in real time by a hacker. We need you to make some decisions."

"Uh oh," Paul said. Wide awake now, he began to go over in his mind what he knew about DDoS (distributed denial-of-service) attacks and what Susan just told him.

"Okay," Paul replied while reaching for the laptop computer on his nightstand. "Give me a minute to get logged in."

For the next few minutes, he carefully scanned the logs on the firewall and border gateway over his VPN connection. He had seen that all the attacks seemed to be within a certain range. "Susan," he finally said, "try adding a rule to filter ports 1400 through 2200."

As she clicked away on her end, something from the back of Paul's mind nagged at him. What was it? Something to do with a new vulnerability he had read about in the last few days.

"*Yes!*" Susan exclaimed. "I think that did it!"

"Okay, pull all the logs and print them out, and we'll go over them when I come in. . ." Paul leaned over to look at the clock, ". . .in just under an hour."

"Okay, I'll have the coffee ready!" Susan said, laughing.

Paul leaned back in bed. "Maybe just a few more minutes of shuteye," he thought.

Then his cell phone went off again.

INTRODUCTION

Contingency planning (CP) addresses everything done by an organization to prepare for an unexpected incident. One of the core elements of CP, incident response (IR) is focused on detecting and evaluating the severity of emerging unexpected events. Whenever possible, the IR process should attempt to contain and resolve incidents according to the incident response plan (IR plan). When incidents arise that cannot be contained or resolved, other elements of the CP process are activated using the documented escalation processes noted throughout the plan. The overall IR process is made up of four phases: preparation; detection and analysis; containment, eradication, and recovery; and post-incident activity.[1] The IR process is complex, so this module will address only the initial preparation phase. Later modules will cover the planning functions of IR, organization and preparation efforts, detection aspects, response strategies, recovery from incidents, and the remaining components of the IR process. This module focuses on creating the IR plan used by organizations to effectively respond to incidents. Defining the thresholds that determine when events become incidents (or even disasters) is a critical part of the CP process.

THE IR PLANNING PROCESS

As the contingency planning management team (CPMT) completes each component of the business impact analysis (BIA), it begins to transfer the information gleaned from the organization to the various subordinate committees and their teams. To assist in this subordinate planning, the IR, disaster recovery (DR), and business continuity (BC) teams each get overlapping information on the adverse events they could face, the prioritization of those events, and the attack scenario end cases. In fact, each committee gets as much of the overall contingency plan as the CPMT has prepared. After committee members have this information, they begin their subordinate plans. In the case of IR planning, the group follows these general stages:

incident

An adverse event that violates the security of an organization and represents a potential risk of loss of the confidentiality, integrity, or availability of its assets and ongoing operations.

incident response (IR)

An organization's set of planning and preparation efforts for detecting, reacting to, and recovering from an incident.

incident response plan (IR plan)

The documented product of incident response planning; a plan that shows the organization's intended efforts in the event of an incident.

1. Form the incident response planning team (IRPT).
2. Develop the IR policy.
3. Integrate the BIA in the incident response mission.
4. Identify preventive controls.
5. Organize the computer security incident response team (the CSIRT, covered in Module 5).
6. Create IR strategies and procedures (covered in Module 8).
7. Develop the IR plan.
8. Ensure plan testing, training, and exercises.
9. Ensure plan maintenance.

To provide an overview of the ways that IR planning is performed at other organizations, two examples of the IR planning life cycle are shown in Figures 4-1 and 4-2. Figure 4-1 shows how the U.S. National Institute of Standards and Technology (NIST) defines the IR planning process. As you can see, this book follows the NIST approach very closely. Figure 4-2 provides a slightly broader perspective, inspired by the CERT Division at Carnegie Mellon University approach to IR planning, which fits into its overall IR model.

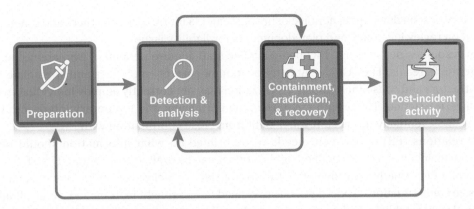

Figure 4-1   NIST incident response life cycle[2]

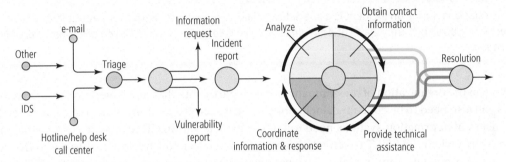

Figure 4-2   CMU CERT Division incident handling cycle[3]

Forming the IR Planning Team (IRPT)

Organizing the IRP process begins with creating and staffing the IR team responsible for development and administration of the IR plan, as well as development and training of the CSIRT. Often, the creation and evolution of the teams that support the overall CP process are centrally coordinated. Much of the preliminary organizing effort is done by the CP team, but the IR group needs to be organized as a separate entity, with its own defined and specialized teams. That process begins by consulting with the CPMT and then identifying and engaging a collection of stakeholders—a representative collection of individuals with a stake in the successful and uninterrupted operation of the organization's information infrastructure. These stakeholders are used to collect vital information on the roles and responsibilities of the IRPT, and will help shape it. The IRPT is then responsible for staffing, developing, and training the CSIRT.

Typical stakeholders often include representatives from the communities of interest described in Module 2, as well as other organizational departments and interest groups:

- General management needs to understand what the IR teams are and what they do. It also needs to preauthorize interaction among the IRPT, the CSIRT, and key business functions, should certain actions be necessary to arrest the spread and impact of an incident.
- IT management needs to understand the specific demands that the IR teams will place on IT, and what resources and access they will require to successfully plan for and respond to incidents. It also needs to preapprove certain CSIRT actions that will affect existing systems, networking functions, and connections.
- InfoSec management needs to understand practical implementation requirements of the CSIRT if the team is called into action on short notice—details like parking, after-hours building access, access to meeting rooms, and office assignments if the response location is not their usual workplace.
- The legal department needs to review the procedures of the IR teams and understand the steps the CSIRT will perform to ensure it is within legal and ethical guidelines for municipal, state, and federal jurisdictions. The legal department can provide guidance on developing contracts and service level agreements for auxiliary and

redundant services, on developing nondisclosure agreements for business partners and other associations as needed, and on reviewing policy and plan documents for liability issues.

- The human resources department (HR) helps InfoSec staff acquire personnel who are not already on hand to complete the IR teams. They can facilitate relocation of current employees and streamline the process to engage contractors and consultants, as the organization may not currently employ individuals with experience in IR planning or reaction. Those who are developing permanent and temporary job descriptions and then interviewing and eventually hiring staff will benefit from close coordination with HR.
- The public relations (PR) department needs to be briefed on what information should be disclosed to the public if an incident occurs. Predefined public notices can be drafted and reviewed by PR to ensure that the proper amount of information is provided to the appropriate agencies, law enforcement, and media when the need arises. In some situations, specialist skills may need to be brought in from media consultants. In all cases, it should be clearly established who will speak for the organization to media outlets; all others are prohibited from making statements.

 Public relations during an incident is a specialized skill. If you want to learn more about it, read a fascinating and entertaining book by Lanny Davis titled *Truth to Tell: Tell It Early, Tell It All, Tell It Yourself: Notes from My White House Education*.

- Depending on the organization of the company, some departments that have overlapping information security interests will also need to be consulted, including physical security, auditing, risk management, and insurance.
- General users of information systems need to know what the various IR teams are responsible for as well as what transpires when the CSIRT is activated. They also need to know how to best assist in the development and testing of procedures and policies. These stakeholders are the most familiar with the functions of the business and can provide additional insight into these areas.
- Other stakeholders include key business partners, contractors, temporary employee agencies, and, in some cases, consultants.[4]

From the communities of interest and the CPMT, the executive leadership of the organization should begin building the team responsible for all subsequent IR planning, development, and administrative activities. The IRPT should consist of individuals from all relevant groups that will be affected by the actions of the front-line response teams, most notably the CSIRT. As a result, the IRPT will typically be composed most heavily of information technology and information security professionals, with representatives from other communities. In any case, the IRPT leader is selected by the team and will serve as a liaison between the IR team and the CPMT.

The IRPT will work to build the IR policy, plan, and procedures that the CSIRT follows during IR actions. As with any organizational team, the group will require a champion—typically the chief information officer (CIO), chief information security officer (CISO), or vice president of IT—as well as a selected or elected group leader to manage the team. The group should meet regularly to build the IR policy and then complete development of the IR plan. This group is also responsible for the structuring, development, and training of the CSIRT at the appropriate stage of the planning process. Its role includes overseeing the ongoing maintenance of the plans.

Developing the Incident Response Policy

One of the first deliverables prepared by the IRP committee should be the IR policy. The IR policy is similar in structure to other policies used by the organization. Just as the enterprise information security policy defines the roles and responsibilities for information security for the entire enterprise, the IR policy defines IR roles and responsibilities for the organization in general and the CSIRT in particular, as well as others who will be mobilized to activate the plan. Note that the composition, roles, and responsibilities of the IRPT are usually defined in the CP policy; however, in the event they are not, they can be included in the IR policy. Table 4-1 provides an overview of a typical IR policy.

IR policy, like all well-written policies, must gain the full support of senior management and be clearly understood by all affected parties. It is especially important to gain the support of communities of interest that will be required to alter business practices or make changes to their IT infrastructures. For example, if the CSIRT determines that

Table 4-1   Incident Response Policy Elements[5]

Statement of management commitment
Purpose and objectives of the policy
Scope of the policy (to whom and what it applies and under what circumstances)
Definition of information security incidents and their consequences within the context of the organization
Organizational structure and delineation of roles, responsibilities, and levels of authority, which should include: • The composition of the CSIRT, including the team lead   • The role of the CSIRT members   • The position and role of a watch commander and any **watchstanders** to identify an incident candidate and activate the IR plan   • The responsibilities of all security professionals to monitor systems for potential incidents, and the methods of reporting   • The responsibilities of all organizational employees to report suspicious activity   • The authority of the IR team to confiscate or disconnect equipment and to monitor suspicious activity   • The requirements for reporting certain types of incidents
Prioritization or severity ratings of potential incidents
Performance measures (as discussed in later modules)
Schedule of IR plan training and testing, which includes the identification of responsible individuals and specifications of minimum standards
Reporting and contact forms
Schedule of review and revision of this policy, to include the identification of responsible individuals

Source: NIST SP 800-61.

the only way to stop a DDoS attack (like the one in the opening scenario) is to sever the organization's connection to the Internet, it should have a signed document locked in an appropriate filing cabinet preauthorizing such action. This prevents any perception of the CSIRT performing actions outside its level of authorization and protects both the CSIRT members and the organization from misunderstanding and potential liability.

Table 4-2 provides additional attributes of the policy beyond its content.

watchstanders

Entry-level InfoSec professionals responsible for the routine monitoring and operation of a particular InfoSec technology. Also known as security staffers.

Table 4-2   Additional IR Policy Elements

Policy Attribute	Objective
Support	All strategic directives must be supported by the entire senior management team. This encompasses the vision statement, the mission statement, and all enterprise-wide policies.
Clarity	Each person expected to comply with policy must be able to understand the policy as it is written. This includes all of the affected groups, including various levels of management, technical staff, and administrative staff. Writing should be free of technical terms when possible and should avoid ambiguity in phrasing and usage. A best practice is to write using short sentences and a restricted vocabulary. When consistent with classification and disclosure policies, representative groups outside the security team should be invited to read drafts and specifically comment on readability. Revise and rewrite as indicated until the prose is understandable by the intended audiences. Some regulatory bodies specify the Flesch-Kincaid reading level for certain types of documents; most word processors can calculate the reading level of a block of text.

(continues)

Table 4-2   Additional IR Policy Elements (*Continued*)

Policy Attribute	Objective
Length	As often quoted from Shakespeare, brevity is the soul of wit. This is also true when writing policy. Policy that is longer than absolutely required is either poorly designed, poorly written, or is actually a procedure (which is not really part of policy). Regrettably, security policies of improper length are frequently implemented because they confuse the real intent of communicating management's aims with the distraction of operational processes. Such detailed process directives are procedures, not policies, and while they are important and need to be written, they are not part of the policy.
Required and sufficient	Written policies must include only what is required and must include all that is required. Redundancy is not an objective in creating policy documents but may be included in supporting procedures and other parts of the managerial process.
Functional	Use concrete language that directs behavior and avoid statements that are subject to individual interpretation. Pleasant phrases that state truisms like "we will always provide world-class security services" serve little purpose to inform policy adherents how they should act. It may be necessary on occasion to include truisms if they lead to concrete actions, such as "stakeholders and customers will be treated with respect," but this only serves a purpose when those expected to follow the policy know what the phrases mean.
Realistic	Unless a policy is realistic in the cultural context of the intended organization, it will fail before it is implemented. In the preceding example that requires respect for customers, additional guidance is needed for how to reach that objective. This guidance might include a directive to provide regular training to all staff to understand how to deal with customers. Unless a policy can be followed to achieve an intended objective, it is not realistic.
Enforceable	Unless a policy has sufficient detail and concrete requirements to aid in its enforcement, it is of limited or no value. Enforceable policies are accompanied by measurement criteria and assessment guidance for those criteria so compliance can be evaluated. These criteria and how they are used to assess performance may often be labeled as standards. An example of a contradictory policy would be one that claims data security as a first priority and requires complete privacy for all stakeholders. The second requirement will preclude any possibility of achieving the first.

Source: Carnegie Mellon University, Software Engineering Institute.

As when developing other policies, the involvement of people responsible for using the policies is critical in their development. In addition, interaction and review by the other CP teams (DR and BC) will aid in the development of clear, consistent, and uniform policy elements and structure. It is useful to look at published policies from other agencies and organizations when developing the policy.[6] Other sources of information for the policies include the following:

- Organization charts for the enterprise and specific business functions
- Topologies for organizational or constituency systems and networks
- Critical system and asset inventories
- Existing DR or BC plans
- Existing guidelines for notifying the organization of a physical security breach
- Any existing IR plans
- Any parental or institutional regulations
- Any existing security policies and procedures[7]

Integrating the BIA

As described in Module 2, the business impact analysis involves three steps designed to allow the organization to prioritize its business functions; define the resources needed to support those functions, including information assets, information technology, and security; and then establish recovery priorities. Within the IR plan, the IRPT must take this information and translate it into priorities for the CSIRT and supporting groups.

When multiple systems are compromised during an incident, the CSIRT must establish a priority of effort for recovery after the incident has been contained. While it typically does not create issues as widespread as those in a disaster, a large-scale incident can still cause multiple systems to be unavailable to support business operations. Consider as an example the Zeppelin ransomware, which often spread throughout an entire organization, locking users out of their systems, encrypting data and applications, and eventually shutting down the entire business. If the CSIRT can halt the spread of ransomware before it completely incapacitates the organization, it may avoid escalation of the incident to disaster classification. However, in the recovery phase or even the reaction phase, the organization will still need to prioritize its efforts, working to protect and recover more critical assets first so the organization can continue its operations.

Much of the information in the IR plan will be derived from the CP plan and then expanded upon. Although the BIA may have established organization-wide recovery priorities, multiple systems within each functional unit will likely be identified as key recovery resources. In addition to prioritizing these systems, the IT and information security groups will need to prioritize their functions and supporting information assets and systems resources. These functions may overlap, so it is important that the two groups perform this task together, or at least collaborate and coordinate extensively.

attack scenario

A description of a typical attack, including its methodology, indicators, and broad consequences.

attack profile

See *attack scenario*.

Attack Scenarios

To apply the information from the BIA and begin to develop detailed procedures that will form the IR plan, the IRPT must examine the various attack scenarios that could arise as incidents. An **attack scenario** or **attack profile** is a description of a potential attack that includes as much information as the IRPT can document on the most likely attack methods, attack points, and attack methodology. The team should also estimate the likelihood and potential impact of a successful attack. After the attack profiles are completed, the team can begin developing detailed procedures for detecting, reacting to, and recovering from each scenario. An example of an attack scenario is presented in Table 4-3.

Table 4-3   Malicious Code Attack Scenario

Date of analysis	*June 23, 2020*
Attack name/description	*Malicious code via e-mail*
Threat/probable threat agents	• *Vandalism/script kiddies*
	• *Theft/experienced hacker*
Known or possible vulnerabilities	• *Emergent weaknesses in e-mail clients*
	• *Inappropriate actions by employees, contractors, and visitors using e-mail clients*
	• *Emergent weakness in e-mail servers or gateways*
Likely precursor activities or indicators	*Announcements from vendors and bulletins*
Likely attack activities or indicators of attack in progress	• *E-mail volume measurements may show variances*
	• *Unusual system failures among clients*
	• *Unusual system failures among servers*
	• *Notification from e-mail recipients who may be ahead of us in attack life cycle*
Information assets at risk from this attack	*All connected systems due to blended attack model now prevalent*
Damage or loss to information assets likely from this attack	• *Denial of service for some clients almost certain*
	• *Denial of service for servers possible*
	• *Possible losses of data depending on nature of attack*

(continues)

Table 4-3 Malicious Code Attack Scenario (*Continued*)

Other assets at risk from this attack	*None likely*
Damage or loss to other assets likely from this attack	*None likely*
Immediate actions indicated when this attack is under way	• *Disconnect e-mail gateway(s)* • *Update e-mail gateway-filtering patterns and apply* • *Update and distribute client-filtering patterns* • *Isolate all infected servers* • *Isolate all infected clients* • *Begin server recovery actions for infected servers* • *Begin client recovery actions for infected clients*
Follow-up actions after this attack was successfully executed	*Review pattern update timing and procedure to ensure adequacy*
Comments	*None at this time*

attack scenario end case

An estimate of the likelihood and impact of the best, worst, and most likely outcomes of an attack.

Potential Damage Assessment

From the detailed scenarios generated in the process just completed, the BIA planning team must estimate the cost of the best, worst, and most likely outcomes by preparing an **attack scenario end case**. This allows the organization to identify what must be done to recover from each possible case. At this time, the team does not attempt to determine how much to spend on the protection of business units—this issue is analyzed during risk management. The costs determined at that point include the actions of the response team members (described in the following sections) as they try to quickly and effectively recover from any incident or disaster. These cost estimates can persuade managers throughout an organization about the importance of planning and recovery efforts. Some of the supporting information used to complete the attack scenario end cases comes from the attack profiles described earlier. The following example uses the attack profile to create potential damage assessments. When added to the attack scenarios, a complete picture of the realistic threat caused by the attacks is possible.

Table 4-4 shows the type of information that can be added to an attack scenario to compose an attack scenario end case. Although each scenario is simplistic, a wealth of information is provided that can be used to evaluate future incidents and help determine how serious an ongoing attack might be.

Table 4-4 Malicious Code Attack Scenario Addendum

Date of analysis	*June 23, 2020*
Attack name/description	*Malicious code (ransomware) via e-mail*
Comments	*None at this time*

Best-case scenario for this attack:

As a best-case scenario for this attack, the end user receives the malicious code via e-mail and recognizes the attack based on the training and awareness information provided quarterly. Virtually all e-mail attacks are launched via an attached file. The current e-mail client in use allows the user to view the attachment name without opening the file. Users trained to recognize questionable file attachments (.pif, .scr, .com, .exe, etc.) immediately delete the file and empty it from their e-mail trash folder.

Scenario risk: *Moderate; only through continued training and awareness programs can we ensure the best-case scenario prevails.*

Scenario cost to organization: *Very low; the only real cost is the time and effort employees must dedicate to filtering their e-mail. It is estimated, however, that somewhere between 40 to 50 hours organization-wide are wasted processing e-mail with potentially malicious content.*

Scenario probability of attack continuing and spreading: *Very low*

(continues)

Table 4-4   Malicious Code Attack Scenario Addendum (*Continued*)

Worst-case scenario for this attack:

As a worst-case scenario for this attack, the end user receives the malicious code via e-mail but has disabled his antivirus and antispyware software (or disabled the automatic signature updates). The user then opens an e-mail attachment that contains malicious code. The code could potentially launch a ransomware payload and encrypt user data and organizational data. The local user could lose all local data and work effort as well as subject organizational assets to ransomware. In the worst case, key organizational files will be held for ransom, which means the files must either be reconstituted or replaced with new effort.

Scenario risk: *Moderate; only through continued training, awareness programs, and enforcement of local user file backups can we ensure that this scenario does not occur.*

Scenario cost to organization: *Moderate; while the overall organization can be protected through the methods described in the other scenarios, there is a loss of local user data and work effort if this scenario prevails. The affected user is forced to restore key files, as described. The potential cost to the organization could be severe if those files were critical to organizational planning and operations. However, with the implementation of a centralized key file repository, which has daily backups, the organization can minimize the effects of this activity. Real costs to the organization could be in thousands of dollars in lost man-hours, and potentially lost customer revenue, if customer service or public image suffers because of the lack of information or exposure.*

Scenario probability of attack continuing and spreading: *Low*

Most likely case scenario for this attack:

As a most likely case scenario for this attack, the end user who receives the malicious code via e-mail may inadvertently open the attachment under the impression that it is an important file and potentially release the attached malicious code. With the current level of antivirus and antispyware software installed, there is a high probability that the protection software will activate and then contain and quarantine the malicious code before any significant damage occurs. A technical control environment with functional unified threat management is also likely to mitigate the spread of such an attack.

Scenario risk: *Moderate; only through continued maintenance and update of antivirus and antimalware programs can we ensure the most likely case scenario prevails.*

Scenario cost to organization: *Low. The only concrete cost is the time and effort employees must dedicate to ensuring that their antivirus and antispyware software signatures are up to date. With the current managed signatures program, this is handled automatically, as are scheduled scans of 100 desktop systems each night. The challenge arises in educating employees not to abort these scans by shutting down their systems at night, as the scans will then be diverted to morning activation, rather than running at 2 a.m. as currently scheduled.*

Scenario probability of attack continuing and spreading: *Very low*

Identifying and Reviewing Preventative Controls

As part of any IR plan development, review, or revision, the IRPT should ensure that all preventative controls implemented in the organization are periodically reviewed and assessed. While this may be conducted as part of the ongoing risk management program, it's also a good idea to reinforce the concept of constantly "checking the wall" to ensure that the organization's information assets are protected and that all implemented controls are functioning as expected. It's also critical to ensure that employees serving as watchstanders are properly trained to recognize potential incidents detected by the organization's technology. It does no good for an intrusion detection and prevention system (IDPS) to detect an ongoing attack if the people monitoring the IDPS don't know how to interpret its displays and notifications.

During an incident, it is also critical to keep an eye on key preventative controls to ensure that an ongoing incident does not open the door to concurrent or subsequent attacks. A crucial part of recovery efforts following an incident is the inspection of all existing controls to ensure that the threat source was not able to compromise additional systems, which might allow a follow-on attack by the primary threat source or other potential threats that may hear of the success of the attack and want to test their skills against the same systems. The organization is perhaps most at risk immediately following a successful attack, even if the CSIRT was able to contain the attack before it progressed to the point of actual data loss. Even the idea that a particular organization is vulnerable and susceptible to attack may cause other threat sources to view the organization as an easy target.

Organizing the CSIRT

In some organizations, the CSIRT may simply be a loose or informal association of IT and InfoSec employees who are called if an attack is detected on the organization's information assets. In other more formal implementations, the CSIRT (also referred to as a *security IRT* or *computer IRT*) is the team of people and their supporting policies, procedures, technologies, and data necessary to prevent, detect, react to, and recover from an incident that could potentially damage the organization's information. At some level, all members of an organization are members of the CSIRT, as every action they take could potentially cause or avert an incident. Development and structure of the CSIRT is covered in detail in Module 5.

DEVELOPING THE IR PLAN

The incident response plan (IR plan) attempts to anticipate, detect, and mitigate the effects of negative events that might compromise information resources and assets. In an organization, unexpected activities or events occur regularly. When those activities or events have the potential to threaten information assets, they are referred to as adverse events. In contingency planning, an adverse event that actually threatens the security of the organization's information assets is called an *incident*. An incident occurs when an adverse event (natural or human made) affects information assets, systems, or other resources, causing actual loss, damage, or disruption. The organization's efforts to deal with incidents must be carefully planned and coordinated because quick and efficient containment and resolution of incidents is necessary to prevent loss. The IR plan is usually activated when an incident is first detected, whether by users, the help desk, a security professional, or some type of security technology, as the incident attempts to cause damage. The criteria for activating the IR plan must be set in advance by the organization to avoid disruption to business operations and loss of information assets. Incidents that cause damage beyond the threshold of the IR plan's ability to contain and recover from the incident would be reclassified as disasters.

adverse events

Events with negative consequences that could threaten the organization's information assets or operations; sometimes referred to as incident candidates.

When one of the threats identified in Module 1 turns into a valid attack, it is classified as an information security incident, but only if it has all of the following characteristics:

- It is directed against information assets owned or operated by the organization.
- It has a realistic chance of success.
- It threatens the confidentiality, integrity, or availability of information resources and assets.

The prevention of threats and attacks has been intentionally omitted from this discussion because guarding against such possibilities is entirely the responsibility of the information security department. It is important to understand that IR procedures are *reactive measures*; excluding the efforts taken to prepare for such actions, they are *not considered preventive controls*.

The responsibility for creating an organization's IR plan often falls to the IRPT leader, who is typically a senior manager from the information security or information technology unit. Depending on the size of the organization, it may be the chief information security officer (CISO). With the aid of other managers and systems administrators on the IRPT, the IRPT leader should select members from each community of interest to form the CSIRT that will execute the IR plan. The roles and responsibilities of IRPT and CSIRT members should be clearly documented and communicated throughout the organization. The IR plan also includes an alert roster that lists critical internal and external agencies to be contacted during the course of an incident. Planning for an incident and the responses to it requires a detailed understanding of the organization's information assets and systems and the threats they face. The IRPT and the CSIRT will work to develop a series of predefined response procedures that will guide the CSIRT and information security staff through the IR steps. Predefining incident responses enables the organization to react to a detected incident quickly and effectively, with less confusion and wasted time and effort.

As part of the IRP process, the IR team creates the IR plan, and from there the IR procedures that are integral to the plan can begin to take shape. For every potential attack scenario, the IR team creates an incident plan, which is made up of three sets of incident-handling procedures. These procedures address steps to be taken during, after, and before an incident:

- *During the incident*—The planners develop and document the procedures that must be performed immediately upon detection of an ongoing incident. These procedures are grouped and include information on the individuals or their assigned roles. A systems administrator's tasks will differ from those of a manager or a firewall administrator, so members of the planning committee must draft sets of function-specific procedures. Provisions must be made for a dedicated scribe or secretary to keep thorough notes of all activity.
- *After the incident*—After the procedures for handling an incident are drafted, the planners develop and document the procedures that must be performed immediately after the incident has ceased. These procedures are also performed if the incident was detected after it concluded. Again, separate functional areas may need different procedures.
- *Before the incident*—The planners draft a third set of procedures, which are tasks that must be performed to prepare for the incident. These procedures include the details of the data backup schedules, training schedules, testing plans, copies of service agreements, and references to DR and BC plans, as needed. At this level, the plan could include information on off-site data storage, and any cloud computing resources contracted by the organization for use in IR planning.

Although it may not seem logical to organize the documentation of the IR plan in the order just described, this is a practical consideration. When the members of the CSIRT reach for the IR plan as they are responding to an incident, the primary concern is what must be done *now*, during the incident. After the incident has been contained, the team will need to access documented procedures on the recovery and follow-up activities. The final section on the procedures used for IR readiness and the steps needed to maintain the plan would be used during regular reviews and updates to plans, controls, and safeguards. Each of these sets of procedures is discussed in detail in the following sections.

Planning for the Response "During the Incident"

Beginning with the end in mind is useful in most planning activities. However, in the specific case of IR, you begin with the middle in mind, the actual incident response. The most important phase of the IR plan is the reaction to the incident, depicted here as "during the incident." When an event escalates to an incident, the team needs quick and easy access to the specific procedures necessary to identify, contain, and terminate the incident. Although the specifics of these actions are covered in other modules, an overview here can assist in understanding the mechanics of developing this phase of the IR plan.

trigger

An activity or event that causes the CSIRT to be activated to respond to an incident.

Each viable attack scenario end case is examined in turn by the IR team. As indicated earlier, representatives from the CSIRT assist as part of this team after the CSIRT has been formed. The IRPT and the CSIRT discuss the end cases and begin to understand the actions that must be taken to react to the incident. The discussion begins with the **trigger**, which causes the CSIRT to be activated and the IR plan to be initiated. This trigger could be any number of situations or circumstances, including the following:

incident response duty officer (IR duty officer)

The on-duty or on-call member of the CSIRT responsible for reviewing adverse events and determining whether an actual incident is ongoing and whether the CSIRT should be activated.

- A phone call from a user to the help desk about unusual computer or network behavior
- Notification from a systems administrator about unusual server or network behavior
- Notification from an intrusion detection device
- Notification from business partners
- Notification from trusted outside sources such as vendors or government agencies
- Review of system log files indicating an unusual pattern of entries
- Loss of system connectivity
- Device malfunctions
- Notification from adversaries either for ransom demands or other motivations

There are many indicators that an intrusion may be occurring. After an indicator has been reported, the IR team leader or the IR duty officer makes the determination that the IR plan must be activated. The **IR duty officer** is a

CSIRT reaction force

A subset of the computer security incident response team responsible for reacting to a specific type of incident.

CSIRT member who is responsible for reviewing any adverse events and determining whether they are actual incidents. After this individual determines an actual incident has occurred or is ongoing, he or she notifies the CSIRT and moves forward with the IR plan.

For each type of incident, a specific set of skills is needed. Therefore, each attack scenario end case requires the IRPT to determine what individuals or specific skills are needed to respond. For example, different skills are probably needed to respond to a physical security threat as compared to a DoS attack or an internal virus infestation. Each unique combination of skills can then be added to the IR plan section dedicated to this particular attack. In addition, the IR plan should specify who the team leader is for the particular incident. Should the incident begin to escalate, the CSIRT leader continues to add resources and skill sets as necessary to attempt to contain and terminate the incident. In addition to specifying the leader, the IR plan should specify the scribe (also known as the archivist or historian) for the incident. This individual is responsible for developing and maintaining a log of events for use in reviewing actions during the after-action review, which is described later. The resulting team represents the CSIRT reaction force for that particular incident.

The next planning component is the determination of what must be done to react to the incident. In the event of a malware infestation, for example, the first action is to verify the presence of the virus by examining the antivirus software, system logs, and other monitoring systems. The help desk also reviews help-desk requests to determine if others have reported strange or unusual system or network behavior. After it is determined that there is a malware attack, the next step is performed: determining the extent of exposure. Is the infestation limited to one computer system, or has it already spread?

After the extent is determined, the team begins to attempt to quarantine the malware—in this example, by first disconnecting infected systems from the network, then by looking for evidence of continued spread, in case the malware has already jumped quarantine. Should isolating infected machines not contain the spread, then additional measures may be necessary, such as isolating network segments, terminating server sessions, disconnecting the Internet connection, and even shutting down the network servers. After the infection is contained, the team continues to look for "flare-ups," which are small pockets of infestation that arise or activate after the primarily infected systems have been isolated. Only after all infected machines or systems have been isolated can the team begin the next phase: decontamination.

In the last phase of *actions during* this example incident, the team begins disinfecting systems by running antimalware software, searching for spyware, and so on. If antimalware software is functional and up to date, the presence of new malware should be documented. When all signs of contamination are eliminated, the *actions during* phase is complete.

Planning for "After the Incident"

After the incident has been contained, the *actions after* or *right-of-bang* phase begins. This descriptive terminology uses *bang* to label the unfolding of the incident; *left-of-bang* refers to events and actions before the incident is declared and *right-of-bang* describes events and actions after the incident is contained. During the "actions after" phase, the extent of the damage is assessed, lost or damaged data is restored, systems are scrubbed of infection, and essentially everything is restored to its previous state. Thus, the IR plan must describe the stages necessary to recover from the most likely events of the incident. It should also detail other events needed for the "actions after" phase, such as the protection from follow-on incidents, forensics analysis, and the after-action review.

Follow-on incidents are highly probable when compromised machines are brought back online or when unprotected computers, which may have been offline at the time of the attack, are brought back up. Such incidents are also likely in the event of a human attacker who retreats to a chat room and describes the attack in specific detail to other potential attackers. Therefore, increased monitoring for potential follow-on attacks should be a high priority. By identifying and resolving the avenues of attacks from forensic analysis, the organization can prevent incidents from reoccurring.

Forensic analysis is the process of systematically examining information assets for evidentiary material that can provide insight into how the incident transpired. Information on which machine was infected first or how a particular attacker gained access to the network provides insight about unknown vulnerabilities or exploits. Care must be taken to use an individual trained in forensic analysis, as the information found during the analysis may be potential evidence in civil or criminal proceedings. Forensic analysis is covered in additional detail later in this textbook.

Before returning to routine duties, the CSIRT must conduct an **after-action review (AAR)** to review what happened during the event. All key players review their notes and verify that the IR documentation is accurate and precise. All team members review their actions during the incident and identify areas where the IR plan worked, didn't work, or could be improved. This allows the team to update the IR plan. The AAR can also serve as a training case for future team members. After the AAR report is delivered to management, the incident is closed and the CSIRT can stand down from its active state.

after-action review (AAR)

A detailed examination and discussion of the events that occurred during an incident or disaster, from first detection to final recovery.

Reaction

The Second Armored Cavalry Regiment (ACR) is the oldest U.S. cavalry regiment on continuous active duty, starting in 1836. It served as the vanguard of the 1st Armored Division in the sweep of Iraqi forces during the 1991 Gulf War. Before the Gulf War, it was responsible for the patrol and protection of the West German/East German/Czechoslovakian border. The regiment, with its approximately 3000 soldiers, three armored cavalry squadrons, a tank company, a howitzer battalion, and an air-cavalry squadron, carried out this mission by placing one troop (a company-sized element) from each of the three front-line squadrons (a battalion-sized element) in various patrol camps along the border for a 30- to 45-day rotation. Each of these border troops conducted constant surveillance, ready to give early warning of potential border violations, political incidents, and even hostile invasions. Within the camp, the border troop consisted of either a cavalry troop of approximately 100 soldiers, 12 M3A1 Bradley Fighting Vehicles (BFVs), and 9 M1A1 Abrams Main Battle Tanks, or a tank company with 14 M1A1s. Occasionally, units from outside the regiment took a shift on the border, but it was ultimately the 2nd ACR's responsibility to guard this stretch of territory, constantly monitoring the border for indications of a pending attack by the former Soviet Union.

The unit occupying the border camp was required to organize a series of elements capable of deploying in reaction to an incident—be it a border crossing by a political defector or an invasion by a military force. The smallest such element was the "reaction force" made up of 8 to 10 soldiers manning two armored vehicles (M3A1s or M1A1s). It was required to be ready to deploy to an area outside the base within 15 minutes in response to an incident. Routine patrols were conducted in HMMWVs (Hum-Vees), but the reaction elements had to deploy in armored vehicles. The next-larger element was the "reaction platoon," the remainder of the reaction force's platoon (two additional M-1s or four additional M-3s, and 8 to 20 additional troops), which had to be ready to deploy within 30 minutes. If the incident warranted it, the remainder of the troop had to be prepared to depart the base within 1 hour. This deployment was rehearsed daily by the reaction force, weekly by the reaction platoon, and at least twice during border camp by the entire troop.

What does this scenario illustrate? An incident is an incident. The employees in an organization who respond to a security incident do not engage in combat against a physical threat, of course. The preparation and planning required to respond to an information security incident is not entirely different from that required to respond to a military incident, however. The same careful attention to detail must be paid, each potential threat scenario must be examined, and a number of responses commensurate with the level of the incident must be developed.

Planning for "Before the Incident"

Planning for *before the incident*, *before actions*, or *left of bang* calls on the planners to implement good IT and information security practices. However, specific incidents may have unique characteristics requiring special prevention methods. "Before actions" include preventive measures to manage the risks associated with a particular attack as well as the preparations of the IR team. As described in the "Reaction" feature, it is only through routine rehearsal that a team can maintain a state of readiness to respond to attacks. This process includes training the CSIRT, testing the IR plan, selecting and maintaining the tools used by the CSIRT, and training users of the systems and procedures controlled by the organization. Risk management was covered in Module 1.

Ensuring Plan Training, Testing, and Exercising

After the IR plan is developed, all users and managers as well as IRPT and CSIRT members must be involved in testing, training for, and exercising the plan. The CSIRT is also trained and tested on the procedures for reacting to incidents, which must also be documented. To clarify, training is the process of providing information and skills to the individuals responsible for implementing the IR plan, while testing is an assessment of their performance and capabilities under simulated attack conditions. Exercising a plan is the process of rehearsing under less strenuous circumstances to ensure that everyone knows their roles and to periodically review and revise the details of the plan.

Training the CSIRT

One of the primary responsibilities of the IRPT is to ensure that the CSIRT is prepared to respond to each incident it may face. This requires a large number of ongoing training and rehearsal activities. Training IR personnel can be conducted in various ways. There are several national training programs that focus on IR tools and techniques. For example, the SANS Institute offers a number of national conferences specifically designed to train information security professionals (see *www.sans.org*). SANS even has a set of conferences—SANSFIRE (Forensics and Incident Response Education)—that is specifically focused on IR. Unlike other conferences, SANSFIRE is not designed for the hacker first and everyone else second. Vendors such as Microsoft, Cisco, and Sun also provide IR training to IT professionals. For government employees, the National Initiative for Cybersecurity Careers and Studies (NICCS) offers security incident response training (*https://niccs.us-cert.gov/training/search/trainace/security-incident-response-training*).

In addition to formal external training, an organization can set up its own training program in which senior, more experienced staff members share their knowledge with newer, less experienced employees. An ongoing training program should include this mentoring-type approach to prevent specific organizational knowledge from leaving when certain employees depart.

Other training methods include a professional reading program, which is a self-created list of trustworthy information sources to read on a regular basis. There are a host of high-quality information security journals and magazines that have articles and columns on IR topics, including:

- CISO Magazine (*www.cisomag.com/*)
- Chief Security Officer (*www.csoonline.com*)
- Information Security Magazine (*www.infosecurity-magazine.com*)
- SANS Information Security Reading Room (*www.sans.org/rr*)—Individuals seeking advanced SANS certification are required to write a practicum paper. Several of these papers include CP topics.
- SC Magazine (*www.scmagazine.com*)

Unfortunately, at the time of this writing, there are no dedicated IR journals or magazines. However, many of the general information security and DR journals identified in later modules have occasional articles on IR. There are a number of online resources for IR, including:

- Forum of Incident Response and Security Teams (FIRST)—*www.first.org*
- U.S. Computer Emergency Readiness Team (US CERT)—*www.us-cert.gov*
- Incident Response Consortium—*www.incidentresponse.com*
- Carnegie Mellon University, Software Engineering Institute CSIRT resources—*www.sei.cmu.edu/education-outreach/computer-security-incident-response-teams/index.cfm*
- NIST Computer Security Resource Center (CSRC)—*csrc.nist.gov*

Training the Users

Training the end user to assist in the IR process is primarily the responsibility of individuals who provide security education training and awareness (SETA) for the organization. As part of the ongoing employee training program, SETA trainers should instruct end users on the following tasks:

- *What is expected of them*—What is expected of members of the organization's security team
- *How to recognize an attack*—Each user is instructed on what to look for in an attack, broken down by category, including the key indicators.

- *How to report a suspected incident and whom to report it to*—By e-mail or phone call to the help desk, information security hotline, *abuse@myorganization.com*, or other designated mechanism
- *How to mitigate the damage of attacks on the desktop*—By disconnecting the system from the network if users suspect an attack is in progress and by reporting incidents promptly
- *Good information security practices*—Tasks that prevent attacks on the desktop, such as:
  - ○ Keeping antivirus/antimalware software up to date
  - ○ Using spyware detection software
  - ○ Working with systems administrators to keep operating systems and applications up to date with patches and updates
  - ○ Not opening suspect e-mail attachments
  - ○ Avoiding social engineering attacks by not providing critical information over the phone or through e-mail to untrusted sources
  - ○ Not downloading and installing unauthorized software or software from untrusted sources
  - ○ Protecting passwords and classified information

Although the specifics of developing a training program are beyond the scope of this text, you will want to develop training for general users, managerial users, and technical users.

Training for general users. One method of ensuring that IR is understood by general users is to provide training on the plan. This allows users to ask questions and receive specific guidance, and it allows the organization to emphasize key points. These general users also require training on the technical details of how to do their jobs securely, including good security practices, password management, specialized access controls, and violation reporting.

A convenient time to conduct this type of training is during employee orientation. During this critical time, employees are educated on a wide variety of organizational policies and procedures and on the expectations the organization has for its employees. Because employees haven't yet established preconceived notions or methods of behavior, they are more likely to be receptive to this instruction. This is balanced against the fact that they are not yet familiar with the organization's systems or their jobs, so they are unaware of work issues and don't yet know what questions to ask.

Training for managerial users. Management may have the same training requirements as those for general users; however, managers expect a more personal form of training, with smaller groups and more interaction and discussion. In fact, managers often resist organized training of any kind. This is another area in which a champion can exert influence; support at the executive level can convince managers to attend training events, which in turn reinforces the entire training program. It is a recommended practice that training be delivered to cohorts based on levels of hierarchical and technical responsibility—executives, mid-level managers, first-line supervisors, technical staff, and non-technical staff.

Training for technical users. Technical training for IT staff, security staff, and technically competent general users is more detailed than general user or managerial training, and it may therefore require the use of consultants or outside training organizations, as described earlier.

Training techniques and delivery methods. Good training techniques are as essential to successful training as a thorough knowledge of the subject area. As explained by Charles Trepper in an article titled "Training Developers More Efficiently":

> Using the wrong method can actually hinder the transfer of knowledge and lead to unnecessary expense and frustrated, poorly trained employees. Good training programs, regardless of delivery method, take advantage of the latest learning technologies and best practices. Recent developments include less use of centralized public courses and more on-site training. Other best practices include the increased use of short, task-oriented modules and training sessions, available during the normal work week, that are immediate and consistent. Newer concepts in training also provide students with the training they need when they need it—a practice often called just-in-time training.[8]

Selection of the training delivery method is not always based on the best outcome for the trainee. Often, other factors come first, like budget, time frame, and the needs of the organization. The most common delivery methods are shown in Table 4-5.

Table 4-5   Training Delivery Methods

Method	Advantages	Disadvantages
One-on-one A dedicated trainer works with each trainee on the areas specified.	• Informal • Personal • Customized to the needs of the trainee • Can be scheduled to fit the needs of the trainee	• Resource intensive to the point of being inefficient
Formal class A single trainer works with multiple trainees in a formal setting.	• Formal training plan, efficient • Trainees can learn from each other. • Interaction with the trainer is possible. • Usually considered cost-effective	• Relatively inflexible • May not be sufficiently responsive to the needs of all trainees • Difficult to schedule, especially if more than one session is needed
Computer-based training (CBT) Prepackaged software provides training at the trainee's workstation.	• Flexible, no special scheduling requirements • Self-paced, can go as fast or as slow as trainee needs • Can be cost-effective	• Can be very expensive • Content not always customized to the needs of the organization • Some employees not motivated to use this format
Distance learning and Web seminars Trainees receive a seminar presentation at their computers. Some models allow teleconferencing for voice feedback; others have text questions and feedback.	• Can be live, or can be archived and viewed at trainee's convenience • Can be low-cost or no cost	• If archived, can be very inflexible, with no mechanism for trainee feedback • If live, can be difficult to schedule
User support group When support is available from a community of users, it is commonly facilitated by a particular vendor as a mechanism to augment the support for products or software.	• Allows users to learn from each other • Usually conducted in an informal social setting	• Does not use a formal training model • Centered around a specific topic or product
On-the-job training Trainees learn the specifics of their jobs while working, using the software, hardware, and procedures that are normal parts of their work.	• Very applicable to the task at hand • Inexpensive	• A sink-or-swim approach in which the trainee usually receives no formal training program • Can result in substandard work performance until trainee gets up to speed
Self-study (noncomputerized) Trainees study materials on their own, usually when not actively performing their jobs.	• Lowest cost to the organization • Places materials in hands of the trainee • Trainees able to select the material they need to focus on the most • Self-paced	• Shifts responsibility for training to the trainee, with little formal support • Some employees not motivated to use this format

IR Plan Testing

A critical part of preparing an IR plan is testing it. An untested plan is no plan at all. Very few plans are executable as initially written; they must be tested to identify vulnerabilities, faults, and inefficient processes and procedures. After problems are identified during the testing process, improvements can be made, and the resulting plan can be relied on in times of need. Some common strategies that can be used to test contingency plans include:[9]

- *Desk check*—The **desk check** is the simplest kind of validation. It involves distributing copies of the IR plan to each individual who will be assigned a role during an actual incident. Each individual performs a desk check by reviewing the plan and creating a list of correct and incorrect components and concerns. Though not a true test, this is a good way to periodically review the perceived feasibility and effectiveness of the plan.
- *Structured walk-through*—In a **structured walk-through**, all involved individuals walk through the steps they would take during an actual event. This can consist of an on-site walk-through, in which everyone discusses their actions at each particular location and juncture, or it may be more of a "chalk talk," in which all involved individuals sit around a conference table and each discusses his or her responsibilities as the incident unfolds.
- *Simulation*—In a **simulation**, each participant goes through the activities and processes they would be expected to perform in an actual incident. The simulation stops short of performing the actual physical tasks required, such as installing a backup or disconnecting a communications circuit. The major difference between a walk-through and a simulation is that in a walk-through, individuals independently work on their own tasks and are responsible for identifying the faults in their own procedures. In a simulation, the entire team goes through the testing together and then reviews the effectiveness of the plan at each stage.
- *Full interruption*—In **full-interruption testing**, individuals follow each and every procedure in the plan, including the interruption of service, restoration of data from backups, and notification of appropriate individuals. In organizations that cannot afford to disrupt or simulate the disruption of business functions, this testing is often performed after normal business hours. Although full-interruption testing is the most rigorous form of testing, it is unfortunately too risky for most businesses.

IR Exercises

Organizations are increasingly looking for low-cost ways of preparing their CSIRTs. One mechanism that can be used as a training or testing tool is the table-top exercise. A **table-top exercise** is a rehearsal for IR that is often considered a gaming simulation. As illustrated in the opening scenario of Module 2, participants walk through scripted scenarios during the exercise and perform their portions of the IR plan. While effective table-top exercises include representatives from each group that would be involved during an actual incident, participants generally simulate interaction with the rest of the business or with outside entities. They also don't typically interact with functional systems. Similar in construction and conduct to a structured walk-through, the table-top exercise involves having a disinterested third party, often a consultant, serve as a moderator. The moderator provides a basic overview of the scenario to participants, who are typically members of the organization, including normal on-duty IT and InfoSec staff, CSIRT members, and select managers. The moderator typically initiates an exercise by providing information to a single member of the group, who must read the provided information and then go through normal communications processes to notify the appropriate internal and external parties. This communication can be simulated by having those parties relocate to a break-out room, or by use of mobile phones, e-mail, or other communications software. Only when the rest of the group is brought into the simulated scenario will they receive any insight to the event.

Each participant is expected to discuss their roles and responsibilities at each stage of the event with the moderator (and any observing members of the organization's leadership), and to communicate with others as needed. The moderator can serve as a proxy for any internal or external party the team would need to

---

desk check

The CP testing strategy in which copies of the appropriate plans are distributed to all individuals who will be assigned roles during an actual incident or disaster; each individual reviews the plan and validates its components.

structured walk-through

The CP testing strategy in which all involved individuals walk through a site and discuss the steps they would take during an actual CP event. A walk-through can also be conducted as a conference room talk-through.

simulation

The CP testing strategy in which the organization conducts a role-playing exercise as if an actual incident or disaster had occurred. The CP team is presented with a scenario in which all members must specify how they would react and communicate their efforts.

full-interruption testing

The CP testing strategy in which all team members follow each IR/DR/BC procedure, including those for interruption of service, restoration of data from backups, and notification of appropriate individuals.

table-top exercise

A simulation of an incident in which the participants work together in a physical or virtual conference room to talk through plans and procedures, without interacting directly with the rest of the business or outside entities and without directly influencing functional systems.

war game

A type of rehearsal that seeks to realistically simulate the circumstances needed to thoroughly test a plan.

contact. As the team works through the process, the moderator keeps the team focused and on a tight timetable, periodically injecting any new information or changes to the scenario. Another consultant or organizational representative keeps track of the group's progress, documenting who does what and all communications.

At a predefined time or a certain point in the scenario script, the moderator terminates the exercise, leads the team in an after-action review of their performance, and reviews the effectiveness of the team plan. The moderator usually writes up a summary of the event and makes recommendations for how to improve the plan and the team's performance.

A favorite pastime of information security professionals is the war game, which is a large-scale simulation of attack and defense activities using realistic networks and information systems. The exercise of IR plans is an important element of the simulation. This valid, effective technique is so popular that there are national competitions at conferences like Black Hat (*blackhat.com*) and DEFCON (*www.defcon.org*). War-gaming competition at the collegiate level includes the National Collegiate Cyber Defense Competition (*www.nationalccdc.org*) for teams and the National Cyber League (*www.nationalcyberleague.org*) for individual participants.

The IRPT can use several methods in training the CSIRT as well as testing the IR plan. These methods are only valid if the CSIRT acts as defenders, using their own equipment or a duplicate environment, and follows the IR plan in the performance of the training. There is little to be gained from simply "going at it." Common war-gaming variations include the following:

- *Capture the flag*—In this variation, a "flag" (token file) is placed on each team's system. The teams are given a predetermined amount of time to protect the systems, with specific rules to keep the game from being unwinnable, such as encrypting the flag. After setting up their protections, each team defends its flag and attempts to capture the opponent's flag. This war game can also be executed on a larger scope with multiple teams in a free-for-all.
- *King of the hill*—In this variation, similar to "capture the flag," one team is designated as king of the hill (KOTH) and has a flag planted in its systems. One or more other teams work independently to breach the KOTH's security and obtain the file "flag". This method of war gaming may be better suited for CSIRT training and testing, as it allows the KOTH team to focus exclusively on defensive tactics and IR plan implementation rather than splitting the team between offensive and defensive operations.
- *Computer simulations*—In this variation, individual users or teams of users work to defend their systems and networks from simulated attacks. Although not many of these types of simulations are currently available, some organizations develop their own as a training technique, customizing them to their own systems and configurations.
- *Defend the flag*—In this combination of KOTH and computer simulations, a number of systems are set up to continually attack or simulate attacks on the target system. The defensive team must react to an escalating level of attacks to successfully defend its systems. The software to create the attacking systems is easily found by searching the Web, and reputable companies such as Cisco use these tools in training their students how to properly configure firewalls, IDSs, and routers. The nearby CCDC box describes a case of defend-the-flag competitions.
- *Online programming-level war games*—For technically advanced programmers, there are online war games for information security education and training like those at *www.hackthissite.org*. At this site, users can go on different "missions" that are designed to help improve skill sets in various areas, like client-side attacks, application attacks, and Web site attacks, to name a few.

Even the CIA and the U.S. military use war games to train and test their troops in information security and information warfare tactics. Unfortunately, hackers also have their own war games (see *roothack.org*), which allow them to practice prior to conducting their attacks.

At a minimum, organizations should conduct a periodic walk-through (or chalk talks) of each part of their CP plans. A failure to update these plans as the business and its information resources change can erode the team's ability to respond to an incident, or possibly cause greater damage than the incident itself.

The CCDC

To facilitate the development of a regular, national-level cybersecurity exercise, the Center for Infrastructure Assurance and Security at the University of Texas at San Antonio (UTSA) hosted the first Collegiate Cyber Defense Competition (CCDC) for the U.S. Southwestern region in May 2005. In June 2005, members of the Kennesaw State University (KSU) Center for Information Security Education attended a presentation by UTSA faculty members and recognized the value of the program. They immediately volunteered to create a similar event at KSU in 2006 to provide a regional competition that recognized the best team in the Southeast. KSU has hosted the Southeast Collegiate Cyber Defense Competition (SECCDC) every year since.

Though similar to other computer security competitions in many aspects, the SECCDC, as part of the CCDC, is unique in that it focuses on the operational aspect of managing and protecting an existing network infrastructure. Unlike "capture-the-flag" exercises, which incorporate both offensive and defensive actions by the teams, this competition is exclusively a real-world *defensive* competition. Students configure, harden, and protect a network over the course of the competition and focus on the task of assuming administrative and protective duties for an existing "commercial" network. Teams are scored based on their ability to:

- Detect and respond to outside threats (from a professional penetration-testing "red team").
- Maintain the availability of existing services, such as mail servers and Web servers.
- Respond to business requests, such as those for adding or removing additional services.
- Balance security needs against business needs.

There are regional and state competitions throughout the United States, with an at-large region for institutions outside a reasonable travel range of a defined region. For more information, visit *www.nationalccdc.org*.

The testing methods described above will be referred to in other sections of the book, as they can be applied to all CP training and testing efforts. If this sounds like a military training effort, note that in his book *Designation Gold*, author Richard Marcinko, a former Navy SEAL, recommends the following:[10]

> *The more you sweat in training, the less you bleed in combat.*
> *Training and preparation hurts.*
> *Lead from the front, not the rear.*
> *You don't have to like it, just do it.*
> *Keep it simple.*
> *Never assume.*
> *You are paid for your results, not your methods.*

ASSEMBLING AND MAINTAINING THE FINAL IR PLAN

Draft plans can be used for the preliminary training of staff and for evaluating the effectiveness of the plan. Any errors or difficulties discovered during training or testing can then be remedied as the draft plans mature. After the desired level of plan maturity is achieved and the drafts have been suitably reviewed and tested, the final assembly can commence.

The testing process does not stop when the final plan is created. As indicated earlier, each scenario of the IR plan should be tested at least semiannually by performing at least a structured walk-through test and a more realistic type of test when possible. Obviously, if the IR plan was executed in response to an actual incident, the sections used during the response may not require the same degree of periodic retesting, assuming of course that no changes were made to the plan in the after-action review. Any plans that are modified should be scheduled for additional testing at the earliest opportunity.

After all the individual components of the IR plan have been drafted and tested, the final IR plan document can be created. Every organization has its own preferences for the format and content of the IR plan. The most important requirement is that the IR plan is developed, tested, and placed in an easily accessible location.

Hard-Copy IR Plans

The following list of recommended practices describes the design and implementation of a hard-copy IR plan that will be easy to locate and use in an emergency. A hard copy is essential, if only as a backup, because plans that are only accessible via digital media may not be available in some incident scenarios.

1. Select a uniquely colored binder. Red or yellow is recommended, as organizations are inundated with white binders.
2. On the spine of the binder, place red and yellow (or red and white) reflective tape. Why? Some incidents involve a loss of power. In a dimly lit environment illuminated by emergency exit lights or flashlights, the binder will shine like a lighthouse, making it easy to identify and use.
3. Under the front slipcover, place a classified document cover sheet. This identifies the book as an element that has been evaluated as nonpublic by the organization's data classification scheme. If the document were to fall into the wrong hands, the finder's knowledge of how an organization responds to a particular attack could reveal procedural vulnerabilities.
4. Place an index on the first inside page, preferably one with a color-coded bar corresponding to a set of tabs.
5. For each category of attack, place the corresponding IR plan documents under a common tab and label the index.
6. Organize the contents so that the first page contains the "during attack" actions, followed by the "after attack" actions and finally the "before attack" actions. In an emergency, you want to be able to see the most important information first.
7. Attach copies of any relevant documents in the back of the plan under a separate tab—for example, copies of service agreements for the ISP, telephone, water, power, gas, and so on.
8. Add more documents as needed.
9. Store the plan in a secure but easily reachable location.

Electronic IR Plans

While organizations may never completely get away from having hard-copy documents, the preferred format for most critical policies and plans is electronic. If the organization has a security operations center (SOC), a team of security professionals will most likely monitor the status of the security systems. After the CSIRT has been notified, they will most likely check in to the SOC, and several individuals might need access to the IR plan. If the organization relies heavily on hard-copy documents, there is a good chance that enough won't be available to go around. Having access to electronic documents allows everyone to use them. The following recommendations apply to the creation and storage of an electronic copy of the IR plan:

1. Create the plan in an easy-to-read, indexed format. Teams that need to read the IR plan during an incident must be able to quickly access the content. Using a hyperlinked HTML or PDF (Adobe) format allows users of an electronic copy to quickly click a link and get to the needed content.
2. Organize the contents appropriately. As recommended for a hard-copy IR plan, organize the content so that the first page for each incident scenario shows the actions to be taken "during the attack," followed by the "after attack" actions and finally the "before attack" actions.
3. Store the plan in an accessible location, but do not make it too accessible. Team members must be able to quickly access the IR plan, but it is equally critical to ensure that unauthorized individuals *cannot*. Knowing how a CSIRT will respond to an incident could give the attacker a tactical advantage. Thus, the electronic IR plan must be stored in a location where only authorized individuals can access it, but the location must be accessible quickly and easily. This could require a document management system or other secure intranet location.

4. Encrypt the document and/or password-protect it. If an attacker does manage to access an electronic copy of the IR plan, it's important to make sure they cannot actually read it. Use of encryption or password protection can slow down or even stop an attacker's ability to read electronic IR documents. Adobe Acrobat version 10 (X) or later employs AES 256 encryption to prevent unauthorized reading, which is sufficient for most organizations.

5. Ensure that the plan has a proper classification cover and page notifications. After being unlocked, the electronic IR plan, just like its hard-copy alternative, must be properly labeled and classified. Because IR plans are almost always confidential or similarly classified, the front cover of the document should include a clear indication of this classification. Similarly, each page should include the classification in the margin along with a complete title so that if a single page is printed, it is still clearly identified as classified content.

6. Save the plan in a scalable format. When saving a document into a format like PDF, it's important to ensure that the final document is scalable and machine-readable. This format is more for the user's convenience than for security. Using a machine-readable and scalable plan means the user can zoom in on a particular section. It also means that employees with disabilities can use their specialized computing platforms to support their reading and comprehension. For example, features in Adobe Acrobat can be selected to ensure that a PDF complies with the Americans with Disabilities Act (ADA).

Maintaining the Plan

Just as every plan and policy within the organization requires formal maintenance, so does the IR plan. The plan should have a documented process for reporting issues and a formal schedule for revision. The revision process should include a mechanism whereby anyone in the organization can submit recommendations for improvement and can identify errors and inaccurate processes to the IRPT. The IRPT should collect this input and use it during scheduled revisions to the IR plan. At a minimum, the plan should be reviewed and revised annually. It should also be reviewed immediately following a testing or training exercise, as those events are likely to highlight problems with the current plan and ways to improve it.

As changes to the plan are made during scheduled or unscheduled revisions, the plan is once again circulated to the entire IRPT and upper management for review and comment. After everyone has had a chance to review the revisions, the IRPT again meets to finalize any recommended changes and updates. They then republish the plan with a new effective date and the date of the next scheduled revision.

Closing Scenario

Eventually, Paul made it into the office.

Susan had called back to advise him that the frequency of source address shifting, ports being used, and volume of traffic from the DDoS attack had all increased. As on-site incident manager, she had decided to disconnect the company from the Internet.

She had formally made the declaration that this was an incident and not just another event. She had pulled the plug.

Discussion Questions

1. What should be the next action taken by the response team?
2. What if the plans had left out the list of people to notify? Who should be informed of this action next, after Paul?
3. When the production network is taken off the Internet, how can essential online response still occur? List three ways that an organization can plan for redundant essential communications.

Ethical Decision Making

Assume that Susan had the authority to terminate the network connection but deferred making that tough call until Paul arrived an hour later so she could avoid being responsible for the disruption. Is that an ethical position to take?

MODULE SUMMARY

- Contingency planning addresses everything done by an organization to prepare for the unexpected. The IR process is made up of several phases: preparation; detection and analysis; containment, eradication, and recovery; and post-incident activity.

- When the contingency planning management team (CPMT) completes each component of the business impact analysis (BIA), it identifies how information flows and how responsibility is shared among subordinate teams. These may include the incident response (IR) team, the disaster recovery (DR) team, and the business continuity (BC) team. In the case of incident planning, the group follows these general stages: form the IR planning team, develop the IR policy, integrate the BIA, identify preventive controls, organize the CSIRT, create IR strategies and procedures, develop the IR plan, ensure plan testing, training, and exercises, and ensure plan maintenance.

- Organizing the IR planning process begins with staffing the IRPT and identifying stakeholders, such as general management, IT management, InfoSec management, and organizational departments—for example, legal, human resources, and public relations. The incident response planning (IRP) team works to build the IR policy, plan, and procedures that the CSIRT will follow during the IR actions themselves.

- One of the first deliverables prepared by the IRPT is the IR policy. The IR policy is similar in structure to other policies used by the organization. Specifically, it will include the roles and responsibilities for the CSIRT and others who will be mobilized in the activation of the plan. IR policy, like all well-written policies, must gain the full support of senior management and be clearly understood by all affected parties.

- The CSIRT (also referred to as the *security IRT* or the *computer IRT*) is the team of people and their supporting policies, procedures, technologies, and data necessary to prevent, detect, react to, and recover from an incident that could potentially damage the organization's information.

- An incident response plan (IR plan) is a detailed set of processes and procedures that anticipate, detect, and mitigate the effects of an unexpected event that might compromise information resources and assets. The IR plan is usually activated when an incident causes minimal damage—according to criteria set in advance by the organization—with little or no disruption to business operations. When a threat turns into a valid attack, it is classified as an information security incident, but only if it is directed against information assets owned or operated by the organization, has a realistic chance of success, and threatens the confidentiality, integrity, or availability of information resources and assets.

- The incident plan usually includes three sets of incident-handling procedures to document the intended actions over time. These are the actions during the incident, after the incident, and before the incident.

- For each type of incident, a specific set of skills is needed. Therefore, each attack scenario end case requires the IRPT to determine what individuals are needed to respond to each particular end case.

- One of the primary responsibilities of the IRPT is to ensure that the CSIRT is prepared to respond to each incident it may face. This requires a large number of ongoing training and rehearsal activities.

- A key part of training the CSIRT is testing the IR plan. Strategies that can be used to test contingency plans include a desk check, structured walk-through, simulation, table-top exercise, full interruption, and war gaming.

- After all the individual components of the IR plan have been drafted and tested, the final IR plan document can be created. A number of recommended practices describe the design and implementation of a physical IR plan that will be easy to locate and use in an emergency.

Review Questions

1. What are the steps of the overall IR development process?
2. What are the general stages followed by the IRP team?
3. What are two external sources for performing IRP that were mentioned in this module?
4. What does the organizational phase of the IRP process begin with?
5. Who are the typical stakeholders of the IR process?
6. Which individuals should be assembled to form the IRP team?
7. What should be among the first deliverables created by the IR planning committee?
8. What is the primary function of the IR policy?
9. In order for IP policy to be effective, what group must give its full support?
10. What are the essential attributes of an IR policy document?
11. What is an incident response plan (IR plan)?
12. What characteristics must be present if an adverse event is to be considered an incident?
13. What are the three sets of time-based procedures that are often part of the IR planning process?
14. What is meant by the "trigger" for an IR-related plan?
15. What is a "reaction force" in terms of IR planning?
16. What is an after-action review (AAR)?
17. What are the ways that training can be undertaken for the CSIRT?
18. Briefly describe the strategies used to test contingency plans.
19. Briefly describe the possible training delivery methods.
20. When should the "final" version of the IR plan be assembled?

Real-World Exercises

Exercise 4-1

Do a Web search to identify at least five sources of information you would want to use when training a CSIRT.

Exercise 4-2

Visit *www.mitre.org*. What information is provided there, and how would it be useful?

Exercise 4-3

Visit *www.securityfocus.com*. What is Bugtraq, and how would it be useful? What additional information is provided under the Vulnerabilities tab?

Exercise 4-4

Visit *www.cert.org*. What information is provided there, and how would it be useful? What additional information is provided at *www.cert.org/csirts/*?

Exercise 4-5

Do a Web search for other methods employed by industry or government to share information on possible incidents.

Hands-On Projects

The hands-on project for this module can be accessed in the Practice It folder in MindTap or through your instructor's LMS. The virtual labs provided with this resource can help you develop practical skills that will be of value as you progress through the course.

References

1. Cichonski, Paul, Tom Millar, Tim Grance, and Karen Scarfone. SP 800-61, Revision 2, "Computer Security Incident Handling Guide." National Institute of Standards and Technology. 2012.
2. Ibid.
3. West-Brown, Moira, Don Stikvoort, Klaus-Peter Kossakowski, Georgia Killcrece, Robin Ruefle, and Mark Zajicek. *Handbook for Computer Security Incident Response Teams (CSIRTs)*. Carnegie Mellon University, Software Engineering Institute. 2003. Accessed 01/11/20 from *https://resources.sei.cmu.edu/asset_files/Handbook/2003_002_001_14102.pdf*.
4. "Create a CSIRT." Carnegie Mellon University, Software Engineering Institute. White paper, March 18, 2016. Accessed 01/06/2020 from *https://resources.sei.cmu.edu/asset_files/WhitePaper/2017_019_001_485695.pdf*.
5. Cichonski, Paul, Tom Millar, Tim Grance, and Karen Scarfone. SP 800-61, Revision 2, "Computer Security Incident Handling Guide." National Institute of Standards and Technology. 2012.
6. Hall, Mary. "Implementing a Computer Incident Response Team in a Smaller, Limited Resource Organizational Setting." SANS (2003). Accessed 8/29/2012 from *www.sans.org/reading_room/whitepapers/incident/implementing-computer-incident-response-team-smaller-limited-resource-organizational-settin_1065*.
7. "Creating a Computer Security Incident Response Team: A Process for Getting Started." Carnegie Mellon University, Software Engineering Institute. 2002. Accessed 8/29/2012 from *www.cert.org/csirts/Creating-A-CSIRT.html*.
8. Trepper, Charles. "Training Developers More Efficiently." *InformationWeek*. Issue 738, P1A, 06/14/99.
9. Krutz, Ronald L., and Russell Dean Vines. *The CISSP Prep Guide: Mastering the Ten Domains of Computer Security*. Page 288. New York: John Wiley and Sons, 2001.
10. Marcinko, Richard, and John Weisman. *Designation Gold*. Preface. New York: Pocket Books, 1998.

INCIDENT RESPONSE: ORGANIZING AND PREPARING THE CSIRT

Upon completion of this material, you should be able to:

1. Describe the purpose and function of the CSIRT
2. Discuss the skills and abilities needed in the CSIRT
3. Explain the standard operating procedures associated with CSIRTs
4. Describe training and deployment of the CSIRT
5. Identify the special circumstances of CSIRT interaction with the security operations center (SOC) and when outsourcing incident response operations

Good plans shape good decisions. That's why good planning helps to make elusive dreams come true.

—Lester Robert Bittel

Opening Scenario

Brody had been enjoying a calm shift in HAL's security operations center. The calm was interrupted, however, when a pop-up notification appeared on his monitor. The network intrusion detection and prevention system had detected malicious traffic on a branch network in Tuscaloosa, Alabama, specifically targeting the branch Web server. That system had fed the events into the SOC management system and began correlating them with data from across the company. When Brody saw the alert, he digested the details and then picked up the telephone to contact the on-call network technician for that office. Meanwhile, the system displayed another pop-up notification, this time reporting malicious traffic on a branch network in Mobile. In short order, it also displayed notifications for branches in Athens, Columbia, Auburn, and Starkville. Even more alarming, the system indicated that all the traffic was coming from other branches within the company.

Brody immediately recognized that this was different from the typical attacks he'd seen in his time with the company and decided to call his boss, Nick Shula.

"Hello?" said Nick, picking up on the first ring.

"Boss, it's Brody. I think we've got a problem. We are showing that Web servers in multiple branch offices are under attack, and the traffic is coming from inside our network. What do you want me to do?"

Nick thought back to the proposal on his desk for the creation of an incident response team within the company. Nick had been so busy with other things that he hadn't been able to consider the proposal at all. Mentally kicking himself, he muttered into the phone, "Why didn't I look at that proposal?"

"What was that, boss?" Brody said.

"Never mind," Nick said. He had to think quickly and organize the team's actions to address the situation. "Call the fire-walls team," he said, "and have them put in a temporary rule to block all inbound traffic to the Web servers from internal IP addresses." After all, not many employees would be doing work that involved the Web servers. This would buy some time to consider the next steps.

"OK boss, will do. I'll keep you in the loop," Brody said.

Nick hoped the team would have a few minutes to gather more information. Then the phone rang again. He took a look at the caller ID and blanched. It was Mal Bryant, the company CEO.

"Nick, it's Mal. Listen, I'm in D.C. and I'm logged into the corporate network via the VPN. For some reason, I can't get to any of our internal Web servers. You have any idea what's going on?"

Nick sighed as he realized it was going to be a long day.

INTRODUCTION

To have a coordinated reaction to unexpected adverse events—in other words, to respond to incidents once they've been detected—an organization must designate a group with primary responsibility for dealing with situations that threaten the organization's information assets. Individuals in this group must be carefully selected so that the appropriate range of skills needed in any possible contingency is available. Also, if a group member is unavailable for some reason (vacation, illness, or off-site responsibilities for work), a capable and prepared alternate needs to be available to assume responsibility. This was the situation facing Nick in the opening scenario.

This group must be distinct from the incident response planning team (IRPT) discussed in Module 4, but it may have some overlap. The IRPT is primarily responsible for developing and implementing the policy and plans associated with incident response, but the IR reaction team—known by a myriad of names, including the computer security incident response team (CSIRT), the security incident response team (SIRT), the computer emergency response team (CERT), or simply the IR team—is responsible for responding to a suspected incident once notified by a person or system. The CSIRT, based on its policies, procedures, and training, then responds to the notification and works to regain control of the information assets at risk, determine what happened, prevent repeat occurrences, and eventually restore operations to normal.

In some organizations, the computer security incident response team (CSIRT) may simply be a loose or informal association of IT and InfoSec staffers who are called if an attack on the organization's information assets is detected. In other, more formal implementations, it is the formal team of active and on-call professionals prepared to respond to an incident notification. In most organizations, the CSIRT is comprised of IT and InfoSec professionals who may have other responsibilities on a day-to-day basis, but drop what they're doing and respond to an incident once notified. This approach is much like that of a volunteer fire department in rural areas. At some level, every member of an organization supports the objectives of the CSIRT, as every action they take could potentially cause or avert an incident.

BUILDING THE CSIRT

As stated earlier, the CSIRT may be informal, which is the case in most small to medium-sized organizations, or it may be a formal group that is part of the information security department, which is common in larger organizations. In more formal situations, Carnegie Mellon University's Software Engineering Institute recommends that the development of the CSIRT involve the following stages, which are shown in Figure 5-1 and discussed in the following sections.

computer security incident response team (CSIRT)

An incident response team composed of technical IT, managerial IT, and InfoSec professionals who are prepared to detect, react to, and recover from an incident. The CSIRT may include members of the IRPT.

Step 1.   Obtain management support and buy-in.
Step 2.   Determine the CSIRT strategic plan.
Step 3.   Gather relevant information.
Step 4.   Design the CSIRT's vision.
Step 5.   Communicate the CSIRT's vision and operational plan.

Step 6. Begin CSIRT implementation.

Step 7. Announce the operational CSIRT.

Step 8. Evaluate the CSIRT's effectiveness.[1]

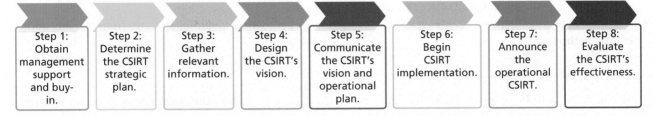

Figure 5-1   Steps in the development of a CSIRT[2]

The following sections have been adapted from a variety of NIST Special Publications, including 800-61, Rev. 2, "Computer Security Incident Handling Guide"[3] (and its earlier versions), and several documents from the Software Engineering Institute at Carnegie Mellon University, including the *Handbook for Computer Security Incident Response Teams*,[4] as well as online materials from both of these sources.

> Carnegie Mellon's Software Engineering Institute has been at the forefront in developing many of the recommended practices for large areas of the information technology industry. Their extensive digital library covers many topics, including resources for creating a CSIRT.
>
> We recommend that you visit *sei.cmu.edu* and find the page titled "Resources for Creating a CSIRT." It contains many interesting and useful resources that provide thorough coverage of this topic.

Step 1: Obtaining Management Support and Buy-In

It should be self-evident that without formal management support at all levels, from the top down to each supervisor, any organization-wide effort will fail. Building the CSIRT is no different. Most organizations create the CSIRT by assigning additional duties to members of the organization who have other responsibilities and who will work on the CSIRT on an as-needed basis or as a temporary assignment. Therefore, care must be taken to ensure that people assigned roles as CSIRT members do not have irresolvable conflicts with their primary job responsibilities. This requires careful coordination and authorization by proper supervisors and higher-level managers. When assigned staff members have other duties, senior management must direct subordinate managers to ensure that the staff members are allowed to spend time away from their primary responsibilities to work on CSIRT activities, such as training and testing the IR plan.

In addition, the time and materials needed to effectively prepare for and react to incidents are but two of the resources that will require formal funding and support. Without these resources, which are discussed later in this module, the team will find itself scrounging for the tools it needs to contain and control incidents when time is critical.

It is important to note that management support is not a one-time activity needed only for the start-up of the CSIRT. Support must be constant and ongoing in order to sustain the efforts of the team and ensure long-term success in its efforts to manage incidents. It is common to appoint a champion for the CSIRT, just as it is important to appoint a champion for the entire contingency planning (CP) function, encompassing IR, DR, and BC planning and operations. The champion for the CSIRT may even be the same person as the champion for the entire IR function—typically, the chief information officer (CIO). In any case, it must be an upper-level executive with enough organizational power and authority to ensure the success of the effort.

Step 2: Determining the CSIRT Strategic Plan

As with any formal effort, developing the CSIRT requires a formal plan, which encompasses the scope and responsibilities of the team as well as its reporting structure and functional processes. This plan should address the following items, which will be discussed in the following sections:

- Time frame for development of the CSIRT
- Gap analysis of needed versus available personnel (skills)

- CSIRT structure and team model
- Available and needed funding for initial and ongoing CSIRT operations
- Training and testing methods and requirements for the CSIRT
- Formal and informal communications requirements between the CSIRT and existing IT/InfoSec operations, organizational management, and other responsible individuals
- Procedures for updating and modifying CSIRT documents and activities, including findings from training and testing methods

Time Frame for Development of the CSIRT

One of the first items to be determined in the CSIRT strategic plan is how soon the team needs to be up and running. Although management will inevitably tell the IR team "yesterday," the cold reality is that it could take weeks or even months before a well-prepared CSIRT is available to actually respond to incidents. Until that time, any informal response procedures that the organization has previously implemented must continue.

Gap Analysis of Needed versus Available Personnel Resources (Skills)

Another harsh reality in most organizations is that few departments have the entire breadth and depth of personnel they would like to support ongoing operations. Whether it is due to budgetary constraints or issues with finding properly prepared personnel, few departments are overstaffed. When the organization begins to look at the skills it needs to effectively respond to incidents, it may quickly come to the conclusion that the entire IT and InfoSec departments are needed to comprise the CSIRT. This is the case in most small to medium-sized organizations. The result is that even when the IT staff is "off duty," they are "on call" and expected to respond to incidents that occur after a normal work shift. When the organization finds that it is constantly calling back its primary IT and InfoSec personnel after normal business hours (for organizations not operating 24/7), it must conclude that additional resources are needed to prevent losing the critical personnel it already has. Also, higher marginal costs of overtime and compensatory time are needed to offset the additional work imposed on critical staff members. Many disgruntled employees change organizations for the simple reason that they feel they can never completely get away from work, even for an evening.

In performing its gap analysis, the organization must first understand what skills are needed to effectively respond to an incident. (These skills are covered in detail later in this module.) It must then determine if it already has those skills on staff. If not, management must decide if it is willing to acquire needed personnel to fill in the gaps, willing to provide the training needed for existing personnel, or willing to live with the consequences of an incident beyond the team's ability to respond. Although few managerial teams are eager to choose and fund either of the first two options, even fewer are willing to accept the consequences of the third. The only other option, also described later in this module, is outsourcing the CSIRT function.

A typical CSIRT needs experience or access to specialized expertise in the following areas:

- Malware scanning, elimination, and recovery
- System administration—Windows and Linux/UNIX as appropriate
- Network protocols (Ethernet, TCP/IP versions 4 and 6, and others as appropriate)
- Network administration (switches, routers, and gateways)
- Firewall administration
- Intrusion detection and prevention systems
- Cryptography
- Network support tools such as packet sniffers, protocol analyzers, and vulnerability scanners
- Data storage and recovery (for example, RAID and/or storage area networks)
- Documentation creation and maintenance

In addition to this technical skill set, experience in creating and following policy and plans is highly desirable. This experience should be aligned with the systems in use by the organization.

CSIRT Structure and Team Model

A CSIRT liaison or other designated team member should be available for contact by employees or business partners who discover or suspect that an incident has occurred. Some organizations prefer that employees contact the help desk (if one is present) and that the help desk determine whether to contact the CSIRT. One or more

CSIRT members, depending on the magnitude of the incident and availability of personnel, then handle the incident. These incident handlers analyze the incident data, determine the impact, and act appropriately to limit the damage to the organization and restore normal services. Although the CSIRT may have only a few members, its success depends on the participation and cooperation of individuals throughout the organization. This section identifies such individuals, discusses CSIRT models, and provides guidance for selecting an appropriate model.

Models used to develop CSIRTs tend to fall into one of three structural categories:

- *Central CSIRT*—A single CSIRT handles incidents throughout the organization. This model is effective for small organizations and for organizations with minimal geographic diversity in terms of computing resources.
- *Distributed CSIRTs*—The organization has multiple CSIRTs, each of which is responsible for handling incidents for a particular logical or physical segment of the organization. This model is effective for large organizations (for example, one team per division) and for organizations with major computing resources at distant locations (for example, one team per geographic region, one team per major facility). However, the teams should report to a single centralized authority and use a common reporting structure and system so that the IR process is consistent across the organization and information is shared among teams. This is particularly important because multiple teams may see components of the same incident or may handle similar incidents. Strong communication among teams and consistent practices should make incident handling more effective and efficient.
- *Coordinating team*—A CSIRT provides guidance and advice to other teams without having authority over them—for example, a department-wide team may assist individual agency teams. This model can be thought of as a CSIRT for CSIRTs. Because the focus of this discussion is on central and distributed CSIRTs, the coordinating team model is not addressed in detail in this module.

CSIRTs are often developed along one of these three staffing models:

1. *Employees*—The organization performs all its own IR work, with limited technical and administrative support from contractors.
2. *Partially outsourced*—The organization outsources portions of its IR work. (Later sections of this module discuss the major factors that should be considered when outsourcing.) Although IR duties can be divided among the organization and one or more outsourcers in many ways, a few arrangements have become commonplace:
   - Organizations often outsource 24-hour-a-day, 7-day-a-week (24/7) monitoring of intrusion detection sensors, firewalls, and other security devices to an off-site managed security service provider (MSSP). The MSSP identifies and analyzes suspicious activity and reports each detected incident to the organization's CSIRT. Because MSSP employees can monitor activity for multiple customers simultaneously, this model may provide a 24/7 monitoring and response capability at a skill and cost level that is preferable to a comparable internal team.
   - Some organizations perform basic IR work in-house and use contractors to assist with handling incidents, particularly those that are more serious or widespread. The services most often performed by the contractors are computer forensics, advanced incident analysis, incident containment and eradication, and vulnerability mitigation.
3. *Fully outsourced*—The organization completely outsources its IR work, typically to an on-site contractor. This model is most likely to be used when the organization needs a full-time, on-site CSIRT but does not have enough available, qualified employees.

Team Model Selection   When selecting the appropriate structure and staffing models for a CSIRT, organizations should consider these factors:

- *Need for 24/7 availability*—Large organizations, as well as small ones that support critical infrastructures with high availability, usually need IR staff to be available 24/7. This typically means that incident handlers can be contacted at any time by phone or text, but it can also mean that an on-site presence is required at all times.

---

incident handler

A member of the organization's CSIRT designated to respond to a specific type of incident.

managed security service provider (MSSP)

An organization that provides security services to client organizations, often remotely, including incident monitoring, response, and recovery.

Real-time availability is the best choice for IR because the longer an incident lasts, the more potential there is for damage and loss. Real-time contact is often needed when working with other agencies and organizations—for example, tracing spoofed traffic back to its source through Internet service providers. A CSIRT that can quickly react to investigate, contain, and mitigate incidents should be genuinely useful to the organization.

- *Full-time versus part-time team members*—Organizations with limited funding, staffing, or IR needs may have only part-time IR team members. When an incident occurs, the team members are contacted rapidly, and those who can assist do so. An existing group such as the IT help desk can act as a first point of contact for incident reporting. The help-desk members can be trained to perform initial investigation and data gathering and then alert the CSIRT if it appears that a serious incident has occurred. Organizations with part-time team members should ensure that they maintain their IR skills and knowledge.
- *Employee morale*—Incident response work is very stressful, as are the on-call responsibilities of most team members. This combination makes it easy for CSIRT members to become overly stressed. Many organizations struggle to find willing, available, experienced, and properly skilled people to participate, particularly in 24-hour support.
- *Cost*—Cost is a major factor, especially if the organization requires on-site teams 24/7. Organizations may fail to include IR-specific costs in budgets. For example, many organizations do not allocate sufficient funding for training and maintaining skills. Because the CSIRT works with so many facets of IT, its members need much broader knowledge than most IT staff members. They must understand how to use the tools of IR, such as network traffic analysis and computer forensics software. The organization should also provide funding for regular team exercises so the team can gain practical experience and improve its performance. Other costs that may be overlooked are up-to-date training on the newest attack vectors, and response tools and methodologies.
- *Staff expertise*—Incident handling requires specialized knowledge and experience in several technical areas; the breadth and depth of knowledge required varies based on the severity of the organization's risks. Service providers may possess deeper knowledge of intrusion detection, vulnerabilities, exploits, and other aspects of security than employees of the organization. Also, managed security service providers may be able to correlate events among customers so they can identify new threats more quickly than any individual customer could. However, technical staff members within the organization usually have much better knowledge of the organization's environment than an outsider, which can be beneficial in identifying false positives associated with organization-specific behavior and the criticality of targets.
- *Organizational structures*—In large organizations that have independent, decentralized departments, IR may be more effective if each department has its own CSIRT. The main organization can host a centralized IR entity that facilitates standard practices and communications among the teams.

Available and Needed Funding for Initial and Ongoing CSIRT Operations

Everything in business costs money. Time is money. People are money. Organizations that build a CSIRT operation must plan for the needed financial support that allows the CSIRT to organize, staff, train, test, and function. It is up to the top management to demonstrate its commitment to the IR function by funding what the CSIRT will need. As discussed throughout this module, team members will need (at a minimum):

- Time away from their current responsibilities, which could require hiring full-time or temporary personnel to cover their normal tasks.
- Formal or informal training for staff members who are deficient in skills, which could entail training classes held off-site through organizations like SANS. Training can also be offered via self-study or online training held on-site or after business hours. Additionally, training will be needed for all team members to stay current on the latest vulnerabilities, attacks, and exploits, and to use the right tools to detect and combat those attacks.
- Equipment needed to detect and manage incidents, such as intrusion detection systems, packet sniffers, and log file analysis tools. Although implementing the purchase of these tools organization-wide is beyond the scope of this CSIRT plan, the acquisition of additional materials and tools to support training is within its funding needs. CSIRT personnel will need tools to rehearse and test procedures before applying them in a real-world situation.
- Special communications equipment, such as cell phones and laptops, and the ability to remotely access and assess on-site systems. Although the organization may or may not have issued these tools to employees, the

CSIRT must at least have a way to be immediately contacted and "brought into the loop" when an incident is suspected. It may be faster to allow response personnel to remotely access and manage key systems, which enables them to more quickly diagnose suspected incidents. If the organization does not want to expend funding on remote access equipment, the CSIRT will be forced to physically return to the office during an incident, which could delay response and result in additional damage.

NIST provides recommendations for tools to be used by incident handlers. These tools should be used in training so respondents can become familiar with them. The worst time to try to learn a new tool is when you really need to … fast.

Training and Testing Methods and Requirements for the CSIRT

The testing and training methods discussed earlier must be defined in the strategic plan for the CSIRT. Although the actual methods are discussed later in this module, it should be noted here that the planning team must enumerate management's expectations for the CSIRT so it can better prepare. Most organizations provide some training for their CSIRTs, even if it is in-house and informal, but few conduct formal testing regimes, partly for fear of creating incidents in the process.

Formal and Informal Communications Requirements

Also included in the CSIRT strategic plan are the formal and informal communications methods to be used between CSIRT personnel and other organizational personnel. There must be clearly defined methods for contacting CSIRT personnel and notifying them of potential incidents. This subject is also discussed later in this module.

A critical consideration here is the upward flow of information needed from the CSIRT to organizational and IT/InfoSec management. When it is operational and reacting to an incident, the CSIRT can determine what exactly is happening and report its preliminary finding to management. This responsibility should also be clearly identified in the IR policy and plan documents.

Procedures for Updating and Modifying CSIRT Documents and Activities

A final component of any formal plan is the mechanism by which the plan can and should be updated. Any plan will become outdated if not routinely reviewed and modified. At a minimum, the CSIRT development plan should be reviewed annually. This is not strictly a start-up plan designed to get the CSIRT up and running; it is an ongoing maintenance document designed to guide CSIRT planning, training, and testing. This document and the actual IR plan are the guiding standards for all CSIRT operations.

Throughout the development or revision of any CSIRT document, the formal incident response policy and the existing CSIRT plans that are derived from it must be the guiding documents. Some of the information needed here will be found in the policy document. The plans, however, are more about the preparation and training of response team members than preparation and response operations of the entire InfoSec and IT departments. In reality, some organizations will combine the CSIRT strategic plan with the IR plan, subjugating the entire CSIRT plan to a section within the IR plan. This is neither a good nor bad idea, as it depends entirely on the organization's ability to develop, deploy, and maintain both components. The organization can choose to manage a single document if it can do so with regular maintenance and due diligence.

Step 3: Gathering Relevant Information

In forming the CSIRT, the IRPT needs to collect as much information as possible about the IR and service needs of the organization. This information is used to craft the CSIRT and ensure that the necessary skills and abilities are brought to bear on any situation the team might encounter. Opinions about how the CSIRT should be organized and about its responsibilities may differ between the various communities of interest. Establishing the scope and responsibilities of the CSIRT is one of the first tasks the IRPT performs when forming the CSIRT. After these are drafted, the team's constituency and abilities should be determined. Again, conversations with stakeholders help identify the necessary skills and abilities of the team, as well as the specific needs of end users.

Resources are available to assist in this step, including NIST special publications and team development materials from Carnegie Mellon University's Software Engineering Institute (*resources.sei.cmu.edu/library/asset-view.cfm?assetid=485643*).

Step 4: Designing the CSIRT's Vision

The following planning elements should be considered when designing the final CSIRT model. Many of these may have been initially developed as part of the strategy described earlier. The broad strokes of the strategic plan for the CSIRT must be fully developed prior to implementation. Here are the steps, which are discussed in detail in the following sections:

- *Identify your constituency*—Who does the CSIRT support and serve?
- *Define your CSIRT's mission, goals, and objectives*—What does it do for the identified constituency?
- *Determine the organizational model*—How will the proposed CSIRT structure be implemented?
- *Select the CSIRT services to provide to the constituency (or others)*—How does the CSIRT support its mission?
- *Identify required resources*—What staff, equipment, and infrastructure are needed to operate the CSIRT?
- *Determine your CSIRT funding*—How is the CSIRT funded for its start-up and its long-term maintenance and growth?[5]

Identifying Your Constituency

To do an effective job, the CSIRT needs to know who it works for and what systems it should focus on. This may not be as simple as it sounds. However, a clear chain of command is critical to make sure that the CSIRT can take charge of the situation once it is on-site and exert its influence to regain control of the organization's systems. This means more top management support is needed to provide emergency authority to the CSIRT leader, who can request and gain access to any organizational system in order to perform incident response.

Another part of identifying the constituency is the "scope of operations"—in other words, the determination of what systems and information assets fall under the CSIRT's responsibility. To make this assessment, organizations must clearly understand the borders of their systems as well as who is responsible for them. The problem becomes more complex when the organization has connected its systems to upstream and downstream partners—in other words, both suppliers and customers are part of in-house computer systems and networks. Thus, the scope of the constituencies may be defined by ownership, geographic boundaries, network assignments, or other criteria defined by the organization. CSIRT members should clearly understand the scope of operations and the supporting details, such as domain, IP, and MAC addresses as well as the locations of the systems they are expected to protect. These definitions help the team delineate which systems are "ours" and which are "theirs."

An example of some items that would be included in an inventory of systems assets is shown in Table 5-1. The creation and maintenance of this type of inventory is a significant task and requires an ongoing effort to keep up to date.

Table 5-1 Sample Inventory of Systems Assets

Asset Class	Asset Type	Example Asset Names/ Identification	Example Valuation Notes
Hardware	Server systems	File server	Replacement cost
	Network devices	Router	Replacement cost
	Endpoint systems	Office desktop	Replacement cost
		Laptop	
		Tablets	
Software	Operating systems	Server systems	Cost to recover operational state
		Endpoint systems	
	Off-the-shelf applications	Transaction processing systems	Cost to recover operational state
		Accounting systems	
	Custom applications		Cost to recover operational state
Intellectual property	Databases	Customers	Cost to recover operational state
		Products	
		Sales	
	Other files	Policies	Cost to recover operational state
		Procedures	
Other assets	To be determined		

The CSIRT must also have a clearly defined scope within which it performs its functions. Those who will rely on the CSIRT must be aware of its existence, and those on the team must know who they serve. The constituents of the CSIRT are most often defined by who provides the funding, whether it comes directly from a company or indirectly, as in the case of a governmental unit. This definition of who is and isn't served by the CSIRT must be made clear to everyone affected, including people on the team, people served by the team, and those who might seek services but are not served by the team.

It is equally important to ensure that constituents know the CSIRT is *not* the help desk, nor do they provide routine technical support. Frustrated users may reach out to every resource at their disposal when confronted with a technology issue, but unless the organization has formally staffed the help desk with CSIRT members, it may be a distraction to have the CSIRT chasing routine help-desk requests instead of monitoring for potential incidents. This is not to say the help desk can't loop in CSIRT members for additional opinions about whether an adverse event constitutes an incident; rather, the CSIRT should only be brought in when a user issue is not clearly a "normal" help-desk issue.

CSIRTs work collaboratively with other CSIRTs in their geographic and logical areas. Each CSIRT serves a group of people known as its constituency. The CSIRT knows who is in its constituency and who is not included. Each CSIRT also knows about other nearby CSIRTs, who they serve, and what issues they can resolve. This knowledge is needed so that when problems are being worked on and a service request comes from someone not served by the CSIRT, a proper referral can be made to move the request to the correct CSIRT.[6] Knowing who the CSIRT supports and reports to removes a layer of complexity from an already multifarious situation.

Defining Your CSIRT's Mission, Goals, and Objectives

After the CSIRT knows who it works for, both in terms of providing services and the reporting relationships it must work within, it needs to know exactly what its mandate is—its mission, goals, and objectives.

Mission of the CSIRT The mission of the CSIRT should be clearly and succinctly stated to make all involved aware of its purpose. A mission statement establishes the tone for the team and provides a path to obtaining its goals and objectives.

There are many CSIRTs in operation, with a variety of constituencies and areas of interest. A common failing among many of them is a lack of precision in defining what mission they seek to fulfill and/or a failure to communicate that mission to members of their constituencies. This can lead to wasted effort, squandered resources, and higher stress in a crisis. When the reality of this failure becomes apparent—sometimes mid-crisis—the CSIRT will try to validate priorities to make sure they are using limited resources based on the most important priority. The team may even fall into crisis itself while deciding if current actions are appropriate and whether the expectations of their constituency are aligned with the CSIRT's intentions. This can lead to the CSIRT revising policy and procedures or constituent expectations on the fly. In other words, the CSIRT may be forced to revise service offerings and service levels in the middle of an incident response. While this is not the most desirable solution, it may be the only viable option in some situations, and it must be available when the alternatives are even more disruptive.

The CSIRT must have a clear and concise mission statement that uses just a few sentences to unambiguously articulate what it will do. Such a statement provides the needed focus and basic understanding to set goals for performance as well as boundaries for services and service levels, and to facilitate communication of those goals and boundaries to its constituents. The mission statement allows the CSIRT to establish a service list, service levels, and a quality framework. It enumerates the full set of services to be provided, defines policies and procedures for CSIRT operations, and enables the expression of the intended quality of service. The mission statement and its derivative service list, service level, and quality framework are combined with a clear definition of the constituency to inform and set boundaries for all CSIRT activities.

It seems obvious that when CSIRTs are created within larger organizations or supported by external parties, the CSIRT mission statement must complement the objectives of those organizations. To add clarity, some CSIRTs prepare a purpose statement to supplement the mission statement and explain the back story that led to the creation of the CSIRT. Equipped with these documents, the CSIRT can articulate its goals and define its services to support its mission. Communicating this basic information makes it easier to define the relationship between the CSIRT and the various constituencies with which it interacts.[7]

protect and forget

The organizational CP philosophy for incident response and digital forensics that focuses on the defense of information assets and preventing reoccurrence rather than the attacker's identification and prosecution.

apprehend and prosecute

The organizational CP philosophy for incident response and digital forensics that focuses on the collection and preservation of potential evidence when responding to and recovering from an incident, with the expectation of possibly finding and prosecuting the attacker.

Integral to the mission is the organization's approach to incident response—its philosophy. At one extreme is a **protect and forget** approach; at the other is an **apprehend and prosecute** approach.[8] With either approach, an organization's responses to an incident are fundamentally the same, but the data collection tasks differ dramatically. In the *protect and forget* approach, the focus is on the defense of the data and the systems that house, use, and transmit it. Tasks performed when pursuing this strategy therefore focus on the detection, logging, and analysis of events to determine how they happened and to prevent reoccurrence. When the current incident is over, the question of who caused it or why is almost immaterial. The *apprehend and prosecute* approach, on the other hand, focuses on the identification and apprehension of the intruder (if a human threat agent is involved), with additional attention given to the collection and preservation of evidentiary materials that might support administrative or criminal prosecution. The key steps used in these two approaches are shown in Table 5-2.

Table 5-2   Key Steps in Reaction Approaches[9]

Key Steps in *Protect and Forget*	Key Steps in *Apprehend and Prosecute*
1. Determine if the event is a real incident.	1. Determine if the event is a real incident.
2. If the event is indeed an incident, terminate the current intrusion.	2. If the event is an incident and the circumstances warrant doing so, contact law enforcement.
3. Discover how access was obtained and how many systems were compromised.	3. Document each action taken, including the date and time as well as who was present when the action was taken.
4. Restore the compromised systems to their pre-incident configuration.	4. Isolate the compromised systems from the network.
5. Secure the method of unauthorized access by the intruder on all systems.	5. If the organization has the capability, entice the intruder into a safe system that seemingly contains valuable data.
6. Document the steps taken to deal with the incident.	6. Discover the identity of the intruder while documenting his or her activity.
7. Develop lessons learned.	7. Discover how the intruder gained access to the compromised systems, and secure these access points on all uncompromised systems.
8. Have upper management briefly evaluate what happened.	8. As soon as sufficient evidence has been collected, or when vital information or vital systems are endangered, terminate the current intrusion.
	9. Document the current state of compromised systems.
	10. Restore the compromised systems to their pre-incident configuration.
	11. Secure the method of unauthorized access by the intruder on all compromised systems.
	12. Document in detail the time (in man-hours) as well as the cost of handling the incident.
	13. Secure all logs, audits, notes, documentation, and any other evidence gathered during the incident, and appropriately identify it to secure the "chain of custody" for future prosecution.
	14. Develop lessons learned.
	15. Have upper management evaluate what happened.

Here is an example of how a CSIRT mission statement might describe its reaction approach:

The mission of the HAL CSIRT is to provide immediate response to events and situations identified by the HAL duty officer; to assess, decide, and respond in an appropriate manner to rapidly protect HAL's information from further loss, damage, or disclosure; and consequently determine the source of the incident and work to prohibit future occurrences, under the overriding approach of security first. The security-first approach means that if it is possible to determine the source or root cause of an incident beyond the bounds of HAL's systems, that information will be passed to HAL's legal team; however, securing HAL's information is the primary responsibility.

Goals and Objectives of the CSIRT   Regardless of which services a CSIRT chooses to provide, the goals of a CSIRT must be based on the business goals of the constituent or parent organizations. Protecting critical assets is key to the success of both an organization and its CSIRT. The CSIRT must enable and support the critical business processes and systems of its constituency. CSIRTs without goals are like security programs without policies. These goals are designed to guide the CSIRT, and when they are coupled with detailed procedures—the "what" of the goals, as enumerated in CSIRT policy—they work with the "how" of the procedures to enable the team to effectively contain and resolve incidents. An absence of clear goals, policies, and procedures results in the organization depending on the expertise of individuals on staff, and possibly individuals on call, in responding to incidents. This results in inconsistent and incomplete response to incidents and creates the potential for erroneous reactions, which could worsen incidents rather than resolve them. NIST has provided the following guidance about the need to give clear goals and objectives:

One thing that is consistent across all CSIRTs is that they do not have sufficient resources to do their job to the ability they would like. Their working day is a continual compromise of priorities. The lack of clearly defined goals makes priority decisions arbitrary at best, opening the possibility for error resulting in mistrust from the community.

Deciding goals generally follows immediately from answering the question about the reason for the CSIRT's existence. Once the goals are defined, they should be communicated to the community being served. Many misunderstandings between a CSIRT and its community have occurred because members of that community misunderstood the role and goals of the CSIRT. Clear and well-defined communication of the goals of the CSIRT is essential if the community is to work with the CSIRT, not against it.

The expression of the goals may be made in the form of a mission statement to the constituency. The day-to-day operation of the CSIRT is then measured against the question, "Does this situation and action fit within the mission statement of the team?" A measure of success of the team's operations may be determined through some empirical measurement of how well these goals are being met.

Examples of goals may include:

- *Raising the bar of Internet security*
- *Assisting sites in proactive security ventures*
- *Increasing the awareness of security incidents*
- *Determining the scope of the security problem*
- *Assisting the community in applying the best security practices available*[10]

Determining the Organizational Model

Carnegie Mellon University has prepared a supporting manual to provide guidance for determining the most suitable model to adopt when an organization is designing its CSIRT.[11] This detailed resource, titled *Organizational Models for Computer Security Incident Response Teams (CSIRTs)*, provides a complete process to be used in this effort. The introduction of the handbook states:

The handbook will focus on the various common organizational structures that a CSIRT might implement, regardless of whether they are from the commercial, educational, government or military sector and regardless of whether they provide an internal service or address an external constituency consisting of many independent organizations. Some of the issues that will be covered for each different model described in this handbook include:

- *Supported constituencies*
- *Organizational structure*
- *Triage*
- *Available services*
- *Resources*

 We recommend that you acquire and make use of *Organizational Models for Computer Security Incident Response Teams (CSIRTs)*. You can find the handbook at *https://resources.sei.cmu.edu/asset_files/Handbook/2003_002_001_14099.pdf.*

Selecting the CSIRT Services to Provide to the Constituency (or Others)

The main focus of a CSIRT is performing incident response; however, it is rare for a team to perform incident response only. In most organizations, the CSIRT members work like volunteer firefighters, going about their primary responsibilities until an incident arises. When news of an event does arise, through word of mouth or electronic notification, the team receives its orders and shifts gears to deal with the threat. In other organizations, the CSIRT is organized to provide IR services, which may significantly overlap with other traditional information security tasks but have an IR focus. By constantly working with IR-based tools and technologies, the CSIRT stays focused on incidents and can better deal with intrusions.

CSIRT services are usually considered as falling into the following categories:

- *Reactive services*—Services performed in response to a request or a defined event, such as a help-desk alert, an IDPS alarm, or a vendor alert of an emerging vulnerability. This category represents most of what the CSIRT does.
- *Proactive services*—Services undertaken to prepare the organization or CSIRT constituents to protect and secure systems in anticipation of problems, attacks, or other events. The performance of these services often reduces the number and severity of future incidents.
- *Security quality management services*—Some of the CSIRT's services enhance existing services beyond the scope of incident handling. These existing services are usually performed by others, such as the IT, audit, or training department. The CSIRT's point of view and expertise can help improve the organization's overall security and identify risks, threats, and system weaknesses by assisting these external services. These services are viewed as proactive and can aid in reducing the number of incidents.[12]

Table 5-3 shows some of the specific services that correspond with these categories.

Additional services that a CSIRT might offer (according to NIST) are discussed in the following sections.

Advisory Distribution   A team may issue advisories that describe new vulnerabilities in operating systems and applications and provide information for mitigating the vulnerabilities. Promptly releasing such information is a high priority because of the direct link between vulnerabilities and incidents. Distributing information about current incidents can also help others identify signs of such incidents. It is recommended that only a single team within the organization distribute computer security advisories, which avoids duplication of effort and the spread of conflicting information.

Vulnerability Assessment   An IR team can examine networks, systems, and applications for security-related vulnerabilities, determine how they can be exploited and what the risks are, and recommend how the risks can be mitigated. These responsibilities can be extended so that the team performs auditing or penetration testing, perhaps visiting sites unannounced to perform on-the-spot assessments. Incident handlers are well suited to perform vulnerability assessments because they routinely see all kinds of incidents and have firsthand knowledge of vulnerabilities and how they are exploited. However, because the availability of incident handlers is unpredictable, organizations should typically assign primary responsibility for vulnerability assessments to another team and use incident handlers as a supplemental resource.

Table 5-3 CSIRT Services[13]

Incident Response	• Incident detection and notification
	• Managing incidents
	  ○ Incident analysis
	  ○ Incident response on site
	  ○ Incident response support
	  ○ Incident response coordination
	• Managing vulnerabilities
	  ○ Vulnerability analysis
	  ○ Vulnerability response
	  ○ Vulnerability response coordination

Preparation	• Assessment activities
	• Managing configuration across the enterprise
	  ○ Frameworks
	  ○ Tools
	  ○ Applications
	• Managing intrusion detection
	• Security information and event management (SIEM) activities

Quality Assurance	• Analyzing risk • Business resumption planning activities • Security consulting • Ongoing awareness, education, and training programs • Evaluation or certification of purchased and developed tools

Intrusion Detection An IR team may assume responsibility for intrusion detection because others within the organization do not have sufficient time, resources, or expertise. Based on knowledge the team gains from using intrusion detection technologies, it can analyze future incidents more quickly and accurately. Ideally, however, primary responsibility for intrusion detection should be assigned to another team, with members of the IR team participating in intrusion detection as their availability permits.

Education and Awareness Education and awareness are resource multipliers—the more the users and technical staff know about detecting, reporting, and responding to incidents, the less drain there should be on the IR team. Educational information can be communicated through many means, including workshops and seminars, Web sites, newsletters, posters, and even stickers on monitors.

Technology Watch A team can perform a technology watch function, which means that it looks for new trends in information security threats. Examples include monitoring security-related mailing lists, analyzing intrusion detection data to identify an increase in worm activity, researching new rootkits that are publicly available, and monitoring honeypots. The team should then make recommendations for improving security controls based on the trends it identifies. A team that performs a technology watch function should also be better prepared to handle new types of incidents.

Patch Management Giving the IR team the responsibility for patch management—acquiring, testing, and distributing patches to appropriate administrators and users throughout the organization—is generally not recommended. Patch management is a time-intensive, challenging task that cannot be delayed every time an incident needs to be handled. In fact, patch management services are often needed most when an organization is attempting to contain, eradicate, and recover from large-scale incidents. Effective communication channels between the patch management staff and the CSIRT are likely to improve the success of a patch management program.

Identifying Required Resources

As mentioned earlier, the CSIRT will need numerous resources to perform its tasks. First and foremost, it will need qualified individuals with technical and non-technical skills to perform the myriad of required tasks. It will also need time, funding, and managerial support.

Incident Response Personnel Regardless of which IR model an organization chooses, a single employee should be in charge of the CSIRT. In a fully outsourced model, this person is responsible for overseeing and evaluating the service provided. In all other models, this responsibility is generally achieved by having a CSIRT manager (or team lead) and a deputy team manager, with the latter assuming authority in the absence of the team manager. The manager typically performs a variety of tasks, including acting as a liaison with upper management and other teams and organizations, defusing crisis situations, and ensuring that the team has the necessary personnel, resources, and skills. Managers should also be technically adept and have excellent communication skills, particularly an ability to communicate with a range of audiences. They should also be able to maintain positive working relationships with other groups, even under times of high pressure.

The CSIRT manager's role is not the same as that of the incident commander, who takes charge when responding to an incident. Depending on the size of the CSIRT, there may be a different incident commander for different incidents. The incident commander has the authority to apply CSIRT resources, direct IT and InfoSec employees, and request changes to the organization's networks and systems as needed to combat an incident.

Depending on the size of the IR team and the magnitude of the incident, the incident commander may not perform any actual incident handling, such as data analysis or evidence acquisition. Instead, the incident commander may coordinate incident handlers' activities, gather information from the handlers, provide updates about the incident to other groups, and ensure that the team's needs are met, such as arranging for food and lodging during extended incidents.

Failure to establish a clear chain of command and pre-authorization for action can result in delays in responding to an incident while someone tries to find a particular manager or executive to get a needed permission. Delays can lead to increased damage and the loss of information assets or systems.

Technical Skills Members of the CSIRT should have excellent technical skills because they are critical to the team's success. Unless the team members command a high level of technical respect across the organization, people will not turn to them for assistance. Technical inaccuracy in functions such as issuing advisories can undermine the team's credibility, and poor technical judgment can cause incidents to worsen. Critical skills for technical areas include system administration, network administration, programming, technical support, and intrusion detection. Every team member should have good problem-solving skills; there is no substitute for real-world troubleshooting experience, such as dealing with operational outages. It is not necessary for every team member to be a technical expert—to a large degree, practical and funding considerations will dictate this—but having at least one highly proficient person in each major area of technology (for example, particular operating systems, Web servers, and e-mail servers) is a necessity.

It is important to counteract staff burnout by providing opportunities for learning and growth. Suggestions for building and maintaining skills include:

- Budget enough funding to maintain, enhance, and expand proficiency in technical areas and security disciplines as well as for less technical topics, such as the legal aspects of incident response. Consider sending each full-time team member to at least two technical conferences per year and each part-time team member to at least one.
- Ensure the availability of books, magazines, and other technical references that promote deeper technical knowledge.

- Give team members opportunities to perform other tasks, such as creating educational materials, conducting security awareness workshops, writing software tools to assist system administrators in detecting incidents, and conducting research.
- Consider rotating staff members in and out of the CSIRT.
- Maintain sufficient staffing so that team members can take vacations.
- Create a mentoring program to enable senior technical staff to help less experienced staff learn incident handling.
- Participate in exchanges in which team members temporarily trade places with others (for example, network administrators) to gain new technical skills.
- Occasionally bring in outside experts and contractors with deep technical knowledge in needed areas, as funding permits.
- Develop incident-handling scenarios and have team members discuss how they would handle the scenarios.
- Conduct simulated incident-handling exercises for the team. Exercises are particularly important because they not only improve the performance of incident handlers, they identify issues with policies, procedures, and communication.

Non-Technical Skills   CSIRT members should have a variety of non-technical skills as well. Teamwork skills are of fundamental importance because cooperation and coordination are necessary for successful incident response. Every team member should also have good communication skills. Speaking skills are particularly important because the team interacts with a wide variety of people, including incident victims, managers, system administrators, and people from human resources, public affairs, and law enforcement. Writing skills are important when team members are preparing advisories, procedures, incident reports, and after-action reviews. Although not everyone on a team needs strong writing and speaking skills, at least a few members should possess them so the team can represent itself well in front of senior management, users, and the public at large.

Determining Your CSIRT Funding

It is crucial that a clearly defined budget be provided to the CSIRT's manager and/or IRPT to guide their efforts in planning preparation, training, and testing of the CSIRT.

Step 5: Communicating the CSIRT's Vision and Operational Plan

An important step in the development of the CSIRT is communication between the IRPT that's building the CSIRT and the general management and employees of the organization. Equally important is a mechanism that allows feedback from these constituencies, which can provide updates and modifications to the various plans as development moves forward. This communication not only keeps the stakeholders informed and involved in the process, it helps to identify issues before they become problems.

Communicating the CSIRT's vision and plan begins with the managerial team or individual serving as champion. This allows the champion to begin cultivating a marketing stance with the rest of the organization's top managers in advance of formally presenting the vision and plan to the entire managerial group. By providing highlights and success stories, as well as presenting issues and concerns to the champion in advance, the CSIRT can promote positive aspects of the process and prepare mitigation strategies for the negative aspects. As a result, the champion can convince top management that the CSIRT operation is a general success and that the team is on top of the situation, opening the doors for additional resources and support.

Next, the team should plan to educate the rest of top management about the CSIRT's actions and activities. This serves two purposes: It closes the loop on the preparation phase of CSIRT building and it moves the group into an operational capacity so the CSIRT can begin normal operations as the organization's response team. In most cases, this is a pro forma notification, given that the CSIRT may have already begun supporting the organization informally, much as a retail venue or restaurant may have a "grand opening" weeks after it officially begins business operations. However, the notification is an important step in updating the group's status within the collective mindset of top management.

It may also be advisable to communicate the creation of the forthcoming CSIRT to all employees. This prepares employees for the final roll-out of the CSIRT and for its operation.

Step 6: Beginning CSIRT Implementation

When the notices, briefings, and postings have been made and completed, the CSIRT goes to work. Before, everything was a planning function, but now, execution of those plans begins. Prior to moving forward, the team should gain management approval with a formal sign-off. This approval assures all parties that potential issues identified in the presentations have been resolved to the satisfaction of all.

This step includes the following substeps, which are illustrated in Figure 5-2:

- Recruit and train initial CSIRT staff as needed.
- Purchase equipment and prepare the required network infrastructure.
- Define and prepare the necessary CSIRT policies and procedures.
- Coordinate with additional IT and InfoSec department members to ensure effective communications during an incident.
- Define and acquire an incident tracking system.
- Prepare incident reporting guidelines and forms.

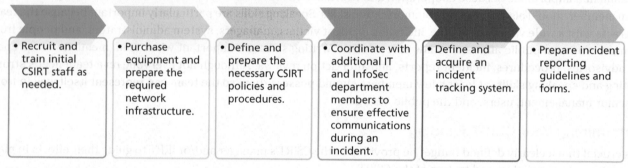

Figure 5-2 Implementing the CSIRT

Incident reporting guidelines are an essential part of what enables a constituency to interact with the CSIRT. The guidelines define what makes up an incident, the types of incidents to report, who should report them, why an incident should be reported, the reporting process, and the process for responding to an incident. The guidelines must be understandable by everyone who will use them.

The process for reporting an incident should be concrete and include directives for how to make reports using telephone, e-mail, the Web, or other means. Guidance for responding to incidents must include how the CSIRT prioritizes requests, what service levels and response times will apply, how notifications and escalations are managed during the incident, and how resolution of incidents is documented and reported.

The definition of guidelines and procedures for responding to an incident is a critical aspect of the IR plan. Given that the CSIRT will be the entity executing these procedures, guidelines, and standards, its development is a prerequisite to that task. The process and its recommended components were covered in Module 4.

Step 7: Announcing the Operational CSIRT

The next notification should be to the remainder of the organization, informing them that the CSIRT is operational and available. This may be done formally, via a letter from the champion to all employees, or informally, through an internal newsletter or Web posting. This is a crucial step in that it notifies employees that CSIRT services are available and lets them know who to call if they notice something untoward in their system operations. In effect, this notification extends and enhances the detection function of the information security department and provides advanced warning to the CSIRT when a potential incident arises.

At a minimum, the announcement should include the CSIRT's:

- Staff members and leadership
- Mission and goals

- Services and functions
- Operating hours
- Contact methods and numbers

A summary of this information should be circulated regularly as part of the organization's security awareness program, if there is one. It is important to keep this information in front of the employees so they know who to contact in the event of an emergency. Information can be distributed via brochures, magnets, flyers, posters, or other awareness mechanisms. The important thing is to make it easy to identify critical information quickly.

Step 8: Evaluating the CSIRT's Effectiveness

Assessing CSIRT effectiveness is done through two key mechanisms: IR plan tests and CSIRT performance measures (also known as metrics). The former serves both as a test of the CSIRT's ability to respond to an incident and as a means to test the suitability and comprehensiveness of the IR plan itself.

Closing the Loop

At the end of every test, exercise, or assessment function, the group should assemble for an *after-action review* (AAR). During the AAR, all key players review their notes, perform a detailed examination of the events that occurred from first detection to final recovery, and verify that the IR documentation is accurate and precise. All team members review their actions during the incident and identify areas for improvement. This review allows the team to recommend updates to the IR plan. The focus during an AAR is not on blame, so the group should avoid pointing fingers. The focus is on learning what worked, what didn't, and where communications and response procedures may have failed. No operation is perfect; however, organizations and operations that use AARs as learning tools can continually improve their ability to respond to incidents.

The AAR can also serve as a training case for future staff, allowing individuals to see what happened in a response operation. Thus, before being "thrown in the fire," a new member of a CSIRT can review how and why the team responded the way it did and see how well the response worked.

The AAR also brings to a close the actions of the CSIRT, signaling a return to normal operations. The AAR is also performed at the end of every actual incident response, disaster operation, or contingency plan execution. It is a useful tool in assessing and improving the operations of any team.

CSIRT Performance Measures

Performance measures (also known as metrics) are methods for assessing the relative worth and operations of a subject of interest. NIST SP 800-55, Revision 1 provides a guide for the development and implementation of a performance measurement program in information security. This document also includes information on IR-oriented measures (see *doi.org/10.6028/NIST.SP.800-55r1*). The process of selecting and implementing performance measures is beyond the scope of this text, but SP 800-55 is a good source for additional guidance. As a summary of the process, however, the organization must identify areas of the operation to assess, collect data from those areas, and then review the data periodically to determine if the organization is improving.

Feedback mechanisms offer the opportunity to measure effectiveness. Options include:

- Comparison of local CSIRT measures to those of other CSIRTs
- Solicitation of comments from the CSIRT's constituency
- Using periodic surveys to gain insight from the CSIRT's constituency
- Definition of a set of empirical measures that can be collected, reported, and audited to evaluate the team

Some CSIRTs may find it useful to build up a baseline of past measures and allow a comparison of current performance to performance levels of the past. Such information may allow a team to determine its effect on the user community. Measurements used for comparison might include:

- Number and types of incidents reported
- Response times
- Resolution rates for reported incidents[14]

These measurements can be used in conjunction with the usual management practice of a cost-benefit analysis, where the benefits of the activities are compared to the costs incurred to perform them.

Final Thoughts on CSIRT Development

The development of a CSIRT can be a tedious, difficult process. The amount of time necessary to build an effective CSIRT varies greatly depending on a number of variables, including the organization's size, the industry, staffing, and the availability of needed skills. It can take months or even years for an organization to feel that it has an effective team. Patience is therefore recommended to allow the organization to build the best team it can, given the constraints on the process. One of the first signals that the organization is making progress in the development of its IR program, specifically in the development of its CSIRT, is a dramatic increase in the number of identified incidents. This is not a negative aspect of the process; it is an increase in the organization's ability to detect incidents as it educates both the CSIRT and the rest of the workforce. This process is commonly recognized as a matter of trust. The more you trust the CSIRT to respond positively to a potential issue, the more likely an employee is to report it.

SPECIAL CIRCUMSTANCES IN CSIRT DEVELOPMENT AND OPERATIONS

Two general areas associated with CSIRTs warrant further examination. The first is the special relationship that may exist between a CSIRT and a security operations center or SOC. The second is the outsourcing of some or all of an organization's CSIRT activities.

With the increase in the size of an organization and its level of security maturity, there is a greater chance it may have established a formal **security operations center (SOC)** to manage and oversee its day-to-day security technologies and operations. SOCs are gaining in popularity as a variety of security applications now have the ability to provide information in aggregate form—using dashboards and executive summaries to provide an overview of operations, with the ability to "drill down" into increasing detail. Depending on how much the organization is willing to invest in the effort, a SOC can look like a NASA control center, with SOC operatives each with multiple computer screens looking at various aspects of the organization's security technologies and related information. At the front is typically a large display showing either a general overview of the organization's security status or details about an area of concern.

SOC operatives each examine a subset of the security effort, such as network operations, firewall administration and activity, help-desk tickets, IDPS status, VPN connections, and malware notifications. SOCs tend to operate 24/7 with multiple shifts. In large organizations, remote SOCs may be coordinated through a centralized global SOC (GSOC) responsible for monitoring and aggregating activities. When SOCs become crucial to the ongoing operations and security of organizations, they begin to need their own CP plans, including disaster recovery and business continuity planning. GSOCs may use regional SOCs for BC operations, or they may choose to employ a "follow the sun" model in which multiple GSOCs use traditional three-shift operations and are sited one-third of the way around the world from the next GSOC. Using this approach, local employees work "9 to 5" from a global perspective, and the organization has 24/7 availability and monitoring.

CSIRT Operations and the Security Operations Center

If an organization has invested heavily in a SOC, an executive may eventually ask, "If we're funding a SOC, do we really need a CSIRT?" It's then up to the IRPT and the point of view from top management (often the CISO or CIO) to clarify the roles of the two entities. While the SOC is designed to *monitor* all security operations, the CSIRT focuses on *responding* to incidents. A SOC can provide a much quicker detection capability for the organization, as multiple individuals in the same room can assist each other in monitoring key areas of security. Without a SOC, an individual administrator may miss a key alert due to other work obligations, such as a meeting. With a SOC, there is usually a SOC supervisor who keeps an eye on the "big picture" along with multiple operatives who examine each area of security.

When a member of a SOC detects an incident, he or she still has to contact the appropriate individual CSIRT representatives to respond to it. It is highly recommended that the CSIRT and SOC share common members, and it makes the most sense for the SOC to be comprised of most CSIRT members, if not all of them. However, the response phase of IR belongs to the CSIRT, while the detection phase may be relegated to the SOC. Overlap is fine, but each group will have different tasks, training, and responsibilities. Due to the "volunteer firefighter" nature of the CSIRT in most organizations, this arrangement may not be an issue at all; CSIRT members can work in the SOC on a day-to-day basis and respond as a CSIRT member if needed. It is important, however, for employees to be able to cover their SOC responsibilities if they are activated as CSIRT members—an incident may simply be part of a multipronged attack in which a highly visible incident is designed as a distraction while a much more dangerous attack occurs concurrently.

Outsourcing Incident Response and the CSIRT

With the increased popularity of managed security services, many organizations are outsourcing at least part of their IR capacity. Companies specializing in this area frequently install equipment such as firewalls and IDSs in the organization and then remotely monitor it from a centralized facility, in much the way a home security company handles fire and burglary monitoring. There are various advantages and disadvantages to this approach, as shown in Table 5-4.

Table 5-4   Advantages and Disadvantages of Outsourcing the IR Process

Advantages	Disadvantages
• Services provided by professionals trained in IR	• Potential loss of control of response to incidents
• 24/7 monitoring	• Possible exposure of classified organizational data to service providers
• Early notification of potential problems in region	• Locked into proprietary equipment and services
• Formal reports and briefings on attacks and response	• Loss of services when contract expires, unless renewed
• Equipment specified and installed by well-trained professionals	• Loss of customization to the needs of each organization
• No additional personnel costs or training requirements	• Organization's needs subjugated to service provider's needs
	• More important/prestigious companies given preference in response over smaller, less prestigious ones

When deciding whether to outsource IR services, organizations should carefully consider the issues discussed in the following sections.[15]

Current and Future Quality of Work

The quality of the service provider's work is a very important consideration. Organizations should consider not only the current quality of work but the service provider's efforts to ensure the quality of future work, such as minimizing turnover and burnout and providing a solid training program for new employees. Organizations should think about how they could audit or otherwise objectively assess the quality of the service provided.

Division of Responsibilities

Organizations are usually unwilling to give an outside resource authority to make decisions for the operating environment, such as disconnecting a Web server. It is important to determine the point at which the service provider hands off incident response to the organization. One model for partial outsourcing addresses this issue by having the service provider deliver an incident report to the organization's internal team along with recommendations for further handling of the incident. The internal team ultimately makes the operational decisions.

Sensitive Information Revealed to the Contractor

Dividing IR responsibilities and restricting access to sensitive information can limit what a contractor knows about an organization. For example, a contractor might be able to determine what user ID was used in an incident but not know what person is associated with the user ID. The contractor can report to the organization that user ID 123456 is apparently being used to download pirated software without the contractor knowing who 123456 is. Trusted employees within the organization can then take over the investigation.

Other examples of sensitive information include personal health information (sometimes labeled as PHI), personal identifying information (often labeled PII), and financial records such as bank and credit account numbers.

Lack of Organization-Specific Knowledge

Accurate analysis and prioritization of incidents are dependent on specific knowledge of the organization's environment. The organization should give the service provider regularly updated documents that define what incidents the organization is concerned about, which resources are critical, and what the level of response should be under various sets of circumstances. The organization should also report all changes and updates made to its IT infrastructure, network configuration, and systems. Otherwise, the contractor has to make a best guess as to how each incident should be handled, inevitably leading to problems and frustration on both sides. Lack of organization-specific knowledge can also be a problem even when incident response is not outsourced—for example, if communications are weak among teams or if the organization simply does not collect the necessary information.

Lack of Correlation

Correlation among multiple data sources is very important. If an intrusion detection system records an attempted attack against a Web server but the service provider has no access to the Web logs, it may be unable to determine whether the attack was successful. To be efficient, the contractor requires administrative privileges to critical systems and security device logs with remote access over a secure channel. However, this increases administration costs, introduces additional access entry points, and increases the risk of unauthorized disclosure of sensitive information.

Handling Incidents at Multiple Locations

Effective IR work often requires a physical presence at the organization's facilities. If the service provider is off-site, the organization should consider how quickly it can have a CSIRT at any facility and how much this will cost. Consider on-site visits, but realize that the organization might have certain facilities or areas where the service provider should not be permitted to work.

Maintaining IR Skills In-House

Organizations that completely outsource IR should strive to maintain basic IR skills in-house. Situations may arise in which the outsourcer is unavailable—for example, a new worm could attack thousands of organizations simultaneously or a natural disaster or national flight stoppage could occur. The organization should be prepared to perform its own incident handling if the service provider is unable to act. The organization's technical staff must also be able to understand the significance, technical implications, and impact of the service provider's recommendations.

 SANS is a highly regarded training organization that provides white papers and analytical reports on many information security topics. We recommend that you visit the SANS Web site (at *www.sans.org*) and set up a free membership account. One of the many resources there covers the use of "SOC as a service," which is an example of how one firm offers services to provide some CSIRT resources without the start-up expenses of building a CSIRT.

Closing Scenario

Two weeks later, Brody got an e-mail from Nick inviting him to attend a meeting later in the week. The meeting was being called to discuss the formation of the company's new CSIRT.

Brody would be one of the employees identified to perform specific actions when events became incidents and the response plans were activated. As a front-line watchstander in the SOC, Brody would play a critical role. In addition to his role as a key member of the response team, Brody was going to be invited to help develop plans and procedures and would then be trained to become a more effective first responder.

Discussion Questions

1. From what you know of the company so far, what various constituencies will the CSIRT serve?
2. Will the company need to hire more employees to meet the needs of the CSIRT, or would you suggest it outsource some of that effort? What do you think should be the factors that influence the decision to outsource incident response operations?

Ethical Decision Making

1. Thinking back to the opening scenario, suppose Brody had been the person responsible for the internal Web-based attack against the branch offices. Was he trying to set up a situation where he could make himself look good? Because there was no real harm done and he was careful not to damage production systems, was his action ethical? Why or why not?
2. Suppose the sequence of events described in the scenario was part of a penetration test by an outside contract assessment team. The test was authorized by Nick's superiors without advising Nick or his team. Do you think this is an appropriate way to test the company's readiness? Why or why not?

MODULE SUMMARY

- Organizations designate groups to have the primary responsibility for dealing with unexpected situations and reestablishing the security of the organization's information assets. The members of these groups are carefully selected to ensure the appropriate range of skills. Redundancy is built in, given that availability may vary. These groups are distinct from the incident response planning team (IRP team), but there may be some overlap. The IR reaction team, often called the computer security incident response team (CSIRT), is responsible for responding to declared incidents. The CSIRT uses its policies, procedures, and training to regain control of the information assets at risk, determine what happened, and prevent repeat occurrences.
- The CSIRT may be informal, or it may be a formal part of the information security department. CSIRT development typically uses the following stages: obtaining management support, determining the CSIRT strategic plan, gathering relevant information, designing the CSIRT's vision, communicating the CSIRT's vision and operational plan, beginning CSIRT implementation, announcing the operational CSIRT, and evaluating CSIRT effectiveness.
- Without formal management support, no organization-wide effort can succeed; management support must be constant and ongoing to ensure long-term success. Developing the CSIRT requires a formal plan. Few departments have the breadth and depth of personnel they would like to have both to support ongoing operations and field a complete CSIRT. Even if the CSIRT assumes that off-duty IT staff could be used for CSIRT functions, much of the IT staff is on call, either in rotation or when exceptions occur. They are already expected to respond to incidents that occur after a normal work shift, and using them for CSIRT duties as well may be a significant overbooking of their time.

- The organization must understand what skills are needed to effectively respond to an incident and must begin determining if it already has those skills on staff. Areas that a typical CSIRT needs skills in include virus scanning, elimination, and recovery; system administration; network administration; firewall administration; administering intrusion detection systems; cryptography; data storage and recovery; and documentation creation and maintenance. In addition to these technical skills, managerial experience with creating and following policy and plans is highly desirable.

- A representative of the CSIRT should be available for contact by employees who discover or suspect that an incident has occurred. One or more team members, depending on the magnitude of the incident and availability of personnel, then handle the incident. Models for IR teams fall into one of three structural categories: the central IR team, distributed IR teams, and coordinating teams. IR teams are often staffed with one of three staffing models: employees, partially outsourced, or fully outsourced. When selecting appropriate structure and staffing models, an organization should consider the need for 24/7 availability, full-time versus part-time teams, employee morale, cost, staff expertise, and organizational structures.

- Organizations that build a CSIRT operation need to plan for adequate financial support so the CSIRT can organize, staff, and train its members. Expenses include employee time away from current responsibilities, formal or informal training, equipment to detect and manage incidents, and special communications and computing equipment.

- Testing and training methods are defined in the strategic plan for the CSIRT, as are the methods for formal and informal communications. There must be clearly defined methods for contacting CSIRT personnel and notifying them of potential incidents.

- A final component of any formal plan is the mechanism by which the plan can and should be updated.

- The IRP team needs to collect as much information as possible about the organization's IR and service needs in order to form an effective plan. Previously, the CSIRT may have existed as a broadly defined plan, but now, all details must be fully developed. This means CSIRT designers have identified that all the details for implementation are complete and that the CSIRT's constituency has been identified; defined the CSIRT's mission, goals, and objectives; determined the organizational model; selected the CSIRT services to provide to the constituency; identified required resources; and determined the CSIRT's funding.

- CSIRT planners must communicate to general management and employees of the organization as well as allow feedback to enable updates and modifications to the various plans.

- When the notices, briefings, and postings have been made and completed, the CSIRT goes to work, moving beyond the planning function. This includes hiring and training initial CSIRT staff, buying equipment and building any necessary network infrastructure, developing the initial set of CSIRT policies and procedures, defining the specifications for and building an incident tracking system, and developing incident reporting guidelines and forms for the constituency.

- The next notification should be to the remainder of the organization, informing them that the CSIRT is operational and available. This announcement should at least include a list of the CSIRT's staff members and leadership, its mission and goals, its services and functions, its operating hours, and its contact methods and numbers.

- Assessing CSIRT effectiveness is done through two key mechanisms: IR plan tests and CSIRT performance measures (also known as metrics).

- The development of a CSIRT can be a tedious, difficult process. The amount of time needed to build an effective CSIRT varies greatly depending on a number of variables, including the organization's size, the industry, staffing, and the availability of needed skills. It can take months or even years for an organization to feel it has an effective team.

- Some organizations consider outsourcing at least part of their incident response capacity. There are several advantages and disadvantages to this approach. Outsourcing may allow the acquisition of highly skilled professionals and free up staff resources that would otherwise be consumed by developing the capacity in-house. On the other hand, these services are often expensive, and the organization loses some control of a critical business process.

Review Questions

1. What is the formal definition of a CSIRT?
2. What is the difference in roles between the CSIRT and the IRPT?
3. What is the most essential reason to involve upper management in the formation of the CSIRT?
4. Is management approval a simple, one-time action?
5. Among the skills needed by the CSIRT staff, what is required beyond technical skill?
6. What structures are most often used to develop CSIRTs?
7. What are the most likely staffing models for CSIRTs?
8. How does the need for 24/7 operations affect staffing decisions?
9. How does the need to manage employee morale affect staffing decisions for CSIRTs?
10. How does the organizational structure impact staffing design for CSIRTs?
11. Once created, must a plan be maintained? How often should it be revisited?
12. What are the guiding documents for CSIRT creation or maintenance?
13. What should be one of the first tasks performed by an IR planning committee when forming a CSIRT?
14. What is meant by the "scope of operations" for a CSIRT?
15. What purpose does the CSIRT mission statement provide?
16. What are the two approaches that define a CSIRT's philosophy for incident response?
17. The services of a CSIRT can be grouped into which three categories?
18. What is an after-action review (AAR), and why is it valuable to organizations?
19. What are the key benefits of the AAR?
20. Why are performance measures collected for CSIRT activities?

Real-World Exercises

Exercise 5-1

Use the Web to search for "incident response training." Look through the first five results and identify one or two companies that offer such training. Pick one company and look at the course offerings. Locate a course that can train you to create a CSIRT. How many days will that course take?

Exercise 5-2

Use the Web to search for "incident response template." Look through the first five results and choose one for further investigation. Take a look at it and determine if you think it would be useful to an organization that is creating a CSIRT. Why or why not?

Exercise 5-3

Use the Web to search for "best practices for creating a CSIRT." Pick three of the resources you discover and find the two practices that are common to all three lists. What are they?

Hands-On Projects

The hands-on project for this module can be accessed in the Practice It folder in MindTap or through your instructor's LMS. The virtual labs provided with this resource can help you develop practical skills that will be of value as you progress through the course.

References

1. CMU/SEI. "Create a CSIRT." Carnegie Mellon University, Software Engineering Institute. Accessed 2/2/2020 at *https://resources.sei.cmu.edu/asset_files/WhitePaper/2017_019_001_485695.pdf.*

2. Ibid.

3. Chichonski, Paul, Tom Millar, Tim Grance, and Karen Scarfone. SP 800-61, Revision 2, "Computer Security Incident Handling Guide." National Institute of Standards and Technology. January 2012. Accessed 2/2/2020 at *https://csrc.nist.gov/publications/detail/sp/800-61/rev-2/final.*

4. West-Brown, Moira J., Don Stikvoort, Klaus Peter Kossakowski, Georgia Killcrece, Robin Ruefle, and Mark Zajicek. *Handbook for Computer Security Incident Response Teams (CSIRTs).* Carnegie Mellon University, Software Engineering Institute. April 2003. Accessed 2/2/2020 at *https://resources.sei.cmu.edu/asset_files/Handbook/2003_002_001_14102.pdf.*

5. CMU/SEI. "Create a CSIRT." Carnegie Mellon University, Software Engineering Institute. Accessed 2/2/2020 at *https://resources.sei.cmu.edu/asset_files/WhitePaper/2017_019_001_485695.pdf.*

6. Smith, Danny. "Forming an Incident Response Team." Australian Computer Emergency Response Team. Accessed 2/2/2020 at *http://all.net/books/standards/NIST-CSRC/csrc.nist.gov/publications/secpubs/form-irt.ps.*

7. West-Brown, Moira J., Don Stikvoort, Klaus Peter Kossakowski, Georgia Killcrece, Robin Ruefle, and Mark Zajicek. *Handbook for Computer Security Incident Response Teams (CSIRTs).* Carnegie Mellon University, Software Engineering Institute. April 2003. Accessed 2/2/2020 at *https://resources.sei.cmu.edu/asset_files/Handbook/2003_002_001_14102.pdf.*

8. Adler, D., and K. Grossman. "Establishing a Computer Incident Response Plan." *Data Security Management.* 2001. Accessed 2/3/2020 at *www.ittoday.info/AIMS/DSM/82-02-70.pdf.*

9. Ibid.

10. Smith, Danny. "Forming an Incident Response Team." Australian Computer Emergency Response Team. Accessed 2/2/2020 at *http://all.net/books/standards/NIST-CSRC/csrc.nist.gov/publications/secpubs/form-irt.ps.*

11. Killcrece, G., K. Kossakowski, R. Ruefle, and M. Zajicek. *Organizational Models for Computer Security Incident Response Teams (CSIRTs).* Carnegie Mellon University, Software Engineering Institute. December 2003. Accessed 4/25/2020 at *https://resources.sei.cmu.edu/asset_files/Handbook/2003_002_001_14099.pdf.*

12. West-Brown, Moira J., Don Stikvoort, Klaus Peter Kossakowski, Georgia Killcrece, Robin Ruefle, and Mark Zajicek. *Handbook for Computer Security Incident Response Teams (CSIRTs).* Carnegie Mellon University, Software Engineering Institute. April 2003. Accessed 2/2/2020 at *https://resources.sei.cmu.edu/asset_files/Handbook/2003_002_001_14102.pdf.*

13. Ibid.

14. Ibid.

15. Grance, Tim, Joan Hash, Marc Stevens, Kristofor O'Neal, and Nadya Bartol. SP 800-35, "Guide to Information Technology Security Services." National Institute of Standards and Technology. Accessed 2/3/2020 at *https://csrc.nist.gov/publications/detail/sp/800-35/final.*

INCIDENT RESPONSE: INCIDENT DETECTION STRATEGIES

Upon completion of this material, you should be able to:

1. Identify the parts of a kill chain and how organizations can use it to disrupt offensive operations
2. Define incidents that pose a risk to the organization
3. Discuss the elements necessary to detect incidents
4. Describe methods of detecting incidents by incident type
5. Discuss methods of detecting incidents in general

> *"Luck is not an acceptable substitute for early detection."*
> —Valerie Harper

Opening Scenario

Emily was at her desk, at home. Her position at HAL, LTD in the Office of Corporate Communications allowed her to work from home three days each week. The title on her business cards read "Director of Social Media," and she spent much of her time working with marketing and advertising staff on ad placement and social outreach to bolster the company's image and keep customers feeling connected with the company.

But she also spent a lot of time reading and responding to posts on the multitudes of social media sites whenever the company was mentioned. She used a number of tools and vendors that identified posts and messages that mentioned the company by name or discussed HAL's competitors and suppliers. Some clever colleagues in the Information Systems office at HAL had created a dashboard that funneled each of the alerts to her attention, with some helpful icons that rated each of them for importance. She did not have a lot of faith in the rating algorithm and still looked at almost all of the alerts.

As she worked her way through the mentions of HAL and the dozens of other businesses on the watch list, she noticed a pattern. Several alerts seemed to be from HAL customers describing illicit charges on payment cards that had been used to make payments to HAL.

She opened a spreadsheet and started making a list of mentions where HAL customers were finding improper charges. By using a few search terms on her dashboard and then doing a few of her own queries in a database of past social media activity that the company subscribed to, she soon had nearly 50 items of interest identified over the past 48 hours of activity.

It was time to turn this issue over to the company's threat intelligence team.

INTRODUCTION

incident classification

The process of evaluating the circumstances of reported events.

incident candidate

An adverse event that is a possible incident.

cyber kill chain

A series of steps that follow stages of a cyberattack from the early reconnaissance stages to the exfiltration of data; it helps you understand, identify, and combat many cyberattack strategies and advanced persistent threats.

Among the earliest challenges that incident response planners must face is determining how an organization classifies events as they occur. Note that some systems are computer-based, whereas others are personnel- or organization-based, so not all events are computer- or network-oriented. Some events are the product of routine system activities, while others are indicators of situations that need an urgent response. When an adverse event becomes a genuine threat to the ongoing operations of an organization, it is classified as an *incident*. Incident classification involves evaluating the circumstances around organizational events, determining which adverse events are possible incidents (incident candidates), and determining whether a particular adverse event constitutes an actual incident. Designing the process used to make this judgment is the role of the incident response planning team (IRPT), but the everyday process of classifying an incident is the responsibility of the CSIRT.

There are a variety of sources for tracking and detecting incident candidates, including reports and other documents from end users, intrusion detection and prevention systems (IDPSs, discussed in Module 7), endpoint protection software (for example, antivirus), and systems administrators. Careful training in the reporting of unusual and adverse events allows end users, the help-desk staff, and all security personnel to relay vital information to the CSIRT. Once an actual incident is properly identified, the members of the CSIRT can effectively execute the corresponding procedures from the IR plan, including the notification of key response resources.

Although any threat category could instigate an incident, NIST SP 800-61, Rev. 1 provides a five-category incident classification scheme for network-based incidents:

- *Denial of service*—An attack that prevents or impairs the authorized use of networks, systems, or applications by exhausting resources
- *Malicious code*—A virus, worm, Trojan horse, or other code-based malicious entity that successfully infects a host
- *Unauthorized access*—When a person, without permission, gains logical or physical access to a network, system, application, data, or other IT resource
- *Inappropriate usage*—When a person violates acceptable use of any network or computer policies
- *Multiple component*—A single incident that encompasses two or more incidents[1]

Organizations looking for a simple method of classifying their network-based incidents could use this list to prepare for and plan for incidents. Those that are not looking should develop their own lists to facilitate incident detection and classification.

 You should take a few minutes to go online and search for the document file for NIST SP 800-61, Rev. 2. Download the PDF and read through it. The Rev. 2 version is significantly different from the Rev. 1 version used for some of the references in this module. We found that some of the approaches in the earlier version are useful and add to the understanding of issues encountered in incident response detection. Although much of the contents of Rev. 2 are explained in this module, you should start collecting your own set of key reference documents.

Anatomy of an Attack—the "Kill Chain"

In order to better understand intrusions and thus know how better to detect them, it's first beneficial to understand the process an attacker goes through in a typical attack. While the concept of a "typical attack" may seem counterintuitive, given the previous discussion of how different each attack is, there are at least commonalities in categories of attacks (for example, virus or malware attacks and hacker intrusions). The term commonly used to understand these attacks is an *anatomy of an attack* or the cyber kill chain.

Some cyberattacks are made against targets of opportunity—vulnerable systems that attackers discover and then use exploits to compromise. Other targets are more purposeful and are sought out for directed attacks by adversaries looking for specific data assets. In some cases, adversaries mount complex and thorough attacks to implement a persistent foothold in an organization's systems, and then wait for the opportunity to complete the exploitation of the organization's assets.

The concept of the kill chain is based on a military planning approach whereby an enemy target is identified and investigated, with strategies for attacks thoroughly planned to effectively engage, attack, and destroy the enemy. This approach can be applied to security threats by investigating the methods and approaches used by attackers to gain access to information assets.

The cyber kill chain shown here is based on the Lockheed Martin framework as part of its Intelligence Driven Defense® model for identifying and preventing cyber intrusions. This widely used model has become the mainstay of many threat intelligence analysts, and it identifies what adversaries must do to achieve their objectives.[2] The Lockheed Martin model identifies seven stages in the cyber kill chain attack strategy shown in Figure 6-1. These stages are discussed in the following sections.

footprinting

The organized research and investigation of Internet addresses owned or controlled by a target organization.

fingerprinting

The process of gathering information about the organization and its network activities and the subsequent process of identifying network assets by a potential attacker.

open source intelligence (OSINT)

Information collected from publicly available sources and used in an intelligence context.

Reconnaissance

During the reconnaissance phase, the attacker attempts to gain information on the organization, its systems, employees, and anything else that may increase the chances of their attacks' success. Most attacks against the organization begin this way, with an exploration of publicly available information and any information the attacker can gain without raising the suspicions of the organization or its security teams. This initial estimation of the defensive state of an organization's networks and systems is conducted first by identifying the range of Internet addresses used by an organization (known as **footprinting**), and then gathering information on and identifying network assets (known as **fingerprinting**). Footprinting typically involves using available Web tools and resources such as the "whois" function, provided as a free service by many Web domain registrars, to identify the network addresses assigned to the organization, as shown in Figure 6-2. It also involves a review of the organization's own Web pages to identify key employees, their e-mail addresses, phone numbers, positions and reporting relationships, access to key information assets and systems, and ultimately, potential for exploitation.

In the intelligence community, the term *open* is used to describe publicly available information that is collected to create **open source intelligence (OSINT)**, which is used to maintain awareness of evolving threats in general and is a resource for researching specific threats as an organization develops usable threat intelligence. OSINT is widely used by attackers and defenders, and the emergence of the Internet has made it possible to collect large amounts of highly relevant information from unclassified sources.

While the organization may never be aware of an attacker's footprinting efforts, fingerprinting is much more intrusive and much more easily detectible. Fingerprinting involves the use of scanning and analysis tools to examine the available resources of an organization and to determine what services are being offered on which computers, what ports are open and possibly exploitable, and what vulnerabilities may be present.

Ports   In the TCP/IP protocol suite, the term *port* is used to specify a numbered interface for communications between hosts. Both the TCP and UDP protocols have provisions for port assignments to differentiate between multiple possible

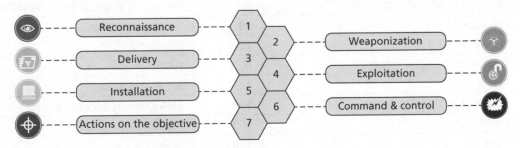

Figure 6-1   Lockheed Martin's cyber kill chain[3]

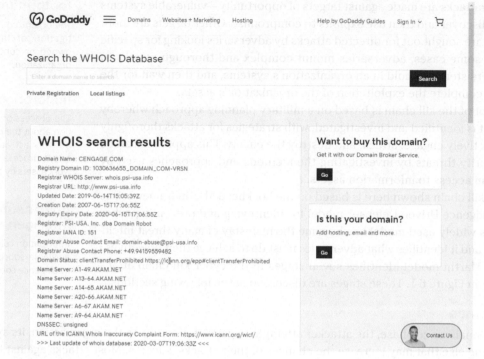

Figure 6-2   GoDaddy.com WHOIS database

Source: GoDaddy.com.

connections needed between hosts and other network devices. The combination of the IP address and the port is usually called a socket. As described in RFC 793 and the IANA Service Name and Transport Protocol Port Number Registry, well-known port numbers range from 0 through 1023, registered port numbers from 1024 through 49151, and dynamic and/or private port numbers from 49152 through 65535.[4]

TCP/IP ports are the mechanism used by the TCP/IP protocol to enable access to a system. Table 6-1 shows the TCP/IP ports that are commonly used by commercial applications, while Table 6-2 shows the TCP/IP ports that are commonly used by hackers and exploits.

Relevant Technologies maintains a list of TCP and UDP ports commonly used by hacker tools, malware, other undesirable applications, and attackers at *www.relevanttechnologies.com/resources_4.asp.*

Table 6-1   Well-Known Ports[5]

Port Number	Description	Port Number	Description
1	TCP Port Service Multiplexer (TCPMUX)	43	WhoIs
5	Remote Job Entry (RJE)	49	Login Host Protocol (Login)
7	ECHO	53	Domain Name System (DNS)
18	Message Send Protocol (MSP)	69	Trivial File Transfer Protocol (TFTP)
20	FTP—Data	70	Gopher services
21	FTP—Control	79	Finger
22	SSH Remote Login Protocol	80	HTTP
23	Telnet	103	X.400 standard
25	Simple Mail Transfer Protocol (SMTP)	108	SNA gateway access server
29	MSG ICP	109	POP2
37	Time	110	POP3
42	Host name server (Nameserv)	115	Simple File Transfer Protocol (SFTP)

(continues)

Table 6-1   Well-Known Ports[5] (*Continued*)

Port Number	Description	Port Number	Description
118	SQL services	389	Lightweight Directory Access Protocol (LDAP)
119	Newsgroup (NNTP)	396	Novell Netware over IP
137	NetBIOS Name Service	443	HTTPS
139	NetBIOS Datagram Service	444	Simple Network Paging Protocol (SNPP)
143	Interim Mail Access Protocol (IMAP)	445	Microsoft-DS
150	NetBIOS Session Service	458	Apple QuickTime
156	SQL Server	546	DHCP client
161	SNMP	547	DHCP server
179	Border Gateway Protocol (BGP)	563	SNEWS
190	Gateway Access Control Protocol (GACP)	569	MSN
194	Internet Relay Chat (IRC)	1080	Socks
197	Directory Location Service (DLS)		

Table 6-2   Ports Commonly Used by Hackers and Exploits[6]

Port Number	Hacker Program/Exploit	Port Number	Hacker Program/Exploit
5	Midnight Commander	5568	Robo-Hack
21	Doly Trojan	5714	WinCrash
25	AntiGen, Email Password Attacks	5741	WinCrash
80	Executer	5742	WinCrash
109	Sekure SDI, b00ger	6006	Bad Blood
137	NetBios exploits	6670	DeepThroat
555	phAse zero, Stealth Spy	6711	Sub-7, DeepThroat
1001	SK Silencer	6969	GateCrasher
1011	Doly Trojan	9989	Ini-Killer
1234	Ultor's Trojan	10167 U	Portal of Doom
1243	Sub-7	10529	Acid Shivers
1245	VooDoo Doll	10666 U	Ambush
1807	SpySender	12345	GirlFriend
1981	ShockRave	19932	DropChute
1999	BackDoor	21544	NetBus
2001	The Trojan Cow	23456	EvilFtp, UglyFtp
2023	Ripper Pro, HackCity	26274	Delta Source
2140	Deep Throat, The Invasor	27374	Sub-7
3024	WinCrash	30100	NetSphere
3129	Master Paradise	31789	Hack'a'Tack
3150	DeepThroat, The Invaser	31337 U	BackOrifice
4092	WinCrash	31338	NetSpy
4950	ICQ Trojan	31339	NetSpy
5321	BackDoorz, Firehotchker	34324	Big Gluck, TN

(continues)

Table 6-2 Ports Commonly Used by Hackers and Exploits[6] (*Continued*)

Port Number	Hacker Program/Exploit	Port Number	Hacker Program/Exploit
40412	The Spy	60000	DeepThroat
47262	Delta Source	61466	TeleCommando
50505	Sockets de Troie	65000	Devil
50766	Fore	65535	RC1 Trojan
53001	Remote Windows Shutdown		

When a review of log files, network scans, or just plain luck turns up one of these ports in use, the next step is to examine who or what is using this port to determine if the traffic is legitimate. Many attacks come through ports and then attack legitimate processes to allow themselves access or to conduct subsequent attacks.

Scanning and Enumeration   As noted earlier, fingerprinting using scanning is the process of collecting information about computers. Passive scanning does this by listening to network traffic. Active scanning does it by sending traffic and observing what traffic returns as a result. Once a target has been identified, enumeration is the process of identifying what resources are publicly available for exploit. These two methods must be used in conjunction with each other. You first scan the network to determine what assets or targets are on the network, and then you enumerate each target by determining which of its resources are available. Without knowing which computers and resources are vulnerable, it is impossible to protect these resources from attack. Later modules of this book contain a number of exercises that will show you how to determine exactly which computers are making resources available on the network and what vulnerabilities exist.

Scanning utilities are tools used to identify which computers are active on a network as well as which ports and services are active on the computers, what function or role the machines may be fulfilling, and so on. These tools can be very specific as to what sort of computer, protocol, or resource they are scanning for, or they can be very generic. It is helpful to understand what sort of environment exists within your network so you can use the best tool for the job. The more specific the scanner is, the more likely it will give you detailed information that is useful later. However, it is also recommended that you make use of one or more generic, broad-based scanners as well. As a system administrator, this may help you to locate and identify nodes on the network of which you might not be aware. In addition, specific utilities can be used as counter-surveillance tools. Some of these tools may be able to help detect packet sniffers that are operating on the network. Many of the scanning tools available today are capable of providing both simple/generic and detailed/advanced functionality.

Some of the tools mentioned in this module are open source and freely available to attackers and defenders alike. Others are proprietary products that must be purchased to gain full access to their capabilities. Many powerful proprietary tools began as open source projects from both attackers and defenders. A little Web-based research can help you identify tools that remain open source.

Some commonly used scanning tools by both information security professionals and hackers include the following:

- Nmap, a widely used port scanner (*https://nmap.org*)
- Zenmap, a GUI front end for Nmap (*https://nmap.org/zenmap/*)
- OpenVAS, a vulnerability scanner (*www.openvas.org/*)
- LanGuard, a client-based vulnerability scanner (*www.gfi.com/products-and-solutions/network-security-solutions/gfi-languard*)
- Ping, a command included in the TCP/IP stack of most operating systems
- Wireshark, a network traffic scanner (*www.wireshark.org/*)

Additional tools are listed and reviewed at one of *Insecure.org*'s sites at *https://sectools.org/*.

Use of these tools by an information security professional is essential in determining what ports are open and thus subject to attack by a hacker.

When the organization is capable of detecting the early warning signs of reconnaissance, much as neighborhood watch volunteers might be capable of detecting potential burglars casing their neighborhoods by testing doors and windows, the administrators may have time to prepare for a potential attack or to take actions to minimize potential losses from an attack.

Weaponization

Weaponization in the literal sense is the conversion of an item into a weapon capable of dealing damage to a target. In the military and government environment, this involves the conversion of explosive, nuclear, biological, and chemical components into destructive weapons. In the cyber kill chain, it's the loading of a payload, such as a virus or rootkit, into an exploit delivery mechanism, such as a phishing e-mail. Other security weaponization efforts involve the development of self-replicating malware and ransomware capable of spreading throughout an organization and infecting as many systems as possible, as quickly as possible.

In many respects, this is the most technically challenging part of the intrusion for the attacker. The degree of programming skill and technical knowledge required to develop effective weaponized exploits is significant. One would think the skill needed to accomplish this would greatly reduce the security threats present in the world. Unfortunately, there are attackers focusing on just this aspect of the kill chain, developing attack exploits that others can freely download and use to attack their own targets. In fact, many of these developers may work for government and organized crime groups.

Delivery

The delivery stage of the cyber kill chain is the transmission of the weaponized delivery mechanism to the intended target or targets. As discussed later in this module, this could be accomplished through the delivery of generic e-mails as part of a phishing attack (such as a 4-1-9 message), or through a very narrowly crafted delivery of an e-mail tailored for a specific target (as in a spear phishing message).

The organization can stop the attack and thus the entire kill chain at this point if all employees are trained well enough to detect the threat, and sufficiently alert and diligent to respond appropriately to these deliveries. For example, employees can delete the messages or forward them to the help desk or CSIRT so they can modify e-mail and firewall technologies to filter future messages. At this point in time, attackers have not succeeded in creating self-activating e-mail attacks, which means that an unsuspecting or less-than-diligent employee must click on a link, download an attachment, or respond to an attack message to initiate the remainder of the kill chain. This process also includes social engineering attacks that are more "old school," such as phone-based social engineering attacks.

Exploitation

The next stage of the cyber kill chain is the "detonation" of the delivered and weaponized exploit. The act of clicking the link in the malicious e-mail, downloading the infected e-mail attachment, or accessing and downloading the corrupt application from the Web will activate and begin the process whereby the crafted exploit gains a foothold and attempts to expand its influence.

There is little the user or organization can do at this point if the local antivirus or antimalware application is unable to recognize the exploitation as an intrusion. If the exploitation was the delivery of malware or a rootkit, the organization may be able to interrupt the kill chain; however, not all exploitations involve these detectable exploits. The exploitation may involve a remote access application not classified as malware by the vendors, or some other approach.

Installation

Once activated, the exploit installs itself onto the local user's systems and attempts to spread throughout the organization. This could involve malware locating the contact list in the user's e-mail app and sending itself to all of the user's contacts, or other methods of distribution. It could also involve the installation of a rootkit on the local user's system.

Because the intrusion is now behind the organization's firewall, detection and resolution of the incident is much more difficult without the assistance of technologies like antivirus/antimalware applications and IDPSs (discussed in Module 7). The use of technologies like two-factor authentication to prevent the automatic log-in of other systems and services in the organization will also deter the exploitation and spread of the attack at this point. In addition, training users to detect "unusual activity" on their systems can assist in quickly diagnosing an attack at this stage. Similarly, the preparation and training of the help desk can assist in recognizing the signs of an intrusion.

indicator

An activity that may signal an adverse event is under way and provide a notification of an adverse event or incident candidate.

precursor

An activity in progress that may signal an incident could occur in the future.

Command and Control

Once the exploit has gained a foothold on the local user's system, the installed exploit will commonly report back to the attacker that the intrusion has succeeded. This could involve the transmission of a message to the attacker that they are now able to log into the system, attempt to access local information, and access additional systems through privilege escalation.

Detection of these outbound communications and inbound responses is possible with vigilant perimeter protection technologies and security staff. Many rootkits have a recognizable signature that a network IDPS (discussed in Module 7) can detect and respond to. Modern unified threat management (UTM) firewall appliances have integrated event and antimalware features that allow them to respond more effectively to inbound intrusions, outbound communications, and data exfiltration.

Actions on Objectives

The final stage of the cyber kill chain is the attacker's end game—the theft, damage, or denial of use of the organization's information assets. We may never know why attackers do what they do; what's more important is the "what" and the "how." By understanding the attack techniques used at this point, the organization can detect the intrusion, respond to contain the attack, and regain control of the systems.

The organization will again rely heavily on technologies such as a network and host IDPS to detect the intruder's activity. While it may be too little, too late, the log monitoring systems discussed later in this module can assist the organization's security and systems administrators in detecting an attack after the fact and preventing future incursions.[7]

INCIDENT INDICATORS

A number of different events occurring in and around an organization signal the presence of an incident candidate. Unfortunately, these same events may occur when a network becomes overloaded, a computer or server encounters an error, or some normal operation of an information asset mimics the appearance of an identified incident candidate. An event that is an indicator or precursor may assist the CSIRT in identifying incidents in progress or before they happen, respectively.[8] To help make the detection of actual incidents more reliable, renowned security consultant Donald Pipkin has identified three broad categories of incident indicators: *possible*, *probable*, and *definite*.[9] This categorization enables an organization to expedite the decision-making process of incident classification as events are evaluated and ensure that the IR plan is activated as early as possible, and that the proper procedures are followed. These categories are explored in the following sections.

A key issue in this evaluation is the ability to quickly differentiate between false positives—events that are not truly a threat—and false negatives, which are events that are actual threats but are not detected. This point is explained further in later sections of this module and in Module 7.

Possible Indicators of an Incident

Using the criteria established by Pipkin, there are four types of indicators that actual incidents are *possibly* under way:

- *Presence of unfamiliar files*—Users might discover unfamiliar files in their home directories or on their office computers. Administrators might also find unexplained files that do not seem to be in a logical location or are not owned by an authorized user. (See the discussion on rootkits in Module 7 for examples of unfamiliar files.)
- *Presence or execution of unknown programs or processes*—Users or administrators might detect unfamiliar programs running, or processes executing, on office machines or network servers. (For more information, see the discussion on "Detecting Incidents through Processes and Services" later in this module.)

- *Unusual consumption of computing resources*—Consumption of memory or hard disk space might suddenly spike or fall. Many computer operating systems, including Windows 7, Windows 10, and many Linux and UNIX variants, allow users and administrators to monitor CPU and memory consumption (see Figure 6-3). Most computers also have the ability to monitor hard drive space. In addition, servers maintain logs of file creation and storage.
- *Unusual system crashes*—Computer systems can crash. Older operating systems running newer programs are notorious for locking up or spontaneously rebooting whenever the operating system is unable to execute a requested process or service. You are probably familiar with system error messages such as "Program Not Responding," "General Protection Fault," and the infamous Windows Blue Screen of Death. However, if a computer system seems to be crashing, hanging, rebooting, or freezing more frequently than usual, the cause could be an incident candidate.[10]

Probable Indicators of an Incident

Pipkin further identifies four types of adverse events that are *probable* indicators of actual incidents:

- *Activities at unexpected times*—If traffic levels on an organization's network exceed the measured baseline values, an incident candidate is probably present. If this activity surge occurs when few members of the organization are at work, the probability becomes much higher. Similarly, if systems are accessing attached devices such as mounted drives or USB media when the end user is not using them, an incident may also be occurring.
- *Presence of unexpected new accounts*—Periodic review of user accounts can reveal one or more that the administrator does not remember creating or that are not logged in the administrator's journal. Even one unlogged new account is an incident candidate. An unlogged new account with root or other special privileges has an even higher probability of being an actual incident.

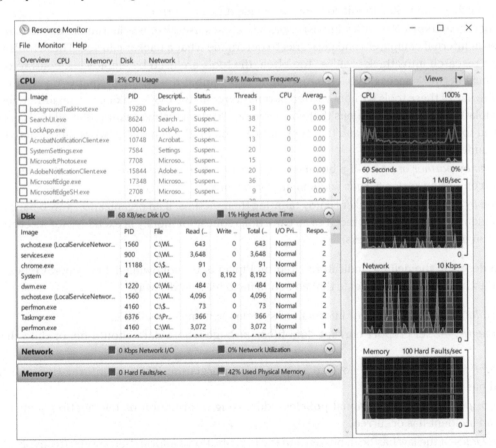

Figure 6-3 Windows 10 Resource Monitor

Used with permission from Microsoft Corporation.

false positive

An alert or alarm that occurs in the absence of an actual attack. A false positive can sometimes be produced when an IDPS mistakes normal system activity for an attack. False positives tend to make users insensitive to alarms and thus reduce their reactions to actual intrusion events.

- *Reported attacks*—If users of the system report a suspected attack, there is a high probability that an attack has occurred, which constitutes an incident. The technical sophistication of the person making the report should be considered.
- *Notification from an IDPS*—If the organization has installed and correctly configured a host-based or network-based IDPS, then notification from the IDPS indicates that an incident might be in progress. However, IDPSs are seldom configured optimally and, even when they are, tend to issue many **false positives** or false alarms. The administrator must then determine whether the notification is real or if it is the result of a routine operation by a user or other administrator.[11]

Definite Indicators

Pipkin's categories continue with a list of five types of adverse events that are *definite* indicators of an actual incident. That is, they clearly and specifically signal that an incident is in progress or has occurred. In these cases, the corresponding IR plan must be activated immediately.

- *Use of dormant accounts*—Many network servers maintain default accounts, and there are often accounts from former employees, employees on a leave of absence or sabbatical without remote access privileges, or dummy accounts set up to support system testing. If any of these accounts begin accessing system resources, querying servers, or engaging in other activities, an incident is almost certain to have occurred.
- *Changes to logs*—The smart systems administrator backs up system logs as well as system data. As part of a routine incident scan, systems administrators can compare these logs to the online versions to determine whether they have been modified. If they have, and the systems administrator cannot determine explicitly that an authorized individual modified them, an incident has occurred.
- *Presence of hacker tools*—Network administrators sometimes use system vulnerability and network evaluation tools to scan internal computers and networks to determine what a hacker can see. These tools are also used to support research into attack profiles. Too often, the tools are used by employees, contractors, or outsiders with local network access to hack into systems. To combat this problem, many organizations explicitly prohibit the use of these tools without written permission from the CISO, making any unauthorized installation a policy violation. Most organizations that engage in penetration testing require that all tools in this category be confined to specific systems, and that they not be used on the general network unless active penetration testing is under way.
- *Notifications by partner or peer*—If a business partner or another connected organization reports an attack from your computing systems, then an incident has occurred.
- *Notification by hacker*—Some hackers enjoy taunting their victims. If an organization's Web pages are defaced, it is an incident. If an organization receives an extortion request for money in exchange for its customers' credit card files, an incident is in progress.[12]

Another way to describe the definite indicators cited by Pipkin is the following list of general types of events that, when confirmed to have occurred, indicate that an actual incident is under way:

- *Loss of availability*—Information or information systems become unavailable.
- *Loss of integrity*—Users report corrupt data files, garbage where data should be, or data that just looks wrong.
- *Loss of confidentiality*—You are notified of sensitive information leaks, or information you thought was protected has been disclosed.
- *Violation of policy*—If organizational policies addressing information or information security have been violated, an incident has occurred.
- *Violation of law*—If the law has been broken and the organization's information assets are involved, an incident has occurred.

Identifying Real Incidents

As noted earlier, one of the first challenges facing IR plan designers is creating a process to collect and evaluate incident candidates to determine whether they are actual incidents (or adverse events likely to become incidents) or nonevents, also called *false positive* incident candidates. This is very important because most organizations will find themselves awash in incident candidates at one time or another, and the vast majority will be false positives.

Each organization must create its own processes to collect and evaluate incident candidates. Some may choose to have an *incident center*, where all incident candidates are sent from the earliest moment of recognition. Others may decide to have a security operations center (SOC), where day-to-day operations of key security technology are monitored, serve to review incident candidates. Still others choose to have geographically separate review locations, perhaps based on time zones, where preliminary determinations about the status of an incident candidate can be assessed. Some organizations choose to isolate incident candidate evaluation based on business units, product lines, or some other criterion.

Many organizations struggle with the relationship between a false-positive incident candidate and noise. In a properly designed system (whether human-based or machine-based), candidate events that are legitimate activities wrongly reported as incident candidates are noise, and should result in the activation of a feedback process that can improve the system so that alerts based on these legitimate activities are suppressed by the data collection procedures or programs and are not flagged as events. Some high-profile breaches, such as the Target breach in 2013, occurred after indicators of an ongoing compromise were dismissed as false positives.

Most data collection systems are implemented with little or no formal training for the users of the process. When done properly, the training needs for incident candidate data collection should be extensive at first and then continue with a less intensive effort for the life of the system. The quality and quantity of the training, and the resulting skills of the staff involved in the data collection, will result in the removal of noise from the process. Even the best-tuned incident candidate collection system generates false positives; usually, they are considered to be inherent in the nature of such systems. However, the ratio of false positive events to actual events needs to be kept to a manageable level through ongoing improvements to the collection processes.

Noise or false positives result from several general causes, including:

- *Placement*—The incident candidate's source is a significant factor. If an automated IDPS is placed outside the trusted subnetwork of the organization, it is likely to see a vast number of attempted attacks, which may be interpreted as incident candidates. Moving the sensor so that it is the first device inside the trusted subnetwork perimeter can reduce the number of events reported, allowing the control devices (firewall rules, in this case) to have the desired effect before sending in the alarm.
- *Policy*—In some situations, organizational policy may allow certain activities by employees that are later detected as incident candidates. For instance, if company policy allows network administrators within the company to use certain tools whose network signatures are classified by automated tools as network attacks (for example, Nmap, Metasploit, or any of the other tools commonly used by hackers), this will be a significant source of noise. Aligning data collection practices with policy parameters minimizes this kind of event.
- *Lack of awareness*—In some cases, users are not aware of policy limitations on certain activities. For example, in the previous situation, if Nmap were disallowed for use within the organization by policy, many systems administrators might not be aware of the policy and might use the tool for routine activities. An awareness program can help minimize the noise generated by this kind of activity.

Many organizations do not deal well with the effort to minimize noise and the false positives it generates. There must be a procedure defined for the data collection tuning process that results in a careful analysis of the effect of each change to the data collection rules. Left to their own devices, many automated IDPS administrators would

security operations center (SOC)

A staffed control room where key security technologies, networks, and critical systems are monitored for incidents.

noise

In incident response, an event that does not rise to the level of an incident.

tuning

The process of adjusting a technical control to maximize its efficiency in detecting true positives while minimizing false positives and false negatives.

false negative

The failure of a technical control to react to the intended stimulus so that it goes unreported.

process

A task being performed by a computer.

simply turn off the reporting of some classes of adverse events rather than perform an analysis of the events and determine if a change in the position of the data collector, an adjustment to policy, or increased awareness might be a better solution.

Although the issue of false positives gets a lot of attention, it is also important to avoid the occurrence of false negatives, which deserve attention but are not reported. One example of a false negative comes from the character of Sherlock Holmes in Arthur Conan Doyle's mystery "Adventure of Silver Blaze." In the story, an expensive racehorse is stolen from its stable. Inspector Gregory of Scotland Yard asks Holmes if there is any particular aspect of the crime calling for additional study. Holmes says there is, then mentions "the curious incident of the dog in the night-time." Inspector Gregory says, "The dog did nothing in the night-time," to which Holmes replies, "That was the curious incident." In this case, the failure of the dog to bark when Silver Blaze was stolen was a false negative report. If a data collection process such as an IDPS fails to warn of a valid network attack, it becomes "the dog that did nothing in the nighttime."

Another factor to add to the tuning process is routine change. When new or modified systems are placed in service or existing systems are updated, the result may be a need for additional tuning of the data collection process. Newer technologies often change the way network traffic appears to both human and automated sensors. For example, some load-balancing appliances may generate significant traffic that probes the availability of the services they are attempting to balance. This traffic, if unanticipated, may be perceived as an incident candidate when in fact it is merely noise. The objective of the tuning process is to reduce the number of false positives while ensuring no false negatives occur.

 Tuning systems have seen many advances to dial-in rules for determining event significance. If this is interesting to you, use a browser to search for "Tuning the False Positive Rate/False Negative Rate." This search will find quite a few popular and scholarly articles on the subject.

INCIDENT DETECTION STRATEGIES

Detecting an intrusion or other incident depends heavily on the preparedness of the organization's employees. Well-trained and aware employees can quickly spot something out of the ordinary. Well-trained and well-organized help-desk employees can detect trends in reporting from these users and alert the CSIRT or SOC staff. Alert and diligent CSIRT and/or SOC staff can react quickly to examine an anomalous situation and determine whether an incident is under way. The security education, training, and awareness (SETA) program discussed in Module 1 therefore becomes critical to early detection and reaction for the organization.

There are a number of approaches the organization can deploy to assist in the definition of incidents. Using the indicators described previously, the organization can use these strategies to greatly speed up the process of sifting through the large number of adverse events and identify those that represent real risk to the organization's information assets. Some of these approaches are manual, time-consuming tasks that require a significant degree of knowledge and skill. Others rely on the support of technologies, like the IDPSs discussed in Module 7, to sift out the incident from the noise.

The development of machine learning and artificial intelligence (AI) to improve the ability to detect incidents from a vast set of reported events has been maturing in recent years. As organizations mature and acquire more advanced tools (see the section on SIEM in Module 7), they can improve the speed and efficiency with which they detect and respond to incidents. Manual efforts to analyze, identify, correlate, and troubleshoot events to detect actionable incidents are slow and cumbersome. Emerging techniques and tools built on machine learning and artificial intelligence can enable improved response times and increased accuracy and allow response teams to automate, customize, and integrate incident detection and management procedures.

Detecting Incidents through Processes and Services

Computer systems are made up of hardware, software, data, and networking devices that enable support for applications programs to be used by people to solve problems. Current computer systems use a series of processes, some in a supervisory mode and others in a user mode. Computer processes are often performed at the same time that the computer system is handling other tasks. Therefore, many processes may be under way at the same time, each of them being handled by the system's processor in turn. Each process is made up of the following:

- *A set of instructions, coded in a machine language held in a state that can be run by the processor*—This set of instructions is commonly called an image. It has a current state that changes over time as the program is run. This image is usually provided with a name or label that corresponds to other versions of the program, such as its source code, its compiled code, or perhaps the code library it came from.
- *A set of memory locations where the image is housed, where process-specific data values are stored, where input and output buffers are placed, and where a special-purpose memory structure stores details about subroutine calls (the call stack), and a memory heap where intermediate computations are staged while the program is in a running state*—This collection of memory assignments usually includes physical memory as well as areas of virtual memory stored on other media, almost always hard disk drives.
- *A list of allocated resources provided from the operating system*—This includes links to files and other data channels.
- *A list of attributes that describe the allowable operations*—This list of attributes describes the allowable operations (called permissions) that the image has been granted by the operating system.
- *A table that identifies the current context of the various parts and pieces of the image*—While the image is running, various registers in the central processing unit track the current processor state (kernel vs. user), point to the next executable instruction (the program counter), map to registers that are associated with the image, and point to physical and virtual memory segments that are part of the image.

All the essential facts about an image are held in these structures, which are collectively called "control blocks." Each image has a root process and then may spawn (or fork) to include subordinate processes sometimes called "daughter" processes. The kernel handles each process of the operating system as a separate element and allocates requested resources to it as they become available. This is done to reduce the likelihood of inter-process interference, such as deadlocking or thrashing. Data structures are sometimes used between processes to facilitate communication between the processes.

To view operational processes provided on a Windows-based PC, use the Windows Task Manager, as shown in Figure 6-4.

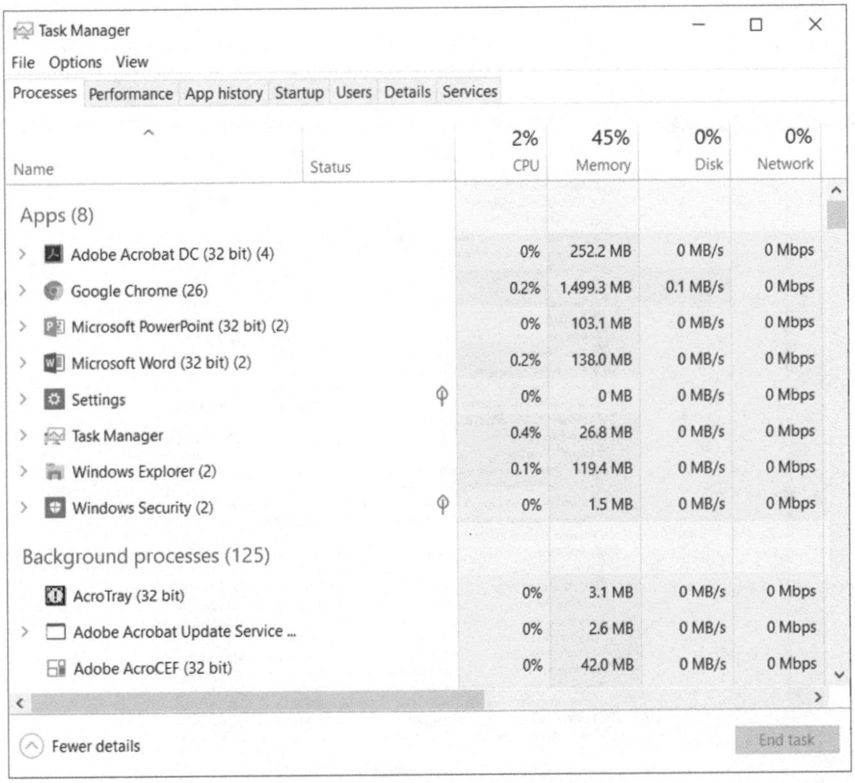

Figure 6-4   Processes tab of Windows 10 Task Manager

Used with permission from Microsoft Corporation.

service

A set of software functionalities with capabilities that different clients can reuse for different purposes; in Linux/UNIX systems, services are referred to as daemons.

In some cases, operating systems can conceal certain critical OS processes from some tools. For instance, Windows Task Manager does not reveal all processes. However, another utility included in most versions of Windows, including Windows 10, is the System Information utility (msinfo32.exe), located in the C:\program files\ common files\microsoft shared\msinfo folder. This utility can detect all processes running on a particular system. Knowing the limitations of operating system tools and interfaces is essential in making informed decisions.

Practitioners in the field have observed that the msinfo32 tool may be used to seek out Trojan programs. This can be done by listing the tasks and **services** that are running and then investigating any that are not recognized. Look at the paths and filenames shown for the listed entries as well as the file properties. If there are anomalies, locate the.dll file linked to the process and run it through your virus checker. If you have reason to believe that a process is suspect, use the Startup Programs editor in the Tools menu to disable that task and then restart the system without starting the questionable task. Note that you should make a system backup before undertaking any of these steps. After restart, if your system still runs, leave the questionable process stopped and continue looking. Once you have eliminated what's unnecessary, you will wind up with only essential processes running on your system and will have removed Trojans, which will also make your PC start and run more quickly.[13]

Microsoft no longer documents the common Windows processes on a system that runs on a typical Windows PC. Because the complete list of processes that could run on a typical PC is too vast to share here, several online sites allow users to search the function of an identified process:

- File Inspect Library (*www.fileinspect.com*)
- *Processlibrary.com* (*www.processlibrary.com*)
- *Tasklist.org* (*www.tasklist.org*)

To view available services provided on a Windows-based PC or server, you can access the services function through the Windows Task Manager (see the Services tab in Figure 6-4) or Services under Administrative Tools in the Control Panel (select System and Security > Administrative Tools > Services), as shown in Figure 6-5.

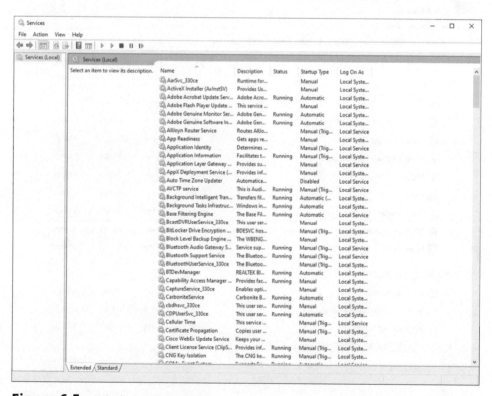

Figure 6-5   Windows 10 services

Used with permission from Microsoft Corporation.

The presence of unexpected processes and services could indicate an intrusion or other incident. It is therefore imperative that incident response and information security personnel become familiar with the services and processes that should be present, which simplifies the task of identifying services and processes that should not be present.

Detection Strategies for Common Incidents

In this section, we'll look at some detection strategies for the most probable occurrences associated with incidents and related adverse events focused on specific systems. In the next section, we'll examine general detection strategies that provide support regardless of the target system.

Phishing

One of the more commonly seen and most easily avoided incidents is the phishing attack. Employees are bombarded with numerous attempts to convince them to activate a link embedded in an e-mail or respond to a request for communications with an unknown outside party, often masquerading as a known entity. The SETA program mentioned previously is the most effective tool in enabling all employees to detect this type of incident. Training employees to distinguish between legitimate and illegitimate communications is key to stopping this threat cold.

More dangerous than the general phishing attack is the spear phishing attack, which results from an attacker custom-tailoring the exploit to the individual or at least the organization. E-mails claim to be from a fellow employee, executive, or business partner, and often have graphics taken from a Web site and modified to link to scripts that will download malicious code. While the "get rich quick" Nigerian 4-1-9 attacks have been around long enough to generally be discredited (see Figure 6-6), many employees are still susceptible to messages asking them to click a link to confirm an order, account status, or request for payment, as shown in the spear phishing attack in Figure 6-7.

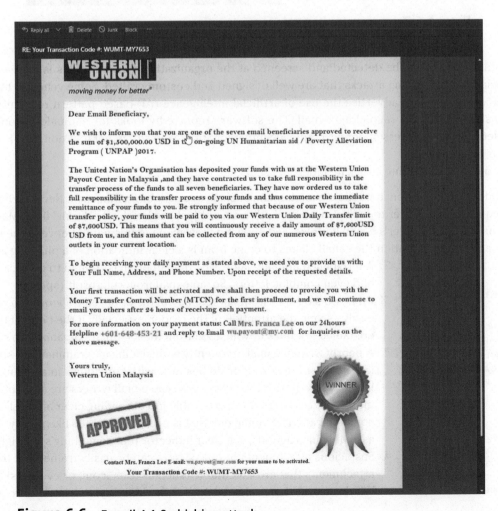

Figure 6-6   E-mail 4-1-9 phishing attack

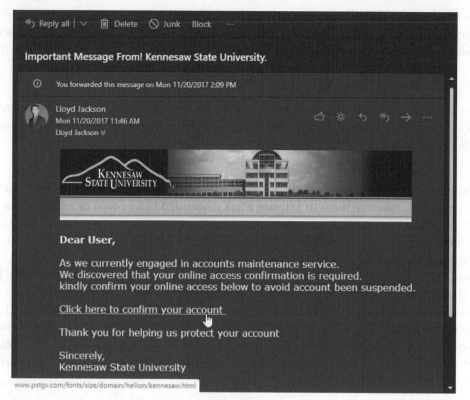

Figure 6-7 E-mail spear phishing attack

Some phishing attacks can be detected and screened at the organization's firewall. This is increasingly difficult, however, especially with phishing attacks that are well designed and custom crafted. Some vendors, like Barracuda's Sentinel (*www.barracuda.com*), advertise the use of artificial intelligence (AI)-based pattern recognition to identify and isolate phishing attacks in suspicious e-mail. The software reportedly looks for anomalous content in e-mail, allowing it to detect e-mail address spoofing, employee impersonation, Web site impersonation, and **business e-mail compromise** or **CEO fraud**.

Five ways to detect a phishing attack include:

1. The sender's e-mail is from a public e-mail domain, such as *live.com* or *hotmail.com*. Recognizing this often requires the receiver to look at the e-mail address, not just the header or "From" field. Many e-mail programs mask the sender's e-mail address, just showing their name. A mismatch between the e-mail domain and the organization the e-mail claims to come from is a clear indication of a phishing attack.

2. A misspelled domain name. The human brain is trained to correct minor typos and even combine letters. So, an e-mail from rnicrosoft (spelled r n i c r o s o f t) or from baracuda.com (as opposed to *barracuda.com*) could easily escape the attention of the reader, especially if the body of the e-mail contained graphics downloaded from the legitimate organization's account.

3. A poorly written e-mail, frequently with significant grammar and spelling issues. Most organizations do business with individuals in a common language. Even with the occasional typo e-mail writers are susceptible to, most business users do a reasonable job of sending clear and well-written communications. Finding one that is not, or that reads like poorly translated assembly instructions, is a clear indicator that something's not right.

4. Suspicious attachments or links. Users can be easily trained not to download attachments that are executable (such as .exe, .com, or even .msi for Windows systems, .run, .out, and .sh for Linux systems, and .osx, .dmg, and

business e-mail compromise (BEC)

The use of e-mail in fraudulent efforts to compromise the organization. BEC is often used to target executives and key employees in the organization.

CEO fraud

The impersonation of executives in an effort to trick an employee into revealing confidential financial information or sending unauthorized financial transfers.

.app for Macs). However, many attachments can be used to cause problems, especially Adobe .pdfs. Suspicious links often have a mismatch between the displayed text and the HTML encoding behind it. This can be verified by hovering the mouse—*without clicking it*—over the text. Links are also suspect if the domain in the revealed code doesn't match the content of the e-mail. In Figure 6-7, the e-mail reported an issue with a Kennesaw State University e-mail account, yet the code behind the "click here" message pointed to a completely different domain.

5. The message is marked URGENT! The more rushed the receiver is, the more likely they are not to pay close attention to one of the flags indicated above. If the sender can prevent a receiver from carefully reviewing the content of the request, they might just overlook a clue and fall into the phish trap (pun intended).[14]

Malware

Another commonly seen incident is the entire set of malicious code known as *malware*. Malware includes viruses, worms, Trojan horses, and an entire library of malicious scripts designed to steal information, deny service to needed resources, and generally wreak havoc in the organization.

The most common detection method for malware is the reaction by the users' antivirus/antimalware software. Current versions of Microsoft Windows now come with Windows Defender as an integral part of Microsoft Security at no additional cost. Similarly, the newest versions of Apple macOS come with "industry-standard antivirus software built in to block and remove malware."[15] There are also numerous freeware antimalware applications available from reputable Web sites, such as Total AV (*www.totalav.com/free-anti-malware*) and AVG (*www.avg.com*), as well as industry-leading commercial products like Symantec Norton (*https://us.norton.com*), shown in Figure 6-8, and McAfee (*www.mcafee.com*). Most organizations deploy an enterprise-wide antimalware solution and manage the necessary subscriptions and updates needed to keep the application current.

Antimalware applications become critical when users visit suspicious Web sites, especially when users are looking for free or open source applications to minimize the drain on security or IT department technology budgets. Effective antimalware can recognize links or downloads that have embedded malicious code, interrupt the downloads, and then delete or quarantine them.

Figure 6-8   Norton Security Suite with antivirus protection

Source: Norton.

ransomware

Software designed to penetrate security controls, identify valuable content, and then encrypt files and data in place in order to extort payment for the key needed to unlock the encryption.

Ransomware

Ransomware attacks are on the rise:

- "Ransomware costs businesses more than $75 billion per year.
- The average cost of a ransomware attack on businesses was $133,000.
- 75% of companies infected with ransomware were running up-to-date endpoint protection.
- 34% of businesses hit with malware took a week or more to regain access to their data.
- A new organization will fall victim to ransomware every 11 seconds by 2021."[16]

The most common detection of ransomware, unfortunately, is a message to a user that they have been locked out of their computer system, and that their files and data have been encrypted. As illustrated in Figure 6-9, most ransomware involves a countdown to permanent encryption, rendering the files and data inaccessible.

It is possible that antimalware or antivirus software could detect a malware attack, especially software that uses AI to review e-mail for potentially malicious links or embedded scripts or malware. However, as the previous statistics show, organizations with antimalware or antivirus software are not immune to ransomware attacks, especially those that are downloaded as a result of user phishing attacks. In response to this new cyber-epidemic, new ransomware protection applications are available, and more are under development. Some are integrated into unified threat management programs that can detect ransomware attacks.

Ransomware attacks attempt to modify large numbers of files in a short period of time. Software that can detect such widespread and high-frequency changes will assist in detecting ransomware, and at a minimum notify an organization's IT or information security administrators about the attack. Because some ransomware variants are designed to spread once an internal system is compromised, early detection can prevent widespread infestation and minimize data loss.

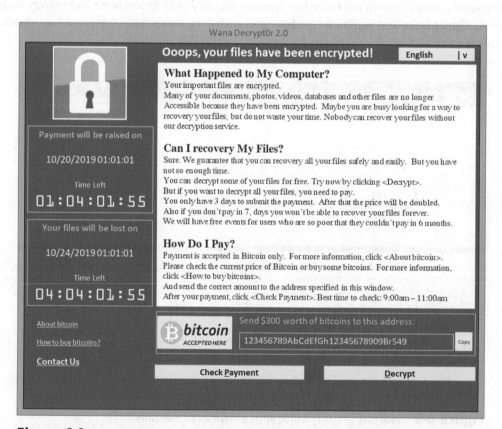

Figure 6-9   Replication of Wana Decryptor ransomware display

In the event a user is notified that a ransomware attack was detected (and hopefully stopped), the notification should be immediately relayed to the SOC or CSIRT as evidence of an attack attempt so that the rest of the organization can be warned of the threat and the IR plan can be activated.

Some additional methods of detecting ransomware include:

- *Monitor known file extensions*—Ransomware has unique file extensions that can be screened for. There are records of the known file extensions (for example, see Figure 6-10 and *www.reddit.com/r/netsec/comments/4ijpu8/ransomware_overview_names_extensions_patterns/*). Host intrusion detection and prevention systems (HIDPSs, like Snort at *www.snort.org*) can be configured to look for and detect these extensions.

- *Monitor for increased file modifications*—As mentioned earlier, ransomware will change a large number of files in a very short time. Again, quality HIDPSs can detect both what is changed and the rate of changes. A rule of thumb to use when configuring these systems is that a rate of change greater than 4 renames per second can indicate a potential ransomware attack.

- *Make your own honeynet*—A network resource that has a large number of unimportant files can serve as a honeynet. A honeynet often comprises a number of honeypots. Network and host IDPSs can monitor these resources to detect any changes. Ransomware that is spreading through an organization can be delayed and detected through the use of these sites. If the organization needs a massive collection of files for these sacrificial networks, it can use document repositories like Project Gutenberg (a library of public-domain ebooks at *www.gutenberg.org*) or even mirror software repositories like github (*www.github.com*). Anything that creates large sets of files can be used; the more files, the better, as the encryption process does take time.

- *Ensure that all IDPSs are configured with "exploit kit detection rules"*—An exploit kit is used to get the ransomware (or other malware) into the target system. Elements of the IDPS can detect the attack vectors used by ransomware and ensure that the IDPS is able to detect and respond to the attack. Even an open source HIDPS like Snort can detect these exploit kits.

- *Deploy antivirus/antimalware software with ransomware detection on all client systems*—All AV/AM software is not created equal; some applications are capable of detecting ransomware and some are not. It is important for the organization to ensure that the solution is deployed on all of its client systems—including mobile technology capable of detecting ransomware.[17]

With ransomware, an ounce of prevention will save your organization's data. Frequent and sequestered backups allow the organization to recover from ransomware attacks. Restoring systems completely from known good, full backups that include the operating system ensures that the ransomware has been removed and the organization can resume operations, as long as the organization knows how the systems were infected and how to avoid a reoccurrence.

Web System Attacks

In this context, a Web attack is an attack on a server that is providing publicly accessible services, like a Web server, ecommerce server, or some other service. An attack on a Web service is typically detected during the attack or after the attack. The most common detection of a Web attack is after the attack. Detection occurs when someone—either a customer or an employee—notices a change in the appearance or behavior of an application or Web site. They report it to the organization and then the SOC or CSIRT investigates.

Another way post-attack detection occurs is when a systems administrator reviews the logs of a system and identifies abnormal entries. They may notify the SOC or CSIRT, and then an investigation begins. The use of log assessment tools can help in the identification of probes across multiple systems, before an attack is successful. Most normal traffic occurs in predictable patterns. Improper HTTP headers, or missing POST data when it is expected, can indicate an attack or attempted exploit.

Of course, IDPSs can also detect unauthorized changes in Web systems; however, many attacks are performed against vulnerabilities in the *use* of a Web system, which an IDPS may not detect. SQL injections, buffer overruns, and cross-site scripting attacks can occur from the user interface. URL manipulation, such as that in the case of the Harvard 119 described in the following feature, wasn't a software-based attack, but was a manipulation of commands displayed in the Web site's URL. There are also applications that scan Web sites to detect vulnerabilities present, but this isn't truly detection as much as it is prevention.

honeynet

A network version of a honeypot; a decoy network simulation that attempts to draw attackers to it and away from actual production networks.

honeypot

A decoy application or systems simulation that attempts to draw attackers to it and away from actual production systems.

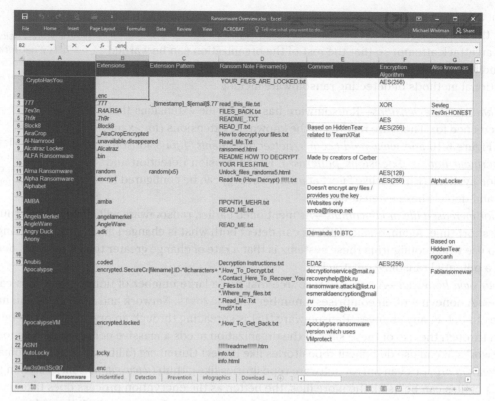

Figure 6-10 Spreadsheet of known ransomware file extensions[18]

Used with permission from Microsoft Corporation.

Case of the Harvard 119

In 2005, dozens of applicants to Harvard, MIT, Stanford, Duke, and Dartmouth made the news when they were accused of hacking, not because they attempted to break into a university system, but because of how they viewed their admissions applications and reviews. The problem was, they weren't supposed to be able to view their admissions reviews. All of these schools shared a third-party admissions review site called ApplyYourself, which is common in higher education. However, someone figured out that if you accessed your account and then cut and pasted your account number into a different Web page, you could see the reviews of your application, if any existed. The applicants weren't able to change anything, and had to log in with their own credentials to see their reviews.

However, some schools, like Harvard, took exception to this "URL manipulation." Harvard summarily rejected the admissions applications of 119 potential students, stating, "Our mission is to educate principled leaders who make a difference in the world ... To achieve that, a person must have many skills and qualities, including the highest standards of integrity, sound judgment, and a strong moral compass—an intuitive sense of what is right and wrong. Those who have hacked into this Web site have failed to pass that test."[19] This story provided the foundation for much discussion in computer ethics courses, considering that many users have modified a Web site's URL at some point or to some degree, either by correcting a typo that prevents accessing a legitimate page or shortening a long URL when looking for additional information. This raises the question: At what point does URL manipulation become hacking?

Internal Systems Intrusions

A related intrusion that is different from a Web attack is an intrusion into the organization's networks and non-public systems. Whereas a Web attack is usually performed on a public-facing system, an intrusion in this context is an attack on an internal system, after the attacker has made it past the firewall. Using phishing or social engineering techniques, an attack may penetrate the organization's networks.

Another method of gaining access is through a physical visit to the organization. Few organizations screen connection requests to systems physically connected to their networks. Others have open wireless networks for their employees. Smart organizations require credentials on both. However, organizations that fail to protect internal connection requests are susceptible to attack by a visitor, friend, or family associate of an employee. This attacker can connect their systems or an exploitation device to the internal network, and then scan and attack systems from the inside (or later from outside the organization).

data exfiltration
The theft of organizational data, either physically or by extraction through the owners' network.

Regardless of whether the attack comes from inside or outside the network, detecting attacks on internal systems presents a challenge. Some applications like IDPSs and antimalware/antivirus programs can detect the use of scanning tools. Organizations should have policies prohibiting the use of such scanning tools by unauthorized employees and allowing the detection of these tools to be immediately classified as a potential incident.

Unlike other intrusions discussed previously, the IT and security departments won't be able to rely on end users for primary detection, unless the intrusion results in a denial of service to an internal asset. The review of systems logs described in the previous section on Web attacks applies equally here.

Detection tools focused on **data exfiltration** can assist in detecting internal systems intrusions. Network IDPSs that are configured to look for excessive numbers of data packets leaving the organization's networks, and not coming from Web sites, can pick up potential intrusions of this nature. Similarly, network administrators using network performance dashboards may detect large amounts of traffic coming from one or a few internal systems that they don't specifically expect to be involved in such traffic, especially when the destination field on the packets is outside the network. Detecting high traffic during off-peak hours is another way to isolate potential data exfiltration incidents. Behavior-based NIDPSs, as discussed in Module 7, are capable of benchmarking "normal" traffic and then alerting administrators when traffic is abnormal.

The same information may be obtained from the organization's firewall and gateway devices. Unless data is physically stolen from the organization—as in someone downloading data to an external USB drive and walking it out—then stolen data has to go through the organization's perimeter. Paying close attention to those chokepoints can help an organization detect the aftereffects of a successful attack on an internal system, as well as detect data theft by an employee. Similarly, network administrators using network performance dashboards may detect large amounts of traffic coming from one or a few internal systems that they don't expect to be involved in such traffic, especially when the destination field of the packets is outside the network. Detecting high traffic during off-peak hours is another way to isolate potential data exfiltration incidents.

Internal attacks on systems by employees become more difficult to detect. Users with authorized accounts may accidentally or intentionally cause the loss of data or damage to the system or data. While *privilege escalation* can be detected by review of system logs and periodic review of user privileges, loss due to normal use is much more difficult to detect. Only through effective backup and recovery methods can the organization reverse the damage from these incidents.

Compromised Software

Who watches the watchers? (*Quis custodiet ipsos custodes?*) If the systems that monitor the network, servers, or other components are compromised, then the organization's incident detection is compromised. This problem can be prevented through verification. Organizations can have a separate HIDPS sensor or agent monitor the HIDPS itself. If you suspect the detection systems have been compromised, you can quarantine them and examine the installation by comparing them to either the original installation files or to an insulated installation.

 The SANS Institute publishes GIAC Certification Papers on every aspect of information security. If you want to know more about current trends in detecting and suppressing data exfiltration, use a browser to search for "GIAC certificate papers on data exfiltration." By quickly scanning the abstracts of the papers you find with the search, you should be able to pick out a paper for study.

General Detection Strategies

While the previous section discussed detection strategies for specific systems, this section examines general detection strategies that provide insight into the operations of the organization's technology infrastructure and assist in detecting incidents, regardless of the target.

Watch the Network for Unexpected Behavior

Whether using manual intrusion detection or IDPSs, it is imperative to constantly monitor networks for signs of intrusion. The Carnegie Mellon University Software Engineering Institute's CERT Division (CMU/SEI CERT) recommends that this be accomplished in the following manner:

- Notify users that network monitoring is being done.
- Review and investigate notifications from network-specific alert mechanisms (such as e-mail, voice mail, or text messages).
- Review and investigate network error reports.
- Review network performance statistics and investigate anything that appears anomalous.
- Identify any unexpected, unusual, or suspicious network traffic and its possible implications.
- If you are reviewing network traffic on a system other than the one being monitored, ensure that the connection between them is secure.[20]

Watch Systems for Unexpected Behavior

Similarly, systems used to store, process, and transmit critical data should be reviewed if they display unusual or abnormal behavior. CMU/SEI CERT recommends that this review include the following:

- Notify users that process and user activities are being monitored.
- Review and investigate notifications from system-specific alert mechanisms (such as e-mail, voice mail, or text messages).
- Review and investigate system error reports.
- Review system performance statistics and investigate anything that appears anomalous.
- Continuously monitor process activity (to the extent that you can).
- Identify any unexpected, unusual, or suspicious process behavior and its possible implications.
- Identify any unexpected, unusual, or suspicious user behavior and its possible implications.
- Identify other unexpected, unusual, or suspicious behavior and its possible implications.
- Periodically execute network mapping and scanning tools to understand what intruders who use such tools can learn about your networks and systems.
- Periodically execute vulnerability scanning tools on all systems to check for the presence of known vulnerabilities.
- If you are reviewing system activities on a host other than the one being monitored, ensure that the connection between them is secure.[21]

Watch Files and Directories for Unexpected Changes

The task of monitoring file systems for unauthorized change is best performed by using an HIDPS. This can be augmented by having a reporting process in place to allow users to alert the monitoring team of suspicious file activity. If a user claims unusual file activity, whether it be modification in size, content, or date, this may be an indicator of an incident. An HIDPS may be configured to perform a scheduled scan of systems to compare the current versions of files against an archive equivalent or hash value. Hash values are extremely useful in performing file verification. However, problems with false positives can occur if the file is routinely used by a user or the system. Choosing what files to monitor is as critical as the actual monitoring.

Investigate Unauthorized Hardware Attached to Your Organization's Network

Existing software is capable of scanning a network and identifying the identity, configuration, and location of any device attached to the network. Unless the networking team, in cooperation with the information security team and the CSIRT, periodically checks the network both electronically and visually, an unauthorized piece of equipment may tap into the system and be redirecting or recording traffic without authorization. Modem sweeps are another method of detecting unauthorized equipment. Visual inspections, while tedious, are the best way to detect an unknown device tapped into the network, such as a wireless access port rebroadcasting to an external receiver.

Inspect Physical Resources for Signs of Unauthorized Access

"Physical access trumps electronic security." This saying, which is all too true, indicates that if an intruder can physically access a device, then no electronic protection can deter the loss of information, save that of a burglar alarm. Periodically, perhaps in conjunction with the networking inspection, the information security team should examine all doors, windows, locks, ceilings, and gates that physically protect the information resources contained within. Signs of tampering, attempted or successful breaching, or other malfeasance should be documented and reported to the appropriate authorities.

An example of physical access trumping logical security comes from a 2017 incident in which a thief broke into a car of a Coplin Health Systems employee and stole a laptop with over 43,000 patients' personal information.[22] This kind of loss is not a new circumstance, as illustrated in an event from 2012 when the associate deputy administrator of NASA had his laptop stolen from his locked car; the laptop contained the personal information of over 10,000 employees and contractors.[23] Those who have worked with computers know that if a person has access to the computer systems, can remove and restore power, and can control the booting devices (USB, hard disk, or DVD/CD media drives), he or she can circumvent all logical security controls added to the system.

Review Reports about Suspicious and Unexpected Behavior

Users can be the front line in intrusion detection. By promptly reviewing all reports to the help desk, anonymous reporting hotlines, and e-mail boxes, the CSIRT and information security teams can detect a problem early enough to prevent it from spreading.

Take Appropriate Actions

Responding to an intrusion appropriately, as discussed in other modules, is absolutely essential. How the organization responds to an intrusion can make or break the end result. An efficient and effective strategy significantly increases the odds that the organization will contain and resolve the incident successfully, while delays in response or ineffective strategies will greatly reduce those odds. Simply having an effective plan is not enough. The plan must be trained, rehearsed, and tested before the organization can have confidence in the process.

Manage Logging and Other Data Collection Mechanisms

When one of the data sources used for incident detection and decision-making is coming from individual or aggregated log files, the management of those sources becomes more critical. The aggregated log files from network devices, servers, and even critical workstations can contain both indicators and documentation of intrusion events. To be effective, logs must first be enabled. (Some systems are enabled by default; others must specifically be activated.) Then, protect your logs through the hardening of servers that create and store logs. Finally, manage your logs. Managing logs involves the following:

- *Be prepared to handle the amount of data generated by logging*—Some systems may produce multiple gigabytes of data that must be stored or otherwise managed.
- *Rotate logs on a schedule*—As indicated, some systems overwrite older log entries with newer entries to comply with the space limitations of the system. Ensure that the rotation of log entries is acceptable, rather than accepting system defaults.
- *Archive logs*—Log systems can copy logs periodically to remote storage locations. There is a debate among security administrators as to how long log files should be maintained. Some argue that log files may be subpoenaed during legal proceedings and thus should be routinely destroyed to prevent unwanted disclosure during this process. Others argue that the information to be gained from analyzing legacy and archival logs outweighs the risk. Still others take the middle ground and aggregate the log information, then destroy the individual entries. Regardless of the method employed, some plan must be in place to handle these files or risk loss.
- *Encrypt logs*—If the organization does decide to archive logs, the logs should be encrypted in storage. Should the log file system be compromised, this encryption prevents unwanted disclosure.
- *Dispose of logs*—Once log files have outlived their usefulness, they should be routinely and securely disposed of.[24]

Challenges in Intrusion Detection

It should now be obvious that the detection of intrusions can be a tedious and technically demanding process. Only those with advanced technical skills within a certain set of hardware and software can manually detect signs of an intrusion through reviews of logs, system performance, user feedback, and system processes and tasks. This underscores the value of two key facets of incident detection: (1) effective use of technology to assist in detection, and (2) the necessity of cooperation between incident response and information security professionals and the entire information technology department. The former is discussed in sufficient detail in the sections on IDPSs and IPSs in Module 7. With regard to the latter, the IT staff is best prepared to understand the day-to-day operations of the hardware, software, and networking components that support organizational operations on an ongoing basis. They can then work with the CSIRT and information security teams to identify anomalies in system performance and administration. This should underscore the necessity to integrate IT systems and network administrators as part of CSIRT operations, if not CSIRT team building.

Collection of Data to Aid in Detecting Incidents

The routine collection and analysis of data is required to assist in the detection and declaration of incidents. Even if an incident is not detected in real time, the data collected by automatic recording systems can assist the teams in better understanding what are normal and routine operations for the systems that process, transmit, and store information for the organization. Good security practices indicate the need to know the current environment—from networks and operating systems to details of how applications solve business problems, and continuing to the policy and procedural environment of the organization. This understanding of the organization's norms can assist in the detection of the abnormal. Some of the information that is beneficial for these teams to collect is presented in Table 6-3.

Table 6-3   Data Categories and Types of Data to Collect[25]

Data Category	Types of Data to Collect
Network performance	• Total traffic load in and out over time (packet, byte, and connection counts) and by event (such as new product or service release) • Traffic load (percentage of packets, bytes, connections) in and out over time, sorted by protocol, source address, destination address, other packet header data • Error counts on all network interfaces
Other network data	• Service initiation requests • Name of the user/host requesting the service • Network traffic (packet headers) • Successful connections and connection attempts (protocol, port, source, destination, time) • Connection duration • Connection flow (sequence of packets from initiation to termination) • States associated with network interfaces (up, down) • Network sockets currently open • Whether or not network interface card is in promiscuous mode • Network probes and scans • Results of administrator probes
System performance	• Total resource use over time (CPU, memory [used, free], disk [used, free]) • Status and errors reported by systems and hardware devices • Changes in system status, including shutdowns and restarts • File system status (where mounted, free space by partition, open files, biggest file) over time and at specific times • File system warnings (low free space, too many open files, file exceeding allocated size) • Disk counters (input/output, queue lengths) over time and at specific times • Hardware availability (modems, network interface cards, memory)
Other system data	• Actions requiring special privileges • Successful and failed logins • Modem activities • Presence of new services and devices • Configuration of resources and devices

(continues)

Table 6-3   Data Categories and Types of Data to Collect[25] (*Continued*)

Data Category	Types of Data to Collect
Process performance	• Amount of resources used (CPU, memory, disk, time) by specific processes over time; top resource-consuming processes • System and user processes and services executing at any given time
Other process data	• User executing the process • Process start-up time, arguments, filenames • Process exit status, time, duration, resources consumed • The means by which each process is normally initiated (administrator, other users, other programs or processes), with what authorization and privileges • Devices used by specific processes • Files currently open by specific processes
Files and directories	• List of files, directories, attributes • Cryptographic checksums for all files and directories • Accesses (open, create, modify, execute, delete), time, date • Changes to sizes, contents, protections, types, locations • Changes to access control lists on system tools • Additions and deletions of files and directories • Results of virus scanners
Users	• Login/logout information (location, time): successful attempts, failed attempts, attempted logins to privileged accounts • Login/logout information on remote access servers that appears in modem logs • Changes in user identity • Changes in authentication status, such as enabling privileges • Failed attempts to access restricted information (such as password files) • Keystroke monitoring logs • Violations of user quotas

Applications	• Application- and service-specific information such as network traffic (packet content), mail logs, FTP logs, Web server logs, modem logs, firewall logs, SNMP logs, DNS logs, intrusion detection and prevention system logs, database management system logs
	• Service-specific information could be:
	  ○ For FTP requests: Files transferred and connection statistics
	  ○ For Web requests: Pages accessed, credentials of the requestor, connection statistics, user requests over time, which pages are most requested, and who is requesting them
	  ○ For mail requests: Sender, receiver, size, and tracing information; for a mail server, number of messages over time, number of queued messages
	  ○ For DNS requests: Questions, answers, and zone transfers
	  ○ For a file system server: File transfers over time
	  ○ For a database server: Transactions over time

Log files	• Results of scanning, filtering, and reducing log file contents • Checks for log file consistency (increasing file size over time, use of consecutive, increasing time stamps with no gaps)
Vulnerabilities	• Results of vulnerability scanners (presence of known vulnerabilities) • Vulnerability patch logging

Closing Scenario

Jovanni is the lead threat analyst at HAL. His business card lists his title as "Manager, Threat Assessment Unit." He likes to think of himself as a threat hunter.

It had been 17 hours since the e-mail arrived from Emily. At first it was an interesting anomaly, an *event*, that piqued his interest just enough to keep looking into it.

But, as he gained more information and he considered the event an *incident candidate*, he called on others. At first, yesterday afternoon, his team identified the details from the list of customers Emily had sent. Then, as they saw patterns in the victims of the breach, they broadened the hunt. They moved on to looking at the tactics, techniques, and procedures the attackers had been using. When the scope and scale began to be apparent, it escalated to an *incident*.

In the past few hours, just as the day shift started up again, Jovanni had handed the evolving response over to an incident manager and the company began to react to the breach. The incident manager began calling up the alert roster even before she knew all the details of the incident.

Jovanni pushed himself back from his desk after making a final tweak to his presentation. He had already changed into his "crisis suit" that he kept in a garment bag in his office closet. As he finished knotting his tie, he rubbed his chin and sighed. "No time for a shave," he muttered.

He was about to inform the company's senior executives of a major breach that his team had discovered and that the company was reacting to with its IR process.

It seems that one of HAL's suppliers had been used by a hacker collective to penetrate and maintain a presence inside of HAL's system for the past 82 days. So far the team had identified over 45,000 customer and vendor accounts that were compromised by this advanced persistent threat (APT).

Jovanni headed for the elevator.

Discussion Questions

1. Did Emily respond properly by referring the event to Jovanni? Should she have informed someone else? If so, who might that have been?
2. What other resources do you think Jovanni reached out to as they began this investigation? The Accounting department? The company's credit card processor? Others?
3. Which company departments do you think would be activated by the incident response team in this case? Make a list of these departments and what they might be focused on.

Ethical Decision Making

1. Suppose Jovanni reached the conclusion that an insider at HAL was at least partly responsible for the APT discovered in this incident. To make it more complicated, he suspected that his longtime friend Jason might be the culprit. Would it be ethical for Jovanni to directly ask Jason about this possibility? Why or why not?
2. One of Jovanni's tasks that he enjoys is data collection and surveillance of the "black side" of the Internet. He has memberships in various groups in the hacker community and usually lurks, but occasionally he participates in online discussions with that community. He thinks he might know one of the perpetrators of this breach from those interactions. Do you think Jovanni should share his suspicion with the law enforcement community?

MODULE SUMMARY

- Among the earliest challenges that incident response planners face is determining how an organization classifies events as they occur. In incident response, an event is an outcome or occurrence that has the potential to disrupt the normal operations of a system. Although any threat category could instigate an incident, NIST SP 800-61, Rev. 1 provides a five-category incident classification scheme for network-based incidents: denial of service, malicious code, unauthorized access, inappropriate usage, and multiple components.
- The cyber kill chain is a series of steps that follow stages of a cyberattack from the early reconnaissance stages to the exfiltration of data; it helps you understand, identify, and combat many cyberattack strategies and advanced persistent threats.
- There are three broad categories of incident indicators: possible, probable, and definite. There are four types of possible incident candidates: the presence of unfamiliar files, the presence or execution of unknown programs or processes, unusual consumption of computing resources, and unusual system crashes. There are four types of probable incident candidates: activities at unexpected times, the presence of unexpected new accounts, reported attacks, and notification from an IDPS. There are five types of definite incident candidates: use of dormant accounts, changes to logs, the presence of hacker tools, notifications by partner or peer, and notification by hacker. Another way to describe the definite indicators is by general types of events: loss of availability, loss of integrity, loss of confidentiality, violation of policy, and violation of law.
- IR plan designers must create a process to collect and evaluate incident candidates to determine whether they are actual incidents (or circumstances likely to become incidents) or nonevents, also called false positive incident candidates. Noise or false positives, which may have to be tuned from the collection system, result from several general causes, including placement, policy, and lack of awareness.
- When one of the data sources used for incident decision-making is coming from individual or aggregated log files, the management of those sources becomes more critical. The aggregated log files from network devices, servers, and even critical workstations can contain both indicators and documentation of intrusion events. To be effective, logs must first be enabled. Then, you protect the logs by hardening the servers that create and store logs. Finally, you manage the logs.

Review Questions

1. From the perspective of incident response, what is an event?
2. What is an incident candidate?
3. What is the cyber kill chain?
4. In the TCP/IP protocol, what is a port?
5. What are the three broad categories of incident indicators?
6. What are the four categories of events that are considered *possible* indicators of actual incidents?
7. What are the four types of events that are considered *probable* indicators of actual incidents?
8. What are the five types of events that are considered *definite* indicators of actual incidents?
9. The occurrences of what general types of events indicate that an actual incident is occurring?
10. What is a false positive?
11. What is noise? Is noise different from a false positive event?
12. What are the general causes of noise?
13. What is tuning?
14. What is a false negative?
15. What is a computer process?
16. What is a computer service?
17. What is the most effective way to stop phishing attacks?
18. What is business e-mail compromise (BEC)?
19. What is data exfiltration?
20. What general approach is recommended to distinguish real incidents from false positive events?
21. What activities go into a complete log management approach?

Real-World Exercises

Exercise 6-1

Do a Web search for "cyber kill chain in breach responses." Look for an article that points out weaknesses in using the cyber kill chain. What are the one or two deficiencies of the cyber kill chain that are pointed out in the article?

Exercise 6-2

Do a Web search on "honeypots" and "honeynets." Search for "honeypot versus honeynet." How are they different? List three reasons why making your own honeypot or honeynet might be a bad idea.

Exercise 6-3

Using Table 6-2, do a Web search on a few of the port numbers known to be used by hacker programs, such as Sub-7, Midnight Commander, and WinCrash. What significant information did you find in your search? Why should the information security manager be concerned about these hacker programs? What can he or she do to protect against them?

Exercise 6-4

Using the list of possible, probable, and definite indicators of an incident, draft a recommendation to assist a typical end user in identifying these indicators. Alternatively, using a graphics package such as PowerPoint, create a poster to make the user aware of the key indicators.

Hands-On Projects

The hands-on project for this module can be accessed in the Practice It folder in MindTap or through your instructor's LMS. The virtual labs provided with this resource can help you develop practical skills that will be of value as you progress through the course.

References

1. Scarfone, Karen, Tim Grance, and Kelly Masone. SP 800-61, Revision 1, "Computer Security Incident Handling Guide." National Institute of Standards and Technology. March 2008. Accessed 2/11/2020 at *https://nvlpubs.nist.gov/nistpubs/Legacy/SP/nistspecialpublication800-61r1.pdf*.
2. Lockheed Martin. "The Cyber Kill Chain®." Accessed 3/7/2020 at *www.lockheedmartin.com/en-us/capabilities/cyber/cyber-kill-chain.html*.
3. Ibid.

4. IANA. "Service Name and Transport Protocol Port Number Registry." Internet Assigned Numbers Authority. Accessed 2/24/2020 at *www.iana.org/assignments/service-names-port-numbers/service-names-port-numbers.xhtml*.

5. Ibid.

6. "Hacker Ports." Relevant Technologies. Accessed 03/07/2020 at *www.relevanttechnologies.com/resources_4.asp*.

7. Spitzner, Lance. "Applying Security Awareness to the Cyber Kill Chain." SANS.org. Accessed 3/7/2020 at *www.sans.org/security-awareness-training/blog/applying-security-awareness-cyber-kill-chain*.

8. Chichonski, Paul, Tom Millar, Tim Grance, and Karen Scarfone. SP 800-61, Revision 2, "Computer Security Incident Handling Guide." National Institute of Standards and Technology. January 2012. Accessed 2/11/2020 at *https://csrc.nist.gov/publications/detail/sp/800-61/rev-2/final*.

9. Pipkin, Donald L. *Information Security: Protecting the Global Enterprise*. Upper Saddle River, NJ: Prentice Hall PTR, 2000.

10. Ibid.

11. Ibid.

12. Ibid.

13. Ktflash. "Malware Detection." Accessed 2/11/2020 at *https://ktflash.gitbooks.io/ceh_v9/65_malware_detection.html*.

14. James, M. "5 Ways to Spot a Phishing Email." StaySafeOnline. Accessed 3/1/2020 at *https://staysafeonline.org/blog/5-ways-spot-phishing-emails/*.

15. "macOS Security." Accessed 2/26/2020 at *www.apple.com/macos/security/*.

16. "Rate of Ransomware Attacks." PhoenixNAP Global IT Services. Accessed 2/29/2020 at *https://phoenixnap.com/blog/ransomware-statistics-facts*.

17. Delaney, Darragh. "5 Methods for Detecting Ransomware Activity." Netfort. 2016. Accessed 2/29/2020 at *www.netfort.com/blog/methods-for-detecting-ransomware-activity*.

18. "Ransomware Overview: names, extensions, patterns, decryptors list." Accessed 2/29/2020 at *www.reddit.com/r/netsec/comments/4ijpu8/ransomware_overview_names_extensions_patterns/*.

19. Weisman, Robert. "Harvard rejects 119 accused of hacking." Boston.com. 2005. Accessed 3/1/2020 at *http://archive.boston.com/business/articles/2005/03/08/harvard_rejects_119_accused_of_hacking_1110274403/*.

20. "Monitor and Inspect Network Activities for Unexpected Behavior." CERT Security Improvement Modules. Accessed 5/29/2005 at *www.cert.org/security-improvement/practices/p094.html*.

21. Ibid.

22. Davis, Jessica. "Data of 43,000 patients breached after theft of unencrypted laptop." Accessed 2/24/2020 at *www.healthcareitnews.com/news/data-43000-patients-breached-after-theft-unencrypted-laptop*.

23. Vijayan, Jaikumar. "NASA breach update: Stolen laptop had data on 10,000 users." Accessed 2/24/2020 at *www.computerworld.com/article/2493084/nasa-breach-update--stolen-laptop-had-data-on-10-000-users.html*.

24. "Managing Logging and Other Data Collection Mechanisms." CERT Security Improvement Modules. Accessed 5/29/2005 at *www.cert.org/security-improvement/practices/p092.html*.

25. Allen, Julia, and Ed Stoner. "Detecting Signs of Intrusion." CERT Security Improvement Modules. Accessed 2/24/2020 at *https://resources.sei.cmu.edu/library/asset-view.cfm?assetid=12943*.

INCIDENT RESPONSE: DETECTION SYSTEMS

Upon completion of this material, you should be able to:

1. Explain the components of an intrusion detection and prevention system

2. Discuss the optimal locations for intrusion detection and prevention system components

3. Describe the processes used in making decisions about incident detection

4. Recognize the functions and capabilities of security information and event management systems and how organizations use them

A little fire is quickly trodden out; which, being suffered, rivers cannot quench.

— William Shakespeare, *King Henry VI. Part III. Act IV. Sc. 8*

Opening Scenario

JJ had become quite bored with the discussion that was taking place in the conference room and had let his mind wander as he stared out the window.

Paul frowned at him while repeating the question JJ had not heard. "Which sensor placement strategy do you think will get us the best network performance? For the IDPS—you know—the project we're working on in this meeting?"

"Well," said JJ, "truth be told, I wonder if the network approach is the right way to go. I think we should move toward a host-based model and limit the network intrusion system to a few critical subnetworks."

Paul thought about it for a second. "Good point," he said, then paused again before saying, "Funny, I thought you were daydreaming, but that's an interesting observation. I would like you to work up a new rough design based on a host-centric approach. We can review it tomorrow when we continue this meeting."

"OK, Paul," said JJ.

Later that day, JJ came into Paul's office. "I've got a couple of ideas that I'd like your opinion on."

"Shoot," said Paul.

"I just attended a presentation where a CIO discussed ways to cut information security spending," JJ said. "There were some, well, radical ideas that paid off for that company."

"I'm all ears," Paul replied. The idea of going into this process with a cost-effective strategy had his undivided attention.

"Well, this CIO indicated that the firm had invested quite a large amount of money in proprietary security technologies—everything from firewalls to scanners to intrusion detectors. They then discovered that the maintenance and upgrade packages were costing more than the initial equipment purchase had."

"I know that feeling," said Paul.

"Well, they discovered that there is a lot of open source software out there; you know, the Linux and UNIX stuff," JJ continued.

"Uh, oh," Paul said, stopping JJ in his tracks. "I see a potential problem there. We don't have any UNIX or Linux people on staff."

"That was the point," JJ said, leaning over and tapping Paul's desk for emphasis. "With the money that could be saved from ending the service contracts, they were able to hire three good systems people and still save about half of the $1 million budget."

"And if I don't have a million-dollar budget?"

"Then we just hire one or two people, or hire one, and send one of our current network admins off to training. At the top of the list is OSSEC for host-based IDPS, and Snort for network-based IDPS. I found several local places that offer open source software training for both right here in town."

"I think you're on to something," Paul said, obviously intrigued by JJ's suggestion. "Tell you what, I want you to write a business case by reviewing the current expenditures, add the projected additions from the meeting earlier today, and then balance those against the cost of a plan for an open source approach, including a new hire and training for one to two of our staff. Be brutally honest; we don't want to chase vaporware on this one. We need solid, tested stuff and the skills to support it."

"Can do, Paul." JJ grinned. He liked it when Paul got behind his ideas.

"And have it to me by the end of business tomorrow," Paul added.

The grin disappeared from JJ's face.

INTRODUCTION TO INTRUSION DETECTION AND PREVENTION SYSTEMS

intrusion detection and prevention system (IDPS)

The general term for a collection of hardware and software that determines whether activity is present that is contrary to organization policy and represents an intrusion. A system with the capability both to detect and modify its configuration and environment to prevent intrusions. An IDPS encompasses the functions of both intrusion detection systems and intrusion prevention technology.

intrusion

An adverse event in which an attacker attempts to gain entry into an information system or disrupt its normal operations, almost always with the intent to do harm.

intrusion detection system (IDS)

A hardware and software system capable of automatically detecting an intrusion into an organization's networks or host systems and notifying a designated authority.

In Module 6, we discussed the detection of a potential incident, specifically intrusions. While the most powerful tool in the security administrator's arsenal is still the vigilance of the people in the organization, there is a set of technologies that can greatly assist in the early detection and even response to an intrusion. The **intrusion detection and prevention system (IDPS)** is a computer data burglar alarm. It is designed to be placed in a network or on a computer server to determine whether the organization's technology is being used in ways that are out of compliance with the organization's policy or whether an attack is in progress. The primary purpose of this technology is to detect an **intrusion**. Whether or not the intrusion is performed with the intent to steal or do harm, it is an unauthorized activity and thus remains outside the intended use of the system or network. Even when such attacks are automated or self-propagating, as in the case of viruses and distributed denial-of-service attacks, they are almost always instigated by an individual whose purpose is to harm the organization. In a later section of this module, we will explore how an IDPS is a critical element of a security information and event management system.

To understand the technologies associated with IDPSs, you must first understand their evolution. **Intrusion detection systems (IDSs)** became commercially available in the late 1990s. An IDS works like a burglar alarm in that it detects a violation (some system activity analogous to an opened or broken window) and activates an alarm. This alarm can be audible and/or visual, producing noise and/or lights, or it can be silent, providing an e-mail message or text alert. With almost all IDSs, systems administrators can choose the configuration of the various alerts and the alarm levels associated with each type of alert. Many IDSs enable administrators to configure the systems to notify them directly of trouble via e-mail or pagers. The systems can also be configured—again, like a burglar alarm—to notify an external security service organization of a break-in. The configurations that enable IDSs to provide customized levels of detection and response are quite complex. An extension of IDS technology is the **intrusion prevention system (IPS)**, which can detect an intrusion and prevent it from successfully attacking the organization by means of an active response. Because the two systems coexist inside the IPS, the combined term *intrusion detection and prevention system (IDPS)* is used to describe current IPS technologies.

intrusion prevention system (IPS)

See *intrusion detection and prevention system (IDPS).*

A valuable source of information about IDPSs is the NIST publication SP 800-94, Rev. 1, "Guide to Intrusion Detection and Prevention Systems." This guide distinguishes between an IPS and IDS as follows:

> *IPS technologies are differentiated from IDS technologies by one characteristic: IPS technologies can respond to a detected threat by attempting to prevent it from succeeding. They use several response techniques, which can be divided into the following groups:*
>
> - *The IPS stops the attack itself. Examples of how this could be done are as follows:*
>   - *Terminate the network connection or user session that is being used for the attack*
>   - *Block access to the target (or possibly other likely targets) from the offending user account, IP address, or other attacker attribute*
>   - *Block all access to the targeted host, service, application, or other resource*
> - *The IPS changes the security environment. The IPS could change the configuration of other security controls to disrupt an attack. Common examples are reconfiguring a network device (for example, firewall, router, switch) to block access from the attacker or to the target, and altering a host-based firewall on a target to block incoming attacks. Some IPSs can even cause patches to be applied to a host if the IPS detects that the host has vulnerabilities.*
> - *The IPS changes the attack's content. Some IPS technologies can remove or replace malicious portions of an attack to make it benign. A simple example is an IPS removing an infected file attachment from an e-mail and then permitting the cleaned e-mail to reach its recipient. A more complex example is an IPS that acts as a proxy and normalizes incoming requests, which means that the proxy repackages the payloads of the requests, discarding header information. This might cause certain attacks to be discarded as part of the normalization process.*[1]

 We recommend that you access and then study SP 800-94, Rev. 1. It was prepared by Karen Scarfone and Peter Mell and is available through NIST's Computer Security Resource Center at *https://csrc.nist.gov/CSRC/media/Publications/sp/800-94/rev-1/draft/documents/draft_sp800-94-rev1.pdf*.

IDPS Terminology

To understand how an IDPS works, it is important to first become familiar with some terminology that is unique to the field of IDPSs. Here is a list of common IDPS terms and definitions:

- *Alarm or alert*—An indication that a system has just been attacked or is under attack. IDPSs create alerts or alarms to notify administrators that an attack is or was occurring and may have been successful. Alerts and alarms may take the form of audible signals, e-mail messages, pager notifications, pop-up windows, or log entries written without taking any action.
- *Alarm clustering*—A process of grouping almost identical alarms that occur nearly at the same time into a single higher-level alarm. This consolidation reduces the number of alarms, which reduces administrative overhead and identifies a relationship among multiple alarms. Clustering may be based on combinations of frequency, similarity in attack signature, similarity in attack target, or other criteria that are defined by system administrators.
- *Alarm compaction*—A form of alarm clustering that is based on frequency, similarity in attack signature, similarity in attack target, or other similarities. Like the previous form of alarm clustering, alarm compaction reduces the total number of alarms generated, reducing the administrative overhead. Alarm compaction can also indicate if a relationship exists between the individual alarm elements when they have specific similar attributes.

- *Alarm filtering*—The process of classifying the attack alerts that an IDPS detects in order to distinguish or sort false positives from actual attacks more efficiently. After an IDPS has been installed and configured, the administrator can set up alarm filtering by first running the system for a while to track what types of false positives it generates and then by adjusting the classification of certain alarms. For example, the administrator may set the IDPS to discard certain alarms that he or she knows are produced by false attack stimuli or normal network operations. Alarm filters are similar to packet filters in that they can filter items by their source or destination IP addresses, but they have the additional capability of filtering by operating systems, confidence values, alarm type, or alarm severity.

- *Confidence value* (or simply *confidence*)—A value associated with an IDPS's ability to detect and identify an attack correctly. The confidence value an organization places in the IDPS is based on experience and past performance measurements. The confidence value, a type of "fuzzy logic," provides an additional piece of information to assist the administrator in determining whether an attack alert is indicating that an actual attack is in progress or the IDPS is reacting to false attack stimuli and creating a false positive. For example, if a system deemed capable of reporting a denial-of-service attack with 90 percent confidence sends an alert, there is a high probability that an actual attack is occurring.

- *Evasion*—The process by which an attacker changes the format of the network packets and/or timing of their activities to avoid being detected by the IDPS.

- *False attack stimulus*—An event that triggers alarms and causes a false positive when no actual attacks are in progress. Testing scenarios that evaluate the configuration of IDPSs may use false attack stimuli to determine if the IDPSs can distinguish between these stimuli and real attacks.

- *False negative*—The failure of a technical control (in this case an IDPS system) to react to an actual attack event. Of all failures, this is the most grievous, as the very purpose of an IDPS is to detect attacks.

- *False positive*—An alarm or alert that indicates that an attack is in progress or that an attack has successfully occurred when in fact there is no such attack. A false positive alert can sometimes be produced when an IDPS mistakes normal system operations or activity for an attack. False positives tend to make users insensitive to alarms, which in turn can make them less inclined and slower to react when an actual intrusion occurs.

- *Filtering*—The process of reducing IDPS events in order to feel more confidence in the alerts received. For example, the administrator may set the IDPS to discard alarms produced by false positives or normal network operations. Event filters are similar to packet filters in that they can filter items by their source or destination IP addresses, but they can also filter by operating systems, confidence values, alarm type, or alarm severity.

- *Noise*—The ongoing activity from alarm events that are accurate and noteworthy but not necessarily as significant as potentially successful attacks. Unsuccessful attacks are the most common source of noise in IDPSs, and some of these may not even be attacks at all—just employees or other users of the local network experimenting with scanning and enumeration tools without any intent to do harm. The main issue with noise is that most of the intrusion events detected are not malicious and have no significant chance of causing a loss.

- *Site policy*—The rules and configuration guidelines governing the implementation and operation of IDPSs within the organization.

- *Site policy awareness*—An IDPS's ability to dynamically modify its site policies in reaction or response to environmental activity. A "smart IDPS" can adapt its reaction activities based on both guidance learned over time from the administrator as well as circumstances present in the local environment. Using a device of this nature, the IDPS administrator acquires logs of events that fit a specific profile instead of being alerted for minor changes, such as when a file is changed or a user login fails. A smart IDPS also knows it does not need to alert the administrator when an attack uses a known and documented exploit against systems that the IDPS knows to be patched against that specific kind of attack. When the IDPS can accept multiple response profiles based on changing attack scenarios and environmental values, it makes the IDPS that much more useful.

- *True attack stimulus*—An event that triggers alarms and causes an IDPS to react as if a real attack were in progress. The attack may be actual when an attacker is at work on a system compromise attempt, or it may be a drill—one of many ongoing tests of a network segment by security personnel using real hacker tools.

- *Tuning*—The process of adjusting an IDPS to maximize its efficiency in detecting true positives while minimizing both false positives and false negatives. This process may include grouping almost identical alarms that happen at close to the same time into a single higher-level alarm. This consolidation reduces the number of alarms generated, thereby reducing administrative overhead, and identifies a relationship among multiple alarms. This type of clustering may be based on combinations of frequency, similarity in attack signature, similarity in attack target, or other criteria that are defined by the system administrators.

Why Use an IDPS?

According to NIST's SP 800-94, Rev. 1, there are several uses for an IDPS:

- *IDPSs are primarily focused on identifying possible incidents.* First and foremost, the IDPS serves to detect a compromised system or a vulnerability exploited by an attacker. The IDPS then notifies its administrators, who notify the CSIRT, who in turn activate the IR plan. The quick and effective notification of these systems, and even direct intervention on the part of the IDPS, can allow the organization to minimize any potential damage to systems or loss of information.
- *Many IDPSs can also be configured to recognize violations of security policies.* Similar to firewalls, some IDPSs can be configured to allow them to detect violations of organizational policies, including unauthorized data modification, duplication, or destruction. This could be useful in preventing or detecting data exfiltration, for example.
- *Many IDPSs can also identify reconnaissance activity, which may indicate that an attack is imminent.* Just as an antivirus program is able to detect a potential virus by matching its signature to a database, some IDPSs can similarly monitor network traffic or systems activities looking for use of a scanning tool or unauthorized data manipulation. This monitoring could look for an attacker performing fingerprinting, for example, or attempting to escalate privilege on a server.[2]

As you can see here, the purpose of an IDPS is to detect and respond to an ongoing intrusion. It identifies unusual activity on the network or a system, depending on the type of IDPS deployed, and then performs its expected response—notification or intervention. Due to the sheer quantity of malicious traffic on the Internet, however, it is recommended that IDPSs generally be deployed inside the organization, on protected networks.

NIST also indicates several secondary uses of an IDPS as valuable in the following cases:

- *Identifying security policy problems*—An IDPS can provide some degree of quality control for security policy implementation, such as duplicating firewall rulesets and alerting when it sees network traffic that should have been blocked by the firewall but was not because of a firewall configuration error.
- *Documenting the existing threat to an organization*—IDPSs log information about the threats that they detect. Understanding the frequency and characteristics of attacks against an organization's computing resources is helpful in identifying the appropriate security measures for protecting the resources. The information can also be used to educate management about the threats that the organization faces.
- *Deterring individuals from violating security policies*—If individuals are aware that their actions are being monitored by IDPS technologies for security policy violations, they may be less likely to commit such violations because of the risk of detection.[3]

One of the secondary uses of IDPSs is to serve as a straightforward deterrent measure. In other words, they increase the fear of detection and discovery among would-be attackers or internal system abusers. If internal users know and external users suspect that an organization has deployed an IDPS, they are less likely to snoop around on the organization's networks or systems, just as criminals are less likely to break into a house that has been clearly marked as having a burglar alarm. Some IDPS implementations display notices of blocked content or actions taken to increase visibility and create awareness.

Another reason for installing an IDPS is to cover the organization when its network fails to protect itself against known vulnerabilities or is unable to respond to a rapidly changing threat environment. The defense of taking "every reasonable precaution" is valid against frivolous lawsuits if the organization's systems are compromised in spite of their best efforts.

defense in depth

A strategic approach to information security in which the organization deploys multiple protection tools and technologies so that if one fails or is compromised, another will be presented between the attacker and the organization's assets. Defense in depth commonly involves multiple layers of policy, technology, and efforts in security education, training, and awareness programs.

Forces Working Against an IDPS

Many factors can delay or undermine an organization's ability to make its systems safe from attack and subsequent loss. For example, even though popular information security technologies such as scanning tools (discussed later in this module) allow security administrators to evaluate the readiness of their systems, they may still fail to detect or correct a known deficiency, or the administrators may perform the vulnerability detection process too infrequently. Even when a vulnerability is detected in a timely manner, it is not always quickly corrected. Because such corrective measures usually involve the administrator installing patches and upgrades, they are subject to delays caused by the administrator's workload and the organization's change management practices.

To further complicate the matter, services that are known to be vulnerable might be so essential to ongoing operations that they cannot be disabled or otherwise protected in the short term. When there is a known vulnerability or deficiency in the system, an IDPS can be particularly effective, given that it can be set up to detect attacks or attempts to exploit existing weaknesses. By guarding against these vulnerabilities, an IDPS can become an important part of the **defense in depth** strategy.

Another potential concern with an IDPS is the use of automated responses. Some IDPSs can be configured to respond automatically if an attack is sensed. Sometimes, these responses can include shutting down access to the outside network. Automated responses can have unintended consequences, however, and should be implemented with care. For example, if an attacker's goal is to cause a denial of service from a Web server, he or she may trip an IDPS alarm, knowing that the IDPS will block access to the port or IP address of that Web server. In effect, the attacker gets the IDPS to accomplish the attacker's objective.

Justifying the Cost

To justify the expenses associated with implementing security technology such as an IDPS (and other controls, such as firewalls), security professionals are frequently required to prepare and defend a business case. Because deploying these technologies is often very expensive, almost all organizations require that proponents document the threat from which the organization must be protected. The most frequent method used is to collect data on the attacks that are currently occurring in the organization and other similar organizations. Although such data can be found in published reports or journal articles, firsthand measurements and analysis of the organization's own local network data are likely to be more persuasive. As it happens, one means of collecting such data is by using an IDPS. Thus, IDPSs are self-justifying systems—that is, they can serve to document the scope of the threat(s) an organization faces and thus produce data that can help administrators persuade management that additional expenditures in information security technologies (for example, IDPSs) are not only warranted but also critical for the ongoing protection of information assets. Measuring attack information with a freeware IDPS tool (such as Snort) may be a method to start this process.

NIST SP 800-94, Rev. 1 notes that when selecting an IDPS from a resource standpoint, it is important to understand two key items:

1. *The total cost of ownership of IDPSs well exceeds acquisition costs. Other costs may be associated with acquiring systems on which to run software components, deploying additional networks, providing sufficient storage for IDPS data, obtaining specialized assistance in installing and configuring the system, and training personnel.*

2. *Some IDPSs are designed under the assumption that personnel will be available to monitor and maintain them around the clock. If evaluators do not anticipate having such personnel available, they may wish to explore those systems that accommodate less than full-time attendance or are designed for unattended use, or they could consider the possibility of outsourcing the monitoring and possibly also the maintenance of the IDPS.*[4]

Budget decisions should not be made based only on the "sticker price" of the technology. As NIST suggests, most organizations evaluate acquisition options based on a total cost of ownership that includes initial costs, such as licensing, hardware, and configuration, and increases to operating costs for an initial period of use, such as 3 to 5 years.

The concepts of quality assurance and continuous improvement are well known to most senior managers. IDPSs are often implemented as a step along the way to improve network security by adding an extra layer between the firewall and the server layers of defense. This means that an IDPS can be justified using the concept of defense in depth—an IDPS can consistently pick up successful attacks that have compromised the outer layers of information security controls, such as a firewall, but have not yet reached the valuable servers residing on the organization's trusted networks. When continuous-improvement methodologies are applied to the results from the IDPS, emergent or residual flaws in the security and network architectures can be identified and repaired. Such efforts expedite the incident response process as well.

Finally, IDPSs can assist in post-attack review by helping a system administrator collect information on how the attack occurred, what the intruder accomplished, and which methods the attacker employed. This information can be used, as discussed in the preceding paragraph, to remedy any deficiency as well as trigger the improvement process to prepare the organization's network environment for future attacks. The IDPS may also provide forensic information that could be useful as evidence, should the attacker be caught and criminal or civil legal proceedings pursued. When handling forensic information, an organization should follow the legally mandated procedures for handling evidence. Foremost among these is that information collected should be stored in a location and manner that precludes its subsequent modification. Other legal requirements and plans the organization has for the use of the data may warrant additional storage and handling constraints. As such, it may be useful for an organization to consult with legal counsel when determining policy governing this situation.[5]

IDPSs operate as network-based, host-based, or application-based systems. A network-based IDPS is focused on protecting network information assets. A host-based version is focused on protecting the server or host's information assets. Figure 7-1 shows an example that monitors both network connection activity and current information states on host servers. The application-based model works on one or more host systems that support a single application and is oriented to defend that specific application from special forms of attack. Regardless of whether they operate at the network, host, or application level, all IDPSs use one of two detection methods: signature-based or statistical anomaly-based. Each of these approaches to intrusion detection is examined in detail in the following sections.

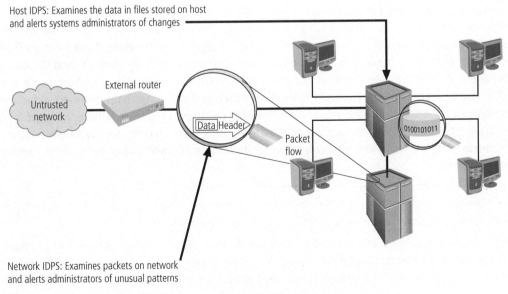

Figure 7-1   Intrusion detection and prevention systems

Technical Details: Rootkits

The following information draws on the work of McAfee, a security company that is a joint venture between Intel Corporation and TPG Capital:

rootkit

A software program or module of code that enables ongoing privileged access to a computer while actively hiding its presence from the system kernel as well as human administrators.

One piece of malware that is important to detect and remove is the **rootkit**. Rootkits are typically inserted into a system through a social engineering attack on an unsuspecting user or during an intrusion by an external attacker. Rootkits allow access and possibly privilege escalation by subverting standard operating system functionality, common utility programs, or other applications. The term *rootkit* is a concatenation of *root* (the traditional name of the privileged account on UNIX operating systems) and *kit*, which refers to the software components that implement the tool. The name or label of *rootkit* is often flagged by filtering software and e-mail scanners; some rootkit code is recognized by pattern filters to block file attachments. The use of rootkits has negative connotations because many people view them as a form of malware.[6]

The Windows Sysinternals Web site defines four categories of rootkits:

- *Persistent rootkits*—Those that become a part of the system bootstrap process and are loaded up every time the system boots. The program elements associated with this type of rootkit must be stored somewhere in the infested system, either as a separate file, within another system file, or as a system configuration store like the Windows registry.
- *Memory-based rootkits*—Those that do not install themselves to the infested computer's file system, have no persistence, and are not reinstalled when the system is rebooted.
- *User-mode rootkits*—Those that insert themselves between the user and the operating system kernel, intercepting the calls to the application programming interface of the operating systems and then reinterpreting the results of all commands to display content chosen by the rootkit. For example, when the user requests a list of all running processes to see if the rootkit is running, the indication of the rootkit's process will be deleted.[7]
- *Kernel-mode rootkits*—Those that insert themselves within the operating system itself and are then able to intercept and manipulate all aspects of the kernel. This allows manipulation of communications to and from the kernel as well as between elements of the kernel. It also means that the rootkit can change the content of kernel memory structures, such as process tables and memory assignments. For example, the program files needed to re-infest the system at boot-up are erased from the file system data structure and are then invisible to system users, systems administrators, and even the kernel itself.[8]

To install a rootkit, attackers must first gain access by attacking through a port, exploiting a vulnerability, or tricking the user into installing the rootkit for them, usually through an e-mail attachment or Web site link. After the attacker gains access, he or she installs or activates the rootkit and gains administrative privileges. Unfortunately, these tools are freely available on the Web for all types of platforms. These tools—Alureon, Cutwail, Datrahere (Zacinlo), Rustock, and Sinowal, to name a few of the Windows varieties[9]—are also able to collect and store user login and password information; some even contain keystroke loggers. The mere presence of these tools indicates that either the system was compromised sometime in the past or the systems administrator has been using tools and capabilities that carry some degree of inherent danger. It may be possible for one attacker to piggyback on another attacker's rootkit, so even using them on one's own system is potentially dangerous. (See *https://docs.microsoft.com/en-us/windows/security/threat-protection/intelligence/rootkits-malware* for more information on modern malware rootkits.)

How do you detect rootkits? There are utilities to find these attacker tools. For example, Microsoft Defender Offline can be launched from the Windows Security Center and will detect most current rootkits. As shown in Figure 7-2, the user just needs to access Scan Options under Windows Security and perform a scan.

Other rootkit-detecting utilities are available that provide free detection and removal of rootkits using simple graphical interfaces, and they work on most modern operating systems—for example, Sophos Virus Removal Tool (*www.sophos.com*). With the increase in attacks that install rootkits, most modern antivirus/antimalware utilities can detect rootkits as well.

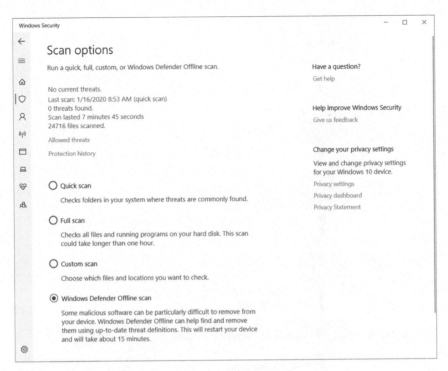

Figure 7-2   Windows 10 Windows Defender offline scan

Source: Microsoft Corporation.

IDPS TYPES

IDPSs are developed to monitor different aspects of the organization's information infrastructure. Depending on the type of IDPS, the placement of the sensor and detection devices or software components will vary dramatically. This in turn will have a significant effect on how the IDPS operates. There are three widely used types of IDPSs: network-based, host-based, and application-based IDPS.

Network-Based IDPSs

A **network-based IDPS (NIDPS)** monitors traffic on a segment of an organization's network and looks for indications of ongoing or successful attacks. When a situation occurs that the NIDPS is programmed to recognize as an attack, it responds. An NIDPS examines the packets transmitted through an organization's networks looking for patterns within network traffic that indicate an intrusion event is under way or about to begin. An example would be recognizing a number of network packets of a type that could indicate a DoS attack is under way. Or, an analyst could note the exchange of a series of packets in a pattern that could indicate a port scan is in progress. When someone is scanning network service ports, it is often a sign that they are looking for weaknesses or for ways to attack computing assets on the local network.

An NIDPS can therefore detect many more types of attacks than a host-based IDPS, but to do so requires a much more complex configuration and maintenance program. An NIDPS can be installed at a specific place in the network (such as on the inside of an edge router or firewall) so that it can watch the traffic going in and out of a particular network segment. Figure 7-3 shows an **inline sensor** deployment

network-based IDPS (NIDPS)

A type of IDPS that monitors network traffic for indications of attacks.

inline sensor

A software or hardware monitor that is placed in the flow of network traffic in order to review the traffic and report back to a management application.

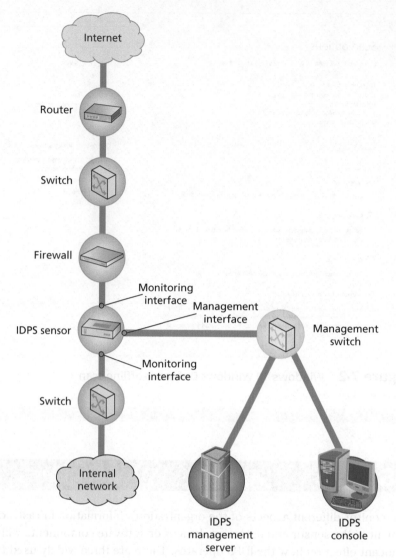

Figure 7-3 Example inline network-based IDPS sensor
architecture[10]

Source: NIST.

on the interior of a firewall, which mandates that all traffic must pass through the sensor and then report back to the NIDPS. This allows the response capability of the NIDPS to terminate detected malicious traffic passing through it, thus protecting all downstream assets.

The NIDPS can also be deployed to watch a specific grouping of host computers on a specific network segment, or it may be installed to monitor all traffic between the systems that make up an entire network. An NIDPS sensor that sits off to the side of a network segment, monitoring traffic without mandating that the traffic physically pass through the sensor, is known as a **passive sensor**. An example is shown in Figure 7-4.

When placed next to a switch or other key networking device, the NIDPS may use that device's monitoring port, also known as a *switched port analysis (SPAN) port* or **mirror port**. The monitoring port is a specially configured connection on a network device that is capable of viewing all the traffic that moves through the entire device. Hubs were used in the early 1990s before switches became the popular choice for connecting networks in a shared-collision domain. A hub receives traffic from one connection port and retransmits it to all the other ports. This

passive sensor

A software or hardware monitor that is connected to a network device, without physically being in the flow of network traffic, in order to review the traffic and report back to a management application.

mirror port

A specially configured connection on a network device that is capable of viewing all traffic that moves through the entire device. See also *switched port analysis (SPAN) port.*

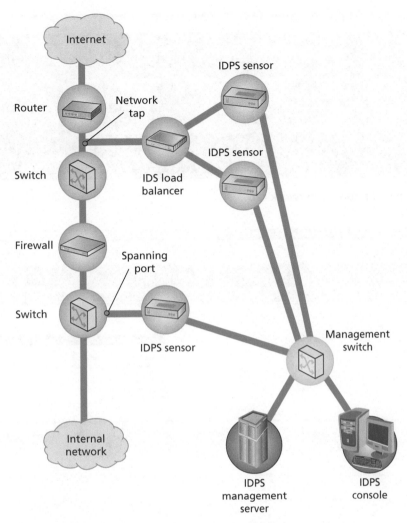

Figure 7-4   Example passive network-based IDPS sensor architecture[11]

Source: NIST.

configuration allowed any device connected to the hub to monitor all traffic passing through the hub, which represented a security risk. Today, hubs are almost nonexistent, and switches are used to connect networks. Switches create dedicated point-to-point links between their ports. This creates a higher level of transmission security and privacy and effectively eliminates the ability to eavesdrop on all traffic. Unfortunately, this ability to capture the traffic is necessary for the use of an IDPS. Monitoring ports allow network administrators to collect traffic from across the network for analysis by the IDPS as well as for occasional use in diagnosing network faults and measuring network performance.

An alternative to using a SPAN port is to use a *tap*. A tap is a device that connects to the network and copies traffic from its network port to a monitoring port. Any device that needs to review network traffic can be connected to the monitoring port. A tap is typically placed inline, allowing multiple network sensors to monitor the network without creating a failure point. Taps like that shown in Figure 7-5 are simple yet powerful tools that have very high reliability. As a specialty device, its only purpose is to read all traffic on a network segment and copy it to the tap's secondary ports.

The use of IDPS sensors and analysis systems can be quite complex. One common approach is to use an open source application like Snort. Once installed and configured, Snort can be managed and queried from a desktop computer using a client interface, as shown in Figure 7-6. The figure shows a sample screen from the Basic Analysis and Security Engine (BASE) displaying events generated by the Snort Network IDPS Engine (see *www.snort.org*).

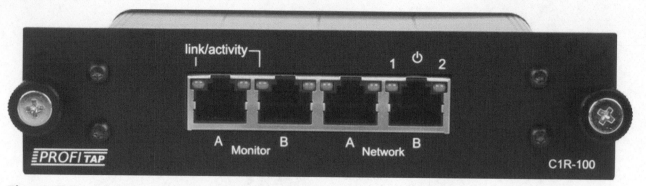

Figure 7-5   Example of a copper network tap

Source: Michael Whitman.

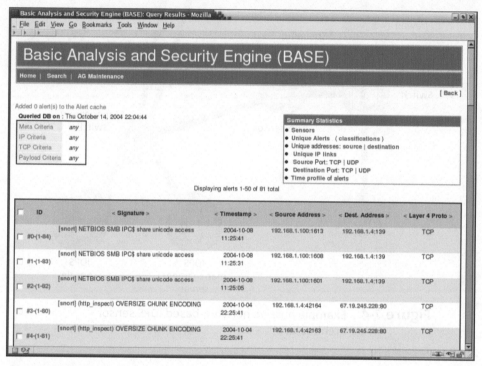

Figure 7-6   Snort BASE example

Source: Snort.

Signature Matching

Using a process known as **signature matching**, NIDPSs look for attack patterns by comparing observed network activity to known signatures in their knowledge base to determine whether an intrusion is under way. This is accomplished by examining network traffic using a special implementation of the TCP/IP stack that reassembles the packets and applies protocol stack verification, application protocol verification, and/or other verification and comparison techniques. An ever-present issue for this approach is the need for continuous updating of signature files to maintain currency with the attack environment. This need for updates leaves systems vulnerable to so-called zero-day exploits—attacks launched using the latest vulnerabilities.

signature matching

Comparing current activity against a library of known malicious activity for purposes of detecting an attack.

protocol stack verification

Examining and verifying current network traffic for packets that do not conform to TCP/IP protocol specifications.

In the process of **protocol stack verification**, the NIDPS looks for invalid data packets—that is, packets that are malformed under the rules of the TCP/IP protocol. A data packet is defined as invalid when its configuration does not match what is defined as valid by the various Internet protocols, such as TCP, UDP, and IP. The elements of the protocols in use (IP, TCP, UDP, and application layers such as HTTP) are combined in a complete set called the protocol stack when the software is implemented in an operating system or application. Many types of intrusions, especially denial-of-service (DoS) and distributed denial-of-service (DDoS) attacks, rely on the creation of improperly formed packets to take advantage of weaknesses in the protocol stack in certain operating systems or applications.

In **application protocol verification**, the higher-order protocols (HTTP, FTP, and Telnet) are examined for unexpected packet behavior or improper use. Sometimes, an intrusion involves the arrival of valid protocol packets but in excessive quantities. In the case of a tiny fragment packet attack, the packets are also excessively fragmented. Although a protocol stack verification looks for violations in the protocol packet structure, the application protocol verification looks for violations in protocol packet use. One example of this kind of attack is **Domain Name System (DNS) cache poisoning**, in which valid packets exploit poorly configured DNS servers to inject false information that corrupts the servers' answers to routine DNS queries from other systems on that network. Unfortunately, however, this higher-order examination of traffic can have the same effect on an IDPS as it can on a firewall—that is, it slows the throughput of the system. Therefore, it may be necessary to have more than one NIDPS installed, with one of them performing protocol stack verification and one performing application protocol verification.

application protocol verification

A type of protocol stack verification that focuses on higher-order protocols such as HTTP, FTP, and Telnet.

Domain Name System (DNS) cache poisoning

An attack against a DNS server that injects false data into the DNS environment so that the service responds to all requests for address resolution with an answer of the attacker's choosing. Also known as DNS spoofing.

Wireless NIDPSs

A wireless NIDPS (or simply wireless IDPS) monitors and analyzes wireless network traffic, looking for potential problems with the wireless protocols (Layers 2 and 3 of the OSI model). Like wireless access points, wireless IDPS sensors have to be deployed physically around the protected site in order to monitor the broad range of wireless signals able to reach the facility. In many cases, this type of functionality can be built into the wireless access point itself.

Wireless IDPSs can help to detect the following:

- Unauthorized wireless LANs (WLANs) and WLAN devices
- Poorly secured WLAN devices
- Unusual usage patterns
- The use of wireless network scanners
- DoS attacks and conditions
- Impersonation and man-in-the-middle attacks[12]

Sensor locations for wireless networks can be located at the access points or on specialized sensor components, or they can be incorporated into selected mobile stations. Centralized management stations collect information from these sensors, much as other network-based IDPs do, and aggregate information into a comprehensive assessment of wireless network intrusions. Issues associated with the implementation of wireless IDPSs include the following:

- *Higher protocol monitoring*—Wireless IDPSs cannot evaluate and diagnose issues with higher-layer protocols like TCP and UDP. As such, wireless IDPSs are unable to detect certain passive wireless protocol attacks, in which the attacker monitors network traffic without active scanning and probing.
- *Physical security*—Unlike wired network sensors, which can be physically secured, many wireless sensors are located in public areas like conference rooms, assembly areas, and hallways in order to attain the widest possible network range. Some of these locations may even be outdoors, as more and more organizations are deploying networks in external locations. Thus, the physical security of these devices is an issue, which may likely require additional security configuration and monitoring. The best-configured IDPS in the world cannot withstand an attack from a well-placed brick.
- *Sensor range*—A wireless device's range can be affected by atmospheric conditions, building construction, and the quality of both the wireless network card and access point. Some IDPS tools allow an organization to identify the optimal location for sensors by modeling the wireless footprint based on signal strength. Sensors are most effective when their footprints overlap.
- *Access point and wireless switch locations*—Wireless components with bundled IDPS capabilities must be carefully deployed to optimize the IDPS sensor detection grid. The minimum range is just that; you must guard against the possibility of an attacker connecting to a wireless access point from a range far beyond the minimum.
- *Wired network connections*—Wireless network components work independently of the wired network when sending and receiving between stations and access points. However, a network connection eventually

integrates wireless traffic with the organization's wired network. Where there is no available wired network connection, it may be impossible to deploy a sensor.

- *Cost*—The more sensors an organization deploys, the more expensive the configuration. Wireless components typically cost more than wired counterparts; thus, the total cost of ownership of wired and wireless IDPSs should be carefully considered.[13]

Advantages and Disadvantages of NIDPSs

Each organization must approach the justification, acquisition, and use of an NIDPS with its own strategic objectives in mind. The advantages and disadvantages of NIDPSs are shown in Table 7-1.

Host-Based IDPSs

A **host-based IDPS (HIDPS)** works differently than a network-based IDPS. Whereas an NIDPS resides on a network segment and monitors activities across that segment, an HIDPS resides on a particular computer or server, known as the host, and monitors activity only on that system. HIDPSs are also known as **system integrity verifiers (SIVs)**, as they benchmark and monitor the status of key system files and detect when an intruder creates, modifies, or deletes monitored files. While all HIDPSs are SIVs, not all SIVs are HIDPSs. Some SIVs have other uses, such as verifying data backups and software installations.

host-based IDPS (HIDPS)

A type of IDPS that monitors a single system for signs of attack by looking for the unauthorized creation, modification, and deletion of monitored files.

system integrity verifier (SIV)

An application that reviews monitored files to detect unauthorized creation, modification, and deletion.

Table 7-1   NIDPS Advantages and Disadvantages[14]

Advantages	Disadvantages
Good network design and placement of NIDPS devices can enable an organization to use a few devices to monitor a large network.	An NIDPS can become overwhelmed by network volume and fail to recognize attacks it might otherwise have detected. Some IDPS vendors are accommodating the need for ever-faster network performance by improving the processing of detection algorithms in dedicated hardware circuits to gain a performance advantage. Additional efforts to optimize ruleset processing may also reduce overall effectiveness in detecting attacks.
NIDPSs are usually passive devices and can be deployed in existing networks with little or no disruption to normal network operations.	An NIDPS requires access to all the traffic that is to be monitored. The broad use of switched Ethernet networks has replaced the ubiquity of shared collision domain hubs. Because many switches have limited or no monitoring port capability, some networks are not capable of providing aggregate data for analysis by an NIDPS. Even when switches do provide monitoring ports, they may not be able to mirror all activity within a consistent and reliable time sequence.
NIDPSs are not usually susceptible to direct attack and, in fact, may not be detectable by attackers.	The increasing use of encryption on some network services (such as SSL, SSH, and VPN) limits the effectiveness of NIDPSs.
	NIDPSs cannot reliably ascertain if an attack was successful or not; this requires an ongoing effort by the network administrator to evaluate the results of the logs for suspicious network activity.
	Some forms of attack are not easily discerned by NIDPSs, specifically those involving fragmented packets; in fact, some NIDPSs are particularly susceptible to malformed packets and may become unstable and stop functioning.

Source: NIST SP 800-31.

The approach of using a list of predefined, approved conditions for actions that can occur is often called *whitelisting*. In such cases, actions and activities are blocked unless they are specifically listed, and then they are allowed to occur as needed. This approach can be contrasted with *blacklisting*, in which all activities are allowed except those identified as harmful.

An HIDPS is also capable of monitoring system configuration databases, such as the Windows registry, in addition to stored configuration files like .ini, .cfg, and .dat files. Most HIDPSs work on the principle of configuration or change management, which means they record the sizes, locations, and other attributes of system files. The HIDPS triggers an alert or alarm when file attributes change, new files are created, or existing files are deleted. An HIDPS can also monitor systems logs for predefined events. The HIDPS examines these files and logs to determine if an attack is under way or has occurred, and if the attack is succeeding or was successful. The HIDPS maintains its own log file so that even when hackers successfully modify files on the target system to cover their tracks, the HIDPS can provide an independent audit trail of the attack. Once properly configured, an HIDPS is very reliable. The only time an HIDPS produces a false positive alert is when an authorized change occurs for a monitored file. This action can be quickly reviewed by an administrator and dismissed as acceptable. The administrator may then choose to disregard subsequent changes to the same set of files. If properly configured, an HIDPS can also detect when individual users attempt to modify or exceed their access authorization and give themselves higher privileges.

An HIDPS has an advantage over an NIDPS in that it can usually be installed in such a way that it can access encrypted information before or after it travels through the network, before the local system encrypts information or after it decrypts the information. In this way, an HIDPS is able to use the content of otherwise encrypted communications to make decisions about possible or successful attacks. Likewise, because the HIDPS is designed to detect intrusion activity on only one computer system, all the information the HIDPS needs to determine whether any specific traffic is legitimate will be present for analysis. The nature of the network packet delivery is not material, regardless of whether it's switched or in a shared collision domain, or whether the packets are fragmented in transit.

HIDPS Configuration

An HIDPS relies on the classification of files into various categories. It then applies various notification actions, depending on the rules in the HIDPS configuration. Most HIDPSs provide only a few general levels of alert notification. For example, an administrator can configure an HIDPS to treat the following types of changes as reportable security events: changes in a system folder (for example, in C:\Program Files or C:\WINNT) and changes within a security-related application (for example, C:\Tripwire). In other words, administrators can configure the system to trigger an alert on any changes within a critical data folder.

The configuration rules may classify changes to a specific application folder (for example, C:\Program Files\Microsoft Office) as being normal, and thus such changes are not reported. Administrators can configure the system not only to log all activity but also to instantly page or e-mail any administrator if a reportable security event occurs. Although this change-based system seems simple, it appears to suit most administrators, who are primarily concerned if unauthorized changes occur in specific and sensitive areas of the host file system. Applications frequently modify their internal files, such as dictionaries and configuration templates, and users are constantly updating their data files. Unless an HIDPS is very specifically configured, these actions can generate a large volume of false alarms.

As shown in Figure 7-7, managed HIDPSs can also monitor multiple computers simultaneously.[15] They do this by creating a configuration file on each monitored host and by making each HIDPS report back to a master console system, which is usually located on the systems administrator's computer. This master console monitors the information provided from the managed hosts and notifies the administrator when it senses recognizable attack conditions.

In configuring an HIDPS, the systems administrator must begin by identifying and categorizing folders and files. One of the most common methods is to designate folders using a classification scheme of red, yellow, and green. Critical systems components are coded red, and they usually include the system registry, any folders containing the key elements of the operating system, and application software. Critically important data should also be included in the red category. Support components, such as device drivers and other relatively important files, are generally coded yellow; user data is usually coded green.

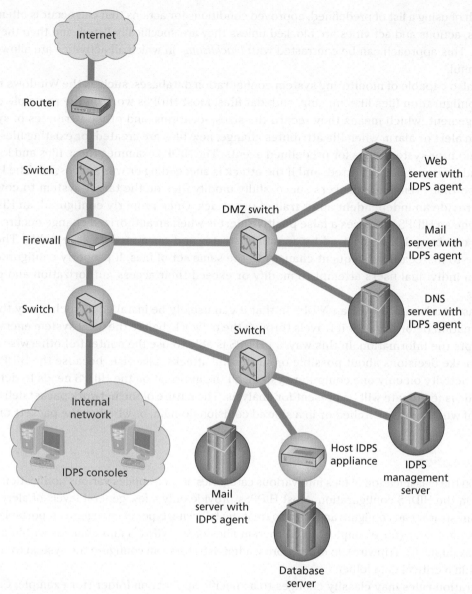

Figure 7-7   Example host-based IDPS agent deployment architecture[16]

Source: NIST.

This is not to suggest that user data is unimportant, but in practical and strategic terms, monitoring changes to user data does have a lower priority. One reason for this is that users are often assigned storage space that they are expected to use routinely to maintain and back up their documents, files, and images. Another reason is that user data files are expected to change frequently—that is, as users make modifications. System kernel files, on the other hand, should only change during upgrades or installations. Categorizing critical system components at a higher level than less important files ensures that the level of response to change is in proportion to the level of priority. Should the three-tier system be overly simple for an organization, there are systems that allow for an alternative scale of 0–100, with 100 being the most mission-critical and 0 being unimportant. It is not unusual, however, for these types of scales to be overly refined and result in confusion; for example, is there really much difference between the prioritization of responses to level 67 and 68 intrusions? Sometimes, simpler is better.

Advantages and Disadvantages of HIDPSs

Each organization must approach the justification, acquisition, and use of an HIDPS with its own strategic objectives in mind. A summary of some of the advantages and disadvantages of HIDPSs is shown in Table 7-2.

Table 7-2   HIDPS Advantages and Disadvantages[17]

Advantages	Disadvantages
An HIDPS can detect local events on host systems, and it can also detect attacks that may elude an NIDPS.	An HIDPS poses more management issues because HIDPSs are configured and managed on each monitored host; this means that more management effort is required to install, configure, and operate several HIDPSs than for a comparably sized NIDPS solution.
An HIDPS functions on the host system, where encrypted traffic is decrypted and available for processing.	An HIDPS is vulnerable to both direct attacks and to attacks against the host operating system. Either circumstance can result in the compromise and/or loss of HIDPS functionality.
The use of switched network protocols does not affect an HIDPS.	An HIDPS is not optimized to detect multihost scanning, nor is it able to detect the scanning of nonhost network devices, such as routers or switches. Unless complex correlation analysis is provided, the HIDPS is not aware of attacks that span multiple devices in the network.
An HIDPS can detect inconsistencies in how applications and systems programs were used by examining records stored in audit logs; this can be used to detect some types of attacks, including Trojan horse programs.	An HIDPS is susceptible to some DoS attacks.
	An HIDPS can use large amounts of disk space to retain the host OS audit logs and may therefore require the addition of disk capacity to the system to function properly.
	An HIDPS can inflict a performance overhead on its host systems and, in some cases, may reduce system performance below acceptable levels.

Source: NIST SP 800-31.

Application-Based IDPSs

A refinement of the host-based IDPS is the **application-based IDPS (AppIDPS)**. Whereas the HIDPS monitors a computer system for file modification in multiple folders, the AppIDPS examines a single application for abnormal events. It usually does this by looking at the files created by the application and checking for anomalous occurrences, such as users exceeding their authorization, invalid

application-based IDPS (AppIDPS)

A type of IDPS that monitors an application for abnormal events.

file executions, or other activities that would indicate a problem in the normal interaction between users, the application, and the data. By tracking the interaction between users and applications, the AppIDPS is able to trace specific activity back to individual users. The AppIDPS also has the advantage of having custom-developed signature databases for specific applications. So, for example, if the organization has a large investment in a SAS implementation, they can implement an AppIDPS that is custom-tailored for SAS files, and will have a much more focused monitoring capability.

One unique advantage of the AppIDPS is its ability to view encrypted data. Because the AppIDPS interfaces with data as it is processed by an application, and because any encrypted data that enters an application is decrypted by the application itself, an AppIDPS does not need to become involved in the decryption process. This allows an AppIDPS to examine the encryption/decryption process and identify any potential anomalies in data handling or user access.

According to the Missouri State Information Infrastructure Protection Center:

Application-based IDPSs may be configured to intercept the following types of requests and use them in combinations and sequences to constitute an application's normal behavior:

- *File system—File read or write*
- *Network—Packet events at the driver (NDIS) or transport (TDI) level*

- *Configuration—Read or write to the registry on Windows*
- *Execution space—Write to memory not owned by the requesting application—for example, attempts to inject a shared library DLL into another process*[18]

As each organization determines its own needs for intrusion detection, some in the industry suggest a blended use of elements from NIDPS, HIDPS, and AppIDPS approaches. A common practice is to implement HIDPSs and AppIDPSs on high-value servers and other critical systems, with the use of a robust NIDPS for global infrastructure protection.

Advantages and Disadvantages of AppIDPSs

Each organization must approach the justification, acquisition, and use of an AppIDPS with its own strategic objectives in mind. The advantages and disadvantages of AppIDPSs are shown in Table 7-3.

Table 7-3   AppIDPS Advantages and Disadvantages[19]

Advantages	Disadvantages
An AppIDPS is aware of specific users and can observe the interaction between the application and the user; this allows the AppIDPS to attribute unauthorized activities to specific and known users.	AppIDPSs may be more susceptible to attack than other IDPS approaches because applications are often less well protected than network and host OS components.
An AppIDPS is able to operate even when incoming data is encrypted because it can operate at the point in the process when the data has been decrypted by applications and has not been reencrypted for storage.	AppIDPSs are less capable of detecting software tampering and may be taken in by Trojan horse code or some other form of spoofing; it is usually recommended that AppIDPSs be used in combination with HIDPSs and NIDPSs.

Source: NIST SP 800-31.

Comparison of IDPS Technologies

Table 7-4 provides a summary comparison of IDPS technology types.

Table 7-4   Comparison of IDPS Technology Types

IDPS Technology Type	Types of Malicious Activity Detected	Scope per Sensor or Agent	Strengths
Network-based	Network, transport, and application TCP/IP layer activity	Multiple network subnets and groups of hosts	Able to analyze the widest range of application protocols; only IDPS that can thoroughly analyze many of them
Wireless	Wireless protocol activity; unauthorized wireless local area networks (WLANs) in use	Multiple WLANs and groups of wireless clients	Only IDPS that can monitor wireless protocol activity
Host-based	Host application and operating system (OS) activity; network, transport, and application TCP/IP layer activity	Individual host	Allows analysis of activity that was transferred in end-to-end encrypted communications
Application-based	Application and operating system (OS) activity; network, transport, and application TCP/IP layer activity	An application deployed across multiple hosts	Allows analysis of activity that was transferred in end-to-end encrypted communications and has context of the application and knowledge of user identities and authenticated privilege level

IDPS DETECTION APPROACHES

The approach used to detect events also has a significant effect on how the IDPS operates. There are two widely used detection options: signature-based and statistical anomaly-based.

Signature-Based IDPSs

A **signature-based IDPS**, also known as a **knowledge-based IDPS**, examines data traffic in search of patterns that match known **signatures**. Signature-based IDPS technology is widely used because many attacks have clear and distinct signatures, including the following:

- *Footprinting* and *fingerprinting* activities, which have an attack pattern that includes the use of ICMP, DNS querying, and e-mail routing analysis
- Exploits involving a specific attack sequence designed to take advantage of a vulnerability to gain access to a system
- DoS and DDoS attacks; an example could include a system that sends significant numbers of synchronization or connection requests but never completes the connection
- A Telnet attempt with a username of "root," which is a violation of an organization's security policy
- An e-mail with the subject line "Free pictures!" and an attachment filename of "freepics.exe," both of which are characteristics of a known form of malware[20]

The problem with this approach is that as new attack strategies are identified, the IDPS's database of signatures must be continually updated. Failure to keep this database current can allow attacks that use new strategies to succeed. An IDPS that uses signature-based methods works much like most antivirus software. In fact, antivirus software is often classified as a form of signature-based IDPSs. This is why experts tell users that if they don't plan on keeping their antivirus software updated, it will not work as effectively as it would with current updates.

Another weakness of the signature-based method is the time frame over which attacks occur. If attackers are purposefully slow and methodical, they may slip undetected through this type of IDPS because their actions do not match signatures that often include the time allowed between steps in the attack. The only way for a signature-based IDPS to resolve this vulnerability is for it to collect and analyze data over longer periods of time, a process that requires substantially larger data storage capability and additional processing capacity.

Anomaly-Based IDPSs

Another approach for detecting intrusions is based on the frequency with which certain network activities take place. The **anomaly-based IDPS** (formerly known as a **statistical anomaly-based IDPS**), which is also known as a **behavior-based IDPS**, collects statistical summaries by observing traffic that is known to be normal. This normal period of evaluation establishes a performance baseline. Next, the anomaly-based IDPS periodically samples network activity and uses statistical methods to compare the sampled network activity to the baseline. When the measured activity is outside the baseline parameters, it is said to exceed the **clipping level**. The data that is measured from normal traffic and used to prepare the baseline can include host memory or CPU usage, network packet types, and packet quantities. Later comparisons of measured traffic might reveal anomalies when compared to the baseline, thus triggering the alert.

The advantage of the anomaly-based approach is that the IDPS can detect new types of attacks because it is looking for abnormal activity of any type. Unfortunately, these systems require much more overhead and processing capacity than signature-based IDPSs, as they must constantly compare patterns of activity against the baseline. Another drawback is that these systems may not detect minor changes to system variables and may generate many false positives. If the actions of users or systems on

---

signature-based IDPS

A type of IDPS that uses signature matching to enable detection of an attack. Also known as a *knowledge-based IDPS*.

knowledge-based IDPS

See *signature-based IDPS*.

signature

A unique value or pattern of an attack that enables detection; it may include the hash of a file or a series of scans or queries commonly used in an attack.

anomaly-based IDPS

A type of IDPS that collects statistical summaries of known valid traffic, then compares current traffic against it in order to detect questionable traffic.

statistical anomaly-based IDPS

See *anomaly-based IDPS*.

behavior-based IDPS

See *anomaly-based IDPS*.

clipping level

The measured activity level at which an IDPS triggers an alert.

a network vary widely, with periods of low activity interspersed with periods of frantic packet exchange, this type of IDPS may not be suitable because the dramatic swings from one level to another will almost certainly generate false alarms. Due to the complexity of the configuration, the depth of commitment needed for ongoing operations, the need for intensive computing capabilities to support real-time analysis, and the large number of false positive results usually generated, this type of IDPS is less commonly used than the signature-based type.

IDPS Implementation

The evaluation procedure implemented in any organization should consider the practices recommended in Table 7-5.

As Table 7-5 shows, there are some practices that each organization should adopt when faced with structuring a process for incident decision classification. When analyzing and validating events to determine which are incidents, NIST recommends the following:

- *Profile networks and systems*—Using an HIDPS to create snapshots of system configurations assists in the detection of unauthorized modifications to those systems. Similarly, examining network usage (bandwidth and traffic) will assist in identifying average and peak usages for pattern analysis.
- *Understand normal behaviors*—Know what "normal operations" are so abnormal operations can be more easily detected.
- *Use centralized logging and create a log retention policy*—Creating centralized logging prevents attackers from "covering their tracks."
- *Perform event correlation*—Event correlation involves examining logs from multiple systems and identifying trends or indicators of attacks across multiple systems.
- *Keep all hosts' clocks synchronized*—This will make looking at multisystem data, such as log data, easier because all systems will have the exact same time.
- *Maintain and use a knowledge base of information*—This will provide a quick and easy method of researching information for incident analysis and response.
- *Use Internet search engines for research*—Use the knowledge of the thousands of other information security professionals out there who post their experiences in forums and on Web sites.
- *Run packet sniffers to collect additional data*—Programs such as Wireshark can help collect traffic data for detailed analysis.
- *Consider filtering the data*—Filtering can reduce the "information overload" that results from the hundreds or thousands of systems sending thousands (or hundreds of thousands) of data packets in a short time frame.

Table 7-5 Summary of Recommended Practices for IDPS Implementation[21]

Area	Recommended Practice
Planning	• Develop/verify policies, procedures, and processes to detect indications of intrusion. • Prepare a business impact analysis of a similar process to define systems and relative importance. This must include identifying the characteristics of systems that would indicate suspicious behaviors. • Ensure system and network logs are enabled, collected, and consolidated for analysis.
IDPS Integrity	• Validate that the IDPS is reliable, accurate, and uncompromised.
Network and System Baseline	Monitor the following for unexpected change and unusual behavior: • Network activities • System activities and configurations • Directory and file systems
Physical Controls	• Validate/update the hardware inventory. • Verify the physical integrity of work and storage spaces.
Implementation	• Perform ongoing detection activities to review the IDPS, help desk, and other reports of suspicious activities. • Act on notifications to triage and then escalate and respond to warranted events, including unauthorized, unexpected, or suspicious activity.

- *Consider experience as being irreplaceable*—The organization's administrators hold a wealth of personal knowledge and experience about the normal operations and "quirks" of the systems. Capture as much of that information as possible and share it with other employees.
- *Create a diagnosis matrix for less experienced staff*—Quick reference guides for administrators who don't have the experience of more senior employees ensure that a potential incident is not overlooked, and that the proper procedures are followed when incidents are detected.
- *Seek assistance from others when needed*—There are state and federal resources as well as industry support centers created specifically to assist an organization in incident response. Use their expertise and knowledge to supplement the organization's.

IDPS-RELATED TOPICS

IDPS technology has become a mainstay in most organizations, and as you will see in this section, it becomes part of a holistic approach to security at many organizations. Some related topics to be considered with IDPSs include a precursor technology, the log file monitor. We will also discuss the roles of automated response in the context of the IDPS.

Log File Monitors

A **log file monitor (LFM)** reviews the log files generated by servers, network devices, and even other IDPSs. These systems look for patterns in the log files that may indicate an attack or intrusion is in process or has already succeeded. Although an individual host IDPS is only able to look at the activity in one system, the LFM can look at multiple log files from a number of different systems. The patterns that signify an attack can be subtle and hard to distinguish when one system is examined in isolation, but they may be much easier to identify when the network and its systems are viewed holistically. Of course, this holistic approach requires the allocation of considerable resources, as it involves the collection, movement, storage, and analysis of very large quantities of log data. An LFM is considered a precursor of a security information and event management system, which is discussed later in this module.

Automated Response

New technologies and capabilities are emerging in the field of incident response beyond the intent of IDPS control models. Some of these build on traditional strategies and extend their capabilities and functions. Traditionally, systems were configured to detect incidents and then notify the human administrator; now, new systems can respond to the incident threat autonomously, based on preconfigured options that go beyond simple defensive actions usually associated with IDPS and IPS systems.

These systems, referred to as **trap and trace**, use a combination of resources to detect an intrusion and then trace it back to its source. On the surface, this seems like an ideal solution; security is no longer limited to defense. Now, the security administrators can take the offensive. They can track down the perpetrators and turn them over to the appropriate authorities. Under the guise of justice, some less scrupulous administrators might even be tempted to "back hack"—that is, hack into a hacker's system to find out as much as possible about the hacker. *Vigilante justice* would be a more appropriate term, and activities in this vein are deemed unethical by most codes of professional conduct. In tracking the hacker, administrators may wander through other organizations' systems. The wily hacker may use IP spoofing, compromised systems, or a myriad of other techniques to throw trackers off the trail. The result is that administrators can become hackers themselves, which defeats the purpose of catching hackers and puts the defender in the role of the unethical lawbreaker.

Honeypots and Honeynets

There are more than legal drawbacks to trap and trace. The trap portion frequently involves the use of honeypots or honeynets. As you learned in Module 6, *honeypots* resemble production systems and contain (usually fake) information just begging to be hacked. If a hacker stumbles into the system, alarms are set off and the administrator is notified.

---

log file monitor (LFM)

A type of IDPS that reviews log files generated by servers, network devices, and other IDPSs for attack indicators.

trap and trace

A system that combines resources to detect an intrusion and then trace its network traffic back to the source.

honeytoken

Any system resource that is placed in a functional system but has no normal use in that system, and instead serves as a decoy and alarm, similar to a honeypot.

honeypot farm

A network version of a honeypot; a decoy network simulation that attempts to draw attackers to it and away from actual production networks. Also known as a *honeynet*.

Honeypots can distract adversaries from more valuable machines on a network, they can provide early warning about new attack and exploitation trends, and they allow in-depth examination of adversaries during and after exploitation of a honeypot. There are two general types of honeypots:

- Production honeypots are easy to use, capture only limited information, and are used primarily by companies or corporations.
- Research honeypots are complex to deploy and maintain, capture extensive information, and are used primarily by research, military, or government organizations.

An example of a honeypot is a system used to simulate one or more network services. This honeypot could log access attempts to particular ports, including an attacker's keystrokes, and could give advanced warning of a more concerted attack.

Even smaller than the honeypot is the honeytoken. If a honeytoken attracts attention, it is from unauthorized access and will trigger a notification or response. An example would be a bogus record placed into a database and monitored by the system. If the record is accessed, it is an indicator of unwanted activity. Another example, this one from the physical world, is a small antitheft tag that bookstores insert in their books for sale. If a customer attempts to take a book without paying, an alarm sounds.

Honeynets (also known as honeypot farms) operate similarly to honeypots, except that they consist of networks or subnets of systems and represent a much richer, high-interaction target. *High-interaction* means a honeynet provides real systems, applications, and services for attackers to interact with. These victim systems (honeypots within the honeynet) can be any type of system, service, or information you want to provide; any interaction with a honeynet implies malicious or unauthorized activity. Any connections initiated inbound to your honeynet are most likely a probe, scan, or attack. Almost any outbound connection from your honeynet implies that someone has compromised a system and initiated outbound activity.

When using honeypots and honeynets, administrators should be careful not to run afoul of any legal issues. The first issue is the line between enticement and entrapment. Enticement is the process of attracting attention to a system by placing tantalizing bits of information in key locations. Entrapment is the action of luring an individual into committing a crime to get a conviction. Enticement is legal and ethical, whereas entrapment is not. It is difficult to gauge the effect that a honeypot system can have on the average user, especially if the individual has been nudged into looking at the information.

The next issue involves problems with the Fourth Amendment to the U.S. Constitution, which protects Americans against unwarranted search and seizure. Organizations that operate in the United States or do business with people in the United States should exercise care to ensure that anyone connecting to the honeypot or honeynet does not inadvertently place information into that environment.

Other issues arise when dealing with the Electronic Communications Privacy Act (18 U.S.C. § 2511), also known as the Wiretap Act, which prohibits recording of wire-based or cable-based communications unless an exception applies. These exceptions include the following:

- Interception required as part of normal work operations—by a systems administrator for an ISP, say, or an employee of a telephone company
- If authorized by court order
- If performed by one of the parties involved, or with the permission of one of the parties involved
- If the transmission is readily accessible to the general public
- If the transmission is radio-based and designed for use by the general public, including amateur or citizens band radio
- Other exceptions defined in the act[22]

Another federal law that specifically deals with the use of devices to collect information from a network user is the Pen Register, Trap and Trace Devices law (the *Pen/Trap statute*). The law governs the real-time collection of non-content traffic information associated with communications, such as the phone numbers dialed by a particular telephone or the destination or source IP address of a computer network user—data that the statute refers to as "dialing, routing, addressing, or signaling information."[23] Like the Wiretap Act's prohibition on intercepting the contents of communications, the Pen/Trap statute creates a general prohibition on the real-time monitoring of traffic data relating to communications.[24]

The downside of enhanced automated response systems may outweigh their upside. Legal issues associated with tracking individuals through the systems of others have yet to be resolved. What if the hacker who is backtracked is actually a compromised system running an automated attack? What are the legal liabilities of a counterattack? How can security administrators condemn a hacker when they themselves may have illegally hacked systems to track the hacker? These issues are complex, but they must be resolved to give security professionals better tools to combat incidents.

SECURITY INFORMATION AND EVENT MANAGEMENT

Many organizations have come to rely on security information and event management (SIEM) as a central element to empower the *security operations center (SOC)* to identify and react to the many events, incidents, and attacks against the organization's information systems. SIEM's roots are in the UNIX syslog approach to log file aggregation; for years, organizations and security professionals have sought ways to leverage existing systems and have them work together to maintain situation awareness, identify noteworthy issues, and enable response to adverse events.

What Are SIEM Systems?

A SIEM system supports threat detection and informs many aspects of threat intelligence. It is also instrumental in managing aspects of compliance vulnerability management. It often plays a pivotal role in an organization's security incident management through data collection and analysis by enabling near real-time and historical analysis of security events. It integrates data from multiple sources, including local events and contextual data sources. SIEM systems are derived from legacy log file monitoring systems and procedures. The basics of SIEM data flows are shown in Figure 7-8.

The core capabilities of SIEM systems leverage the broad scope of log event collection and management from point sources across the organization, including firewalls, endpoint defenses, and IDPS systems. They give the organization the ability to analyze log events and other data from varied sources. The correlated results derived from advanced data analysis techniques enable several operational capabilities, including dashboards for situational awareness, reporting of trends, and incident management.

SIEM systems have been a mainstay in larger organizations for many years, evolving from locally developed LFM systems whose capabilities have been

security information and event management (SIEM)

An information management system specifically tasked to collect and correlate events and other log data from a number of servers or other network devices for the purpose of interpreting, filtering, correlating, analyzing, storing, reporting, and acting on the resulting information.

threat intelligence

A process used to develop knowledge that allows an organization to understand the actions and intentions of threat actors and develop methods to prevent or mitigate cyberattacks.

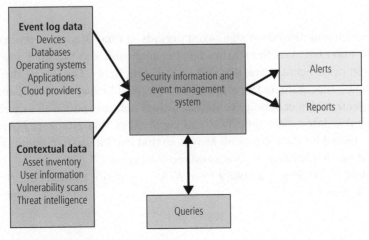

Figure 7-8   SIEM data flows

integrated into commercially developed platforms. This has allowed organizations with large numbers of devices used in information systems to collect and act on events from these devices, including servers and networking equipment, endpoint defense systems, desktop computing systems, and laptops. The reliance on cloud-based computing solutions has added significant complexity to larger information technology systems, and current-generation SIEM platforms have evolved to include those environments as well.

As the volume and complexity of data flowing into the SIEM system have multiplied, analysis of that data using data analytics techniques has been included in SIEM solutions. This has enabled organizations using SIEM solutions to keep pace as they monitor for intrusions and attacks against a mixed environment of on-premises systems, cloud hosted services, and hybrid system models that include both enabling technologies. The current level of capability is made possible by the analytics-driven SIEM system.

Larger organizations are faced with several needs that SIEM platforms can address:

- Aggregation of security-related events from across the organization regardless of the source technology
- Correlation of events with context from external sources, including vendor-specific updates and cooperative industry associations
- Integration of events from devices, systems, and technologies from disparate sources deployed throughout the organization
- Detection of known threats when patterns of attack behavior are known
- Possible detection of emerging threats when analysis is coupled with threat analysis techniques designed into the SIEM system
- Enablement of ad hoc searches and reporting from recorded events to enable advanced breach analysis during and after incident response and provide support for forensic investigation into breach events
- Tracking the actions of attackers and allowing sequencing of events to provide an understanding of what happened and when it occurred

The essential capabilities that an analytics-driven SIEM system should provide include:

- *Real-time monitoring*—Enable flexible and timely reaction to attacks.
- *Incident response*—Information about the incident response process improves the ability of the organization to detect and respond to attacks to reduce the degree of damage and enable more rapid containment and recovery.
- *User monitoring*—The monitoring of user activity can identify breaches and reveal insider misuse, which is often a requirement for compliance to external regulators.
- *Threat intelligence*—The development of threat intelligence can enable the recognition of abnormal events and prioritize the response process.
- *Analytics* and *threat detection*—Advanced query and reporting tools enable analysis of past events and make it possible to detect threats and vulnerabilities that are not otherwise apparent.

These capabilities give the organization the ability to identify and respond to a wide variety of situations.

Real-Time Monitoring

Many successful attacks remain undetected for significant periods of time. Mandiant reports that in 2019, an attack's median dwell time—the duration between the start of a cyber intrusion and the time it is detected—was 56 days.[25] While this is an improvement over recent years, it is still a significant delay. The longer the dwell times are, the more likely it is that attackers can be successful in the exfiltration of data and causing other damage.

Improvement in an organization's capability to detect intrusions can reduce the dwell time and allow containment and recovery to be implemented more quickly. Reducing the time that attackers operate undetected inside the organization reduces the potential for data loss. A SIEM system that can integrate contextual data and ongoing events may be able to reduce the time attackers can operate and reduce losses.

An example of a real-time monitoring capability from AT&T Security's Unified Security Management Anywhere demonstration is shown in Figure 7-9.

Figure 7-9   Example SIEM system real-time display

Source: AT&T

Incident Response

A properly implemented SIEM platform can enable the ability to identify incidents and enable a process to track and respond to them. SIEM systems enable responders to track and document ongoing incidents and perform record-keeping and reporting on the incident response activities. In addition, the system can automatically or manually aggregate multiple events, interact with other systems, and assist in the collection of evidentiary materials. Some SIEM platforms can integrate response playbooks that guide staff on how to respond to specific incident categories.

In some circumstances, a SIEM system can initiate predefined defensive scripts to automatically disrupt ongoing cyberattacks. An effective SIEM system can be a central service to coordinate the response workflow, combining predefined automatic response with notifications to enable a coordinated defensive reaction with a unified flow of information to the CSIRT and the SOC staff.

An example of a SIEM capability that assists in incident response and event investigations is shown in Figure 7-10; it is part of AT&T Security's Unified Security Management Anywhere demonstration.

Figure 7-10   Example of a SIEM system supporting an incident response

Source: AT&T.

User Monitoring

An effective SIEM system can analyze user access and authentication activities and provide alerts for suspicious behaviors and violation of policy. This is of particular importance for privileged user accounts and is often a requirement for many compliance reporting functions. To be effective, these functions must be implemented to provide alerts of reporting and alerts in near real time.

Threat Intelligence

To enable the threat intelligence function of the organization, the SIEM system must be able to integrate threat intelligence services that provide current information on compromise indicators and adversary tactics, techniques, and procedures (TTP) with knowledge of organizational asset criticality and usage behaviors. These will enable analysts to recognize abnormal behaviors and assess the risks and impact of various forms of attack.

Threat intelligence information can then be integrated with data from the IT infrastructure to create watch lists and enable correlation of event data with the nature of the infrastructure to identify and prioritize threats to organizational assets.

Analytics and Advanced Threat Detection

SIEM systems should have capabilities to analyze event data to detect anomalies and track the interactions between users and data repositories. The SIEM system should be able to correlate and visualize events to support incident investigations. By using machine learning, the SIEM system can learn to distinguish normal behavior from abnormal user behaviors. As the threat landscape evolves, a SIEM system should have the capacity to identify and respond to new and more advanced threats.

Selecting a SIEM Solution

Many SIEM platforms are available. Some are available from open source vendors and others are proprietary solutions. An organization must determine which options provide the necessary level of capability within the availability of resources to deploy the solution. When trying to determine the best SIEM solution for an organization, you should consider the following questions:

- Which type of SIEM technology offers the right balance between protection and cost for the needs of the organization? Would a SIEM system with fewer data source options and less functional analytics provide the capabilities needed?
- What features are included in the base price? What features are available at extra cost? Are all cost factors known?
- How easy is it to set up and configure the technology? Does the organization have staff on hand that are trained to configure the software, or would the hiring of additional employees (or contractors or managed service providers) be required?
- Can the SIEM system adapt to the current and immediate future capacity requirements of the organization?

The most important factor, of course, is the extent to which the SIEM system provides the required features the organization needs and perhaps to meet compliance needs. The next important factor is cost, which may keep a certain make, model, or type of SIEM system out of reach. As with all security decisions, certain compromises may be necessary to provide a viable solution under the budgetary constraints stipulated by management.

There are several methods available to help you gain further insight into the feature choices for a SIEM solution. One widely used advisory service is the Gartner Group. Gartner Research offers an advisory document by subscription titled *Critical Capabilities for Security Information and Event Management* that can assist you in developing your list of critical capabilities and then guide you through an analysis of the SIEM products that are on the market.

For organizations with staff that possess the requisite skills, some open source SIEM products are available to implement at a low cost of initial investment. It is important to consider the total cost of ownership when comparing open source solutions to proprietary SIEM solutions. Some proprietary systems can be prohibitively expensive, but when all categories of expense are considered, including acquisition, configuration, maintenance, and operating costs, some can compare well to open source options without the need for the depth of staff knowledge implied for open source solutions.

 To see a reasonably complete list of SIEM vendors, you can visit eSecurity Planet's Web page on top SIEM products. You can find a list of widely available open source SIEM products at *www.dnsstuff.com/free-siem-tools*.

Many proprietary SIEM software vendors, service integrators, and consulting companies offer helpful tools to identify SIEM features and show off their products' capabilities. Several products you can use as a starting point for a Web search include Splunk, Exabeam, and Rapid7.

Closing Scenario

"Good work, JJ!"

Amanda Wilson, HAL's CIO, was pleased. And when Amanda was pleased, everybody was pleased. Only a few days after seeing JJ's preliminary findings, Paul took JJ to present again to Amanda at her request.

"So, we can save almost $150,000 using these open source packages?" she asked.

"Yes, ma'am," JJ replied. "I wouldn't recommend using all of them at once, but I think we could implement the top two or three within six months, once we get a new hire and a couple of our staff trained up."

"And you have a personal interest in being involved in the Snort transition and in getting the corresponding training?" Amanda asked, looking at JJ across the conference table. She smiled at Paul.

JJ suppressed a groan. "Uh, I would be happy to help out wherever needed," he managed to reply.

"Just kidding!" Amanda laughed. "Paul said that UNIX gave you headaches. I thought I'd test the theory."

"Thanks, Paul," JJ said, visibly relieved.

"So, how soon can you and Paul start the job hunt for the new person?" Amanda asked.

Paul spoke up. "I have drafted a job description for your review," he said. "Then it goes to Personnel. We could start interviewing by the end of next week."

"Great," she said. "Get us a good one. He or she has a lot of work to do. If we're going to use Snort for the NIDPS, we still need to determine if we are going to stick with our HIDPS or look at alternatives," Amanda added.

"We'll get on that right away," Paul said. As the meeting came to a close, Paul stood up and looked over at JJ to congratulate him. When he saw the look in JJ's eyes, though, he looked for a back door to the conference room.

Discussion Questions

1. What is one reason to avoid using open source software?
2. If open source software is free to use without licensing costs, what other factors should be considered when evaluating the total cost of operating such software?
3. What technologies could JJ recommend to Paul?
4. Where could JJ go for more information on open source software? Training?

Ethical Decision Making

Suppose JJ had a close personal friend who was a very experienced IDPS specialist, with broad and deep experience with a specific IDPS software vendor. JJ thought she would be an excellent candidate for the new position. JJ told her about the opportunity, but she was not quite as enthused about applying for it as JJ had hoped. You see, there was a referral bonus, and JJ would get a tidy sum of cash if she were hired based on his recommendation.

JJ told her that she needed to get on board and that he would split the referral bonus with her. Do you think that is an ethical way to encourage the candidate to apply?

MODULE SUMMARY

- An intrusion detection and prevention system (IDPS) is a network burglar alarm. It is designed to be placed in a network to determine whether the network is being used in ways that are out of compliance with the organization's policy. An intrusion is a type of attack on information assets in which the instigator attempts to gain unauthorized entry into a system or network or disrupt its normal operations.

- There are several compelling reasons to acquire and use an IDPS: to prevent problem behaviors by increasing the perceived risk of discovery and punishment for people who would attack or abuse the system; to detect attacks and other security violations that are not prevented by other security measures; to detect and deal with the preambles to attacks (commonly experienced as network probes and other "doorknob rattling" activities); to document the existing threat to an organization; to act as quality control for security design and administration, especially in large and complex enterprises; and to provide useful information about intrusions that do take place, allowing improved diagnosis, recovery, and correction of causative factors.

- The placement of sensor and detection devices or software programs has a significant effect on how the IDPS operates. There are three widely used placement options: network-based, host-based, and application-based IDPSs. Each option has a number of advantages and disadvantages.

- A network-based IDPS (NIDPS) monitors traffic on a segment of an organization's network. An NIDPS looks for indications of ongoing or successful attacks and resides on a computer or appliance connected to the network segment it monitors.

- A host-based IDPS (HIDPS) resides on a particular computer or server, known as the host, and monitors activity only on that system. HIDPSs are also known as system integrity verifiers because they benchmark and monitor the status of key system files and detect when an intruder creates, modifies, or deletes monitored files.

- A refinement of the host-based IDPS is the application-based IDPS (AppIDPS). Whereas an HIDPS examines a single system for file modification, the AppIDPS examines an application for abnormal events. It usually does this by looking at the files created by the application and looking for anomalous occurrences within the context of the application.

- The approach used to detect events also has a significant effect on how the IDPS operates. There are two widely used detection options: signature-based and statistical anomaly-based. A signature-based IDPS, also known as a knowledge-based IDPS, examines data traffic in search of patterns that match known signatures—that is, preconfigured, predetermined attack patterns. Signature-based IDPS technology is widely used because many attacks have clear and distinct signatures. Another approach for detecting intrusions is based on the frequency with which certain network activities take place. The anomaly-based IDPS (formerly known as a *statistical anomaly-based IDPS*), also known as a behavior-based IDPS, collects statistical summaries by observing traffic that is known to be normal. This normal period of evaluation establishes a performance baseline. Next, the anomaly-based IDPS periodically samples network activity and uses statistical methods to compare the sampled network activity to the baseline. When the measured activity is outside the baseline parameters, it is said to exceed the clipping level—the level at which the IDPS triggers an alert to notify the administrator.

- A log file monitor (LFM), a type of IDPS that is similar to an NIDPS, reviews the log files generated by servers, network devices, and even other IDPSs. These systems look for patterns in the log files that may indicate that an attack or intrusion is in process or has already succeeded.

- Organizations rely on security information and event management (SIEM) to support threat detection and threat intelligence, manage vulnerabilities, and support security incident management processes by integrating data from multiple sources. The essential capabilities that an analytics-driven SIEM system should provide include real-time monitoring, incident response, user monitoring, threat intelligence, analytics, and threat detection. When trying to determine the best SIEM solution for your organization, you should consider the extent to which the SIEM system provides the required features your organization needs and perhaps how it meets compliance needs as well as cost requirements.

Review Questions

1. What is an intrusion?
2. What is an IDPS?
3. What is an intrusion detection system and how does it differ from an IDPS?
4. Describe alarm clustering and alarm compaction. Why are these actions performed?
5. What is a confidence value in the context of an IDPS?
6. What are the compelling reasons to acquire and use an IDPS?
7. What is defense in depth?
8. What are the three dominant placements for IDPSs? Give one advantage and one disadvantage to each approach.
9. What is the relationship between an IDPS's total cost of ownership and its acquisition cost?
10. What is a rootkit and why is the presence of a rootkit concerning?
11. What are the dominant approaches used to detect intrusions in IDPSs? Give one advantage and one disadvantage to each approach.
12. What is a SPAN port and how is it different from a tap?
13. What is the clipping level?
14. What is a log file monitor? What is it used to accomplish?
15. What does the term *trap and trace* mean?
16. What is a honeypot? What is a honeynet? How are they different?
17. What are the core capabilities of a SIEM system?
18. What is dwell time?
19. What are the principal questions to ask when selecting a SIEM solution?

Real-World Exercises

Exercise 7-1

Do a Web search for open source and freeware intrusion detection tools. Identify a commercial equivalent of one of the no-cost choices. What would the estimated cost savings be for an organization to use the open source or freeware versions? What other expenses would the organization need to incur to implement this solution?

Exercise 7-2

Find out more about defense in depth. Visit *youtube.com* and search for "network defense in depth." Select one or two of the options and watch the videos. What is the primary value or justification for using this approach?

Exercise 7-3

Visit the site *www.honeynet.org*. What is this Web site, and what does it offer the information security professional? Visit the "Know Your Enemy" white paper series and select a paper based on the recommendation of your professor. Read it and prepare a short overview for your class.

Exercise 7-4

The OSSIM product from AT&T Security (formerly AlienVault) offers an interesting and useful online demonstration version you can use to learn more about SIEM tools. After you try the demo, the company offers the open source SIEM tool for downloading. You can access the online demo of the USM Anywhere application at *https://cybersecurity.att.com/products/usm-anywhere/demo*.

Hands-On Projects

The hands-on project for this module can be accessed in the Practice It folder in MindTap or through your instructor's LMS. The virtual labs provided with this resource can help you develop practical skills that will be of value as you progress through the course.

References

1. Scarfone, Karen, and Peter Mell. SP 800-94, Rev. 1, "Guide to Intrusion Detection and Prevention Systems (IDPS)." National Institute of Standards and Technology. July 2012. Accessed 2/24/2020 at *https://csrc.nist.gov/CSRC/media/Publications/sp/800-94/rev-1/draft/documents/draft_sp800-94-rev1.pdf*.
2. Ibid.
3. Ibid.
4. Ibid.
5. IANA. "Service Name and Transport Protocol Port Number Registry." Internet Assigned Numbers Authority. Accessed 2/24/2020 at *www.iana.org/assignments/service-names-port-numbers/service-names-port-numbers.xhtml*.
6. "Rootkits, Part 1 of 3: The Growing Threat." McAfee. April 2006. Accessed 2/24/2020 at *http://download.nai.com/products/MCAFEE-AVERT/whitepapers/akapoor_rootkits1.pdf*.
7. Russinovich, Mark. Microsoft Sysinternals. RootkitRevealer v.1.71. Accessed 2/24/2020 at *https://docs.microsoft.com/en-us/sysinternals/downloads/rootkit-revealer*.
8. Ibid.
9. Microsoft. "Rootkits." Accessed 2/11/2020 at *https://docs.microsoft.com/en-us/windows/security/threat-protection/intelligence/rootkits-malware*.
10. Scarfone, Karen, and Peter Mell. SP 800-94, Rev. 1, "Guide to Intrusion Detection and Prevention Systems (IDPS)." National Institute of Standards and Technology. July 2012. Accessed 2/24/2020 at *https://csrc.nist.gov/CSRC/media/Publications/sp/800-94/rev-1/draft/documents/draft_sp800-94-rev1.pdf*.
11. Ibid.
12. Ibid.
13. Ibid.
14. Bace, Rebecca, and Peter Mell. SP 800-31, "Intrusion Detection Systems." National Institute of Standards and Technology. November 2001. Accessed 2/24/2020 at *https://nvlpubs.nist.gov/nistpubs/Legacy/SP/nistspecialpublication800-31.pdf*.
15. Scarfone, Karen, and Peter Mell. SP 800-94, Rev. 1, "Guide to Intrusion Detection and Prevention Systems (IDPS)." National Institute of Standards and Technology. July 2012. Accessed 2/24/2020 at *https://csrc.nist.gov/CSRC/media/Publications/sp/800-94/rev-1/draft/documents/draft_sp800-94-rev1.pdf*.
16. Ibid.
17. Bace, Rebecca, and Peter Mell. SP 800-31, "Intrusion Detection Systems." National Institute of Standards and Technology. November 2001. Accessed 2/24/2020 at *https://nvlpubs.nist.gov/nistpubs/Legacy/SP/nistspecial-publication800-31.pdf*.
18. "Application-Based IDPS, Compliance Component." Missouri State Information Infrastructure Protection Center. Accessed 3/21/2004 at *http://siipc.mo.gov/PortalVB/uploads/CC%20-%20Application%20Based%20IDPS%2004-03-03.doc*.

19. Bace, Rebecca, and Peter Mell. SP 800-31, "Intrusion Detection Systems." National Institute of Standards and Technology. November 2001. Accessed 2/24/2020 at *https://nvlpubs.nist.gov/nistpubs/Legacy/SP/ nistspecialpublication800-31.pdf*.

20. Scarfone, Karen, and Peter Mell. SP 800-94, Rev. 1. "Guide to Intrusion Detection and Prevention Systems (IDPS)." National Institute of Standards and Technology. July 2012. Accessed 2/24/2020 at *https://csrc.nist .gov/CSRC/media/Publications/sp/800-94/rev-1/draft/documents/draft_sp800-94-rev1.pdf*.

21. "Application-Based IDPS, Compliance Component." Missouri State Information Infrastructure Protection Center. Accessed 3/21/2004 at *http://siipc.mo.gov/PortalVB/uploads/CC%20-%20Application%20Based%20 IDPS%2004-03-03.doc*.

22. 18 USC 2511. Accessed 2/24/2020 at *www.govinfo.gov/app/details/USCODE-2011-title18/ USCODE-2011-title18-partI-chap119-sec2511*.

23. 18 U.S.C. §§ 3121–3127. Accessed 2/24/2020 at *www.govinfo.gov/app/details/USCODE-2011-title18/ USCODE-2011-title18-partII-chap206-sec3121*.

24. 18 USC 206. Accessed 2/24/2020 at *www.govinfo.gov/app/details/USCODE-2011-title18/ USCODE-2011-title18-partII-chap206*.

25. "FireEye Mandiant M-Trends 2020 Report Reveals Cyber Criminals are Increasingly Turning to Ransomware as a Secondary Source of Income." FireEye. Accessed 4/27/2020 at *www.fireeye.com/company/ press-releases/2020/fireeye-mandiant-m-trends-2020-report-reveals-cyber-criminals-are-increasingly-turning-to- ransomware.html*.

INCIDENT RESPONSE: RESPONSE STRATEGIES

Upon completion of this material, you should be able to:

1. Explain what an IR reaction strategy is and list general strategies that apply to all incidents

2. Define *incident containment* and describe how it is applied to an incident

3. List some of the more common categories of incidents that may occur

4. Discuss the IR reaction strategies unique to each category of incident

The most extreme conditions require the most extreme response.

— Diana Nyad, U.S. long-distance swimmer

Opening Scenario

It was the middle of the night when Osbert Rimorr finished his programming assignment. Osbert was taking a university class that included a unit on how to write worm programs in order to defend against them. Now, he was about to set into motion events that would affect the lives of numerous people all over the planet (including the employees at HAL), even though he was working in a small computer lab at a relatively unknown campus.

Osbert's assignment was to create a multivector, self-replicating module that could take a payload module across a network. Although there are legitimate uses for such a module—to deploy patched versions of programs or perform unscheduled version upgrades for distributed applications, for example—many IT professionals frown on this type of programming. It is far too easy to lose control, and the consequences could be devastating.

Osbert was a conscientious student. He took great care to make sure the test payload was harmless. It was a little bigger than it needed to be, as he wanted to be able to trace it around the test lab easily. Actually, it was a lot bigger than it needed to be. It seems that Osbert really liked the fun parts he had written into his program and couldn't bring himself to streamline the test payload. He had also varied the timing parameters from those specified by his professor, making the program replicate itself much more quickly than the recipe called for. He did not want to wait around the lab all night to see the results of his test run.

The small computer lab Osbert was using had quite an impressive network built by his professors specifically for this project. Several racks of server computers were running many virtual systems, representing a large number of computers of almost every possible type. Variations in capabilities were built in to test the virulence of efforts like Osbert's. To keep the project under control, the whole test network was isolated from the campus network. Osbert could reset each virtual system to its initial state with a simple command. A single status display showed all of the virtual systems in the lab, with a small colored dot to represent each system. Osbert noticed that all the dots were a steady green, which meant that each system was in its original, uncorrupted state.

As he prepared to click the Start icon on his screen, Osbert carefully checked all the lab network's software settings one last time. Everything seemed to be in order, so he started the test. Almost too fast to see, the individual indicator dots on the master display turned red; each red light meant that a virtual computer had become compromised by Osbert's worm.

"Amazing," Osbert said out loud. The display showed him that the entire lab had been compromised in under 600 milliseconds. No one in his class had even approached that level. Being able to get half of the widely varied systems to accept a worm was the best record so far. Getting 100 percent so quickly meant that the results of his effort were quite impressive.

Feeling almost euphoric with his efforts, Osbert scooted his chair to the administrator's console and clicked the button to reset all the virtual machines to their initial state.

The command had no effect.

"No matter," Osbert thought. "I'll come back early tomorrow and restart all the servers."

Unfortunately for him, another student had made a slight but unauthorized change to the test network a few hours before Osbert began his test. The student had forgotten to disconnect a network cable that was running from the test network to a wall plate that connected to the general campus network. Osbert did not know it yet, but he had just unleashed his potent new worm on the Internet.

INTRODUCTION

incident response (IR) reaction strategies

Procedures for regaining control of systems and restoring operations to normalcy.

The most critical question on the minds of an organization's management team is "What do we do once we've detected an incident?" Known as **incident response (IR) reaction strategies**, or simply IR strategies, these procedures are the heart of the IR plan and the CSIRT's operations.

As mentioned in Module 5, how the CSIRT responds to an incident relies in part on its mission philosophy—*protect and forget* or *apprehend and prosecute*. With either approach, an organization's responses to an incident are fundamentally the same, but the data collection tasks differ dramatically.

Although there are overarching preparation and detection activities for the CSIRT and IR processes, each type of incident has its own unique characteristics that will dictate specific preparations.

IR REACTION STRATEGIES

After the CSIRT has been notified and arrives, whether physically or virtually, the first task that must occur is an assessment of the situation. During this task, the CSIRT leader (also known as the incident commander) determines what type of incident, if any, has occurred and what reaction strategies are appropriate. The CSIRT leader's second task is to begin asserting control over the situation and make positive steps to regain control over the organization's information assets. As shown in Figure 8-1, the process of detection and analysis fuels the containment, eradication, and recovery efforts of the response strategies. Without effective preparation and detection, some types of reaction and recovery would be impossible.

Incident reaction in the age of cloud computing remains a matter of preparation; the ability to react is dependent on having plans and processes in place. It may be useful to revisit the "Cloud Technologies for Backup and Recovery" section in Module 3, which discusses disaster recovery as a service. When organizations make use of cloud services for production, it becomes essential to coordinate and integrate disaster recovery planning with their cloud service provider. Many organizations now implement incident response integrated solutions using cloud service providers to add flexibility to the strategies they already have in place.

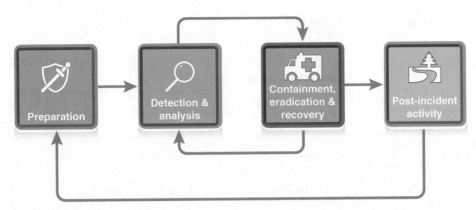

Figure 8-1 NIST IR strategy[1]

Response Preparation

"An ounce of prevention is worth a pound of cure" is especially true within the area of IR. The better the organization prepares for an incident, including prevention strategies, the easier the CSIRT's job becomes. Most of the prevention strategies an organization should pursue are simply good security practices. These would include the following:

- Using risk assessment to make informed decisions
- Acquiring and maintaining good host security
- Acquiring and maintaining good network security
- Implementing comprehensive malware prevention
- Thorough and ongoing training to raise user awareness[2]

A number of sources provide insight into implementing effective security. (See the Cengage Web site for a few of these sources, including *Principles of Information Security* and *Guide to Network Security*.) Preparation, as opposed to prevention, is specifically designed to get both the CSIRT and the rest of the organization ready to detect, respond to, and recover from incidents. Much of that subject was covered in previous modules and will not be discussed here.

To manage an incident, NIST recommends using a checklist like the one shown in Table 8-1.

Incident Containment

It is imperative that the CSIRT immediately begin to contain a confirmed incident. This is the first phase of this part of the IR—the response function. Once containment is achieved, eradication and recovery can occur.

There are a number of ways a trained CSIRT can conduct **incident containment**; however, the methods that the team uses to stop an incident can have an adverse effect on the organization and its operations. If an incident is internal, the simplest solution may be to shut down the affected systems. If it is external, the simplest solution may be to disconnect the affected systems from the Internet or other external network. Yet, some organizations cannot afford to have certain systems or network connections disconnected. These organizations invest heavily in redundancy of systems, power, and networking to avoid just such an occurrence. Although shutting down and shutting off may solve an immediate, short-term problem, it may create a much bigger long-term problem, such as damage to customer relationships, market perceptions about reliability and competence, and other forms of image and brand erosion.

Containment planning should include guidance from senior management to incident response managers about the trade-off between short-term needs and long-term objectives. If a brief interruption of Internet access can gain time to improve incident response outcomes, plan guidance should account for how much disruption can occur and how additional needs can be approved. Such pre-approved containment actions can provide more flexibility with less stress for incident response managers.

In some cases, an external attacker may simply want to disrupt normal operations. For example, if the attacker can scan an organization's information assets and cause the CSIRT to overreact and shut down the network connection, the CSIRT has

incident containment

The process by which the CSIRT acts to limit the scale and scope of an incident and begins to regain control over the organization's information assets.

Table 8-1   Incident Handling Action Checklist[3]

	Action	Completed
	Detection and Analysis	
1.	Determine whether an incident has occurred.	
1.1	Analyze the precursors and indicators.	
1.2	Look for correlating information.	
1.3	Perform research (e.g., search engines, knowledge base).	
1.4	As soon as the handler believes an incident has occurred, begin documenting the investigation and gathering evidence.	
2.	Prioritize handling the incident based on the relevant factors (functional impact, information impact, recoverability effort, etc.).	
3.	Report the incident to the appropriate internal personnel and external organizations.	
	Containment, Eradication, and Recovery	
4.	Acquire, preserve, secure, and document evidence.	
5.	Contain the incident.	
6.	Eradicate the incident.	
6.1	Identify and mitigate all vulnerabilities that were exploited.	
6.2	Remove malware, inappropriate materials, and other components.	
6.3	If more affected hosts are discovered (e.g., new malware infections), repeat Detection and Analysis steps 1.1 and 1.2 to identify all other affected hosts, then contain (5) and eradicate (6) the code that caused the incident for them.	
7.	Recover from the incident.	
7.1	Return affected systems to an operationally ready state.	
7.2	Confirm that the affected systems are functioning normally.	
7.3	If necessary, implement additional monitoring to look for future related activity.	
	Post-Incident Activity	
8.	Create a follow-up report.	
9.	Hold a "lessons learned" meeting (mandatory for major incidents, optional otherwise).	

Source: NIST.

been tricked into doing what the attacker may not have been able to accomplish on his or her own. Therefore, the CSIRT's operational guidance should at least include the following applicable containment strategies, as well as when they may be employed. Note that these guidelines are ranked from least to most intrusive for users of the systems.

- Verifying that redundant systems and data have not been compromised
- Monitoring system and network activities
- Disabling access to compromised systems that are shared with other computers
- Changing passwords or disabling accounts of compromised systems
- Disabling system services, if possible
- Disconnecting compromised systems or networks from the local network or the Internet
- Temporarily shutting down compromised systems[4]

Depending on its response philosophy, the CSIRT may not want to "tip off" attackers that they have been detected, especially if the organization is following an *apprehend and prosecute* approach. However, that approach sometimes requires a lot of patience and subterfuge (see the feature titled "The Cuckoo's Egg"), making it much more difficult than simply disconnecting the attacker. Also, it can completely change how the CSIRT responds to the incident, requiring a measure of "acceptable loss" while the CSIRT collects information for later prosecution. In the case of unauthorized use by internal users, such as when employees seek to access information beyond their authorization, it may be much more desirable to monitor their use while physically tracking down their access in an attempt to "catch them red-handed." This adds greater support to the prosecution phase, whether it consists of formal, external legal charges or administrative internal responses.

The Cuckoo's Egg[5]

Although you may think it is a bit dated, Clifford Stoll's book *The Cuckoo's Egg* still provides an excellent perspective about a real incident that turned into an international tale of espionage and intrigue. In 1986, Stoll, a graduate student and employee of the Lawrence Berkeley National Laboratory at the University of California, Berkeley, was asked to trace the origin of a $0.75 accounting error. At that time, most computer centers charged for computer use, and the error represented approximately 9 seconds of unaccounted-for computer time. After tracing the computer use to the account of someone who was outside the country on business, Stoll began tracking the unauthorized user who had hacked the account. After he had determined that the hacker was looking for information of national strategic value, he contacted the FBI, the CIA, and the NSA.

With the help of the phone company, Stoll eventually tracked the hacker to West Germany. Because of the antiquity of the phone switches there, the hacker never stayed on the dial-up Internet connection long enough for the trace to be completed. Stoll concocted a honeypot of fabricated documents that supposedly described the Strategic Defense Initiative (SDI), also known as the "Star Wars" program, and was able to keep the hacker online long enough to trace the computer modem connection to a man named Markus Hess. Eventually, Stoll traveled to Germany to testify at Hess's trial and found that Hess had been selling secrets to the Soviet Union's KGB.

Stoll first published an account of his real-life adventure in a *Communications of the ACM* article titled "Stalking the Wily Hacker." In 1990, *The Cuckoo's Egg* was turned into a NOVA documentary called *The KGB, the Computer and Me*, which is widely available for viewing online.

The CSIRT leader may also be required to notify upper management—or at least a specific member of upper management, such as the CIO or CISO—before executing a response beyond a predetermined level. For example, the CSIRT leader may be authorized to execute specific containment actions but be expected to obtain executive approval before executing others, such as disabling services or shutting down systems or connections that may affect the organization as a whole. In this instance, close communication is a must to provide quick and effective authorization in response to the CSIRT's findings.

Identifying the Attacking Hosts

When the IR plan has been activated and the CSIRT is actively responding to the threat, it must be able to identify the systems and network connection being used by the attacker. Although there is a strong urge to identify the attacker, it is almost always a better strategy to focus the team's energies on containment, eradication, and recovery efforts. The processes used to identify attacking networks and systems are time-consuming, and most attackers will have implemented countermeasures to prevent having their identities revealed. Time spent trying to identify the attacker can keep the CSIRT from attaining its primary objective, which is to minimize the impact of the emerging incident on the business.

On the other hand, it is sometimes necessary to identify the attacker, in which case the following activities should be done:

- *Verification of the IP address of the attacking system*—Even if this is not a dynamically assigned address (which is probably being rotated quickly through a list of alternate addresses during the attack), the attacker is likely to have disabled pings and traceroutes as part of his or her attack protocol. If an attacking host does respond to a ping or traceroute, it probably will not provide valid or useful information.

- *Web-based research of the attacking host IP address*—Using the apparent IP address of an attacker might lead to information about similar attacks if the attacker has used the same means of attack before. Sometimes, shared resources on the Internet can contain the means and methods of prior attacks, which could help diagnose the situation.
- *Incident/attack database searches*—There are affinity groups that collect and consolidate intrusion event data along with event details. These entries may include IDPS and firewall log files along with commentary and the outcome from the incident. Your own organization may have a searchable history from past events that, if properly organized and accessible, can help diagnose a current incident.
- *Attacker back-channel and side-channel communications*—It is possible to monitor communications channels that attackers sometimes use. For example, many attackers direct bots being used to facilitate attacks to employ IRC (Internet relay chat) channels for their command and control functions. Less disciplined attackers sometimes use social media or known IRC channels to claim credit for an attack. This type of information is of limited value but may provide some information to assist with the ongoing event.[6]

Incident Eradication

After the immediacy of incident containment has passed, the organization is still faced with the contamination that inevitably results after an unauthorized access to a system. The attacker, who may not have been careful in accessing the system, will most likely have left a wide swath of damage and destruction. In addition, most successful attackers leave behind rootkits and back doors to allow future returns. Others, using a "scorched earth" approach, leave malware behind to continue the damage long after the attacker has either left or been extricated from the system. In some instances, attackers have modified systems logs, files, user accounts, and data. All of these problems must be identified, removed to prevent recurrence, and the components restored to their pre-incident status. Many practitioners feel that a compromised system can never be restored to a trusted state. They believe that rebuilding the system image from known and trusted media is the only way to recover from these types of intrusions.

Preventing Concurrent Recurrence

While working to contain an incident, the CSIRT must ensure that the attacker (or another attacker or instigator who knows of the incident) does not initiate a new incident before the current incident is resolved. When a second attack uses the same means and methods of the first attack and is undertaken while the first attack is still under way, this is considered a *concurrent recurrence*. To prevent it, the team must continuously monitor not just the assets associated with the current incident but also the remaining assets that may be susceptible to attack using the same or similar attack methods.

One key problem with a successful intrusion is the high probability that the attacker will immediately inform his or her peers about it, either through posting in hacker discussion lists, chat rooms, e-mail, or in other ways. Not only do attackers want to gloat over their victories, they want to allow others to benefit from their wisdom and success. Unless the problem that resulted in the intrusion is remedied, the CSIRT should expect another wave of attacks by other intruders. However, as described earlier, determining the cause of the attack may take some time. In that case, the organization's monitoring teams should be on high alert, carefully examining communications and systems activities to determine if another attack has occurred.

Incident Recovery

Incident recovery may take a substantial amount of time. A full recovery is defined as the time needed for the organization to verify that all traces of an incident are erased from its systems. The emotional scars associated with a successful incident, whether natural or man-made, may never fully heal. IT and InfoSec professionals who have never

incident recovery

The reestablishment to pre-incident condition of all organizational systems.

been successfully attacked may develop a feeling of invulnerability as they work with their systems, but a successful attack will dramatically change that perspective. Although actual counseling may be neither needed nor warranted, it will take some time for the team's confidence to return. A successful and effective IR plan, properly executed, will help mitigate the aftermath of such an event.

Incident recovery involves implementing the backup and recovery plans that should already be in place before the attack. Many of the strategies described in earlier modules come into play. Any data that is suspected of corruption or modification must be recovered.

The difficult part of recovery is the identification of data that may have been disclosed. Although damaged data may be recovered, disclosed data may never be recovered. The process requires that the organization understand what data may have been disclosed and what impact it will have on the operations of the company, then determine what further actions must be taken if the disclosure includes data held by the organization that affects external stakeholders. For insight into what *not* to do in this situation, see the feature titled "Egghead."

Egghead

Established in 1984, Egghead Software began as a traditional, bricks-and-mortar computer software and hardware store. In early 2000, it merged with *Onsale.com*, creating *Egghead.com* and providing the company with a major online sales infrastructure. Among their offerings were discount auctions for older versions of software and hardware that were left over in stores when new versions were released. These auctions were very popular, as they started with bids of $1. Among the customers were the authors of this textbook.

In December 2000, the company was hacked and customer information was stolen. But, the problem wasn't just that *Egghead.com* was hacked; it was also how the entire incident was handled. One of this textbook's authors received a letter stating, in effect, "Regardless of what you might have heard, Egghead has not been successfully attacked. . . . Please feel free to continue to shop with confidence at *Egghead.com*." Nevertheless, the author immediately called his credit card companies and canceled all credit cards used on the Egghead Web site.

According to reports in the British technology newspaper *The Register*, *Egghead.com* stated that its security team had stopped the attack while it was under way. At the time, the company did not reveal whether its customers' credit card numbers were stolen in the attack or it was stopped before the data was stolen. *Egghead.com* also claimed that fewer than 7,500 accounts had experienced fraudulent activity. Industry observers reacted by saying that 7,500 compromised accounts seemed like a lot of fraudulent activity, but *Egghead.com* dismissed the number as a normal amount of fraud claims in routine credit operations. In its public statement, *Egghead.com* observed that it was difficult to make the link between any specific data spill and any fraudulent actions on a small subset of its customer accounts, and that those activities may have occurred from credit card number theft elsewhere. The vendor further maintained it had no evidence that the fraud victims' card numbers were stolen from its Web site.

A week after the article ran in *The Register*, one of the authors received another letter, this one stating, "You may have heard that *Egghead.com* has had a minor breach. We are confident that none of the data that may have been accessed involves your personal information. . . . Please feel free to continue to shop with confidence at *Egghead.com*." Two weeks after that, a third letter was received: "*Egghead.com* regrets to inform you that it has experienced a major breach of its customer database. We advise you to immediately take whatever actions you feel are necessary to protect your credit cards and other personal information. . . . Please feel free to continue to shop with confidence at *Egghead.com*."

In other words, it took almost a full month before the organization acknowledged that over 3.6 million customer accounts, including credit card information, were compromised. Many customers didn't even get the courtesy of the letters that the author received. They were notified by their banks, which were notified by Visa, which in turn had been notified by Egghead once the company confirmed that it had indeed been hacked. The resulting fallout and media attention was the end of Egghead. In 2001, it was torn apart and sold piecemeal. Amazon purchased most of the company for just over $6 million, a fraction of the company's previous worth.

While you might think that a business failure from 20 years ago is too old to study, consider that the situation has become a timeless problem, with company after company learning the same lessons again and again. The key point is that the larger part of the destruction sometimes comes from how the aftermath is handled after the attack is identified. Delayed breach disclosures in recent years have shown that this point is still true—consider Target in 2013, Equifax in 2017, and First American in 2019. As Lanny Davis, former Special Counsel to President Clinton, advises others on how to deliver bad news, "Tell it all, tell it early, tell it yourself."

Films can often be an entertaining way to get context for serious topics of information security and incident response. You may have access to some of the films listed here; they might inform your understanding of attackers and incident response strategies as organizations deal with attacks:

- *Algorithm* (2014)—A procedural that shows much of what happens from the hacker's perspective.
- *Blackhat* (2015)—An action thriller with a hacker protagonist and a global geopolitical backdrop.
- *Takedown* (2000)—How the notorious hacker Kevin Mitnick was apprehended.
- *The Matrix* (1999)—A fanciful depiction of virtual reality with a hacker cultural backdrop.
- *WarGames* (1983)—A classic depiction of hacking before the Internet and the potential for global thermonuclear war.

INCIDENT CONTAINMENT AND ERADICATION STRATEGIES FOR SPECIFIC ATTACKS

Selecting the appropriate reaction strategy is an exercise in risk assessment in which the CSIRT leader must determine the appropriate response based on a number of variables, including the following aspects of the incident:

- Type
- Method of incursion
- Current level of success
- Expected or projected level of success
- Current level of loss
- Expected or projected level of loss
- Target
- Target's level of classification and/or sensitivity
- Any legal or regulatory impacts mandating a specific response

The complexity of the resulting decision thus mandates clear and effective CSIRT reaction procedures, which enable the CSIRT leader to take quick and appropriate actions to contain the incident.

For example, different strategies will be needed for an incident involving a contractor-supplied laptop that infects local network hosts because it did not have proper malware defenses and for an incident involving a network-based DDoS attack. Each major type of incident that can be foreseen should have a separate containment strategy defined as part of the organization's planning process. Each complete containment strategy should include details about how the organization will handle the following:

- Theft or damage to assets
- Whether to preserve evidence for potential criminal prosecution
- Service-level commitments and contract requirements to customers
- Allocation of necessary resources to activate the strategy
- Graduated responses that may be necessary—for example, whether a partial containment should be used if a full containment is not achievable
- Duration of containment efforts—for example, whether some aspects of containment can be lifted as the threat is reduced

One strategy is to engage in watchful waiting, a tactic that deliberately permits the attack to continue while the entire event is observed and additional evidence is collected. The use of this type of delayed containment may need to be previewed with legal counsel to see if it is feasible. Knowingly allowing an attacker to continue the attack may give rise to liability, or it may prevent the prosecution of the attacker. The liability may result if an attacker is allowed to continue and then uses the compromised system to attack others, resulting in downstream liability. Also, waiting may result in escalation of the attack's intensity, leaving responders unable to interrupt the attack after all. Only experienced CSIRTs should contemplate delayed containment because it requires a lot of discipline and skill to interrupt an escalated attack in only a few seconds. In most cases, even the most capable CSIRT will forego delayed containment; most often, the risks far outweigh any benefits.

Another thing to consider regarding containment is that attackers can devise means to cause further damage when containment steps are initiated. For example, an attacker may implement a "heartbeat" process that monitors the ongoing attack; if network traffic between the attacker and the compromised system is interrupted, a malicious script can be triggered, wiping out all the data on the compromised host. Disconnecting a compromised system does not mean it is safe from further damage.

Just as each incident has its own issues that must be understood, each plan needs to be designed to react appropriately. The following sections provide insight into some of the more common attack incidents. Most of this material has been adapted, at least in part, from NIST's Special Publication 800-61, Revision 2, "Computer Security Incident Handling Guide," and its predecessors.[7]

Handling Denial-of-Service (DoS) Incidents

As it was defined in Module 1, a *denial-of-service (DoS)* attack is designed to prevent the legitimate users of a system or network from using it—for example, by consuming the resources that a service normally provides. DoS attacks might use a large number of network connections or excessive network bandwidth from a network service or use a large quantity of processor time, disk capacity, or computer memory. A *distributed denial-of-service (DDoS)* attack is usually much more impactful than a DoS attack; a DDoS attack results from the use of multiple systems to simultaneously attack a single target.

Before the DoS Incident

Long before a DoS (or DDoS) attack occurs, certain tasks should be performed to maximize the organization's response capability. These include the following:

- *Coordinating with the ISP*—The most important partner in a DoS attack is the organization's Internet service provider. Although not all DoS attacks involve the organization's ISP, most do; if an organization is experiencing a DoS attack, so is its ISP. Preconfiguring ISP resources for expected versus unexpected traffic monitoring and filtering can shut certain attacks off before they start. The ISP may also have guidelines for responding to DoS incidents, including contact numbers and emergency points of contact.
- *Collaborating and coordinating with professional response agencies*—There are a number of professional IR agencies, such as US-CERT, which was discussed in Module 4. Coordination with these agencies and involvement in industry partnerships can provide additional resources to help prevent and detect DoS incidents.
- *Implementation of prevention technologies*—The use of IDPS technologies can help detect and respond to DoS attacks with little or no additional intervention on the organization's part. However, with the level of false positives that can occur from these systems, careful configuration and monitoring is still crucial.
- *Monitoring resources*—In order to determine when a DoS attack is occurring, the organization must understand normal and peak operation resource utilization. Monitoring system performance, as described in previous modules, allows the organization to see when it is experiencing traffic beyond what it can reasonably handle.
- *Coordinating the monitoring and analysis capabilities*—Internal coordination between divisions such as systems, servers, and networking groups is important for sharing resources and information when responding to DoS-style incidents.
- *Setting up logging and documentation*—Key system and networking equipment should be configured to report critical facts to systems logs. Logging should be hardened by establishing backup and offline logging capabilities. To avoid situations in which an attacker purposefully conceals attack activities, it is important to configure logging functions to store copies in read-only media like CDs or DVDs and to offline log monitors, in which the logs are copied into a different system. Documentation of current system configurations at a recorded baseline is also critical to determining if any unauthorized changes have been made.
- *Configuring network devices to prevent DoS incidents*—Unneeded and unused services should be blocked, with traffic routed to approved destinations and carefully managed. In essence, best practices should be followed in the configuration of key devices.

During the DoS Incident

The first step in responding to a DoS incident is the detection of the incident. If the organization has done an effective job of preparing for and preventing such an incident, then detecting it should be straightforward.

Table 8-2 provides a list of DoS attack precursors—conditions that often lead to a DoS attack—and suitable responses. Table 8-3 provides a list of indicators that a DoS attack is under way.

The next step in responding to a DoS incident is selecting the appropriate containment strategy. Although it may be possible to simply shut off the network connection that the incident is using as a conduit, sometimes it may not be possible or even feasible. In fact, the incident could cause more damage if it forces the organization to cease online operations than if the incident were simply managed without shutting down the network connection. The next idea may be to block the address that the attacks are coming from. In the case of a simple DoS incident, this may be effective,

Table 8-2   DoS Attack Precursors and Suitable Responses[8]

Precursor	Response
Reconnaissance activity to determine which attacks would be effective; often, this is a lower volume of the traffic that will be used in the attack.	Attempt to block the attack by quickly altering the security posture—for example, altering firewall rule sets to block a particular protocol from being used or to protect a vulnerable host.
Newly released DoS tool.	Investigate the new tool and, if possible, alter security controls so that the tool will not be effective against the organization.

Source: NIST.

Table 8-3   Indicators of a DoS Attack[9]

Malicious Action	Indicators
Network-based DoS attack against a network	• User reports of system and network unavailability • Unexplained connection losses • Network intrusion detection alerts • Increased network bandwidth utilization • Asymmetric network traffic pattern (large amount of traffic entering the network, little traffic leaving the network) • Firewall and router log entries • Packets with unusual source addresses • Packets with nonexistent destination addresses
DoS attack against the operating system of a particular host	• User reports of system and application unavailability • Network and host intrusion detection alerts • Operating system log entries • Packets with unusual source addresses
DoS attack against an application on a particular host	• User reports of application unavailability • Network and host intrusion detection alerts • Application log entries • Packets with unusual source addresses

Source: NIST.

but keep in mind that most DoS sources are spoofed and may therefore represent the address of a legitimate source that the organization may not want to permanently block. In the case of a complex DoS attack, there may be thousands of addresses representing compromised attack sources. Some attackers will frequently shift source addresses, which makes response even more difficult. So, in addition to blocking (at least temporarily) incoming addresses, the organization may want to consider the following strategies:

- *Trying to fix the source problem*—Correct the underlying issue that is allowing the DoS or DDoS. The attack may be the result of an unfiltered protocol or service, or of an unpatched server. Resolution not only stops the current incident but will prevent repeat incidents.
- *Changing the organization's filtering strategy*—Altering the filtering rules, either temporarily or permanently, may resolve the issue. Be aware of the possibility of service disruption for legitimate customers. Also, the attacker may not only shift spoofed addresses, he may also shift source protocols. Also be aware that the more rules a device has, the slower it will run. Thus, changing the organization's filtering strategy should only be done on a temporary, emergency basis if it causes issues. For long-term solutions, the organization may want to consider upgrades to critical network technologies to make such responses insignificant.
- *Trying to filter based on characteristics of the attack*—For example, if the attack is using ICMP echo requests, an organization could alter its perimeter security to temporarily keep such requests from entering the network. Unfortunately, this is not always practical. For example, if an attacker is sending a SYN flood to a Web server's Hypertext Transfer Protocol (HTTP) port, blocking SYN packets destined for that port will itself cause a DoS for users. In addition, most DoS attack tools are versatile, so if one attack method is blocked, attackers can easily switch to another method. Another strategy is rate limiting: permitting only a certain number of packets per second to use a specific protocol or contact a certain host. Although filtering techniques can be valuable in containing incidents, they can introduce additional problems. For example, adding new rules to a router or firewall may have a substantial negative impact on the device's performance, causing network slowdowns or even a DoS. Organizations should carefully consider where filtering should be implemented (for example, a border router or firewall) and should be prepared to upgrade networking devices if necessary to facilitate filtering of long-term attacks.
- *Engaging upstream partners*—Having the organization's ISP prescreen traffic can dramatically reduce the DoS's impact on the organization's networking equipment. The attacks coming over the ISP's networks can just as easily be filtered at the ISP as in the organization. By having the ISP handle the incident, it can prevent the same attacker from affecting other customers and thus improve relations with its customers as well.
- *Eliminating or relocating the target system*—If an incident is focused on a particular target, such as an e-commerce server, it may be advantageous to move the system to a location that is more difficult for the attacker to reach. Using proxy servers to act as intermediaries may reduce some of the issues; however, the attack may simply shift to the proxy, resulting in the same DoS issues. The target service may also be relocated to a different IP address. Again, however, if the attacker is actively managing the attack, he or she may simply shift the focus.

The organization may have to go through a trial-and-error process until it finds a solution that eliminates the issues associated with the attack without disrupting normal operations. In any instance, it should at least inform its ISP to enable the needed resources and facilitate the response.

After the DoS Incident

After the organization has responded to the DoS incident, it should consider its overall philosophy of *protect and forget* or *apprehend and prosecute*. In either case, the organization will want to collect some evidence to see how the incident occurred and to provide insight into how to avoid future recurrences. Table 8-4 provides a checklist for handling a DoS incident.

Table 8-4 Incident Handling Action Checklist for DoS Attack[10]

	Action	Completed
	Detection and Analysis	
1.	Prioritize handling the incident based on the business impact.	
1.1	Identify which resources have been affected, and forecast which resources will be affected.	
1.2	Estimate the current and potential technical effect of the incident.	
1.3	Find the appropriate cell(s) in the prioritization matrix, based on the technical effect and affected resources.	
2.	Report the incident to the appropriate internal personnel and external organizations.	
	Containment, Eradication, and Recovery	
3.	Acquire, preserve, secure, and document evidence.	
4.	Contain the incident; halt the DoS if it has not already stopped.	
4.1	Identify and mitigate all vulnerabilities that were used.	
4.2	If not yet contained, implement filtering based on the characteristics of the attack, if feasible.	
4.3	If not yet contained, contact the ISP for assistance in filtering the attack.	
4.4	If not yet contained, relocate the target.	
5.	Eradicate the incident; if Step 4.1 was not performed, identify and mitigate all vulnerabilities that were used.	
6.	Recover from the incident.	
6.1	Return affected systems to an operationally ready state.	
6.2	Confirm that the affected systems are functioning normally.	
6.3	If necessary and feasible, implement additional monitoring to look for future related activity.	
	Post-Incident Activity	
7.	Create a follow-up report.	
8.	Hold a "lessons learned" meeting.	

Source: NIST.

Malware

Deliberate software attacks occur when an individual or group designs and deploys software to attack a system. Most of this software is referred to as **malicious code**, **malicious software**, or as it was defined in Module 1, *malware*. Malware is designed to steal information, do damage, or deny service to the target systems. According to the 2019 McAfee Quarterly Threats report, almost 1 billion malware instances were detected in early 2019, with over 65 million instances of new malware, continuing the trend of increased numbers and types of malware threats.[11] The 2020 FireEye M-Trends report indicates that 25 percent of the malware observed in 2019 was publicly available, meaning any attacker could download and use it. The report also indicates that the varieties of malware types and instances continue to expand with the identification of new malware families.[12]

As you learned in prior modules, some of the more common instances of malicious code are viruses and worms, Trojan horses, logic bombs, back doors, and rootkits. Many malware attacks are blended attacks, which involve more than one type of malware and more than one type of transmission method, and are usually

malicious code

Computer software specifically designed to perform malicious or unwanted actions. Synonymous with *malware*.

malicious software

See *malware*.

prefaced with a type of social engineering attack, as in the case of a phishing attack. Blended attacks can occur via any type of Internet or network service, such as e-mail, Web servers or clients, and Windows shares.

A type of malware that has become less of a concern—in fact, many people do not consider it malware at all—is the cookie. The term *cookie* is short for *cookie crumb*, evoking Hansel leaving crumbs behind as he walked from his parents' house through the forest in the Grimm's fairy tale "Hansel and Gretel." A session cookie is a data file that is valid for just one session at a Web site, which uses it to "make notes" about that session. A persistent cookie, on the other hand, is stored on the client computer for a much longer time. This type of storage allows the Web site to identify the system on any return visits. Usually, a persistent cookie is meant to enable the Web site to customize or enhance the user's experience on subsequent visits to the site. However, persistent cookies can be misused as a form of spyware called "tracking cookies." A tracking cookie collects valuable personal information and then sends it along to the attacker, who can sell it to identity thieves for a profit. When malware-control applications are concerned with cookies, they usually focus on the removal of these tracking cookies.[13] In recent years, there has been a dramatic increase in the expectation (and in some jurisdictions, the legal requirement) that Web sites notify users when cookies are being used, as shown in Figure 8-2.

cookie
A small quantity of data stored on the user's computer by a Web site as a means of recording that the user has visited that Web site.

Before the Malware Incident

If at all possible, malware incidents should be detected in advance through antivirus and antimalware applications, as well as through effective security awareness programs designed to educate employees on how to handle suspicious events. Other ways to prepare for a malware incident include the following:

- *Awareness programs informing users about current malware issues*—This could be done through e-mails, newsletters, or regular meetings.
- *Keeping up on vendor and IR agency postings and bulletins*—Many agencies, such as the Department of Homeland Security's Cybersecurity and Infrastructure Security Agency (CISA), formerly known as US-CERT (*www.us-cert.gov*), and SecurityFocus (*www.securityfocus.com*), inform the public about new malware threats. Mitre (*http://cve.mitre.org*) maintains a massive database of vulnerabilities that describes known issues with applications, including those associated with malware. Having security personnel keep up with their professional reading will help the organization prepare for an incident in these areas.
- *Implementing appropriate IDPSs*—Both network-based and host-based IDPSs can help screen for malware on the organization's networks and systems. Utilities such as file integrity checkers, if used regularly, can help ensure that systems are in an expected state, with no unauthorized modifications or deletions of critical system files.
- *Effective inventory and data organization*—The organization should inventory, document, and constantly reassess its current systems and network—their configuration, implementation details, and critical information assets. By knowing what the organization has, it becomes easier to detect inserted assets, modifications, or damage to existing assets and stolen assets.
- *Implementing and testing data backup and recovery programs*—Malware most commonly corrupts files it is targeted toward, including inserting new files and replacing existing critical system files. Being able to quickly and reliably replace those corrupted files with known, trusted, archived versions is imperative. This includes any installation materials needed, such as install kits, update files, and patch files.

Figure 8-2   Example of notice that cookies are being used

malware hoax

A message aimed at causing users to waste time reacting to a nonexistent malware threat.

With regard to malware prevention, NIST recommends the following:

- *Use antivirus/antispyware software.*
- *Block suspicious files by configuring servers and networking devices to prevent distribution of certain file extensions (for example, .exe, .com, .msi, .pif), especially in e-mail and Web traffic.*
- *Filter unwanted e-mail traffic and prohibit open relays*—As you learned in Module 1, *spam* is both a common carrier for malware and a source of phishing attacks that attempt to lead users to a location where malware exists. Effective network spam filters prevent these potential incidents from reaching the users. Some malware attacks use organizational e-mail systems to forward the malware's payload via e-mail messages. Prohibiting open relays prevents the use of these systems as a relay for messages that neither originate from internal users nor are designated for them. In general, the organization should configure e-mail clients and servers to be as secure as possible to greatly reduce the spread of malware if a single system is infected.
- *Minimize file transfer capabilities to those essential to business operations*—Most organizations don't need file transfer capability, deferring instead to e-mail attachments or physical data transfers via USB drives or optical media. If the organization doesn't need a file transfer service, it should be disabled and its use prohibited. This includes peer-to-peer applications, file and music sharing, instant messaging, IRCs, and even private Web servers within the organization. If there is concern for malware distribution via physical media, systems can be configured to prohibit read/write functions from external media such as USB devices.
- *Eliminate or prohibit file sharing and print sharing*—Windows open shares are a well-known avenue of attack for malware. If these shares aren't absolutely essential to the organization, they should be removed and operating systems should be configured to prohibit their implementation.
- *Educate, inform, and involve users at all stages*—Keeping users informed of current threats, educated on what to do when facing a potential incident, and involved in organizational IR planning can help mitigate the risk of incidents across the board.[14]

Of particular note is the malware hoax. Essentially a DoS attack, the malware (or virus) hoax is commonly used in phishing attacks aimed at getting users to visit a fake Web site; others are designed to work as human malware devices, tricking users into manually deleting or modifying key files. Well-meaning people can disrupt the harmony and flow of an organization when they send group e-mails warning of supposedly dangerous viruses that don't actually exist. When people fail to follow virus-reporting procedures, the network becomes overloaded, and much time and energy is wasted as users forward a warning message to everyone they know, post the message on bulletin boards, and try to update their antivirus protection software.

A number of Internet resources enable individuals to research viruses and determine if they are fact or fiction. For the latest information on real, threatening viruses and hoaxes, along with other relevant and current security information, visit one of the addresses in the nearby information box.

For more information on viruses and malware threats, visit the following sites:
- Norton's Internet Security Center—*https://us.norton.com/internetsecurity-emerging-threats.html*
- McAfee Labs Threat Center—*www.mcafee.com/enterprise/en-us/threat-center/mcafee-labs.html*
- Microsoft Security Intelligence—*www.microsoft.com/en-us/wdsi/*
- Hoax-Slayer—*www.hoax-slayer.com*

During the Malware Incident

Early detection of a malware incident relies heavily on the preparations described in the previous section. Antivirus programs, antimalware, and IDPSs are the front line in detection. However, the end users are the first line in reporting. Notifications to the organization's help desk of suspected malware infestation should be the first clue of a serious malware incident. The help desk then becomes the notification agency responsible for activating the CSIRT. Table 8-5 provides a list of malicious-code precursors and suitable responses. Unfortunately, malware doesn't always trip these indicators. Therefore, the organization's personnel should be aware of indicators of malicious code, as listed in Table 8-6. Although these indicators are strong warnings of possible malware incidents, they are not necessarily guarantees. Many of the indicated events could be the results of other more normal problems, such as system or infrastructure failures (cabling, power, ISP).

Table 8-5 Malicious Code Precursors and Suitable Responses[15]

Precursor	Response
An alert warns of new malicious code that targets software that the organization uses.	Research the new virus to determine whether it is real or a hoax. This can be done through antivirus vendor Web sites and virus hoax sites. If the malicious code is confirmed as authentic, ensure that antivirus software is updated with virus signatures for the new malicious code. If a virus signature is not yet available, and the threat is serious and imminent, the activity might be blocked through other means, such as configuring e-mail servers or clients to block e-mails matching characteristics of the new malicious code. The team might also want to notify antivirus vendors of the new virus.
Antivirus software detects and successfully disinfects or quarantines a newly received infected file.	Determine how the malicious code entered the system and what vulnerability or weakness it was attempting to exploit. If the malicious code might pose a significant risk to other users and hosts, mitigate the weaknesses that the malicious code used to reach the system and would have used to infect the target host.

Source: NIST.

Table 8-6 Indicators of Malicious Code[16]

Malicious Action	Indicators
A virus that spreads through e-mail and infects a host	• Antivirus software alerts of infected files • Sudden increase in the number of e-mails being sent and received • Changes to templates for word-processing documents, spreadsheets, and so on • Deleted, corrupted, or inaccessible files • Unusual items on the screen, such as odd messages and graphics • Programs that start slowly, run slowly, or do not run at all • System instability and crashes • If the virus achieves root-level access, see the indications for "Root compromise of a host" as listed in Table 8-10, "Indicators of Unauthorized Access."
A worm that spreads through a vulnerable service and infects a host	• Antivirus software alerts of infected files • Port scans and failed connection attempts targeted at the vulnerable service (e.g., open Windows shares, HTTP) • Increased network usage • Programs that start slowly, run slowly, or do not run at all • System instability and crashes • If the worm achieves root-level access, see the indications for "Root compromise of a host" as listed in Table 8-10, "Indicators of Unauthorized Access."
A Trojan horse that is installed and running on a host	• Antivirus software alerts of Trojan horse versions of files • Network intrusion detection alerts of Trojan horse client-server communications • Firewall and router log entries for Trojan horse client-server communications • Network connections between the host and unknown remote systems • Unusual and unexpected ports open • Unknown processes running • High amounts of network traffic generated by the host, particularly if directed at external host(s) • Programs that start slowly, run slowly, or do not run at all • System instability and crashes • If the Trojan horse achieves root-level access, see the indications for "Root compromise of a host" as listed in Table 8-10.

(continues)

Table 8-6   Indicators of Malicious Code[16] (*Continued*)

Malicious Action	Indicators
Malicious mobile code on a Web site that is used to infect a host with a virus, worm, or Trojan horse	• Indications listed earlier in this table for the specific type of malicious code • Unexpected dialog boxes requesting permission to do something • Unusual graphics, such as overlapping or overlaid message boxes
Malicious mobile code on a Web site that exploits vulnerabilities on a host	• Unexpected dialog boxes requesting permission to do something • Unusual graphics, such as overlapping or overlaid message boxes • Sudden increase in the number of e-mails being sent and received • Network connections between the host and unknown remote systems • If the mobile code achieves root-level access, see the indications for "Root compromise of a host" as listed in Table 8-10
A user who receives a virus hoax message	• Original source of the message a government agency or important official person rather than an authoritative computer-security group • No links to outside sources • Tone and terminology that attempt to invoke a panic or sense of urgency • Recipients urged to delete certain files and forward the message to others

Source: NIST.

These tables are a start toward understanding the precursors and indicators an organization may encounter, but this information must be augmented with an ongoing threat intelligence process, which you learned about in Module 7. Attackers have many ways to gain a foothold in your systems, and these methods will leave markers that can be detected. A comprehensive threat intelligence program will let you update tables of precursors and indicators to match the current threat environment.

 Many widely available open source sites can help you gain insight into the threats you face. One well-regarded source for up-to-date threat intelligence is the OWASP Top Ten page at *https://owasp.org/www-project-top-ten/*.

Containment strategies for malware begin with the prevention strategies outlined earlier: antimalware and IPDSs. These applications will not only detect malware, they will quarantine it and handle it in the manner in which the applications are configured, which ranges from simple annotation of log files to notification of organizational personnel to automatic deletion. After an infection has been detected, it is up to the CSIRT to look for other possibly undetected infections. Ways to accomplish this include the following:

- Scanning internal systems to look for active service ports that are not supposed to be present on internal systems. These service ports may be Trojan horse or back-door access mechanisms placed by malware or other attacks.
- Prompt and aggressive use of updated scanning and cleanup tools.
- Analysis of the logs from e-mail servers, firewalls, IDPSs, and individual host log files for anomalous items. This may be part of a broader log analysis initiative often undertaken for network security purposes.
- Giving network and host intrusion systems access to signature files that can indicate when the behavior characteristics of malware infection have occurred. The alerts can be screened for possible infections.
- Periodic and ongoing audits of the running processes on systems to validate that all running processes are expected and legitimate.[17]

The CSIRT should also consider notifying appropriate entities, including antimalware and IDPS vendors, if it encounters malware that is not commonly known or understood, or if the malware was not automatically detected by the antimalware or IDPS. Catching malware "in the wild" often helps official agencies and vendors better detect the malware in the future, especially new strains of malware. In 2019 alone, FireEye's IR division detected 1268 families of malware, of which 500 were new, with each family consisting of one or more related malware variants.[18]

Response strategies for malware outbreaks include the following:

- *Filtering e-mail based on subject, attachment type using malware signatures, or other criteria*—Though not fool-proof, given that patterns are not always known in advance, filtering can intercept some attacks and lower the likelihood of a successful attack.
- *Blocking known attackers*—Once again, this is not foolproof, given that attackers are always changing their attack parameters, but the ability to block specific addresses may offer a tactical means of control while incidents are under way.
- *Interrupting some services*—During severe outbreaks of mail-based malware, it may be useful to quarantine e-mail for a period until malware filters are updated and pattern files are distributed.
- *Severing networks from the Internet or each other*—Because some malware may involve host-to-host infection using worms or other means, disconnecting the network connections selectively can limit this spread. Well-designed systems may have isolated network segments that enable more graceful disconnection or may have segmentation that allows some types of network service to continue—for example, local file servers and printers may continue to operate when Internet access has been disrupted.
- *Engaging the users*—Users can be trained and provided with the means to identify infections and react appropriately. This may be as simple as calling the help desk when they see unusual behavior.
- *Disrupting service*—By selective disruption of services, it may be possible to disrupt malware attack vectors; however, it also may disrupt essential services. Each organization, as part of the BIA used earlier in the IR planning process, should have a list of interdependent services that will enable CSIRT members to avoid inadvertently disrupting critical services.[19]

After the Malware Incident

The standard actions common to all incidents should be followed when the malware incident is over—specifically, reporting and AARs (after-action reviews). The most critical action after a malware incident has been handled is to constantly monitor to prevent reinfection. Distribution of warnings that a malware incident occurred and was successfully handled will further educate the organization's users as well as remind them of the necessary steps in responding to a malware incident and whom to notify (and when) if they suspect they have experienced one. Table 8-7 provides a summary checklist to use when handling a malicious code or malware incident.

Table 8-7   Malicious Code Action Checklist[20]

	Action	Completed
	Detection and Analysis	
1.	Prioritize the handling of the incident based on its business impact.	
1.1	Identify which resources have been affected and forecast which resources will be affected.	
1.2	Estimate the current and potential technical effect of the incident.	
1.3	Find the appropriate cell(s) in the prioritization matrix, based on the technical effect and affected resources.	
2.	Report the incident to the appropriate internal personnel and external organizations.	
	Containment, Eradication, and Recovery	
3.	Contain the incident.	
3.1	Identify infected systems.	
3.2	Disconnect infected systems from the network.	
3.3	Mitigate vulnerabilities that were exploited by the malicious code.	
3.4	If necessary, block the transmission mechanisms for the malicious code.	
4.	Eradicate the incident.	
4.1	Disinfect, quarantine, delete, and replace infected files.	
4.2	Mitigate the exploited vulnerabilities for other hosts within the organization.	

(continues)

Table 8-7   Malicious Code Action Checklist[20] (*Continued*)

	Action	Completed
5.	Recover from the incident.	
5.1	Confirm that the affected systems are functioning normally.	
5.2	If necessary, implement additional monitoring to look for future related activity.	
Post-Incident Activity		
6.	Create a follow-up report.	
7.	Hold a "lessons learned" meeting.	

Source: NIST.

unauthorized access (UA)

A circumstance in which an individual, an application, or another program, through access to the operating systems or application programming interface (API), attempts or gains access to an information asset without explicit permission or authorization.

Unauthorized Access

When the term **unauthorized access** is mentioned, the inclination is to use it as a synonym for hacking. However, the term also refers to attempts by insiders to escalate their privileges, access information, and access other assets to which they do not explicitly have authorization. The legal term for these attempts is *exceeding authorized access*. This includes both internal and external efforts as well as virtual attempts (over the network) and physical incidents. According to NIST, examples of UA include the following:

- Gaining unauthorized administrative control of any server or service
- Gaining unauthorized access to any network or computing resource, including connection to inadvertently open service ports or dialing into unsecured modems
- Defacing or unauthorized modification of any public-facing or internal information service, including Web-based content
- Guessing or cracking passwords, or subverting or bypassing multifactor authentication procedures, to gain unapproved access to any server or service
- Viewing or copying any nonpublic information without proper authorization
- Sniffing network traffic without explicit authorization
- Using network and computing resources to distribute pirated content, including music and software
- Using social engineering techniques, such as impersonating another person to gain unauthorized access
- Using unattended or unsecured workstations without permission of the authorized user[21]

Verizon's 2019 Data Breach Investigations Report indicated that over 52 percent of investigated breaches involved some type of hacking, a value that has remained relatively constant since 2013. Of particular note is the prominent target—mostly Web applications on servers (63 percent).[22]

Before the UA Incident

Preparation and prevention of UA incidents involves a process that addresses industry-recommended security efforts. Preparing to handle these incidents requires much the same effort as preparing for other incidents in installing, configuring, and maintaining effective IDPSs. Other strategies that specifically target UA incidents include the centralization and protection of log servers and implementing an effective password policy.

Using a common central log server and placing it in a more highly protected area of the network may not prevent UA incidents, but it will certainly assist in the post-event analyses that are needed to prevent reoccurrence. If a skilled individual seeks to gain UA, she may attempt to cover her efforts, successful or not, by erasing or corrupting logs stored on the target systems or intermediate systems, such as network routers. Copying log files in real time or using centralized log servers can negate this attempt to "cover one's tracks."

Implementing an effective password policy and having a complete and usable management policy as well as technology-enforced password requirements is critical. Use of an industry de facto standard password policy is recommended. One example is the 10+4 model (at least 10 characters, with at least one uppercase letter, one lowercase letter, one number, and one special character), which will go a long way toward preventing certain types of UA attacks. Coupled with policies on changing passwords regularly, storing passwords securely, and other safe practices, the written policy is an effective first step in UA mitigation. Enforcing those policies—ensuring they are distributed, read, understood, agreed to, and uniformly applied—will further improve the organization's readiness for UA incidents. The second half of the strategy—implementing the written policies as systems policies—will cement the strategies in place. Making the user agree to a defined password strength is one thing, but configuring the system to not allow a password that doesn't comply is quite different. In the event of a reported password breach, the organization should plan to implement an immediate password change to prevent the widespread use of ill-gotten passwords and password files. Table 8-8 provides an overview of additional actions to prevent UA incidents.

Table 8-8   Actions to Prevent UA Incidents[23]

Category	Actions
Network security	• Configure the network perimeter to deny all incoming traffic that is not expressly permitted. • Properly secure all remote access methods, especially VPNs. When securing remote access, carefully consider the trustworthiness of the clients; if they are outside the organization's control, they should be given as little access to resources as possible, and their actions should be closely monitored. • Put all publicly accessible services on secured demilitarized zone (DMZ) network segments. The network perimeter can then be configured so that external hosts can establish connections only to hosts on the DMZ, not internal network segments. • Use private IP addresses for all hosts on internal networks. This will restrict the ability of attackers to establish direct connections to internal hosts.
Host security	• Perform regular vulnerability assessments to identify serious risks and mitigate the risks to an acceptable level. • Disable all unneeded services on hosts. Separate critical services so they run on different hosts. If an attacker then compromises a host, immediate access should be gained only to a single service. • Run services with the least privileges possible to reduce the immediate impact of successful exploits. • Use host-based/personal firewall software to limit individual hosts' exposure to attacks. • Limit unauthorized physical access to logged-in systems by requiring hosts to lock idle screens automatically and asking users to log off before leaving the office. • Regularly verify the permission settings for critical resources, including password files, sensitive databases, and public Web pages. This process can be easily automated to report changes in permissions on a regular basis.
Authentication and authorization	• Create a password policy that requires the use of complex, difficult-to-guess passwords, forbids password sharing, and directs users to use different passwords on different systems, especially external hosts and applications. • Require sufficiently strong authentication, particularly for accessing critical resources. • Create authentication and authorization standards for employees and contractors to follow when evaluating or developing software. For example, passwords should be strongly encrypted using a FIPS 140-validated algorithm when they are transmitted or stored. • Establish procedures for provisioning and deprovisioning user accounts. These should include an approval process for new account requests and a process for periodically disabling or deleting accounts that are no longer needed.
Physical security	• Implement physical security measures that restrict access to critical resources.

Source: NIST.

During the UA Incident

Table 8-9 highlights some possible precursors and suitable responses to a UA incident.

Table 8-9   UA Incident Precursors and Suitable Responses[24]

Precursor	Response
Reconnaissance activity to map hosts and services and identify vulnerabilities. Activity may include port scans, host scans, vulnerability scans, pings, traceroutes, DNS zone transfers, OS fingerprinting, and banner grabbing. Such activity is detected primarily through IDPS software, secondarily through log analysis. Look for distinct changes in reconnaissance patterns—for example, a sudden interest in a particular port number or host.	If the activity points out a vulnerability that appears to be exploitable, the organization may have time to block future attacks by mitigating the vulnerability (e.g., patching a host, disabling an unused service, modifying firewall rules).
A new exploit for gaining UA is released publicly, and it poses a significant threat.	Investigate the new exploit and, if possible, alter security controls to minimize the potential impact of the exploit.
Users report possible social engineering attempts—attackers trying to trick them into revealing sensitive information, such as passwords, or encouraging them to download or run programs and file attachments.	The IR team should send a bulletin to users with advice on handling the social engineering attempts. The team should determine what resources the attacker was interested in and look for corresponding log-based precursors because it is likely that the social engineering is only part of the reconnaissance.
A person or system may observe a failed physical access attempt (for example, an outsider attempting to open a secured door or an unknown individual using a canceled ID badge).	If possible, security guards should detain the person. The purpose of the activity should be determined, and it should be verified that the physical and computer security controls are strong enough to block the apparent threat. (An attacker who cannot gain physical access may perform remote computing-based attacks instead.) Physical and computer security controls should be strengthened, if necessary.

Source: NIST.

Table 8-10 provides a list of indicators that a UA has occurred.

Table 8-10   Indicators of Unauthorized Access[25]

Malicious Action	Indicators

Root compromise of a host	• Existence of unauthorized security-related tools or exploits
	
	• Unusual traffic to and from the host (e.g., an attacker who uses the host to attack other systems)
	
	• System configuration changes, including:
	  ○ Process/service modifications or additions
	  ○ Unexpected open ports
	  ○ System status changes (restarts, shutdowns)
	  ○ Changes to log and audit policies and data
	  ○ Network interface card set to promiscuous mode (packet sniffing)
	  ○ New administrative-level user account or group

(continues)

Table 8-10   Indicators of Unauthorized Access[25] (*Continued*)

Malicious Action	Indicators
	• Modifications of critical files, time stamps, and privileges, including executable programs, OS kernels, system libraries, and configuration and data files
	• Unexplained account use (e.g., idle account in use, account in use from multiple locations at once, unexpected commands from a particular user, large number of locked-out accounts)
	• Significant changes in expected resource use (e.g., CPU, network activity, full logs or file systems)
	• User reports of system unavailability
	• Network and host intrusion detection alerts
	• New files or directories with unusual names (e.g., binary characters, leading spaces, leading dots)
	• Highly unusual operating system and application log messages
	• Attacker who contacts the organization to say that he or she has compromised a host
Unauthorized data modification (e.g., Web server defacement, FTP "warez" server providing the hacker community with unauthorized software)	• Network and host intrusion detection alerts
	• Increased resource utilization
	• User reports of data modification (e.g., defaced Web site)
	• Modifications to critical files (e.g., Web pages)
	• New files or directories with unusual names (e.g., binary characters, leading spaces, leading dots)
	• Significant changes in expected resource use (e.g., CPU, network activity, full logs or file systems)
Unauthorized use of standard user account	• Access attempts to critical files (e.g., password files)
	• Unexplained account use (e.g., idle account in use, account in use from multiple locations at once, commands that are unexpected from a particular user, large number of locked-out accounts)
	• Web proxy log entries showing the download of attacker tools
Physical intruder	• User reports of network or system unavailability
	• System status changes (restarts, shutdowns)
	• Hardware completely or partially missing (i.e., a system was opened and a particular component removed)
	• Unauthorized new hardware (e.g., an attacker connects a packet-sniffing laptop to a network or a modem to a host)
Unauthorized data access (e.g., database of customer information, password files)	• Intrusion detection alerts of attempts to gain access to the data through FTP, HTTP, and other protocols
	• Host-recorded access attempts to critical files
Unexpected data movement	• Unexpected data flows between network segments could indicate that data exfiltration is under way

Source: NIST.

Containment strategies for a UA may be as wide and varied as the types of incidents that fall under this name. The organization will most likely respond differently to an internal user attempting to escalate privilege than to an external hacker. NIST recommends the following containment strategies:

- *Isolate*—Disconnecting each affected system from any network access will usually contain the incident. The challenge is in identifying all the affected systems, given that they may be physically separated and it may therefore be difficult to precisely locate where the attacker has been. At the first sign of this type of intrusion, internal port scanning procedures should commence to look for back doors and unauthorized services inside the compromised network services.
- *Disable network port*—If an attack uses a particular service port, it may be possible to filter that service at the network perimeter, permanently or temporarily. For example, if an attacker is using unsecured Simple Network Management Protocol (SNMP) to attack an internal system, the service protocol should be blocked at the network.
- *Block*—Disrupt the attacker's path into the environment. When possible, use precise means like blocking specific IP addresses. If necessary, block entire classes of service while minimizing disruption to authorized users. For example, temporarily blocking incoming connections to a specific network segment could stop the attacker.
- *Disable user account*—If specific user accounts have been leveraged for the attack, shut them down. Users may have used the same password on multiple systems, so all instances of that identity should be disabled until the password can be reset. Likewise, during an incident, all new accounts should be verified or even disabled until confirmed because they may have been created by the attacker. Until responders determine what actions the attacker has performed, accounts should be disabled instead of simply changing passwords.
- *Lockdown*—When an incident includes a breach of physical security, escalate all aspects of physical security in a measured response. For example, if an attacker may have gained unauthorized access to a server room, that room should be resecured, but tightening of general building security and a search for unauthorized people throughout the building should occur as well. When a breach is confirmed to have occurred once, it is likely to have happened before and could happen again.[26]

After the UA Incident

After the UA has been contained, the task of identifying the avenue of attack and closing any still-open repeat mechanisms begins. At the same time, the organization must identify the extent of the damage done by the UA and look for any residual effects, such as rootkits or back doors. The forensic analysis (described in later modules) of the incident may take some time; however, it is imperative to determine exactly how much damage is done so the CSIRT can effectively advise management about what internal and external actions to take, especially if critical files were accessed. The CSIRT should always presume that if a critical information asset was accessed, the data stored within it is compromised.

As mentioned earlier, one task that must occur after a UA involving a lost, stolen, or hijacked user account is a reset of all passwords, including those for administrator accounts. If a UA is successful in accessing server password files, those files are not to be trusted and should be restored from backup, with a corresponding requirement for all users to change their passwords immediately. Although some may advocate rebuilding the entire system from scratch after such an incident, this should not be done until the system is copied for later analysis, when the organization can ensure that the replacement system is more secure than the former. With the advent of virtualization technologies, this task has become greatly simplified, allowing the IT team to fix the replacement image offline and then swap out the hardened image for the compromised one in a very short time.

Table 8-11 presents a checklist for handling UA incidents.

Table 8-11 Incident Handling Checklist for UA[27]

	Action	Completed
	Detection and Analysis	
1.	Prioritize handling the incident based on its business impact.	
1.1	Identify which resources have been affected and forecast which resources will be affected.	
1.2	Estimate the current technical effect of the incident.	
1.3	Find the appropriate cell(s) in the prioritization matrix, based on the technical effect and affected resources.	
2.	Report the incident to the appropriate internal personnel and external organizations.	
	Containment, Eradication, and Recovery	
3.	Perform an initial containment of the incident.	
4.	Acquire, preserve, secure, and document evidence.	
5.	Confirm the containment of the incident.	
5.1	Further analyze the incident and determine if containment was sufficient (including checking other systems for signs of intrusion).	
5.2	Implement additional containment measures, if necessary.	
6.	Eradicate the incident.	
6.1	Identify and mitigate all vulnerabilities that were exploited.	
6.2	Remove components of the incident from systems.	
7.	Recover from the incident.	
7.1	Return affected systems to an operationally ready state.	
7.2	Confirm that the affected systems are functioning normally.	
7.3	If necessary, implement additional monitoring to look for future related activity.	
	Post-Incident Activity	
8.	Create a follow-up report.	
9.	Hold a "lessons learned" meeting.	

Source: NIST.

Inappropriate Use

Distinct from UA incidents, **inappropriate use (IU)** incidents are predominantly characterized as a violation of policy rather than an effort to abuse existing systems. Attempting to access unauthorized information or to escalate one's access privileges would be a UA violation, whereas attempting to download, install, or use software, hardware, or services in violation of organizational policy constitutes inappropriate use.

Traditionally, IU incidents are identified by IT personnel or CSIRT teams but regulated and controlled by management. Although a technician installing a new printer in an employee's office may note that the user is playing a computer game on organizational equipment, for example, the user's immediate supervisor typically enforces the policy prohibitions. However, with the increased need to protect systems from internal attacks, including those resulting from Trojan horses hiding in freeware and shareware, CSIRTs are increasingly treating these types of IU policy violations the same as other categories of incidents and responding accordingly.

inappropriate use (IU)

A category of incidents that covers a spectrum of violations by authorized users of a system who nevertheless use it in ways specifically prohibited by management; these incidents are predominantly characterized as a violation of policy rather than an effort to abuse existing systems.

Things that can be considered IU incidents include the following:

- *Inappropriate or unauthorized software or services*—Employees downloading software in violation of organizational policy can result in internal security issues. Policy specifically prohibiting such actions should already be in place. This type of software generally includes anything not formally offered or authorized by management. Examples include computer games, freeware or shareware, security tools not provided by the InfoSec group, music-sharing and file-sharing software, and especially pornography. Another example is setting up a personal or private business Web site on organizational equipment.
- *Organizational resources used for personal reasons*—Most organizations take a dim view of employees using resources specifically purchased to support the mission of the organization for their own affairs. Whether it is in support of personal enterprises or part of an employee-supported nonprofit activity, using company resources—e-mail, photocopying, office mail, and the like—may constitute an IU incident if the organization has specifically prohibited such action.
- *Organizational resources used to harass coworkers*—Technically speaking, e-mail, instant messaging, video-conferencing tools like Skype, and other organizational communications equipment qualify as telecommunications devices. As such, their use in harassing employees is a violation of U.S. federal law, especially if such use occurs across state borders, as during company travel. In any instance, harassing coworkers is a specific problem that must be dealt with, or the organization risks litigation from the offended party.
- *Restricted company information and other assets stored in external sites*—An issue that many organizations struggle with is the presence and ease of using external data storage locations, many of which are free. Well-meaning and hard-working employees may create IU incidents by storing restricted organizational information on sites that may not provide the level of security the organization needs. File-sharing platforms like Microsoft Mesh, Dropbox, and Google Cloud provide free or low-cost storage capabilities that allow employees to work with company files anywhere, anytime. However, this means that information may be at risk because it is outside the control of the organization.

What the organization and its employees must remember is that for the preceding actions to be considered IU violations, they must be counter to established policy. Although ignorance of the law is no excuse, ignorance of policy is. If an organization hasn't explicitly told employees that they can't play a computer game in their office, any actions taken against them must be tempered or the organization opens itself up to litigation.

Before the IU Incident

Organizational policy is the primary strategy in preparing for and preventing IUs. As mentioned earlier, policies function as organizational laws, complete with penalties, judicial practices, and sanctions to require compliance. Because these policies function as laws, they must be crafted with the same care in order to ensure that they are complete, appropriate, and fairly applied to everyone in the workplace.

The difference between a policy and a law is that ignorance of a policy is an acceptable defense. Thus, for a policy to become legally enforceable and defendable, it must meet the following criteria:

- *Dissemination (distribution)*—The organization must be able to demonstrate that the relevant policy has been made readily available for review by the employee. Common dissemination techniques include hard copy and electronic distribution.
- *Review (reading)*—The organization must be able to demonstrate that it disseminated the document in an intelligible form, including versions for illiterate, non-English-reading, and reading-impaired employees. Common techniques include audio recordings and translations of the policy in English and alternate languages, including Braille.
- *Comprehension (understanding)*—The organization must be able to demonstrate that the employee understands the requirements and content of the policy. Common techniques include quizzes and other assessments.
- *Compliance (agreement)*—The organization must be able to demonstrate that the employee agrees to comply with the policy, through act or affirmation. Common techniques include logon banners that require a specific action (a mouse click or keystroke) to acknowledge agreement or a signed document clearly indicating that the employee has read, understood, and agreed to comply with the policy. Organizations can make acceptance

of the policy a requirement and may choose to block system access for employees that balk at such approval, which could lead to their termination.

- *Uniform enforcement*—The organization must be able to demonstrate that the policy has been uniformly enforced, regardless of employee status or assignment. Special treatment for executives or other classes of employees can lead to legal challenges.

Only when all these conditions are met can an organization penalize employees who violate the policy without fear of legal retribution.

When the organization has effective policies in place, it should establish a security education, training, and awareness (SETA) program to fully integrate those policies. Training and awareness efforts will make the policy effective and provide benefit to the organization. Employees attend classes, formally or informally, where the policies are presented and discussed. Upon completion of the classes, the employees are tested and then sign compliance forms to ensure that the organization has met any legal requirements for implementation. As you might have noticed, the SETA program helps reinforce the criteria in the preceding list. Follow-up messages in newsletters, e-mails, and other announcements can serve to keep the information fresh in the employees' minds.

Other preparation strategies fall under the category of good security practices, such as the proper configuration of IDPSs, log management systems, and filtering rules on network devices. In order to detect policy violations, however, the organization should consider periodic scans of internal systems as part of a configuration management program. If the organization has a clear set of documentation for how systems should be configured, any variations on that configuration will be much easier to detect in cases of unauthorized installations of inappropriate software or services.

The organization should also prepare itself to deal with the administrative fallout from policy violations. Presuming that the policies are well designed and effectively implemented, representatives from management as well as the human resources and legal departments should be involved in discussions about detection, reaction to, and recovery from IU incidents. The CSIRT must be prepared to brief these representatives on the type, scope, and extent of any incident and provide needed documentation, especially if the incident may result in legal action. Coordination may also be needed with physical security agencies, as they may be called upon to assist in internal investigations and subsequent administrative actions.

The primary prevention tools are written policies, as discussed earlier, and configuration management policies. These management policies are often elements of broader organizational policy. They serve both to inform users of what is allowed when implementing software and to provide recourse if an employee violates the policy. Organizations may want to consider content filters on Web usage to prevent users from visiting sites where they might access inappropriate software for downloading and installation.

During the IU Incident

Table 8-12 provides a list of indicators that an IU incident has occurred. One important thing to consider when investigating a potential IU incident is the level of authority an individual manager has when responding. If a manager suspects an employee of an IU incident and notifies the CSIRT, clear policies must be in place to specify what level of direct investigation the CSIRT may undertake. Comparable to law enforcement's need for search warrants based on probable-cause affidavits, an organization should clearly define the circumstances under which the CSIRT and management may investigate a piece of the organization's equipment that a particular employee commonly uses, especially if the organization allows the employee to connect personal systems to its networks. There is legal precedence for privacy violations that arise when an organization's CSIRT seizes an employee's office or personal computer for purposes of determining IU violations; not all cases have ended well for the organization. The key is whether the organization has created an expectation of privacy for the employee. In most privately owned organizations, there is little expectation of employee privacy, unless one is created intentionally. However, in public organizations, especially academic institutions, there is enough ambiguity to require very specific clarification and extensive permissions before the organization should attempt a search and seizure. If the organization's senior management has clearly outlined when, how, and under which conditions the CSIRT may investigate an IU, then the organization is better prepared and protected. Making employees aware of this information means they are better prepared and protected as well, and it may serve as a deterrent to IU incidents.

Table 8-12 Indicators of IU Incidents[28]

Inappropriate Action	Indicators
Unauthorized service use (e.g., Web server, file sharing, music sharing)	• Network intrusion detection and network behavior analysis software alerts • Unusual traffic to and from the host • New process/software installed and running on a host • New files or directories with unusual or nonstandard names • Increased resource use (e.g., CPU, file storage, network activity) • User reports • Application log entries (e.g., Web proxies, FTP servers, e-mail servers)
Accessing inappropriate materials (e.g., downloading pornography, sending spam)	• Network intrusion detection alerts • User reports • Application log entries (e.g., Web proxies, FTP servers, e-mail servers) • Inappropriate files on workstations, servers, or removable media
Attack against external party	• Network intrusion detection alerts • Outside party reports • Network, host, and application log entries

Source: NIST.

Table 8-13 presents NIST's recommendations on the "service levels" for IU incidents—in other words, how quickly the organization should respond to general types of incidents. The recommendations are based on two classification criteria: whether the activity is criminal in nature and to what extent it might damage the organization's reputation, if disclosed.

Table 8-13 Sample Service Levels for IU Incidents[29]

Current Impact or Likely Future Impact of the Incident	Nature of Incident	
	Criminal Activity	**Noncriminal Activity**
Major damage to the organization's reputation	Within 15 minutes, initial response begins. Within 1 hour, team contacts Public Affairs, Human Resources, and Legal departments as well as law enforcement.	Within 1 hour, initial response begins. Within 2 hours, team contacts Public Affairs and Human Resources departments.
Minor damage to the organization's reputation	Within 2 hours, initial response begins. Within 4 hours, team contacts Human Resources and Legal departments as well as law enforcement.	Within 4 hours, initial response begins. Within 8 hours, team contacts Human Resources Department.
No damage to the organization's reputation	Within 4 hours, initial response begins. Within 8 hours, team contacts Human Resources and Legal departments as well as law enforcement.	Within 1 day, initial response begins. Within 2 days, team contacts Human Resources Department.

Source: NIST.

Containment strategies for IU incidents predominantly focus on detecting the incident through technical means or managerial reports, then removing the offending technology. For incidents in which employees are using systems for purely personal concerns that do not otherwise violate appropriate use guidelines, a determination whether to stop the activity or proceed with administrative punishment typically falls to the individual's supervisor. For instance, an employee asked to work outside normal hours may have some flexibility to use organizational systems for shopping or interacting with family members. Here are some examples of these types of infractions and possible reactions:

- *Inappropriate or unauthorized software or services*—The offensive software or service is removed from systems by the CSIRT or follow-up IT teams; the matter is then referred to management.
- *Personal use of an organizational resource*—Evidence is collected by the CSIRT; the matter is then referred to management.
- *Organizational resources used to harass coworkers*—Evidence is collected by the CSIRT; the matter is then referred to management.
- *Restricted company information and other assets stored in external sites*—Company information is removed from external storage with assistance from the offending employee; the matter is then referred to management.

After the IU Incident

After an incident, the CSIRT typically turns copies of all documentation over to management for administrative handling, then monitors the affected systems for possible recurrences. At this point, the CSIRT goes through standard activities to document the end of the incident, including discussion and AARs.

Table 8-14 provides a checklist for handling IU incidents.

Hybrid or Multicomponent Incidents

CSIRTs would greatly prefer incidents to cleanly fall into only one of the just-described categories. In the real world, however, it's seldom so neat and tidy. Many incidents begin with one type of event, then transition to another. What may begin as an IU incident, for example, may quickly change into a malware incident. These hybrid or multicomponent incidents may create complex response operations that involve multifaceted investigations and responses. Critical

Table 8-14 Incident Handling Checklist for Inappropriate Use[30]

	Action	Completed
	Detection and Analysis	
1.	Prioritize the handling of the incident based on its business impact.	
1.1	Determine whether the activity is criminal in nature.	
1.2	Forecast how severely the organization's reputation may be damaged.	
1.3	Find the appropriate cell(s) in the prioritization matrix, based on the criminality and damage to reputation.	
2.	Report the incident to the appropriate internal personnel and external organizations.	
	Containment, Eradication, and Recovery	
3.	Acquire, preserve, secure, and document evidence.	
4.	If necessary, contain and eradicate the incident (for example, remove inappropriate materials).	
	Post-Incident Activity	
5.	Create a follow-up report.	
6.	Hold a "lessons learned" meeting.	

Source: NIST.

among the tasks in responding to a hybrid incident is the prioritization of the response. To continue with the previous example, the CSIRT must respond to the threat posed by the malware before dealing with the administrative issues associated with the IU incident or incident phase.

Dealing with these incidents requires that all the previous recommendations for preparation and prevention, containment, and response and recovery have been considered. CSIRTs must be flexible in responding to any incident and ever vigilant to the possibility that the incident can spawn another type of attack or possible loss scenario. Getting too focused on one incident type—having tunnel vision—can lead the CSIRT into overlooking a prerequisite or follow-on incident. If a team is investigating a malware incident, someone should be asking how it started in order to determine if the malware issue is the result of an IU event or possibly a UA event, such as an attack by a remote hacker.

Timeliness is also a factor in prioritizing the response. A report from a help desk that a user "saw something unauthorized" on a coworker's system last week may be processed after a malware event that has just been reported by a centralized antivirus application. If the organization has deployed a ticketing system to manage ongoing help-desk operations, that system may be adapted to support the CSIRT's efforts as well, facilitating the identification and classification of incidents, tracking incident components as they arise, and generally helping to make sure that no component is unresolved or overlooked.

Here are some key recommendations for handling hybrid incidents:

- *Using software to support incident management*—Along with help-desk software, log management software, and specialized software designed to manage incidents, the CSIRT should use every resource at its disposal.
- *Prioritizing each incident component as it arises*—First come is not first served. As each new component or category of incident is detected in the response process, the entire collection of incidents must be reprioritized to focus assets on the task with the highest risk. This may mean pulling staff off current IR tasks and reassigning them to other more dangerous tasks.
- *Containing each incident, then scanning for others*—As each incident is processed, the CSIRT continually looks for other incidents, whether they are predecessors, parallel incidents, or follow-on events. Each should be immediately documented, prioritized, and addressed in turn.

Table 8-15 provides a checklist for handling hybrid or multiple-component incidents.

Table 8-15   Incident Handling Checklist for Hybrid or Multiple-Component Incidents[31]

	Action	Completed
	Detection and Analysis	
1.	Prioritize handling the incident based on its business impact.	
1.1	Follow the Step 1 instructions for each applicable incident category.	
1.2	Determine the proper course of action for each incident component.	
2.	Report the incident to the appropriate internal personnel and external organizations.	
	Containment, Eradication, and Recovery	
3.	Follow the Containment, Eradication, and Recovery steps for each component, based on the results of Step 1.	
	Post-Incident Activity	
4.	Create a follow-up report.	
5.	Hold a "lessons learned" meeting.	

Source: NIST.

AUTOMATED IR SYSTEMS

As you learned throughout this module, the CSIRT must document and preserve every action, file, event, and item of potential evidentiary value. The documentation will serve multiple purposes, both to the CSIRT and to the organization as a whole. This documentation must be designed by the organization; it can be physical paperwork or electronic in nature. Integration with a help-desk ticketing system will help to ensure that user issues are properly organized, documented, and tracked through to the CSIRT's response.

Automated IR systems to facilitate IR documentation are available through a number of vendors. Some of the capabilities to perform these tasks are found in security information and event management (SIEM) systems, which were described in Module 7. Other options for these types of capabilities are designed to be an integrated configuration management component of a forensic management toolkit. Guidance Software's Endpoint Security (*www.guidancesoftware .com*) is an example of such a tool.

Depending on the tools selected, they might be able to track actions, monitor the configuration of systems, integrate antivirus and IDPS feedback, and scan systems for events and policy violations. They are also capable of looking for industry-specific regulatory compliance issues. With developments in predictive analytics, monitored networks and systems can have incidents detected earlier with automated response using these very capable tools.

 Take the opportunity to learn more about SIEM application systems by visiting *youtube.com* and searching for "SIEM explained." You can find several short videos that will get you up to speed quickly.

Closing Scenario

Ninety seconds after Osbert started his lab-based exercise, the first attempt was made to compromise a computer on the HAL company network. Just as in the lab, Osbert's worm took over the HAL mail server and quickly infected every system in the company. As the worm copied itself over and over again, the servers at HAL quickly stopped doing their assigned tasks and spent all their resources copying the worm to every computer they could reach.

Discussion Questions

1. Who is responsible for this catastrophe? Osbert? His professor? The student who changed the network configuration? The university? On what do you base your position?
2. Osbert had read, understood, and signed the white hat agreement his university required. He had followed all of the rules and never had an intent to do harm. Do you think his position in this matter is defensible if he were to face criminal charges? What if he is sued by the many organizations that might have been affected by his worm?

Ethical Decision Making

1. Was Osbert acting ethically when he wrote his worm program? On what do you base your position?
2. Was Osbert's professor acting ethically by assigning him the worm program? On what do you base your position?

MODULE SUMMARY

- IR reaction strategies are plans for regaining control of systems and restoring operations to normality in the event of an incident. How the CSIRT responds to an incident relies in part on whether its mission philosophy is *protect and forget* or *apprehend and prosecute*. Each type of incident will have its own unique characteristics.

- Once the CSIRT is active, the first task that must occur is assessment of the situation. The CSIRT leader (or incident commander) determines what type of incident has occurred, if any, and what reaction strategies are appropriate. The second task is to begin asserting control over the situation and begin regaining control over the organization's information assets.

- Prevention strategies include using risk assessment to make informed decisions, acquiring and maintaining good host security, acquiring and maintaining good network security, implementing comprehensive malware prevention, and thorough and ongoing training to raise user awareness.

- It is imperative to contain a confirmed incident. Once containment is achieved, eradication and recovery can occur. Incident containment seeks to limit how widespread and intense an incident may become. The CSIRT should plan for one of the following containment strategies: monitoring system and network activities, disabling network access to compromised systems, changing passwords or disabling logon access of compromised systems, disabling system services, if possible, disconnecting the compromised systems, shutting down the compromised systems, and verifying that redundant systems and data have not been compromised. Notification of upper management before executing a response beyond a predetermined level is often a requirement of IR planning. Once an incident is contained, the organization must deal with actual and potential contamination, which must be identified and removed to prevent recurrence. In each case, systems must be restored to their pre-incident status.

- Incident recovery is the reestablishment of pre-incident status of all organizational systems. Incident recovery involves implementing the backup and recovery plans that should be in place before the attack. Any data that is suspected of corruption or modification must be recovered. A difficult part of recovery is the identification of data that may have been disclosed. Although damaged data may be recovered, disclosed data may never be recovered.

- The selection of the appropriate reaction strategy is an exercise in risk assessment in which the CSIRT leader must determine the appropriate response based on a number of variables, including the incident's type, method of incursion, current level of success, expected or projected level of success, current level of loss, expected or projected level of loss, the target, the target's level of classification and/or sensitivity, and any legal or regulatory impacts.

- Each complete containment strategy should include details about how the organization will handle the following: theft or damage to assets, whether evidence needs to be preserved for potential criminal prosecution, service-level commitments and contract requirements to customers, allocating necessary resources to activate the strategy, graduated responses that may be necessary, and duration of containment efforts.

- Denial of service (DoS) occurs when an attacker's action prevents the legitimate users of a system or network from using it. Unauthorized access (UA) refers to an individual or an application program that attempts or gains access to an information asset without explicit permission or authorization to do so. This includes both internal and external efforts as well as virtual attempts (over the network) and physical incidents. Inappropriate use (IU) is a category of incidents that covers a spectrum of violations by authorized users of a system who nevertheless use it in ways specifically prohibited by management. CSIRTs would greatly prefer incidents to cleanly fit into neat categories, but many incidents begin with one type of event, then transition to another. These hybrid or multicomponent incidents may create complex response operations that involve multifaceted investigations and responses.

Review Questions

1. What is an IR reaction strategy?
2. If an organization chooses the *protect and forget* approach instead of the *apprehend and prosecute* philosophy, what aspect of IR will be most affected?
3. What is the first task the CSIRT leader will undertake on arrival?
4. What is the second task the CSIRT leader will undertake?
5. What is the best thing an organization can do to make its CSIRT most effective?
6. What is the first imperative of the CSIRT when there is a confirmed incident?
7. Why might an organization forego trying to identify the attacking host during an incident response?
8. What is the phase after containment during incident response?
9. What is a concurrent recurrence?
10. What is the phase after eradication during incident response?
11. What is the primary determinant of which containment and eradication strategies are chosen for a specific incident?
12. What is watchful waiting and why might we use it?
13. Why is delayed containment not recommended for most CSIRTs?
14. What is a DoS attack and how does it differ from a DDoS attack?
15. What is the first and most important step in preparing for DoS and DDoS attack responses?
16. What is malware?
17. What is spam? Can it cause an incident?
18. What is unauthorized access?
19. What is inappropriate use?
20. What is a hybrid incident?

Real-World Exercises

Exercise 8-1

Learn more about denial-of-service attacks by visiting *youtube.com*. Enter the search term "DoS versus DDoS attacks." Choose at least two of the options and view the videos. (Note that you may be required to view advertisements unless you have a YouTube service account.) As you watch, look for the reasons why DDoS attacks are usually more impactful.

Exercise 8-2

Depending on where you live and copyright requirements, the documentary "The KGB, the Computer and Me" may be available for viewing on public video-streaming services. Use a search engine to find the title and watch the documentary if it is available. (The video remains available as of 2020; its run time is about 57 minutes.) As you watch the film, note what makes Cliff start the search for the hacker.

Exercise 8-3

One example of unauthorized access occurs when a relatively low-level account is used to gain access and then the commandeered account has its privileges escalated. To learn more about this, visit *youtube.com*. Enter the search term "privilege escalation demonstration." Choose at least two of the options and view the videos. (Note that you may be required to view advertisements unless you have a YouTube service account.) As you watch, look for the techniques used to achieve the desired result.

Hands-On Projects

The hands-on project for this module can be accessed in the Practice It folder in MindTap or through your instructor's LMS. The virtual labs provided with this resource can help you develop practical skills that will be of value as you progress through the course.

References

1. Cichonski, P., T. Millar, T. Grance, and K. Scarfone. SP 800-61, Rev. 2, "Computer Security Incident Handling Guide." National Institute of Standards and Technology. 2012. Accessed 3/15/20 at *https://nvlpubs.nist.gov/nistpubs/SpecialPublications/NIST.SP.800-61r2.pdf*.

2. Ibid.

3. Ibid.

4. Kossakowski, K-P, et al. "Responding to Intrusions." CERT Security Improvement Modules. 1999. Accessed 03/16/20 at *https://resources.sei.cmu.edu/asset_files/SecurityImprovementModule/1999_006_001_16679.pdf*.

5. Stoll, Clifford. *The Cuckoo's Egg: Tracking a Spy Through the Maze of Computer Espionage*. New York: Doubleday, 1989.

6. Cichonski, P., T. Millar, T. Grance, and K. Scarfone. SP 800-61, Rev. 2, "Computer Security Incident Handling Guide." National Institute of Standards and Technology. 2012. Accessed 3/15/20 at *https://nvlpubs.nist.gov/nistpubs/SpecialPublications/NIST.SP.800-61r2.pdf*.

7. Ibid.

8. Scarfone, Karen, Tim Grance, and Kelly Masone. SP 800-61, Rev. 1, "Computer Security Incident Handling Guide." National Institute of Standards and Technology. March 2008. Accessed 3/16/20 at *https://csrc.nist.gov/publications/detail/sp/800-61/rev-1/archive/2008-03-07*.

9. Ibid.

10. Ibid.

11. McAfee Labs Threat Report. August 2019. Accessed 3/15/2020 at *www.mcafee.com/enterprise/en-us/assets/reports/rp-quarterly-threats-aug-2019.pdf*.

12. FireEye M-Trends. 2020. Accessed 3/16/2020 at *https://content.fireeye.com/m-trends/rpt-m-trends-2020*.

13. Cichonski, P., T. Millar, T. Grance, and K. Scarfone. SP 800-61, Rev. 2, "Computer Security Incident Handling Guide." National Institute of Standards and Technology. 2012. Accessed 3/15/20 at *https://nvlpubs.nist.gov/nistpubs/SpecialPublications/NIST.SP.800-61r2.pdf*.

14. Ibid.

15. Scarfone, Karen, Tim Grance, and Kelly Masone. SP 800-61, Rev. 1, "Computer Security Incident Handling Guide." National Institute of Standards and Technology. March 2008. Accessed 3/16/20 at *https://csrc.nist.gov/publications/detail/sp/800-61/rev-1/archive/2008-03-07*.

16. Ibid.

17. Ibid.

18. Kovacs, E. *Security Week*. "FireEye Spotted Over 500 New Malware Families in 2019." Feb 21, 2020. Accessed 3/19/2020 at *www.securityweek.com/fireeye-spotted-over-500-new-malware-families-2019*.

19. Scarfone, Karen, Tim Grance, and Kelly Masone. SP 800-61, Rev. 1, "Computer Security Incident Handling Guide." National Institute of Standards and Technology. March 2008. Accessed 3/16/20 at *https://csrc.nist.gov/publications/detail/sp/800-61/rev-1/archive/2008-03-07*.

20. Ibid.

21. Cichonski, P., T. Millar, T. Grance, and K. Scarfone. SP 800-61, Rev. 2, "Computer Security Incident Handling Guide." National Institute of Standards and Technology. 2012. Accessed 3/15/20 at *https://nvlpubs.nist.gov/nistpubs/SpecialPublications/NIST.SP.800-61r2.pdf*.

22. "2019 Data Breach Investigations Report." Verizon. Accessed 3/21/2020 at *https://enterprise.verizon.com/resources/reports/2019-data-breach-investigations-report.pdf*.

23. Scarfone, Karen, Tim Grance, and Kelly Masone. SP 800-61, Rev. 1, "Computer Security Incident Handling Guide." National Institute of Standards and Technology. March 2008. Accessed 3/16/20 at *https://csrc.nist.gov/publications/detail/sp/800-61/rev-1/archive/2008-03-07*.

24. Ibid.

25. Ibid.

26. Ibid.

27. Ibid.

28. Ibid.

29. Ibid.

30. Ibid.

31. Ibid.

INCIDENT RESPONSE: RECOVERY, MAINTENANCE, AND INVESTIGATIONS

Upon completion of this material, you should be able to:

1. Describe how an organization plans for the incident recovery process

2. Explain how the organization performs incident recovery

3. Describe the steps involved in maintaining an IR plan

4. Explain the importance of digital forensics investigations as part of incident response

5. Discuss the steps involved in collecting and analyzing digital evidence

> *You were sick, but now you're well again, and there's work to do.*
>
> —Kurt Vonnegut, *Timequake*

Opening Scenario

Osbert Rimorr had released a potent malware attack into the wild. It was simple bad luck that Osbert's worm took over the primary HAL mail server. From there, it quickly infected every system in the company. As the worm copied itself over and over again, the servers at HAL quickly stopped doing their assigned tasks and spent all their resources copying the worm to every computer they could reach.

It was nearing dawn when Susan Carter, the third-shift help-desk supervisor, was informed of the attack, first by the technicians in the network operations center and then by the application support team. Once she heard what was happening, Susan wasted no time. She directed the application support team to shut down the mail server, then she initiated the incident response plan by calling the help-desk supervisor to activate the call tree.

Susan called Paul Alexander, the HAL incident commander on call, to advise him of the incident.

Paul answered after taking a sip of his second cup of coffee.

"Good morning. What's up, Susan?" Paul asked.

"We're down," Susan replied. "All systems. All networks. It looks like a worm that just bogs everything down. No data exfiltration that we can see, just a massive denial of service through consumption of systems resources, and it's everywhere," Susan said, sounding worried.

"Okay," Paul replied. He opened the cover on his tablet, tapped on the browser, and then on the tab for the dashboard that would show him every system and its current status. "Let me see . . ." The screen stayed frozen. "Oh, wait, all networks are down! Okay, start to assemble all the facts you can. I guess the containment options didn't pan out very well; it's time for recovery operations. Work the IR plan with the CSIRT. I'll be at the SOC as soon as I can."

"Okay, we'll start getting what we know together," said Susan.

The IR plan worked as expected and the CSIRT assembled quickly. While the worm was good, HAL's IR team was better. They quickly identified the threat, isolated the malware by severing the connections between infected systems, and disrupted its spread.

System by system, the CSIRT brought each infected computer up—they isolated it in a controlled environment, wiped the system clean, and re-installed the applications and available data from backup. Fortunately for HAL, the CISO's insistence on near-real-time data backups paid off. Within two hours, every system had been scrubbed, reset, and was available for business, with only a few hours of lost data. Considering the fact that the worm hit almost every system in the company, the loss was negligible.

"We were lucky this time," Susan said, handing Paul his fourth cup of coffee since he arrived. "What's next?"

"I'd rather be lucky than good any day," Paul responded, "but in this case, the team was lucky *and* good. Next we formalize our recovery, try to figure out how this happened with the incident forensics team, start the after-action processes, and prepare to brief the bosses."

INTRODUCTION

After an incident has been contained and system control has been regained, incident recovery can begin. As in the response phase, the first task is to inform the appropriate people—most importantly, executive management. Almost simultaneously, the CSIRT must assess the full extent of the damage to determine what must be done to restore the systems. The CSIRT must also examine the appropriate systems and network logs and try to determine exactly how the attack began and spread. Each involved individual should begin recovery operations based on the appropriate incident recovery section of the IR plan.

RECOVERY

Recovery from an incident or incidents begins with incident damage assessment, which can take days or weeks, depending on the extent of the damage. The damage can range from a minor incident caused by a curious hacker or employee who snooped around to a severe infection of hundreds of computer systems by uncrackable ransomware. System logs, IDPS logs, configuration logs, and documentation from the response phase can provide information on the type, scope, and extent of damage. Using this information, the CSIRT assesses the current state of the organization's information and systems and compares them to their last known state. The individuals who are expected to document incident damage must be trained to collect and preserve evidence in case the incident is determined to be part of a crime or results in a civil action.

The organization ensures that the appropriate systems and data recovery procedures are initiated, working to restore all systems from backup to usable condition. Concurrently, teams begin investigating what happened and how, trying to determine how the attack began and spread throughout the organization's systems. They also seek to ensure the organization knows the full extent of any loss of data, damage, or destruction of resources and to ensure no residual effects remain, such as a rootkit or hijacked employee account that could allow an attacker to return and resume their efforts, or a malware-infected system that begins to infect other systems when it is powered on.

incident damage assessment

The initial determination of the scope of a breach as it applies to the confidentiality, integrity, and availability of information and information assets.

The following sections detail the appropriate steps to be taken in the recovery process.[1]

Identify and Resolve Vulnerabilities

Although it may appear to be a simple and straightforward process, the task of identifying and resolving vulnerabilities can prove to be a major challenge in reestablishing operations. At this point, many sources of guidance on intrusion detection practices direct the investigator to delve into the megabytes or even gigabytes of forensic data that will have been collected. Digital forensics can be used both for intrusion analysis and as part of evidence collection and analysis, but it can also be used to assess how the incident occurred and what vulnerabilities were exploited to cause the assessed damage. In some cases—for example, natural disasters—digital forensics may not be necessary, but in cases that involve digital attacks from hackers, worms, and other systems violations, digital forensics is extremely beneficial in helping an organization understand exactly what happened and how. Given the size of the forensic footprint from most events, this can sometimes be a daunting process.

If the process results in the discovery of evidentiary material that could be used in legal proceedings, it is imperative that the individuals performing the analysis are trained to recognize and handle the material in a way that does not violate its value as evidence in civil or criminal proceedings. As described later in this module, organizations must have access to competent and well-trained personnel who are responsible for any digital forensics efforts, in order to avoid "doing more harm than good."

After any incident, an organization should address the safeguards that failed to stop or limit the incident, or that were missing from the system in the first place. Safeguards must then be installed, replaced, or upgraded as needed. Whether the incident was caused by a malfunctioning or misconfigured network security device, such as a firewall, router, or VPN connection, or by a breach in policy or data protection procedures, any safeguards that were already in place must be examined to determine if they were part of the incident. If the incident was caused by a missing safeguard, the organization should assess why the safeguard was not in place. It may be determined that the incident occurred because a planned safeguard had not been procured yet, or because a safeguard that could have prevented or limited the incident was previously assessed as being unnecessary. In any event, the findings should clearly document which safeguards and controls were not present or performing as specified, and the safeguards should be repaired, reconfigured, replaced, or procured.

The organization should evaluate monitoring capabilities when they are present and improve the detection and reporting methods as needed. If necessary, new monitoring capabilities should be installed. Many organizations do not have automated intrusion detection systems; some of them feel that the negative impact on performance does not justify the benefit of having such monitoring systems. Also, the hesitance to use these systems may be founded on a perception of invulnerability that exists only because an attack has not yet occurred. Interestingly, vendors of residential burglar alarms and monitoring services know that the best time to sell their products and services is right after an incident has occurred in a neighborhood. Small warning signs that a property is being monitored pop up in neighborhoods where someone's home has been broken into or vandalized. The sad fact is that some organizations have to experience the loss caused by an incident before they are willing to commit to the expenses of intrusion monitoring. In some cases, open source software can provide many of the capabilities needed with little or no additional hardware or software expense to the organization. Examples of this software include Snort, found at *www.snort.org*, or the Security Onion at *www.securityonion.net*. Although each set of circumstances needs to be carefully analyzed, in many cases the increased expense to train staff and provide support for open source solutions costs much less than replacing existing proprietary solutions.

If you don't have monitoring capabilities, get them. If you have them, review their implementation and configuration to determine if and how they failed to detect an incident. IDPSs cannot detect all incidents, no matter how well built they are or how carefully implemented. Even when network and host monitoring systems are implemented to keep track of events in the virtual world, remember that burglar and fire alarm systems are also needed to detect adverse events that happen in the physical world.

Restore Data

Unfortunately, many organizations associate the entire IR process with simple data backup and recovery schemes. Although they are important at this phase of the recovery plan, they are not enough. The IR team must understand the backup strategy used by the organization, must restore the data contained in backups, and then must use the appropriate recovery processes from incremental backups or database journals, or even individual transaction records, to re-create any data that was created or modified since the last backup.

It is equally important at this point to emphasize the need to regularly test backups. The worst time to discover a problem with the backup and recovery systems is when you're desperately and quickly trying to recover from an incident. Routine testing will identify issues and allow the organization to resolve them before critical backups are needed to restore business operations.

Restore Services and Processes

Compromised services and processes must be examined, verified, and then restored. If services or processes were interrupted in the course of regaining control of the systems, they need to be brought back online. Fully documented system configuration specifications combined with good backup processes and well-rehearsed restore procedures will enable the restoration to proceed smoothly and quickly. The same testing requirements for backups apply to documented system services and processes. It may not be sufficient to simply back up a system unless the processes necessary to administer that system are also backed up. Having a key administrator out of contact due to illness, injury, or vacation may result in a lack of on-site expertise when restoring and bringing key systems back online after a loss. Having multiple personnel trained on critical tasks and having effective documentation will shorten the recovery time after an incident.

It is a given that an organization should continuously monitor its systems; however, the organization is especially vulnerable after an incident. If an incident happens once, it can easily happen again. Hackers frequently boast of their exploits in chat rooms and dare their peers to match their efforts. If word gets out, others may be tempted to try the same or different attacks on your systems. Therefore, it is important to maintain vigilance during the entire IR process.

Restore Confidence Across the Organization

With management's permission, the IR team may want to issue an announcement outlining the incident and assuring everyone that it was handled and the damage was controlled. If the incident was minor, that should be communicated. If the incident was major or severely damaged systems or data, users should be reassured that they can expect operations to return to normal as soon as possible. The objective of this communication is to prevent panic or confusion from causing additional disruption to the operations of the organization. If the organization denies the occurrence of a successful incident and is later discovered to have lied or misguided key stakeholders, real problems can occur.

There may also be a legal requirement to notify select stakeholders, depending on the organization's industry. There are breach notification requirements in HIPAA for healthcare organizations, requirements in the Gramm-Leach-Bliley (GLB) Act for financial organizations, and a host of state requirements for public and private organizations. Failure to follow the mandated notification requirements of a breach law could cause more problems than the actual incident.

 Performing a damage assessment as part of an incident response, either during or after the incident, is a specialty skill area that is often outsourced to consultants with long experience in that task.

You can learn more about damage assessments in general by looking at how damage to physical assets is assessed at the Federal Emergency Management Agency. Use their *Preliminary Damage Assessment Guide*, which can be found at *www.fema.gov/media-library/assets/documents/109040*.

MAINTENANCE

The maintenance of the IR plan is not a trivial commitment for an organization. It includes procedures to complete effective after-action review meetings, a process to complete comprehensive, periodic plan review and maintenance, efforts to continue the training of staff members who will be involved in IR, and a continuing process of rehearsing plan actions in order to maintain readiness for all aspects of the incident plan.

After-Action Review

An absolutely essential activity is the *after-action review (AAR)*. As defined and discussed in Module 4, all key players review their notes during an AAR and verify that the IR documentation is accurate and precise. All team members review their actions during the incident and identify areas where the IR plan worked, didn't work, or should improve. This exercise allows the team to update the IR plan. AARs are conducted with all "players" in attendance. The CSIRT leader presents a timeline of events and highlights who was involved at each stage, with a summary of their actions. Ideally, the involved individuals relate what they discovered or did, and any discrepancies between what they say and what the documentation says are noted. The entire AAR is recorded for use as a training case for future staff. All parties should treat the AAR not as an inquisition but as a discussion group to relate their own part of the experience and to learn how others dealt with it. If properly structured and conducted, the AAR can have a positive effect on the organization's IR capacity and employee confidence in responding to incidents. If poorly handled, the AAR can actually reduce the organization's ability to react because users and other employees may prefer to sweep potential future incidents "under the rug" rather than risk improperly responding and having to face "the firing squad." The AAR formally brings the IR team's actions to a close after an incident. The benefits of an effective AAR are described in the following sections.

AAR to Document Lessons Learned and Generate IR Plan Improvements

At the end of the incident review, the AAR serves as a review tool, allowing the team to examine how it responded to the incident. Examining the documentation of the incident should reveal the point at which the incident was first detected, the point in time that the IR plan was enacted, and how the first responders and CSIRT reacted. This review is not done to cast blame on an individual or group for substandard performance, but to ensure that the best methods of reacting were employed and that any mistakes made during the process, whether from a failure to follow the IR plan or from errors in the IR plan, are not made again. The IR plan is continually reexamined during the AAR to ensure that the included procedures are the best method of responding to the particular incident. Should the AAR reveal that the incident represents a new type or variation of incident, additional material can be added to the IR plan to better prepare the team for future interactions.

AAR as Historical Record of Events

An additional use of the AAR is as a historical record of events. This may or may not be a requirement for legal proceedings, depending on the laws that apply to the industry and location where the organization operates. In any case, it is useful to be able to establish a timeline of events, drawn from a number of different sources, to show the evolution of the incident from first identification to final resolution. This timeline then serves other purposes, as described next. Important information can be gained from examining the amount of time it took to respond to an incident and the CSIRT's response effectiveness.

AAR as Case Training Tool

On the more positive side, an old adage applies when it comes to incidents: "That which does not kill us makes us stronger."[2] By examining the events of past attacks, future IR employees and students of information security and IR can learn from others' actions, whether correct or incorrect, or whether successful or unsuccessful. As Thomas Edison said: "I have not failed. I've just found 10,000 ways that won't work."[3]

Honest effort in the pursuit of one's goals is not failure. By studying the AAR reports from an organization's past incidents, not only do new members of the team become familiar with the system, plans, and responses of the organization, they get a lesson in how to deal with the challenges of IR in general. Part of this process is knowing how the team handles defeats. Even in defeat, however, as in the case of a successful and painful attack, the organization must continue forth, recovering from its battles and rebuilding its defenses to fight another day.

AAR as Closure

One final quote that applies to the AAR is from Yogi Berra: "It ain't over 'til it's over."[4] People require closure to events, especially traumatic events, and the AAR serves as closure to the incident. Even though there may be a great deal of work left to recover data and systems and to train and retrain users and CSIRT members, the incident has come to a close, for the most part, once the AAR report is filed. The team goes back to its normal routine and responsibilities associated with protecting information and preparing for the next incident.

As part of the closure aspect of the AAR, the organization must address any shortcomings in personnel, training, technology, and procedures identified during the incident. While the AAR itself may not seek to apply blame to an individual during the process, it's the responsibility of management after the AAR has concluded to resolve any issues that emerged as discrepancies during the AAR. If staff are undertrained, or if technology is outdated or poorly configured, these issues must be resolved. The unfortunate side effect of a large breach is that individuals are commonly blamed for the success of the breach, whether or not it is their fault. Even when attempting to maintain a positive approach after a breach, management cannot shirk its responsibility if the current personnel proved ineffective in doing their jobs. If an individual is undertrained or underequipped to perform a task, it's management's fault. If individuals are unable to perform their tasks even with the proper training and equipment, it may be necessary to re-assign them to a less critical responsibility or even let them go. Not everyone is able to handle the stress of working on the CSIRT.

 Learn more about how to conduct an effective AAR by looking at how law enforcement structures the process. A manual called *How to Conduct an After Action Review* by the U.S. Department of Justice can be found at *https://cops.usdoj.gov/RIC/Publications/cops-w0878-pub.pdf*.

Plan Review and Maintenance

The specific processes used by organizations to maintain the IR plan vary from one organization to another, but some commonly used maintenance techniques can be noted. When shortcomings are noted in the plan, they should be reviewed and revised to repair or remediate the deficiency. Deficiencies may come to light based on AARs when the plans are used for actual incidents, during rehearsals when plans are used in simulated incidents, or by review during periodic maintenance. It is recommended that at periodic intervals, such as one year or less, an assigned member of management should undertake some degree of review of the IR plan. Some questions that might be useful in this review include the following:

- Has the plan been used during the past review period?
- Were any AAR meetings held, and have the minutes of any such meetings been reviewed to note deficiencies that may need attention?
- Have any other notices of deficiency or related feedback been submitted to the plan owner, and if so, have they been addressed yet?

Depending on the answers to these questions, the plan may need to be reviewed and amended by the CPMT. All changes proposed to the IR plan must be coordinated with the CPMT so that the changes stay aligned with other contingency planning documents used by the company.

Training

A systematic approach to training is needed to support the IR plan. Because the nature of the IR plan dictates that any number of people may be called upon to fill the roles identified in the plan, the organization must undertake training programs to ensure that a sufficient pool of qualified staff members is available to meet the needs of the plan when it is activated. Cross-training is also needed to ensure that enough staff members with the proper skills are available for all realistic scenarios. Remember that in some cases, the IR plan, the DR plan, and the BC plan may all be functioning concurrently. Staff members should be sufficiently cross-trained, and authorization provision should be in place to allow a sufficient employee response to all likely scenarios, regardless of current staffing levels.

The training plan should also include references to the provisioning of actual or contingent credentials needed to execute the containment and recovery steps in the plan. It does little good to have trained and qualified staff on hand to restart servers as part of the IR plan if the staff does not have the proper credentials to access the systems and effect those actions.

Rehearsal

The ongoing and systematic approach to planning requires that plans be rehearsed until responders are prepared for the actions they are expected to perform. When structured properly, rehearsals can also supplement training events by pairing less experienced staff members with more experienced staff members as understudies. Whenever possible, all major planning elements should be rehearsed. Rehearsal adds value by exercising the procedures, identifying any shortcomings, and providing the opportunity to improve the plan before it is needed. In addition, rehearsals make people more effective when an actual event occurs.

As mentioned in Module 4, rehearsals that closely match reality are called *war games*. War games or simulations use a subset of the IR plan to create a realistic testing environment, which adds to the value of the rehearsal and can enhance training. Some organizations hold significant rehearsal events with high degrees of realism. Others make do with less realistic conference room rehearsals.

Law Enforcement Involvement

When an incident violates civil or criminal law, it is the organization's responsibility to notify the proper authorities. Selecting the appropriate law enforcement agency depends on the type of crime committed. The Federal Bureau of Investigation (FBI), for example, handles computer crimes that involve federal offenses—those committed crossing state boundaries. The U.S. Secret Service investigates crimes involving U.S. currency, counterfeiting, and certain cases involving credit card fraud and identity theft. The U.S. Treasury Department has a bank fraud investigation unit, and the Securities and Exchange Commission has investigation and fraud control units as well.

The heavy caseloads of these federal agencies mean that they typically prioritize incidents in favor of those that affect the national critical infrastructure or that have significant economic impact. The FBI Web site, for example, has this to say about the FBI Cyber Division:

> The FBI is the lead federal agency for investigating cyber attacks by criminals, overseas adversaries, and terrorists. Our nation's critical infrastructure, including both private and public-sector networks, are targeted by adversaries. American companies are targeted for trade secrets and other sensitive corporate data, and universities for their cutting-edge research and development. Citizens are targeted by fraudsters and identity thieves, and children are targeted by online predators. Just as the FBI transformed itself to better address the terrorist threat after the 9/11 attacks, it is undertaking a similar transformation to address the pervasive and evolving cyber threat. This means enhancing the Cyber Division's investigative capacity to sharpen its focus on intrusions into government and private computer networks.[5]

If the crime is not directed at the national infrastructure or doesn't affect it, the FBI may not be able to assist the organization as effectively as state or local agencies, or the FBI might not have jurisdiction and the ability to investigate. However, in general, a crime that crosses state lines becomes a federal matter. The FBI, if it has the resources to spare, may also become involved at the request of a state agency.

Each state, county, and city in the United States has its own law enforcement agencies. These agencies enforce all local and state laws, handle suspects, and secure crime scenes for state and federal cases. Local law enforcement agencies rarely have computer crime task forces, but the investigative (detective) units are quite capable of processing crime scenes and handling most common criminal violations, such as physical theft, trespassing, damage to property, and the apprehension and processing of suspects. They can then bring in additional expertise as needed to handle cybercrime.

Involving law enforcement agencies has both advantages and disadvantages. For example, such agencies are usually much better equipped at processing evidence than a business organization. Unless the security forces in the organization have been trained in processing evidence and digital forensics, they may do more harm than good when attempting to extract information that can lead to the legal conviction of a suspected criminal. Law enforcement agencies are also prepared to handle the warrants and subpoenas necessary when documenting a case. They are adept at obtaining statements from witnesses, search warrants, and other required documents. For all these reasons, law enforcement personnel can be a security administrator's greatest allies in prosecuting a computer crime. Therefore, it is important to become familiar with the appropriate local and state agencies before you have to make a call announcing a suspected crime. Most state and federal agencies offer awareness programs, provide guest speakers at conferences, and offer programs such as the FBI's InfraGard program (*www.infragard.org*). These agencies clearly understand the challenges facing security administrators.

The disadvantages of law enforcement involvement include possible loss of control of the chain of events following an incident, including control over the collection of information and evidence and the prosecution of suspects. An organization that wants to simply reprimand or dismiss an employee should not involve a law enforcement agency in the resolution of an incident. Additionally, the organization may not hear any new information about the case for weeks, or even months, because of the agency's heavy caseloads or resource shortages. A very real issue for commercial organizations when involving law enforcement agencies is the evidence tagging of equipment that is vital to the organization's business. Valuable assets can be removed, stored, and preserved to prepare the criminal case. Despite these difficulties, if the organization detects a criminal act, it has the legal obligation to notify appropriate law enforcement officials. Failure to do so can subject the organization and its officers to prosecution as accessories to the crime or for impeding the course of an investigation. It is up to the security administrator to ask questions of law enforcement agencies to determine when each agency needs to be involved and which crimes are addressed by each agency.

Reporting to Upper Management

After the CSIRT has conducted a preliminary assessment of the incident, its impact on the organization, the organization's success or failure in responding to the incident, and the progress of the recovery, the CSIRT leader should make a report to upper management—typically the CISO and CIO. As mentioned earlier, the first notification that an incident is in progress should occur only after the incident has been confirmed, but before media or other external sources learn of it. At this point, executive management above the CIO level will most likely be pressing for details in case they are approached by the media for information. After the event has been contained and recovered from, upper management may request assistance in drafting a press release to notify the general public and in providing specific notification to any stakeholders affected by the event.

Loss Analysis

One of the first questions that upper management has for the investigative team is "How much was lost, and how much will it cost us to recover?" This question may take some time to accurately answer. Fortunately, in most cases, an incident's costs are limited to those associated with internal recovery. In determining the costs associated with an incident, the following should be considered:

- Cost associated with the number of person-hours diverted from normal operations to react to the incident
- Cost associated with the number of person-hours needed to recover data
- Opportunity costs associated with the number of person-hours that could have been devoted to working on more productive tasks
- Cost associated with reproducing lost data (if possible)
- Legal cost associated with prosecuting offenders (if possible)
- Cost associated with loss of market advantage or share due to disclosure of proprietary information
- Cost associated with acquisition of additional security mechanisms ahead of budget cycle

If the incidents were acts of nature, then any additional costs associated with the repair or replacement of facilities will also need to be considered. If the incidents involved power problems, additional costs might include replacing computers or other electrical equipment damaged in the incident.

incident impact assessment

A quick determination of the extent of damage or loss and the associated cost or value associated with an incident.

After an incident, management will need an immediate **incident impact assessment**. In the event of a minor or moderate incident, the report may be short. In more complex situations, the analysis of an incident may be much more extensive and could include details about how the intruder gained access to a system, how the intruder established or elevated access privileges until he or she was able to gain control of the system, and whether the intruder compromised databases, deleted or destroyed files, or modified log entries. These types of assessments may find damages in the hundreds of thousands or even millions of dollars, especially if intellectual property is compromised or customer data is stolen. A sample impact analysis might look like this:

Impact of virus infestation in ABC Corp. was minor, with two infected user systems and no infected servers. Infestation was contained at 2300 June 20, with no loss of data. Estimated cost was 12 person-hours used to identify and contain the outbreak, and 10 person-hours of lost productivity as the two individuals were denied access to their systems as a result of the virus. It was determined that the outbreak occurred when a user downloaded and opened an e-mail attachment from a spoofed managerial account, infecting her system and that of one of her workmates, whose e-mail was CC'd on the original infected e-mail. Recommend additional awareness training for users on e-mail viruses. Total cost/loss to organization is under $500 (in personnel costs).

INCIDENT INVESTIGATIONS AND FORENSICS

As a critical component of the recovery phase of IR, it is important to understand how computer and network forensics can be used to assist in the determination of **root cause analysis** and incident effect—in other words, what happened and how. The word **forensics** comes from the Latin word *forensis*, which in ancient Rome referred to the public forum—the precursor to today's courts of law.[6] Forensics involves the collection and presentation of materials in a legal proceeding. When its information resources have been affected in the course of an incident and it decides to apprehend and prosecute the offender(s), the organization must collect information in such a way that it will be usable in a criminal or civil proceeding. This information is usually called "evidence," but only what a judge admits in court can truly be considered evidence; the correct term is **evidentiary material**. During legal proceedings, opposing counsel usually will challenge the admission of this material on any available ground. Even something as simple as taking a look at a compromised computer may allow opposing counsel to challenge the information gathered from it, on the grounds that it might have been modified or otherwise tainted.[7]

In law enforcement, forensics is used to examine a crime scene and determine what happened and how. **Computer forensics** applies the procedures and techniques of forensics to the computer world. **Digital forensics** further expands the use of forensics to any digital device, such as a cell phone or digital music player. Like information security in general, digital forensics involves as much art as science. However, the use of established methodologies can facilitate the collection of legally defensible evidentiary material. Why "legally defensible"? Even though the process may be initiated in response to an incident or as part of routine procedures for an outgoing employee, you never know when you might stumble across evidentiary material that requires reporting to law enforcement; therefore, each investigation should be treated as if it will end in legal proceedings. Digital forensics is still relatively new, as electronic evidence has only been admissible in legal proceedings for the past few decades.

The field of digital forensics combines skills from a number of disciplines but has its roots in two: computer science and criminal justice. Although the latter provides detailed knowledge in the handling and presentation of evidentiary material, the former is needed to successfully obtain the material—a computer system has a myriad of digital nooks and crannies in which to hide information. Even the deletion of information and the reformatting of data storage units do not hinder the acquisition of evidence by a skilled forensic analyst. An expert in digital forensics can gain employment as a corporate forensics analyst, a member of a law enforcement agency, or a freelance investigator and expert witness.

root cause analysis

The determination of the initial flaw or vulnerability that allowed the incident to occur by examining the systems, networks, and procedures that were involved.

forensics

The use of methodical technical investigation and analysis techniques to identify, collect, preserve, and analyze objects and information of potential evidentiary value so that they may be admitted as evidence in a court of law, used to support administrative action, or simply used to further analyze suspicious events.

evidentiary material (EM)

Any information stored electronically or on physical media that could potentially support the organization's legal or policy-based proceeding against a suspect. Also known as "items of potential evidentiary value."

computer forensics

The use of forensic techniques when the source of evidence is a computer system.

digital forensics

The use of forensic techniques when the source of evidence is a digital electronic device.

Legal Issues in Digital Forensics

Investigators should consider the objectives for the collection of forensic information and determine whether the investigation is for law enforcement or policy enforcement. The laws governing search and seizure in the private sector to ensure policy compliance are much more straightforward than those for collecting evidence in a criminal case. However, certain conditions must be met in order to ensure that any evidentiary material found is admissible in any legal proceedings that follow, whether administrative or judicial. In general, law enforcement agents must have either a search warrant or the employer's consent in order to search for evidentiary materials. For a private organization to search an employee's computer, the following procedure is usually employed:

1. Verify that organizational policy allows such a search to occur. This policy must have been distributed to, read, understood, and agreed to by all employees. The policy is also uniformly applied across the organization and is applicable to all levels of staff. It is also useful to have included recurring notifications in network and system banners that remind users such searches may occur.

2. Verify that the search is "justified at its inception." This means that there was a legitimate business reason for the search; for example, it may have been done specifically to locate a legitimate work product or as part of an investigation into work-related misconduct involving organizational resources. In the former case, if the organization routinely searches every employee's computer or conducts truly random searches and then uncovers potential evidentiary material, the findings are admissible. If the employee was working on a product for the organization and an authorized individual—that is, a supervisor, manager, or assistant—was looking for that product and discovered evidence of misconduct, then such evidence is equally admissible. In the latter case, if the InfoSec department received information that someone was conducting unauthorized activities using organizational resources, the search may be justified.

3. Verify that the search is "permissible in its scope," meaning that it has a specific focus and is constrained to that focus. One cannot look for Word documents on a system's e-mail server unless there is a clear link between the two, such as that the employee reported having e-mailed the document. This requirement does not prohibit the use of materials found during a normal business search, but it prohibits a total inventory search when the search should have been constrained to one or two folders or directories.

4. Verify that the organization has clear ownership over the container the material was discovered in. This precludes searches of the employee's person, personal belongings, and personal technologies, but it does not exclude containers provided by the organization for the employee's use, such as a tablet, smartphone, cellular phone, telephone, or laptop. One gray area is the use of employee-purchased briefcases, satchels, and backpacks used to transport work. Also, an area that has not yet been challenged in court is the ability of an organization to search a personal computer used by a telecommuter; however, such a challenge may occur in the near future, given the increase in telecommuting and remote computing, especially in the wake of the "shelter-in-place" instructions to work from home during the COVID-19 pandemic of 2020.

5. Verify that the search has been approved by a manager or administrator who is authorized to approve it. For systems, the senior system administrator must allow the search unless this individual is a suspect in an internal investigation. For most organizational equipment, a designated manager or executive must provide written authorization. Forward-thinking organizations designate a senior executive officer such as the CIO to authorize organizational searches. Even then, the search itself should be conducted by a designated, disinterested individual, such as the CISO or some other employee or external professional recommended by legal counsel.

6. Once these conditions are met, an organization should have a reasonable degree of confidence in its ability to look for and collect potentially evidentiary material. This does not mean that any administrative or judicial actions will go unchallenged; however, it does mean that the organization has a much stronger case to refute any allegations of impropriety.

Digital Forensics Team

The type of digital forensics team an organization should have, if any, depends on the size and nature of the organization and its available resources. Sometimes, the need for a forensics unit is obvious, as in the case of large organizations that are subject to frequent network attacks—for example, governmental agencies or high-profile companies like Microsoft. However, with the increasing criticality of digital information for business operations, organizations of all types and sizes may be required to engage in some form of forensic investigation, as you saw in the opening scenario of this module.

Technical Details

When planning a forensics operation, an organization should consider the following:[8]

- *Cost*—This includes the costs of the tools, hardware, and other equipment used to collect and examine digital information as well as the costs for staffing and training.
- *Response time*—Although an outside forensic consultant may seem cheaper because the service is only paid for when actually used, the interruption to normal business operations while the consultant gets into place and up to speed may turn out to be more expensive than maintaining an in-house forensic capability.
- *Data sensitivity*—Providing access to outside consultants may complicate their use. Forensic data collection can expose highly sensitive information, such as personal health records, credit card information, and business plans.

Resolving these issues can be challenging, which is why many organizations divide the forensic functions as follows:

1. *First response*—Assessing the "scene," identifying the sources of relevant digital information, and preserving it for later analysis using sound processes
2. *Analysis and presentation*—Analyzing the collected information to identify material facts that bear on the subject of the investigation; preparing and presenting the results of the analysis to support possible legal action

Although analysis and presentation require significant expertise (gained through extensive training and experience) and specialized tools that most IT professionals do not have, first-response skills are more common among IT professionals and can be supplemented by sound processes and documentation to preserve the collected information's evidentiary potential, which is sought in the second phase.

It is also very easy to get lost in the terabytes of data, the thousands of images, and the veritable storm of network packets that are the raw data of a forensic investigation; however, it is critical to remember that the investigation is about making a determination of fact in the real world. As Inman and Rudin have noted, forensics is about translating a real-world problem into one or more questions that can be answered by means of forensic analysis.[9] For example, Joe may be suspected of having violated his organization's intellectual property policy by disclosing details of a new product to a competitor in hopes of gaining a position with that competitor. The challenge for the forensic analyst is to translate the question "Did Joe violate the IP policy by disclosing the product details to a competitor?" into a series of questions answerable by digital forensic investigation, such as:

- Did Joe access the new product information during the relevant time period?
- Are there indications of a quid pro quo agreement between Joe and the competitor?
- Did Joe send e-mails to the competitor containing product information?
- Did Joe transmit the information to the competitor over the network?

The answers to these questions might be found on the drive image of Joe's computer, network logs, access logs for a file server, or within other digital sources.

First Response Team

The size and makeup of a first-response team will vary based on the size of the organization and other factors, but the team often includes the following roles and duties:

- *Incident manager*—Surveys the scene and identifies sources of relevant information; orchestrates the work of the other team members and usually produces any photographic documentation
- *Scribe*—Produces the written record of the team's activities and maintains control of the field evidence log and locker
- *Imager*—Creates forensically sound copies of digital evidence as well as collecting photocopies or photographic images of non-digital media

Consider a situation in which a forensics team has the objective of performing on-site data collection at an employee's company office. After securing the scene, the scribe begins the written record and the incident manager enters the scene to make the overall photographic survey as well as identify and photographically document major items, such as computers and external media, where evidentiary material might be located. An important part of this survey is prioritizing the sources of information. Some considerations that guide the selection of evidence to collect and the relative priority of that collection include the following:

- *Value*—The likely usefulness of the information
- *Volatility*—The stability of the information over time. Some types of information are lost when the power is cut, and others are lost by default over time (for example, log records that may be overwritten with newer data)
- *Effort required*—The amount of time required to acquire a copy of the information[10]

The incident manager then identifies an area for the imager to set up equipment and directs him or her in removing items to image. Equipment removals are documented both photographically and in the written record by the scribe. As the imager finishes imaging each digital item, a description and a hash value are documented in the written record. A hash value, as discussed later in this module, is a form of integrity assurance that can determine if a digital file has been altered between the time it is duplicated and when it is referenced. Photographic images are also documented. Each item is then logged into the field evidence locker, and the original item is replaced. When all the items have been imaged, the exit process begins; the incident manager will compare the scene's appearance to the initial photographic survey to ensure that the team has left little trace of its presence.

Analysis Team

Whether performed in-house or outsourced to a third party, the analysis and reporting phases must be performed by people who are specially trained in the use of digital forensic tools to analyze the collected information and address the questions that gave rise to the investigation. These tools help forensic analysts to recover deleted files, reassemble file fragments, and interpret operating system artifacts.

Forensic analysis is sometimes broken into two parts: examination and analysis. The examination phase involves the use of forensic tools to recover the content of files that were deleted, operating system artifacts such as event data and logging of user actions, and other relevant facts. The analysis phase uses those materials to answer the questions that led to the investigation. Larger organizations may even delineate these two functions as job descriptions: forensic examiners, who are skilled in the operations of particular tools, and forensic analysts, who know about operating systems and networks as well as how to interpret the information gleaned by the examiners. Often, an incident requires subject-matter expertise beyond that of the dedicated forensic analysis team. In these cases, the team should be able to draw upon a pre-identified pool of resources that can be pulled to help with forensic analysis. For example, the team may not have experience analyzing data from an Oracle application server that has been compromised, so they ask for assistance from a wider team of experts.

The analysis function includes reporting and presenting the investigation's findings. Forensic reports serve a variety of audiences ranging from upper management to legal professionals and other forensic experts who may use the findings to build a case in court; therefore, forensic examiners and expert witnesses must be able to clearly communicate highly technical matters without sacrificing critical details. Effective communication becomes even more critical when the forensic analyst is called into court, where the audience includes a judge and jury who likely have only a nodding acquaintance with technology and an opposing counsel whose job is to undermine the analyst's findings and expertise.

Presenting a forensic analysis to a nontechnical audience can be quite challenging. If the analyst's presentation is ineffective, the findings are likely to be regarded as technical gobbledygook; worse, members of the jury may perceive that the analyst is talking down to them. In this way, analogies play an important part in communication; a common analogy is referring to a library card catalog to illustrate how deleted files are recovered. A computer drive is like a large library wherein books (files) are shelved according to the information in a card catalog or electronic book database (a file system directory). Deleting a file is like removing the book's card from the card catalog or its entry from the book database. The pointer to the book is gone, but the book itself can still be found in the library shelves, although it might take some searching. This analogy aptly illustrates how a technical process can be explained to a nontechnical audience. Sometimes, the most challenging part of presenting the results of forensic analysis is finding a relevant analogy that helps the audience grasp the technical details.

Digital Forensics Methodology

As shown in Figure 9-1, a digital investigation usually begins with some allegation of wrongdoing—either a policy violation or commission of a crime. Based on that allegation, authorization is sought to begin the investigation by collecting relevant evidence. In the public sector, this authorization may take the form of a search warrant; in the private sector,

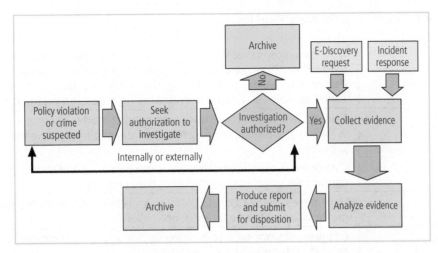

Figure 9-1   Overall flow of a digital investigation

it takes whatever form is specified by the organization's policy. Many private-sector organizations require a formal statement called an affidavit, which furnishes much of the same information usually found in a public-sector search warrant. In the private sector, it is more common to authorize the collection of digital images, but in the public sector, the warrant authorizes seizure of relevant items *containing* the information.

Forensic Field Kit

Most digital forensic teams have a prepared field kit, also known as a jump bag, which contains a portable set of all the equipment and tools needed for an investigation. This preplanning ensures that the team can leave at a moment's notice to perform the necessary response and analysis. The key is that, in order to keep the kit at the ready, the equipment in the kit should never be borrowed or used. The contents of a field kit are typically as personal as the individual investigator, but those shown in Figure 9-2 are often encountered.

A forensic field kit may include the items listed in Table 9-1.

Assessing the Scene

Before the forensics team moves in to collect evidence, it is important to assess the overall scene and document its state. This process typically involves interviewing the key contacts who are present, including the initial complainant, informant, or witness, the relevant system owner or business unit manager, and others with material knowledge of the alleged event or incident. The assessment also requires documenting the scene as it exists at the time of arrival. To do so, forensics teams typically use two methods: photography and field notes.

Figure 9-2   Example of a forensic field kit

Table 9-1   Possible Contents of a Forensic Field Kit

Portable computers	Forensic laptops that have multiple operating systems and can be dedicated to the field kit. They are often built from a baseline image for each incident to ensure that no prior evidence from using the laptops contaminates the investigation. Tablet devices can also be used for taking notes and photographs.
Call list	Telephone number directories with subject-matter experts in various IT technologies, management, and other stakeholders in the incident management process
Mobile phones	One or more mobile phones with extra batteries and charging devices for continuous communication during the investigation
Blank media	Hard drives, blank CDs, blank DVDs, and USB flash drives (sanitized and free from prior evidence) to use for evidence collection
Imaging tools	Imaging software on a computing device or use of dedicated hardware imaging devices with built-in write blockers
Forensic software	Forensic software that includes tools to perform forensic data collection and analysis
Network tap	Ethernet tap to sniff network traffic; this can be done using a simple switch or using a dedicated high-speed product
Network cables	Cables to provide access to other devices; these can be crossover cables for system-to-system communication, Ethernet cables, USB cables, or serial cables
Power extensions	Extension cords and power strips to power all the equipment in areas that have few or hard-to-reach outlets
Evidence containers and labels	Evidence bags, seals, and permanent markers used to store and label evidence; the bags should be antistatic and might need desiccants to absorb any moisture
Cameras	A digital camera with photographic markers and scales to take detailed photos of an investigation area—also, tie-on labels (for identifying cables, etc.). Tablet devices can be used to take photographs and notes, and video cameras can provide a continuous record of the data collection process.
Forms	Incident forms (if used), extra notebooks, and a generous supply of pens for detailed logging of the investigation
Tools	A toolkit with various tools to handle a wide variety of computer attachment devices, including specialty security screws, antistatic mats and straps, mechanics' mirrors, telescoping lights and grabbers, and other tools that may come in handy for opening computer equipment

Photography   Photographic record keeping and its supporting documentation play a major role in documenting evidence and its provenance. Like forensic analysis of computer systems, capturing the state of the scene can help investigators go back for reference during the analysis phase. For example, photographs can help answer questions like whether the server had both network cables plugged in at the time of the incident or was only connected to one network. The best tool for photography is the digital camera, which is much more convenient than a traditional field camera but requires some preparation and sound processing, including the following steps:

1. Sterilize the digital photographic media (memory card). Forensic sterilization can easily be performed by formatting the card to destroy the directory information and then using a tool such as sdelete.exe to clear all free space on the card of existing content. (The sdelete.exe and sdelete64.exe tools are available from Sysinternals at *https://live.sysinternals.com/*.)
2. Set the camera's clock to ensure that the dates and times recorded for the digital photographs are accurate.
3. Verify that the camera's EXIF recording option is turned on to ensure that all metadata is being recorded, including date, time, location, and camera settings.
4. Make the photographic media "self-documenting" by taking the first exposure of a "Begin Digital Photography" image, which shows the date and time and identifies that the investigation is under way. This also starts the sequential numbering of digital images being created.

5. Ensure that the digital photographic media (DPM) number—a tracking number assigned to the particular card—is identified in the digital photography log as each photograph is taken.

6. At the conclusion of the on-site activities, make an "End Digital Photography" exposure that marks the end of the photography session.

7. Remove the card from the camera, package it in an antistatic bag, and seal it in an evidence envelope, like any other piece of digital evidence.

8. Do not make hashes of digital photographs until the first time the evidence envelope is opened.

Field Notes   A valuable companion to the digital photographs is the collection of field notes. Field notes can be any notes that help investigators remember key aspects of a scene and the evidence collected. These notes are normally assembled into a case file that travels with the investigation team and becomes a permanent part of the investigation's documentary record.

A number of forms can aid an investigation or just help the team keep important notes:

- *Scene sketch*—The scene sketch is the only item that can be done in pencil. Its purpose is to show the general locations of items.
- *Field activity log*—The field activity log documents the activities of the team during evidence collection.
- *Field evidence log*—The field evidence log identifies each item collected by filename number.
- *Photography log*—The photo log tracks each picture taken and the context of the picture for later reference.

Acquiring the Evidence

An organization's IR policy must spell out the procedures for initiating the investigative process, including management approvals. This is particularly critical in the private sector, as private organizations do not enjoy the broad immunity accorded to law enforcement investigations. In general, a law enforcement organization cannot be sued for its conduct during an investigation unless police officers acted negligently, whereas a private organization can become the target of a retaliatory lawsuit for damages arising from an investigation that proves to be groundless.

Once the authorization to conduct an investigation is obtained, the collection and analysis of evidence can begin. As shown earlier, this is also the point where IR begins to interface with the forensics process. Prior to the digital forensics analysis, the organization must appropriately secure any potential digital media in which evidentiary material may reside.

Identifying Sources   Although identifying sources of evidence is somewhat straightforward in the physical world of bloodstains and fingerprints, it's much more complex in the digital world. Simple data collection in a suspect's corporate office may involve hundreds of gigabytes of information residing on one or more of the following:

- Drives in a desktop or laptop computer
- Drives in external storage enclosures (USB drives)
- Memory drives or cards (for example, USB flash/thumb drives, SD, microSD, xD, CompactFlash)
- Tablet computers and book readers (possibly with additional removable memory cards installed)
- Smartphones (including any memory cards installed in them)
- Storage devices, such as MP3 players
- Optical storage, such as CDs and DVDs
- Networked storage

When identifying evidence in a data center, perhaps as part of an intrusion or complex fraud investigation, the sources of potential evidence multiply to include the following:

- Drives attached to servers
- Storage attached to a storage network, such as a fiber channel or iSCSI SAN
- Files on NAS (network-attached storage) devices
- Cloud-based storage locations such as Dropbox, OneDrive, and Google Drive
- Logs on servers, routers, firewalls, or centralized logging servers
- Connected Internet of Things (IOT) devices

One of the more perplexing problems in collecting digital data concerns *volatile* information, such as the contents of a computer's memory. Traditional forensic practice calls for photographing a running computer's screen and then disconnecting the power, but this leads to loss of volatile information. Should investigators sacrifice the evidence stored on a drive by running tools to collect the volatile information, or should they sacrifice the volatile information in favor of the information on the drive? In time, better tools will make this less of a quandary, but currently it is a challenge.

Authenticating Evidence   Unlike objects in the physical world that have characteristics that set them apart from other similar items, one binary digit looks pretty much like another. This presents a significant challenge in the practice of digital forensics, as the legal system demands assurances that the information presented in court must be demonstrably authentic—for example, the genuine image of the drive in John Doe's workstation or a true copy of the log records from the RADIUS server collected on January 15th.

One way to identify a particular digital item (collection of bits) is by means of a cryptographic hash or hash value. These mathematical functions are ideal for this purpose because of their following properties:

- Each input (of a nontrivial size, at least) will produce an almost unique value.
- The hash value is easily stored and can be searched and compared quickly.
- Regardless of the size of its input, each hash operation produces a fixed-size output (128 bits for MD-5, 160 bits for SHA-1, and 256/512 bits for SHA-256/SHA-512, respectively).
- It is extremely unlikely that any contrived input could produce a specific hash value without an obvious manipulation of the input document file. This means that, although it is theoretically possible that two inputs could produce the same hash value, the attempted manipulation would be detectable in the source files.

As the following example shows, simply changing the case of two letters generates very different hash values:

```
: echo hello there > test.txt
: md5sum test.txt
782a482a8ba848cec578e3006678860c *test.txt
: echo Hello There > test.txt
: md5sum test.txt
937e9f428b23c367247b2c29318093b0 *test.txt
```

When a piece of digital evidence is collected, its hash value is calculated and recorded. At any subsequent point, the hash value can be recalculated to show that the item has not been modified since its collection. This technique can also authenticate copies of the original item as true and accurate copies. Two commonly used hashes are Message Digest (MD-5) and the Secure Hash Algorithm (SHA-1, SHA-256, SHA-512, and SHA-3), although other algorithms and variants like BLAKE and SHAKE are gaining in popularity. Command-line and GUI tools for calculating hashes are widely available.

Weaknesses of these hash algorithms have been described in the research literature.[11] In a case that occurred in Australia, a court decided to invalidate the use of a hash value to ensure positive identification so that digital evidence was excluded.[12] Regardless of these specific shortcomings, the general consensus remains that hashes are acceptable for demonstrating integrity of digital evidence.[13]

Collecting Evidence   There are many things to consider when collecting digital evidence. The investigator must decide on the mode of acquisition, as in *live* (power on) or *dead* (powered off), and how to package and image the collected material. The investigator must also accurately and thoroughly document all activities undertaken. Most importantly, the investigator must make no changes to the evidence.

The emphasis on not changing evidence during a digital forensic investigation may seem overstated, but it is justified by the potentially serious consequences. Digital forensic findings can cost (or save) the organization millions of dollars, can lead to employees being fired, and if used in criminal proceedings, can lead to a person being deprived of freedom or even their life.

When a piece of digital information is altered, the legal question arises as to exactly what was changed. Did an investigator inadvertently boot up a computer, or did the investigator plant evidence and cover the modification by booting up the computer? Although it is possible to minutely describe every change that occurred during boot-up and verify that only those changes were made in the image, such an effort is not likely to be rewarded, given the time and expertise involved, the difficulty in explaining such changes to a judge and jury, and the possibility of lingering doubts that might cause the evidence to be discounted.

To prevent doubts about evidence handling, evidence labels and seals are crucial. Although any secure package will serve, the use of packaging specifically designed for this purpose aids proper documentation and storage. An evidence envelope is preprinted with a form that shows where the information was collected, by whom, and when. The evidence seal is designed for single use and is very difficult to remove without breaking it. Evidence label and tape examples are shown in Figure 9-3.

Grounds for challenging the results of a digital investigation can also come from claiming possible contamination—that is, alleging that the relevant evidence came from somewhere else or was somehow tainted in the collection process. For this reason, media that are used to collect digital evidence must be forensically sterile, meaning that they contain no residue from previous use. There are various ways to prepare sterile media, but a common method is to write 0s to every block on the device, which erases any previous contents, and then to format the device with a file system if needed.

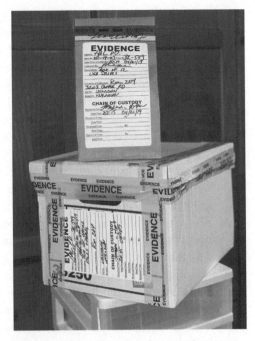

Figure 9-3   Examples of evidence containers and labels

All sterilization procedures must be codified, and all media sterilization processes must be documented. For such uses, most forensic teams maintain an inventory of sterilized media, which should be packaged, sealed, and documented through tagging to preclude the possibility of undisclosed tampering before use.

When an investigator is faced with a running system that may have been compromised, valuable information such as open network connections and other running processes may reveal the attacker's intentions and mode of entry. The investigator may conclude that this volatile information is important enough that a live acquisition should be conducted, and thus sacrifice the durable information that might be obtained by powering the system down. The investigator can later shut the computer down and image its drive(s) to gather information that may be useful in identifying the mode of entry and other activities of the attacker. However, because the live response tools modified the state of the system, it is very unlikely that the information collected from the drives will be admissible in any legal proceeding.

In a live acquisition, the investigator has no idea what the attacker did to the system during the compromise. Common system tools may have been replaced with malicious versions, or various traps may have been put in place to destroy information if the system was disturbed. For these reasons, the investigator will typically use a trusted set of tools from external media, such as Kali Linux, Helix3, KNOPPIX, or Forensic and Incident Response Environment (F.I.R.E.). These tools are available on live CDs, DVDs, USB drives, or external media with full bootable operating systems, and they contain a collection of scripts that automate the process of running a series of validated tools and preserving their output.

There are also a large number of stand-alone tools that help investigators gather evidence from live acquisition. Some examples of these tools are Windows Forensic Toolchest (WFT), which can be found at *www.foolmoon.net/security/wft*; SANS Investigative Forensic Toolkit (SIFT), which can be found at *http://computer-forensics.sans.org/community/downloads*; and Autopsy from *https://www.sleuthkit.org/autopsy/*. These tools can capture volatile information that might be useful in investigating a system compromise.

Although live acquisition is usually thought of in the context of a running host, the need to acquire the state of an active process arises in at least two other situations. First, because system log records are generated on a continuous basis, capturing their states at one point in time for an investigation requires a live acquisition. Second, some devices, such as tablets and smartphones, do not have boot-up sequences that correspond to traditional hosts, and live acquisition offers the best mechanism to collect evidentiary materials.

A continuously changing process presents challenges in acquisition, as there is not a "fixed" state that can be collected, hashed, and so forth. This has given rise to the concept of "snapshot forensics,"[14] which captures a point-in-time picture of a process, much like a photograph freezes an action.

Consider the log files on a centralized syslog server that is continually receiving log records from firewalls, intrusion detection systems, authentication servers, application servers, and other sources. Because log records are arriving on a continual basis, there is no fixed state of the log file that can be collected and hashed. For this reason, a snapshot is taken of the active log file by copying it, perhaps using a normal file copy. This copy is then acquired, perhaps by another copy, and hashed to verify that an accurate copy was acquired. The investigator should be prepared to produce good documentation and fully justify the actions in testimony, if necessary—perhaps using the analogy of extracting a single frame from a motion picture or taking a still photo of a running child, explaining and demonstrating that a copy operation does not "add" information to the item copied.

Often, an intrusion is detected by its effect, such as drive devices being deleted, and the investigator must work backwards to identify the sources of evidence. In situations like this, the information in log records often provides critical evidence of how the situation developed over time. For example, logs from VPN and authentication servers might show an intruder logging in from outside the corporate network; also, records generated by management applications might reveal the exact operations performed in deleting drives from a storage array.

Active devices, such as tablets, wireless phones, and other mobile technology, present similar challenges because as long as they have power, they actively monitor the status of tasks and appointments, check for e-mail or instant messages, and manage connections with the cellular network, so their internal state is continually changing.[15] They also maintain a lot of volatile information in memory that is lost if the batteries are removed.

These types of small wireless devices are increasingly critical to modern forensic investigations because almost everyone has at least one and because they are increasingly used for a variety of business and personal communications, including e-mail and instant messaging. They are also fairly promiscuous; if there is a compatible network available, they will connect to it. A smartphone or tablet seized from a suspect might be accessed wirelessly to modify or delete information, and a cellphone could continue to receive calls, instant messages, and e-mails after its seizure.

For these reasons, it is critical to protect wireless devices from accessing the network (or being accessed) after seizure and during analysis. Because removing power to the device would lose the volatile information, a better solution is to block wireless access using a Faraday cage. A Faraday cage is a continuous electrically conducting surface that surrounds a three-dimensional area so that no electromagnetic radiation can enter or exit.

Equipping an organization to handle forensics for wireless devices can easily cost tens of thousands of dollars just in specialized hardware and software. For this reason, and because of the rapid changes in technology, forensic analysis of wireless devices may be an excellent candidate for outsourcing to a specialist consultant.

In a dead acquisition, the computer is typically powered off so that its drives can be removed for imaging; the information on the devices is static ("dead") and durable. Although dead acquisition processes and procedures were developed for computer drives, they apply equally well to similar devices, such as thumb drives, memory cards, and MP3 players.

In a dead acquisition, an investigator seeks to obtain a forensic image of the drive or device. This image must include active files and directories as well as deleted files and file fragments. Figure 9-4 shows a snapshot of a portion of a file system.

A normal file system copy of the drive shown in Figure 9-4 would obtain File 1 and File 3, which are the only active files. However, there is more information on the device, including the following:

- The deleted entry in the directory, which might contain useful information about the deleted file
- The remnant of File 2 that was not overwritten by File 3, which might retain useful file fragments

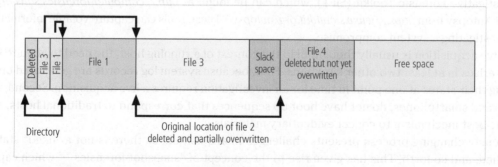

Figure 9-4   Small portion of a file system

- File 4, which has been deleted but not yet overwritten, so its contents should still be recoverable
- The free space, which might contain other files or fragments

To make sure this potentially valuable information is acquired, forensic investigators use bit-stream or sector-by-sector copying when making a forensic image of a device. Bit-stream copying reads a sector or block from the source drive and writes it to the target drive; this process continues until all sectors on the suspect drive have been copied.

Forensic imaging can be accomplished using specialized hardware tools or software running on a laptop or other computer. The advantage of using hardware tools specialized for the single purpose of copying drives is that they are generally faster. When performing a large imaging task (for example, imaging drives from 150 desktop computers involved in a complex fraud investigation), a hardware imaging solution will speed up the process. One example of a hardware imaging solution is the Image MASSter Solo, shown in Figure 9-5. The disadvantages of hardware imaging platforms are their cost and the fact that they support only certain interfaces.

There are many software imaging tools. Popular software products include EnCase, UNIX/Linux's dd, and Paraben's Forensic Replicator. These software packages run on a standard laptop or other system and support any drive interface supported by the host. In the model shown in Figure 9-5, the suspect drive on the left is enclosed for imaging in a protective rubber "boot" and is connected to the laptop through a forensic bridge, which serves two purposes:

- It bridges the IDE drive interface to the laptop USB interface.
- It blocks any write requests the laptop might generate.

It is critical that the information on the suspect media not be changed during the imaging process; otherwise, its value as evidentiary material may be compromised. For example, because the Helix tool is specialized for forensic use, it does not mount file systems or create swap partitions on any of the attached drives; an experienced investigator following correct procedure should not need any additional write block protection. However, investigators are human, and most will admit to having at least once confused the suspect and destination drives when performing imaging (say, at 4 a.m., while imaging the 72nd of 83 drives). For this reason, and to preclude any grounds for challenging the image output, it is common practice to protect the suspect media using a write blocker.

Write blockers are devices that allow acquisition of information on a drive without creating the possibility of accidentally damaging the drive contents. They do this by allowing read commands to pass but blocking write commands—hence their name. Write blockers may be software programs or hardware devices. The hardware write blocker has the advantage of having been in use longer, which means the legal community is more familiar with it. It can also perform the bridging function just described. For example, a write blocker kit (such as the UltraKit sold by Digital Intelligence) may contain bridges for IDE, SCSI, and SATA devices, which provide the write blocking function both to protect the suspect media and "bridge" the connection to a USB or FireWire device that's compatible with the laptop. Software write blockers have the advantage of eliminating a piece of hardware from the investigator's kit, but they add to the burden of proof for examiners, who will have to document that they were properly trained in the use of the software and that it was used properly in a particular instance.

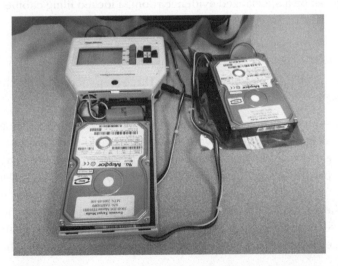

Figure 9-5 Example hardware imaging solution

chain of custody

A legal record of the location of evidentiary materials and the people responsible for them.

Before imaging a piece of drive media, its origin, vendor name, model number, and serial number are documented in both written and photographic form. This establishes the provenance of the drive image and helps to ensure its authenticity. Also, the media used as the target for forensic imaging should be forensically sterile, and that fact should be documented.

After the suspect piece of media is attached to the imaging setup, the general imaging process is as follows:

1. Calculate and record a baseline cryptographic hash of the suspect media.
2. Perform a bit-stream image of the suspect media.
3. Calculate and record a hash of the target. (Optionally, another hash of the suspect media can be calculated to verify that it was not modified by the imaging process.)
4. Compare the hashes to verify that they match.
5. Package the target media for transport.

Maintaining a Documented Chain of Custody   Although documentation of processes and procedures, digital fingerprints, and secure packaging help demonstrate the authenticity of digital evidence, there are additional requirements for demonstrating that the evidence has been protected from accidental or purposeful modification at every point from its collection through analysis and then its presentation in court. This protection is called maintaining the chain of custody.

In principle, the chain of custody is a record of who is responsible for the protection of evidentiary materials. As shown previously, the chain of custody is duplicated on the evidence label as well as managed through a secured document. The usual process is that the field investigator maintains personal custody and control of the sealed item until it is logged in the chain of custody book at the evidence storage room. Each time the item is removed for analysis, copying, or other purposes, it is logged out, which forms a documented trail of who accessed the information and when.

Collected evidence must be stored and handled appropriately to protect its value, especially because items may sometimes be stored for weeks, months, or even years before they are analyzed. If the investigation results in legal proceedings, the evidence may be stored for years before the matter is heard in court.

Proper storage requires a protected, controlled access environment coupled with sound processes governing access to its contents. For example, access must be limited to specifically authorized personnel and documentation of every access must be maintained in the chain of custody book. The storage facility must also maintain the proper environment for holding digital information, which requires the following:

- Controlled temperature and humidity
- Freedom from strong electrical and magnetic fields that might damage the items
- Protection from fire and other physical hazards

The evidence storage facility can be a specialized evidence room, a locked filing cabinet in an office, or something in between.

The Digital Forensics Investigation Process

At its heart, a digital forensics investigation follows a simple three-step methodology that begins when digital media have been seized for analysis:[16]

1. *Preparation/extraction*—After the organization determines there is sufficient cause to proceed, the investigators validate all hardware and software and then proceed to duplicate all electronic media, creating forensic images. The investigators then validate the integrity of the images, recording the hash values, and develop a plan to extract the needed evidentiary materials. Figure 9-6 shows the flow of this phase.
2. *Identification*—With the extraction plan in hand, investigators use digital forensic tools to search for and document relevant evidentiary materials. Any additional evidentiary materials uncovered in the process are also documented, even if they are unrelated to the primary investigation. The investigators may submit

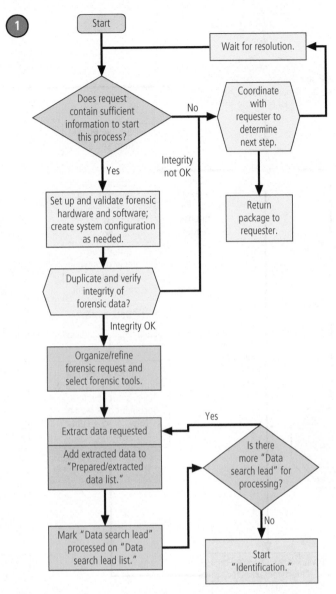

Figure 9-6   Forensic preparation and extraction[17]

a preliminary findings report to management and legal counsel. At that point, the investigator may be directed to return to the search and document any additional materials based on the preliminary findings. Figure 9-7 shows the flow of this phase.

3. *Analysis*—With the findings from the identification phase in hand, the investigators develop a formal findings report, explaining what was found, where, and how it was located. They also attempt to explain how the material was introduced into the system and by whom. As part of an incident investigation, the investigators will attempt to understand what happened and how, and provide that information back to the CSIRT and management. Figure 9-8 shows the flow of this phase.

Analyzing Evidence   To answer the question that originated in the physical world and triggered the digital investigation, an analyst must translate that question into a series of questions that are answerable through forensic analysis. These "digital world" questions will guide the analysis and set its scope.

The first step in the analysis process is to obtain the evidence from the storage area by signing it out in the chain of custody book and then performing a physical authentication. This involves verifying the written documentation against the actual item of evidence—that is, verifying the manufacturer, serial number, and other identifying

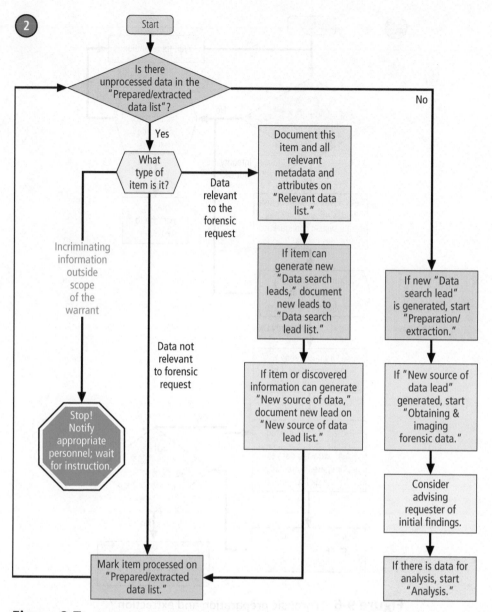

Figure 9-7   Forensic identification[18]

information. Next, a copy of the evidence is made for analysis and the original is returned to storage; it is crucial that the analysis never take place on the original evidence. The copy of the evidence can then be authenticated by recomputing its hash and comparing it to the written record to verify that an accurate copy of the original evidence has been obtained.

Drive images must be loaded into the appropriate forensic tool used by the organization. This typically involves processing the image into the format used by the tool; performing preprocessing, such as undeleting files and data carving (recovering files and images from fragments in free space); and comparison against known hashes.

The two dominant industry tools used in forensic analysis are Forensic Toolkit (FTK) from AccessData and EnCase from Guidance Software. One of the most popular open source tools is Autopsy from SleuthKit, shown in Figure 9-9.

Searching for Evidence   With the increasing sizes of drive devices, identifying relevant information is an important task for analysts. For example, when investigating a computer image in a case involving widespread identity theft, credit card numbers and Social Security numbers are highly relevant.

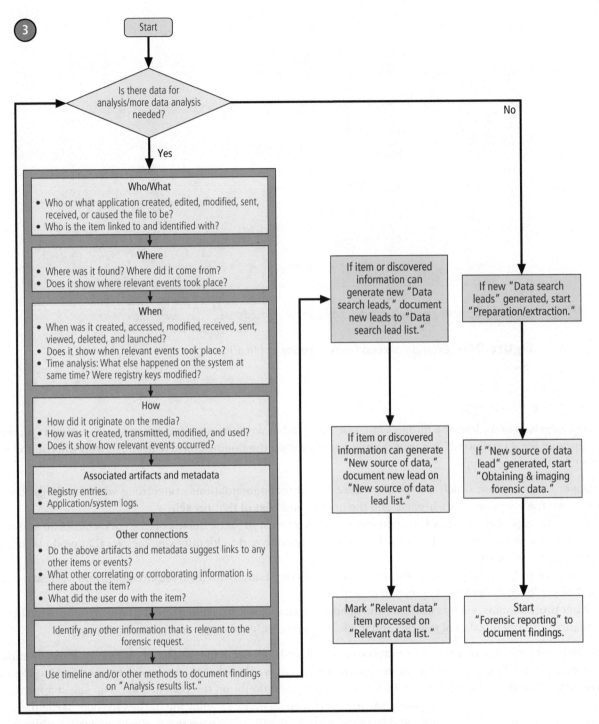

Figure 9-8   Forensic analysis[19]

As part of their preprocessing, forensic search tools will construct an index of terms found in the image. Developing relevant search terms can be challenging; a technique from the legal profession called cartwheeling,[20] in which a term is extended with links to subsidiary terms, can help. These tools also offer a flexible search interface and include predefined filters for common items, such as e-mail and Web addresses and Social Security numbers. As relevant items are located, they are "bookmarked" for inclusion in the final report.

Upon completion of the collection process, the evidence awaits presentation and reporting in some formal proceedings. During this time, the organization must maintain a documented chain of custody to ensure that the material's integrity is protected. A recommended procedure for acquiring this type of evidentiary material is discussed in the following sections.

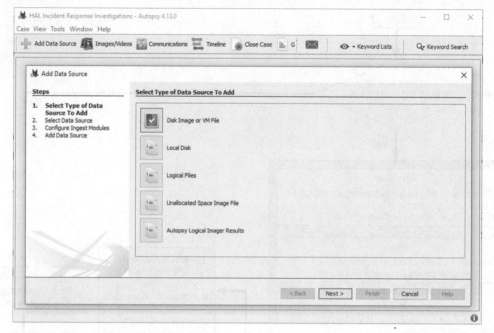

Figure 9-9   Example screen from Autopsy application

Source: sleuthkit.org.

Reporting the Findings

After the analysis is complete, the findings must be reported in written and often spoken form, either in a presentation or through legal testimony. This report must communicate the findings clearly to those who will use the report, including the following groups:

- Upper management, which is typically interested in recommendations concerning whether allegations are correct, the scope of a data breach, and the impact and cost of that breach
- A forensic expert retained by the opposition, who is interested in the details of evidence collection and analysis in order to determine if the analysis was properly done and to identify weaknesses that could be used to challenge it in court
- Attorneys, judges, and juries, which are interested in compliance with legal requirements and the real meaning of the evidence in deciding a question of fact
- Other professionals, such as auditors and heads of human resources departments, who are interested in compliance with organizational policies and in identifying possible changes to those policies

It is tempting to prepare a series of reports, each tailored to a particular audience. However, if the investigation leads to legal proceedings, all these various reports are discoverable—that is, they must be disclosed to the opposing side. Any differences among the various versions could cast doubt on the conclusions. The safest approach is to prepare a single report with an index to point the parties to their particular areas of interest. The report should identify what gave rise to the investigation, the sources of the evidence that was analyzed, the tools and processes that were used to analyze the evidence, the specific findings, and an interpretation of the findings (in other words, did the evidence support or disprove the allegation?). In general terms, the report summarizes the detailed records contained in the case file, the analyst's notebooks, and other documentation, which can be produced to address detailed questions.

eDiscovery

The search for, collection, and review of items stored in digital format that are of potential evidentiary value based on criteria specified by a legal team.

anti-forensics

An attempt made by potential subjects of digital forensic techniques to obfuscate or hide items of evidentiary value.

eDiscovery and Anti-Forensics

A newer element of the digital forensics field is the areas of electronic discovery (**eDiscovery**) and **anti-forensics**. As a field, eDiscovery is related to digital forensics, and they are often combined as associated disciplines. Whereas digital forensics focuses on the entirety of the collection process, from data collection to data analysis, eDiscovery involves a smaller portion of the digital forensics process.

Discovery is the component of law that allows one party to request information from another party. This usually requires formal legal requests, such as subpoenas. With the wide range of electronic (digital) media used today, traditional legal fields that have been associated with discovery of documentation have had to expand their capabilities to manage the onslaught of gigabytes of digital records that are subject to such searches. eDiscovery is different from discovery, as it involves the search for digital information on a specific topic from a larger body of information, such as searching for items related to a specific purchase or communications from an organization's entire set of digital data.

eDiscovery may involve using a digital forensics team to perform the actual tasks; however, the search criteria and subsequent review of findings fall under eDiscovery. This is not to imply that digital forensics is a subset of eDiscovery; rather, the two fields overlap when legal teams require technical teams to collect the information they need for their litigation. People who seek to hide information are typically engaged in anti-forensics; however, forensic tools excel at retrieving information that has been deleted through normal means or that resides in places hidden by the operating system. This deleted or hidden information is valuable to investigators, but its recovery can pose a significant threat to the privacy and confidentiality of an organization's information assets.

Actions in the digital world leave many traces, such as records of Web sites visited or archived e-mail messages, and these items can be easily retrieved from discarded or recycled computer equipment. As a result, the use of anti-forensics techniques is of value to organizations to prevent accidental disclosure of data. Simson Garfinkel did an empirical study in which he purchased used computers and drives from online merchants and analyzed what was left on the devices by their previous owners, either inadvertently or due to poor deletion processes.[21] Garfinkel found medical records, business records, and many other types of confidential information.

In SP 800-88, Rev. 1, "Guidelines for Media Sanitization," NIST has recommended practices for anti-forensics to help keep data that should be protected from being disclosed. These practices range from overwriting drive media with 0s or random data to physically destroying the equipment.[22] Organizations must be aware that forensic tools are not just in the hands of honest professionals, but are available to everyone. Therefore, organizations must have policy and procedures to ensure that discarded digital information is destroyed beyond forensic recovery.

An increasing concern for privacy and widespread availability of encryption products has led to the use of encryption for individual files and even entire devices. Although some encryption is poorly done and is easily broken, high-quality products increasingly use good encryption algorithms that are beyond the current capability to reverse encryption by trying all possible combinations. Encrypted information poses significant challenges to forensic investigators because, by its nature, encryption conceals the content of digital material. Many encryption products require input of an encryption key when the user logs on and then decrypt the user's information on the fly. When the system goes into screensaver mode or is powered down, the encryption key is deactivated and must be reentered. Unfortunately, data needed by the forensic investigator will be encrypted and will not be readable without the proper key.

Some forensic products offer brute force attacks against encrypted information, using dictionaries of common passphrases. These attacks are sometimes successful, but they can be defeated by the use of strong passphrases. One element of modern computers that forensic investigators can leverage is the possible presence of unencrypted copies of encrypted information in temporary "work files" or the systems paging file. So, although the original or master copies are concealed through encryption, the temporary copies may be usable by the forensic examiner.

 You can learn more about anti-forensics in an article available at *https://resources.infosecinstitute.com/anti-forensics-part-1/*.

discovery

The component of civil law whereby one party can obtain evidence from the opposing party through specific requests for information, which usually requires formal legal requests, such as subpoenas.

Closing Scenario

After a very long morning, HAL's servers and client systems were fully functional, verified, and back online, with minimal downtime and loss of data. The CSIRT had been able to get a copy of the worm early in the process, for reverse engineering and research purposes. A brief e-mail was sent to explain what had happened and to let everybody know that things were now back to normal.

On the afternoon of the incident, Paul had a meeting with Sheila Wentworth and Jorge Hernandez, both from the legal department. They wanted a briefing on what had occurred in order to assess potential liability issues for the company. After the three of them assembled in the conference room and exchanged pleasantries, Sheila got down to business and started questioning Paul.

"Paul, what in the world happened? I thought we had firewalls in place to prevent stuff like this from attacking our network! How could you let this happen?"

Still focused on his active day responding to the incident, he resisted the urge to start yelling at Sheila over the implied accusation. He took a deep breath, composed himself, and said, "Let's begin at the top, shall we?"

Discussion Questions

1. Was the CSIRT response appropriate, given the circumstances? On what do you base your position?
2. Was Paul being unjustly accused of allowing the incident to happen? On what do you base your position?
3. Was there anything else Paul could have done to prevent the incident? On what do you base your position?

Ethical Decision Making

Suppose the forensic investigation at HAL was able to backtrack the worm attack and found that the worm first appeared in the special projects lab at Osbert's university. The team reaches out to the university and is given access to lab-door access records that identify Osbert. Almost at once, they realize that Osbert is a close friend of one of the forensic team members.

1. How does the team approach this aspect of the investigation to get the best results and to avoid conflicts of interest?
2. Can the team access Osbert's personal devices to examine them? Under what constraints? How might the team accomplish this legally?
3. During the investigation and forensic effort in response to the worm outbreak, you are examining a hard drive and find "love letters" between two employees of the organization who are not married to each other. This activity is not illegal, and it is not related to the worm attack. Do you report it in the investigation?
4. Suppose the examiner is friends with the spouse of one of the lovers, and the examiner shows the friend evidence of the affair. Would that be ethical behavior? Why or why not?

MODULE SUMMARY

- After an incident has been contained and system control has been regained, IR begins by informing the appropriate human resources. The CSIRT must assess the full extent of the damage to determine what must be done to restore the systems. This may take days or weeks.
- After any incident, an organization should address the safeguards that failed to stop or limit the incident or that were missing from the system. Safeguards must be installed, replaced, or upgraded as needed. The organization should evaluate monitoring capabilities and either improve detection and reporting methods or install new monitoring capabilities.

- Compromised services and processes must be examined, verified, and then restored. If services or processes were interrupted in the course of regaining control of the systems, they need to be brought back online.
- Ongoing maintenance includes after-action review (AAR) meetings, plan review and maintenance, training of staff members who will be involved in IR, and ensuring ongoing rehearsal of the plans in order to maintain readiness. The AAR is a detailed examination of the events that occurred, from first detection to final recovery. All key players review their notes and verify that the IR documentation is accurate and precise. At the end of the incident review, the AAR serves as a review tool, allowing the team to examine how it responded to the incident. An additional use of the AAR is as a historical record of events. By examining the events of past attacks, the organization may learn as much from mistakes as from successes.
- When shortcomings are noted in the plan, they should be reviewed and revised. Plans should be periodically reviewed.
- A systematic approach to training is needed to support the IR plan. Cross-training is also needed to ensure that enough staff members with the proper skills are available for all reasonably realistic scenarios. This ongoing and systematic approach to planning requires that plans be rehearsed until responders are prepared for the actions they are expected to perform.
- When an incident violates civil or criminal law, it is the organization's responsibility to notify the proper authorities and work with them throughout the investigation and resolution of the matter.
- After the incident, the CSIRT leader should make a report to upper management—typically the CISO and CIO. One of the first questions that upper management has for the investigative team is "How much was lost, and how much will it cost us to recover?"
- Computer forensics is the use of computer investigation and analysis techniques to identify, collect, preserve, and analyze electronic items of potential evidentiary value so that they may be admitted as evidence in a court of law or used to support administrative action. The term *digital forensics* refers to all modern electronic devices, including computers, mobile phones, personal digital assistants (PDAs), and portable music players.
- A digital investigation begins with an allegation of wrongdoing—either a policy violation or the commission of a crime. Based on that allegation, authorization is sought to begin the investigation by collecting relevant evidence; once authorization has been obtained, the collection of evidence can begin.
- The first-response digital forensics team secures and collects the devices, media, or media images that are potentially evidentiary. Later, analysis and reporting techniques are performed by people who are specially trained in the use of forensic tools to analyze the collected information and answer the questions that gave rise to the investigation.
- To settle the issue that prompted an investigation, the analyst must translate the issue into a series of specific questions that are answerable through forensic analysis, then use the proper tools to answer those specific questions.
- Forensic tools can be used by investigators even to obtain information that has been deleted from digital media. These tools can also be used for nefarious purposes—that is, to illegitimately obtain private or proprietary information from discarded digital media.
- eDiscovery is the search for, collection, and review of items stored in digital format that are of potential evidentiary value based on criteria specified by a legal team.
- Anti-forensics involves the attempt by potential subjects of digital forensics techniques to obfuscate or hide items of evidentiary value.

Review Questions

1. What is an incident damage assessment?
2. What are some of the reasons a safeguard or control may not have been successful in stopping or limiting an incident?
3. What must be done with interrupted services during the recovery process?
4. What procedures should occur on a regular basis to maintain the IR plan?

5. What is digital forensics?

6. What legal issues guide an organization in setting up a forensic capability?

7. How do organizations often divide the practice of digital forensics?

8. What are the common roles and duties of a digital forensic first-response team?

9. What factors determine which digital evidence should be collected and in what order?

10. In forensic analysis, what are the differences between examination and analysis?

11. What type of document is usually required when an organization other than a law enforcement agency obtains authorization for a search?

12. In what important way does search and seizure differ in the public and private sectors?

13. What are the four steps in acquiring digital evidence?

14. What two hash functions are the most commonly used?

15. What is the purpose of sterile media?

16. What type of forensics is used for practices that continue to operate while being examined?

17. What types of information are missed by a normal copying process but included in a forensic image?

18. What is the relationship between forensics and anti-forensics, and why is it important to the forensics investigator?

19. Why is encryption a good thing for IT workers but bad for forensic investigators?

20. When is the involvement of law enforcement optional in a forensics investigation? Who should make this determination?

Real-World Exercises

Exercise 9-1

Do a Web search for "Trojan horse defense." How can it be used to question the conclusions drawn from a forensic investigation?

Exercise 9-2

At the end of 2006, a new edition of the Federal Rules of Civil Procedure (FRCP) went into effect. Do a Web search to learn more about the FRCP. What likely effect will its emphasis on electronically stored information (ESI) have on an organization's need for a digital forensic capability?

Exercise 9-3

Do a Web search to identify some common certifications for digital forensic practitioners. Identify one certification that is vendor-neutral and one that is targeted at a specific investigation toolset.

Exercise 9-4

Do a Web search to identify cases in which private information was disclosed when computer equipment was discarded. Recent examples have included smartphones (like BlackBerries) that were sold without proper data cleansing and hard drives that were sold without data cleansing after the computers they were originally used in were upgraded. Provide a short report that details the cases and identifies the technology involved.

Hands-On Projects

The hands-on project for this module can be accessed in the Practice It folder in MindTap or through your instructor's LMS. The virtual labs provided with this resource can help you develop practical skills that will be of value as you progress through the course.

References

1. Pipkin, Donald L. *Information Security: Protecting the Global Enterprise.* Upper Saddle River, NJ: Prentice Hall PTR, 2000, 285.
2. Nietzsche, Friedrich. "Friedrich Nietzsche Quotes." BrainyQuote. Accessed 04/04/20 at *www.brainyquote .com/quotes/friedrich_nietzsche_101616.*
3. Edison, Thomas Alva. "Thomas A. Edison Quotes." BrainyQuote. Accessed 04/04/20 at *www.brainyquote .com/quotes/thomas_a_edison_132683.*
4. Berra, Yogi. "Yogi Berra Quotes." BrainyQuote. Accessed 04/04/20 at *www.brainyquote.com/quotes/ yogi_berra_110034.*
5. Federal Bureau of Investigation. "Cyber Crime." Accessed 04/06/20 at *www.fbi.gov/investigate/cyber.*
6. Merriam-Webster Dictionary. Accessed 4/6/20 at *www.merriam-webster.com/dictionary/forensics.*
7. Lewis, Paul G. "Curiosity May Kill the Case." New Jersey Law Journal 182:11: 1030–1031.
8. Kent, Karen, Suzanne Chevalier, Tim Grance, and Hung Dang. SP 800-86, "Guide to Integrating Forensic Techniques into Incident Response." National Institute of Standards and Technology. Accessed 04/21/20 at *https://csrc.nist.gov/publications/detail/sp/800-86/final.*
9. Inman, Keith, and Norah Rudin. *Principles and Practice of Criminalistics: The Profession of Forensic Science.* Boca Raton, FL: CRC Press, 2001.
10. Ibid.
11. Schneier, Bruce. "More Hash Function Attacks." Schneier on Security. March 10, 2005. Accessed 04/16/20 at *www.schneier.com/blog/archives/2005/03/more_hash_funct.html.*
12. McCullagh, Declan. "MD5 Flaw Pops Up in Australian Traffic Court." CNET. August 2005. Accessed 04/16/20 at *www.cnet.com/news/md5-flaw-pops-up-in-australian-traffic-court/.*
13. "RFC 6151." Internet Engineering Task Force. Accessed 04/16/20 at *http://tools.ietf.org/html/rfc6151.*
14. Kipper, Gregory. *Wireless Crime and Forensic Investigation.* Boca Raton, FL: Auerbach, 2007.
15. Cohen, Tyler, and Amber Schroader. *Alternate Data Storage Forensics.* Burlington, MA: Elsevier, 2007.
16. Carroll, O., S. Brannon, and T. Song. "Computer Forensics: Digital Forensics Analysis Methodology." *Computer Forensics.* Jan. 2008, Vol. 56, No. 1. pp. 1–8. Accessed 04/21/20 at *www.justice.gov/sites/default/ files/usao/legacy/2008/02/04/usab5601.pdf.*
17. Ibid.
18. Ibid.
19. Ibid.
20. Statsky, William P. *Legal Research and Writing.* West Publishing, 1982.
21. Garfinkel, Simson. "New Directions in Disk Forensics." Accessed 04/16/20 at *www.blackhat.com/ presentations/bh-federal-06/BH-Fed-06-Garfinkel.pdf.*
22. Kissel, R., A. Regenscheid, M. Scholl, K. Stine. SP 800-88, Rev. 1, "Guidelines for Media Sanitization." National Institute of Standards and Technology. Accessed 04/16/20 at *https://nvlpubs.nist.gov/nistpubs/ SpecialPublications/NIST.SP.800-88r1.pdf.*

DISASTER RECOVERY

Upon completion of this material, you should be able to:

1. Identify the classifications for various types of disasters
2. Describe the various disaster recovery teams and their composition
3. List the key elements found in a disaster plan
4. Outline the key challenges an organization faces when engaged in DR operations
5. Explain the actions organizations should take to prepare for the activation of the DR plan
6. Recognize the phases in the development and use of the DR plan

Our disaster recovery plan goes something like this: Throw your hands up and shout "HELP! HELP!"

— Dilbert, *by Scott Adams*

Opening Scenario

Susan pulled into her usual parking place near the HAL offices and wondered what was going on. Fire trucks and police cars were scattered all around the building, and there was even an ambulance waiting nearby.

Grabbing her briefcase and jacket, she walked quickly over to the fire department command truck and asked, "What's going on?"

The fireman who seemed to be in charge asked, "Who might you be?"

"Susan Carter, I am the third-shift IT supervisor here at HAL."

"Not tonight," he said. "There was a major structural fire in this building. We just about have it under control, but we need to make sure there are no flare-ups. Everyone is out of the structure, and as far as we know, no one was seriously injured. There were only a few of your employees inside. All of them are out and accounted for by the second-shift supervisor. But no one is going into the structure at this time. It'll be several hours before the inspectors are done and you can get started with your recovery."

"Okay," Susan said. She walked over to the ambulance where the employees from the second shift in the HAL data center were being looked over by the paramedics. She saw the second-shift supervisor breathing from an oxygen mask. Now that she had quickly appraised the situation, she turned back toward her car. After she sat down in her car, she pulled out her company cell phone and hit the speed dial for her boss, Amanda Wilson.

"Hello," said a voice, clearly awakening from a deep sleep.

"Amanda? Susan Carter here. I am just getting to work, and there was a significant fire in the building. We have a disaster on our hands. Everyone is out safely, and it seems we don't have any serious injuries, but the offices are in a bad state."

"Oh, no!" Amanda said. "I'm glad that everyone is okay. Do you think the on-site backups are going to be usable?"

"I wouldn't bet on it," Susan said.

"Okay," Amanda said. She paused for a moment, then said to Susan, "Declare a disaster and activate continuity plan A and recovery plan B immediately. I will be there in 20 minutes."

Susan next called the HAL automated phone system, knowing it was based off-site at a secure service provider's location. When the HAL greeting started, she entered her PIN code to authenticate herself. She then recorded a brief message outlining the disaster and the disaster and continuity plans that were to be followed. When she finished the message, she confirmed that the alert roster was to be processed with the message she had just recorded. Everyone who needed to know about this catastrophe would be called in the next few minutes. The system would keep trying every person at each of their possible phone numbers until they were reached.

INTRODUCTION

The disaster recovery (DR) elements of the contingency planning (CP) process are often taken for granted in many organizations. An organization should operate on the premise that it is only a matter of time until a disaster strikes. Only through meticulous preparation and ongoing diligence can an organization properly respond when a disaster occurs. Each area of the world has its own challenges and risks of disaster, whether natural or man-made. Organizations that plan to succeed after a disaster will need to react quickly and decisively to restore operations at their primary locations. When that is not possible, or in the event of a total loss, an organization must be prepared to promptly reestablish operations at a new permanent location.

While the organization's chief operations officer (COO) is generally responsible for the overall DR effort, the information technology (IT) community of interest, under the leadership of the CIO, is usually given responsibility for the IT aspects of DR planning, as they are keenly interested in keeping IT systems available during and immediately following disasters. Unfortunately, some organizations then abdicate the overall responsibility for disaster readiness to the IT department, including aspects that are not necessarily related to IT. In a perfectly balanced approach, the IT department focuses on IT-system disaster preparations while the other business units make preparations in their own areas.

Because the plans and procedures used for DR are very similar to those undertaken for incident response (IR) and business continuity (BC), material in this module will seem similar to that in other modules. An organization can interchangeably use many of the approaches discussed with respect to contingency planning: IR, BC, and **disaster recovery planning (DRP)**. In some cases, actual incidents detected by the IR team escalate to the level of disaster, and the IR plan is no longer adequate to handle the effective and efficient recovery from the loss. For example, if a malicious

disaster recovery planning (DRP)

The preparation for and recovery from a disaster, whether natural or man-made; DRP is focused on restoring operations at an organization's primary site or at a new permanent site.

disaster recovery plan (DR plan)

A plan that deals with the preparation for and recovery from a disaster, whether natural or man-made.

program evades containment actions and infects and disables all of an organization's systems and their ability to function, the **disaster recovery plan (DR plan)** is activated. By their nature, some events are immediately classified as disasters—for example, fires, floods, storms, and earthquakes.

As discussed in earlier modules, the contingency planning management team (CPMT) forms the DR team, then assists in the development of the DR plan. In general, an incident is categorized as a disaster when the organization is unable to contain or control its impact or when the level of damage or destruction from the incident is so severe that the organization is unable to quickly recover. The distinction between an actual incident and an immediate disaster may be subtle. The CPMT must document in the DR plan whether an event is classified as an incident or a disaster. This determination is critical, as it determines which plan is activated. The key role of a DR plan is defining how to reestablish operations at the organization's usual location.

The compelling need for DR contingency plans is documented by industry reports:

- *Seventy-five percent of small businesses have no disaster recovery plan objective in place.*
- *Hardware failure is the primary cause of data loss and/or downtime.*
- *According to Dynamic Technologies, hardware failures cause 45 percent of total unplanned downtime, followed by the loss of power (35 percent), software failure (34 percent), data corruption (24 percent), external security breaches (23 percent), and accidental user error (20 percent). Note that these percentages do not add up to 100 percent because some respondents identified multiple causes for failures.*
- *Ninety-three percent of companies without a disaster recovery plan that suffer a major data disaster are out of business within one year.*
- *Ninety-six percent of companies with a trusted backup and disaster recovery plan were able to survive ransomware attacks.*
- *More than 50 percent of companies experienced a downtime event in the past five years that lasted longer than a full workday.*
- *Corero Network Security found that organizations spend significant amounts of money when dealing with a denial-of-service attack—in many cases, tens or hundreds of thousands of dollars.*
- *Estimates are that unplanned downtime can cost up to $17,244 per minute, with a low-end estimate of $926 per minute.*
- *Forty to sixty percent of small businesses that lose access to operational systems and data and that do not have a DR plan close their doors forever. Companies that can recover do so at a much higher cost and with a more extended time frame than companies that had formal backup and disaster recovery plans in place.*
- *Ninety-six percent of businesses with a disaster recovery solution in place fully recover operations.*
- *More than 50 percent of businesses don't have the budget to recover from an attack.*
- *By 2021, cybercrimes will cost $6 trillion per year worldwide.*
- *Cryptojacking attacks are increasing by over 8000 percent as miners exploit the computing power of unsuspecting victims.[1] Cryptojacking refers to an attack that penetrates a network not to steal information but to hijack computing resources and use them to perform complex block-chain calculations that create new blocks for use as cryptocurrencies.*

These kinds of estimates are revealing, and serve as a warning to organizations that don't have a DR plan in place. Even organizations that do are warned to regularly train, rehearse, test, and revise their plans lest they grow outdated and useless.

Disaster Classifications

A DR plan can classify disasters in a number of ways. The most common way is to separate **natural disasters**, such as those described in Table 10-1, from **man-made disasters**. Another way of classifying disasters is by their speed of development; for example, **rapid-onset disasters** include earthquakes, floods, storm winds, tornadoes, and mud flows, while **slow-onset disasters** include droughts, famines, environmental degradation, desertification, deforestation, and pest infestation.

 In an earlier module, we recommended that you visit the U.S. Federal Emergency Management Agency (FEMA) Web site to learn more about planning for natural disasters. The European Union has a similar organization named European Civil Protection and Humanitarian Aid Operations. To compare and contrast these agencies, you can visit *https://ec.europa.eu/echo/what/humanitarian-aid/disaster_preparedness_en*.

The events of the COVID-19 pandemic in 2020 illustrate the need for organizations to be prepared for all types of hazards to continuity of operations. Even though planners often include natural disasters in their preparations, threats such as worldwide health emergencies must be included as well. Few planners in 2020 expected their organizations to be prepared for shelter-in-place orders and disruption of the global supply chain.

natural disaster

A disaster caused by natural occurrences, such as a fire, flood, earthquake, lightning, landslide, tornado, hurricane, tsunami, electrostatic discharge, dust, or excessive rainfall.

man-made disaster

A disaster caused by people, including acts of terrorism (cyberterrorism or hactivism), acts of war, and acts that begin as incidents and escalate into disasters.

rapid-onset disaster

A disaster that occurs suddenly and with little warning, taking the lives of people and destroying the means of production.

slow-onset disaster

A disaster that occurs over time and slowly deteriorates the organization's capacity to withstand its effects.

Table 10-1   Natural Disasters and Their Impacts on Information Systems

Disaster Type	Description
Fire	Can damage the building housing the computing equipment that comprises all or part of the information system. Also encompasses smoke damage from the fire and water damage from sprinkler systems or firefighters. Can usually be mitigated with fire casualty insurance or business interruption insurance.
Flood	Can cause direct damage to all or part of the information system or to the building that houses all or part of it. May also disrupt operations through interruptions in access to the buildings that house all or part of the information system. Can sometimes be mitigated with flood insurance or business interruption insurance.
Earthquake	Can cause direct damage to all or part of the information system or, more often, to the building that houses it. May also disrupt operations by interrupting access to the buildings that house all or part of the information system. Can sometimes be mitigated with specific casualty insurance or business interruption insurance, but is usually a specific and separate policy.
Lightning	Can directly damage all or part of the information system or its power distribution components. Can also cause fires or other damage to the building that houses all or part of the information system. May also disrupt operations by interrupting access to the buildings that house all or part of the information system as well as the routine delivery of electrical power. Can usually be mitigated with multipurpose casualty insurance or business interruption insurance.
Landslide or mudslide	Can damage all or part of the information system or, more likely, the building that houses it. May also disrupt operations by interrupting access to the buildings that house all or part of the information system as well as the routine delivery of electrical power. Can sometimes be mitigated with casualty insurance or business interruption insurance.
Tornado or severe windstorm	Can directly damage all or part of the information system or, more likely, the building that houses it. May also disrupt operations by interrupting access to the buildings that house all or part of the information system as well as the routine delivery of electrical power. Can sometimes be mitigated with casualty insurance or business interruption insurance.
Hurricane or typhoon	Can directly damage all or part of the information system or, more likely, the building that houses it. Organizations located in coastal or low-lying areas may experience flooding (see above). May also disrupt operations by interrupting access to the buildings that house all or part of the information system as well as the routine delivery of electrical power. Can sometimes be mitigated with casualty insurance or business interruption insurance.
Tsunami	Can directly damage all or part of the information system or, more likely, the building that houses it. May also cause disruption to operations by interrupting access or electrical power to the buildings that house all or part of the information system. Can sometimes be mitigated with casualty insurance or business interruption insurance.
Electrostatic discharge (ESD)	Can be costly or dangerous when it ignites flammable mixtures and damages costly electronic components. Static electricity can draw dust into clean-room environments or cause products to stick together. Loss of production time in information processing due to ESD impact is significant. Though not usually viewed as a threat, it can disrupt information systems and is not usually covered by business interruption insurance.
Dust contamination	Can shorten the life of information systems or cause unplanned downtime.
Excessive precipitation	Rain, freezing rain, sleet, snow, hail, and fog can all cause losses, such as through property damage when a roof collapses under the weight of excessive snow. Sometimes, excessive precipitation leads to another listed type of disaster, such as floods or mudslides. Still other circumstances can lead to losses that are not as obvious, such as intense fog causing roadways to be closed or public transportation systems to be shut down.

FEMA is a valuable resource for organizations that want to integrate concerns about pandemics into their continuity plans. For example, the Web page at *www.fema.gov/media-library/assets/documents/93250* offers a DRP template for global viral pandemics. Planners can gain additional insight from a template for an emergency action plan from the U.S. Centers for Disease Control and Prevention (CDC); see *www.cdc.gov/niosh/docs/2004-101/emrgact/emrgact.pdf.*

The plan templates from FEMA and CDC include many of the elements of the planning approach presented in this module, but they contribute additional depth to the unique aspects of planning for global pandemics.

FORMING THE DISASTER RECOVERY TEAM

The CPMT begins with assembling the DR team. Although the IT and information security (InfoSec) departments contribute representatives to this team, it must also include members from outside these two groups. Because much of the work of the DR team is about the reestablishment of business operations at the primary site, the team leader and many of the members should be drawn from the organization's functional areas. Not only is this team responsible for the planning for DR, it also leads the DR process when the disaster is declared. Key considerations in developing the DR team include its organization, the planning needed to identify essential documentation and equipment, and training and rehearsal so the team is able to perform when needed.

The nature of the organization may influence the composition of DR teams. For example, government agencies may have access to shared resources, and some commercial organizations collaborate through the use of information sharing and advisory centers (ISACs) specialized for their industry segment.

 For more information about member-driven organizations collaborating through the use of industry-segment ISACs, visit *www.nationalisacs.org/.*

Organization of the DR Team

The DR team consists of a team leader, who is also a member of the CPMT, and representatives from every major organizational unit. Members are selected for their particular skills, their ability to be a liaison between organizational elements, or other specialized qualities. The membership of the DR team should be distinctly separate from that of any other contingency-related team, as each has differing responsibilities when activated in a real disaster, and it is very possible that more than one team will be active at the same time. Therefore, it is important that DR team members do not serve with either the IR team or the BC team, as their duties may overlap if an incident escalates into a disaster that requires the implementation of the BC plan. The primary DR team includes representatives from some or all of the following groups, depending on the organization and industry:

- Senior management
- Operations
- Corporate support units, including human resources, legal, and accounting
- Facilities
- Fire and safety
- Maintenance staff
- IT technical staff, including database, systems, and networking
- IT managers
- InfoSec technicians
- InfoSec managers

Depending on the size of the organization, there may be many subteams within the DR team that are responsible for separate sequences of activities. The subteams needed for IT disaster response are often much more specific. These specialties are explained in the following sections.

Disaster Management Team

This is the command-and-control group responsible for all planning and coordination activities. It consists of members of the primary DR team who will manage the planning and coordination, as opposed to those who provide skilled specialty services. During a disaster, this group coordinates all the efforts, receives reports from the other teams, and assigns work to them.

Communications Team

The communications team contains representatives from the public relations and legal departments, if the organization has such departments. It serves as the voice of management, providing feedback to anyone who wants additional information about the organization's efforts in recovering from the disaster. Members of this team interface with upper management, the disaster management team, law enforcement, the press, employees and their families, and the general public. All communications are directed from and to this team.

Computer Recovery (Hardware) Team

The hardware team works to recover any physical computing assets that might be usable after the disaster. In smaller organizations, this team may be combined with other IT-related teams. The findings of this team are incorporated into any insurance claims or post-disaster recovery purchases for restoration of operations.

Systems Recovery (OS) Team

The OS team works to recover operating systems and may contain one or more specialists on each operating system that the organization employs. This group works closely with the hardware and applications teams to reestablish systems functions during recovery. It also works to reestablish user accounts and remote connectivity in conjunction with the network team.

Network Recovery Team

The network team works to determine the extent of damage to network wiring and hardware (hubs, switches, and routers) as well as to Internet and intranet connectivity. It works to reestablish functions by repairing or replacing damaged or destroyed components. It also works closely with the Internet service provider (ISP) to reestablish connectivity.

Storage Recovery Team

Should the organization have storage area networks or network-attached storage, the storage recovery team works with the other teams to recover information and reestablish operations. In some cases, this group may have to wait until the hardware, systems, and applications teams have completed their operations before it can begin its efforts. It may also interface with the data management team to restore data from backups to their storage areas.

Applications Recovery Team

The applications team works to reestablish operations, just like the hardware and OS teams. After the other groups have systems backed up and running, the applications team recovers applications and reintegrates users back into the systems.

Data Management Team

Working with all the other teams, the data management team is primarily responsible for data restoration and recovery. Whether data is on-site, off-site, or online, this group is expected to quickly assess the recoverability of data from systems on-site and then make recommendations to the management team as to whether off-site data recovery is needed.

Vendor Contact Team

This team works with suppliers and vendors to replace damaged or destroyed materials, equipment, or services, as determined by the other teams. Based on recommendations by the management team, this group can work from preauthorized purchase orders to quickly order replacement equipment, applications, and services as the individual teams work to restore recoverable systems.

Damage Assessment and Salvage Team

This specialized team provides initial assessments of the extent of damage to materials, inventory, equipment, and systems on-site. It is responsible for physically recovering salvageable items to be transported to a location where the other teams can evaluate them. Items that are obviously beyond recovery are identified by the salvage team and reported to the management team. This team is also responsible for coordinating physical security with law enforcement and any private security service through the communications and vendor teams.

Business Interface Team

This team works with the remainder of the organization to assist in the recovery of non-technical functions. Careful coordination of effort is required to comply with the findings of the business impact analysis (BIA) in determining the priorities of the various business functional areas that need to be reestablished. As the liaison between business and IT, this team ensures that each team can work on its own recovery efforts without interfering with the others.

Logistics Team

This team consists of members responsible for providing any needed supplies, space, materials, food, services, or facilities at the primary site. Although the vendor contact team may order needed services and supplies, this team serves as the go-to group for physically acquiring and transporting the needed resources to the appropriate locations. This team also performs the minute tasks that make operations move smoothly.[2]

Other Teams as Needed

The other business functions may require specialized teams to assist in the recovery of their operations. Therefore, these teams would focus on the reestablishment of key business functions as determined by the BIA.

Special Documentation and Equipment

All members of the DR team should have multiple copies of the DR and BC plans in their homes, vehicles, and offices, as they cannot predict when they will receive an emergency call and be required to activate the plans. Organizations must have a plan to manage distribution of these documents as they are updated so out-of-date versions are replaced in all locations where they are staged.

It is also important for the responsible team members to have access to certain DR materials should the need arise. The equipment that team members need differs based on their roles and responsibilities. In general, the equipment may include the following:

- Data recovery software to recover information data from damaged systems
- Redundant hardware and components to rebuild damaged systems
- Copies of building blueprints to direct recovery efforts. On these blueprints, the following locations should be indicated:
  - Key server cabinets or closets
  - Data communications cabinets or closets
  - Power distribution and UPSs
  - Important document storage (paper copies)
  - Data backup storage
  - Keys and access cards to secure undamaged areas after the disaster has passed
  - Communications lines
  - Fire suppression systems and access points
  - Water lines
  - Gas lines
  - Flammables and combustibles
- Key phone numbers (or complete phone books or directories), including those for:
  - Fire, police, and rescue (other than 911)
  - Insurance contacts
  - Building inspectors

- Service providers, such as:
  - Water
  - Gas
  - Power
  - Data communications
  - Telecommunications
  - Sewer
  - Alert roster first contacts—These employees initiate contact with the rest of the employees to inform them of the disaster and advise them whether to report for work or not.
  - Fire and water damage specialists
- Emergency supplies:
  - Flashlight and extra batteries
  - Two-way radios used for emergency communications (not cellular phones)
  - Poncho
  - First-aid kit
  - Toilet paper
  - Snacks
  - Drinking water
  - Toolkits

Some of these items seem frivolous, but when these teams spend 12- to 24-hour shifts for days on end working at a disaster site, with inoperable facilities and services, these items may prove invaluable.

DISASTER RECOVERY PLANNING FUNCTIONS

DR planning is an important part of the CP process, as described in detail in earlier modules. All the various pieces of CP that an organization undertakes should be guided by the approach used in this book, which is drawn from the National Institute of Standards and Technology's (NIST's) Special Publication 800-34, Revision 1, "Contingency Planning Guide for Federal Information Systems."[3] This document includes elements designed to implement incident, disaster, and continuity recovery efforts as part of a comprehensive planning function. The specifics of developing plans and policies for each of these three components are similar; this module focuses on DR.

 Aspects of the NIST approach that apply to IR planning have been discussed in earlier modules, and topics that belong exclusively to business continuity are discussed in other modules.

Although policies may differ from company to company, the approach taken here is that the first step in the effort to craft any contingency plan is the development of enabling policies. The focus then shifts to developing the requisite plans. Both of these elements are part of the broader CP process.

Module 2 introduced the CP process recommended by NIST. The same steps are used within the narrower context of the DRP process. Here are the brief descriptions of the steps, followed by several sections that discuss the context of DRP:

1. *Develop the DR planning policy statement*—A formal department or agency policy provides the authority and guidance necessary to develop an effective contingency plan.
2. *Review the business impact analysis (BIA)*—The BIA was prepared to help identify and prioritize critical IT systems and components. A review of what was discovered is an important step in the process.
3. *Identify preventive controls*—Measures taken to reduce the effects of system disruptions can increase system availability and reduce contingency life-cycle costs.
4. *Create DR contingency strategies*—Thorough recovery strategies ensure that the system may be recovered quickly and effectively following a disruption.

5. *Develop the DR plan*—The DR plan should contain detailed guidance and procedures for restoring the organization and its system after a disaster.

6. *Ensure DR plan testing, training, and exercises*—Testing validates recovery capabilities, training prepares recovery personnel for plan activation, and exercises identify planning gaps; together, these activities improve plan effectiveness and overall organizational preparedness.

7. *Ensure DR plan maintenance*—The DR plan should be a living document that is updated regularly to remain current with system enhancements and organizational changes.[4]

Not every organization is fully prepared to sustain the effort and expense to keep plans updated and rehearsed. Smart organizations are aware of the value of keeping plans current and ensuring that their teams are trained and prepared.

Develop the DR Planning Policy Statement

The DR team, led by the business manager designated as the DR team leader, begins with the development of the DR policy. The policy provides an overview of an organization's philosophy on the conduct of DR operations and serves as the guide for developing the DR plan. The DR policy itself may have been created by the organization's CPMT and handed down to the DR team leader. Alternatively, the DR team may be assigned the role of developing the DR policy. In either case, the DR policy contains the following key elements, which are described in the subsequent sections:

- Purpose
- Scope
- Roles and responsibilities
- Resource requirements
- Training requirements
- Exercise and testing schedules
- Plan maintenance schedule
- Special considerations, such as information storage and maintenance

The preferred solution is for an organization-wide, business-focused DR policy to be established at the highest level of the organization and then passed down through its subordinate units, so that each unit may prepare its own complementary DR process and plan. The organization's DR group may require a universal planning approach, but this can only occur after the business DR policy is completed, thus creating the context to ensure that all planning processes can interoperate.

Purpose

The purpose of the DR policy is to provide for the direction and guidance of all DR operations. In addition, the policy provides for the development and support of the DR plan. As with any major enterprise-wide policy effort, it is important for the DR policy to begin with a clear statement of executive vision. The purpose statement includes a summary of what the policy addresses. Here is an example of the purpose section of a DR policy:

> *The purpose of this policy is to ensure that business and information resource investments made by the organization are protected against service interruptions, including large-scale disasters, by the development, implementation, and testing of disaster recovery (DR) plans.*
>
> *For purposes of this policy, disaster recovery planning includes, but is not limited to, the documentation, plans, policies, and procedures that are required to restore normal operation at the organization's primary or permanent alternate site when a division is impacted by man-made or natural outages or disasters.*
>
> *The policy assists the organization to:*
>
> - *Identify business resources that are at risk*
> - *Implement useful plans to protect against identified threats and mitigate risk*
> - *Implement tested emergency procedures when a service outage occurs*
> - *Implement and test procedures that enable reestablishment of services at the primary site or permanent alternate site following a disaster*
> - *Develop a plan that enables full recovery and the resumption of normal operations[5]*

Scope

This section of the policy identifies the organizational units and groups of employees to which the policy applies, as well as what specific issues, technologies, and activities the policy addresses. This clarification is important in case the organization is geographically dispersed or is creating different policies for different organizational units.

Here is an example of the scope section in a DR policy:

This policy applies to all corporate information technology, division information technology, each operational unit of the company designated as DR mission critical, and the individuals employed in those business units.

The policy applies to the preparation, implementation, and operation of disaster recovery activities by designated individuals within the organization.

Roles and Responsibilities

This section identifies the roles and responsibilities of the key players in the DR operation, ranging from executive management down to individual employees. You will notice in the following examples that some sections are duplicated from the organization's contingency planning policy. For smaller organizations, this redundancy can be eliminated, as many of the functions are performed by the same group. Here is an example of the Roles and Responsibilities section of a DR policy:

The chief operations officer, as the organization's contingency planning officer, appoints a disaster recovery planning officer from his or her office.

The chief financial officer appoints an individual to assist the disaster recovery planning officer in securing service agreements necessary to reestablish operations at the organization's primary place of business, or at a permanent alternate site, as dictated by the situation.

The appointed disaster recovery planning officer oversees all phases and functions of the disaster recovery planning process and reports divisional readiness directly to the contingency planning officer.

Each division must have a disaster recovery plan that identifies and mitigates risks to critical functions and sensitive information in the event of a disaster.

The plan shall provide for contingencies to restore operations and information if a disaster occurs. The disaster recovery plan for each division may be a subset of the organization's comprehensive disaster recovery plan. The concept of disaster recovery focuses on business resumption at the primary place of business.[6]

Each division shall:

- *Develop disaster recovery plans*
- *Maintain and update disaster recovery plans annually*
- *Test disaster recovery plans annually*
- *Train their employees to execute the recovery plans[7]*

Division heads are responsible for the oversight of their respective divisions' management and use of IT resources. An annual confirmation letter for the disaster recovery and business continuity plan must be submitted to the CIO by August 31 of each year. With this letter, the head of each division confirms to the executive management that a disaster recovery and business continuity plan has been reviewed, updated, and tested.

The auditor may audit division disaster recovery and business resumption plans and tests for compliance with policy and standards.

Resource Requirements

Should the organization desire, it can specify the resources needed for the development of its DR plans. These resource requirements may include directives for individuals, or individual requirements can be included in the preceding Roles and Responsibilities section with the other resources delineated in the following example for emphasis and clarity.

The chief financial officer provides the necessary contractual agreements and funds to ensure the availability of financial resources should they be required to rebuild the organization's primary business site or to select a suitable permanent alternative. The CFO also ensures suitable funds to support the development and annual testing of the DR plan.

Training Requirements

In this section of the policy, the training requirements for the various parts of the organization and the various types of employee categories are defined and highlighted. Here is an example:

> *Training for the DR plan consists of:*
>
> - *Making employees aware of the need for a disaster recovery plan*
> - *Informing all employees of the existence of the plan and providing procedures to follow in the event of an emergency*
> - *Training all personnel who have responsibilities identified in the plan to perform the disaster recovery procedures*
> - *Providing the opportunity for recovery teams to practice disaster recovery skills[8]*

Exercise and Testing Schedules

The section that stipulates the frequency of the exercises and tests for the DR plan can include both the type of exercise or testing and the individuals involved. Here is an example:

> *A quarterly walk-through of all DR plans is conducted with all key DR team representatives.*
> *Annually, the DR officer, in coordination with the CP officer, conducts an unannounced disaster recovery exercise. Each key individual is provided with a specific type of disaster scenario and asked to function as if the disaster were genuine. Results are discussed in an after-action review with the executive management team.*

Plan Maintenance Schedule

All good plans include a schedule and instructions for reviewing and updating the plan. This section should address the frequency of reviews and list the people who are involved in the review. It is not necessary for the entire DR team to be involved, and the review can be combined with a periodic test of the DR plan (usually performed as a desk-check, talk-through, or walk-through) as long as the resulting discussion includes areas for improvement for the plan. Here is an example of a section that describes the plan maintenance schedule:

> *The disaster recovery policy must be reviewed at least annually to ensure its relevance.*
> *Just as in the development of the policy, a planning team that consists of upper management and personnel from information security, information technology, human resources, or other operations should be assembled to review the disaster policy.[9]*

Special Considerations

One or more additional sections may be included. For example, a policy section might be included to direct organizational efforts on the topic of information storage and retrieval plans. This section may be referred to as "Data Storage and Recovery" or "Data Backup and Recovery," and would be the part of the policy where the general on-site and off-site backup schemes are highlighted. The use of off-site but online data storage may also be specified. Although the specifics do not have to be covered, the individuals responsible should be able to implement the strategy based on this guidance. Here is an example:

> *The CIO, in conjunction with the CISO, ensures that a generally accepted data storage and recovery scheme is implemented, with weekly off-site data storage using a secure transportation method.*
> *The CIO evaluates and implements appropriate off-site but online data storage to record transactional data, with a recovery time objective of no longer than four hours once hardware has been recovered.*

Review the Business Impact Analysis

Returning to the second of the seven steps in the DR-focused CP planning process, a DR-centric review of the BIA requires only a close examination of the BIA that was developed by the CPMT. This review ensures compatibility with DR-specific plans and operations. Because much of the work done by the CPMT included business managers as well as IT and InfoSec representatives, the BIA document is usually acceptable as it was prepared and released by the CPMT.

The business priorities identified in the BIA will serve to prioritize recovery efforts in the event of an actual disaster. If the organization's production or service activities were identified as the most important in the BIA, then recovery efforts will attempt to restore that function first. It then follows that the systems, data, and other resources necessary to perform that function will be the top priority of IT, InfoSec, and other recovery teams.

Identify Preventive Controls

The third of the seven steps is to identify preventive controls. It is performed as part of the ongoing information security posture. Effective preventive controls implemented to safeguard online and physical information storage also facilitate their recovery. At a minimum, the DR team should review and verify that the generally accepted data storage and recovery techniques discussed in previous modules are implemented, tested, and maintained. The team should also ensure that sufficient and secure off-site data storage is implemented, tested, and maintained, including any remote transactional or journaling functions. Because it is difficult to prevent the loss of physical assets during a disaster, it becomes critical to ensure that business continuity activities are in place to allow key business functions to continue until the primary site is recovered. Business continuity is discussed in Module 11.

Develop Recovery Strategies

The fourth step is to develop thorough recovery strategies to ensure that systems can be recovered quickly and effectively following a disruption. Although it may be virtually impossible to prepare for all contingencies, ranging from floods to fires to tornadoes or even man-made disasters, it is important to have recovery strategies in place for the disasters most likely to occur. Based on the BIA conducted early in the process, the *after the disaster* efforts must be thoroughly documented, developed, and tested.

It is important to understand, and to explain to management, that the DR strategies go substantially beyond the *recovery* portion of *data backup and recovery* and must include the elements necessary to fully restore the organization to its operational status. This includes personnel, equipment, applications, data, communications, and support services such as power and water. Only through close coordination with these services can the organization quickly reestablish operations back at its principal location, which is the primary objective of the DR plan.

One key aspect of the DR strategy is the enlistment and retention of qualified general contractors capable of quickly assessing any physical damage the organization may have experienced and pulling in the necessary subcontractors to rebuild the facility if it is damaged. It is useful to include this general contractor in DR training and rehearsals, allowing the contractor to determine what resources are needed to rebuild part or all of the organizational structure. If the facilities the organization occupies are leased, the leasing agency may also need to play a role in acting as intermediary between the DR team and any contractors needed.

Develop the DR Plan Document

The next step is to develop the DR planning document so that it contains the specific and detailed guidance and procedures for restoring lost or damaged functionality. The procedures previously developed and tested are formally written out. The responsibility for creating the DR plan itself, unlike for the IR plan, does not usually fall to the CISO. As a general business activity, the disaster team leader may be from upper management, such as the chief operations officer, or one of his or her senior managers.

When the BIA was initially integrated in the overall contingency plan and then used to plan for incident responses, the IRP team developed incident-handling procedures for every attack scenario, based on the BIA. The DR team (or management team, as described previously) takes the same information, plus the information from the IRP team, and begins developing its own procedures for the DR plan. The DR team documents details that help identify when an escalation of incidents will be designated as a disaster and then does a comprehensive review to discover any events that are not documented by the IRP team but might be declared a disaster. This list of disaster initiation points is then reviewed so that very similar entries can be removed or combined.

This list then becomes a set of disaster scenarios. The **disaster scenario** summarizes the disasters that may befall an organization and their potential effects. The DR team will then develop three sets of activities for each disaster scenario. Recall that

disaster scenario

A description of the disasters that may befall an organization, along with information on their probability of occurrence, a brief description of the organization's actions to prepare for that disaster, and the best case, worst case, and most likely case outcomes of the disaster.

the activities are presented in sections in the sequence in which they are most frequently used. Because the activities used *during* a disaster are most urgently needed in the event of plan activation, they are placed in the binder first. The activities that are part of the *follow-up* plan, to be used after the disaster has been resolved, are placed second, and the *planned* activities that should be integrated into every daily procedure and activity, and which are only occasionally referenced for change management purposes, are placed third. These three sets of activities will be briefly explained and then discussed in additional detail in the sections that follow.

1. *During the disaster*—The planners develop and document the procedures that must be performed during the disaster. These procedures are grouped and assigned to individuals. Systems administrators' tasks differ from managerial tasks, so members of the planning committee must draft a set of function-specific procedures. All plans need to be readily available to those who will use them. Obviously, some disasters start so quickly and have such a devastating effect on local infrastructure that response may be completely dependent on staff who are at work when the disaster strikes. For these types of disasters, the safety of staff may preclude any intentions to preserve business operations. The effort shifts to crisis management and evacuation plans and other emergency reactions. Of course, these plans must also be organized and placed into documents that are easy to access, easy to read, and can be referred to during the disaster.

2. *After the disaster*—Once procedures are drafted for handling or reacting to a disaster, the planners develop and document the procedures that must be performed immediately after the disaster has ceased. Again, separate functional areas may develop different procedures. If the damage from the disaster is substantial enough, business continuity and crisis management procedures may be needed, as described in other modules.

3. *Before the disaster*—The planners draft a third set of procedures to list the tasks that must be performed to prepare for the disaster. These procedures include data backup information, DR preparation, training schedules, testing plans, copies of service agreements, and business continuity plans, if any.

Similar to the incident plan addendum created in the IRP process, the DR team should create as many **DR plan addendums** as needed. As shown in Figure 10-1, addendums are created for each disaster scenario by taking the information for the anticipated disaster (whether an escalated incident or original disaster scenario) and adding more items. This additional information includes the trigger, the notification method, and the response time. The notification method describes the manner in

DR plan addendum

A supplemental document to the DR plan that provides information on a disaster scenario, including the trigger, notification method, and desired response times.

DR Plan Addendum to Disaster Scenario	
Disaster type:	
Trigger:	
Team lead:	
Notification method:	
Response time:	
Actions during disaster:	
1.	
2.	
N.	
Actions during disaster are complete when:	
Actions after disaster:	
1.	
2.	
N.	
Actions after disaster are complete when:	
Actions before disaster:	
1.	
2.	
N.	
Actions before disaster are complete when:	

Figure 10-1   Format of a DR plan addendum

trigger

In CP, the point at which a management decision to act is made in reaction to data or a notification of an incident or disaster.

which the team is notified that a disaster has occurred and the way the plan is to be executed. As discussed earlier in this textbook, this notification could be by phone, text, e-mail, loudspeaker, or word of mouth.

The response time represents the amount of time in which the team should respond; it typically ranges from *immediately* to 48 hours, depending on the disaster. Some natural disasters, such as fires, lightning, earthquakes, or tornadoes, may strike with little or no warning and require an immediate response, while the response to floods, hurricanes, and other disasters may be deferred for 24 to 48 hours, depending on their impact.

Planning for Actions Taken during the Disaster

DR, like IR, usually begins with a trigger. In DR, the trigger is the point at which management responds to a notification of an impending or ongoing disaster, such as a weather report or an activity report from IT indicating the escalation of an incident. In DR, most triggers occur in response to a natural event. Some of these events have a long build-up, such as a tropical depression growing to a tropical storm and finally a hurricane. The hurricane may take days to reach full strength and then make landfall. Some inland cities may have sufficient time to prepare for the actual disaster, whereas others may have very little time, as it is often difficult to accurately predict a storm's impact. The best way to plan for actions during the disaster is to develop disaster end cases, which are reaction scenarios that direct employees to safety, and then develop training programs for the "before the disaster" phase.

The next planning component is the determination of what must be done to react to the scenario. The dominant reaction may be to warn employees not to come to work or to direct them to a shelter, which requires identifying a safe location as part of the planning process. For IT-based disasters, especially those that have escalated from incident to disaster, the IR team works closely with the DR team leader to determine what is required from both groups. In the event of a widespread, disastrous technology attack, the IR group works primarily on restoring internal systems, whereas the DR group activates the groups responsible for data, applications, systems, networking, and communications to assist in handling the event and providing information to other organizational units and external parties. Once all signs of the disaster have ceased, the "actions during" phase is complete.

Planning for Actions Taken after the Disaster

After the disaster has passed and its effects no longer directly impact the organization, the "actions after" phase begins. During this phase, for natural disasters, facilities and physical assets are assessed for damage or destruction and the process of planning to replace any affected equipment and technology is initiated. Also, a determination is made whether to activate the business continuity plan, depending on the extent to which the organization can continue operations at the primary site immediately, or whether reconstruction is needed.

For IT-based disasters, lost or damaged data is restored, systems are scrubbed of infection, and all systems and data are restored to their previous state. The DR plan must describe the actions needed to recover from the most likely aftereffects of the disaster. It should also detail other elements necessary to the "actions after" phase, such as possible follow-on disasters, forensic analysis, and the after-action review (AAR).

Like incidents, follow-on disasters are highly probable when infected technologies are brought back online or when other infected computers that may have been offline at the time of the attack are brought back up. Follow-on disasters are also likely in the event of a large-scale hacker attack; for example, attackers might retreat to a chat room and describe in specific detail to their associates the method and results of their latest conquest. Therefore, identifying potential follow-on attacks should be a top priority. By identifying and resolving the avenues of attacks based on the forensic analyses, the organization can prevent these disasters from reoccurring.

Forensic analysis is the process of systematically examining information assets for evidentiary material that can provide insight into how an incident transpired. Information on which machine was infected first or how a particular attacker gained access to the network can indicate unknown vulnerabilities or exploits. Care must be taken to use an individual trained in forensic analysis, given that the information found during the analysis may be potential evidence in civil or criminal proceedings. Forensic analysis is covered in additional detail in other modules.

Before returning to routine duties, the DR team must also conduct an AAR. All key players review their notes and verify that the DR documentation is accurate and precise. All team members review their actions during the incident and identify areas where the DR plan worked, didn't work, or should improve. This allows the team to update the DR plan. The AAR can serve as a training case for future staff, and it brings to a close the actions of the DR team.

Planning for Actions Taken before the Disaster

Planning for "before the disaster" consists of all the actions found in common business and information security practices. However, specific disasters may have specific preparation requirements that go beyond the normal actions. "Before actions" for IT-based disasters include preventive measures to manage the risks associated with an attack and the actions taken to enhance the preparedness of the DR team. For natural disasters, the need to carefully plan the location of physical facilities used for operations will influence the organization's susceptibility to a particular type of disaster. For example, placing the data center on the top floor would be best for flooding, but not as good for fires, earthquakes, and other events that affect the structure. Effective planning for disasters may also involve the acquisition of insurance and the selection and implementation of redundancies for power, Internet services, and other utilities. Because each disaster scenario identifies the specific actions needed to best prepare for it, predicting what is required is a challenge. However, DR planning usually includes actions in the areas of staffing, training, equipping, stocking of critical consumables, and executing service and support contracts to enable rapid responses.

One important note for both DR and IR planning: When selecting an off-site storage location for data backups or equipment, extra care should be taken to minimize the risk at that storage location. In many instances, a large-scale disaster may destroy or damage both the primary location and the off-site storage location, if the latter is not carefully selected. The use of cloud-based data backups can minimize the potential impact of a disaster on the organization's off-site data storage.

Plan Testing, Training, and Exercises

By training management and staff in the proper performance of their roles described in the DR plan, the organization can test the validity and effectiveness of the DR plan as well as prepare the various teams to use it. Any problems identified during training can be incorporated into the draft document. After the drafts have been reviewed and tested, the final assembly can begin. As with the IR plan, testing the DR plan is an ongoing activity, with each scenario tested at least semiannually, at least at a walk-through level.

A recent survey from Spiceworks, an IT industry network, indicates that at least "23 percent of companies never test their disaster recovery plan."[10] Why? "Some 61 percent said they simply didn't have enough time. Inadequate resources were cited by 53 percent, and 34 percent said that DR just wasn't a priority."[11] What was the result of not testing their plans? "Within the last 12 months, 30 percent of the 762 IT professionals surveyed said they had lost revenue due to a business or service outage, the release said. In that same time frame, 77 percent said they had experienced at least one outage, while 59 percent experienced 1 to 3 outages."[12] AT&T reports that 65 percent of businesses say they fail their own DR tests.[13]

After all the components of the DR plan have been drafted and tested, the final DR plan can be created, similar in format and appearance to the IR plan. This format is described in greater detail in other modules.

Plan Maintenance

The plan should be a dynamic document that is updated regularly to remain current with system enhancements. The organization should revisit the DR plan at least annually in order to update its procedures, contracts, and agreements, and to make the necessary personnel and equipment modifications dictated by the business operations. Unfortunately, according to AT&T, only 30 percent of businesses plan to update their DR plan in the next year, even though 75 percent believe their DR plans are inadequate.[14]

If the organization changes its size, location, or business focus, the DR management team and the other management teams should begin anew with the CP plan, and it should also reexamine the BIA. The maintenance process used for DR plans is discussed in greater detail in other modules.

IMPLEMENTING THE DR PLAN

Part of the challenge with disaster planning is that disasters are not confined to the IT department, nor are they limited to the information assets of an organization. Frequently, a disaster is widespread enough to affect multiple departments and levels of authority in the organization, as well as the community that comprises the organization, including the organization's customers and suppliers. It is inconvenient when an organization loses its electrical power, but it can be even worse when an entire neighborhood or city goes dark. It is important to realize that in the midst of reestablishing operations, there may be ongoing challenges associated with local emergency services and service providers as well as community issues. In many disasters, outside help may be unavailable for days or even weeks. During that time, the following may be affected:

- Emergency services, such as fire calls and ambulance requests, may be delayed under triage requirements so that only the most critical calls are answered.
- Public services and routine local government services, such as trash pickup or debris clearing, may be significantly delayed.
- Groceries and other goods may become unavailable as local demand for staples and basic emergency supplies, such as bottled water, batteries, or plywood, exceeds the local supply. Local shortages of these products are quite common.
- Utility services, including electricity, gas, water, and sanitation, may be disrupted if local power supplies are unavailable or become damaged.
- Private services, such as taxi service and other vendor services, may be delayed because of a variety of factors, including traffic disruptions and high demand.
- Telecommunications services (both landline and cellular) may experience spikes in demand or damage, making communications difficult, delayed, or impossible.
- Air and surface transportation is often affected, with canceled flights and many roads quickly becoming gridlocked.[15]

A seemingly routine event can quickly spin out of control, creating a *worst-case scenario*. This situation could result in service disruptions for weeks or months, requiring a government to declare a state of emergency. In dire circumstances, local or national governments could declare martial law to prevent or combat social disorder. Even if people are not confined to their homes, only some of an organization's employees may be available for work. This was true worldwide during the 2020 COVID-19 pandemic and the "shelter-in-place" orders given in most U.S. states.

Organizations must communicate to their employees what is expected of them during a disaster. The reality is that most disaster-related loss occurs because of the inability to react properly to the disaster. If the organization is to survive, it may have to improvise, adapt, and overcome obstacles, including reassigning employees and other resources as needed to meet the most critical needs. In many scenarios, as few as one-third of the staff may be available in the early stages of the recovery period.[16] As additional resources are reclaimed or become available, the balancing act will continue, allowing more functions to be restored and more operations to resume.

Fortunately, most disasters are short-lived, lasting only hours or a few days. For example, even the worst winter storms tend to clear up within a week. Whether employees are at work or home, a DR plan should be prepared to deal with various contingencies over various durations. Depending on the scope of the disaster, implementing the DR plan typically involves the following phases, which may or may not overlap with the BC plan:

- *Preparation*—The planning and rehearsal necessary to ready the organization to deal with a disaster
- *Response*—The identification of a disaster, notification of appropriate individuals, and immediate reaction to the disaster
- *Recovery*—The recovery or salvage of necessary equipment, technology, and data from the affected site
- *Restoration*—The reconstruction of facilities and reinstallation of technologies and equipment at the primary site, or selection and preparation of a new permanent site
- *Resumption*—The reestablishment of normal operations at the primary site or new permanent site as they were before the disaster

Preparation: Training the DR Team and the Users

Aside from the planning requirements discussed earlier, there is a great deal of work to be done in preparing for disasters. Note that in DR planning, unlike in IR planning, there is no prevention phase because the vast majority of disasters cannot be prevented. However, some organizations can minimize the probability of being hit with certain disasters by preparing for them. Here are some examples of geographically based disasters that organizations should prepare for:

- In California, organizations should prepare for earthquakes. Depending on the location, the organization may also need to prepare for mudslides and wildfires.
- In "Tornado Alley," which includes parts of Texas, Louisiana, Oklahoma, Kansas, South Dakota, Iowa, and Nebraska, organizations should prepare for tornadoes and high winds.

- On the Gulf Coast and along the southeastern seaboard, organizations should prepare for hurricanes and the accompanying floods.
- In Alaska, Hawaii, and Washington, organizations should prepare for volcanoes.
- In the northern United States and along the Canadian border, organizations should prepare for large snow-storms and the accompanying loss of infrastructure.
- Almost all organizations should prepare for electronic disasters, such as massive denial-of-service attacks and concentrated hacking attempts.

Preparation means making an organization ready for possible contingencies that can escalate to become disasters. Module 2 described the development of the BIA, which is one of the first preparation steps. Earlier, this module described the organizing and staffing of the various teams necessary to assist in DR, and the development of the DR plan, which focuses DR efforts if a disaster strikes.

Plan Distribution

Once the plan has been fully developed, it's critical to get copies into the hands of people who need the plan the most. How the plan is distributed is not as important as making sure that all personnel have access to the plan, have fully read it, and understood it. The same techniques used to ensure compliance with policy can be used to track dissemination and comprehension of the DR plan.

During an organization's day-to-day operations, it would be easy to misplace a physical copy of the IR, DR, or BC plan; however, electronic disruptions could also prevent access to online storage locations. In order to cover all bases, password-protected copies of critical contingency plans should be stored wherever employees may need access to them. This means the plans must be stored in the following three locations at a minimum:

- *At the office*—Physical copies in the employees' offices, electronic copies on all organizational computer systems. Traveling employees would be covered if they are using laptops or tablets owned by the organization.
- *Away from the office*—Physical copies in employees' homes, electronic copies available on home systems.
- *Online (anytime, anywhere)*—Electronic copies stored on services leased by the organization.

By password-protecting all electronic files and requiring employees to store physical copies in secure locations, the organization can ensure that no matter where the employees are, they can locate copies of the plan and react accordingly when notified of a disaster, without worrying that sensitive details will fall into the hands of people who would abuse this information.

Plan Triggers and Notification

The preparation phase is a continuous one; however, other phases are activated by triggers that can originate from a number of sources, including the following:

- *Management notification*—If management has been keeping track of an imminent disaster, it may choose to implement the DR plan before the disaster actually occurs in order to move its employees out of harm's way or to areas of increased safety and security. This is common when natural disasters such as hurricanes, tornadoes, and wildfires threaten large areas.
- *Employee notification*—As described in the module's opening scenario, an employee may simply happen upon the disaster, or the disaster may occur in the area where an employee is currently working. If a fire breaks out during the workday or an employee arrives at work and finds evidence of a disaster, employee notification will likely be the source.
- *Emergency management notification*—FEMA or a state equivalent, the Centers for Disease Control and Prevention (CDC), or other state or federal agencies may notify individual organizations or entire areas of an imminent or ongoing disaster.
- *Local emergency services*—Local fire departments, police departments, or medical personnel may provide information that allows the organization to react to imminent or ongoing disasters. With the ongoing emphasis on emergency preparedness from the Department of Homeland Security, even local communities are beginning to establish disaster management programs.
- *Media outlets*—Depending on the circumstances and the organization's policy on press and public relations, official statements should be carefully coordinated for release to local media so that employees know where to look for such notices. Many organizations will specify one or a few media outlets for news items such as weather-related closures.

Disaster Recovery Planning as Preparation

Developing an effective DR plan is the cornerstone of preparation. The primary goals of the DR plan are to do the following:

1. Eliminate or reduce the potential for injuries, loss of human life, damage to facilities, and loss of assets and records. A comprehensive assessment of each department is required to ensure that the following steps are taken:

   - Minimize disruptions of services to the institution and its customers.
   - Minimize financial loss.
   - Provide for a timely resumption of operations in case of a disaster.
   - Reduce or limit exposure to potential liability claims filed against the institution and its directors, officers, and other personnel.

2. Immediately invoke the emergency provisions of the DR plan to stabilize the effects of the disaster, allowing for appropriate assessment and the beginning of recovery efforts. Staff and other resources then minimize the effects of the disaster and provide for the fastest possible recovery.

3. Implement the procedures contained in the DR plan according to the type and impact of the disaster. When implementing these procedures, recovery efforts must be emphasized as follows:

   - *Employees*—An organization must ensure the survival of its employees not just as a basic human concern but because they will help other people who are on the premises when the disaster strikes.
   - *Customers*—As with employees, customers affected by the disaster must be cared for physically, mentally, emotionally, and financially.
   - *Facilities*—After the safety of employees and customers has been ensured, each facility should be secured both as a shelter for people and as an asset.
   - *Assets*—Conducting a damage assessment determines which assets have been destroyed, which ones are at risk, and what resources are left.
   - *Records*—Documenting the disaster and the actions taken by the organization's personnel, when combined with comprehensive videotapes obtained during routine facility inspections, reduces the likelihood of legal actions while helping to assess the responsibility for losses.

To plan for disaster, the CP team engages in scenario development and impact analysis, which categorizes the level of threat that each potential disaster poses. When generating a DR scenario, an organization starts with the most important asset: people. Are the human resources with the appropriate knowledge available to restore business operations? The process of cross-training employees ensures that operations and a sense of normality can be restored as quickly as possible. In addition, the DR plan must be tested regularly so that the DR team can lead the recovery effort quickly and efficiently.

Key Features of the DR Plan   The key points that the CP team must build into the DR plan include the following:

- Clear delegation of roles and responsibilities
- Execution of the alert roster and notification of key personnel
- Use of employee check-in systems
- Clear establishment and communication of business resumption priorities
- Complete and timely documentation of the disaster
- Preparations for alternative implementations

Everyone assigned to the DR team should be aware of their duties during a disaster. Some may be responsible for coordinating with local services, such as fire, police, and medical care. Some may be responsible for the evacuation of personnel, if required. Some may be responsible for shutting down non-essential systems and equipment. Others may be tasked to simply pack up and leave. Key personnel may include external groups such as fire, police, or medical services as well as insurance agencies, disaster teams like the Red Cross, and other specialized management teams within the organization. Organizations should make provisions for manual or automated procedures to verify the status of employees, contractors, and consultants who are affected by a disaster.

During a disaster response, the first priority is always the preservation of human life. Data and systems protection is subordinate when the disaster threatens the lives, health, and welfare of employees and members of the community.

Only after employees and neighbors have been safeguarded can the DR team attend to protecting organizational assets. As with IR, the disaster must be carefully recorded from the onset. The documentation is used later to determine how and why the disaster occurred.

Mitigation of impact is the inclusion of action steps to minimize the disaster's damage on the operations of the organization. The DR plan should specify the responsibilities of each DR team member, such as the evacuation of physical assets or making sure all systems are securely shut down to prevent further loss of data.

Plans should include alternative implementations for various systems components if primary versions become unavailable. This includes standby equipment, whether it is purchased, leased, or under contract with a DR service agency. Developing systems with excess capacity, fault tolerance, auto-recovery, and fail-safe features facilitates a quick recovery. Something as simple as using Dynamic Host Configuration Protocol (DHCP) to assign network addresses instead of using static addresses allows systems to quickly and easily regain connectivity without technical support. Networks should support dynamic reconfiguration; restoration of network connectivity should be planned. Organizations should implement secure VPNs to allow employees to work from home or while travelling should on-site operations be unavailable. Data recovery requires effective backup strategies and flexible hardware configurations. System management should be a top priority. All solutions should be tightly integrated and developed in a strategic plan to provide continuity. Piecemeal construction can result in another disaster after the first one as incompatible systems are thrust together.

Additional Preparations As part of DR readiness, all employees should have two types of emergency information in their possession at all times. The first is personal emergency information—who to notify in case of an emergency, medical conditions, and a form of photo identification. The second is a set of instructions on what to do in the event of an emergency. This snapshot of the DR plan should contain a contact number or hotline for calling the organization during an emergency, emergency numbers for fire, police, and medical services, evacuation and assembly locations (storm shelters, for example), the name and number of the DR coordinator, and any other needed information. This information is often encapsulated into a wallet-sized, laminated card for convenience and portability, as shown in Figure 10-2.

The DR plan must also include references to another process that many organizations plan for separately: crisis management. **Crisis management** during disaster recovery is a set of focused steps that deal primarily with the safety and state of the people from the organization who are involved in the disaster. The DR team works closely with the crisis management team to ensure complete and timely communication during a disaster. Crisis management is covered in additional detail in Module 12.

DR Training and Awareness

Training all the people who have an interest in the disaster planning process involves a number of different approaches, as discussed in the following sections. Training focuses on the particular roles each individual is expected to execute during an actual disaster. For most employees, disaster preparation is limited to awareness training, which is conducted as part of an annual or semiannual security education,

crisis management (CM)
An organization's set of planning and preparation efforts for dealing with potential human injury, emotional trauma, loss of life, or damage to an organization's reputation or image as a result of a disaster.

Front

ABC Company Emergency ID Card

Name:________ DOB:________
Address:________
City:________ St:____ Zip:________
Blood Type:________
Allergies:________
Organ Donor?:________
Emergency Contacts:________
>
>

Call 800-555-1212 for updates and to report status

Back

ABC Company DR Plan Codes

CODE	ACTION
1a	Shelter in Place – do not report to work
1b	Shelter in Place – DR team to work
2a	Evacuate immediately – do not report to work
2b	Evacuate immediately – DR team to work
3	Lockdown – Secure all doors/windows – do not report to work if off-site

Call 800-555-1212 for updates and to report status

Figure 10-2 Emergency ID card with DR plan information

training, and awareness (SETA) program for all employees. During this session, employees are made aware of general procedures for responding to disasters, including the use of the alert roster.

General Training for All Teams   For most teams, the best preparation for a disaster is to be well trained and comfortable in completing their normal tasks. It is also important to note that these individuals may be a bit rusty when it comes to certain tasks and technical skills. Some managers may not have installed or configured a server or networking device in some time and may require assistance. Therefore, the training and rehearsals should identify individuals with less than ideal technical skills and allow them to brush up on their responsibilities. Note that not all systems may be recovered during the disaster; the priorities are established during the BIA.

In addition to being well prepared for normal tasks, a business activity that can assist DR efforts is job (or task) rotation. By routinely training all employees to do at least one other job, the organization prepares itself to handle normal personnel shortages or outages, such as those caused by maternity and paternity leave, sick days, injuries, vacations, conferences, and training programs. Job rotation can be vertical, meaning that employees learn their boss's job, or horizontal, which means they learn a colleague's job. If all positions have at least two employees prepared to perform them, responding to a disaster is that much easier. Task rotation is similar, but focuses on individual tasks rather than the entirety of a position's responsibilities.

Most organizations don't tend to train employees to operate under adverse conditions, also known as degraded mode. Military personnel spend far more hours working in less than ideal circumstances than under optimal conditions. When training, an organization should periodically try working in degraded mode—without power and communications—to see how employees can adapt to adverse conditions. During a disaster, it is very likely that some utilities will be unavailable. Each specialized team needs to train in tasks unique to its responsibilities, and it needs to cross-train in other tasks, as discussed in the following sections.

Disaster Management Team Training   This is the command and control group responsible for all planning and coordination activities. Training, rehearsal, and testing for the management team is predominantly communicative in nature. This team must be able to quickly and effectively communicate the need for resources required by their subordinate teams. It must also be able to communicate directives from the higher teams (the CP management team) and peer teams (the IR and BC planning teams).

Communications Team Training   This group is responsible for interacting and communicating with external stakeholders and constituents. The communications team trains by preparing information notices, news releases, internal memorandums, and directives sent to all groups and teams, letting them know what their tasks and responsibilities are. Because the members of this group may also be responsible for the alert system, they should be involved in the routine rehearsal and testing of that system to better prepare them to handle information requests from employees during actual disasters.

Computer Recovery (Hardware) Team Training   Ideally, the hardware recovery and reconstitution team practices and trains during normal operations. However, if a computer sustains even minor damage during normal business operations, the organization may simply opt to replace it rather than rebuild it. This team requires advanced training to rebuild systems by scavenging parts from a number of damaged systems and getting as many back up and running as quickly as possible. Training should also include how to deal with systems damaged by water, heat, and dust. This team should work closely with the other technology teams (OS, applications, network, and data) in their preparation. If systems are not too badly damaged, a local repair capability, such as the one shown in Figure 10-3, may come into play.

Systems Recovery Team Training   This is the team responsible for recovering and reestablishing operating systems (OSs). As with the hardware team, the OS team may rehearse its DR duties during normal operations. Its DR training most likely consists of being able to quickly recover a system's OS in preparation to reinstall applications and data. The responsibilities of this team may be combined with those of the other IT teams. However, if the organization stores its OSs, applications, and data separately, each team requires at least one individual who can acquire the archived copy and reestablish each information asset to a usable state.

degraded mode

The conduct of operations under adverse conditions.

Network Recovery Team Training   This is the team responsible for reestablishing connectivity between systems and to the Internet, if applicable. Network recovery teams physically repair damaged systems. Therefore, much of their DR training should focus on establishing ad hoc networks quickly but securely. The most convenient networking tools available today are wireless networks—encrypted, of course.

Figure 10-3   Computer repair bench

Although some organizations have already converted to a completely wireless infrastructure for client systems, others have not; network recovery teams at such organizations need training on quickly converting recovered systems to wireless operations, installing and configuring wireless access points, and securely distributing connection information to all users who need to connect. The leader of the network recovery team should have a "stash" of wireless networking components stored outside the organization so they can be quickly relocated to assist in recovering internal connectivity. Internet connectivity may be much more difficult, and interaction with the vendor through the vendor team or the communications team may be necessary. With the increased popularity of wireless Internet connectivity, the organization may want to contract for any services that are available in the area as part of a contingency plan that can be scaled up when needed. The team requires training in the use and implementation of this technology as well.

It may also fall to this team to establish voice communication networks during a disaster. Should some or all employees be issued mobile phones, a directory of the numbers can be used if the need arises. In the event that local circuits are affected, short-range handheld FM radios (walkie-talkies) or even satellite phones should be stored for distribution when needed. The team also needs to provide training to others on the use and implementation of networking technology.

Storage Recovery Team Training   This team is responsible for the recovery of information and the reestablishment of operations in storage area networks or network-attached storage. Like the hardware team, this team may need training in rebuilding damaged systems. For example, Figure 10-4 shows a fixed-media drive damaged by a head crash, as indicated by the scarred disk surfaces. This team's function may be subsumed by the hardware team's responsibilities or those of the networking team. Along with the data management team, this team needs training in recovering data from off-site locations.

Figure 10-4   Damaged hard drive

Applications Recovery Team Training   This is the team responsible for recovering and reestablishing the operations of critical business applications. Like the others, the team's performance during normal operations requires coordination and training so they can perform under adverse circumstances. This team will almost certainly have user representation, and the effectiveness of the team is heavily influenced by its ability to create an effective liaison with the business units that use the applications.

Data Management Team Training   This is the team primarily responsible for data restoration and recovery. Its training correspondingly focuses on quick and accurate restoration of data from backup. The training should also include the recovery of data from damaged systems. Recovering transactional information recorded on local systems since the last routing backup may be necessary, and therefore it is useful to know how to extract information from systems that have sustained some damage. There are vendors capable of extracting data from all but the most catastrophically damaged systems, but these services are expensive. Even durable optical-media formats are not invulnerable. Figure 10-5 shows a CD damaged by excessive heat, as indicated by the cracking of the silver data layer.

Vendor Contact Team Training   This team is responsible for working with suppliers and vendors to replace damaged or destroyed equipment or services, as determined by the other teams. Training is best obtained through normal work in equipment procurement, whether as an IT employee or a professional purchasing agent. This team should contain representatives from both groups if possible. Training should focus on methods of obtaining resources as quickly as possible, as well as familiarity with preferred vendors for each piece of equipment and type of service. Should any of these be unavailable, team members should be trained in obtaining comparable products from other vendors. Vendor relationships are crucial during a disaster. A poor relationship or a questionable supplier may result in hardships such as expensive or unavailable replacements.

Damage Assessment and Salvage Team Training   This team is responsible for providing initial assessments of the extent of damage to equipment and systems on-site and for physically recovering equipment that gets transported to a location where other teams can evaluate it. The basic background needed is in hardware repair. Individuals who have repaired computers for the general public—for example, the technical support staff in a large retail chain—have likely seen many of the problems that are encountered in DR activities, such as water and physical damage. The average organization may not have damage assessment and salvage expertise on staff and thus might have to outsource to get it. Programs are available to describe how to conduct salvage and assessment of technology systems.

Figure 10-5   Damaged optical media

Business Interface Team Training This team is responsible for working with the remainder of the organization to assist in the recovery of non-technical functions. This team's training could also combine technical and non-technical functions to ensure that the technology needs of the business groups are met. Training involves interfacing with the various business groups to determine their routine needs. Representatives from the help desk may be well suited for this team.

Logistics Team Training This team is responsible for providing any needed supplies, space, materials, food, services, or facilities at the primary site, other than vendor-acquired technology and other material obtained by the vendor team. Individuals may need only basic training in local purchasing to serve on this team, as their primary function is to serve as health, welfare, and morale support for the other teams as they do their jobs. Simply being ready to prepare and provide meals, a rest area, and someone to talk to may be the best qualifications.

DR Plan Testing and Rehearsal

In practice, the testing of DR plan elements can overlap with the training and rehearsal of the plan. In the strictest sense, an organization rehearses when it simply practices the steps to be performed during a disaster—like a fire drill. Testing, on the other hand, involves assessment, whether internal or external. Internal testing can include employees conducting self-assessments after an exercise by completing feedback surveys, indicating what they thought worked well and what didn't. Other methods include peer evaluations and formally appointing internal assessors who serve as performance evaluators, drafting formal reports for their department or division manager. External testing can come from standardization boards or consultants (for example, ISO 9000), certification or accreditation groups, or a group selected by the organization's management from a sister company.

Ideally, employees should receive formal, structured training before being expected to perform in a large-scale exercise. Jumping straight into large-scale rehearsals or testing can cause more problems than it solves. Although it is beneficial for employees to see what a large-scale disaster reaction looks like (based on the axiom that "sweating in training can prevent bleeding in combat"), it will only be confusing rather than educational if the employees are not prepared for it. Rehearsing the plan should start small and escalate to larger-scale exercises. Many organizations never test and rehearse beyond the desk check or structured walk-through; although some rehearsal is better than none, organizations that can progress further along the scale of rehearsal and testing will be better off when an actual disaster occurs.

Because DR uses the same basic types of rehearsal and testing as those for IR, the following information may appear similar to that in prior sections of this book. An organization can interchangeably use the following strategies in both DR and IR:

- *Desk check*—Copies of the DR plan are provided to all teams and team members for review. Although the desk check is not a true test, it is a good way to review the perceived feasibility and effectiveness of the plan.
- *Structured walk-through*—All involved individuals walk through the steps they would take during an actual disaster, either on-site or as a conference-room discussion.
- *Simulation*—Each involved individual or team works independently rather than in conference, simulating the performance of each task but stopping short of the actual physical tasks required, such as restoring the backup or rebuilding a particular server or communications device.
- *Full-interruption*—Involved individuals follow each and every procedure, including interruption of service, restoration of data from backups, and notification of appropriate individuals. It is not uncommon for state and local agencies to request the assistance of nearby organizations in preparing local first responders and government agency staff for disasters, such as chemical contamination, biological warfare, or nuclear emergencies. Even so, the probability that an organization is mature enough in its rehearsal and testing methods to attempt full-interruption exercises is quite slim.
- *War gaming*—Unlike the IT community's fascination with IR war gaming, which was discussed in Module 4, there are few venues for DR war gaming. Therefore, there is little work in this arena. Some state and federal agencies do host inter- and intra-agency exercises that allow representatives and liaison officers to work together on state and national emergencies. However, there is little effort or interest on the part of organizations in this area. An exception is larger corporations that are part of the national infrastructure—power, gas, communications, and other vital service providers. Their war gaming falls under the realm of state and federally mandated emergency readiness to prepare for terrorist strikes, rather than a corporate effort to maintain business functions for continuity of the organization.

Rehearsal and Testing of the Alert Roster

One last area of rehearsal and testing is the use of an alert roster. It is also used during IR planning, BC planning, and crisis management. Contact information for the individuals to be notified during an actual incident or disaster is included in an alert roster. The alert roster must be tested more frequently than other components of the plans because it is subject to continual change from employee turnover. In the military, as well as in many corporate settings, alert rosters are tested at least quarterly.

One of the two activation methods discussed elsewhere in this textbook, *sequential* and *hierarchical*, is selected based on the organization's preferences and structure. For smaller, more informal organizations, the sequential roster may be preferred; this method requires that a contact person call every person on the roster. For larger, more formal organizations, the hierarchical roster may be more appropriate. It requires that the first person call other designated people on the roster, who in turn call other designated people, and so on. For example, the CEO may call the members of the executive team, who call their senior managers, who contact their individual employees or subordinate managers. This would make the alert process closely follow the organization chart. In either activation method, it is important to ensure that the alert message is properly formed and distributed. In this context, the **alert message** is a scripted description of the disaster that consists of just enough information so that each responder knows what portion of the DR plan to implement without impeding the notification process. Unlike the IR plan's alert roster, the DR plan's alert roster must have a mechanism to contact everyone in the organization, especially if part of the message is "don't report to work today, but call this number for more information."

Some organizations can make use of an **emergency notification system**, which is sometimes called an **auxiliary phone alert and reporting system**. This is an information system with a telephony interface that can be used to automate the alert process. Such a system can use predefined notification strategies updated with specific details at the time of use to perform rapid and effective notification. This type of system can be used both to distribute information about the disaster and to collect information about the status of employees. It can also greatly streamline the process and complete it in much less time than a manual alert system.

A related usage of telecommunications technology is the "I'm okay" automated emergency response service. This service allows employees to call a predetermined number when notified of a disaster, either by the alert system or through the public media, and obtain additional information or just let the organization know their status. Some organizations have their employees put this information on a card in their wallet or purse. Employees report their status by entering their employee numbers into an automated system, then obtain information about whether they should attempt to show up for work and where. This system is also extremely useful when critical individuals must be informed that they are needed at an alternate location but are not currently home and thus are out of reach through normal alert procedures.

Systems and processes to verify the status of employees have practical value. Not only do they demonstrate the organization's concern for the well-being of its employees, contractors, and vendors, they allow the organization to begin responding to potential gaps in available skill sets as response and recovery plans are activated.

Once all employees have been trained, rehearsed, and tested on their DR responsibilities, they should be ready to implement the plan during an actual disaster. Be cognizant of the fact that no matter how prepared you think you are for a particular disaster, you really aren't. The key skills to retain from the rehearsals are flexibility, decisive decision making, and professionalism.

alert message

A scripted description of the disaster that avoids impeding the notification process by consisting of just enough information so that each responder knows what portion of the DR plan to implement.

emergency notification system

An information system with telephony, messaging, and e-mail integration that can be used to automate the alert notification process.

auxiliary phone alert and reporting system

See *emergency notification system*.

disaster response phase

The phase of the disaster response process associated with implementing the initial reaction to a disaster; it is focused on controlling or stabilizing the situation to the greatest degree possible.

Disaster Response Phase

After a source has indicated the presence or threat of a disaster, the organization initiates the DR plan and begins the next phase, the response phase. The **disaster response phase** is designed to do the following:

- Protect human life and physical safety.
- Attempt to limit and contain damage to the organization's facilities and equipment.
- Manage communications with employees and other stakeholders.

The response phase involves activating the DR plan and following the steps outlined therein. Organizations without such a plan will find themselves attempting to perform these steps ad hoc in the midst of the disaster. The diversity of possible disasters and the plans for reacting to them can result in disparate responses, so preparation for one type of disaster, such as a fire, might not be sufficient in reaction to other disasters, such as hurricanes or tornadoes.

Disaster Recovery Phase

The third phase of disaster recovery, or the second phase of the implemented disaster plan, is the recovery phase. During the **disaster recovery phase**, the organization works to salvage what it can from the affected site. In the event the organization doesn't suffer a total loss, it may be able to recover hardware, office equipment, furniture, and supplies from the disaster site. The teams described previously work to identify what can be salvaged and then document what replacement components will be needed to restore operations in later phases.

In the disaster recovery phase, the organization begins with rebuilding the most critical business operations; the less critical operations may have to wait until later. In most cases, the production or service functions that generate revenue for the organization are most crucial. The primary goals of the recovery phase include the following:

- Salvage any feasible equipment, technology, and data.
- Recover critical business functions.
- Coordinate recovery efforts.
- Begin acquiring resources to replace damaged or destroyed materials and equipment.
- Evaluate the need to implement the BC plan.

Restoration Phase

In the fourth phase of disaster recovery, the **disaster restoration phase** finds the organization conducting the tasks necessary to rebuild its primary facilities and preparing to reestablish operations there. Should the disaster cause more damage at any of the primary sites than the organization can repair, then this phase involves the selection of a new permanent home. Organizations must also consider that this phase may represent the end of a business too damaged by the disaster to recover. Organizations don't like to think about it, but it is a possibility.

The restoration phase formally begins after all assessments of the damage have been accomplished and the decision has been made either to rebuild the primary site or select a new permanent location. As stated earlier, the change from the previous phases to this phase may be subtle and the phases may overlap.

The primary goals for the restoration phase are:

- Repair all damage to the primary site *or* select or build a replacement facility.
- Replace the damaged or destroyed contents of the primary site, including supplies, equipment, technology, and material.
- Restore all technology with appropriate operating systems, applications, and data.

Repair or Replacement

There are two possibilities in the restoration phase: Reestablish operations at the primary site or establish operations at a new permanent site. The respective actions taken are obviously very different.

Reestablish Operations at the Primary Site   The organization might be able to rebuild damaged facilities at the primary site. Given the probability that a disaster will not completely destroy a facility, the organization may be able to continue at least partial operations at the primary site while repairs are being made. Administrative offices are the easiest to relocate, considering the complexities of data centers, manufacturing facilities, and customer service offices.

Depending on the level of damage from the disaster, it may be in the organization's best interest to activate the BC plan and move operations off-site to allow construction teams to have access to the facility. That way, the noise and space demands of the reconstruction efforts will not affect operations.

disaster recovery phase

The phase of the disaster response plan associated with the salvage of equipment and data from the affected sites.

disaster restoration phase

The phase of the disaster response plan associated with the restoration of business facilities, beginning with those most critical to the organization's operations.

Move to a New Permanent Site   If the disaster is so severe that the primary site becomes uninhabitable, the organization is faced with two choices: Bulldoze and rebuild or select a new location. If the organization owns the land, then the first option may be the better one. The downside is that it may be months before the organization can return to its original location. The business continuity solution may not be feasible for such a long-term stay, and an intermediate location may be required. In this case, the organization may have to lease temporary facilities until the new building is constructed.

Alternatively, the organization may choose to select a new location. This may be necessary when the organization cannot relocate for an extended stay at temporary locations while the primary site is reconstructed, or when the organization does not own the primary structure. After Hurricane Katrina, for example, some organizations first moved temporarily, then had to permanently move their operations. Also, the facility owner may not choose to rebuild in a timely manner, leaving the organization stuck in temporary facilities. It may be easier to find a new suitable location. The downside is that if the organization has customers that visit the primary site, they will require redirection, by mail or other means of communication. The selection of a new permanent site is a complex decision and requires a management team to identify candidate sites, coordinate on-site visits, and review the facilities before selecting a suitable replacement. Because of the scope of a disaster, permanent and temporary staff may not be available because they have had to relocate their families.

Restoration of the Primary Site

After the physical facilities are rebuilt or new space is leased, the contents must be installed. Office furniture, desktop computers, photocopying equipment, filing systems, office supplies, and a host of other materials must be acquired, delivered, and set up. Most employees don't realize exactly how much "stuff" they need to run their operations.

Office supplies aside, the organization may need substantial reinvestment in office equipment. Care should be taken to determine what insurance will cover and to examine service contracts to determine if damage or destruction to leased equipment is covered by the provider.

At the end of this phase, an organization has a building ready for occupancy, with the needed technology, equipment, supplies, and data ready to go to resume operations.

Disaster Resumption Phase

Whereas the restoration phase focuses on rebuilding business facilities, the disaster resumption phase focuses on reestablishing business functions—returning to work. The BIA should be the guiding document in creating the prioritized list of primary and secondary functions the organization can use when setting back up at their recovered facilities. This list may differ dramatically from one organization to another. The goals of the resumption phase are:

- Coordinate the relocation from temporary offices to the primary site or a suitable new replacement facility.
- Restore normal operations at the primary site, beginning with critical functions and continuing with secondary operations.
- Stand down the DR teams and conduct the after-action review.

Some of these goals are implemented according to the BC plan, and may be delayed until a specific point in that plan. The interaction that must exist between the DR plan and BC plan is complex and difficult to execute. There is often confusion and even conflicting opinions about when to engage the various parts of the plan. In these circumstances, strong executive leadership is required to keep the organization focused on the best mixture of continuing operations and progress toward restoration at the primary site.

The restoration phase formally begins after all assessments of the damage have been made and the rebuilding of the primary site has concluded, or when a new permanent site has been selected and equipped. After the decision has been made to return to work at the permanent location, the movement of personnel, technology, and data must be carefully coordinated.

disaster resumption phase

The phase of the disaster response plan associated with the return to normal business operations, beginning with those most critical to the organization.

Relocation from Temporary Offices

As indicated earlier, the organization may have relocated to an alternate site or to temporary facilities at the primary site. The movement back to the primary site signals the end of disaster operations for most members of the organization. Getting employees settled back into their offices and normal routines must be carefully coordinated. If the organization has been operating out of temporary facilities for an extended period of time, this may not be a simple transition. Even during short-term functions, an administrative office generates an inordinate amount of paperwork that inevitably gets scrambled during relocation. If data functions were relocated, the restoration of computing equipment is even more difficult, as damage to systems and components can occur in transit.

Data management practices are even more crucial before and after moves. In some cases, it may be advantageous to have a movement coordinator who plans the relocation of personnel, equipment, materials, and data from the alternate location back to the primary location.

Resumption at the Primary Site

As indicated earlier, the organization may not be able to reestablish critical functions on-site, hence the need for a BC plan. If an organization has tried and failed to reestablish functions at the primary site and has relocated critical functions to another location, the next challenging step is to reestablish normal operations at the primary site. There may have been a number of tertiary operations and functions that were suspended while the organization worked to keep afloat at the temporary location. Routine, day-to-day operations help to stabilize the organization and keep it running efficiently. These functions can include the following:

- Management of employee benefit packages
- Employee training and awareness programs
- Organizational planning retreats and meetings
- Routine progress meetings and reports
- Long-term planning activities
- Research and development activities

These activities are important, but in the overall scope of a disaster, they can wait until normal operations have been reestablished.

At this point, the business has been reconstituted and is functioning as it did before the disaster. The only task remaining is to review what happened during the disaster and determine how the organization handled it.

Standing Down and the After-Action Review

Standing down involves the deactivation of the DR teams and releasing individuals back to their normal duties. In an ideal situation, these individuals will have focused exclusively on their DR roles until they are released. The reality, however, is that these employees have probably worked double duty, handling their DR jobs while keeping an eye on their normal duties to make sure nothing suffered from their absence.

Perhaps the last formal activity the organization performs before declaring the disaster officially over is the after-action review (AAR). As described in previous modules, the AAR provides a way for management to obtain input and feedback from representatives of each team. Team leaders first obtain feedback from their team members about the specifics of the disaster and the suitability of the DR plan. This information is then combined with the official disaster log, which has been maintained by a designated representative and used to update the DR plan and procedures. The official log serves as both a legal and planning record of the event and as a training tool for future team members. One of the ongoing challenges of organizational training is turnover. Eventually, employees get promoted, are relocated, move to different organizations, or are released outright. The team that gains valuable experience during one disaster will not be the same team that faces the next. Thus, it is important to capture as much organizational knowledge as possible about the disaster to help train the next generation.

The last step is the creation and archiving of the official report. Outcomes from the AAR are combined with the reports of the individual teams and archived for future use in training. The official report may also be a legal requirement if the insurance company, the legal department, or the parent organization requires a record of what happened to ensure there was no negligence. If an individual was injured or killed during the disaster or events that followed, the legal proceedings that inevitably ensue require as much documentation as possible to determine if liability exists.

When the official report has been archived, the members of the various teams can go back to their normal jobs and, except for periodic training, put the disaster behind them.

BUILDING THE DR PLAN

The planning process for the DR plan should be tied to that for the IR plan, but distinct from it. As discussed earlier in this module, an incident may escalate into a disaster when it grows dramatically in scope and intensity. It is important that the IR, DR, and BC functions be so tightly integrated that the reaction teams can easily transition from IR to DR and BC planning.

The form the actual DR plan takes will vary dramatically for each organization. In general, the typical DR plan will include the following sections, based on the BIA:

- Sets of procedures to be performed during, after, and before each disaster, organized by type of disaster. Just as the incident response plan was organized with a focus on actions during, after, and before the incident, the DR plan is focused on personnel safety first, then recovery efforts. During a disaster, there will be little for the organization's personnel to do except seek shelter, avoid the area of the disaster, and notify emergency services as needed.
- Names, positions, roles, and responsibilities of individuals assigned to help with disaster recovery
- Contact lists for management so employees can make contact, let managers know they're OK, and request additional instructions after the disaster
- Contact information for all needed emergency services, including fire, police, and medical services as well as electrical, gas, and water suppliers for shut-offs as needed
- Locations of in-house emergency supplies, which help provide some degree of response in the event a disaster starts as an incident (like a fire); first-aid materials and other resources can sustain personnel until emergency services arrive
- Locations of emergency shelters both inside and outside the organization's facilities
- Salvage priority lists for use after the disaster has passed, should there be physical loss of organization assets

Even though the DR plan may be unique for each organization, it's often useful to locate and adapt an exemplar from a public resource. One useful resource is NIST Special Publication 800-34, Revision 1 (see *https://csrc.nist.gov/publications/detail/sp/800-34/rev-1/final*), which includes contingency planning templates. Other government and business sites provide similarly structured plans that are suitable to adapt to an organization's needs. For example, *Ready.gov*, which is part of the U.S. Department of Homeland Security, provides guidance on writing an IT disaster recovery plan based on the recommendations of NIST (see *https://www.ready.gov/business/implementation/IT*). Note that *Ready.gov* uses the term *business continuity plan* to describe what this text refers to as a business resumption plan—the combination of DR and BC, as described below.

Regardless of the terminology used, these resources will assist the organization in developing the plan. When the plan is completed, it needs to be stored and kept available in as many locations and formats as possible, given the need for access by key staff while maintaining control of the content. The plan can contain a wealth of sensitive data that would be a significant loss to the organization if it fell into the wrong hands. Planners need to make arrangements for the ways that planning documents are copied and stored to accommodate the availability requirement while making sure the necessary confidentiality is maintained. Other useful information can be found at the Disaster Recovery Journal's download site (*https://drj.com/resources/sample-plans/*) and at other sites that are easy to find with a Web search.

Although templates can be useful in preparing plans, an organization must also collect the basic information needed to address complex DR planning problems. The following areas represent information that must be collected and organized before beginning formal development of the DR plan itself:

- The goals of the DR plan
- A roster of personnel associated with DR plan development and implementation, including their roles and responsibilities
- An inventory of all critical information assets
- Detailed documentation of the organization's data backup and recovery processes and procedures, including data backup storage locations
- Documentation of the selected BC contingency strategies to support DR

The Business Resumption Plan

Because the DR plan and the BC plan are closely related, many organizations prepare the two at the same time and may combine them into a single planning document, as described earlier in Module 3. Such a comprehensive plan—often referred to as a *business resumption plan (BR plan)* or simply a contingency plan—must support the immediate reestablishment of operations at an alternate site and eventual reestablishment of operations back at the primary site. Therefore, although a single planning team can develop a BR plan, execution of the plan requires separate teams.

INFORMATION TECHNOLOGY CONTINGENCY PLANNING CONSIDERATIONS

This section, adapted from NIST SP 800-34, Rev. 1, discusses the contingency planning needs of IT systems in organizations. The document is targeted at U.S. federal agencies, but the content is applicable to organizations of all types and sizes. The focus is on business resumption planning for organizations, which integrates the contingency planning elements of DR and BC.[17] Note that a typical organization's DR plan will address the entire organization and its information, not just the IT systems. However, the information presented here should be included to ensure continuity of operations of IT systems and the information they support, and then supplemented with additional business-specific DR information.

Deciding which technical contingency strategies are selected, developed, and implemented is most often based on the type of information system being used. Because each organization is unique and makes use of many types of systems, SP 800-34, Rev. 1 describes actions for a wide variety of systems to provide guidance that will be useful to many readers of the report. Rather than attempt to enumerate all the possible systems, this section discusses the types of systems that are commonly found in production or development settings:

- *Client/server systems*—Systems designed to work in a client/server environment may have storage and processing of data at any level: client, intermediate server, or database server. Historically, the client level includes desktop, laptop, or netbook systems; today, it may also include tablets as well as specialty devices, such as barcode readers and smartphones. These clients are supported by application and authentication servers that provide business processing and security services. Database servers are often isolated to optimize data throughput performance. The network is used to provide connectivity to the various parts of the system.
- *Telecommunications systems*—There are two classes of telecommunications systems: local area networks (LANs) and wide area networks (WANs). A LAN is used for an office or small campus, with segment distances measured in tens of meters. A WAN is a collection of nodes in which the segments are geographically dispersed. The physical link is often a data communications channel provided by a public carrier or a virtual private network (VPN) tunnel carried by an ISP. These backbone connections enable one LAN to interact with another, forming the WAN.
- *Mainframe systems*—Mainframe architectures remain in use in many organizations. Whereas client/server systems leverage data communications to decentralize or distribute capacity, mainframe systems rely on centralization of key capabilities. Mainframes seldom rely on hardware-based terminals, instead using client hosts to emulate terminal functionality. The mainframe is a large, multiuser system designed to provide both computational capacity and high-volume data storage support for large organizations.
- *Cloud-based systems*—Many organizations have cloud-based platforms or are planning to move IT service delivery to them. While many cloud service providers have robust and complete disaster planning built into their offerings, it is important that individual subscribing organizations validate the disaster resiliency promised by the vendor. While the use of a cloud service provider may lessen the complexity and depth of the planning and preparations needed, verifying that services will be available and accessible is still an essential aspect of an organization's resilient plan to ensure ongoing operations.

Each of these system types can be approached from two perspectives: the technical requirements that must be met to recover the needed functionality and the technology-based solutions that will meet those technical requirements.

There is quite a bit of commonality in what can be done to prepare to recover from disasters. In many cases, the cause of a disruption to services at the primary site of operations is not relevant to how the service will be restored. When the common elements of the most likely disaster scenarios are considered, they form a foundation of capabilities that address technical contingencies for most contingency plans and for most types of systems. This foundation of capability, if incorporated into the everyday IT processes, is likely to address most disaster responses for most core business systems:

- Make the information collected and assembled during the BIA process a current and vital part of IT operations.
- Make certain that general data security, data integrity, and data backup policies, procedures, and practices are integral to all IT operations at all locations all the time.
- Verify that physical protective measures for hardware, supporting infrastructure, and other system resources are current and that staff do not fall out of practice with essential procedures.
- The engineering specifications used to configure primary and alternate sites with appropriate power management systems and environmental controls must always be current and valid.
- Everyday operations should use high-availability systems and processes to ensure a resilient business process by striving for architectures and implementations that can sustain a measured uptime of 99.999 percent or better.

Systems Contingency Strategies

The focus of any system contingency strategies must be on the availability, confidentiality, and integrity of the data being processed. The primary recovery control is regular and frequent backup of the data using a validated process, which is rehearsed periodically with a complete cycle of backup and recovery. In general, strategies must include the following:

- Backup data stored in the cloud, off-site, or at an alternate site
- Use of standardized hardware, software, and peripherals to enable backup and recovery to and from replacement systems
- Documentation of all supported system configurations, with local copies of key vendor information
- Coordination with security policies and system security controls used in the organization
- Reliance on the systems' priority and key data needs, as documented in the BIA
- Processes that aggressively limit the placement of data on client systems, with any local data kept for the minimum possible time
- When local storage of data cannot be eliminated, sound procedures established to back up and periodically test restoration of local data and standardization of local data storage locations
- To the greatest degree possible, automation of backup processes and proactive validation of the automated backup by repeatable processes
- Coordination of all contingency solutions with cyber IR plans and team operations

The sensitive nature of network connectivity to systems means that CP must provide replacement network functionality that is robust and able to be restored with minimal efforts. A complete replacement network solution will require the following:

- Standardization of the required hardware, software, and peripherals so recovery using replacement devices is straightforward
- Documentation of all systems configurations to include details unique to specific vendor implementations
- Coordination across an organization's security policies and security controls
- Coordination of all contingency solutions with organizational IR plans and team operations
- Sequencing of replacement networking capabilities to make sure that access is restored to systems in the order needed based on the BIA requirements

Systems Contingency Solutions

Many solutions are available to meet the technical needs of contingency planning. Encryption tools are widely used to ensure the confidentiality and integrity of communication between clients and servers and for backup media. These tools may include digital signatures to gain nonrepudiation and assurance of integrity, as well as certificate-based encryption and decryption to ensure the confidentiality of backup media if they are lost or stolen. Recovery will rely on complete planning, training, and rehearsals. The procedures used by replacement systems must enable users to read in the backup media and recover the data. The similarities and differences in CP for each of these systems is summarized in Table 10-2.

Table 10-2   Summary of Contingency Considerations

	Client/Server System	Telecommunications System	Mainframe System
Contingency Consideration			
Document system, configurations, and vendor information.	X	X	X
Encourage individuals to back up data.	X		
Coordinate contingency solution with security policy.	X	X	X
Coordinate contingency solution with system security controls.	X	X	X
Consider hot site and reciprocal agreements.	X		X
Coordinate with vendors.		X	X
Institute vendor service-level agreements.	X	X	X
Provide guidance on saving data on personal computers.	X		
Standardize hardware, software, and peripherals.	X		
Store backup media off-site.	X	X	X
Store software off-site.	X	X	X
Contingency Solution			
Back up system, applications, and/or data.	X	X	X
Ensure interoperability among components.	X		
Identify single points of failure.		X	
Image disks.	X		
Implement fault tolerance in critical components.			X
Implement load balancing.	X		X
Implement redundancy in critical components.	X	X	X
Implement storage solutions.			X
Integrate remote access and wireless technologies.	X	X	
Replicate data.	X		X
Use uninterruptible power supplies.	X		X

Closing Scenario

Susan pulled out her laptop and inserted the USB stick with all of HAL's IR, DR, and BC plans. She quickly pulled up her master planning document, selected the continuity plan, clicked option A, and began to read. She then pondered her next action.

Discussion Questions

1. What do you think Susan's next action should be if her plan is like the recommendations in this module?
2. What are the priorities for Susan in the next 30 minutes?

Ethical Decision Making

1. Part of Susan's responsibilities is to notify a number of company leaders. One of them, shown near the end of the priority list, is a good friend who may have been in the office at the time of the fire. Susan chooses to call her friend first to make sure she's OK before starting at the top of the priority list. "It'll only take a minute," she thinks. How could this choice go wrong?
2. Suppose that one of HAL's contractors was issued a copy of the company alert roster. Suppose further that the contractor has family members who sell recovery services, and the contractor passed them a copy of the roster with all personal contacts and critical skills listed. Is this an ethical action by the contractor? Why or why not?
3. Suppose Susan had a friend with a small business that offered some services similar to those provided by HAL Inc. During a discussion of DRP and HAL's plan, Susan's friend asked to see how a "big" company would plan for disasters. Susan decided to provide her friend with a copy of the DR plan. Was this an appropriate action? Why or why not?

MODULE SUMMARY

- DR planning is the preparation for and recovery from a disaster. The DR team, working with the CPMT, develops the DR plan. The key role of a DR plan is defining how to reestablish operations at the organization's usual location.
- A DR plan can classify disasters as either natural disasters or man-made, such as acts of terrorism or war. The DR plan can also classify disasters by their speed of development: rapid-onset or slow-onset disasters.
- The CPMT assembles the DR team, which is tasked with the reestablishment of business operations at the primary site; this team is responsible for the planning for DR and leadership after a disaster is declared.
- The DR team consists of representatives from every major organizational unit, plus specialized members selected for their unique capabilities or perspectives. Members of the DR team do not serve with either the IR team or the BC team because the duties of these teams may overlap if an incident escalates into a disaster, requiring implementation of the BC plan. The organization of the DR team should be distinct from that of the BC team, as each team has different responsibilities when activated in a real disaster. The DR team may have many subteams.
- All members of the DR team should have multiple copies of the DR and BC plans in their homes, vehicles, and offices, as they cannot predict when they will receive a call and be required to activate the plans. It is also important for the responsible team members to have access to certain DR materials should the need arise.
- The first step in the effort to craft any contingency plan is the development of enabling policy or policies. The focus then shifts to developing the requisite plans.
- The NIST planning process adapted for DR planning is as follows: develop the DRP policy statement; conduct or review the BIA; identify preventive controls; develop recovery strategies; develop a contingency plan; ensure plan testing, training, and exercises as well as maintenance of the plan.

- The DR team, led by the business manager designated as the DR team leader, begins with the development of the DR policy. The policy provides an overview of the organization's philosophy on the conduct of DR operations and serves as the guide for developing the DR plan.
- Effective preventive controls implemented to safeguard online and physical information storage also facilitate their recovery.
- Thorough recovery strategies ensure that the system may be recovered quickly and effectively following a disruption.
- The DR plan should contain detailed guidance and procedures for restoring lost or damaged information. It is prepared in three sections with guidance for actions during the disaster, after the disaster, and before the disaster.
- Training in the DR plan can be used to test its validity and effectiveness as well as to prepare the various teams to use it.
- Testing the DR plan is an ongoing activity, with each scenario tested at least semiannually, at least at a walk-through level.
- An organization should operate on the premise that it is only a matter of time until a disaster strikes. Only through meticulous preparation and ongoing diligence can an organization properly respond when a disaster occurs. The worst-case scenario occurs when service is disrupted for weeks or months.
- Implementing the DR plan typically involves five phases: preparation, which is the planning and rehearsal necessary to respond to a disaster; response, which is the identification of a disaster, notification of appropriate individuals, and immediate response to the disaster; recovery of necessary business information and systems; restoration, the reconstruction of facilities and reinstallation of technologies and equipment at the primary site, or selection and preparation of a new permanent site; and resumption, the reestablishment of normal operations at the primary site or new permanent site as they were before the disaster.
- The goals of DR and business resumption planning are to eliminate or reduce the potential for injuries, loss of human life, damage to facilities, and loss of assets and records; stabilize the effects of the disaster; and implement the procedures contained in the DR and business resumption plans, according to the type and impact of the disaster, to resume operations.
- During the recovery phase, the organization begins the recovery of the most critical business functions as quickly as possible. Resumption focuses on the remaining unrestored functions.
- The goals of the restoration phase are to repair all damage to the primary site or arrange for a replacement facility, and to replace the damaged or destroyed contents of the primary site.

Review Questions

1. Why might some organizations abdicate all responsibility for DR planning to the IT department?
2. How can you classify disasters based on how they may emerge and become an issue for an organization?
3. What entity is responsible for creating the DR team? What roles should the DR team perform?
4. Discuss the limitations on the number and type of CP teams to which any one individual should be assigned.
5. What key elements should be included in the DR policy?
6. Why are the DR activity groups presented out of sequence (during, after, before) instead of in chronological order?
7. What are the major activities planned to occur during the disaster?
8. What are the major activities planned to occur after the disaster?
9. What are the major activities planned to occur before the disaster?
10. What is a DR plan addendum, and why will one or more of them be prepared?
11. What is a DR after-action review (AAR), and what are the primary outcomes from it?
12. Why should DR planning documents be classified as confidential and have their distribution tightly controlled?
13. What is a worst-case scenario? What role does it play in an organization's planning process?
14. What are the primary goals of the DR plan?
15. What are the key features of the DR plan?
16. Describe the phases in a DR plan.

17. What is job rotation? Why is it a useful practice from a DR plan perspective?
18. What does it mean when operations are in degraded mode? Should organizations prepare to operate in this mode?
19. What should be the primary focus of the training that is provided to the network recovery team?
20. What are the primary duties of the business interface team?
21. Describe the various rehearsal and testing strategies that an organization can employ.

22. Why must the alert roster and the notification procedures that use it be tested more frequently than other components of the DR plan?
23. What are the primary objectives of the response phase of the DR plan?
24. What are the primary objectives of the recovery phase of the DR plan?
25. What are the primary objectives of the restoration phase of the DR plan?

Real-World Exercises

Exercise 10-1

Imagine that a fire or other disaster has befallen your home, damaging your belongings and some of the interior walls. What would your priorities be in assessing the damage and working to reoccupy your home? Create a prioritized list and timetable to accomplish this task.

Exercise 10-2

This module listed several natural disasters that routinely occur in various parts of the United States. Using a Web browser or library research tool, identify the disasters that occur regularly in your area. Prioritize this list based on probability of occurrence and potential damage. What should organizations in your area do to prepare for these disasters?

Exercise 10-3

Do a Web search for organizations in your area that offer DR training. What topics do they cover in their training? Create a list of the topics covered by each organization and look for common topics covered across the offerings.

Exercise 10-4

Using a Web browser or local directory, search for organizations that provide DR services. Make a list, then scratch out the organizations that only provide data backup services or alternate-site services (BC services). How many are left? Why is this list so much shorter than the first? What services do the remaining organizations offer?

Exercise 10-5

Do a Web search to access the online version of Disaster Recovery Journal (*www.drj.com*). Review the articles in the latest issue; this may require some form of user registration. Identify articles that might help the individuals described in the opening scenario. Bring the articles to class to discuss.

Exercise 10-6

Do a Web search for "disaster recovery plan." Identify three or four examples of what appear to be comprehensive plans. What do these have in common? Create an outline for a DR plan using these examples. Bring them to class to discuss.

Hands-On Projects

The hands-on project for this module can be accessed in the Practice It folder in MindTap or through your instructor's LMS. The virtual labs provided with this resource can help you develop practical skills that will be of value as you progress through the course.

References

1. phoenixNAP. "2020 Disaster Recovery Statistics That Will Shock Business Owners." Accessed 04/28/2020 at *https://phoenixnap.com/blog/disaster-recovery-statistics*.
2. Marcus, Evan, and Hal Stern. "Beyond Storage: 12 Types of Critical Disaster Recovery Teams." SearchStorage. December 30, 2003. Accessed 04/30/2020 at *https://searchdisasterrecovery.techtarget.com/tip/Beyond-storage-12-types-of-critical-disaster-recovery-teams*.
3. Swanson, Marianne, Pauline Bowen, Amy Wohl Phillips, Dean Gallup, and David Lynes. SP 800-34, Revision 1, "Contingency Planning Guide for Federal Information Systems." National Institute of Standards and Technology. November 2010. Accessed 04/30/2020 at *https://csrc.nist.gov/publications/detail/sp/800-34/rev-1/final*.
4. Ibid.
5. "IT Disaster Recovery Planning." Accessed 04/30/2020 at *https://ocio.wa.gov/policy/information-technology-disaster-recovery-planning*.
6. Nebraska IT Commission Standards and Guidelines. "Security Architecture Complete Set of Policies." Accessed 04/30/2020 at *https://nitc.nebraska.gov/technical_panel/meetings/documents/20020108/security_completesetofpolicies.pdf*.
7. "IT Disaster Recovery Planning." Accessed 04/30/2020 at *https://ocio.wa.gov/policy/information-technology-disaster-recovery-planning*.
8. Nebraska IT Commission Standards and Guidelines. "Security Architecture Complete Set of Policies." Accessed 04/30/2020 at *https://nitc.nebraska.gov/technical_panel/meetings/documents/20020108/security_completesetofpolicies.pdf*.
9. "Disaster Recovery Policy Template." Accessed 04/30/2020 at *http://templatezone.com/pdfs/DisasterRecoveryPolicy.pdf*.
10. Forest, C. "Why 23% of companies never test their disaster recovery plan, despite major risks." Accessed 04/30/2019 at *www.techrepublic.com/article/why-23-of-companies-never-test-their-disaster-recovery-plan-despite-major-risks/*.
11. Ibid.
12. Ibid.
13. AT&T. "Disaster Recovery & The Cloud." Accessed 04/30/2020 at *www.business.att.com/content/dam/attbusiness/infographics/att-disaster-recovery-and-the-cloud-infographic.pdf*.
14. Ibid.
15. Turner, Dana. "Disaster Recovery & Business Resumption Planning." BankersOnline.com. Accessed 05/05/2020 at *www.bankersonline.com/tools/42715*.
16. Ibid.
17. Swanson, Marianne, Pauline Bowen, Amy Wohl Phillips, Dean Gallup, and David Lynes. SP 800-34, Revision 1, "Contingency Planning Guide for Federal Information Systems." National Institute of Standards and Technology. November 2010. Accessed 04/30/2020 at *https://csrc.nist.gov/publications/detail/sp/800-34/rev-1/final*.

BUSINESS CONTINUITY

Upon completion of this material, you should be able to:

1. List the elements of business continuity (BC) planning
2. Identify the type and composition of the BC planning and response teams
3. Describe the development and content of the BC policy and plan
4. Explain the strategies for creating effective BC plans
5. Recognize the methods used to maintain and continuously improve the BC process

> *Human history becomes more and more a race between education and catastrophe.*
>
> —H. G. Wells

Opening Scenario

"This floor can be set up with about 15 office cubicles, one manager's office, a conference room, and a break room area," Amy Novak said as she guided the HAL team through the building that the company might someday occupy. "That brings the total to 32 available office cubicles, five conference room areas, and three break room areas. If you add one or two open floors, you can have data centers or even small-scale production facilities. The building has power, heating, and air conditioning at all times—even when you don't need it. Telephone lines and a high-speed Internet connection can be activated within six hours."

HAL's business continuity planning committee had been tasked with finding suitable yet affordable accommodations for contingencies in which the company would have to relocate any or all of its operations.

A member of the group asked, "Is it easily reconfigurable?"

"Yes!" Amy said. "Completely. I know it doesn't look like much, but these renovated textile plants make perfect temporary sites; the wide-open floors, coupled with the movable cubicle walls, can be reconfigured within an hour or so to match the customer's needs."

Amy represented Contingencies, Inc. (CI), a business that specialized in renovating older industrial buildings and turning them into suitable business continuity alternate sites. Amy and the group from HAL were standing in an old textile mill that had shut down in the 1960s and had been scheduled for conversion into loft apartments. When the real estate market bottomed out in the 1990s, CI had bought the building along with several truckloads of surplus office equipment. Right now, the purchase looked more like a disaster than a business continuity site.

"I know what you're thinking," Amy said, smiling, "but our crews, given almost any organization's floor plan, can re-create the location and layout of your offices and work areas." With a sly grin, she waved them toward another open bay, where the movable cubicles were already set up. "Look around," she said.

The group was walking through the area when one member exclaimed, "That's my name." Each cubicle had the name of a HAL employee, taken from the reservation form that Juan Vasquez had submitted before setting up the on-site tour. The group quickly realized that the room had been laid out exactly like the third floor of HAL's administrative offices. The interesting part was that all of the power, data, and telephone cabling was dangling from the room's 20-foot-high ceiling among the exposed rafters.

"The secret is in the floor plan," Amy continued. "We laid out a scaled replica of your floor plan on the bay floor with tape. We then dropped the cabling in using a lift, and then we moved in the walls and desks. Our crew did this in about two hours. Obviously, you wouldn't be the only ones reserving space in the building, but this grand old millhouse can hold about four companies of your size. If it fills up, we have another building we've converted about 10 miles away. If for some reason this building isn't available, we will provide you with space in the other facility at a 10 percent discount to compensate you for the drive. If you sign with us, whatever the disaster, you give us a call and you can occupy the next business day."

INTRODUCTION

Business continuity planning (BCP) represents the final response of the organization when faced with any interruption of its critical operations. Because of a lack of effective planning, over half of all the organizations that close their doors for more than a week after a disruption never open them again. **Business continuity (BC)** is specifically designed to get the organization's most critical services up and running as quickly as possible to enable continued operation and minimize financial losses from the disruption.

business continuity planning (BCP)

The process of completing a set of specialized team plans that document backups, continuity strategies, and associated actions needed to restore or relocate a business.

business continuity (BC)

The efforts of an organization to ensure its long-term viability when a disaster precludes normal operations at the primary site. BC usually involves the rapid relocation of an organization's critical business functions to an alternate location until it can return to the primary site or relocate to a new permanent facility.

business continuity plan (BC plan)

A plan that describes how critical business functions will continue at an alternate location after a disaster while the organization recovers its ability to function at the primary site—as supported by the DR plan.

This module parallels Module 10, which covers preparations for the DR process and its implementation. Because DR and BC are similar in structure and both play a part in the business resumption (BR) plan, it follows that there will be repetition in the underlying preparations and planning if the organization follows an integrated approach. However, although the two may look similar in structure and perhaps even in content, they have very different objectives. DR focuses on resuming operations at the normal operating facility (or facilities), known as the primary site. BC concentrates on resuming critical functions at an alternate site until DR efforts are complete.

As in DR planning, the identification of critical business functions and the resources to support them is the cornerstone of the process used to create the **BC plan**. The processes performed during the business impact analysis (BIA) are the source of this information. When a disaster strikes, making it impossible to function at the primary site, these critical functions are the first to be reestablished at the alternate site. The CP team needs to appoint a group to evaluate and compare the various alternatives and recommend which strategy should be selected and implemented. The selected strategy often uses some form of off-site facility, which must be inspected, configured, secured, and tested on a periodic basis. The selection should be reviewed periodically to determine if a better alternative has emerged or whether the organization needs a different solution.

Many organizations with operations in New York had their BC efforts tested critically on September 11, 2001. Similarly, organizations in the Gulf Coast region of the United States saw the effectiveness of their BC plans tested during the 2005 hurricane season. After the September 11 attacks, Chuck Tucker and Richard Hunter, representing Gartner, Inc., an information technology research and advisory firm, reported that parts of the business continuity process functioned as expected, and maybe even better than planned.

Organizations are still awaiting full evaluation of the results of their efforts to provide BC during the 2020 COVID-19 pandemic. While organizations were prepared for most natural disasters, the possibility that their facilities wouldn't be damaged but their entire workforce would nevertheless be sequestered and work off-site wasn't on the list of probable outcomes for most BC planning committees. The number of employees affected by state and regional shelter-in-place orders in response to COVID-19 was massive. The number of organizations that were unable to adjust on the fly and sustain critical business functions remains to be tallied, but many small businesses, especially those in personal and hospitality services, may never recover.

It is common for disasters to reveal unforeseen complications whenever reality triggers contingency plans, regardless of whether the disaster was natural or man-made. Some lessons can be gleaned from the fallout from these catastrophes. First, plans must be kept current with emerging realities. The planning assumptions can change and the scenarios used to consider alternatives may become stale. Also, training should never cease, and rehearsals should be as realistic as possible. The real recovery will almost certainly be different from the recovery time objective (RTO) and recovery point objective (RPO) forecasted in any plan. Also, resilience built into IT systems will improve recovery performance, and an organization's assumptions should include the loss of access to existing workspaces, including desktop systems, local area networks, and locally stored data such as e-mail. Finally, coordination relies on communications using internal and external channels that are consistent and accurate.[1]

As discussed previously, the RTO is the amount of time the business can tolerate until alternate capabilities are available. Reducing RTO requires mechanisms to shorten start-up times or provisions to make data available online at a failover site. The RPO is the point in the past to which recovered applications and data at the alternate infrastructure will be restored. In database terms, this is the amount of data loss that will be experienced as a result of resumption at the alternate site. Reducing RPO requires mechanisms to increase the synchronicity of data replication between production systems and their backup implementations.

Not everything always works as planned, however. There is a general consensus about enterprise vulnerability that has been brought home by recent catastrophes, including 9/11, cementing a rising awareness among corporate contingency planners. Every sector of the industry has pushed for improved contingency planning, especially business continuity. However, although many improvements to BC planning have been ongoing, few organizations made plans for a global pandemic. Many organizations large and small are reassessing basic business needs. Senior management at more and more organizations are focusing on contingency planning as they seek to gain assurance that they will remain viable when events challenge them to retain customer loyalty and keep the confidence of their stakeholders. It is fairly certain that future planning efforts will include preparations for pandemics.

Unfortunately, Gartner predicts, "The momentum of digital transformation projects will outpace the ability of organizations to accommodate the changes, introducing additional complex threats. Neither the pace of change nor the evolving risk landscape will wait for business continuity management and organizational resilience strategies to evolve and catch up."[2]

One outcome of high-profile events is the scrutiny of contingency plans and the requirement that planners defend their work to be ready for the non-technical challenges they will face. Sound planning for data, hardware, and software resilience is being recognized as insufficient if the human resource aspects of the plans are not equally valid. Plans prepared without senior executive support may face repudiation. Managers in non-technical roles will also be challenged to become more integrated into the planning process; without proper training, they may come to believe that contingency planning is just another boondoggle from headquarters.

BUSINESS CONTINUITY TEAMS

As is the case when developing a DR plan, the BC plan should be created by a team of specialists. Under the overall direction of the contingency planning management team (CPMT), the BC team leader—most likely a senior manager from the organization's operations division—begins by assembling the BC planning and response teams. As with the DR teams, the information technology and information security departments contribute representatives to the BC teams to provide guidance in the development of plans for the planning team and technical services for the various response teams when the organization begins relocation to an alternate site. The real advantage provided by a properly assembled BC response team is in the breadth and depth of non-technical members drawn from business units in the organization. Because the BC planning team so closely mirrors the structure and activities of the DR planning team, its composition will not be discussed here. The following section provides an overview for organizing an effective BC response team.

Organization of BC Response Teams

Like the DR team, the BC response teams should consist of representatives from every major organizational unit as appropriate. Unlike the DR team, the need for specialized, technology-focused members is significantly reduced, and the emphasis instead should be placed on generalized business and technology skills. Members of the BC response teams need to be able to set up preliminary facilities to support the relocation of critical business functions, as specified in the BIA. Therefore, the teams should include needed representatives from the following:

- Senior management
- Corporate functional units, specifically the human resources, legal, and accounting departments
- IT managers, plus a few technical specialists with broad technical skill sets
- Information security managers, with a few technical specialists

As discussed in previous modules, the BC and DR response teams should contain different members. The BC response teams will be required to immediately relocate off-site and begin the transition to the alternate location, while the DR response teams must remain behind and work at the primary site to determine what is salvageable, what is not, and what needs to be done to reestablish operations at the primary site. Depending on the size of the organization, there may be many BC response teams or just a few. A list of typical BC response teams may include the following:

- *BC management team*—This is the command and control group responsible for all planning and coordination activities. The management team consists of organization representatives working together to facilitate the transfer to the alternate site. During relocation, this group coordinates all efforts, receives reports from the other teams, and assigns work to them. The BC management team handles the functions performed by the communications, business interface, and vendor contact teams under the DR model.
- *Operations team*—This group works to establish the core business functions needed to sustain critical business operations. The specific responsibilities of this team vary dramatically between organizations, as their operations differ.
- *Computer setup (hardware) team*—This team works to quickly set up the hardware needed to establish operations at the alternate site. It is typically responsible for desktop PCs, mobile and tablet devices, and server hardware. In smaller organizations, this team may be combined with other IT-related teams.
- *Systems (OS) team*—The OS team works to install operating systems on the hardware installed by the hardware team. It works closely with the hardware, apps, and data teams to establish system functions during relocation. It also sets up user accounts and remote connectivity in conjunction with the network recovery team.
- *Network team*—The network recovery team works to establish short-term and long-term networks, including the network hardware (hubs, switches, and routers), wiring, and Internet and intranet connectivity. It also typically installs wireless networks in the short term to provide immediate connectivity, unless wired services can be brought online quickly. Companies that provide services, as in this module's opening scenario, already have the cabling ready and connected to a central rack or cabinet; when the installation of firewall, router, server, and Internet connections is complete, the company can be brought online securely.
- *Applications team*—This team works with the hardware and OS teams to get internal and external services up and running to begin supporting business functions.
- *Data management team*—The data management team works with other teams for data restoration and recovery, including on-site, off-site, and online transactional data, to support the relocated business functions.
- *Logistics team*—This team is responsible for providing supplies, materials, food, services, equipment, or facilities needed at the alternate site. It is also the go-to team when it comes to physically acquiring and transporting the needed resources to the alternate site. This team performs the smaller tasks that make the operations move smoothly.[3]

As with the DR response teams, some organizations may consolidate these functions into a smaller number of teams or even into a single team. At a minimum, the organization needs the ability to set up hardware, software, and data; handle the purchasing of needed supplies; and then coordinate with the organization's executive management team at the primary site to determine which functions should be relocated to the BC site. This information, coupled with the BC plan, allows the BC response teams to prepare for operations with all business and IT-based pieces in place.

Special Documentation and Equipment

All members of the BC teams should have multiple copies of the BC plan readily available in all locations from which they may be asked to respond in the event of mobilization. This might include ready access to copies stored securely in their homes, vehicles, and offices, as team members cannot predict when they will receive a call and be required to activate the plans. It is also important for the responsible team members to have access to certain prepositioned BC supplies, materials, and equipment should the need for them arise. The equipment that team members need will differ according to their roles and responsibilities. The needed equipment includes all of the items described in Module 10 as well as the modifications described next:

- The specifics of the hardware elements on the list depend on the type and degree of coverage provided by the BC alternate site strategy and enabling contracts. In a fully designed strategy, only portable computers, software media, licenses, and backup copies of data need to be ready for deployment.
- Replacement or redundant computers, networks, power, telecommunications hardware, and spares are not usually staged for BC deployment; instead, they are specified for provisioning by the BC site provider or issued to employees in the case of mobile technologies.
- Arrangements for utilities infrastructure are usually included in the provision specification for the BC site provider.
- BC versions of contact information need to be carefully planned and created, given that the location from which they will be used may prove to be a complicating factor; for instance, the local policy contact number may be different at the BC site.
- Emergency supplies are still required, but the nature and quantity may be adjusted to take into account the need for a high degree of portability.

Many of these items may seem frivolous, but when you have to reconstitute a functioning enterprise far from your home base of operations, the supplies, materials, and equipment you bring may make a difference. Many of the items listed are not suitable for preplacement or transportation to the BC site and may need to be acquired as needed. As a result, one key requirement for BC operations is a purchasing card (sometimes called a *P-card*)—essentially, a credit card owned by the organization that can be used to purchase needed office supplies and various equipment.

Unless the organization contracts for a hot site or equivalent (as described in Module 3), office equipment such as desktop computers, phones, and faxes are not provided. As a result, these items either need to be purchased or leases need to be signed in advance to allow for on-demand delivery. Some BC vendors provide this equipment as an option, but some organizations prefer to contract with their current service providers to have extra equipment shipped on short notice.

One technique an organization can employ to simplify the equipment needed at a remote BC site is to provide all employees with a secure, networked laptop computer and mobile phone and require them to use the laptop to back up essential files before returning home with it at the end of each day. As a result of this requirement, fewer systems will be needed if the organization needs to relocate, given that employees can work off their laptops and use them for Internet connections. With the rapid spread of enhanced broadband and wireless networking technologies, organizations can be even more flexible and prepared. One organization that adopted this model of BC readiness was the New York Police Department. In the aftermath of the September 11 attack, the department's High Tech Crimes unit found itself in a real bind. Not only were valued officers lost in the attack, but most of their active case files were lost, along with critical evidence. To provide some measure of business continuity in the event of future disasters, the agency issued laptops to all agents and required them to take all active case files home on these securely encrypted systems.

Most of the world discovered the need to be prepared to work from home during the 2020 COVID-19 pandemic. All noncritical employees were sent home, with most required to work from their residences as part of the shelter-in-place strategy to slow the spread of the virus. The pandemic required most organizations to rethink how they do business. Demand for remote collaboration applications like Microsoft Teams, Webex, Skype, and Zoom skyrocketed, as did the load on most residential Internet bandwidth. Smaller organizations moved to social media communications like Facebook Messenger and Apple FaceTime. Everyone contributed to effective business continuity efforts, regardless of whether a formal plan was in place. In some cases, plans were developed and revised on the fly. Most major universities transitioned to online instruction. While the total impact of the pandemic may not be known for years, the U.S. unemployment rate was almost 15 percent at the time of this writing, with many millions of Americans out of work and a large number of small businesses closing. Some 77 percent of businesses were rethinking their workplace safety before allowing workers to return to the office, with 65 percent reconfiguring workplaces to support social distancing and 52 percent modifying work schedules to reduce the threat of exposure. Overall, almost 75 percent of U.S. businesses have been significantly impacted by the pandemic.[4]

BUSINESS CONTINUITY POLICY AND PLAN

BC is an element of contingency planning (CP), and it is best accomplished using a repeatable process or methodology. In Module 2, you learned that NIST SP 800-34, Rev. 1, "Contingency Planning Guide for Federal Information Systems,"[5] includes planning guidance for incidents, disasters, and other situations that call for BC. The approach used in the NIST document has been adapted for BC use in the section that follows.

The first step in all contingency efforts is the development of policy, and then the effort moves to plans. In some organizations, these are considered corequisite operations, whereas other organizations argue that policy must precede planning. Still other organizations argue that the development of policy is a function of planning. In this text, the approach is to develop the BC policy prior to developing the BC plan, both of which are part of BC planning. As you will recall from Module 2, the NIST approach used in SP 800-34, Rev. 1 defines a process for developing and maintaining a viable CP program. The steps from the NIST approach have been adapted here for the BC planning process:

1. *Develop the BC planning policy statement.* A formal organizational policy provides the authority and guidance necessary to develop an effective continuity plan.
2. *Review the BIA.* The BIA helps to identify and prioritize critical IT systems and components.
3. *Identify preventive controls.* Measures taken to reduce the effects of system disruptions can increase system availability and reduce continuity life-cycle costs.
4. *Create BC contingency (relocation) strategies.* Thorough relocation strategies ensure that critical system functions may be recovered quickly and effectively following a disruption.
5. *Develop the BC plan.* The BC plan should contain detailed guidance and procedures for restoring a damaged system.
6. *Ensure BC plan testing, training, and exercises.* Testing the plan identifies planning gaps, whereas training prepares recovery personnel for plan activation; both activities improve plan effectiveness and overall preparedness.
7. *Ensure BC plan maintenance.* The plan should be a living document that is updated regularly to remain current with system enhancements.[6]

These seven steps are discussed in more detail from a BC perspective in the following sections.

Develop the BC Planning Policy Statement

As with the process employed in DR planning, the BC planning team, led by the business manager designated as the BC planning team leader, begins with the development of the BC policy. The policy provides an overview of the organization's philosophy on the conduct of BC operations and serves as the guiding document for the development of BC planning. Developing the BC policy may be a function of the CP team that is handed down to the BC planning team leader, or it may be developed with the team leader's assistance to guide in subsequent operations. In either case, the BC policy contains eight key elements, all of which are described in the following sections:

- Purpose
- Scope, as it applies to the organization's functions subject to BC planning
- Roles and responsibilities

- Resource requirements
- Training requirements
- Exercise and testing schedules
- Plan maintenance schedule
- Special considerations, such as information storage and maintenance

You may have noticed that this process is virtually identical in structure to that of the DR policy and plans laid out in Module 10. This is intentional, as the processes are generally the same, with minor differences in implementation.

Purpose

The purpose of the BC program is to provide the necessary planning and coordination to facilitate the relocation of critical business functions if a disaster prohibits continued operations at the primary site.

As with any major enterprise-wide policy document, it is important to begin with the executive vision. The primary policy that directs the BC effort is the BC policy that applies to the entire organization.

Here is an example of the purpose section of a BC plan:

> *The purpose of this policy is to ensure that business and information resource investments made by ABC Company are protected against service interruptions, including large-scale disasters, by the development, implementation, and testing of business continuity (BC) plans.*
>
> *For purposes of this policy,* business continuity planning *includes, but is not limited to, the documentation, plans, policies, and procedures that are required to establish critical business functions at the organization's temporary alternate site for a division affected by man-made or natural outages or disasters.*
>
> *The policy will assist the organization to:*
> - *Identify business resources that are at risk*
> - *Implement and test plans and procedures that enable reestablishment of critical services at the alternate site following a disaster[7]*

Scope

This section of the BC plan identifies the organizational units and groups of employees to which the policy applies. This clarification is important in case the organization is geographically dispersed or is creating different policies for different organizational units.

Here is an example of the scope portion of a BC plan:

> *This policy applies to all organizational divisions and departments within ABC Company, and to the individuals employed therein.*

Roles and Responsibilities

This section identifies the roles and responsibilities of the key players in the BC operation. This listing can range from the responsibilities of executive management down to those of individual employees. Note in the following examples that some sections may be duplicated from the organization's CP policy. For smaller organizations, this redundancy can be eliminated because many of the functions are performed by the same group.

Here is an example of the Roles and Responsibilities section of a BC plan:

> *The chief operations officer, as ABC Company's contingency planning officer, will appoint a business continuity planning officer from his or her office.*
>
> *The chief financial officer will appoint an individual to assist the business continuity planning officer in securing service agreements necessary to establish operations at an alternate site as dictated by the situation.*
>
> *The appointed business continuity planning officer will oversee all phases and functions of the business continuity planning process and will report divisional readiness directly to the contingency planning officer.*

Each division must have a business continuity plan that identifies critical functions. The plan shall provide for contingencies to restore operations and information if a disaster occurs and relocation to the alternate site is deemed necessary. The business continuity plan for each division may be a subset of the organization's comprehensive disaster recovery plan. The concept of disaster recovery focuses on business resumption at the primary place of business.[8]

Each organization shall:

- *Develop business continuity plans.*
- *Maintain and update business continuity plans annually.*
- *Test business continuity plans annually.*
- *Train their employees to execute the continuity plans.[9]*

Division heads are responsible for the oversight of their respective divisions' management and use of IT resources. An annual confirmation letter for the disaster recovery and business continuity plan must be submitted to the CIO by August 31 of each year.

With this letter, the head of each division confirms to the executive management that a disaster recovery and business continuity plan has been reviewed, updated, and tested.

The auditor may audit the organization's disaster recovery and business continuity plans and tests for compliance with policy and standards.

Resource Requirements

Should the organization desire, it can allocate specific resources for the development of BC plans in this section. Although this section may include directives to individuals, it can be separated from the previous section for emphasis and clarity.

Here is an example of the Resource Requirements section of a BC plan:

The chief financial officer will provide the necessary contractual agreements and funds to warranty availability of resources should they be required to re-establish operations at a suitable alternative site. The CFO will also ensure suitable funds to support the development and annual testing of the BC plan.

Training Requirements

In this section, the training requirements for the various employee groups are defined and highlighted. Here is an example of the Training Requirements section of a BC plan:

Training for the BC plan will consist of:

- *Making employees aware of the need for a business continuity plan*
- *Informing all employees of the existence of the plan and providing procedures to follow in the event of an emergency*
- *Training all personnel who have responsibilities identified in the plan to perform the business continuity procedures*
- *Providing the opportunity for recovery teams to practice business continuity skills[10]*

Exercise and Testing Schedules

This section specifies the type of BC exercise or testing needed, the frequency, and the individuals involved. Here is an example of the Exercise and Testing Schedules section of a BC plan:

An annual walk-through of all BC plans will be conducted with all key BC team representatives.

The BC officer, in coordination with the CP officer, will conduct an annual unannounced business continuity exercise. Each key individual will be provided with a specific type of relocation request and asked to function as if the relocation were genuine. Results will be discussed in an after-action review with the executive management team.

Plan Maintenance Schedule

All good plans include a schedule and instructions for reviewing and updating the plan. This section should address the frequency of reviews and list the people who will be involved in them. It is not necessary for the entire BC team to be involved, and the review can be combined with a periodic test of the BC plan (as in a talk-through) as long as the resulting discussion includes areas for improvement.

Here is an example of the Plan Maintenance Schedule section of a BC plan:

> *The business continuity policy must be reviewed at least annually to ensure its relevance. As in the development of the policy, a planning team that consists of upper management and personnel from information security, information technology, human resources, or other operations should be assembled to review the BC policy.*[11]

Special Considerations

The DR and BC plans can overlap in extreme situations. Thus, this section provides an overview of the information storage and retrieval plans for the organization. The use of off-site but online data storage is also specified. Although the specifics do not have to be covered, the individuals responsible should be able to implement the strategy based on this guidance.

Here is an example of the Special Considerations section of a BC plan:

> *The CIO, in conjunction with the CISO, will ensure that a generally accepted data storage and recovery scheme is implemented, with weekly off-site data storage using a secure transportation method.*

> *The CIO will evaluate and implement appropriate off-site but online data storage to record transactional data, with a recovery time objective of no longer than six hours, once hardware has been installed.*

Review the BIA

During the second step of the seven-step NIST approach, the BIA is reviewed. This is a review of the version developed by the CP team to ensure compatibility with BC-specific plans and operations. Because much of the work done by the CP team includes business managers as well as IT and information security representatives, the document will usually be acceptable as is. The most important aspect of the BIA applicable to BC is the scenarios developed. For each scenario, the organization can begin to determine the probability that it will have to relocate to an alternate site and thus associate the BC plan with the DR plan.

Identify Preventive Controls

This step is part of a review of the current environment to ensure that the organization's information security posture is being implemented effectively and is fully understood by the BC planners. Planners should know about the existing controls because effective preventive controls implemented to safeguard online and physical information storage also facilitate their recovery. At a minimum, the BC team should review and verify that the generally accepted data storage and recovery techniques discussed in Module 3 are implemented, tested, and maintained. The BC team should also ensure that sufficient and secure off-site data storage is implemented, tested, and maintained, including any remote transaction or journaling functions.

Create BC Contingency (Relocation) Strategies

Thorough recovery strategies ensure that the company's operations will be recovered quickly and effectively following a disruption, whether at the primary site using the DR plan or at an alternate site using the BC plan. Although it may be virtually impossible to prepare for all contingencies, it is important to have BC strategies in place for the most widely expected events. Based on the BIA conducted early in the process, the "after action" activities must be thoroughly developed and tested. These strategies offer a number of relocation options for the organization:

- Relocating a single department (not IT or Production) internally—that is, moving employees around within the organization

- Relocating a single department (not IT or Production) externally—that is, moving employees outside the organization if no internal space is available
- Relocating a specialized department (IT or Production) externally, given that its special needs require separate planning, especially if it's a data center
- Relocating two or more departments (not IT or Production) to a location outside the organization
- Relocating the entire organization to an external but on-site location, if the location is usable but the building is not
- Relocating the entire organization to an external, distant location, if the entire location is unusable

Develop the BC Plan

The BC plan includes detailed guidance and procedures for moving the organization's operations and personnel into and out of the contracted alternate site. The procedures that were previously developed and tested are documented and formalized in the plan. As with the DR plan, the responsibility for creating the BC plan does not usually fall to the CISO. The BC team leader is most likely a general manager from the operations or production division, and is appointed by the chief operations officer, chief finance officer, or chief executive officer. The BC team leader guides the management team in the development of specific plans to execute after the CEO declares such a move to be necessary. In most cases, the trigger for such a decision is the evaluation of the damage to the primary site and determination that it is unusable until restored; the evaluation is conducted by the DR team and reported to the CPMT, which in turn advises the organization's executive management group.

After the trigger has been tripped, the extent of the BC move depends on the extent of damage to the organization. This is why subordinate BC plans are so important. An organization may sustain sufficient damage to move some, but not all, of its functions. Each subordinate group must then be prepared to pack whatever it can salvage and relocate to the alternate site. The BC team should have already arrived and begun designating the locations for each function.

The BC plan consists of three distinct phases of operation, the first of which must be done prior to any disaster that requires relocation. These phases are preparation for BC actions, relocation to the alternate site, and return to the primary site.

 Although you will notice similarities between the following subsections and those in "Implementing the BC Plan" later in this module, the two sections treat the same points from different perspectives and for different purposes. The following subsections discuss BC prospectively from a planning perspective, while the latter section discusses BC operations.

Preparation for BC Actions

The developers of the BC plan must first specify what has to be done before the relocation occurs. Unlike the DR plan, the type of disaster does not affect the method of relocation, nor does the selection of services; only the extent of the disaster does. The more devastating and damaging the disaster is, the more parts of the organization must be relocated to the alternate site.

In this phase of the BC plan, the organization specifies what type of relocation service is desired and what data management strategies are deployed to support relocation. From the variety of relocation services available—hot, warm, or cold sites, as well as the three time-share and mobile site options described in Module 3—the plan specifies what types of resources are needed to support ongoing operations.

Relocation to the Alternate Site

This phase of the BC plan is the official beginning of actual BC operations. The plan should specify how the organization relocates from the primary site to the alternate site and under what conditions. Items to be covered include the following:

- *Identification of advance party and departure point*—At a minimum, the BC plan should specify the BC team that will serve as the advance party—the group responsible for initiating the occupation of the alternate facility. The plan should also include information about the trigger that will signal the relocation of the advance party to the BC site. This is usually done by a verbal directive from the CPMT leader, as directed by the CEO.
- *Notification of service providers*—One of the advance party's first tasks is to notify a number of individuals, including the BC site owner and providers of power, water, gas, telephone, and Internet services, so that they

can begin activating the necessary resources to get the BC site up and running. The plan should contain this critical information and designate who should notify the service providers and when. As the BC advance party arrives at the BC site, it should meet with the site manager and conduct a detailed walk-through to assess the status of the facility and identify any problems. This is the same type of inspection performed when leasing an apartment or home. If the organization does not identify any problems, it may be charged for any needed repairs when it leaves. Of course, the contract stipulates whether this assessment is necessary.

- *Notification of BC team to move to BC site*—The next group to relocate to the BC site is the main part of the BC team. Although the two or three individuals who make up the BC advance party move to the site first, the remainder of the team follows as soon as the BC team leader directs them to do so. The BC plan should reflect this information.
- *Acquisition of supplies, materials, and equipment*—Before the BC team arrives at the site, some members may have preliminary tasks, such as purchasing supplies, materials, and equipment or acquiring them from off-site storage. The BC plan should contain information on what should be purchased or obtained from off-site storage and who is responsible for acquiring it. Some of this material, such as replacement computing equipment, may need to be ordered from a vendor. The BC plan should contain this information and ensure that preapproved purchasing orders or purchasing cards are available to the BC team.

  Some organizations may want to have all BC team members meet at the BC site prior to beginning their procurement activities. This allows the BC team leader to conduct a face-to-face coordination session to ensure that everyone knows their responsibilities and to issue the purchasing orders or cards. Again, the BC plan should contain this information. To prevent abuses of this emergency procurement operation, it may be best to have all BC team members working in two-person teams, one with acquisition authority and the other with approval authority.

- *Notification of employees to relocate to BC site*—At some point during the BC process, the rest of the organization's employees report to the BC site. They receive notification through a predetermined mechanism at a predetermined time, both of which must be specified in the BC plan. It is also useful for each employee to receive a summary document or card that contains the location of the BC site along with directions for how to get there and phone numbers of a few of the individuals who will already be on site, in case additional information is needed.
- *Organization of incoming employees*—For medium-sized and large organizations, the move of employees to the BC site will typically not be done at one time. For larger organizations, a schedule might be needed to indicate when various groups will move in; the schedule will provide a sequence to prevent too many employees from moving into the BC site at one time. As a result, any scheduling of employee movement is contained in the BC plan. This information varies depending on whether the organization experiences a disaster that requires relocation during the business day or after business hours. Some organizations prefer to simply send employees home until it can be determined that the BC site is ready to be occupied. At that time, they begin notifying employees to arrive at a specific date and time, based on the criticality of business functions those employees fill.

  As employees arrive at the new site, it is helpful to have a reception area established where they can be directed to their new work areas and provided with any other needed information. To facilitate this process, it is useful to have an "in-processing" packet prepared for employees or stored electronically off-site. That way, the organization can quickly draft needed instructions for individual employees. Because not all employees may know the extent of the damage to the organization's facilities, a summary of the disaster and the assessed damage should be provided to employees as soon as possible, perhaps in the in-processing document set. Supplementary information, including what organizational elements have been relocated and contact numbers for them, should be directly distributed or placed in the new work areas. Preprinted signage can be used to direct incoming employees as they arrive at the new site.

  In addition to the in-processing package, each arriving employee should receive a briefing that answers any questions not covered in the document set. At a minimum, this briefing should address safety issues, including emergency relocation from the BC site. It should also provide information about the facility's layout, parking, and local food establishments. It should conclude with a positive message about the ability of the organization to survive, thanks to the BC planning that was done.

The BC plan should identify how staffing operations will function and who is responsible for overseeing and implementing them.

Return to the Primary Site

At some point, the organization is notified that the primary site has been restored to working order. At that time, it prepares to relocate employees back to the primary site. To accomplish this relocation in an orderly fashion, the BC plan should have documented procedures for "clearing" the BC site and redirecting employees back to their normal work offices. The operations that must be specified in the BC plan to support returning to the primary site include the following:

- *Scheduling of employee moves*—Note that not all business functions may return at the same time, just as not all will relocate to the BC site in the same order or time. The organization may have the most critical functions continue to work out of the BC site until all support personnel are relocated and support services are functional at the primary site. The organization may also want to wait for a natural break in the business week, like the weekend. In any case, the BC plan should contain information about who will begin directing the move back to the primary site and the order in which business functions and associated personnel will move.
- *Vanguard clearing responsibilities*—The term *clearing* is used in the military and government sectors to represent the process of moving out of temporary facilities and returning them to their owners or managers. The concept is the same here. The BC team, as temporary stewards of the facilities, are responsible for coordinating the shutdown of services, packing and moving the temporary equipment and supplies, and returning the facilities to the BC site owner. The BC plan should contain information about these critical details. The subordinate activities include the following:
  - *Disconnecting services*—Each of the service providers contacted during the move-in need to be notified of the date the organization will no longer need the services (power, water, gas, telephone, and Internet). Not all services may be needed, depending on the arrangements with the BC site owners.
  - *Breaking down equipment*—All the equipment used by the organization at the BC site must be made ready for transportation back to the primary site or to storage locations. The timing on this shutdown is critical, as the organization most likely requires a backup to off-site storage before shutting down the equipment. The DR team at the primary site can then bring its equipment online and download the most recent backups, thus preventing loss of information in transition.
  - *Packing up supplies, materials, and equipment and putting it in storage or transporting it to the primary site*—All supplies, materials, and equipment that was purchased or obtained at the BC site needs to be packed up and shipped back to the primary site or put in storage in anticipation of the next relocation. Unless the BC plan includes details on who is responsible for specific material, valuable supplies, materials, and equipment may be lost in the shuffle. Prior to packing, a detailed inventory must be made to prevent pilferage and to assess any damage that may occur in transit. An important issue to consider is whether individuals will be permitted to relocate their own supplies, materials, and equipment. Although it may be easier to allow employees to clean out their own offices and take their supplies back to the primary site using their personal vehicles, the damage, loss, and liability issues associated with such actions may make them prohibitive. If an employee were injured while loading or unloading equipment from personal vehicles, or if equipment was damaged, destroyed, or stolen from a personal vehicle, complications could arise. Therefore, the organization may prefer to hire professional movers or at least lease moving vehicles. This process must be specified in the BC plan.
  - *Transferring the building to the BC service provider and clearing the building*—The final activity at the BC site is the walk-through with the site manager to identify any damage to the facility that the organization caused. The BC team then documents its findings, compares them with the list made during the move-in, and coordinates any needed expenses with the manager. After all parties are satisfied with the clearing, the keys are returned to the manager and the BC team moves back to the primary site.

BC After-Action Review

Just as the other CP teams do, the BC team must conduct an after-action review, or AAR, before returning to normal operations. All key players review their notes and verify that the BC documentation is accurate and precise. All team members review their actions during the incident and identify areas where the BC plan worked, didn't work, or should be improved. This allows the team to update the BC plan. The AAR is then stored to serve as a training case for future staff. This formally ends the BC team's responsibilities for the BC event.

Ensure BC Plan Testing, Training, and Exercises

Training employees and management to use the BC plan tests the validity and effectiveness of the plan and prepares the various teams to use it. Any problems found in the plan during training can be noted for incorporation into the draft document. Once the drafts have been reviewed and tested, the final assembly of the plan can commence. As with the IR plan and the DR plan, testing the BC plan is an ongoing activity, with each scenario tested periodically—at least annually at a walk-through level or higher. After all the components of the BC plan have been drafted and tested, the final BC plan document can be created, similar in format and appearance to the IR and DR plan documents.

Ensure BC Plan Maintenance

The plan should be a dynamic document that is updated regularly to remain current with system enhancements. The organization should revisit the BC plan at least annually in order to update its procedures, contracts, and agreements and to make the necessary personnel and equipment modifications dictated by the business operations. If the organization changes its size, location, or business focus, the BC team and the other teams should begin anew with the CP plan and reexamine the BIA.

Sample Business Continuity Plans

Several online references are available to assist in writing a BC plan or adapting a BC plan based on a template. A quick Web search may reveal a template that is suitable for the organization to adapt to its needs. When searching for a template, it helps to specify the target organization's industry—for example, "business continuity plan template for manufacturing" or "BC plan template for computer service organizations."

   In addition, the U.S. Department of Homeland Security's Federal Emergency Management Agency has developed a support Web site at *www.ready.gov* that includes a suite of tools to guide the development of DR and BC plans.[12]

 The *Ready.gov* site offers resources to assist small businesses and individuals in preparing for adverse events. This resource is among the best in offering a starting point for developing DR and BC plans.

IMPLEMENTING THE BC PLAN

An organization implements the BC plan when it experiences an event that disrupts and precludes continued operations at the primary site. An organization may reach a predetermined state, known as a *trigger point* or *set point*, when the responsible executive or senior manager indicates that the organization will relocate to a preselected alternate site. This is not a decision to be taken lightly. In addition to the substantial expenses the organization incurs to lease the alternate site, there are inevitably additional expenses associated with establishing and using duplicate utilities and services, additional office supplies, and temporary equipment. Thus, the organization should ensure that the benefits of implementing the BC plan justify the expense. On the other hand, if the damage from the disaster is severe enough to disrupt business operations, the decision to implement the BC plan is straightforward.

   Implementation of the BC plan involves relocation to the alternate site—first by the BC advance party, then the main team, and then the affected employees. Next, the plan involves establishment of operations and, once DR efforts have been completed, a return to the primary site or new permanent alternate site, as described in the previous section.

Preparation for BC Actions

Unlike the DR team, whose reactions are based on the nature of the disaster that has befallen the organization, the BC team can expect that its functions will always be generally the same: to prepare to duplicate one or more of the organization's critical business functions at an alternate site. Which specific alternate site the organization uses and which critical business functions it implements will depend on which functions are disrupted by the disaster and whether it took the primary site completely out of service or only partially. Planning and training encompass the bulk of the preparation activities. From desk checks to walk-throughs to full-blown interruption testing, all the organization's teams and members should be prepared to play their roles in a BC operation.

Preparing Action Plans for Critical Functions

Preparing for all possible contingencies is usually not practical. The organization can develop general training programs that focus on a specific BC operation that implements critical business functions at an alternate off-site facility. These preparations can be made with minimal disruption to normal business functions.

The critical functions that need to be prepared for deployment at an alternate site are designated as *command and control* (sometimes noted as C&C). They are the core administrative and operational functions that the organization needs to perform to remain in business. After the critical functions have been designated, the BC team should rehearse setting up one or more of these functions at an alternate site. Because of the complexities of these individual functions, the size and scale of the operations, the ways in which they interoperate, and depending on which functions are to be implemented, they may or may not be able to coexist at the BC alternate site. As a result, each function may have its own separate BC site that is coordinated with the others.

Integrating Routine Operations to Improve BC Effectiveness

For general operating efficiency and to improve resiliency in the event of disaster or the need for continuity operations, organizations may choose to make any number of changes in routine policies and procedures and perform activities in ways that improve the effectiveness of the BC preparations. When implementing a BC strategy at an alternate site, the IT staff must sustain the backup strategies and practices used at the primary site; good backup practices can safeguard against losses that occur while operating in challenging conditions, when errors or faults can cause additional disruptions. Also, employees will eventually need to relocate to the primary site.

Other preparations include issuing P-cards to designated BC team members. One model suggests issuing P-cards to a small group of employees who are part of the BC advance party or deployment group, so that they can make emergency purchases of critical supplies. In the event that critical functions are relocated, these employees can coordinate the acquisition of a predefined list of supplies, materials, and equipment from a local office supply store.

Another preparation is the off-site storage of key forms used by the company. Even when an organization employs an intranet to conduct most functions using electronic forms rather than paper forms, hard-copy documents allow the organization to function until the intranet is reestablished.

The preparation undertaken by an organization will typically pay off in an efficient operation after the BC plan is implemented. The hours spent walking through rehearsals, discussions, and improvements of the plan will result in much smoother functions under pressure. The worst time to develop the BC plan is while activating the critical business functions in response to a disaster.

Relocation to the Alternate Site

The decision to move specific critical functions initiates a series of carefully choreographed subordinate activities. An initial decision about whether essential functions will be started at the alternate site is followed by deciding which services will be activated. This is followed by determining when each service must be available. Should damage be severe enough, or if the disaster is ongoing (as in a hurricane or flood), the decision to implement BC operations may have to be deferred until reliable information is available or until the primary site can be accessed for a damage assessment. After the decision is made, the advance party is deployed to begin coordinating the move, key service providers are notified, the remainder of the BC team is directed to the site, and needed supplies and materials are acquired.

Next, the affected employees are relocated to the BC site; as they arrive, they are organized and then directed to begin work. The initial work will be to remediate any remaining issues with the site. This will give way to the setup activities, a final review of the alternate site, and the eventual establishment and routine execution of the critical service being resumed. These activities are described in the following sections.

The Advance Party

The identification of the advance party is an important part of the BC plan. The advance party should include members or representatives of each of the major BC teams. The role of the advance party is to prepare the site for the arrival of the rest of the organization's BC teams, and eventually the rest of the organization designated to be working from the BC site. The advance party is the team that will interface with the alternate site owners and BC vendors and ensure that the necessary services are requested, including power, water, data, and phones. They also begin establishing work areas and preparing checklists for the full BC team. If the organization is lucky, the advance party will have several hours to prepare for the arrival of the main BC response teams. If not, they may arrive with the response teams or just minutes ahead of them.

Notifying Service Providers

It is often necessary to alert service providers to get their services activated at the alternate site. Some or all of these service providers may be notified by the BC vendor. If these notifications are not managed by the contingency site's operator, the BC team leader should contact the necessary vendors. When mobile contingency facilities are part of the plan, on-site coordination is often needed to get these services connected at the mobile offices.

Activating the BC Site

After a BC plan is activated, one of the first responsibilities of the BC team leader is to notify the individuals involved in the plan to begin implementing it. The advance party teams immediately begin working their checklists, preparing the site for the imminent arrival of the rest of the staff.

Supplies and Equipment

Organizations need supplies to make work happen. Sometimes, the lack of the most mundane supplies can substantially hinder operations. As a well-known proverb states: "For want of a nail, the shoe was lost. For want of a shoe, the horse was lost. For want of a horse, the knight was lost. For want of a knight, the battle was lost. For want of a battle, the kingdom was lost. And, all for the want of a nail."[13]

It may not be easy to determine what supplies and equipment a particular function needs to conduct operations. However, it would be troublesome to find out after the organization has settled into the alternate site that someone needs to make a list of supplies and equipment and then begin procurement. The creation of a checklist for each function should be part of the planning process. This may result in either the pickup of previously purchased and positioned supplies or a shopping trip to a local supplier. But, some equipment is either too expensive or too unique to allow prepurchasing, prepositioning, or purchasing locally. The need for computer equipment, whether servers, end-user systems, peripherals, or storage devices, can be predetermined, and then the equipment can be ordered with a rush request to a reliable vendor. If the need is dire enough, then local purchasing may be the only viable option. Some vendors offer services to quickly drop-ship a specific list of equipment selected to closely match the needs of each planned contingency option. One simple notification is all it takes to have this order on its way to the alternate site. The catch is acquiring the necessary technical equipment on short notice. This is one reason organizations should consider the distribution of laptops and cell phones: to minimize last-minute purchases, delays, and excessive expenses.

Staff Relocation to BC Site

The next step in implementing the BC plan is getting word to the necessary employees that the alternate site is ready for their occupancy. At the earliest point that a reliable prediction is possible, a notification of the occupancy time can be given to the affected staff members. The staffing packets prepared earlier will be used to guide the employees when they show up. Some organizations may prefer to wait until the beginning of the next scheduled shift or the start of the next business day to move the employees to the alternate site. Other organizations with more time-critical missions can't wait that long, and may require employees to start at the alternate site in the middle of a scheduled shift.

Organization of Relocated Staff

As the employees begin relocating to the alternate site, there will inevitably be confusion. Not every employee will have been able to participate in BC planning events. As a result, the calming influence of a friendly face and well-planned check-in procedures will improve their ability to quickly assimilate to the new environment and begin working productively. The staffing packets should contain information about the location of assigned workspaces, office support equipment and resources, new phone lists, locations of colleagues and supervisors, and so forth.

Returning to a Primary Site

The last event that occurs at the BC alternate site is the preparation for relocating to the primary site or a new permanent site, once it is restored and ready for resumption of operations. This task involves scheduling the employees' move and clearing the BC site. Finally, an AAR is conducted to incorporate lessons learned into the plan and bring closure to the process.

Scheduling the Move

The simplest way to handle the relocation back to the primary site is to schedule the move to occur over a quiet period in the production schedule if one exists, with some employees working extra hours to shut down the alternate site and others loading office supplies, materials, and equipment for transportation back to the primary site. If the relocation can be done on a weekend, employees should use the last few hours of the preceding Friday afternoon to pack up their offices and prepare to have their supplies, materials, and equipment relocated back to the primary site. They should carefully label boxes containing their work papers and other effects, and then leave the material on top of their desks or in a clearly marked area on their way out of the building. In large organizations, the collection and transportation of work supplies, materials, and equipment may take longer than a two-day weekend. If the organization has to relocate production facilities and data centers—anything other than administrative functions, basically—it may take weeks to relocate all the supplies, materials, and equipment back to the primary site. However, in an ideal scenario, employees will stop work on Friday afternoon and resume work on Monday morning back at the primary site, with little break in their work regimes. Data center workers or other IT employees can conduct backups on Friday afternoon after the business closes, and then reload data and transactions at the primary site so that it is available Monday morning as well. Although each organization has its own requirements, those that operate seven days a week may not be able to leverage weekend downtime; still, each situation should be managed to minimize disruption from the move. For organizations that run 24/7, management must determine when the "cut-over" occurs to shift work back to the primary site. As an aside, it is important for the organization to collect the extra office supplies purchased for the move. Expendable supplies should be relocated to the primary site's supply closets, whereas "durable" goods, such as staplers, scissors, phones, and typewriters, can be placed in off-site storage in anticipation of the next disaster.

Clearing Activities

The final steps involve closing down the organization's presence at the alternate site. Among the activities that occur during this phase are disconnecting temporary services, disassembling equipment, packaging recovered equipment and supplies, storing or transporting recovered equipment and supplies, and transferring control of the assigned space to the BC service provider. Most of these steps will be spelled out in the contract with the alternate site provider and in the BC plan.

Settling in at the Primary Site

Even in the ideal scenario, with employees leaving the BC site on Friday and reporting to the primary site on Monday, there will be a settling-in period at the primary site or a new permanent site. If the employees were relocated to the BC site for an extended period of time and it was not in the same area as their primary residences, they may have had to live in temporary housing. If the root cause of the contingency operation was a widespread incident at the organization's primary location, it likely affected the employees' personal lives as well. For instance, if a severe storm caused the relocation, not only was work damage a factor, employees may have experienced property damage and family distress from the event.

On top of that, alternate work conditions during the emergency might have caused interpersonal issues—for example, some employees might have reported to temporary supervisors because their primary supervisor was working on the DR team. Also, some staff may have ignored routine tasks that used to be performed at the primary site because only critical functions were being performed at the BC site. In any event, there is a transition period in which employees reestablish their normal routines.

There may even be challenges associated with learning new business functions or operations. Some managers may take advantage of the transition to implement new procedures or policies designed to streamline operations. If managers found that they were able to work effectively at the BC site without certain responsibilities, policies, or procedures, managers may elect to eliminate them altogether. The organization may have suspended upgrades or updates to business functions or information storage and processing, and may elect to integrate them as the primary facility is reestablished. Employees returning to the primary site will require any retraining or awareness activities the organization feels is necessary to streamline reintegration.

BC After-Action Review

As with the IR and DR processes, after the BC activities have come to a close and the organization has reoccupied its primary facility or a new permanent alternate facility, the BC team should meet to discuss what worked and what didn't. Prior to this meeting, each team member should create a summary of what happened from his or her perspective, including comments on what went well and what needs improvement. These comments will all be included in a master report that is compiled upon completion of the AAR and eventually used to update the BC plan.

The AAR is usually created by using the timeline from contemporaneous documents prepared by the incident manager. This detailed timeline provides a sequence for the events, along with the ability to determine if actions were performed on schedule. Everyone gets to speak at an AAR; no one should be restricted from voicing an unbiased opinion. The smallest detail can derail future efforts, if not corrected. The resulting additions should be incorporated into a final report, called a "Summary of Events," that is presented to the executive management and then archived for posterity.

CONTINUOUS IMPROVEMENT OF THE BC PROCESS

If there is one constant in business, it is that change is inevitable. Even the best BC planning projects will produce plans that leave room for improvement and need to be maintained. The best organizations make continuous improvement a key factor in their BC planning. The following sections discuss maintenance activities in the BC environment and how CP processes can be improved.

Improving the BC Plan

How much today's organizations rely on their information systems goes far beyond what was common only a few years ago. The continuing convergence of business systems as well as the integration of networks and the Internet into everyday business activities have made business and e-business nearly synonymous. This reliance on technical infrastructure leaves most organizations concerned about BC planning. Circumstances have reached the point, however, that merely having prepared a plan is not adequate to the challenges. The process used for initial continuity planning often results in the following shortfalls from the intended outcomes:

- *Reliance*—Relying on a comfortable BC process and the resulting BC plan can lead to a false sense of security and potential business failure if the plan is not updated regularly and fully tested. An untested plan is no plan at all, and a plan in which the organization does not have confidence will not survive a real continuity operation.
- *Scope*—Companies often limit the scope of their systems recovery. When structuring, funding, and reviewing their BC approaches, organizations should pay attention both to the needs of information systems recovery and the continuity of critical business functions. Far too many organizations limit BC processes to IT systems recovery, assuming that if the IT systems are working, they will find a way to make the business systems function around them.
- *Prioritization*—A formal process that prioritizes key business processes is a critical step that often does not get sufficient attention from senior management. As part of the BIA, identification and prioritization of critical business functions ensures that they will be supported in the event of a disaster that requires implementation of the BC plan. The failure to properly prioritize may result in situations that appear absurd in retrospect, such as a data center with working computers but no functioning network circuits, or an e-commerce site that works but cannot ship products from the warehouse.
- *Plan updates*—Formal mechanisms are often not in place to force a plan update on a regular basis or when significant changes have been made to systems or business processes. Periodic review and maintenance of the plan is essential in keeping the document current. In normal operations, core business processes evolve over time, and the continuity plan must be kept up to date if it is to serve any purpose when invoked.
- *Ownership*—Senior management often appoints the wrong person—or at least not the best person—to manage the BC planning process. As stated in earlier modules, a champion is needed—someone high enough in the organization to provide the needed leadership, management, influence, and resources to make the project succeed, and who is sufficiently detail-oriented and motivated to make sure the BC process is in place and up to date.
- *Communications*—Communications issues are often overlooked or viewed as peripheral to the core issues. It is important to establish planned communications with all stakeholders, including employees, service providers, and customers. In fact, redundant communications procedures are often a good idea because BC plans are almost always activated under less than optimal conditions.

- *Security*—This is often not considered a key deliverable in BC processes. Information systems security controls are often disregarded or fall by the wayside during plan development, resulting in a greater risk of exposure during recovery operations.
- *Public relations*—Business and IT professionals tend to focus on the practical aspects of business resumption and may fail to plan for public relations and investor considerations, thereby missing the opportunity to influence the perceptions of these key stakeholders. The communications team described in Module 10 has the specific responsibility for addressing public relations requirements. The public and the press can be valuable aids in recovery.
- *Insurance*—Many BC processes fail to adequately plan for the filing of insurance claims, which results in delayed or reduced settlements. Insurance is a critical part of both DR and BC. Involving the organization's risk management team and closely coordinating its interactions with insurance agents is essential in expediting reimbursements from insurance claims, which is better than having to offset the cost of recovery with the organization's earnings.
- *Service evaluation*—Many companies poorly evaluate recovery products such as hot sites, cold sites, and planning software, partially because they rely too much on vendor-supplied information. This often leads to a solution that does not adequately address a company's needs.

This list of shortcomings has led many practitioners to note problems with the way BC processes are performed. For example, the following comments are from Kathleen Lucey, a Fellow at the Business Continuity Institute:

> *Just yesterday, I said to a professional chef with 20-plus years of high-level experience in his industry that I was beginning to feel like business continuity was becoming like cooking: Everyone thinks that all they need is a "secret recipe" and they can turn out professional dishes, achieve their lifelong dream of opening a restaurant, and so forth. Somehow, businesspeople have become universal "do it yourselfers," failing to understand that the deep and broad knowledge and the painfully honed skills gained from experience are far more important than the business continuity recipe.*
>
> *Here are some important points to consider when developing a business continuity plan:*
>
> 1. *A business continuity plan is NOT a single unified plan. It is a set of specialized team plans documenting the backup and continuity strategies decided upon, based on the company's needs collected through a BIA or other method, and the actions required to implement that strategy to re-create/restore/relocate a business. There are several types of plans, each with some differences in content, but no team plan includes information about policy, history, and so on. Each includes only that information necessary for that team to accomplish its functions. I am getting pretty discouraged with those who think that the plan IS the strategy. I have found that companies tend to do rather well on IT recovery plans, less well on business unit plans, and abysmally on logistics/communication plans and overall coordination. This makes sense since technical recovery is relatively simple, once you have got the bugs out through testing and your data is available; business unit recovery is more complex, but still not terribly difficult. Logistics and coordination processes are definitely not easy, particularly when you leave the military or emergency sectors. A very small percentage of private sector organizations do logistics well.*
> 2. *Within each plan, the individual default response (IDR) of each team member during work hours and outside of work hours is listed by team member name. People pay attention to information associated with their names, not with roles, such as team member. The IDR can also be coded, along with other critical information, on individualized wallet cards that each person will carry at all times.*
> 3. *Use an automated notification system that allows for preprogrammed messages, ad hoc messages, and voice-text translation. We all know that call trees are like passwords: They just don't work and never have. Remember that you can use these systems to do regular notification tests painlessly—reports are automatically generated. Add up the time that you and everyone else spends on this and the product starts to look very good, even as a testing tool, and obviously such a system will perform much better than any manual call tree during an emergency. So, do not put the contact information of team members in the team plan; put it in an ASP-based, high-performing automated notification system. Sell this kind of system to your management based on higher business continuity program productivity and ROI, not just on superior performance during the catastrophic emergency that they suspect will never happen. One caveat: Make sure that the service you subscribe to has fully redundant sites far from each other and that it can*

be accessed through phone or the Internet; make sure nothing goes on your site, because your emergency communication system will disappear when your site does! Sounds pretty obvious, but until the current generation of products, companies in fact put emergency communication boxes in their primary sites!

4. *Keep your detailed reference information—electronic and non-electronic—off-site and out of your plan. A good place for technical recovery information—past tests, command-level system re-creation scripts, and the like—is the site where you plan to re-create your systems. Coordination information and contractual information can be in your command center. If you have more than one command center, replicate the information in each and store a copy off-site as well, just in case. Just DO NOT put it in the plans. Make your maintenance requirements minimal and you will have a chance to have current information.*

5. *Don't forget that the best recovery is one that does not have to happen. Make sure that you identify all risks in mission-critical resources (not just IT) in a risk assessment. Then, eliminate those risks where it is reasonable to do so and lower their probability or occurrence, where feasibility allows. No, you never get 100 percent, but the 80/20 rule applies here. Painful experience teaches that MANY interruptions are self-generated and fully avoidable. This is another topic entirely, but one that you NEED ABSOLUTELY to address.*

6. *One more hint: More and more of us in the profession are understanding that recovery planning for the total catastrophic event (the so-called "worst-case scenario") is NOT the best way to go. If you plan to deal with the interruptions that have a high probability of occurrence, you will get more immediate payback from your business continuity efforts. Work up to worst case gradually; don't start with it. But again, this is a whole other subject.*

My advice to someone who is new to business continuity but is nonetheless charged with doing a "business continuity plan" for regulatory or other purposes: Hire someone to advise you and take their advice. There is no reasonable justification for any enterprise to expect you to do something well that you have never done before and where you have no training or knowledge. Knowing the business and knowing IT does not equal knowing business continuity. This is a complex professional skill that takes time and pain to acquire, and guess what, it is continually evolving. Sorry, there are no silver bullets here. If your organization is too small to pay someone to advise you, at least get some training. Just remember that you need a whole lot more than a recipe! And, that you will truly get nowhere if you are expecting to do this in your spare time.[14]

Improving the BC Staff

The most likely way to improve an organization's BC capabilities is to provide training and encourage professionalism among employees assigned to the role. Several organizations provide professional training for BC team members. This training ranges from managerial to technical, depending on the provider. Although most organizations can train their own personnel, it helps if at least one team member, preferably the team leader or CISO, has attended formal BC planning training.

BC Training

The choices in BC training range from classes taught through continuing education programs to private professional training institutions to national conferences. Table 11-1 presents a list of BC institutions that are known to offer training opportunities. Of course, there are many more than those shown here; you may be able to locate local training providers in your area.

Note that some of the institutions listed in Table 11-1 provide services only to their members at annual conferences and events. Several other organizations host annual conferences at which academic and practitioner presentations on BC are conducted. This book's authors have presented papers on BC topics at regional and national conferences, such as those for the Association for Information Systems (*www.ais.org*), the Colloquium for Information Systems Security Education (*www.cisse.info*), and the Conference on Cybersecurity Education, Research and Practice (*https://cyberinstitute.kennesaw.edu/ccerp/*). An organization should use care in selecting conferences to ensure that appropriate topics are part of the agenda.

BC Professional Certification

Many organizations and working professionals believe that professional associations and certifications work together to improve the results of the BC processes in their organizations. It is not always necessary to achieve a professional certification in order to join an association. However, the acquisition of a widely recognized certification is one way for

Table 11-1 BC Training Institutions

Institution	URL
Association of Contingency Planners	www.acp-international.com
Business Continuity Institute	www.thebci.org
Disaster Recovery Institute International	www.drii.org
Disaster Recovery Journal	www.drj.com
Institute for Business Continuity Training	www.ibct.com
Management Advisory Services & Publications	www.masp.com
Sentryx	www.sentryx.com

a person to receive independent acknowledgment of the knowledge, skills, and possible background needed to lead the BC processes in an organization.

There are two predominantly recognized professional institutions that certify business continuity professionals: the Business Continuity Institute (*thebci.org*), headquartered in the United Kingdom, and DRI International (*drii.org*), headquartered in Falls Church, Virginia. Both are member-owned, non-profit organizations. Both offer certification at different grade levels, and both agree on the "Common Body of Knowledge"—10 specific disciplines—as the basis for certification.

The disciplines are listed here:

1. Project Initiation and Management
2. Risk Evaluation and Control
3. Business Impact Analysis
4. Developing Business Continuity Management Strategies
5. Emergency Response and Operations
6. Developing and Implementing Business Continuity Plans
7. Awareness and Training Programs
8. Exercising and Maintaining Business Continuity Plans
9. Crisis Communications
10. Coordination with External Agencies[15]

Both the BCI and DRII have an international presence: The BCI has approximately 8,000 members in over 100 countries, and DRII has certified approximately 15,000 people in over 100 countries. Each institution offers various professional certifications, which are discussed in the next sections.

Disaster Recovery Institute International (DRII)

DRII offers a number of certification options:

- Continuity certifications
  - Associate Business Continuity Professional
  - Certified Functional Continuity Professional
  - Certified Business Continuity Professional
- Advanced continuity certifications
  - Master Business Continuity Professional
- Healthcare continuity
  - Associate Healthcare Provider Continuity Professional
  - Certified Healthcare Provider Continuity Professional
- Public sector continuity
  - Associate Public Sector Continuity Professional
  - Certified Public Sector Continuity Professional
- Risk management
  - Associate Risk Management Professional
  - Certified Risk Management Professional

- Audit
  - Associate Business Continuity Auditor
  - Certified Business Continuity Auditor[16]

Business Continuity Institute (BCI)

The Business Continuity Institute (BCI) offers one certification and one diploma:

- Certificate of the Business Continuity Institute
- The Business Continuity Management BCI Diploma, offered in cooperation with Buckingham New University[17]

Maintaining the BC Plan

As with the IR and DR plans, the BC plan requires a formal maintenance and update strategy. When the organization rehearses the plan and follows the preparatory steps to make the plan ready for deployment, it may discover suggestions for improvement. These ideas should be documented for later use in the maintenance process. The AARs will also provide valuable ideas for improving the plan. The plan should be formally reviewed at least once each year. Note that in a dynamic environment, this review may need to be more frequent.

Periodic BC Review

The BC review is conducted by the planning team with input from all necessary stakeholders. The review serves the following purposes:

- A refresher on the content of the plan
- An assessment of the suitability of the plan
- An opportunity to reconcile BC activities with other regulatory activities
- An opportunity to make needed minor changes that have been documented but not implemented since the last formal review

Just because an organization conducts an exercise and finds areas for improvement in the BC plan does not mean that the document needs to be immediately revised. Although this would be ideal, it would also mean the document is in a constant state of flux, with employees unsure of which version is "official."

As a result, it is important to collect recommendations for improvement through the events discussed previously, but it is also important to queue them for consideration at the next formal review. Recommendations are not automatically implemented; instead, they must be carefully weighted to determine if the changes represent true improvement in the overall plan.

Sometimes, a modification in one team's actions can have unforeseen consequences for other teams or even the overall organization. For example, if someone recommends that an organization postpone updating the automated notification system until the BC team has completed all its preparation tasks at the alternate site, there may be a delay of hours, if not days, before the organization can resume operations.

BC Plan Archival

One of the requirements of the BC plan is to have an individual—the BC team leader or someone who works for the BC team leader—responsible for the maintenance of the document. This individual also schedules the meetings for periodic reviews. Upon completion of the meeting, the responsible scribe, historian, or archivist will also be responsible for updating the master document and redistributing copies for approval. After the document is formally approved, the new master will be distributed to the appropriate individuals.

An additional requirement for archival is the collection and secure destruction of all old versions of the document. As described in earlier modules, the BC plan must be managed as if it is a classified document. Outdated copies must be collected, accounted for, and shredded or otherwise securely disposed of. After the new copies are in the proper hands and the old copies properly handled, the archivist returns to the ongoing job of collecting and storing recommendations for the next iteration.

 ASIS International is a leader in industrial security and offers many resources for employees at medium-sized and larger organizations to respond to adverse events, including those discussed in this module. Visit the organization at *www.asisonline.org/*.

FINAL THOUGHTS ON BUSINESS CONTINUITY AND THE COVID-19 PANDEMIC

The events of 2020 and the COVID-19 pandemic offer a unique and historical perspective on business continuity efforts. Unlike most BC events, which are typically constrained to a small geographic area in the event of a natural disaster or a computer attack, COVID-19 was a global event. It involved a combination of immediate BC activities associated with lingering effects. Many organizations were able to allow some or all employees to isolate themselves and work from home. Some planned response was blocked by government regulation. The expected response that would have seen employees relocate to work at alternate sites was not permitted.

In fact, in almost all cases there was nothing wrong with the facilities, technologies, or infrastructures normally affected by a disaster. The viral biohazard that caused COVID-19 was an unusual circumstance that was outside the planned response of most organizations. Even organizations that practice biohazard-based DR and BC focus on single and isolated incidents constrained to a small geographic area, like biological organisms or a chemical agent attack. The pandemic that effectively paralyzed much of the world's commerce limited the immediate effectiveness of traditional DR and BC plans and responses. Instead, organizations had to adapt, quickly changing their strategies and operations to maintain key functions and continue as a going concern.

At the time this book was written, the pandemic was ongoing, with businesses slowly beginning to return to operation, still implementing alternative strategies involving social distancing, and encouraging work at home for employees who could do so. Some organizations will adapt and adjust, using options from companies like Twitter and Facebook to enable permanent remote work options for some employees. Other organizations have already failed or will soon; unlike situations from many past DR and BC events, their plans offered little assistance in forestalling failures from COVID-19. All organizations can do at this point is move forward, try to recover, and be vigilant. When future incident responses, disaster recovery plans, and business continuity plans are updated, there will be lessons to learn from the COVID-19 disaster.

 The Security Executive Council is a corporate security advisory consultancy that has been at the forefront of the COVID-19 response. Many of the lessons from this global pandemic have been documented and are available to the general public. You can visit the council's Web site at *www.securityexecutivecouncil.com*. Details of these lessons are found at *www.securityexecutivecouncil.com/spotlight/?sid=32018*.

Closing Scenario

Juan ran through his checklist one last time. The building had everything he expected in a cold site, at a substantially lower price than he had anticipated. If he contracted with this organization and worked with the vendors that supplied HAL's hardware, he could guarantee his boss, Robert Xavier, a 4-hour recovery point objective (RPO) for administration, a 6-hour RPO for the help desk, and a 12- to 24-hour RPO for the entire data center, with critical functions established in 4 to 6 hours. This was significantly better than he had hoped, and he knew Robert would be pleased.

"We'll take it," he said, extending his hand.

Discussion Questions

1. Why is it important for an organization such as HAL to have a cold site like the one described?
2. What features would HAL be looking for in a cold site like this?
3. What major items should be on Juan's checklist?

Ethical Decision Making

Suppose that as the negotiations for the recovery site proceeded, Ms. Novak informed Juan that she would like to "make some adjustments" to the contract that would make it cost "just a little bit more" for HAL in the event the recovery plan was activated. She would give Juan an envelope of gift cards worth about $1000 if he would "look the other way" on these changes during the contracting process. Is this an ethical thing for Juan to do? Do you think it is legal?

MODULE SUMMARY

- BC planning is the set of actions an organization takes to prepare for circumstances that could lead to the interruption of critical operations. The BC process is designed to get the organization's most critical services up and running as quickly as possible; these critical services are identified in the BIA.

- The BC plan is created by a team of specialists drawn from the IT and information security departments, plus a selection of non-technical members from business units across the organization. Depending on the size of the organization, the BC team might have many subteams responsible for individual actions, including the BC management team, the operations team, the computer setup (hardware) team, the systems (OS) team, the network team, the applications team, the data management team, and the logistics team.

- All members of the BC team should have access to the BC plan at all locations from which they may be asked to respond. BC is an element of contingency planning, and it is best accomplished by using a repeatable process or methodology. The BC team develops the BC policy, which includes the following elements: purpose, scope, roles and responsibilities, resource requirements, training requirements, exercise and testing schedules, plan maintenance schedule, and other special considerations.

- Initiation of the BC plan occurs when an organization concludes that it cannot reasonably expect to resume essential operations at its primary site. Implementation of the BC plan involves preparations, relocation, establishment of operations, and the eventual return to the primary site or a new permanent alternate site.

- Preparing for all possible contingencies is usually not practical. However, one or several general training programs should focus on a specific BC operation that implements critical business functions at an alternate off-site facility. These preparations can be made with minimal disruption to normal business functions.

- The advance party should include members or representatives of each of the major BC teams.

- Organizations need supplies and equipment to make work happen; sometimes, the lack of the most mundane supplies can substantially hinder operations.

- After the BC activities have come to a close and the organization has reoccupied its primary facility or new permanent alternate facility, the team should meet to discuss what worked and what didn't in a process called the after-action review (AAR).

- Many organizations and working professionals believe that professional associations and certification work together to improve the results of the BC processes in their organizations.

Review Questions

1. What is BCP?
2. What is the difference between disaster recovery and business continuity?
3. What are the primary and alternate sites in the context of contingency planning?
4. What are RTO and RPO, and why is it essential to define them early in the BC planning process?
5. What parts of the organization should the BC team draw on for its members?
6. List the subteams that support the BC team.
7. What is similar about the DR and BC planning processes with respect to special documentation and equipment needs?
8. What should be the first step in business continuity planning? Which NIST document is used to inform this process?
9. List and describe the components of the BC policy document.
10. List and describe the phases of the BC plan.

11. What are the advantages of including an AAR process in the BC plan?
12. At what point does an organization implement the BC plan, and what is this point called?
13. What are the critical steps in BC implementation?
14. Is it practical to prepare for all possible contingencies? How can this best be handled?
15. Why must the staff at the alternate site continue to observe backup strategies that are in place at the primary site?
16. What is an advance party and what does it accomplish?
17. Why may all the needed equipment not be prepositioned at the alternate site?
18. What steps should be followed in a return to the primary site?
19. What is continuous improvement, and why does it apply to BC processes?
20. Name and describe two BC-related training providers and certifications.

Real-World Exercises

Exercise 11-1

Visit the SunGard Web site at *www.sungardas.com*. Look for options that map to the alternatives in this module. Does the organization offer hot, warm, or cold services? Mobile services? What other services does it offer?

Exercise 11-2

Using your local telephone directory or a Web search, look for companies in your region that offer business continuity services. Which of them offer hot-site services? Which of them offer mobile services?

Exercise 11-3

Visit Continuity Central's Web site at *www.continuitycentral.com*. Click the "Jobs" link at the top of the Web page. What topic listings would be of interest to someone writing a BC plan? To someone focusing on BC management? What skills and attributes are organizations seeking in a candidate? Select a position announcement for each topic and bring it to class for discussion.

Exercise 11-4

Using a Web browser or your library's article-search tool, look for articles describing the impact of recent major events on businesses in your area. Look for details on how the businesses dealt with the disaster through BC planning. Is there any discussion of companies without BC plans that went out of business due to loss of facilities? What about companies that did have BC plans?

Exercise 11-5

Do a Web search on the terms "business continuity" and "certification." What do you find? Are there any certifications other than those listed in this module? What core skills are promoted in the certifications you find?

Hands-On Projects

The hands-on project for this module can be accessed in the Practice It folder in MindTap or through your instructor's LMS. The virtual labs provided with this resource can help you develop practical skills that will be of value as you progress through the course.

References

1. Tucker, Chuck, and Richard Hunter. "September 11: Business Continuity Lessons." Gartner. May 2002. EXP Premier, pp. 1–5.

2. Gartner. "2020 Strategic Road Map for Business Continuity Management." Accessed 5/11/2020 at *www.lumapps.com/content/2020-strategic-road-map-for-business-continuity-management*.

3. Marcus, Evan, and Hal Stern. "Beyond Storage: 12 Types of Critical Disaster Recovery Teams." SearchStorage. December 30, 2003. Accessed 05/11/2020 at *https://searchdisasterrecovery.techtarget.com/tip/Beyond-storage-12-types-of-critical-disaster-recovery-teams*.

4. PwC. "PwC's COVID-19 CFO Pulse Survey." April 27, 2020. Accessed 5/11/2020 at *www.pwc.com/us/en/library/covid-19/pwc-covid-19-cfo-pulse-survey-4.html*.

5. Swanson, Marianne, Pauline Bowen, Amy Wohl Phillips, Dean Gallup, and David Lynes. SP 800-34, Revision 1, "Contingency Planning Guide for Federal Information Systems." National Institute of Standards and Technology. November 2010. Accessed 5/11/2020 at *https://nvlpubs.nist.gov/nistpubs/Legacy/SP/nistspecialpublication800-34r1.pdf*.

6. Ibid.

7. "IT Disaster Recovery Planning." Accessed 04/30/2020 at *https://ocio.wa.gov/policy/information-technology-disaster-recovery-planning*.

8. Nebraska IT Commission Standards and Guidelines. "Security Architecture Complete Set of Policies." Accessed 04/30/2020 at *https://nitc.nebraska.gov/technical_panel/meetings/documents/20020108/security_completesetofpolicies.pdf*.

9. Ibid.

10. Swanson, Marianne, Pauline Bowen, Amy Wohl Phillips, Dean Gallup, and David Lynes. SP 800-34, Revision 1, "Contingency Planning Guide for Federal Information Systems." National Institute of Standards and Technology. November 2010. Accessed 5/11/2020 at *https://nvlpubs.nist.gov/nistpubs/Legacy/SP/nistspecialpublication800-34r1.pdf*.

11. "Disaster Recovery Policy Template." Accessed 04/30/2020 at *http://templatezone.com/pdfs/DisasterRecoveryPolicy.pdf*.

12. "Business Continuity Planning Suite." U.S. Department of Homeland Security. Accessed 05/11/2020 at *www.ready.gov/business-continuity-planning-suite*.

13. Davis, A., and M. Farmer. "JLA: The Nail # 1." DC Comics. ISBN 1563894807. August 1998.

14. Lucey, Kathleen. "Business Continuity Plan Development Explored." Continuity Central. Accessed 05/11/2020 at *www.continuitycentral.com/feature0106.htm*.

15. DCAG. "Professional Practices for Business Continuity Planners." Accessed 7/30/2020 at *www.dcag.com/images/ppintro.pdf*.

16. DRII. "Get Certified." Individual Certifications. Accessed 5/13/2020 at *https://drii.org*.

17. BCI. "Education & Training." Accessed 5/13/2020 at *www.thebci.org/training-qualifications/training-calendar.html*.

CRISIS MANAGEMENT IN IR, DR, AND BC

Upon completion of this material, you should be able to:

1. Describe the role of crisis management in the organization
2. List the development process and structure of the crisis management plan
3. Discuss issues in dealing with post-crisis trauma, including the process of getting people back to work after a crisis
4. Describe the impact of law enforcement involvement during a crisis
5. Explain how to manage crisis communications
6. Discuss succession planning
7. List and describe key international standards in incident response (IR), disaster recovery (DR), and business continuity (BC)

> *The easiest period in a crisis situation is actually the battle itself. The most difficult is the period of indecision—whether to fight or run away. And the most dangerous period is the aftermath. It is then, with all his resources spent and his guard down, that an individual must watch out for dulled reactions and faulty judgment.*
>
> —Richard M. Nixon

Opening Scenario

When the phone rang and the caller ID showed the area code for Boulder, Colorado, Marie LeFleur expected to hear the voice of Alan Hake. He was scheduled to meet with a key supplier of HAL's networking equipment later that day in Littleton. But it wasn't Alan; it was the police.

After Marie identified herself as Alan's assistant, she was informed that the business jet HAL rented for the trip had crashed in poor weather at the small airstrip close to the supplier's offices. There were no survivors.

After this disastrous news, Marie began to mechanically answer the questions from the police investigator. She was told what would happen next and what to expect as the crash investigation proceeded. Marie hung up the phone feeling numb and disoriented from the news. She stared for a moment at the cup of coffee she had poured herself only moments ago. Suddenly, nothing seemed important except thinking about her boss and those who had traveled with him to Colorado.

The meeting they had planned to attend would have included five HAL employees: Alan Hake, CEO; Amanda Wilson, CIO; Bill Freund, the manager of systems; Tina Mann, senior network administrator; and the newest HAL employee, Janet Dasher, who had been hired just last week as a network technician. Using the chartered jet had been a matter of economics; the whole group could get to the meeting and back to headquarters in a single day for the price of just two people flying commercial. It had seemed like a good idea at the time.

Marie thrust her head into her hands, crying. What was she supposed to do now?

INTRODUCTION

Organizations typically respond to crisis by focusing on economic priorities and operational issues, overlooking the steps needed to preserve the most critical assets of the organization: its people. Whether employees, vendors, customers, or neighbors, the people involved in a threat to the organization are often not addressed first. Where data and the preservation of financial stability are concerned, companies spend large amounts of their resources in planning for off-site backup, alternate sites, incident responses, and disaster recovery exercises. However, the events of September 11, 2001, reinforced a tragic lesson: People cannot be replaced readily. Many of the organizations ravaged by the 2001 attack were prepared to some extent for a crisis because of the 1993 bombing at the World Trade Center. Those organizations had contingency plans, off-site data backup, responses planned to the expected types of incidents, and all the disaster and contingency preparations that could be developed. The blind spot, because no such event in recent memory had seen it, was the massive loss of human life that resulted from the collapse of the twin towers at the World Trade Center. Such catastrophes set new benchmarks that readdress scope of devastation, intensity of damage, and severity of impact.

These lessons were reinforced during the COVID-19 pandemic in 2020. Many organizations lost employees, either temporarily due to illness or permanently. Even those who weren't infected were impacted in other ways—they were shut in their homes, with limited interaction with their coworkers, vendors, and clients, and in many cases with reduced access to information. Although disaster management plans are capable of dealing with the loss of property and data, and although business continuity plans are capable of relocating the organization to sustain continuity of operations, neither one can truly prepare for the devastating impact of the loss of people.

Crises also involve events that can adversely affect an organization's reputation and impact its operations from a personal perspective. Employees involved in unethical, illegal, or illicit activities can have a dramatic impact on the perceptions of an organization. Even formal investigations of an organization's actions, such as through the Securities and Exchange Commission, FBI, EPA, or state law enforcement, can constitute a crisis.

CRISIS MANAGEMENT IN THE ORGANIZATION

Crises can arrive at organizations at any time, regardless of whether they are expected and whether contingency plans and crisis management preparations are in place. Before you learn about planning for crises and ideas on how to manage them, you should understand the terminology of crisis management and a few of the myths that surround the subject.

Crisis Terms and Definitions

If you ask any 10 people what a *crisis* is, odds are you will get 10 different answers. For this reason, organizations should develop a clearly defined idea of what constitutes a crisis and what must be done when a crisis occurs. The Institute for Crisis Management (ICM) has defined a business crisis this way:

> *Any issue, problem or disruption which triggers negative stakeholder reactions that can impact the organization's reputation, business and financial strength. Crises can be situations threatening or doing harm to people and property, serious disruptions to operations, product recalls, labor issues, social media attacks, lawsuits, highly negative media coverage or allegations of wrongdoing against employees or leaders.*[1]

For our purposes, we've adapted the ICM definition of a **business crisis**. Crises can be caused by the same events that cause incidents and disasters: natural disasters such as those caused by bad weather and earthquakes; man-made disasters from bad decisions, human mistakes, and mechanical failures; and inappropriate actions by employees or negative media attention. The critical difference between disasters and crises is in the personnel aspect of these events. If a tornado destroys an organization's building but no employees are present, it is simply a disaster. If a tornado destroys an organization's building and kills or harms several employees, it is both a disaster and a crisis. Many crises fall into the category of bad decisions by employees that are exacerbated as a result of management not taking action when it is informed about the problem. Based on the rate of occurrence and amount of time the organization has as a warning, crisis events can be categorized into two types: a sudden crisis and a smoldering crisis.

business crisis
Any personnel-focused issue, problem, or disruption that triggers negative stakeholder reactions and potentially affects the organization's reputation, business, and financial strength.

Sudden Crisis

A sudden crisis occurs when an organization's operations are disrupted without warning. It is an event that has a high probability of drawing news coverage and could cause problems for stakeholders, including employees, investors, customers, and suppliers. A sudden crisis could include events that threaten the health or welfare of the organization's personnel, such as:

- A rapid-onset disaster like a tornado, flash flood, earthquake, or building fire
- Active shooter occurrences that involve employees or other constituents of the organization
- Industrial or personal accidents
- Out-of-control labor disputes or job actions
- Regional violence that impacts the organization

Smoldering Crisis

A smoldering crisis is a problem that may not be initially recognized as a crisis inside or outside the organization. If or when it is revealed, it may generate unfavorable news coverage and cause unanticipated expenses or penalties. Smoldering business crises that prompt a call to the crisis management team may include events that threaten the health or welfare of the organization's personnel, such as:

- A slow-onset disaster like a hurricane, pandemic, wildfire, or flooding
- Notification of employee investigations or arrests
- Negative viral media stories about organizational or employee misconduct
- Media or law enforcement investigations
- Negative product or service effects on customers that gain media attention
- A disgruntled employee's acts of retaliation for perceived mistreatment

Figure 12-1 shows the percentages of sudden and smoldering crises observed by the Institute for Crisis Management after reviewing over 760,000 news reports of crises from around the world.

Crises will happen. Some crises are unavoidable or at least outside the organization's ability to influence. As a result, *crisis management (CM)* becomes an important part of CP planning to deal with the unique situations associated

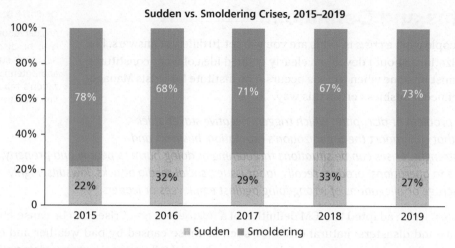

Figure 12-1   Sudden versus smoldering crises, 2015–2019[2]

Source: Institute for Crisis Management

with crises. Although there is a clear association of the role of InfoSec in IR, DR and BC, there is no clear association in CM between the protection of information assets and the preparation and response to crises. The subject is included here in part because some of the personnel impacted by the crisis, or even causing the crisis, may be InfoSec personnel. As such, any good security manager should be prepared to deal with crises and thus participate in CM and **crisis management planning (CMP)**. In general, CM involves three key interactions with external stakeholders:

- *Emergency response*—Actions taken to manage the immediate physical, health, and environmental impacts of an incident. These may include providing first aid and emergency medical services, controlling fires, containing hazardous materials that may have been released, securing sites, and evacuating bystanders.
- *Crisis communications*—Steps taken to communicate what is happening or has happened to internal and external audiences. This includes informing various stakeholders, such as employees, shareholders, media, customers, suppliers, and surrounding members of the community, about the timeline of events, the actions taken, and sometimes the reasons for the communications. Communications might be needed during the crisis and in its immediate aftermath.
- *Humanitarian assistance*—Actions taken to meet the psychological and emotional needs of various stakeholders. In contrast to emergency response, which focuses on the immediate safety of those affected, humanitarian assistance addresses the services needed to get the organization and its stakeholders back to original levels of productivity or satisfaction.[3]

Thus, the emphasis in the CMP process is on the planning function during the "preparing for" stage. The primary document that guides the organization's CM efforts is the **crisis management plan (CM plan)**.

crisis management planning (CMP)

The process of preparing for, responding to, recovering from, and managing communications during a crisis.

crisis management plan (CM plan)

The result of the crisis management planning process; a plan designed to support the preparation for, response to, recovery from, and management of communications during a crisis.

Crisis Misconceptions

There are a number of misconceptions about crises that should be dispelled. The first is that the majority of business crises are sudden, such as industrial accidents or terrorist attacks. Some studies have indicated that there are significantly more smoldering crises than sudden crises. Another myth is that crises are most commonly the result of employee mistakes or acts of nature. Unfortunately, the most prevalent crises are the direct or indirect result of management actions, inaction, or decisions. Figure 12-2 illustrates crises by category for 2019. As you can see, mismanagement is the largest group, with sexual harassment events a close second. Many people would argue that allowing sexual harassment to rise to the level of a crisis could be mismanagement.

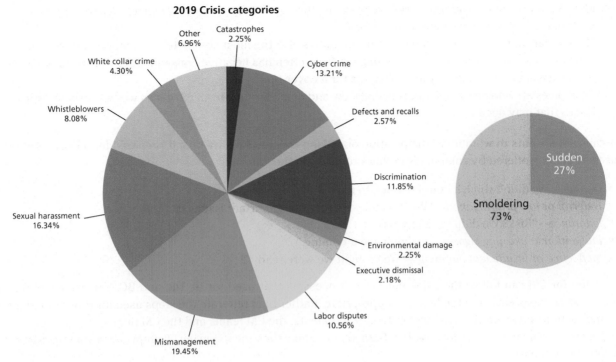

Other: *Casualty accidents 0.68%, Class actions 1.19%, Activism 1.82%, Hostile takeovers 1.17%, Workplace violence 1.59%*

Figure 12-2   2019 crisis categories[4]

Source: Institute for Crisis Management

 The Institute for Crisis Management (ICM) was founded in 1990 as one of the first crisis management consulting firms in North America. It offers a wealth of resources for CM planners. This organization provides access to information about crisis planning and prevention as well as training for crisis response. You can learn more by visiting *www.crisisconsultant.com*.

PREPARING FOR CRISIS MANAGEMENT

Crisis management requires preparation, just like IR, DR, and BC. Unlike the issues involved in contingency planning (CP), which hopefully come up infrequently, crises are something that managers have to deal with on a regular basis, whether the crises are small and innocuous or large and catastrophic. Some would argue that the role of an executive management team should specifically include dealing with crises. The most effective executives are those who have learned to deal successfully with crises. This is often the result of careful planning executed decisively to deal with issues quickly before harm comes to the organization. Keeping the various crises that arise well managed and, when possible, out of the media promotes the strategic objectives of the organization.

General Crisis Preparation Guidelines

Here are some tips for an organization that is preparing to improve its CM processes:

1. Build contingency plans, identify teams, train staff, and rehearse scenarios before a crisis occurs.
2. Verify that all staff members throughout the organization know that only designated members of the crisis management team may represent the company.
3. React as quickly as possible because the first few hours establish the baseline narrative that the media will use for most ongoing reporting.

4. Make sure your plans and processes are of the highest quality by employing expert reviews and professional crisis management consultants.

5. Make it part of your organizational culture to always give the most complete and accurate information possible in a given situation. Manipulating the facts often has negative consequences—far worse than the embarrassment or whatever the reason was for a cover-up.

6. As choices are considered, adopt the long view and consider long-term effects as well as the short-term losses that may occur.[5]

No organization wants to wind up in the position of making excuses for why it isn't prepared for a crisis. Among the excuses frequently offered by companies in this situation are the following:

- *Denial*—"We didn't think it could happen to us."
- *Deferral or low prioritization*—"We thought we had more important issues to handle."
- *Ignorance*—"Risk? We didn't see any risks."
- *Inattention to warning signs*—"We didn't see it coming."
- *Ineffective or insufficient planning*—"We thought we were ready!"[6]

Preparation for CM can follow the same multistep process as that used for IR, DR, and BC. You are encouraged to review those sections earlier in the book, as appropriate. Rather than reiterate the steps used for those functions, the following sections focus on the two most critical components: the CM teams and the CM plan.

Crisis management consultant Jonathan Bernstein recommends the following 10 steps in preventing crises, or at least mitigating their impact:[7]

1. *Reverse-engineer your industry's crises*—This is a fancy way of saying that you should research what crises are common in your industry. Find out what your organization's peers have gone through and try to learn from their experiences.

2. *Conduct a vulnerability audit*—Review your existing CM policies, plans, and activities and look for ways to improve. Conduct CM exercises with executives and confidential interviews with all employees to try to identify potential crises before they occur.

3. *Engage in crisis planning and training*—As recommended in this text, formally perform CM planning as well as training, exercises, and testing.

4. *Collect intelligence*—Periodically review social media for comments on the organization. Have staff members create accounts for the organization, and listen to the comments and complaints made by others.

5. *Optimize physical systems for crisis prevention and response*—Make sure the communications infrastructure can handle a crisis—especially external communications. If customers hear negative information about an employee or the organization, they may flood it with information requests. The organization must be able to quickly expand its telephone and electronic communications capabilities.

6. *Make sure that key personnel can talk to each other during a crisis*—Provide redundant communications methods for your critical CM personnel. Consider issuing them mobile phones, and even hand-held radios or satellite phones, so that in a crisis they don't have to contend with flooded phone networks.

7. *Create crisis response teams by capability, not just by position*—It's important to put the right people in CM positions of responsibility. Regardless of the person's political stature in the organization, it's better to have a person in charge who everyone knows is calm, cool, and collected in an emergency.

8. *Backup, backup, backup*—Not just data backup is needed, but personnel backup. As you will learn later in this module, organizations need to cross-train employees to ensure key skills are available in a crisis. Also, organizations need backups for critical vendors, facilities (as in alternate sites), and critical personnel such as CM response team members.

9. *Ensure that all employees' crisis-related knowledge and skills remain current*—Critical knowledge can get stale or outdated. CM personnel should undergo regular refreshers to ensure they're ready to respond when needed. All employees also need regular retraining on CM, so it should be included in the organization's periodic employee training schedule.

10. *Regroup regularly to reverse-engineer, self-audit, and adapt plans accordingly*—As the organization changes, people come and go, so everything related to CM should be regularly revisited, rechecked, and revised.[8]

Organizing the Crisis Management Teams

As with other CP functions, CM has both a planning team and one or more response teams. The CM planning team is responsible for some critical tasks, including the gathering of information about existing vulnerabilities, analyzing the current state of systems and network vulnerabilities, collecting current plans, and assessing how they impact the anticipated crisis plans. In addition, the CM planning team must lay out the comprehensive future plans that are intended to supplant what is now in place.

In some cases, members of the CM planning team become part of the CM response team. Most often, however, the membership shifts once the plans are put into action. The CM planning team should include broad representation from the parts of the organization that will be most impacted when the plans are put into effect. The team should also include sufficient management representation in the form of a champion who can accomplish necessary tasks and marshal the proper level of support from senior ranks of management. The best results come from a mixed group of creative, technical, and analytical people, and the planning committee may also benefit from the expertise of outside consultants who can guide the process and offer objective advice.

The CM response team includes staff members who will be engaged in the actual response that uses the plan in a crisis. They must be trained in the use of the plan beyond the technical knowledge of their own work assignments. The training must be sharpened and kept current with ongoing rehearsals and realistic simulations. This team adds a protective control for an organization's critical assets when adverse events make decisive action necessary. The members must also work well as a team, with clear lines of responsibility and the commensurate authority to act.[9]

Unlike other teams, the CM response team may consist of only a few individuals empowered to speak for the company. Team members won't necessarily be strong in technical or business management areas, but they should include communications professionals skilled in public relations. The primary focus of this group is the command and coordination of human resources in an emergency and managing the release of information about unfolding events. CM is focused on the physical, mental, and emotional well-being of the people in the organization. The CM response team typically includes the following members:

- *Team leader*—Responsible for overseeing the actions of the CM response team and coordinating all CM efforts in cooperation with DR and BC planning as needed. A natural fit for the team leader would be a senior manager or an executive in human resources.
- *Communications coordinator(s)*—Responsible for managing all communications among the CM response team, management, employees, and the public, including the media and local and state governments. Several individuals might work in this area with an intermediate supervisor. The larger the organization, the more communications there are to be coordinated. A manager or supervisor from the organization's internal communications department, if one exists, would be a natural fit for this position.
- *Emergency services coordinator(s)*—Responsible for initiating and managing all interaction between the organization's management and staff and any needed emergency services, including utility services. During an emergency that puts employees' lives or health at risk, someone skilled in interacting with emergency services is needed to serve as a liaison or contact person. These emergency services include not only traditional police, fire, and ambulance services, but any utilities or services that might be disrupted in an emergency to create a further danger to employees (for example, natural gas or propane). A manager or supervisor in corporate security would be prepared to handle this type of responsibility.
- *Other members as needed*—In certain organizations, representatives from different business areas might need to assist in the coordination of employees, the CM response team, and any external agencies or authorities. In some cases, each manager or supervisor may be a team member responsible for conducting head counts, identifying possible missing or injured personnel, or distributing information on an as-needed basis.

Although it would be ideal to have a separate team for CM, the organization will probably identify critical individuals on the CPMT and the DR team to handle CM responsibilities.

Keeping track of personnel is especially important during and after a crisis. A **head count** is the responsibility of the first-line supervisor, who reports the information to his or her manager, who in turn aggregates the totals for reporting up the corporate chain of command. The old Army phrase "present or accounted for" describes head-count information that must be reported to prevent leaving an injured or unconscious employee inside a building during an emergency.

head count

The process of accounting for all personnel—that is, determining each individual's whereabouts—during and after an emergency.

Preparing the Crisis Management Planning Team

The CM planning team is responsible for developing the CM plan, which will guide the team's actions during a crisis.

In preparing for the first meeting of the CM planning team, it is helpful to pose a number of questions and then get useful answers to assist in the team's organization and initial strategies. Possible questions include the following:

1. What kind of notification system do we have or need? Is it automated or manual? Is it able to reach all employees or just management and the crisis team during business hours? What about after business hours? How long does it take?
2. Do we have an existing CM plan? If so, how old is it, and when was it last used or tested?
3. What internal operations must be kept confidential to prevent embarrassment or damage to the organization? How are we currently protecting that information?
4. Do we have an official spokesperson for the organization? Who is our alternate?
5. What information should we share with the media if we have a crisis? What information should we share with our employees?
6. What crises have we faced in the past? What crises have other organizations in our region faced? In our industry? Have we changed how we operate as a result of these crises?

These questions and others from the planning team should stimulate conversation. This information, along with the business impact analysis (BIA) provided to the IR, DR, and BC teams, can provide the foundation for shaping the CM plan. The use of scenarios, complete with best-case, worst-case, and most likely outcomes, can provide insight into the preparation of the CM plan.

Crisis Management Critical Success Factors

Critical success factors (CSFs), according to Andrew Boynton and Robert Zmud, are "those few things that must go well to ensure success for a manager or an organization, and, therefore, they represent those managerial or enterprise areas that must be given special and continual attention to bring about high performance."[10] The "CSF Perspective" was defined by John Rockart in 1982.[11] Since then, it has been applied to a number of diverse managerial challenges. The factors critical to the success of CM boil down to seven areas that are vital to CMP.[12] These areas are discussed in the following sections.

Leadership

There is a clear distinction between leaders and managers that arises in the execution of organizational tasks. Leaders influence employees so that they are willing to accomplish objectives. They lead by example and demonstrate personal traits that instill a desire in others to follow. In other words, leaders provide purpose, direction, and motivation. Managers, on the other hand, administer the organization's resources. They create budgets, authorize expenditures, and hire employees. The distinction between leaders and managers is important, given that leadership may not always be a manager's responsibility and that nonmanagers are sometimes assigned to leadership roles. Managers often fulfill both management and leadership roles. During a crisis, however, leaders perform in one of two ways: successfully or unsuccessfully. Successful leaders rise to the challenge, providing effective leadership. Unsuccessful leaders fail to provide guidance, fail to make the right decisions, and fail to manage resources so the organization can ride out the crisis with minimal impact on itself or its employees. Skills that are important for a leader to have during CM include the following:

- *Ability to multitask*—Can handle multiple tasks concurrently
- *Rational under pressure*—Even when things get hectic, can remain calm, cool, and collected
- *Empathy*—Listens and relates to his or her employees
- *Quick, effective decision making*—Makes the best possible decision quickly
- *Delegation*—Assigns appropriate tasks to others best suited to assist
- *Good communication*—In communication with all parties involved
- *Ability to prioritize*—Handles most critical tasks first

Speed of Response

In the medical field, the first hour after an injury is referred to as the "golden hour." A person treated by medical personnel during this hour has the highest probability of full recovery. The same can be said of CM. If a large part of the CM plan is mobilized in the first hour—such as the removal of personnel from harm, the notification of emergency services, and the delegation of other identified CM tasks—then the organization and its personnel will have the highest probability of coming out of the crisis with minimal impact.

A Robust Plan

The plan is the heart of the CM response. A good plan that's clearly defined, rehearsed, and managed provides the organization with the best possible chance of surviving a crisis.

Adequate Resources

When a crisis occurs, having the right resources available at the right place can mean the difference between success and catastrophe. Critical resources include the following:

- Access to funds, especially cash
- Communications management, for the flood of incoming information requests
- Transportation to and from the crisis area
- Legal advice
- Insurance advice and service
- Moral and emotional support
- Media management
- An effective operations center

Funding

When a disaster strikes, it is not the time to be cheap. Spend what you need when you need to do so, and you will be much better off than if you attempt to save money. The organization that cuts corners in a crisis may find itself spending substantially more in legal fees and punitive damages if an injured employee or the family of a deceased employee convinces a court that the organization didn't do everything it could to prevent the injury or death. Expenses that may arise during or after a crisis include the following:

- Employee assistance programs, including counseling
- Travel expenses, including lodging
- Employee overtime for hourly staff
- Replacement of lost, damaged, or destroyed property for employees
- Compensation for those who were injured

Caring and Compassionate Response

During a crisis, people need to know the organization cares about them. This means that the crisis team and management need to be able to demonstrate that they understand the personal issues employees are dealing with. Sometimes, a hot cup of coffee and a kind ear are more valuable than overtime and a memo indicating that the company will survive. Having comfort items such as warm food, beverages, and blankets may prove as beneficial psychologically as they are physically.

Excellent Communications

Not knowing what is going on can be construed as a form of torture. Keeping employees, the community, and the media informed of events and the organization's efforts can serve to alleviate anxiety and assure everyone that the organization is doing its best to make things right. Things to consider when planning the communications portion of the CM plan include the following:

- Have key personnel undergo training to understand the media and learn how to work with them.
- Know who your stakeholders are and keep them apprised.

- "Tell it all, tell it fast, and tell the truth."
- Have information ready to distribute, either orally or in writing.
- Express pity, praise, and promise.[13]

Developing the Crisis Management Plan

The CM team must put together a document that specifies the roles and responsibilities of individuals during a crisis. This document provides instruction not only for the CM team but for individual employees. It can serve as both policy and plan, although some organizations may choose to have separate documents for each. The specifics of a good CM plan may vary, but a typical document will contain the sections described next.

Purpose

The introduction to the document should declare its purpose and scope by defining crises, defining crisis management, and identifying the individuals to whom the plan applies.

Crisis Management Planning Committee

The identification of the CM planning committee is an important section in any CM document. It not only identifies the individuals on the committee, it defines the difference between the planning committee and the operating team. Identification of CM personnel can be by name or by position. By indicating individuals by name, the organization can avoid any ambiguities in the assignment of responsibilities. However, this requires frequent updates, and the personnel list can be extensive in larger organizations. Identification by position requires clarification in the event of similar job titles, but it ensures that whoever holds the position is responsible for the corresponding CM activities.

This section of the document may also specify the frequency and location of planning committee meetings.

Crisis Types

To avoid confusion, it is helpful to have a definitions section to identify the types of crises that could result in implementation of the plan. A simple method of defining crises is to group them into three or four categories, each with a corresponding level of response required of the organization. For example:

- *Category 1*—Minor risk of minor injury to personnel or organizational reputation, addressable with on-site resources or limited off-site assistance. Category 1 crises may not require implementation of the plan but simply assistance in coordinating with emergency services.
- *Category 2*—Major risk of minor injury to personnel or organizational reputation, requiring considerable off-site assistance. Category 2 events last longer than Category 1 events and may affect more than a few personnel.
- *Category 3*—Organization-wide crisis requiring evacuation of facilities, if possible, and cessation of the organization's functions pending resolution of the crisis. Category 3 crises represent the highest level of impact on the organization and may be addressed in conjunction with local, state, or federal emergency relief efforts.

Organizations may prefer a more granular scheme with more levels to permit a more appropriate response. For small to medium-sized organizations, three levels may be sufficient. In any case, each category must be very clearly defined, with examples to ensure that employees correctly classify a crisis.

Crisis Management Response Team Structure

The next section of the document identifies the CM response team and its responsibilities. This is not the planning team but the group of individuals that handles the crisis in the event the CM plan is activated. In industry and government terms, these are the *first responders*. The CM response team is created to enable management to gain and maintain control of ongoing emergency situations, to provide oversight and control to designated first responders, and to incorporate IR, DR, and DC plans and resources as needed.

executive-in-charge

When the crisis or emergency arises, the ranking executive on-site who is authorized to initiate the CM plan.

Responsibility and Control

This section may be included with the previous one. However, it is important to note whether the CM response team leader or an **executive-in-charge** assumes overall responsibility. In some organizations, especially state and federal emergency management agencies, the CM response team leader has authority in a declared emergency over all public and private organizations until the emergency is resolved. This allows the team leader to pull any resources that are needed to deal with the problem. The team leader would have a number of liaison officers from various emergency services to provide advice, but would retain ultimate authority.

chain of command
The list of officials ranging from an individual's immediate supervisor to the top executive of the organization.

The concept of the executive-in-charge is from the military **chain of command**. In the United States, the military infrastructure has a well-defined chain of command that has been detailed in legislation. The Goldwater-Nichols Department of Defense Reorganization Act of 1986 documents that the president is the commander-in-chief, but when the president is unable to command, control devolves next to the Secretary of Defense and then to the military chain of command. Having unambiguous rules in place for who takes control when normal links in the hierarchy are disrupted is very important.

Because of the travel-intensive positions of most senior executives, it is entirely possible that one or more senior managers—the chief executive officer, the president, or the senior vice president—may not be available for consultation when a crisis arises. As a result, it is important for organizations to have a clearly defined executive-in-charge roster that indicates levels of executive seniority. The first few levels are straightforward:

1. Chief executive officer or president
2. Senior vice president
3. Vice president for operations or chief operations officer (or VP for production or services; whoever is most critical to the organization's operations)

After that, the list can vary radically depending on the organization. Should the chief finance officer be next or the vice president of human resources? If the organization hasn't defined this seniority ranking, the CM plan may not be implemented in a crisis; worse, people could be injured or killed. Formal inclusion of the list in the CM plan allows the identification of an individual who can declare an emergency or crisis and begin the reaction process. This individual becomes the executive-in-charge.

The chief executive officer is primarily responsible for the implementation and control of the CM plan. If the CEO is unavailable or incapacitated, the vice president of operations, normally the second in command, takes over. The remainder of the chain of command flows according to the seniority of other vice presidents in the organization. Should all vice presidents be unavailable or incapacitated, the CM team leader serves as the executive-in-charge.

After the executive-in-charge has received notification of a crisis event, he or she determines whether to implement the CM plan, along with DR, BC, and other needed plans. The CM team then begins working to minimize the threat to personnel safety and to identify any potential loss of life or health.

Implementation

The next section provides information about the implementation of the plan, including contingencies. The organization cannot assume that telephones or data communication networks will be functional. The real skill in developing CM plans is the ability to prepare for contingencies. A good plan provides alternatives both for optimal situations—fully functioning phones, electricity, and so on—and less than optimal situations with reduced services. Actions to be taken in each situation should be identified. Key tasks include communicating with emergency services, management, and employees. Initial responsibilities for the CM team are also identified.

Crisis Management Protocols

This section provides detailed notification protocols for individuals in the organization in response to a number of common crisis or emergency events. Such events could include any of the following:

- Active shooter events
- Bomb threats
- Environmental or natural disasters
- Medical emergencies
- Off-site incidents or accidents involving employees
- Political situations such as riots or demonstrations
- Violent crime or behavior off-site that extends to the organization's facilities

Initial notification instructions should be provided for each of these emergencies so that each employee knows whom to contact and when. These initial response protocols are the first step in deploying the complete CM plan.

Crisis Management Plan Priorities

The next section details the priorities of effort for the CM team and other responsible individuals in the event a crisis or emergency is declared. This requires the establishment of a number of general priorities, each of which has subordinate priorities. This section also details the objectives for each priority level. First-level priority objectives must be accomplished as quickly as possible after the CM plan is implemented, followed by second-level and third-level priorities.

Appendices

Appendices can be attached to the CM plan. Some of the more important are the following:

- *Communications roster*—This roster contains office, home, and mobile phone numbers of key individuals, including management, the CM team, and emergency services and utilities.
- *Building layouts or floor plans, with emergency exits, fire suppression systems, fire extinguishers, and other emergency equipment clearly marked*—**Assembly areas** (AAs, also known as **rally points**) should also be designated. An AA could be in the parking lot in the event of a fire, in the basement or internal storm shelter in the event of a severe storm or tornado, or on the top floor or roof in the event of a flood. AAs allow the organization to quickly account for its entire staff in an area that is out of harm's way, minimizing the risk of additional injury. The crisis may also involve a criminal act, such as a terrorist attack, so the AA provides a mechanism for getting everyone out of the crime scene, thereby preventing contamination of possible evidentiary material. AAs also facilitate communication with the staff, the assessment of individual needs, and ease of access by emergency services.
- *Planning checklists detailing who should prepare what*—With proper planning, the organization knows who is responsible for what tasks, and during execution everyone knows who has the most current information. Because these checklists may be prepared for many different roles and have contingencies included for each, they often become verbose and might best be documented in the supplemental materials.

Sample CM Plan

As with the development of other CP planning documents, the organization can begin by researching CM plans from other organizations or CM planning groups. The Department of Homeland Security/FEMA site at *ready.gov* has resources to help as well.

Crisis Management Training and Testing

Training in CM follows the same blueprints and procedures that IR, DR, and BC follow. Use of regular desk checks, talk-throughs, walk-throughs, simulations, and other exercises helps prepare the organization for crises and helps keep the CM plan up to date. Training exercises that are unique to CM are described in the following sections.

Emergency Roster Tests

Emergency roster tests, also known as notification tests or alert roster tests, are performed after hours or on weekends to determine how well employees respond to a notification system, whether automated or manual. For tests to work properly, the organization should ask employees to let their supervisors know if they are leaving town for the weekend or other predetermined period of time. Tests could be conducted in one of two fashions. In the first, employees are notified by phone that they are to call a predetermined number and report in. The exercise is concluded when all employees still in the area have called in. In the second method, employees are notified by phone that they are to assemble at a predetermined place and time. On the following weekend, the alert roster is tested. To ensure that panic does not ensue, the organization may elect to include a code word or phrase to indicate that the exercise is only a test. After the employees show up, they may be given a quick overview of what the next logical step would be in a real crisis. Employees are then either dismissed or rewarded with an impromptu picnic or barbeque.

The following example case describes a test of the alert roster at HAL.

assembly area

An area where people should gather during an emergency to facilitate a quick head count.

rally point

See *assembly area*.

Examples of an Alert Roster Test at HAL

Version 1

Notice from the automated notification system:

Attention HAL employees: This is a test of the emergency notification system. All HAL employees are directed to immediately report in using the HAL-Alert application on your smartphone. Text or call to report your name and employee ID to 123-555-1212. Use a different phone if your smartphone is unavailable. This is a test; however, all employees are required to report in, even if they are traveling.

Version 2

Notice from the automated notification system:

Attention HAL employees: This is a test of the emergency notification system. All HAL employees are directed to assemble in the civic center parking lot (1234 West Avenue) at 11:00 a.m. today. This is a test; however, all employees are required to assemble unless they are out of town with prior notification to their supervisors.

Tabletop Exercises

Another common CM rehearsal involves a scenario-driven talk-through, also known as a "tabletop exercise" because most employees involved assemble around a conference table. In a technique like that presented in Module 2's opening scenario, employees are given a general scenario and a sequence of unfolding events or "injections," and then are asked to describe how they would respond. Messages can be passed around the table, simulating coordination and communication, and the entire activity can be documented. An organization could go as far as setting up temporary e-mail accounts and having all employees bring laptops to send their communications via e-mail, providing a record of the exercise. Unlike emergency roster tests, tabletop exercises are usually scheduled so employees can plan to be out of their offices for the duration of the exercise. However, it is possible to schedule an emergency roster test with a tabletop exercise immediately following it. To help smooth stressed employee nerves, however, the organization might provide some notice, as in "Keep the first weekend of the month free for the next four months, in case we need an emergency budget meeting."

Simulations

During military training exercises, individual soldiers are periodically "killed" or "wounded" by being issued "casualty cards." These cards are simulation injections to inform particular soldiers that they are the victims of some injury or illness. The soldiers then drop in place and simulate the injected condition. The soldier's team is expected to diagnose the situation, apply first aid, and process each "injured" soldier appropriately, including continuing the mission without the affected soldier.

Organizations can conduct similar simulations by first notifying employees that on one of several preselected days, a crisis can occur. The crisis will affect one or more of the organization's staff members, no notice will be given, and the remaining employees will be expected to respond accordingly, short of notifying emergency services. Some organizations may even schedule a simulation in conjunction with a fire department training exercise, notifying their local emergency response unit to provide more realism to the simulation. In either event, employees will be notified that a crisis has occurred and that they have been affected in some manner. These employees then simulate the situation, and other employees respond.

These simulations work equally well with small-scale events, such as an employee injury or illness, and with large-scale events, such as an unknown powder appearing in someone's mail. The larger the event is, the more coordination is needed and the more disruption that will occur to the business. However, disruption during a simulation is good practice for disruption during a crisis.

First-Aid Training

Although most organizations are not expected to provide emergency medical services, clinic services, or other on-site healthcare, many larger organizations have developed training and formal procedures to assist first responders in the event of medical emergencies. Although these services are most often activated to deal with individual health incidents and support local authorities and emergency medical services, they can also come into play during crisis response.

First-aid kits are useful to have available at any organization, but they do little good if people do not know how to use them properly. Whenever possible, some employees should be encouraged to have first aid and cardiopulmonary resuscitation (CPR) training. The contents of prepositioned first-aid kits need to be routinely checked to ensure that they are not outdated or missing, as it is common for employees to use first-aid items such as bandages, aspirin, or adhesive tape for everyday problems.

Beyond ubiquitous and routine first-aid kits, relatively inexpensive and easy-to-use heart defibrillators have become available in recent years. They can be strategically located within a facility and should also be checked on a set schedule. While these devices include integrated instructions, employees should still receive training for when and how to use them.

Other Crisis Management Preparations

In addition to the planning activities that the organization conducts during CM preparation, a number of elements can benefit the organization should the CM plan be needed. These include emergency kits, emergency identification cards, and medical condition notifications.

Emergency Kits

If you've ever had the lights go out in your home at night, did you remember where you stored a working flashlight? What about matches and candles? Assembling or purchasing emergency kits is a proactive way to ensure that the organization is ready for a crisis. Similar to the DR kits discussed in Module 10, these kits provide some essential components that will probably be needed in the event of a disaster or crisis. Common items found in emergency kits include the following:

- Copies of the DR, BC, and CM plans
- Laminated checklist of preliminary steps in the CM plan, for easy access during the crisis
- Laminated map with marked assembly areas and shelters, to provide information about safe places to gather in the event of emergency
- Laminated card with emergency numbers (gas, power, water, and so on) for quick reference
- Flashlight and spare batteries
- Reflective vests to allow personnel to work in low-light or adverse weather conditions
- Warning triangle to mark off potentially dangerous areas from traffic
- Caution tape to mark off potentially dangerous areas from foot or automobile traffic
- First-aid kit with rubber gloves to assist those injured in the crisis and protect those rendering assistance
- Clipboard, notepad, and pens to record important information
- Permanent markers to mark anything that needs it—even people
- Spray paint or other high-visibility markers

A permanent marker has many uses in a crisis. For example, it is a common practice among medical personnel in the military to mark the forehead or hands of people who are injured and have received first aid. Emergency services personnel arriving on the scene will then know that some medical attention has been provided. In some cases, if a person has a tourniquet applied or has a medical condition such as an allergy or diabetes, noting their condition by writing it on their body ensures that it will be noticed if no one is available to stay with the person or if the person is unconscious. Likewise, when an evacuation is under way, emergency personnel use spray paint to indicate which buildings, floors, or rooms have been searched or cleared and to indicate the status of any identified hazards.

ID and Emergency Notification Cards

A recent trend in corporate settings is to provide each employee with a crisis management identification card. This card serves two purposes. First, it serves as a quick reference for critical information in a crisis by providing an automated information notification number and emergency phone numbers. Second, it provides critical personal information if the cardholders cannot communicate the information themselves. This card is similar to the BC card from Module 11; in fact, they can be combined into a single card.

Medical Alert Tags and Bracelets

Although the protection of personal privacy is of the utmost importance to most organizations, employees who have medical conditions should provide detailed information to the organization so it can be relayed to medical staff in a crisis. Although this is covered in part by the emergency ID cards discussed in the preceding section, the use of medical alert tags or bracelets can also assist emergency service personnel. These medical notification devices should be encouraged for all personnel with allergies, diabetes, or other special conditions. Tags and bracelets help ensure that any injuries suffered during the crisis are not compounded by improper medical assistance.

POST-CRISIS TRAUMA

Soldiers aren't the only people who suffer from post-traumatic stress disorder. As organizations found out immediately after 9/11, anyone can suffer side effects from a severe traumatic episode. It is important for organizations that have just emerged from a crisis to realize that their work is not done. It is important to look out for the well-being of all individuals, not just those directly affected by the crisis. Some people might not show signs of trauma until several days after a crisis.

Post-Traumatic Stress Disorder

Post-traumatic stress disorder (PTSD) is a condition that has been known in the past by different names: shell shock, battle fatigue, or battle neurosis. The following definition comes from the National Center for PTSD:

> *PTSD is a mental health problem that some people develop after experiencing or witnessing a life-threatening event, like combat, a natural disaster, a car accident, or sexual assault. It's normal to have upsetting memories, feel on edge, or have trouble sleeping after this type of event. If symptoms last more than a few months, it may be PTSD.*[14]

Because it is a widely recognized psychiatric disorder, PTSD is not something that the typical organization will deal with. The CM plan should make preparations for fallout from PTSD, either through a specific plan within the context of CM or by using a program such as an EAP, which is discussed in the following section.

 You may find it useful to see the resources offered by the U.S. Federal Emergency Management Agency. Their page on "Coping with Disaster" can be found at *https://www.fema.gov/coping-disaster*.

Employee Assistance Programs

Even before a traumatic event, an organization should have an employee assistance program (EAP). Some institutions carry EAPs as part of their health benefits, whereas others contract on an as-needed basis. EAPs can provide a variety of counseling services to assist employees in coping with the changes in life that result from surviving a crisis. Although organizations should not simply shunt their responsibilities onto an EAP, they recognize that the EAP can be a vital component of the recovery process.

EAPs are helpful when people need to talk through issues that they are unable to deal with on their own. A humanitarian response team may be part of the CM team, and can be staffed with counselors, legal aids, medical professionals, and even interpreters.

Immediately after the Crisis

As mentioned earlier, assembly areas should be used after a crisis to gather employees, conduct head counts, and assess injuries and needs of employees. In addition to automated notification systems and supervisor head counts, the organization should consider using a buddy system to help account for employees. Pairing up employees can provide additional assistance in identifying missing or injured staff. It also ensures that employees are not left alone without at least one person to talk to.

After the crisis has passed and employees are accounted for and treated, they can be formally released by management. Organizations should resist the urge to move employees out of AAs as quickly as possible. The constant flow of employees through the AAs can result in some individuals "falling between the cracks." This occurs when a supervisor or manager thinks an employee has been accounted for by another supervisor or manager. By marshaling all employees in the AAs, a positive accountability can be obtained, ensuring that no individual is left behind and that no one leaves without needed medical assistance. The stress of the crisis may also cause shock and lead to lingering adverse effects if allowed to develop unchecked, as described in the section on PTSD. Employees suffering from shock should not be allowed to drive themselves home and should be escorted by a friend or appropriate emergency personnel.

Before allowing employees to leave, it is helpful to hold one final information briefing to provide them with an overview of what happened, who was affected, and what the organization's next course of business will be. If the crisis caused the implementation of the DR plan or BC plan, now is the time to advise the staff when and where they should report for work next. It is also beneficial to advise employees not to speak with the media. Although people may desire their "15 minutes of fame," the media have a tendency to report the worst of an incident, so all communications should be routed through the CM communications officer via formal press releases.

Dealing with Families

A complete CM plan prepares the organization's management and staff to interact with family members, especially if serious injury or loss of life has occurred. These family members will be angry and frustrated by insufficient information. They may lash out at anyone they believe is responsible for their loved one's situation. In some cases, professional assistance may be needed from legal counsel, grief counselors, and employees formally trained to deal with these situations. Organizations should always try to follow up with employees who receive medical care at clinics or hospitals. The "we care" attitude that organizations wish to portray can only be reinforced through personal interaction. Visiting injured employees or grieving families can serve to reassure people that the organization is committed to helping them through their issues.

GETTING PEOPLE BACK TO WORK

After the organization has called employees back to work following a crisis, whether at the primary site or an alternate site, it is helpful for executive management to again conduct a briefing of all employees, either directly or through managers and supervisors. Employees will be starved for information, and without the facts, the rumor mill will run rampant. Providing employees with facts about the crisis, management's response, the impact on the organization, and plans to recover will ease employees' concern about the security of their jobs and the welfare of their coworkers, and it will assist in providing closure to the crisis. The inclusion of timetables for recovery further alleviates anxiety.

Some organizations routinely use internal counseling sessions, both for individuals and groups, to allow employees to vent their feelings about the crisis. In years past, organizations would hold "critical incident stress debriefing" (CISD) sessions, in which employees were asked to recount what they had experienced. However, ongoing research of PTSD has found that, even with the best of intentions and the full engagement of those affected, the debriefing process itself may exacerbate problems following a stressful event. While no direct linkage can be shown that debriefing causes a higher rate of PTSD diagnoses, there is also no conclusive evidence that debriefing helps reduce the level of stress, nor has it been proven to shorten the period of time needed to recover from the stress.

What is fairly well understood is that crisis counseling is not a role for amateurs. Most organizations that commit to following recommended practices will use skilled crisis management professionals to monitor the affected workforce and follow up as it returns to normal operations. When needed, additional support services can be deployed to manage recovery.

Because there are mixed opinions about the value and outcomes of debriefing activities, each organization has to develop policies and practices that work within its own culture.

Dealing with Loss

One unfortunate consequence of a crisis is the loss of coworkers, supervisors, and subordinates. Whether as a reaction to a death or serious injury or simply an unwillingness to return to the workplace where the crisis occurred, some employees may leave the organization. As a result, vital skills and organizational knowledge may be lost. If organizations are not prepared for the inevitable loss of these vital assets, they may find themselves suffering from additional effects of a crisis. How can organizations prepare for the loss of skills and knowledge? Several techniques can help, including cross-training, job and task rotation, and redundancy, which are discussed in the next sections. Also, when attrition occurs in the chain of command, succession planning can shorten the time it takes to return the organization to effective operation. That topic is discussed later in this module.

Training for Crises

Cross-training is a critical responsibility: In the event of an emergency that removes employees from their jobs, others can step in during the short term to cover needed duties. Cross-training can be done using many of the formal training techniques covered in earlier modules, but it usually occurs through on-the-job training and one-on-one coaching. The challenge of preparing for cross-training is in ensuring employees that they are not being prepared for termination. This is best done by advising all employees about the cross-training program ahead of time and involving them in identifying their critical job functions. Various critical job functions within a department can then be crossed to other employees. It is not essential for the organization to cross-train all of an employee's work, but only the portion that is critical to the continued operation of the company. After a master list of critical functions is created, the supervisor can document all employees who are primarily trained to perform each function and specify which employees are qualified to perform a function should the primary person be unavailable. This list should be reviewed periodically and updated as personnel change.

Job rotation is another approach to minimize the loss of personnel from an organization. In many industries, there is a clear career progression from a lower-level position to a higher one. For example, a software developer may be initially employed as a QA analyst, then promoted to code writing, then to software analysis, and finally to project management. In an emergency, however, this person could be called upon to perform a lower-level job he used to have. This is called **vertical job rotation**.

Horizontal job rotation is the movement of employees among positions at the same level rather than through progression and promotion. In this case, employees hired to assist in one area, such as manning a help desk, could be rotated to another area, such as assisting in the installation and configuration of client workstations. The key consideration is whether the employee's movement is representative of typical career progression or is simply a change in position to prevent burnout and provide interest.

Task rotation is functionally similar to job rotation, but it only involves training in a portion of a job. Employees may rotate certain tasks, such as a software development team rotating responsibilities to document the development process or systems administrators rotating backup management responsibilities. Task rotation may be preferred for independent responsibilities but may not cover all tasks performed by an individual employee.

cross-training
The process of ensuring that every employee is trained to perform at least part of the job of another employee.

job rotation
The movement of employees from one position to another so they can develop additional skills and abilities.

vertical job rotation
A form of job rotation that involves the movement of employees to positions in the organization that are above or below their current position.

horizontal job rotation
A form of job rotation that involves the movement of employees from one position to another at the same level.

task rotation
The training of employees in a particular task so multiple employees are capable of performing it.

personnel redundancy
Hiring individuals above and beyond the minimum number of personnel needed to perform a business function.

Personnel Redundancy

Another method of providing coverage of critical skills and knowledge is through **personnel redundancy**. Personnel costs are one of the largest expenses for a business, so hiring redundant personnel may not be the best option for all of them. However, if an organization can hire a few key personnel and use them to provide redundancy to two or more key staff positions, they may find themselves better suited to handle the loss of personnel in a crisis.

 If you do not have a human resources background and want to quickly get up to speed, you may want to locate a copy of the textbook *HR*, 5th Edition, by Angelo DeNisi and Ricky Griffin. This textbook provides complete coverage of job and task rotation as well as human resources planning for crisis management.

LAW ENFORCEMENT INVOLVEMENT

Organizations should not hesitate to contact law enforcement during a crisis. These professionals are trained in skills that are specifically geared to crisis management, including crowd control, search and rescue, first aid, and physical security. For the most part, organizations only involve law enforcement in their affairs when they contact emergency services, such as by dialing 911. However, in some crises, the level of involvement may escalate quickly through state investigative agencies to federal agents and officers.

Federal Agencies

A number of federal agencies might be involved in responding to a crisis, depending on its type and scope. A few of the key agencies are discussed in the following sections.

Department of Homeland Security

The Department of Homeland Security (DHS) is the federal agency most specifically organized to handle crises, especially those that threaten the safety of U.S. citizens and potentially damage this country's infrastructure. If a crisis involves a threat to the American people, DHS (*www.dhs.gov*) is at the forefront.

Federal Emergency Management Agency

The Federal Emergency Management Agency (FEMA) was created in 1979 and integrated into DHS in 2003. Its stated mission is "Helping people before, during, and after disasters."[15] In support of its mission, FEMA has three strategic goals:

1. *Build a Culture of Preparedness—Every segment of our society, from individual to government, industry to philanthropy, must be encouraged and empowered with the information it needs to prepare for the inevitable impacts of future disasters.*
2. *Ready the Nation for Catastrophic Disasters—FEMA will work with its partners across all levels of government to strengthen partnerships and access new sources of scalable capabilities to quickly meet the needs of overwhelming incidents.*
3. *Reduce the Complexity of FEMA—FEMA must continue to be responsible stewards of the resources we are entrusted to administer. We must also do everything that we can to leverage data to drive decision-making, and reduce the administrative and bureaucratic burdens that impede impacted individuals and communities from quickly receiving the assistance they need.*[16]

FEMA also sponsors an awareness and education site to provide information on preparing for crisis: *ready.gov*, which the agency refers to simply as "Ready." FEMA describes the Ready campaign as follows:

> *Launched in February 2003, Ready is a national public service campaign designed to educate and empower the American people to prepare for, respond to, and mitigate emergencies, including natural and man-made disasters. The goal of the campaign is to promote preparedness through public involvement.*
>
> *Ready and its Spanish language version Listo ask individuals to do four key things:*
>
> 1. *Stay informed about the different types of emergencies that could occur and their appropriate responses*
> 2. *Make a family emergency plan*
> 3. *Build an emergency supply kit*
> 4. *Get involved in your community by taking action to prepare for emergencies.*[17]

In 2004, FEMA launched Ready Business, an extension of the Ready campaign that focuses on business preparedness. Ready Business provides owners and managers of small to medium-sized businesses with materials and guidance to prepare their employees, operations, and assets for an emergency. (See *www.ready.gov/business*.)

Federal Bureau of Investigation

The Federal Bureau of Investigation (FBI) deals with many crimes that are potential crises. Its mission is "to protect the American people and uphold the Constitution of the United States."[18] To fulfill that mission, it has been assigned jurisdiction over more than 200 categories of federal law, including counterterrorism, counterintelligence, cybercrime, public corruption, civil rights violations, organized crime, white-collar crime, major thefts, and violent crime.

If the crime isn't directed at the national infrastructure or doesn't affect it, the FBI may not be able to assist as effectively as state or local agencies. As a rule of thumb, however, if the crime crosses state lines, it becomes a federal matter. The FBI may also become involved at the request of a state agency, if it has the manpower to spare.

Federal Agencies for Industrial Incidents and Accidents

A number of federal agencies are tasked with intervention and investigation in the event of an accident or incident involving an organization. In the event of a criminal or terrorist act, either DHS or the FBI leads the investigation. The following federal agencies might also be involved in these types of investigations:

- The Occupational Safety and Health Administration (OSHA, at *www.osha.gov*) inspects workplaces and has regulations and guidance concerning incident investigations by employers.

- If the incident or accident involves a public transportation carrier, like a bus, train, or aircraft, the National Transportation Safety Board (NTSB, at *www.ntsb.gov*) would be the principal investigator.
- Hazardous material (HAZMAT) agencies are trained to deal with radiological, biological, or chemical threats. Whether the threat is caused by terrorists or an accident such as a train derailment, these agencies assist to contain contamination and restrict exposure to the contaminant. When these incidents are the result of a transportation accident, they are usually handled by the Pipeline and Hazardous Materials Safety Administration's Office of Hazardous Materials Safety, which is part of the U.S. Department of Transportation. (See *www.phmsa.dot.gov/about-phmsa/offices/office-hazardous-materials-safety*.)
- The Chemical Safety Board (CSB, at *www.csb.gov*) is an independent federal agency that investigates incidents and accidents involving chemicals.
- If an incident involves potentially radioactive materials, a special group from the U.S. Department of Energy's Nuclear Emergency Support Team (NEST, at *www.energy.gov/nnsa/nuclear-incident-response*) is responsible for assessment and control.
- For organizations operating on waterways and coastlines around the United States, the U.S. Coast Guard (USCG at *www.uscg.mil*) provides support, including search and rescue during emergencies, disasters, and other crises.

The Red Cross

The American Red Cross was founded by Clara Barton in 1881 and is normally associated with blood drives and donations. However, they have a long and respected history of assisting in disaster relief, support, and services for the armed forces and their families. They also provide training and certification in first aid and swimming safety, and have provided care packages to families in times of crisis. They support federal and state relief efforts to provide information, food, shelter, and counseling. They provide international efforts through partnerships with the Global Red Cross and Red Crescent societies to give vaccinations, help connect displaced families, and provide food and clean water where needed.

 For more information on the American Red Cross, visit *www.redcross.org*.

State Agencies

Most likely, an organization will interact with state agencies more frequently than federal agencies in a crisis. State agencies are willing to work with trade associations, individual businesses, and local governments to assist in emergency preparations and actual crisis management. These agencies are discussed in the following sections.

State Emergency Management Agency

Most states have some form of emergency management agency as their point of interaction with the federal DHS and FEMA. As an example, in Georgia, the mission of the Georgia Emergency Management and Homeland Security Agency (GEMA/HS) is "the protection of life and property against man-made and natural disasters by directing the state's efforts in the areas of prevention, preparedness, mitigation, response, and recovery."[19] Some states have also created agencies that are aligned with the U.S. DHS in terms of functions and roles and may have corollary relationships with state FEMA agencies. For example, GEMA/HS has a "Ready Georgia" Web page to support disaster preparation. (See *https://gema.georgia.gov/plan-prepare/ready-georgia*.)

State Investigative Services

Many states have their own versions of the FBI: a state bureau of investigation (SBI). There is a great deal of variance in the names of these agencies. In Texas, the primary state-level investigatory agency is the Texas Rangers; in Georgia, it is the GBI, and in several states, the agency is simply called the state police. These agencies may be associated with the state highway patrol, or they may be a separate entity. In most states, the SBI arrests suspects, serves warrants, and enforces state laws. The SBI may also assist local law enforcement officials in pursuing criminals if local authorities ask for help. However, the state investigative office may not have a special agency dedicated to computer crime.

State Hazardous Materials Agency

Just like the Department of Energy's HAZMAT groups, each state may have a team within its transportation department that is prepared to handle emergency spills from trucks, trains, and aircraft. Many substances carried on roadways, railways, and airways can be hazardous to local residents and businesses if spilled, incinerated, or exploded.

State Search and Rescue Agencies

A number of organizations in most states assist in the location of individuals and groups after a disaster or other crisis. Wikipedia lists a number of national and state groups at *https://en.wikipedia.org/wiki/Search_and_rescue_in_the_United_States*. These organizations work with federal agencies and local teams to coordinate emergency services, support the recovery of displaced personnel, and help provide emergency aid.

Local Agencies

Some crises may only involve local entities or agencies. Even local agencies may have special training or preparation to assist with emergencies.

Local Law Enforcement

Each county and city has its own law enforcement agency. These agencies enforce all local and state laws and handle suspects and crime scenes for state and federal cases. Local law enforcement agencies seldom have dedicated units for computer crimes, but their investigative (detective) units are usually quite capable of processing crime scenes and handling most common criminal activities, such as physical theft or trespassing, damage to property, and the apprehension and processing of suspects in computer-related crimes. Local agencies often have access to state-level agencies that can assist with the intricacies of computer crime cases.

Police Special Weapons

When an organization is confronted with terrorists or disgruntled employees, a police special weapons unit such as a SWAT (special weapons and tactics) team or SORT (special operations response team) may be called upon to handle the situation. These teams consist of elite police officers with extensive training in special weapons and tactics, and they are prepared to handle situations involving hostages, snipers, terrorists, and other high risks.

Bomb Detection and Removal

Another special police unit is the bomb detection and removal squad, also known as the bomb disposal unit or just the bomb squad. In some jurisdictions, these officers may be part of the special weapons unit; in others, they may have their own department. They are trained to deal with incendiary, explosive, or contaminating devices, including radiological, biological, and chemical agents. Their job is straightforward: Secure and remove any suspect item to a secure facility.

Search and Rescue

In addition to state and federal search and rescue organizations, many local governments and private organizations provide search and rescue support, which is useful when members of the organization remain unaccounted for after a crisis. These individuals (and specially trained animals) are also prepared to solicit and coordinate local volunteers to assist in their efforts. Search and rescue organizations also often provide first-aid and field survival training for individuals and groups. These groups are often affiliated with fire and rescue departments and services.

MANAGING CRISIS COMMUNICATIONS

An essential part of keeping the organization together and functioning during and after a crisis is maintaining control of communications, both internally and externally. Some communications can be managed, including those among the crisis team, management, and employees. However, other communications may prove to be beyond the control of the organization altogether. These could include communications with law enforcement, emergency services, and especially the media.

Crisis Communications

Jonathan Bernstein of Bernstein Crisis Management, LLC offers 11 steps of crisis communications, which are reprinted here from his 2005 essay with permission.[20]

The 11 Steps of Crisis Communications

By Jonathan Bernstein

Crisis: An unstable or crucial time or state of affairs whose outcome will make a decisive difference for better or worse (Webster's New Collegiate Dictionary).

Every organization is vulnerable to crises. The days of playing ostrich are gone. You can play, but your stakeholders will not be understanding or forgiving because they've watched what happened with Bridgestone-Firestone, Bill Clinton, Arthur Andersen, Enron, WorldCom, 9-11, the Asian tsunami disaster and—even as I write this—Hurricane Katrina.

If you don't prepare, you *will* take more damage. And when I look at existing "crisis management" plans when conducting a "crisis document audit," what I often find is a failure to address the many communications issues related to crisis and disaster response. Organizations do not understand that without adequate communications:

- Operational response will break down.
- Stakeholders (internal and external) will not know what is happening and will quickly be confused, angry, and negatively reactive.
- The organization will be perceived as inept at best and criminally negligent at worst.

The basic steps of effective crisis communications are not difficult, but they require advance work in order to minimize damage. The slower the response, the more damage is incurred. So if you are serious about crisis preparedness and response, read and implement these 11 steps of crisis communications, the first eight of which can and should be undertaken before any crisis occurs.

Step 1: Identify your crisis communications team. A small team of senior executives should be identified to serve as your company's crisis communications team. Ideally, the team is led by the company CEO, with the firm's top public relations executive and legal counsel as his or her chief advisers. If your in-house PR executive does not have sufficient crisis communications expertise, he or she may choose to retain an agency or independent consultant with that specialty. Other team members should be the heads of major company divisions, to include finance, personnel, and operations.

Let me say a word about legal counsel. Sometimes during a crisis, a natural conflict arises between the recommendations of the company's legal counsel and those of the public relations counsel. Although it may be legally prudent not to say anything, this kind of reaction can land the company in public relations "hot water" as damaging as any financial or legal ramification. Fortunately, more and more legal advisors are becoming aware of this fact and are working in close cooperation with public relations counsel. The importance of this understanding cannot be overestimated. Arthur Andersen lost its case and went out of business due to the judgment rendered by the court of public opinion, not the judgment of a court of law.

Step 2: Identify spokespersons. Within each team, there should be individuals who are the only ones authorized to speak for the company in times of crisis. The CEO should be one of those spokespersons, but not necessarily the primary spokesperson. The fact is that some chief executives are brilliant business people but not very effective in-person communicators. The decision about who should speak is made after a crisis breaks, but the pool of potential spokespersons should be identified and trained in advance.

Not only are spokespersons needed for media communications, but for all types and forms of communications, internal and external, including on camera, at a public meeting, at employee meetings, and so on. You really don't want to be making decisions about so many different types of spokespersons while "under fire."

Step 3: Train spokespersons. Two typical quotes from well-intentioned company executives summarize the reason why your spokespersons should receive professional training in how to speak to the media:

"I talked to that nice reporter for over an hour and he didn't use the most important news about my organization."

"I've done a lot of public speaking. I won't have any trouble at that public hearing."

Regarding the first example, there are a good number of segments from *60 Minutes* showing people who *thought* they knew how to talk to the press. In the second case, most executives who have attended a hostile public hearing have gone home wishing they had been better prepared.

All stakeholders—internal and external—are just as capable of misunderstanding or misinterpreting information about your organization as the media, and it is your responsibility to minimize the chance of that happening.

In one example of such confusion, a completely healthy, well-managed $2 billion company's stock price dropped almost 25 percent in one day because Dow Jones reported that a prominent securities firm had made a "sell" recommendation which it later denied ever making. The damage, of course, was already done.

Spokesperson training teaches you to be prepared to respond in a way that optimizes the response of all stakeholders.

Step 4: Establish communications protocols. Initial crisis-related news can be received at any level of a company. A janitor may be the first to know there is a problem or maybe someone in the personnel department, or notification could be in the form of a midnight phone call from an out-of-town executive. Who should be notified, and where do you reach them?

An emergency communications tree should be established and distributed to all company employees, telling them precisely what to do and who to call if there appears to be a potential for crisis or an actual crisis. In addition to appropriate supervisors, at least one member of the crisis communications team, plus an alternate member, should include their cell phone, office, and home phone numbers on the emergency contact list.

Some companies prefer not to use the term *crisis*, thinking this may cause panic. Frankly, using *potentially embarrassing situations* or similar phrases doesn't fool anyone. Particularly if you prepare in advance, your employees will learn that *crisis* doesn't even necessarily mean "bad news," but simply "very important to our company, act quickly."

Step 5: Identify and know your stakeholders. Who are the stakeholders that matter to your organization? Most organizations care about their employees, customers, prospects, suppliers, and the media. Private investors may be involved. Publicly held companies have to comply with Securities and Exchange Commission and stock exchange information requirements. You may answer to local, state, or federal regulatory agencies.

Step 6: Decide on communications methods. For each stakeholder group, you need to have complete lists of e-mail addresses, postal addresses, fax numbers, and phone numbers prepared to accommodate rapid communication in time of crisis. You also need to know what type of information each stakeholder group is seeking, as well as the best way to reach each of your contacts.

Another thing to consider is whether you have an automated system established to ensure rapid communication with those stakeholders. You should also think about backup communications options, such as toll-free numbers for emergency call-ins or special Web sites that can be activated in times of crisis to keep various stakeholders informed and to conduct online incident management.

Consider these factors in advance and rapid communication during crises will be relatively easy.

Step 7: Anticipate crises. If you're being proactive and preparing for crises, gather your crisis communications team for long brainstorming sessions on all the potential crises that can occur at your organization. There are at least two immediate benefits to this exercise:

- You may realize that some of the situations are preventable by simply modifying existing methods of operation.
- You can begin to think about possible responses, about best-case and worst-case scenarios, and so on. Better now than when under the pressure of an actual crisis.

In some cases, of course, you know that a crisis is going to occur because you're planning to create it, such as laying off employees or making a major acquisition. Then, you can proceed with Steps 9 through 11 below, even before the crisis occurs.

There is a more formal method of gathering this information that I call a "vulnerability audit," about which more information is available at my Web site, *www.bernsteincrisismanagement.com*.

Step 8: Develop holding statements. Although full message development must await the outbreak of an actual crisis, "holding statements"—messages designed for use immediately after a crisis breaks—can be developed in advance to be used for a wide variety of scenarios to which the organization is perceived to be vulnerable, based on the assessment you conducted in Step 7 of this process. An example of holding statements by a hotel chain with properties hit by a natural disaster—before the company headquarters has any hard factual information—might be:

- "We have implemented our crisis response plan, which places the highest priority on the health and safety of our guests and staff."
- "Our hearts and minds are with those who are in harm's way, and we hope that they are well."
- "We will be supplying additional information when it is available and posting it on our Web site."

The organization's crisis communications team should regularly review holding statements to determine if they require revision and whether statements for other scenarios should be developed.

Step 9: Assess the crisis situation. Reacting without adequate information is a classic "shoot first and ask questions afterwards" situation in which you could be the primary victim. But, if you've done all of the above first, it is a "simple" matter of having the crisis communications team on the receiving end of information coming in from your communications tree, ensuring that the right type of information is being provided so that you can proceed with determining the appropriate response.

Assessing the crisis situation is, therefore, the first crisis communications step you can't take in advance. But if you haven't prepared in advance, your reaction will be delayed by the time it takes your in-house staff or quickly hired consultants to run through Steps 1 to 8. Furthermore, a hastily created crisis communications strategy and team are never as efficient as those planned and rehearsed in advance.

Step 10: Identify key messages. With holding statements available as a starting point, the crisis communications team must continue developing the crisis-specific messages required for any given situation. The team already knows, categorically, what type of information its stakeholders are looking for. What should those stakeholders know about the crisis? Keep it simple—have no more than three main messages for all stakeholders and, as necessary, some audience-specific messages for individual groups of stakeholders.

Step 11: Ride out the storm. No matter what the nature of a crisis … no matter whether it's good news or bad … no matter how carefully you've prepared and responded … some of your stakeholders are not going to react the way you want them to. This can be immensely frustrating. What do you do?

- Take a deep breath.
- Take an objective look at the reaction(s) in question. Is it your fault, or their unique interpretation?
- Decide if another communication to those stakeholders is likely to change their impression for the better.
- Decide if another communication to those stakeholders could make the situation worse.
- If, after considering these factors, you think it's still worth more communication, then take your best shot!

Final words. "It can't happen to me." When a healthy organization's CEO or CFO looks at the cost of preparing a crisis communications plan, either a heavy investment of in-house time or retention of an outside professional for a substantial fee, it is tempting for them to fantasize that *it can't happen to me* or *if it happens to me, we can handle it relatively easily*.

I hope that type of ostrich playing is rapidly becoming a thing of the past. Yet I know that thousands of organizations hit by Hurricane Katrina will have, when all is said and done, suffered far more damage than would have occurred with a fully developed crisis communications plan in place. This has also been painfully true for scores of clients I have served over the past 23 years. Even the best crisis management professional is playing catch-up—with more damage occurring all the time—when the organization has no crisis communications infrastructure already in place.

I would like to believe that organizations worldwide are finally "getting it" about crisis preparedness, whether we're talking about crisis communications, disaster response, or business continuity. Certainly client demand for advance preparation has increased dramatically in the past several years, at least for my consultancy. But I fear that there is, in fact, little change in what I have said in the past, that 95 percent of American organizations remain either completely unprepared or significantly underprepared for crises. And my colleagues overseas report little better, and sometimes worse statistics.

Choose to be part of the prepared minority. Your stakeholders will appreciate it!

Avoiding Unnecessary Blame

An unfortunate consequence of any crisis is the human need to place blame. Whether a crisis comes from nature or is caused by human action, the media seek to assign responsibility, especially if there are casualties. For example, some may say that the organization's management didn't do enough to prepare for the crisis, they reacted too slowly, they reacted inappropriately, or they just didn't react. Sometimes, accountability is entirely appropriate, especially if negligence is a factor. But accidents do happen and people get hurt or killed. The organization's challenge is to stay prepared to respond.

There is a significant difference between fault and blame. Fault occurs when management had a responsibility to do something in line with due diligence or due care, but didn't do anything or did the wrong things. Blame is simply a human response that is part of dealing with the inexplicable tragedy associated with loss. If an organization experiences a disaster for which it feels it is not at fault, there are steps to take to avoid being blamed. These are discussed in the following sections.[21]

Examine Your Vulnerabilities

Look for situations that could be interpreted as blameworthy if they escalated to crises. Start with the BIA and then move through the CM plan. Is there anything more the organization could reasonably be expected to do to prevent an event or better prepare for one? Will the planned reaction create further risk to employees or to others? If the CM plan goes as expected for each crisis, would the organization be satisfied with how it is portrayed in the media, or would the media aftermath be embarrassing?

Manage Outrage to Defuse Blame

An organization should be ready to show off how prepared it was for an emergency. Whether the emergency is caused by a natural event or human action, the ability to demonstrate preparedness can go a long way toward warding off blame. If the crisis occurs on company property or is in some way related to the functions of the organization, one way it can defuse the outrage that will follow is to be seen as seeking and accepting responsibility for the event. For example, Tylenol's actions in the 1980s not only saved the company, they served as a case study for how to handle a crisis.

Press reports from the period reveal how McNeil Consumer Products, a subsidiary of Johnson & Johnson, dealt with a major crisis in 1982. It emerged when seven people from Chicago died after using the company's Extra-Strength Tylenol product. Later, an investigation found that the capsules had been contaminated with cyanide. The news created a nationwide panic as consumers quickly heard about the event with little in the way of facts about how and why the poisoning had occurred.

Professionals in the field of consumer product marketing announced their collective opinion that the Tylenol brand was doomed. McNeil believed otherwise and crafted an aggressive public relations campaign backed up with even more aggressive actions by the senior management at Johnson & Johnson. Those managers spared no expense in issuing a massive recall to demonstrate that customer safety was the company's top priority, ahead of profit. The initial phase involved a product recall and advertising to alert consumers to the concern. The company told customers to avoid consuming the product until the exact nature of the poisoning could be determined. In the meantime, product advertising and marketing programs were stopped and all product was removed from the market—31 million bottles of the product with a retail value of over $100 million was put at risk.[22]

Johnson & Johnson went even further, offering to swap new Tylenol tablets for the old ones that customers had in their homes. Also, its executives were seen mourning at the funerals of the poisoned victims. After the first phase of the Johnson & Johnson plan was complete, less than six weeks after the poisonings, the company set out to recover from the crisis. It began by reintroducing Tylenol capsules in industry-leading, triple-seal, tamper-resistant packaging, becoming the first organization to comply with the Food and Drug Administration's mandates. As the *Kansas City Times* described it, "The package has glued flaps on the outer box, which must be forcibly opened. Inside, a tight plastic seal surrounds the cap and an inner foil seal-wraps over the mouth of the bottle…. The label carries the warning: 'Do not use if safety seals are broken.'"[23]

Johnson & Johnson continued to manage the public's outrage by flooding the market with discount coupons and discounted retail pricing. A new, bold advertising campaign was launched. The company directed some heavy marketing at medical professionals, asking for testimonials to support the new packaging campaign. In the end, Johnson & Johnson returned to its trusted position, perhaps stronger than it was previously. Its handling of the Tylenol crisis is still being studied in schools around the world as an example of what to do in a crisis.

Questions to Help Avoid Blame

To further address issues that could cause blame and thus affect the organization after a disaster, it should finalize its planning by asking the following questions, even of the training scenarios it undertakes:

- Should you have foreseen the incident and taken precautions to prevent it?
- Were you unprepared to respond effectively to the incident after it occurred?
- Did management do anything intentionally that caused the incident to occur or that made it more severe?
- Were you unjustified in the actions you took leading up to and following the incident?
- Is there any type of scandal or cover-up related to your involvement in the incident?[24]

The answers to these questions may reveal inadequacies in the planning or training process. Fortunately, if these inadequacies are discovered in time before an actual emergency, the organization can avoid unnecessary blame and react more quickly to a crisis.

 As mentioned in earlier modules, some valuable first-person advice on dealing with crisis communications can be found in Lanny Davis' 2002 book, *Truth To Tell: Tell It Early, Tell It All, Tell It Yourself: Notes from My White House Education*. Used copies are widely available and offer a glimpse into this fascinating area of professional communications.

SUCCESSION PLANNING

When a loss of life occurs during a crisis, it is extremely difficult for individuals to function afterward, particularly when the death was witnessed by other members of the organization. When the organization's chain of command is broken and post-traumatic stress among the survivors hampers action, there are several key plans an organization can use to help employees continue to function and allow it to continue operating. One such plan is called **succession planning (SP)**, whereby the organization prepares for the possibility of losing key leadership by specifying who takes charge if the top executive is unavailable. At the federal level, succession for the U.S. presidency is specified in the 25th Amendment of the Constitution and subsequent laws. The following material explains the key elements of succession planning and then discusses the two ways that SP is typically used.

Elements of Succession Planning

SP is widely recognized in corporate settings as an essential executive-level function. Ensuring the orderly succession of promotions through the ranks does not happen smoothly unless carefully managed. The approach to SP discussed here draws heavily from the work of Dr. Michael Beitler, an academic researcher and industry consultant. Beitler recommends a six-step model to direct what senior management of an organization should do:

1. Ensure alignment between the strategic plan of the organization and the intent of the SP process.
2. Strive to identify the key positions in the organization's staffing plan that should be protected by SP processes.
3. Seek out the current and future candidates for these critical positions from the members of the organization.
4. Develop training programs and development opportunities to make sure that potential successors to key positions are ready when needed.
5. Integrate the SP process into the organization's culture to make sure that line management implements the intent of the SP process, and not merely the minimum requirements.
6. Make sure that the SP process is complementary to staff development programs throughout the HR functions of the organization.[25]

Each of these management objectives is discussed in the following sections.

Alignment with Strategy

Every aspect of an organization's structure and operations should be aligned with its strategic planning needs, as articulated by the organization's values statement and mission statement. The SP and CP processes are no exceptions. The best SP process is created to meet the current and future needs of the organization's strategic plan as well as the needs indicated by the CP process. The strategic plan of the modern organization is not a static one. Likewise, the SP must maintain its alignment with the organization's other planning initiatives. For instance, if a company reorganizes into three divisions instead of four, the SP should be revised to reflect the new structure. One way of improving the plan's chances for success is to make the same people responsible for the strategic plan and for verifying the currency of the alignment with interconnected plans, specifically the SP.

Like all well-formed planning tools, the SP must include its own mission statement or statement of purpose and represent a uniquely customized approach for the needs of the specific organization for which it is developed.

Identifying Positions

After alignment with the overall strategic and CP needs is assured, the SP process identifies the key positions that should be included. The metrics typically used to identify these key positions are that the loss of an incumbent will cause great economic loss, result in significant disruption of operations, or create a significant risk to secure operations of critical systems. The thresholds for economic loss, degree of disruption, and increased risk must be established by the executives responsible for the SP process.

succession planning (SP)

A process that enables an organization to cope with any loss of personnel with a minimal degree of disruption by predefining the promotion of internal employees.

After the key positions have been identified, the critical competencies and skills for each position must be identified. This step should not simply be a restatement of the incumbents' credentials, nor should it be an elaborate upgrading to some desired degree of competence in future candidates. Rather, it needs to be a reasoned assessment of needs stated in general terms to permit a reasonable degree of success in matching future candidates while ensuring successful deployment of selected candidates for key positions.

Identifying Candidates

As a rule, managers tend to seek out and advance candidates who are similar to themselves. In itself, this is not a bad thing to do, as long as it is not the sole criterion for identifying candidates. Performance appraisals, especially those that include subordinates and peers, must be a significant part of the assessment process. Top-down evaluations of performance are not adequate to the task, as they leave a blind spot in the process where the self-perpetuating nature of the executive community comes to dominate.

When possible, validated psychological assessments of viable candidates should be collected and considered as part of the assessment process. A more complete picture of the candidates is revealed by documenting their goals and objectives and reviewing their self-assessments. This process will yield a very useful in-depth chart showing multiple candidates for each key position.

Developing Successors

Members of the organization who are identified in the SP process as potential successors to key positions should have career development plans defined by their managers and by the HR department. These objectives are not separate from routine goal-setting and assessment activities undertaken for all members of the organization; rather, SP objectives should be added to and then integrated with routine objective setting and HR assessment. In addition to expected training and development activities, such as skills training, seminars, and education, SP candidates should have access to company-specific development activities, including mentoring and other real-time learning opportunities. Employees designated for the SP process are usually informed of the organization's intentions, which are a factor in planning their career progression.

Integration with Routine Processes

To get the maximum value out of the SP process, it must be operated by line managers who form the core of the organization's executive team. The key tasks of identifying positions and candidates and developing them to be ready when needed cannot be delegated to the HR department. Rather, line managers must be held accountable for these tasks.

Balancing SP and Operations

The SP process is part of the fabric of management execution in an organization. As such, it is but one of many things that managers are accountable for—in other words, it is important, but no more so than many of the planning, organizing, leading, and controlling activities common to managers everywhere. The challenge is to make sure that SP is considered no less important than other management activities and that each part of the SP process is integrated into the daily fabric of management decision making.

Succession Planning Approaches for Crisis Management

Most large and many medium-sized organizations already have SP programs in place. Organizations that do not are cautioned that all CM plans must include provisions for dealing with losses in key positions, as described earlier. A more complete CM plan should include a more complete approach to SP. Regardless of the degree of SP being deployed, however, one decision that should be built into the plan is the degree of visibility the SP process will have within the organization.

Visibility—or, as some call it, transparency—is the amount of information about SP that members of the organization have prior to their need to know about it. The two extremes of transparency discussed in the following sections illustrate the concepts involved. One extreme is an approach in which all employees who participate in SP (and many who don't) are aware of the process, know how they fit into it, and have a set of preconceived notions about how succession works in the organization. At the opposite extreme is an approach in which the SP process is kept from members' awareness until they need to know the details.

Operationally Integrated Succession Planning

In the more visible of the two approaches, the SP process is one or more of the following:

- Fully developed as a supervisory process in the organization
- Fully integrated into the routine management processes of the organization
- Well known to the current incumbents of key positions
- Well known to potential successors to those key positions

Organizations that take this approach do not need to make special provisions for SP when integrating it into their contingency processes. They are well on their way to creating resilient organizations that can sustain themselves in the face of great adversity and even the most trying of crises.

Crisis-Activated Succession Planning

At the other end of the spectrum is the concealed version of SP. One of the issues facing organizations that take this approach is the desire to conceal details about SP for critical business roles. Some organizations may choose not to reveal their SP processes for a variety of valid reasons, including a desire to avoid alarming employees or revealing critical information to competitive intelligence-gatherers. These organizations must develop contingent SPs using less open methods than an integrated plan would use. If a concealed SP process is used, the mechanisms for filling vacant key positions must become part of the CM plan, and the complexities this process creates must be built into the plan.

 If you want to learn more about succession planning, the book *Effective Succession Planning: Ensuring Leadership Continuity and Building Talent from Within* by William Rothwell will help you.

INTERNATIONAL STANDARDS IN IR, DR, AND BC

Until now, this module has focused on crisis management. This final section shifts gears a bit to discuss international standards that affect incident response, disaster recovery, and business continuity. Why are these standards important? In general, the larger the organization is, the more likely it is to have global reach. Many of these standards are governed by laws from other countries and worldwide organizations. Organizations that operate internationally may find that compliance with global standards is one way to meet the requirements of most or all of the countries in which they operate. Also, in the current commercial climate of globalization, organizations benefit from having contingency and continuity plans that incorporate variations in laws and standards; this approach can help ensure compliance to the greatest extent possible in each country where the organization operates.

A number of U.S. and international standards provide guidance for various certifications and implementation of contingency planning. Although organizations within the United States are advised to consider the guidance of the NIST series, given that it is specifically focused on U.S. organizations and agencies, knowledge of other standards may provide additional perspectives and insights into the organization and structure of CP groups.

NIST Standards and Publications in IR, DR, and BC

NIST offers a number of documents to support the development of contingency teams and planning groups. The primary document for IR is SP 800-61, Revision 2, "Computer Security Incident Handling Guide" (*https://nvlpubs.nist.gov/nistpubs/SpecialPublications/NIST.SP.800-61r2.pdf*). NIST notes that in recent years, threats have become more stealthy and slower to spread, but they lead to larger losses. The early detection of these kinds of crises is essential in countering the potential for loss that they represent.[26] The primary NIST document for DR and BC is SP 800-34, Revision 1, "Contingency Planning Guide for Federal Information Systems" (*https://nvlpubs.nist.gov/nistpubs/Legacy/SP/nistspecialpublication800-34r1.pdf*).

ISO Standards and Publications in IR, DR, and BC

The ISO is headquartered in Geneva, Switzerland, and represents standards-setting organizations from 163 nations. It develops and publishes international standards for a wide variety of subject areas. The ISO seeks to develop consensus solutions to meet business and government needs while serving the broader needs of society. Because the organization is international, it named itself using the Greek word *isos*, which means "equal." The name of the organization is ISO, regardless of the language being used.[27]

ISO/IEC 27031:2011

ISO/IEC 27031:2011, "Guidelines for information and communication technology readiness for business continuity," is the ISO standard that focuses on the IT aspects of IR and BC. It describes readiness activities for information and communication technology (ICT); these activities encompass all the actions organizations take to continue operations when the unexpected happens. It is meant to apply to organizations of all sizes and types, including government agencies and private enterprises. The scope of the standard includes all events and incidents that might threaten the continued operation of the ICT infrastructure. Even though the document is from 2011, ISO reports that it was reviewed in 2020 and confirmed as current.[28]

Sections of this document include the following:

- *Overview of IR/BC*—The role of IR/BC in BC management, the principles and elements of IR/BC, and its outcomes and benefits. This section also addresses managerial responsibilities and commitment to the IR/BC program.
- *IR/BC planning*—Resources, staff competencies, IR/BC strategies, and organizational IR/BC capabilities. This section also addresses readiness performance criteria.
- *Implementation and operation*—Implementing elements of the IR/BC strategies, planning documents, and IR/BC document controls.
- *Monitor and review*—Monitoring, detection, and analysis of threats; testing and exercises; audits and managerial reviews; and readiness-performance criteria measurement.
- *IR/BC continuous improvement*[29]

ISO 22301:2019

ISO 22301:2019, "Business continuity management systems — Requirements," specifies what must be done to implement a BC management system (BCMS) that can be certified as complying with the requirements of the standard. It is meant to apply to organizations of all sizes and types, including government agencies and private enterprises. The standard emphasizes meeting business needs, having capacity and resilience to manage events that may occur, describing how the BCMS can be measured for performance and effectiveness, and ensuring ongoing improvement of the BCMS.[30]

Whereas the 27031 standard focuses on the IT aspects of BC management, the 22301 standard focuses more on organizational aspects.

The structure of the standard is as follows:

- *Section 1*—The scope of the plan
- *Section 2*—Normative reference
- *Section 3*—Terms and definitions
- *Section 4*—Context of the organization, including understanding the organization, its needs, and the scope of the management system relative to the business
- *Section 5*—Leadership, including organizational roles, responsibilities, and authorities
- *Section 6*—Planning, including objectives and plans to achieve them
- *Section 7*—Support, including resources, competence, awareness, and communication
- *Section 8*—Operation of the BCMS
- *Section 9*—Performance evaluation, including monitoring, measurement, analysis, and evaluation
- *Section 10*—Continuous improvement[31]

ISO 22320:2018

ISO 22320:2018 is ISO's primary standard for crisis management. Even though it is labeled as "Emergency management – Guidelines for incident management," it is intended to help organizations respond to disasters, social disruptions, or other significant incidents. It contains recommendations for crises and disasters. It also presents summaries of recommended global practices for maintaining organizational command and control as well as essential business cohesion in the face of disruptive events. In addition, it specifies processes and techniques that can assist organizations in preparing plans that help maintain operational stability.[32]

ISO 22320:2018 focuses on establishing and operating an incident management process and structure. The incident management process is shown in Figure 12-3.

The ISO 22320:2018 incident management structure includes the following basic functions.

a. *Command: authority and control of the incident; incident management objectives structure and responsibilities; ordering and release of resources.*

b. *Planning: collection, evaluation, and timely sharing of incident information and intelligence; status reports, including assigned resources and staffing; development and documentation of incident action plan; information gathering, sharing, and documentation.*

c. *Operations: tactical objectives; hazard reduction; protection of people, property, and environment; control of incident and transition to recovery phase.*

d. *Logistics: incident support and resources; facilities, transportation, supplies, equipment maintenance, fuel, food service, and medical services for incident personnel; communications and information technology support.*

e. *Finance and administration: compensation and claims; procurement; costs and time. (Depending on the scale of an incident, a separate financial and administrative function may not be necessary.)[33]*

Other Standards and Publications in IR, DR, and BC

NIST and ISO are not the only agencies in the world that have functional standards for IR, DR, and BC. A few of the better-known standards are introduced next.

BSI

The British Standards Institute (BSI) is the British equivalent of ISO. According to the organization's Web site:

BSI is appointed by the UK Government as the national standards body, holds the Royal Charter, and represents UK interests at the International Organization for Standardization (ISO), the International Electrotechnical Commission (IEC), and the European Standards Organizations (CEN, CENELEC, and ETSI). Formed in 1901, BSI was the world's first national standards body.[34]

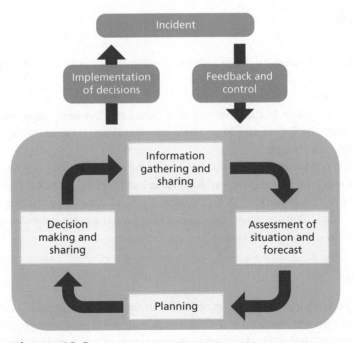

Figure 12-3   ISO 22320:2018 incident management process[35]

Source: ISO

BSI is a nonprofit organization with over 31,000 standards and is considered by many people as the father of several international standards, including the ISO 27000 series (information security management systems), the ISO 9000 series (quality management), and ISO 14000 (environmental management systems). The standards important to the topic of crisis management include the following:

- *PD 25666:2010, Business Continuity Management: Guidance on Exercising and Testing for Continuity and Contingency Programs*—PD 25666 shares practical guidelines to help organizations and enterprises run effective business continuity programs, including testing and specific arrangements for information technology systems. PD 25666 provides a best practice framework for the management of any organization that would like to engage in exercise activities. This standard also describes the processes to define the aim and objectives of exercises, present a business case, and build a program to develop the competence of personnel through training.[36]
- *PD 25111, Business Continuity Management: Guidance on Human Aspects of Business Continuity*—PD 25111 gives best practice guidelines for the planning and development of human resource strategies and policies after an incident to ensure business continuity. This includes coping with immediate effects, managing people and their families during the continuity stage, and supporting employees after normal business practices have been restored. The causes of disruption or incidents are diverse, so it's important for the management of enterprises and organizations to develop plans that minimize the consequences to the best of their ability.[37]
- *BS 25999, Business Continuity Management*—BS 25999 is made up of two parts. Part 1, "Code of Practice," provides best practice recommendations to help organizations put the requirements for BCMS in place.[38] Part 2, "Specification," describes the requirements for a BCMS.[39] This standard evolved into ISO 22301, which was described earlier.

FFIEC

Another document worth mentioning is "Business Continuity Management" from the Federal Financial Institutions Examination Council's (FFIEC) IT Examination Handbook InfoBase (*https://ithandbook.ffiec.gov/media/296178/ffiec_itbooklet_businesscontinuitymanagement_v2.pdf*). This free document provides a valuable resource for anyone looking for additional information on a range of community topics, such as risk management, IR, and CM. Although not a formal standard, it is a useful supplemental reference in developing continuity programs.

Closing Scenario

A few days after attending Alan Hake's funeral, Marie LeFleur, Alan's former assistant, was sitting at home on a Sunday morning. The phone rang.

"Hello?" Marie said, without much enthusiasm.

"Marie, this is Jake Blues," the voice on the other end of the line said. "I've been appointed interim CEO by the HAL board of directors. They have retained my firm to step in and help with this crisis. I realize this is probably a bad time for you, but can you meet me at the office in an hour?"

"I guess so," Marie said. "I don't know you. Do you have anything in writing? Why are we meeting on a Sunday?"

"I can't get into it over the phone, Marie," Jake replied. "Please just meet me at the office as soon as you can. I will have the verification you need. We have a lot of work to do, and quickly, if HAL wants to stay open as a viable business. I've been told by the board that I have 72 hours to reconstitute senior leadership from the current ranks or they will liquidate the company. I need your help contacting key members of the staff."

Discussion Questions

1. Review the organizational charts shown in Figures 12-4 through 12-7. Who should be in charge of the company at this moment, in your opinion? Why do you think that person is not now acting for the board?
2. Who decides which executive should take charge when senior managers are lost? Is that answer different in the short term than in the long term?

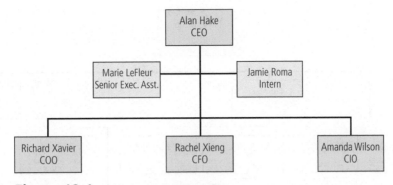

Figure 12-4   HAL's top-level staff

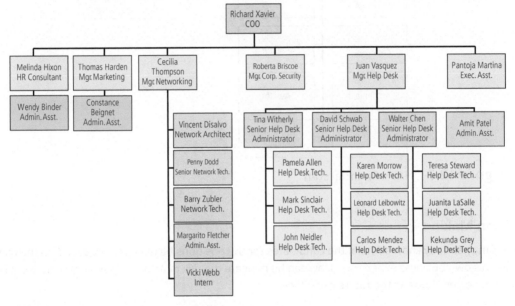

Figure 12-5   HAL's operations staff

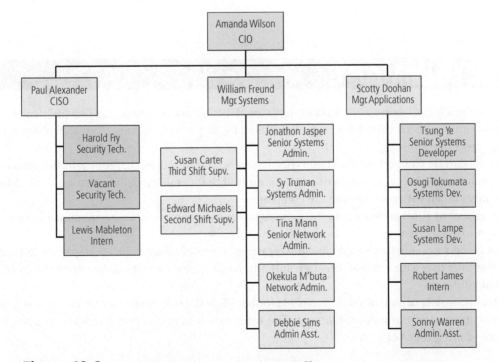

Figure 12-6   HAL's information technology staff

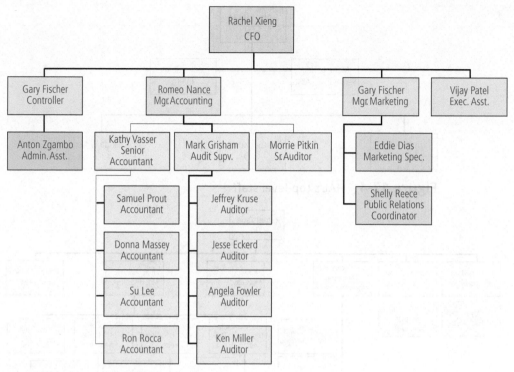

Figure 12-7   HAL's financial staff

Ethical Decision Making

Clearly, Jake Blues may already know some of the candidates for the positions he needs to fill, based on the company's organization chart and his own business experience. How can he mitigate the risk of actual or perceived conflicts of interest as he makes contacts and begins choosing the future executives?

MODULE SUMMARY

- A crisis is a significant business disruption that stimulates media coverage and has political, legal, financial, or governmental impacts. Crises are typically caused by acts of nature, mechanical problems, human error, or management decisions.
- Crisis events can be categorized into two types based on the rate of occurrence and the amount of warning time the organization has. A sudden crisis is a disruption that occurs without warning. A smoldering crisis is not generally known within or outside the company.
- Crisis management (CM) is defined as the actions taken by an organization to minimize injury or loss of life in response to an emergency.
- The crisis planning committee should include representatives of all appropriate departments and disciplines and is most effective with a mix of creative and analytical types. An outside consultant can offer objective advice and guidance.
- The CM team consists of individuals responsible for handling the response in a crisis situation. Team members are trained and tested through simulations. The team exists to protect core assets—people, finances, and reputation—during times of crisis.

- The CM team needs to know what kind of notification system the organization requires, the state of any existing CM plans, which internal operations must be kept confidential to prevent embarrassment or damage to the organization's reputation, current appointments of official spokespersons for the organization, what information should be shared with the media in the event of a crisis, and details about crises the organization has faced in the past.
- The critical success factors for CM are leadership, speed of response, a robust plan, adequate resources, funding, caring and compassionate response, and excellent communications.
- The CM team must work from a document that serves as both policy and plan and that should contain the following sections: the purpose, identification of a CM planning committee, a list of crisis types, the CM team structure, the team's responsibilities and control, implementation, CM protocols, CM plan priorities, and appendices.
- Training exercises unique to CM include emergency roster tests, tabletop exercises, and simulations.
- In addition to planning activities, other efforts can benefit the organization should the CM plan be needed, including emergency kits, emergency identification cards, and medical alert notifications.
- After the organization has called employees back to work following a crisis, the executive management should brief all employees. Providing employees with facts about the crisis, management's response, the impact on the organization, and plans to recover will ease employees' concerns about the security of their jobs and the welfare of their coworkers.
- A number of techniques deal with keeping critical staff available during crisis situations, including cross-training, job and task rotation, and redundancy.
- Organizations should not hesitate to contact law enforcement during a crisis. U.S. federal agencies that are important to CM activities include the Department of Homeland Security, the Federal Emergency Management Agency, the Federal Bureau of Investigation, and federal hazardous materials agencies.
- Succession planning (SP) is the process that enables an organization to cope with the loss of key personnel with a minimum of disruption. It is based on a six-step model that directs an organization to ensure alignment between its strategic plan and the SP process, identify key positions, seek out candidates for critical positions, develop training programs and development opportunities, integrate the SP process into the organization's culture, and make sure the SP process complements development programs.
- NIST, ISO, and other organizations have prepared a variety of standards and supporting documents that may be needed for CM planning.

Review Questions

1. What is a business crisis?
2. What is crisis management?
3. How are crises related to incidents and disasters?
4. What is a sudden crisis? How is it different from a smoldering crisis?
5. What is emergency response?
6. What is crisis communications?
7. What is humanitarian assistance?
8. List the general CM recommended practices.
9. What is the CM planning committee, and how does it differ from the CM team?
10. Who should be on the CM planning committee? Who should be on the CM team?
11. What is a head count? How and when is it used in crisis management?
12. What are the critical success factors for CM planning?
13. What sections should be included in a CM plan?
14. What is the chain of command?
15. What is an assembly area? When and how is it used in CM?
16. What is PTSD?
17. What are EAPs? How are they used in CM?
18. When dealing with the loss of staff, what strategies can be employed?
19. What federal agencies may be involved during a crisis? What role does each play?
20. What is succession planning (SP)? Why is it an important part of CM planning?

Real-World Exercises

Exercise 12-1

Go to the Web site for the American Red Cross at *www.redcross.org*. What disaster services does it offer? Which would be beneficial for an organization in a crisis?

Exercise 12-2

Go to *www.r3c.com* and select the Our Services option. Make a list of the services this firm offers. Which of those services could a medium-sized or large company use during a situation like the COVID-19 global pandemic? Which of their services could be used even if there is no emergency or crisis? Bring your comments to class for discussion.

Exercise 12-3

Using a Web search tool or your library's electronic resources, look for stories on crises that have happened in the past six months in your region. What CM efforts, if any, mitigated the effect on local businesses and residents?

Exercise 12-4

Go to the Department of Homeland Security's Web site at *www.dhs.gov*. On the Topics menu, select Disasters. What are some of the services that the DHS offers to organizations? Locate the DHS National Response Plan brochure. Download it and read it. What information would be beneficial to organizations in CM planning?

Exercise 12-5

Do a Web search for "school crisis management plan." What information would be valuable to your institution in planning for a crisis? Does your institution have a CM plan?

Hands-On Projects

The hands-on project for this module can be accessed in the Practice It folder in MindTap or through your instructor's LMS. The virtual labs provided with this resource can help you develop practical skills that will be of value as you progress through the course.

References

1. Institute for Crisis Management. Accessed 05/14/20 from *https://crisisconsultant.com/*.
2. Institute for Crisis Management. ICM Annual Crisis Report. May 2020. Accessed 5/14/2020 from *www.crisis-consultant.com*.
3. "Integrated Crisis Management Defined." Crisis Management International. Accessed 5/14/20 from *www.prweb.com/releases/2004/05/prweb127847.htm*.
4. Institute for Crisis Management. ICM Annual Crisis Report. May 2020. Accessed 5/14/2020 from *www.crisis-consultant.com*.
5. "Summary of Contingency Planning: Crisis Management." Value Based Management.net. Accessed 5/14/20 from *www.valuebasedmanagement.net/methods_crisis_management_advice.html*.
6. Blythe, B. "The Human Side of Crisis Management." Questia. V. 66, No. 7. July 2004. Accessed 5/14/20 from *www.questia.com/magazine/1G1-120098232/the-human-side-of-crisis-management-catastrophic*.
7. Bernstein, J. "The 10 Steps of Crisis Prevention." Accessed 05/18/20 from *www.bernsteincrisismanagement.com/10-steps-crisis-prevention/*.
8. Ibid.
9. "Integrated Crisis Management Defined." Crisis Management International. Accessed 5/14/20 from *www.prweb.com/releases/2004/05/prweb127847.htm*.
10. Boynton, A., and Zmud, R. "An Assessment of Critical Success Factors." *Sloan Management Review*, 25 (Summer 1984): 17–27.
11. Rockart, J. "The Changing Role of the Information Systems Executive: A Critical Success Factors Perspective." *Sloan Management Review*, 24 (Fall 1982): 3–13.
12. Perl, D. "Critical Success Factors for Effective Crisis Management." Bernstein Crisis Management, Inc. Accessed 05/18/20 from *www.continuitycentral.com/feature0224.htm*.
13. Ibid.
14. PTSD. National Center for PTSD. U.S. Department of Veterans Affairs. Accessed 05/18/2020 from *www.ptsd.va.gov*.
15. FEMA. "About the Agency." Accessed 05/18/20 from *www.fema.gov/about-agency*.
16. FEMA. "Strategic Plan." Accessed 05/18/20 from *www.fema.gov/strategic-plan*.
17. Ready.gov. "About Ready." Accessed 5/18/20 from *www.ready.gov/about-us*.
18. FBI. "Mission & Priorities." Accessed 5/18/20 from *www.fbi.gov/about/mission*.
19. GEMA/HS. "What We Do." Accessed 5/18/20 from *gema.georgia.gov/what-we-do*.
20. Bernstein, J. "The 11 Steps of Crisis Communications." Bernstein Crisis Management, Inc. September 1, 2005. Accessed 05/18/20 from *www.bernsteincrisismanagement.com/newsletter/crisismgr050901.html*.
21. Blythe, B. "How to Avoid Blame in the Aftermath of a Crisis." Accessed 10/21/2012 from *www.cmiatl.com/news_article51.html* (now available from *web.archive.org/web/20110316035427/http://www.cmiatl.com/news_article51.html*).
22. Haberman, C. "How an Unsolved Mystery Changed the Way We Take Pills." *New York Times*. September 16, 2018. Accessed 05/18/2020 from *www.nytimes.com/2018/09/16/us/tylenol-acetaminophen-deaths.html*.
23. Goodman, H. "PR Effort Launches New Tylenol Package." *Kansas City Times*. November 12, 1982.
24. Blythe, B. "How to Avoid Blame in the Aftermath of a Crisis." Accessed 10/21/2012 from *www.cmiatl.com/news_article51.html* (now available from *web.archive.org/web/20110316035427/http://www.cmiatl.com/news_article51.html*).
25. Beitler, M. "Succession Planning." Mikebeitler.com. Accessed 05/19/2020 from *https://docplayer.net/1318014-Succession-planning-michael-beitler-ph-d-www-mikebeitler-com.html*.
26. Cichonski, P., T. Millar, T. Grance, and K. Scarfone. SP 800-61, Revision 2, "Computer Security Incident Handling Guide." National Institute of Standards and Technology. Accessed 05/19/2020 from *https://nvlpubs.nist.gov/nistpubs/SpecialPublications/NIST.SP.800-61r2.pdf*.
27. ISO. "About Us." Accessed 05/19/2020 from *www.iso.org/about-us.html*.
28. ISO. "ISO/IEC 27031:2011." Accessed 05/19/2020 from *www.iso.org/standard/44374.html*.
29. ISO. "ISO/IEC 27031:2011." Accessed 05/19/2020 from *webstore.iec.ch/publication/11304*.
30. ISO. "ISO 22301:2019." Accessed 05/19/2020 from *www.iso.org/standard/75106.html*.

31. ISO. "ISO 22301:2019(en)." Accessed 05/19/2020 from *www.iso.org/obp/ui/#iso:std:iso:22301:ed-2:v1:en*.

32. ISO. "ISO 22320:2018." Accessed 05/19/2020 from *www.iso.org/standard/67851.html*.

33. ISO. "ISO 22320:2018(en)." Accessed 05/19/2020 from *www.iso.org/obp/ui/#iso:std:iso:22320:ed-2:v1:en*.

34. BSI. "UK national standards body: The world's first national standards body." Accessed 05/19/2020 from *www.bsigroup.com/en-GB/about-bsi/uk-national-standards-body/*.

35. ISO. "ISO 22320:2018(en)." Accessed 05/19/2020 from *www.iso.org/obp/ui/#iso:std:iso:22320:ed-2:v1:en*.

36. BSI. "PD 25666:2010, Business Continuity Management: Guidance on Exercising and Testing for Continuity and Contingency Programmes." July 2010. Accessed 05/19/2020 from *shop.bsigroup.com/ProductDetail/?pid=000000000030203702*.

37. BSI. "PD 25111:2010, Business Continuity Management: Guidance on Human Aspects of Business Continuity." July 2010. Accessed 05/19/2020 from *shop.bsigroup.com/ProductDetail?pid=000000000030229830*.

38. BSI. "PD 25999-1:2006 (USA Edition), Business continuity management. Code of practice." November 2007. Accessed 05/19/2020 from *shop.bsigroup.com/ProductDetail?pid=000000000030211016*.

39. BSI. "PD 25999-2:2007 (USA Edition), Business continuity management. Specification." November 2007. Accessed 05/19/2020 from *shop.bsigroup.com/ProductDetail?pid=000000000030211018*.

GLOSSARY

acceptance risk treatment strategy The risk treatment strategy that indicates the organization is willing to accept the current level of residual risk; a conscious decision to do nothing else to protect an information asset from risk and to accept the outcome from any resulting exploitation.

access A subject's or object's ability to use, manipulate, modify, or affect another subject or object.

advance-fee fraud (AFF) A form of social engineering, typically conducted via e-mail, in which an organization or some third party indicates that the recipient is due an exorbitant amount of money and needs only a small advance fee or personal banking information to facilitate the transfer.

adverse events Events with negative consequences that could threaten the organization's information assets or operations; sometimes referred to as incident candidates.

after-action review (AAR) A detailed examination and discussion of the events that occurred during an incident or disaster, from first detection to final recovery.

alarm or **alert** An indication that a system has just been attacked or is under attack.

alarm clustering A process of grouping almost identical alarms that occur nearly at the same time into a single higher-level alarm.

alarm compaction A form of alarm clustering that is based on frequency, similarity in attack signature, similarity in attack target, or other similarities.

alarm filtering The process of classifying the attack alerts that an IDPS detects in order to distinguish or sort false positives from actual attacks more efficiently.

alert message A scripted description of the disaster that avoids impeding the notification process by consisting of just enough information so that each responder knows what portion of the DR plan to implement.

American Recovery and Reinvestment Act (ARRA) of 2009 In the privacy and security area, this law contains new reporting requirements and penalties for breaches of protected health information (PHI).

anomaly-based IDPS A type of IDPS that collects statistical summaries of known valid traffic, then compares current traffic against it in order to detect questionable traffic.

anti-forensics An attempt made by potential subjects of digital forensic techniques to obfuscate or hide items of evidentiary value.

application protocol verification A type of protocol stack verification that focuses on higher-order protocols such as HTTP, FTP, and Telnet.

application recovery A system failover strategy using software to detect the failure of the primary application server and then activate a secondary application server to accept and service client requests.

application-based IDPS (AppIDPS) A type of IDPS that monitors an application for abnormal events.

apprehend and prosecute The organizational CP philosophy for incident response and digital forensics that focuses on the collection and preservation of potential evidence when responding to and recovering from an incident, with the expectation of possibly finding and prosecuting the attacker.

archive See *data archive*.

assembly area An area where people should gather during an emergency to facilitate a quick head count.

asset The organizational resource that is being protected; can be logical, such as a Web site, software information, or data, or can be physical, such as a person, a computer system, hardware, or other tangible objects.

attack An intentional or unintentional act that can damage or otherwise compromise information and the systems that support it; can be active or passive, intentional or unintentional, and direct or indirect.

attack profile See *attack scenario*.

attack scenario A description of a typical attack, including its methodology, indicators, and broad consequences.

attack scenario end case   An estimate of the likelihood and impact of the best, worst, and most likely outcomes of an attack.

auxiliary phone alert and reporting system   See *emergency notification system*.

availability   An attribute of information that describes how data is accessible and correctly formatted for use without interference or obstruction.

availability disruption   A reduced level of service in an element of the critical infrastructure.

avoidance strategy   See *defense risk treatment strategy*.

B

back door   A malware payload that provides access to a system by bypassing normal access controls. A back door is also an intentional access control bypass left by a system designer to facilitate development.

bare metal recovery   A data recovery technique whereby the user is able to restore the entirety of a computer's operating system, applications, and data without any requirements of previously installed operating system software, essentially re-creating the computer from "bare metal" (hardware only).

behavior-based IDPS   See *anomaly-based IDPS*.

blackouts   Long-term interruptions (outages) in electrical power availability.

bot   An abbreviation of *robot*, an automated software program that executes certain commands when it receives a specific input; also called *zombie*.

breach law   A law that specifies a requirement for an organization to notify affected parties when they detect the loss of a specified type of information; may be state or local or part of an international agreement.

brownouts   Long-term decreases in the quality of electrical power availability.

brute force password attack   An attempt to guess a password by trying every possible combination of characters and numbers in it.

business continuity (BC)   The efforts of an organization to ensure its long-term viability when a disaster precludes normal operations at the primary site; usually involves the rapid relocation of an organization's critical business functions to an alternate location until it can return to the primary site or relocate to a new permanent facility.

business continuity plan (BC plan)   A plan that describes how critical business functions will continue at an alternate location after a disaster while the organization recovers its ability to function at the primary site—as supported by the DR plan.

business continuity planning (BCP)   The process of completing a set of specialized team plans that document backups, continuity strategies, and associated actions needed to restore or relocate a business.

business crisis   Any personnel-focused issue, problem, or disruption that triggers negative stakeholder reactions and potentially affects the organization's reputation, business, and financial strength.

business e-mail compromise (BEC)   The use of e-mail in fraudulent efforts to compromise the organization. BEC is often used to target executives and key employees in the organization.

business impact analysis (BIA)   An investigation and assessment of adverse events that can affect the organization, conducted as a preliminary phase of the contingency planning process, which includes a determination of how critical a system or set of information is to the organization's core processes and its recovery priorities.

business process   A task performed by an organization or one of its units in support of the organization's overall mission.

business resumption plan (BR plan)   The documented product of business resumption planning; a plan that shows the organization's intended efforts in the event of a disaster coupled with the requirement to relocate key business functions to an alternate site until the primary site can be recovered.

business resumption planning (BRP)   The actions taken by senior management to develop and implement a combined DR and BC policy, plan, and set of recovery teams.

C

C.I.A. triad   The industry standard for computer security since the development of the mainframe, based on three characteristics that describe the utility of information: confidentiality, integrity, and availability.

CEO fraud   The impersonation of executives in an effort to trick an employee into revealing confidential financial information or sending unauthorized financial transfers.

chain of command The list of officials ranging from an individual's immediate supervisor to the top executive of the organization.

chain of custody A legal record of the location of evidentiary materials and the people responsible for them.

clipping level The measured activity level at which an IDPS triggers an alert.

cloud storage See *storage as a service.*

clustering services See *application recovery.*

cold site An exclusive-use resumption strategy that provides only rudimentary services and facilities; no computer hardware or peripherals are provided.

computer forensics The use of forensic techniques when the source of evidence is a computer system.

Computer Fraud and Abuse (CFA) Act of 1986 The cornerstone of many computer-related federal laws and enforcement efforts, the CFA formally criminalizes "accessing a computer without authorization or exceeding authorized access" for systems that contain information of national interest as determined by the U.S. government.

computer security incident response team (CSIRT) An incident response team composed of technical IT, managerial IT, and InfoSec professionals who are prepared to detect, react to, and recover from an incident; may include members of the IRPT.

confidence value (or simply *confidence*) A value associated with an IDPS's ability to detect and identify an attack correctly.

confidentiality An attribute of information that describes how data is protected from disclosure or exposure to unauthorized individuals or systems.

contingency planning (CP) The actions taken by senior management to specify the organization's efforts and actions if an adverse event becomes an incident or disaster; includes incident response, disaster recovery, business continuity, and crisis management efforts, as well as preparatory business impact analysis.

contingency planning management team (CPMT) The group responsible for the overall planning and development of the contingency planning process, including the organization of subordinate teams and oversight of subordinate plans.

control, safeguard, or countermeasure A security mechanism, policy, or procedure that can successfully counter attacks, reduce risk, resolve vulnerabilities, and otherwise improve security within an organization.

cookie A small quantity of data stored on the user's computer by a Web site as a means of recording that the user has visited that Web site.

copy backup A backup of a set of specified files, regardless of whether they have been modified or otherwise flagged for backup.

crisis management (CM) An organization's set of planning and preparation efforts for dealing with potential human injury, emotional trauma, loss of life, or damage to an organization's reputation or image as a result of a disaster.

crisis management plan (CM plan) The result of the crisis management planning process; a plan designed to support the preparation for, response to, recovery from, and management of communications during a crisis.

crisis management planning (CMP) The process of preparing for, responding to, recovering from, and managing communications during a crisis.

cross-training The process of ensuring that every employee is trained to perform at least part of the job of another employee.

CSIRT reaction force A subset of the computer security incident response team responsible for reacting to a specific type of incident.

cyber kill chain A series of steps that follow stages of a cyberattack from the early reconnaissance stages to the exfiltration of data; it helps you understand, identify, and combat many cyberattack strategies and advanced persistent threats.

cyberactivists See *hacktivists.*

cyberterrorism The conducting of terrorist activities by online attackers.

D

daily backup A backup of files that were modified within a defined 24-hour period.

data archive The duplication of systems data to external media or a secondary location for the purpose of long-term retention; archival is typically mandated by policy or regulation.

data as a service A cloud computing service model whereby storage capability for data, data sets, and databases associated with the organization's applications is provided as a turnkey, on-demand service.

data backup   The duplication of systems data to external media or a secondary location to provide recovery capability in the event of data loss.

data classification scheme   A formal access control methodology used to assign a level of confidentiality to an information asset and thus restrict the number of people who can access it.

data exfiltration   The theft of organizational data, either physically or by extraction through the owners' network.

data recovery   The restoration of data from a backup or archive to a system or user who needs it.

database replication   The backup of multiple copies of a database for recovery purposes.

database shadowing   The storage of duplicate online transaction data, along with the duplication of the databases, at a remote site on a redundant server; it combines e-vaulting with remote journaling, writing multiple copies of the database simultaneously in two separate locations.

defense in depth   A strategic approach to information security in which the organization deploys multiple protection tools and technologies so that if one fails or is compromised, another will be presented between the attacker and the organization's assets; commonly involves multiple layers of policy, technology, and efforts in security education, training, and awareness programs.

defense risk treatment strategy   The risk treatment strategy that attempts to eliminate or reduce any remaining uncontrolled risk through the application of additional controls and safeguards in an effort to change the likelihood of a successful attack on an information asset; also known as the *avoidance strategy*.

degraded mode   The conduct of operations under adverse conditions.

denial-of-service (DoS) attack   An attack that attempts to overwhelm a computer target's ability to handle incoming communications, prohibiting legitimate users from accessing those systems.

desk check   The CP testing strategy in which copies of the appropriate plans are distributed to all individuals who will be assigned roles during an actual incident or disaster; each individual reviews the plan and validates its components.

dictionary password attack   A variation of the brute force password attack that attempts to narrow the range of possible passwords by using a list of common passwords and possibly including attempts based on the target's personal information.

differential backup   The storage of all files that have changed or been added since the last full backup.

digital forensics   The use of forensic techniques when the source of evidence is a digital electronic device.

disaster recovery as a service   A cloud computing service model based on provisioning of both data and computing resources on demand.

disaster recovery phase   The phase of the disaster response plan associated with the salvage of equipment and data from the affected sites.

disaster recovery plan (DR plan)   A plan that deals with the preparation for and recovery from a disaster, whether natural or man-made.

disaster recovery planning (DRP)   The preparation for and recovery from a disaster, whether natural or man-made; focuses on restoring operations at an organization's primary site or at a new permanent site.

Disaster Recovery Reform Act of 2018   These reforms acknowledge the shared responsibility for disaster response and recovery, aim to reduce the complexity of the U.S. Federal Emergency Management Agency (FEMA), and build the nation's capacity for the next catastrophic event.

disaster response phase   The phase of the disaster response process associated with implementing the initial reaction to a disaster; focuses on controlling or stabilizing the situation to the greatest degree possible.

disaster restoration phase   The phase of the disaster response plan associated with the restoration of business facilities, beginning with those most critical to the organization's operations.

disaster resumption phase   The phase of the disaster response plan associated with the return to normal business operations, beginning with those most critical to the organization.

disaster scenario   A description of the disasters that may befall an organization, along with information on their probability of occurrence, a brief description of the organization's actions to prepare for that disaster, and the best case, worst case, and most likely case outcomes of the disaster.

discovery   The component of civil law whereby one party can obtain evidence from the opposing party through specific requests for information, which usually requires formal legal requests, such as subpoenas.

disk duplexing   An approach to disk mirroring in which each drive has its own controller to provide additional redundancy.

disk mirroring   A RAID implementation (typically referred to as RAID level 1) in which the computer records all data to twin drives simultaneously, providing a backup if the primary drive fails.

disk striping   A RAID implementation (typically referred to as RAID level 0) in which one logical volume is created by storing data across several available hard drives in segments called stripes.

disk striping with parity   RAID disk striping that includes redundant data for error correction and allows reconstruction of data if some of the data or parity information is lost.

disk striping without parity   RAID disk striping without data redundancy to provide error correction.

distributed denial-of-service (DDoS) attack   A DoS attack in which a coordinated stream of requests is launched against a target from many locations at the same time using bots or zombies.

Domain Name System (DNS) cache poisoning   An attack against a DNS server that injects false data into the DNS environment so that the service responds to all requests for address resolution with an answer of the attacker's choosing; also known as DNS spoofing.

DR plan addendum   A supplemental document to the DR plan that provides information on a disaster scenario, including the trigger, notification method, and desired response times.

E

eDiscovery   The search for, collection, and review of items stored in digital format that are of potential evidentiary value based on criteria specified by a legal team.

Electronic Communications Privacy Act (ECPA) of 1986   A collection of statutes that regulate the interception of wire, electronic, and oral communications; frequently referred to as the "federal wiretapping acts."

electronic vaulting   A backup method that uses bulk batch transfer of data to an off-site facility; this transfer is usually conducted via leased lines or secure Internet connections.

emergency notification system   An information system with telephony, messaging, and e-mail integration that can be used to automate the alert notification process.

enterprise information security policy (EISP)   The high-level information security policy that sets the strategic direction, scope, and tone for all of an organization's security efforts; also known as a security program policy, general security policy, IT security policy, high-level InfoSec policy, or simply an InfoSec policy.

evasion   The process by which an attacker changes the format of the network packets and/or timing of their activities to avoid being detected by the IDPS.

evidentiary material (EM)   Any information stored electronically or on physical media that could potentially support the organization's legal or policy-based proceeding against a suspect; also known as "items of potential evidentiary value."

executive-in-charge   When the crisis or emergency arises, the ranking executive on-site who is authorized to initiate the CM plan.

expert hacker   A hacker who uses an extensive knowledge of the inner workings of computer hardware and software to gain unauthorized access to systems and information; also known as elite hackers, expert hackers often create automated exploits, scripts, and tools used by other hackers.

exploit   A technique used to compromise a system; can make use of existing software tools or custom-made software components.

exposure   A condition or state of being exposed; in information security, exposure exists when a vulnerability is known to an attacker.

F

false attack stimulus   An event that triggers alarms and causes a false positive when no actual attacks are in progress.

false negative   The failure of a technical control to react to the intended stimulus so that it goes unreported.

false positive An alert or alarm that occurs in the absence of an actual attack; can sometimes be produced when an IDPS mistakes normal system activity for an attack.

faults Short-term interruptions in electrical power availability.

Federal Trade Commission Act (FTCA) This law was recently used to challenge organizations that allegedly made deceptive claims regarding the privacy and security of customers' personal information.

filtering The process of reducing IDPS events in order to feel more confidence in the alerts received.

fingerprinting The process of gathering information about the organization and its network activities and the subsequent process of identifying network assets by a potential attacker.

footprinting The organized research and investigation of Internet addresses owned or controlled by a target organization.

forensics The use of methodical technical investigation and analysis techniques to identify, collect, preserve, and analyze objects and information of potential evidentiary value so that they may be admitted as evidence in a court of law, used to support administrative action, or simply used to further analyze suspicious events.

full backup A complete backup of the entire system, including applications, operating systems components, and data.

full-interruption testing The CP testing strategy in which all team members follow each IR/DR/BC procedure, including those for interruption of service, restoration of data from backups, and notification of appropriate individuals.

G

Gramm-Leach-Bliley (GLB) Act of 1999 (also known as the Financial Services Modernization Act) This law repeals the restrictions on banks that affiliate with insurance and securities firms; it has significant impact on the privacy of personal information used by these industries.

guest (in virtualization) See *virtual machine*.

guidelines Nonmandatory recommendations the employee may use as a reference in complying with the policy.

H

hacker A person who accesses systems and information without authorization and often illegally.

hacktivists Hackers who seek to interfere with or disrupt systems to protest the operations, policies, or actions of an organization or government agency; also called *cyberactivists*.

head count The process of accounting for all personnel—that is, determining each individual's whereabouts—during and after an emergency.

Health Information Technology for Economic and Clinical Health (HITECH) Act of 2009 (part of ARRA-2009) This law addresses privacy and security concerns associated with the electronic transmission of PHI, in part through several provisions that strengthen HIPAA rules for civil and criminal enforcement.

Health Insurance Portability and Accountability Act (HIPAA) of 1996 Also known as the Kennedy-Kassebaum Act, this law attempts to protect the confidentiality and security of healthcare data by establishing and enforcing standards and by standardizing electronic data interchange.

honeynet A network version of a honeypot; a decoy network simulation that attempts to draw attackers to it and away from actual production networks.

honeypot A decoy application or systems simulation that attempts to draw attackers to it and away from actual production systems.

honeypot farm A network version of a honeypot; a decoy network simulation that attempts to draw attackers to it and away from actual production networks; also known as a *honeynet*.

honeytoken Any system resource that is placed in a functional system but has no normal use in that system, and instead serves as a decoy and alarm, similar to a honeypot.

horizontal job rotation A form of job rotation that involves the movement of employees from one position to another at the same level.

host machine See *host platform*.

host platform The physical server (and operating system) that the virtualization application and all virtual machines run on.

host-based IDPS (HIDPS) A type of IDPS that monitors a single system for signs of attack by looking for the unauthorized creation, modification, and deletion of monitored files.

hot site An exclusive site resumption strategy that consists of a fully configured computer facility, with all services, communications links, and physical plant operations capable of being established at a moment's notice.

hot swap   A hard drive feature that allows individual drives to be replaced without powering down the entire system and without causing a fault during the replacement.

hypervisor   The specialized software that enables the virtual machine to operate on the host platform.

I

impact   An understanding of the potential consequences of a successful attack on an information asset by a threat.

inappropriate use (IU)   A category of incidents that covers a spectrum of violations by authorized users of a system who nevertheless use it in ways specifically prohibited by management; these incidents are predominantly characterized as a violation of policy rather than an effort to abuse existing systems.

incident   An adverse event that violates the security of an organization and represents a potential risk of loss of the confidentiality, integrity, or availability of its assets and ongoing operations.

incident candidate   An adverse event that is a possible incident.

incident classification   The process of evaluating the circumstances of reported events.

incident commander   The CSIRT representative in charge of the team's response to a specific incident; not to be confused with the CSIRT manager or lead.

incident containment   The process by which the CSIRT acts to limit the scale and scope of an incident and begins to regain control over the organization's information assets.

incident damage assessment   The initial determination of the scope of a breach as it applies to the confidentiality, integrity, and availability of information and information assets.

incident handler   A member of the organization's CSIRT designated to respond to a specific type of incident.

incident impact assessment   A quick determination of the extent of damage or loss and the associated cost or value associated with an incident.

incident recovery   The reestablishment to pre-incident condition of all organizational systems.

incident response (IR)   An organization's set of planning and preparation efforts for detecting, reacting to, and recovering from an incident.

incident response duty officer (IR duty officer)   The on-duty or on-call member of the CSIRT responsible for reviewing adverse events and determining whether an actual incident is ongoing and whether the CSIRT should be activated.

incident response plan (IR plan)   The documented product of incident response planning; a plan that shows the organization's intended efforts in the event of an incident.

incident response (IR) reaction strategies   Procedures for regaining control of systems and restoring operations to normalcy.

incremental backup   The duplication of only the files that have been modified since the previous incremental backup.

indicator   An activity that may signal an adverse event is under way and provide a notification of an adverse event or incident candidate.

information asset   Within the context of risk management, any collection, set, or database of information or any asset that collects, stores, processes, or transmits information of value to the organization.

information extortion   The act of an attacker or trusted insider who steals information from a computer system and demands compensation for its return or for an agreement not to disclose the information; also known as cyberextortion.

information security (InfoSec)   Protection of the confidentiality, integrity, and availability of information assets, whether in storage, processing, or transmission, via the application of policy, education, training and awareness, and technology.

information security policies   Written instructions provided by management that inform employees and others in the workplace about proper behavior regarding the use of information and information assets.

Infrastructure as a Service (IaaS)   A cloud computing service model whereby an entire computing infrastructure, including computers, operating systems, application software, and any needed network equipment, are provided as a turnkey, on-demand service.

inline sensor   A software or hardware monitor that is placed in the flow of network traffic in order to review the traffic and report back to a management application.

integrity   An attribute of information that describes how data is whole, complete, and uncorrupted.

intellectual property (IP)   Original ideas and inventions created, owned, and controlled by a particular person or organization; IP includes the representation of original ideas.

intrusion   An adverse event in which an attacker attempts to gain entry into an information system or disrupt its normal operations, almost always with the intent to do harm.

intrusion detection and prevention system (IDPS)   The general term for a collection of hardware and software that determines whether activity is present that is contrary to organization policy and represents an intrusion; also, a system with the capability both to detect and modify its configuration and environment to prevent intrusions.

intrusion detection system (IDS)   A hardware and software system capable of automatically detecting an intrusion into an organization's networks or host systems and notifying a designated authority.

intrusion prevention system (IPS)   See *intrusion detection and prevention system (IDPS)*.

issue-specific security policy (ISSP)   An organizational policy that provides detailed, targeted guidance to instruct all members of the organization in the use of a resource, such as one of its processes or technologies.

J

job rotation   The movement of employees from one position to another so they can develop additional skills and abilities.

K

knowledge-based IDPS   See *signature-based IDPS*.

L

likelihood   The probability that a specific vulnerability within an organization will be attacked by a threat.

log file monitor (LFM)   A type of IDPS that reviews log files generated by servers, network devices, and other IDPSs for attack indicators.

loss   In this context, a single instance of an information asset that suffers damage or destruction, unintended or unauthorized modification or disclosure, or denial of use.

M

maintenance hook   See *back door*.

malicious code   Computer software specifically designed to perform malicious or unwanted actions. Synonymous with *malware*.

malicious software   See *malware*.

malware   Computer software specifically designed to perform malicious or unwanted actions.

malware hoax   A message aimed at causing users to waste time reacting to a nonexistent malware threat.

managed security service provider (MSSP)   An organization that provides security services to client organizations, often remotely, including incident monitoring, response, and recovery.

man-in-the-middle   A group of attacks whereby a person intercepts a communications stream and inserts himself in the conversation to convince each of the legitimate parties that the attacker is the other communications partner.

man-made disaster   A disaster caused by people, including acts of terrorism (cyberterrorism or hactivism), acts of war, and acts that begin as incidents and escalate into disasters.

maximum tolerable downtime (MTD)   The total amount of time the system owner or authorizing official is willing to accept for a business process outage or disruption; includes all impact considerations.

media   Hardware, integral operating systems, and utilities that collect, store, process, and transmit information.

mirror port   A specially configured connection on a network device that is capable of viewing all traffic that moves through the entire device.

mirrored site   The ultimate in hot sites; it is identical to the primary site and includes live or periodic data transfers.

mitigation risk treatment strategy   The risk treatment strategy that attempts to reduce the impact of the loss caused by an incident, disaster, or attack through effective contingency planning and preparation.

mobile site   A site resumption strategy based on a service contract with a specialized vendor capable of deploying portable office facilities based on tractor-trailer recovery units that include integral power, phone, data, and HVAC cabling and services; additional options include furniture, telephones, and computer systems.

mutual agreement A shared-site resumption strategy that consists of a contract between two organizations, whereby one organization is obligated to provide necessary facilities, resources, and services until the receiving organization is able to recover from the disaster.

N

natural disaster A disaster caused by natural occurrences, such as a fire, flood, earthquake, lightning, landslide, tornado, hurricane, tsunami, electrostatic discharge, dust, or excessive rainfall.

network sniffers See *packet sniffers*.

network-attached storage (NAS) A data storage and recovery system that consists of a single device or server that attaches to a network and uses common communications methods to provide an online storage environment.

network-based IDPS (NIDPS) A type of IDPS that monitors network traffic for indications of attacks.

noise In incident response, an event that does not rise to the level of an incident; the presence of additional and disruptive signals in network communications or electrical power delivery.

novice hackers Relatively unskilled hackers who use the work of expert hackers to perform attacks.

O

open source intelligence (OSINT) Information collected from publicly available sources and used in an intelligence context.

P

packet monkeys Script kiddies who use automated exploits to engage in denial-of-service attacks.

packet sniffers Software programs or hardware appliances that can intercept, copy, and interpret network traffic.

passive sensor A software or hardware monitor that is connected to a network device, without physically being in the flow of network traffic, in order to review the traffic and report back to a management application.

penetration tester An information security professional with authorization to attempt to gain system access in an effort to identify and recommend resolutions for vulnerabilities in those systems.

personally identifiable information (PII) Information about a person's history, background, and attributes that can be used to commit identity theft; typically includes a person's name, address, Social Security number (SSN), family information, employment history, and financial information.

personnel redundancy Hiring individuals above and beyond the minimum number of personnel needed to perform a business function.

pharming The redirection of legitimate user Web traffic to illegitimate Web sites with the intent to collect personal information.

phishing A form of social engineering in which the attacker provides what appears to be a legitimate communication (usually e-mail), but it contains hidden or embedded code that redirects the reply to a third-party site in an effort to extract personal or confidential information.

Platform as a Service (PaaS) A cloud computing service model whereby one or more computing platforms suitable for use in application development and testing are provided as a turnkey, on-demand service.

policy In business, a statement of managerial intent designed to guide and regulate employee behavior in the organization; in IT, a computer configuration specification used to standardize system and user behavior.

polymorphic threat Malware (a virus or worm) that over time changes the way it appears to antivirus software programs, making it undetectable by techniques that look for preconfigured signatures.

practices Examples of actions that illustrate compliance with policies.

precursor An activity in progress that may signal an incident could occur in the future.

pretexting A form of social engineering in which the attacker pretends to be an authority figure who needs information to confirm the target's identity, but the real object is to trick the target into revealing confidential information; commonly performed by telephone.

privilege escalation The unauthorized modification of an authorized or unauthorized system user account to gain advanced access and control over system resources.

procedures Step-by-step instructions designed to assist employees in following policies, standards, and guidelines.

process   A task being performed by a computer.

process communications   The necessary information flow within and between the governance group, RM framework team, and RM process team during the implementation of RM.

process monitoring and review   The data collection and feedback associated with performance measures used during the conduct of the process.

professional hacker   A hacker who conducts attacks for personal financial benefit or for a crime organization or foreign government; not to be confused with a penetration tester.

protect and forget   The organizational CP philosophy for incident response and digital forensics that focuses on the defense of information assets and preventing reoccurrence rather than the attacker's identification and prosecution.

protected health information (PHI)   A set of information about an individual's physical or mental health, healthcare providers, or health insurance.

protocol stack verification   Examining and verifying current network traffic for packets that do not conform to TCP/IP protocol specifications.

R

rainbow table   A table of hash values and their corresponding plaintext values that can be used to look up password values if an attacker is able to steal a system's encrypted password file.

rally point   See *assembly area*.

ransomware   Software designed to penetrate security controls, identify valuable content, and then encrypt files and data in place in order to extort payment for the key needed to unlock the encryption.

rapid-onset disaster   A disaster that occurs suddenly and with little warning, taking the lives of people and destroying the means of production.

recovery point objective (RPO)   The point in time before a disruption or system outage to which business process data can be recovered after an outage, given the most recent backup copy of the data.

recovery time objective (RTO)   The maximum amount of time that a system resource can remain unavailable before there is an unacceptable impact on other system resources, supported business processes, and the MTD.

redundant array of independent disks (RAID)   A system of drives that stores information across multiple units to spread out data and minimize the impact of a single drive failure.

remote journaling   The backup of data to an off-site facility in close to real time based on transactions as they occur.

residual risk   The risk to information assets that remains even after current controls have been applied.

retention schedule   An organizational policy specifying requirements for data retention, including what must be retained, where it will be stored and for how long, and the method of disposal.

risk   The probability of an unwanted occurrence, such as an adverse event or loss.

risk analysis   A determination of the extent to which an organization's information assets are exposed to risk.

risk appetite   The quantity and nature of risk that organizations are willing to accept as they evaluate the trade-offs between perfect security and unlimited accessibility.

risk appetite statement   A formal document developed by the organization that specifies its overall willingness to accept risk to its information assets, based on a synthesis of individual risk tolerances.

risk assessment   An approach to combining risk identification, risk analysis, and risk evaluation into a single strategy.

risk control   See *risk treatment*.

risk evaluation   The process of comparing an information asset's risk rating to the numerical representation of the organization's risk appetite or risk threshold to determine if risk treatment is required.

risk identification   The recognition, enumeration, and documentation of risks to an organization's information assets.

risk management (RM)   The entire program of planning for and managing risk to information assets in the organization.

risk management plan   A document that contains specifications for the implementation and conduct of RM efforts.

risk threshold   See *risk tolerance*.

risk tolerance   The assessment of the amount of risk an organization is willing to accept for a particular information asset, typically synthesized into the organization's overall risk appetite.

risk treatment   The selection of a strategy to address residual risk in an effort to bring it into alignment with the organization's risk appetite.

RM framework   The overall structure of the strategic planning and design for the entirety of the organization's RM efforts.

RM process   The identification, analysis, evaluation, and treatment of risk to information assets, as specified in the RM framework.

root cause analysis   The determination of the initial flaw or vulnerability that allowed the incident to occur by examining the systems, networks, and procedures that were involved.

rootkit   A software program or module of code that enables ongoing privileged access to a computer while actively hiding its presence from the system kernel as well as human administrators.

S

sags   Short-term decreases in electrical power availability.

Sarbanes-Oxley (SOX) Act of 2002 (also known as the Public Company Accounting Reform and Investor Protection Act)   This law enforces accountability for executives at publicly traded companies and is having ripple effects throughout the accounting, IT, and related units of many organizations.

script kiddies   Hackers of limited skill who use expertly written software to attack a system. Script kiddies are also known as skids, skiddies, or script bunnies.

security   A state of being secure and free from danger or harm. Also, the actions taken to make someone or something secure.

security information and event management (SIEM)   An information management system specifically tasked to collect and correlate events and other log data from a number of servers or other network devices for the purpose of interpreting, filtering, correlating, analyzing, storing, reporting, and acting on the resulting information.

security operations center (SOC)   A staffed, centralized control room where the organization's key security technologies, networks, and critical systems are monitored for incidents by dedicated technicians.

service   A set of software functionalities with capabilities that different clients can reuse for different purposes; in Linux/UNIX systems, services are referred to as daemons.

service agreement   A contractual document that guarantees certain minimum levels of service provided by vendors.

service bureau   A shared-site resumption strategy in which a service agency provides physical facilities for a fee in the event of a disaster.

service level agreement (SLA)   A document or part of a document that specifies the expected level of service from a service provider; usually contains provisions for minimum acceptable availability and penalties or remediation procedures for downtime.

sextortion   A spear-phishing and blackmail attack that demands payment to preclude the distribution of hacked recordings of the target visiting pornographic Web sites.

shoulder surfing   The direct, covert observation of individual information or system use.

signature   A unique value or pattern of an attack that enables detection; it may include the hash of a file or a series of scans or queries commonly used in an attack.

signature matching   Comparing current activity against a library of known malicious activity for purposes of detecting an attack.

signature-based IDPS   A type of IDPS that uses signature matching to enable detection of an attack. Also known as a *knowledge-based IDPS*.

simulation   The CP testing strategy in which the organization conducts a role-playing exercise as if an actual incident or disaster had occurred.

site policy   The rules and configuration guidelines governing the implementation and operation of IDPSs within the organization.

site policy awareness   An IDPS's ability to dynamically modify its site policies in reaction or response to environmental activity.

slow-onset disaster   A disaster that occurs over time and slowly deteriorates the organization's capacity to withstand its effects.

social engineering   The process of using social skills to convince people to reveal access credentials or other valuable information to an attacker.

Software as a Service (SaaS)   A cloud computing service model whereby applications and the necessary computer resources to run them are provided as a turnkey, on-demand service.

software piracy   The unauthorized duplication, installation, or distribution of copyrighted computer software, which is a violation of intellectual property.

spam   Unsolicited commercial e-mail, typically advertising transmitted in bulk.

spear phishing   Any highly targeted phishing attack.

spikes   Short-term increases in electrical power availability, also known as swells.

spoofing   A technique for gaining unauthorized access to computers using a forged or modified source IP address to give the perception that messages are coming from a trusted host.

standards   Detailed statements of what must be done to comply with the policy, sometimes viewed as the rules governing policy compliance.

statistical anomaly-based IDPS   See *anomaly-based IDPS*.

storage area network (SAN)   A data storage and recovery system that uses fiber-channel direct connections between the systems that need the additional storage and the storage devices themselves.

storage as a service   A cloud computing service model whereby storage capability for data backup and archiving is provided as a turnkey, on-demand service.

structured walk-through   The CP testing strategy in which all involved individuals walk through a site and discuss the steps they would take during an actual CP event; can also be conducted as a conference room talk-through.

subjects and objects of attack   A computer can be either the subject of an attack—an agent entity used to conduct the attack—or the object of an attack: the target entity.

succession planning (SP)   A process that enables an organization to cope with any loss of personnel with a minimal degree of disruption by predefining the promotion of internal employees.

surges   Long-term increases in electrical power availability.

system integrity verifier (SIV)   An application that reviews monitored files to detect unauthorized creation, modification, and deletion.

systems diagramming   A common approach in the discipline of systems analysis and design, used to understand how systems operate, chart process and information flows, and understand interdependencies.

systems-specific security policies (SysSPs)   Organizational policies that often function as standards or procedures to be used when configuring or maintaining systems.

T

table-top exercise   A simulation of an incident in which the participants work together in a physical or virtual conference room to talk through plans and procedures, without interacting directly with the rest of the business or outside entities and without directly influencing functional systems.

task rotation   The training of employees in a particular task so multiple employees are capable of performing it.

termination risk treatment strategy   The risk treatment strategy that eliminates all risk associated with an information asset by removing it from service.

theft   The illegal taking of another's property, which can be physical, electronic, or intellectual.

threat   Any event or circumstance that has the potential to adversely affect operations and assets. The term *threat source* is commonly used interchangeably with the more generic term *threat*.

threat agent   The specific instance or a component of a threat.

threat assessment   An evaluation of the threats to information assets, including a determination of their likelihood of occurrence and potential impact of an attack.

threat event   An intentional or unintentional act that can damage or otherwise compromise information and the systems that support it; commonly used interchangeably with the term *attack*.

threat intelligence   A process used to develop knowledge that allows an organization to understand the actions and intentions of threat actors and develop methods to prevent or mitigate cyberattacks.

threat source   A category of objects, people, or other entities that represents the origin of danger to an asset—in other words, a category of threat agents.

time-share   A shared-site resumption strategy that operates like a hot, warm, or cold site, but is leased in conjunction with a business partner or sister organization.

transference risk treatment strategy   The risk treatment strategy that attempts to shift risk to other assets, other processes, or other organizations.

trap and trace   A system that combines resources to detect an intrusion and then trace its network traffic back to the source.

trap door   See *back door*.

trespass   Unauthorized entry into the real or virtual property of another party.

trigger   In CP, the point at which a management decision to act is made in reaction to data or a notification of an incident or disaster; an activity or event that causes the CSIRT to be activated to respond to an incident.

Trojan horses   Malware programs that hide their true nature and reveal their designed behavior only when activated.

true attack stimulus   An event that triggers alarms and causes an IDPS to react as if a real attack were in progress.

tuning   The process of adjusting a technical control to maximize its efficiency in detecting true positives while minimizing false positives and false negatives.

U

unauthorized access (UA)   A circumstance in which an individual, an application, or another program, through access to the operating systems or application programming interface (API), attempts or gains access to an information asset without explicit permission or authorization.

uncertainty   The state of having limited or imperfect knowledge of a situation, making it less likely that organizations can successfully anticipate future events or outcomes.

V

vertical job rotation   A form of job rotation that involves the movement of employees to positions in the organization that are above or below their current position.

virtual machine   A hosted operating system or platform running on a host machine.

virtual machine monitor   See *hypervisor*.

virtualization   The development and deployment of virtual systems rather than physical implementations of systems and services.

viruses   Types of malware that are attached to other executable programs and when activated, replicate and propagate to multiple systems, spreading by multiple communications vectors.

vulnerability   A potential weakness in an asset or its defensive control system(s).

W

war game   A type of rehearsal that seeks to realistically simulate the circumstances needed to thoroughly test a plan.

warm site   An exclusive site resumption strategy that provides some of the same services and options as a hot site, but the software applications are typically not included, installed, or configured.

watchstanders   Entry-level InfoSec professionals responsible for the routine monitoring and operation of a particular InfoSec technology; also known as security staffers.

work recovery time (WRT)   The amount of effort (expressed as elapsed time) needed to make business functions work again after the technology element is recovered. This recovery time is identified by the RTO.

worms   Types of malware that are capable of activation and replication without being attached to an existing program.

Z

zombie   See *bot*.

INDEX